PLACE NAMES OF
ILLINOIS

EDWARD CALLARY

UNIVERSITY OF ILLINOIS PRESS
Urbana and Chicago

Library of Congress Cataloging-in-Publication Data
Callary, Edward.
Place names of Illinois / Edward Callary.
p. cm.
Includes bibliographical references.
ISBN 978-0-252-03356-8 (cloth : alk. paper)
1. Names, Geographical—Illinois.
2. Illinois—Geography. I. Title.
F539.C35   2009
917.73—dc22   2008012691

TO MY WIFE, JEAN,
AND OUR CHILDREN, LAURA AND RAYCHEL

PLACE NAMES ARE THE ARCHIVES
IN WHICH THE HISTORY AND CULTURE
OF A PEOPLE ARE STORED.

CONTENTS

PREFACE

In the mid-1990s, at one of the annual meetings of the American Name Society, Kelsie Harder distributed an extensive bibliography of state place name studies. Most states (more than thirty at that time) had at least one comprehensive book dealing with the origins and significance of their place names; neighboring states were well represented, but there was only occasional and partial coverage for Illinois. Although there had been a number of forays into Illinois names, for the most part these were incomplete or outdated and frequently inaccurate, often little more than uncritical repetitions of hearsay and unreliable anecdotes. The most recent serious study, Virgil Vogel's *Indian Place Names in Illinois,* was published in 1962. In the intervening years a great deal has been learned about the origins and evolution of names and the often-contentious, often-indirect processes of naming and name-changing, largely through the efforts of such professional organizations as the American Name Society and its sponsored projects, including the Place-Name Survey of the United States (now the Toponymy Interest Group) created by the ANS to stimulate interest in the collection and classification of names and aid in promoting and publishing the results of place name research.[1]

One of the main reasons that a study of place names in Illinois had lagged behind that in other states was the lack of an umbrella organization to facilitate and act as a clearing house for name research. The situation was remedied in 1980 when Laurence Seits, then at Waubonsee Community College in Sugar Grove, founded the Illinois Name Society. Through annual symposia and its publication programs, the

INS, later reorganized and expanded as the North Central Name Society (NCNS) provided an outlet for like-minded persons to gather, discuss, and share the results of their research into the sources and development of names, primarily those of Illinois. During the 1980s and early 1990s the INS and NCNS published ten volumes of proceedings and sponsored the *Journal of the North Central Name Society.* My work in onomastics, especially this book, owes a great deal to the opportunities provided by these organizations.

What, we may well ask, is the value of understanding the origins and development of place names? The simple answer is that our history and culture, our beliefs, ambitions, and dreams, are encapsulated in the names we give our communities, schools, churches, and the myriad natural and artificial features that surround us. The lives of Native Americans (Appanoose, Shabbona, and Waubonsee); French priests and explorers (Mermet, Marquette, and La Salle); national and local leaders (Douglas, Jefferson, and Grant); and less-well-known people from all walks of life (Percy, Songer, and Raymond) are compressed into Illinois place names. When we know the sources of the names and how they came to be applied, we gain useful insights into the political, cultural, and social forces that create and define society. As Donald Orth, former executive secretary of the U.S. Board on Geographic Names, has said, "Place names are the language in which the nation's autobiography is written." My aim in writing this book is to contribute to the autobiography of Illinois.

ACKNOWLEDGMENTS

Among the many people who made this book possible, I would like to recognize Kelsie B. Harder, one of America's foremost scholars of names, for unfailing encouragement and friendship and Laurence E. Seits, founder of the Illinois Name Society. I am indebted to Michael McCafferty of Indiana University for generous assistance with names likely originating in Native American languages. I have not always followed his advice, but I am much wiser for his enlightening opinions and informed suggestions. I also owe a debt of gratitude to the Interlibrary Loan Department at Northern Illinois University and the directors of the Illinois history collections at Northern Illinois University, Western Illinois University, Southern Illinois University, and the University of Illinois, Champaign-Urbana.

I am grateful as well to the following organizations, scholars, local historians, librarians, and resource people for providing specific information and offering many helpful suggestions and apologize to those I may have accidently overlooked:

Marilyn Ames
Dean and Nelda Anthony, Bond County Genealogical Society
Thelma Bishop
Clayton W. Brown, Kildeer
Frank Burkett, Hancock County Historical Society
Kathy Butcher, Illiana Genealogical and Historical Society
the Case-Halstead Library, Carlyle

ACKNOWLEDGMENTS

Jennie Cisna, Mattoon Public Library
the Coles County Historical Society
Barbara Collins, Moweaqua Public Library
Linda Eder, Kane County Genealogical Society
Angela Garrett, Flora Public Library
Betty Gibboney, Lewistown
Cheryl Wixon Gocken, Iroquois County Genealogical Society
Stella Grobe, Lee County Historical Society
Wanda Groennert
Gary Hacker, Johnson County Genealogical and Historical Society
Lori Hall, La Salle County
the Hamilton County Historical Society
Linda Hanabarger, Fayette County
Lecta Hortin, White County Historical Society
Martha Hotchkiss, McDonough County Genealogical Society
Noel E. Hurford, Historical Society of Hardin County
Betty J. Irwin, Athens, Georgia
the Jackson County Historical Society
Jenan Jobst, La Salle County Genealogy Guild
Sue Jones, Crawford County Historical Society
Fred Katko, Peoria County Genealogical Society
Jean Kay, Historical Society of Quincy and Adams County
the Kentucky Historical Society
Barbara A. Kessler, Putnam County Historical Society
Larry Lock, Kewanee Historical Society
Lois Lock, Jersey County Historical Society
the Logan County Historical Society
Curt Mandrell, Franklin County Historical Society
Virginia Mansker, Randolph County Genealogical Society
Michael McCafferty, Indiana University, Bloomington
Mildred B. McCormick, Pope County Historical Society
Hugh McMaster
Jan McGowan, Mt. Carroll Township Public Library
Marietta Nolte, Calhoun County Historical Society
Louise Ogg, Unity
Vickie Oliver, White County Historical Society
L. K. Ortman
Craig Pfannkuche, McHenry County Genealogical Society
Piatt County Historical and Genealogical Society
Carol Pirtle, Randolph County

Nancy Reed, Palermo
Lewis E. Retzer, Calhoun County Historical Society
Dorothy Riegel, Kankakee Valley Genealogical Society
Kay Rippelmeyer-Tippy, Carbondale
the Saline County Genealogical Society
Helen L. Sears, Kendall County Historical Society
Patricia Shepherd, Schuyler-Brown Genealogical Society
Mary L. Storm, Moultrie County Historical and Genealogical Society
the Tazewell County Genealogical and Historical Society
D. Kenneth Tucker, Manotick, Ontario
the Versailles Area Genealogical and Historical Society
Norma Walker, St. Clair County Historical Society
Jeni Venker Weidenbenner, Bourbonnais Public Library
the Williamson County Historical Society
Mabel M. Wilson, Knox County Genealogical Society

Finally, I thank my wife, Jean, the world's best proofreader.

INTRODUCTION

As of April 7, 2008, the database of the Geographic Names Information System (GNIS) contained slightly over sixty-two thousand geographic names (place names) for Illinois, and of these just over five thousand were the names of populated places.[1] This number is but a fraction (probably fewer than 20 percent) of all current Illinois names and an even smaller fraction of all Illinois names if we include those which have disappeared from the landscape and those which never appeared on maps or were otherwise documented. Natural questions concern the origins of the names, who chose the names, and—most interesting but hardest to determine— why they were chosen.

It is customary to think of place names as layers on the land, and, much as archaeologists speak of strata or layers of habitation at a particular site, we can speak of layers of names, with each layer attesting to the presence of a particular group of people or the existence of a particular naming practice. Before the twentieth century, names in Illinois composed five distinct layers: names used by Native Americans; names used by early French explorers and settlers; names transferred from Europe or from the eastern states, a practice that flourished in the middle years of the nineteenth century; patriotic names given in commemoration of political and military leaders or names from history; and self-memorializing names given by people who established (or sought to establish) communities in what was then the American West.[2]

The deepest layer, that of Native American names, is, from our limited perspective due to the lack of written materials, thinner than the others. By the time of the arrival of French explorers in the 1670s, much of the Illinois landscape, especially such major features as streams and hills, had probably been named by the Peorias, Kaskaskias, and other groups of Native Americans, but what these names were and what they designated is largely lost to us. If by Native American names we mean names from a Native American language that were probably used by Native Americans for purposes of geographic reference, only a handful are found on modern maps. These would include Chicago, Kankakee, Kishwaukee, Nippersink, Pecatonica, and Sinnissippi; probably Shokokon, Somonauk, and Maquon; and possibly others. Most of what we tend to think of as "Indian names," such as Shabbona, Mettawa, Nachusa, and names with the word *Indian* itself (more than thirty streams in Illinois are named Indian Creek), were applied by Europeans, in many cases decades after Native American occupation had ended.[3]

Even before the historic expedition of Jacques Marquette and Louis Jolliet along the Mississippi and Illinois rivers, names given by French explorers had begun to appear on maps of the western Great Lakes. One of the earliest of these was Illinois. Maps drawn as early as 1671 refer to present Lake Michigan as Lac des Ilinois. Marquette's own map, drawn during or shortly after the expedition of 1673, records not only Lac des Ilinois but also the tribal names *Pana, Maroa, Pe8area* (Peoria, the numeral eight represents a [w] or [oo] sound), and *Kachkaska* (Kaskaskia), all of which became Illinois place names.

The first French names were brought to Illinois primarily from French Canada by hunters, trappers, and traders later accompanied by priests who established missions at Kaskaskia and Cahokia. Because these early explorers traveled mainly by water and kept to the verges of navigable streams, the first French names related to riverine features and to water travel, names such as Aux Sable and Grand Detour. (In Mississippi Valley French, a bend in a river was known as a *detour,* and a large horseshoe bend, such as that on the Rock River north of Dixon, was a *grand detour.*) Later French names were descriptions of the landscape (Prairie du Rocher, Fondulac) or references to aspects of occupation and settlement (Canteen, Saline). Perhaps the most confusing French name to contemporary readers is *embarras,* which gave us the name of the Embarras River in eastern Illinois and (with a slight change in spelling) the community of Embarrass in Coles County and Embarrass Township in Edgar County. The word had nothing to do with shame or humiliation but referred to an obstruction in a stream or lake, often a mass of uprooted trees and debris that made navigation hazardous.

Transfer naming, which began in a limited way in the eastern states and became characteristic of naming in the Midwest in the nineteenth century, provided a means by which early settlers could maintain emotional if not physical ties with farms, homes, and towns left behind. New communities in the Midwest were regularly named for old ones in the East, often with the prefix *new* but more often without. Such naming, in the words of Allen Walker Read, created a network of "gossamer threads" that connected new names with old names and new places with old places, binding communities and families together in spite of the physical distance between them. Names such as Aurora, York, and Wyoming were progressively transferred westward with advancing American civilization. When settlers from Ohio established twin cities in east central Illinois they named one Champaign for their former home, Champaign County, Ohio, and the other Urbana, for the seat of Champaign County, Ohio. The desire to preserve social ties in this fashion was so strong that frequently one group would compete with another over the "right" to a name. When DeKalb County voted to form civil townships in 1849, residents in four of the projected townships chose the name Clinton, for their former home, Clinton, New York. Because none of the four would agree to give up their interests, present Clinton Township was awarded the name by lot.

Transfer names were especially attractive to settlers from Europe; Germans in particular brought their place names with them. There have been at least ten Hanovers in Illinois, nine Berlins, nine Hamburgs, and nine Bremens.

Many Illinois place names were bestowed in the early and middle decades of the nineteenth century, and they reflect major events of the time as well as namers' values and aspirations. Despite the economic hardships of the 1830s, for most people the mid-nineteenth century was a time of optimism, not only for Illinois but also for much of the country. (It is no accident that the name *Young America,* with all the exuberance and promise it connotes, sprang up in a number of the new states, including Indiana, Minnesota, Wisconsin, and at least twice in Illinois.)

By the time Illinois became a state in 1818, both the Revolutionary War and the War of 1812 had been won, the size of the country had been doubled by the Louisiana Purchase, and the Midwest was open to American settlement. What better way for Americans to confirm themselves and demonstrate to the world that they had developed their own identity and history than commemorate those who created the United States: the Revolutionary generation and the founders of the country. Even Christopher Columbus was appropriated as part of U.S. history. The major figures of early America were honored, national heroes such as George Washington and Thomas Jefferson, signers of the Declaration of Independence such as John Hancock and Charles Carroll of Carrollton, and Europeans such as the Marquis de La Fayette and Johann DeKalb who had figured prominently in American history, particularly during the Revolution. Commemorative naming on such a grand scale was unprecedented, and throughout the nineteenth century, historic events as well as historic figures were memorialized, often several times over: Concord and Bunker Hill from the Revolution; Cerro Gordo and Buena Vista from the Mexican War; later, Corinth and Iuka from the Civil War; and, above all, Union. There have been more than fifty post offices, communities, townships, or precincts in Illinois named Union. With few exceptions these were named for the federal union of states, several around the time Illinois was being considered for statehood. Not only were historic figures commemorated but also their nicknames (Buck, Young Hickory) and even their estates (Ashland, Monticello, La Grange).

In one of the more sweeping acts of commemorative naming, in January 1825 the Illinois legislature created eight new counties, all of them named for men who had achieved fame at the time of the American Revolution: Patrick Henry, John Adams, John Hancock, Henry Knox, Hugh Mercer, Israel Putnam, Joseph Warren, and Philip Schuyler.

Commemorative naming became so popular that it was soon extended from honoring national heroes to regional and local figures and then to ordinary citizens, especially those who created communities by laying off building lots on their property. It became the custom to name an embryonic community for the person who owned the town site or for an early settler or postmaster. These nascent metropolises failed by the hundreds; many never evolved beyond a town plat, and their names are all that remain of a land owner's dream.

Although Native American names, French names, transfer names, and commemorative names constitute the major naming patterns in Illinois, there are, as we might expect, a number of complementary practices: names from literature (Dahinda, Nokomis, and Ponemah, all from Henry Wadsworth Longfellow's *The Song of Hiawatha*); names associated with religion (Zion, Salem, and Azotus); names from the classics and mythology (Pomona and Odin); names from nature (Mosquito and Kildeer); and names describing natural features (Grand Rapids and Long Point). These, too, have contributed, although less significantly, to the mosaic of Illinois place names.

WHAT IS AND WHAT IS NOT
INCLUDED IN THIS BOOK

To keep *Place Names of Illinois* to a manageable length I have focused on the names of populated places, and I have included to the extent possible the names of current Illinois communities, of which there are about 3,300, according to DeLorme's *Illinois Atlas and Gazetteer*. To these I have added the names of counties, townships, and precincts and a number of other names that are of historical or cultural importance or interesting in one way or another.

I have also included the names of several dozen former communities because in many instances only their existence can explain the names of current roads, schools, cemeteries, or other features. Blood's Point Road south of Belvidere in Boone County and Blood's Point Cemetery are now the only reminders of the former community of Blood's Point, named for Arthur Blood, the first settler in what is now Flora Township. Canada Road, southwest of Mount Morris in Ogle County, originally led to the Canada Settlement, founded by a group of Torontonians in the late 1830s.

I have generally omitted the names of land forms such as cliffs, islands, and caves; the names of streams, lakes, and swamps; and the names of valleys, forests, and reserves. Reluctantly, I have omitted as well the names of colleges and universities, radio and television stations, bridges, airports, and military bases. I have, however, included several summits that bear directly on the state's history or geography, such as Charles Mound, which at about 1,230 feet is the highest point in Illinois.

A NOTE ON RAILROAD NAMES

The names of Illinois railroads present a confusing, even bewildering, picture. Railroads proliferated in the latter half of the nineteenth century, when scores of new lines were created; some existed only on paper; others operated for a time and went bankrupt; still others were sold to competitors, leased to other operators, or absorbed by parent corporations. Rather than try to sort out pre- and postmerger names, name changes, names of branch lines, and the like I have reproduced the names as they appeared in the sources cited. Thus in one source the line from Flagg Center to Rockford may be called the Chicago, Rockford and Northern; in another, the Chicago and Iowa; and in still another, the Chicago, Burlington and Quincy. All three names are in this book.

A NOTE ON POPULAR ETYMOLOGY

When faced with an esoteric word of which they do not know the meaning, people often resort to a process known as popular etymology (also called folk etymology) in which they recast the unfamiliar word in familiar terms. Thus, Spanish *cucaracha* (wood louse) became "cockroach." When the origin of a name is unknown there is a similar human tendency to invent a plausible story to explain it. Quiver, a township in Mason County on the south shore of the Illinois River, takes its name from Quiver Creek, itself so named, according to local stories, by early settlers, who, when they stood near the stream and rocked back and forth, saw the land around them quiver. It is an engaging etymology, to be sure, but without a grain of truth. The real story behind the name is not nearly so entertaining. An earlier name for the stream was Cuivre River, from *cuivre* (copper), given by French explorers or traders. The unfamiliar French word sounded a bit like the word *quiver*, and that became the new etymology. Several dozen names included here, such as Future City (from Futrell City) and Rose Hill (from Roe's Hill), have generated popular etymologies, often quite imaginative.

A NOTE ON SOURCES

Because there have been few systematic studies of Illinois names, information relating to the origins of the names and the circumstances surrounding the act of naming is widely scattered. Partial accounts appear in newspapers, local and regional magazines, county and community histories, church records, personal memoirs and diaries, travel accounts, and state publications. The following sources are easily located and should be consulted by anyone wishing to elaborate on the entries given here or wishing to extend coverage into other areas such as church names or stream names.

Several series of county histories were published in the late nineteenth and early twentieth centuries. One of the better known is the series edited by Newton Bateman and Paul Selby, the *Historical Encyclopedia of Illinois*. Between 1899 and 1921 more than forty histories were published in two parts, a common encyclopedia of Illinois and an individual county history. Additional county histories were subsequently published when the county was celebrating its hundredth birthday and for the 1976 U.S. bicentennial. Although county histories are important resources for genealogists, historians, and names researchers, they must be used with caution. The older ones in particular tend to copy (often verbatim) from one another, and yet are frequently at odds, even with the most straightforward facts. Conflicting accounts may be found not only between publications but sometimes also within the same volume. In the *Encyclopedia of Illinois* history for Montgomery County, for example, Bateman and Selby (actually, Alexander T. Strange, the editor of the

Montgomery County history) give three different dates for the founding of the village of Donnellson.

The first serious work that dealt with Illinois names directly was that of William D. Barge and Norman H. Caldwell. Barge was a native of Lee County, a respected local historian, and an attorney for the Chicago, Burlington and Quincy Railroad, so he wrote with the archives of the CB&Q at his disposal. Barge's work was edited by Caldwell and published as "Illinois Place Names," a compilation of the sources of some nine hundred names, in the *Journal of the Illinois State Historical Society* in 1936–37. Barge and Caldwell's work, although laudable for its time, is outdated and provides sketchy accounts of the origins of the names and little of substance beyond a brief "was named for so and so," "was named for the city in Italy," and the like. The dynamics of the naming process are omitted, such as who chose the name and why, the date of naming, other names considered at the time, previous names the community may have had, and popular stories invented post hoc to explain the name; in short the very spirit and soul of naming is missing.

A more comprehensive account of a portion of Illinois names is *Indian Place Names in Illinois,* in which Virgil Vogel considers some 270 names with Native American associations. Vogel was a historian by training and vocation and his primary purpose was to demonstrate the impact of ethno-history on the Illinois namescape, in particular the legacies of the relationships between Native Americans and Europeans as revealed through place names. Thus, Vogel is concerned more with history and ethnography than with the dynamics of names and naming, and for that reason he defined "Indian name" in the broadest of terms. For Vogel, an Indian name was any name that originated in any native language, any name derived from any aspect of native culture and given or adapted by Europeans, or any name that resulted from contact between Europeans and Native Americans.

Thus, in addition to such names as Merrimac, Moccasin, and Tampico, derived from native languages, Vogel includes *calques* (translations of native terms) such as Sycamore (from Kishwaukee) as well as more remotely associated names such as Okaw, from French *aux Kas* (at the village of the Kaskaskias) and even Stillman's Run, a stream in north central Illinois near which Isiah Stillman, in command of a troop of Illinois militia, was routed by a small band of Sauk warriors in one of the early skirmishes of the Black Hawk War. Published in 1962, *Indian Place Names in Illinois* is seriously outdated and in need of revision. Vogel's research, however, is remarkably thorough and comprehensive through the 1950s and is thus valuable as a summary of scholarship to that time. In many instances Vogel's entries are more extensive than those in this volume and often contain more cultural and human interest information than space has allowed me to provide.

An indispensable companion to the study of Illinois names is James N. Adams's *Illinois Place Names,* first published in 1968. Adams was employed by the Illinois

State Historical Library from 1943 until 1965, and during that time he became interested in Illinois postal history, an interest which led him to compile a list of all post offices in Illinois, current and historical, along with their location by county, dates of operation, original name(s), and dates of any name changes. To that base Adams subsequently added the names of many communities, townships, and precincts gathered from state maps, county histories, and county atlases and gazetteers. Adams's final compilation ran to some fourteen thousand names, a truly impressive collection. For a comprehensive list of Illinois place names, past and present, Adams is unsurpassed. With the exception of a small number of communities (primarily those named for early postmasters), however, there are no sources of the names, no etymologies, no suggestions of who bestowed the names, and no mention of the circumstances surrounding the naming.

I have relied on Adams for information on the establishment and name changes of post offices through 1961. I disregarded post offices established after 1961 because they are relatively few and largely named for the communities they serve.

Post offices moved frequently, and many were discontinued and reestablished on several occasions, so it should not be assumed that a post office with the name of a given community originated in that community. I have given the earliest name by which the post office that eventually became the community's post office was know (but not necessaarily where it may have been located), followed by any name changes preceding the change to the name of the host community. I have not included information on the current status of the post offices, so some of those mentioned here may no longer be in operation.

For information on the corporate status of communities and date or dates of incorporation I used *Illinois Counties and Incorporated Municipalities* and the *Illinois Blue Book 2005–2006*. For information on the establishment of townships and the location or locations of county seats I employed Sheila Kelly's *County and Township Gazetteer*. Finally, maps mentioned in the text are found in Sara Jones Tucker's *Indian Villages of the Illinois Country: Atlas*.

It should not be assumed that the references provided in the individual entries are where I simply "looked up" the origin of a name. If that were true, it would not have taken me four years to conduct the research for this book. Rather, they provide information I found useful in writing the entries and should be starting points for anyone wanting more details regarding the name (or the names of associated churches, parks, schools, and the like) than I am able to provide. They must be used with caution, however, because their quality varies widely. Some locally produced booklets are excellent, but others are less trustworthy, and even basic information such as dates of founding must be confirmed through other sources.

THE FORM OF ENTRIES

Each name headword is followed by its pronunciation (if necessary and available); the county in which the feature is located; the type of feature (a populated place if not otherwise specified); its corporation status if incorporated; the date or dates of incorporation; its location relative to a larger community for a community of fewer than 2,500 residents; the text of the entry; references; and post office information.[1] The entry for Albion is typical:

> Albion [AL bee uhn]. Edwards. City (1869, 1908) fifteen miles west of Mount Carmel. Formerly known as Edwards Courthouse, English Settlement, and New Albion. Founded in 1818 by George Flower and Morris Birkbeck, well-to-do Englishmen who sought to establish in America a progressive community built upon modern methods of farming and animal husbandry. Birkbeck may have been attracted to Illinois through a meeting in London with Edward Coles about 1817. Coles, as governor, appointed Birkbeck to be Illinois secretary of state in 1824. Birkbeck was also the founder of Wanborough (q.v.). Flower named the colony Albion, an ancient and poetic name for England derived from Latin *albus* (white) (Harper, ed., *History of Edwards County*, 7–8). Post office established Aug. 5, 1819.

A PRONUNCIATION GUIDE

Where I have been able to determine local pronunciation to my satisfaction I have included the pronunciation of those names whose pronunciation is not obvious from the spelling or where the local pronunciation is different from what the spelling would suggest—thus, San Jose [SAN JOZ], Jo Daviess [JO DAYVIS], and Berlin [BER luhn].

The symbols used to indicate pronunciation have their "expected" values with the following exceptions, here illustrated first by a common English word and then by an Illinois place name. Stressed (accented) syllables are in capital letters:

[a] as in cat, Addieville [AD ee vil]
[ay] as in say, Naplate [NAY playt]
[ah] as in father, Mazon [muh ZAHN]
[e] as in bet, Beneld [ben ELD]
[ee] as in me, Hebron [HEE bruhn]
[i] as in fifty, Bingham [BING uhm]
[eye] as in nice, Farina [fuh REYE nuh]
[o] as in slow, Degognia [duh GON yuh]
[oo] as in boot, Colusa [kuh LOO suh]
[u] as in foot, Bushnell [BUSH nuhl]
[uh] as in cut, Blount [BLUHNT]
[yoo] as in cute, Buda [BYOO duh]

[er] as in heard, Ursa [ER suh]
[ehr] as in fair, Herrin [HEHR uhn]
[ahr] as in are, Onarga [o NAHR guh]
[or] as in tour, Orion [OR ee uhn]
[ow] as in now, Lowder [LOW der]
[aw] as in raw, Saunemin [SAW nuh muhn]
[oy] as in toy, Beloit [buh LOYT]
[ch] as in itch, Chana [CHAY nuh]
[g] as in egg, Goins [GO uhnz]
[j] as in wedge, Vergennes [ver JENZ]
[k] as in catch, Wasco [WAS ko]
[kw] as in quaint, Maquon [muh KWAN]
[ng] as in sung, Chemung [shuh MUHNG]
[sh] as in shoe, Rochelle [ro SHEL]
[th] as in bath, Dunleith [duhn LEETH]
[z] as in easy, Albers [AL berz]
[zh] as in measure, Andalusia [an duh LOO zhuh]

PLACE NAMES OF
ILLINOIS

A

ABINGDON [A bing duhn]. Knox. City (1857, 1920) eight miles south of Galesburg. Founded in 1836 by Abraham D. Swartz and named for his former home, Abingdon, in Harford County, Md., itself named for Abingdon, Oxfordshire, England (Perry, *History of Knox County*, 419). Post office established June 30, 1837, as Oregon; changed to Hartford Aug. 12, 1839; changed to Abingdon May 12, 1852.

ABSHER. Williamson. Nine miles west-southwest of Harrisburg. Alternate name for Dykersburg. Named for William A. Absher, the first postmaster (Adams, comp., *Illinois Place Names;* Hubbs, *Pioneer Folks and Places*). Post office established July 27, 1892.

ADAIR. McDonough. Nine miles east-southeast of Macomb. Laid out in 1870 as Reedyville, a station on the St. Louis, Rock Island and Chicago Railroad, by site owners John Reedy and Jacob Grimm. The community later took the name of the Adair post office. The source of the name is unknown (Chenoweth and Semonis, comps., *The History of McDonough County*, 108). Post office established May 22, 1867.

ADAMS. County. Created Jan. 13, 1825, from Pike County. Named for John Quincy Adams, at the time a candidate for president of the United States. The name was probably suggested by John Wood, a future governor of Illinois. After Adams was elected by the U.S. House of Representatives in February 1825, the name for the county seat was discussed, and someone in the audience reportedly remarked, "Let us take another slice from the President's name and call our County Seat 'Quincy.'" A local story claims that Adams's name was fully appropriated when the first town park was called John's Square; thus, in the words of an early county historian, the "learned and popular John Quincy Adams [was given] all that was coming to him" (Wilcox, *Quincy and Adams County*, 106; Genosky, ed., *People's History*, 49, 50, 250).

ADAMS. Adams. Ten miles east-southeast of Quincy. Founded about 1838 and named for early settler Elias Adams and for its location in Adams county (Genosky, ed., *People's History*, 696). Post office established Feb. 21, 1850.

ADAMS CORNER. Wabash. Six miles north of Mount Carmel. Named for early settler Daniel Adams (*Combined History of Edwards, Lawrence, and Wabash Counties*, 283).

ADAMSBURG. Adams. Laid out about 1835 near the center of Adams County. The founders thought Adamsburg would become the county seat, but it never materialized beyond a town plat (www.rootsweb.com/~iladams/places/placenames.htm).

ADDIEVILLE [AD ee vil]. Washington. Village (1896) six miles northwest of Nashville. Founded in 1870 by Col. James Lowery Donaldson Morrison (q.v. Morrisonville), a lawyer and land developer, and named for his wife Adele, known as Addie (*History of Washington County,* 27). Post office established Dec. 12, 1870.

ADDISON. DuPage. Village (1884). Previously known as Duncklee's Grove, named for first settler Hezekiah Duncklee. Formally established about 1840 and probably named by settlers from Addison, Steuben County, N.Y., itself named for English author Joseph Addison (1672–1719). The choice of the name may have been influenced by other notable Addisons, especially Dr. Thomas Addison (1793–1860), the British physician best known for his description of a disease of the adrenal glands now called Addison's Disease and for whom Addison Street in Chicago is named (Hayner and McNamee, *Streetwise Chicago;* Richmond and Vallette, *A History of the County of DuPage,* 149; Vasiliev, *From Abbotts to Zurich*). Post office established April 4, 1839, as Dunkley's [*sic*] Grove; changed to Addison May 28, 1842.

ADELINE [AD uh leyen]. Ogle. Village (1882) seven miles northwest of Mount Morris. Founded in 1845 and named for Adeline Turner, wife of Thomas J. Turner of Freeport, U.S. representative in the late 1840s (*History of Ogle County,* 296). Post office established March 31, 1841, as Mt. Morris; changed to Leaf River March 13, 1844; changed to Adeline Dec. 29, 1848.

ADEN [AYD uhn]. Hamilton. Ten miles north-northeast of McLeansboro. Formerly known as Lower Hills. The name was changed to Aden about 1890. The source of the name is unknown (*Hamilton County,* 37). Post office established Dec. 1, 1875.

ADRIAN. Hancock. Eight miles north of Carthage. Founded in the early 1870s and named for Adrian, Lenawee County, Mich., by Arthur Rice, a postal clerk on the Burlington Railroad (Bateman and Selby, eds., *Historical Encyclopedia of Illinois and History of Hancock County,* 1096). Post office established May 24, 1870.

AETNA [ET nuh]. Logan. Township. Named from Aetna Station, a stop on the Illinois Central Railroad. Probably named by officials of the IC for Mount Aetna in Sicily about the time of a particularly destructive eruption of the volcano in 1852 (Ackerman, *Early Illinois Railroads,* 128).

AFRICA. Williamson. Established in the northeast corner of Williamson County by Robert McCreery as a settlement for freed slaves. McCreery, upon inheriting his father's slaves in the slave state of Missouri, brought them into the free state of Illinois, manumitted them, and settled them on land next to his own, which he called Africa. The area was later known as Willow Bend Farm (Hale, comp. and ed., *Williamson County,* 121; Hubbs, *Pioneer Folks and Places*).

AFTON [AF tuhn]. DeKalb. Township. Named by John A. Hayden, who called Little Rock Creek, which ran through his property, Sweet Afton after the Scottish river popularized by Robert Burns's poem, "Flow Gently, Sweet Afton." Coincidentally, Burns's poem was set to music in Illinois in 1836 by Jonathon

Edwards Spilman, pastor of the First Presbyterian Church in Carmi (Boies, *History of DeKalb County*, 496).

AGNEW [AG noo]. Whiteside. Four miles west of Sterling. Originally known as Rock Island Junction. Named for Lord D. Agnew, station agent for both the Burlington and Chicago and North Western railroads in the 1910s (Bastian, *A History of Whiteside County*, 470).

AKIN [AY kin]. Franklin. Eight miles west of Benton. Laid out about 1875 and named from the Akin post office, itself probably named for postmaster George W. Akin. Possibly named for local land owners Walter S. Aiken and/or Aiken McLean (Adams, comp., *Illinois Place Names*; Aiken, *Franklin County History*, 96; *History of Gallatin, Saline*, 363). Post office established June 15, 1860.

AKRON [AK ruhn]. Peoria. Nine miles north of Peoria. The Chicago and North Western station was established about 1901 as Akron, taking its name from the Akron post office, itself named for Akron Township, which was named by early settlers from Akron, Ohio. Ultimately from the Greek *akron* (summit) (Bateman and Selby, eds., *Historical Encyclopedia of Illinois and History of Peoria County*, 647; Stennett, *A History of the Origin*, 35). Post office established Sept. 23, 1858.

ALBA [AL buh]. Henry. Township. Early county historians were at a loss to explain the name. One went so far as to call it "one of the unaccountable inventions of the Commissioners selected to give baptismal names to the . . . townships. . . . It is a case, perhaps, of purely poetic fancy." Alba Township, however, was established as Elba, a name transferred by settlers from Elba, Genesee County, N.Y. The spelling *Alba* probably represents a local pronunciation of "Elba" (*Portrait and Biographical Album of Henry County*, 764).

ALBANY [AWL buh nee]. Whiteside. Village (1869, 1877) three miles south of Clinton, Iowa. Founded about 1837 as Port Newbury. The name was changed in 1838 by settlers from Albany, N.Y., itself named in 1664 in honor of the Duke of York and Albany, later King James II. Albany is also a poetic name for Scotland. There were also short-lived Albanys in Greene and Logan counties and New Albanys in Scott and Douglas counties (Davis, *History of Whiteside County*, 68; Stewart, *American Place-Names*). Post office established Feb. 7, 1837, as Port Newbury; changed to Albany July 6, 1838.

ALBANY PARK. Cook. North Chicago community. Founded in the early 1890s by a consortium of land developers that included Chicago streetcar magnate De Lancey Louderback, who named the community for his former home, Albany, N.Y. (Hayner and McNamee, *Streetwise Chicago*).

ALBERS [AL berz]. Clinton. Village (1954) four miles east of New Baden. Established about 1860 by J. W. Dugger as Damiansville Station on the Air Line Railroad. The name was changed to Albers Station for site owner F. H. Albers in the early 1890s (*Commercial History of Clinton County*, 5). Post office established May 25, 1893.

ALBION [AL bee uhn]. Edwards. City (1869, 1908) fifteen miles west of Mount Carmel. Formerly known as Edwards Courthouse, English Settlement, and New Albion. Founded in 1818 by George Flower and Morris Birkbeck, well-to-do Englishmen who sought to establish in America a progressive community built upon modern methods of farming and animal husbandry. Birkbeck may have been attracted to Illinois through a meeting in London with Edward Coles about 1817. Coles, as governor, appointed Birkbeck Illinois secretary of state in 1824. Birkbeck was also the founder of Wanborough (q.v.). Flower named the colony Albion, an ancient and poetic name for England derived from Latin *albus* (white) (Harper, ed., *History of Edwards County*, 7–8). Post office established Aug. 5, 1819.

ALDEN [AWL duhn]. McHenry. Five miles northeast of Harvard. Founded about 1844 and named by settlers from Alden, Erie County, N.Y. (Nye, ed., *McHenry County Illinois*, 348). Post office established June 21, 1843, as Wedgewood, named for first postmaster Thomas Wedgewood; changed to Alden Jan. 30, 1844.

ALEDO [uh LEE do]. Mercer. City (1855). Established in the mid-1850s as DeSoto, a station on the Great Western Railroad. By one account, letters of the alphabet were placed in a hat and drawn at random until an acceptable combination was found. More likely, however, the name was chosen by John S. Thompson, one of the founders of Aledo, who is reported as saying that he took a *Webster's Dictionary*, opened it to the section on geographic names, and was favorably struck by the name *Aledo* (presumably Aledo, Spain) (Bassett and Goodspeed, *Past and Present of Mercer County*, 376). Post office established Sept. 24, 1856.

ALEXANDER. County. Created March 4, 1819. Named for (and probably by) Dr. William M. Alexander, who was instrumental in the formation of the county. Alexander was a physician with a practice at America who served as an Illinois state representative and speaker of the Illinois House in the early 1820s. The seat of Alexander County was established at America, moved to Unity in 1833, to Thebes in 1843, and to Cairo in 1860 (*Alexander County*, 8).

ALEXANDER. Morgan. Nine miles east of Jacksonville. Founded about 1857 by site owner John T. Alexander (*History of Morgan County*, 433). Post office established July 15, 1857.

ALEXIS [uh LEK sis]. Mercer, Warren. Village (1873) ten miles north-northeast of Monmouth. Founded in 1870 as Alexandria, a station on the St. Louis branch of the Chicago, Burlington and Quincy Railroad and named for J. E. Alexander, one of the site owners. The name was changed in 1872 in honor of the visit to the United States of the Russian Grand Duke Alexis, who spent part of the winter of 1871–72 in Illinois (Bateman and Selby, eds., *Historical Encyclopedia of Illinois and History of Warren County*, 993; *Portrait and Biographical Album* *of Warren County,* 742). Post office established Dec. 30, 1870, as Alexandria; changed to Alexis Jan. 22, 1872.

ALGONQUIN [al GAHNG kwin]. Kane, McHenry. Village (1890). First known as Denny's Ferry and later as Cornish's Ferry and Cornishville, named for Andrew Cornish, who operated a ferry across the Fox River near the site in the early 1840s. The community was organized about 1847 as Osceola. To avoid duplicating an existing Osceola post office, the name was changed at the suggestion of Samuel Edwards, a local land owner, who proposed the name *Algonquin,* claiming that this was the name of a ship on which he had served (Nye, ed., *McHenry County Illinois,* 365). Post office established July 12, 1839, as Denny's Ferry; changed to Cornish's Ferry July 23, 1840; changed to Cornishville Jan. 3, 1842; changed to Algonquin Dec. 23, 1847.

ALHAMBRA [al HAM bruh]. Madison. Village (1884) twelve miles northeast of Edwardsville. Founded in 1849 by Louis F. Shep(p)ard and Levi Harnsberger and named by their wives, who took the name from Washington Irving's *Tales of the Alhambra.* The Alhambra was the citadel of the Moorish kings of Grenada, Spain (*Alhambra,* 7; Norton, ed., *Centennial History of Madison County,* 462). Post office established April 9, 1850, as Lowryville; changed to Alhambra March 25, 1851.

ALLADIN. Perry. Founded in 1921 by the Alladin Coal and Mining Company. Now part of Cutler (q.v.) (*Perry County,* 6).

ALLEN. LaSalle. Township. Formed from Bruce Township about 1858 and named for Allen Stevens, who immigrated from Scotland to Canada about 1857 and from there to LaSalle County (*History of LaSalle County,* 32). The Allen post office was established and discontinued several times between July 13, 1866, and July 18, 1876.

ALLENDALE. Wabash. Village (1917) eight miles north-northeast of Mount Carmel. Platted in 1869 and named for Col. C. M. Allen, a contractor for the Cairo and Vincennes Railroad (*Wabash County,* 25). Post office established Dec. 25, 1829, as Armstrong, named for first postmaster Abner Armstrong; changed to Allendale July 19, 1870.

ALLENS SPRING. Pope. Two miles southeast of Dixon Springs State Park. Named for George M. Allen, the first postmaster and an early proprietor of the springs (Allen, *Pope County Notes,* 68). Post office established April 6, 1857, as Allen's Springs.

ALLENTOWN. Tazewell. Three miles southeast of Morton. Named for James Allen of Pekin (Adams, comp., *Illinois Place Names*). Post office established Jan. 27, 1879.

ALLERTON [AL er tuhn]. Champaign, Vermilion. Village (1902) sixteen miles west-southwest of Georgetown. Founded in 1887 by Samuel A. Allerton and William G. Herron, partners in the Allerton Herron Grain Company. Allerton was a principal stockholder in the First National Bank of Chicago and founder of the Chicago Union Stock Yards (Morris, *Allerton, Illinois 1887–1987,* 2). Post office established Dec. 5, 1877, as Broadlands (q.v.); changed to Allerton Dec. 15, 1887.

ALLERTON PARK. Piatt. Four miles southwest of Monticello. Part of the estate of Samuel A. Allerton; donated to the University of Illinois by his son, Robert, in 1946 (Adams, comp., *Illinois Place Names;* West, *A Heritage Reborn,* 17).

ALLIN. McLean. Township. Named for James Allin, the founder of Bloomington. Previously known as Mosquito Grove (*History of McLean County,* 320). Post office established Jan. 7, 1868, as Allin Station.

ALLISON. Lawrence. Township. Named from Allison's Prairie, itself named for the Allison family. Samuel, Jonathan, and Ezra Allison filed for 160 acres of land in 1815. The name was changed from Thompson in 1857 (Bateman and Selby, eds., *Illinois Historical Lawrence County Biographical,* 629). Post office established Aug. 30, 1827.

ALMA. Marion [AL muh]. Village (1855, 1897) eight miles north of Salem. Laid out in 1854 by John S. Martin as Rantoul, named for Robert Rantoul (q.v. Rantoul). The name was changed in 1855 at the suggestion of John B. Calhoun, a land commissioner for the Illinois Central Railroad, for the Alma River, a stream in the Crimea where allied forces had defeated a Russian army the year before. Largely because of the news coverage given to the Crimean War, Alma became popular both as a place name and as a fashionable name for girls in the middle of the nineteenth century (Ackerman, *Early Illinois Railroads,* 131; Brinkerhoff, *Brinkerhoff's History of Marion County,* 200). Post office established Dec. 22, 1884, as Grand Mound City; changed to Alma April 13, 1855.

ALMORA [al MOR uh]. Kane. West of Elgin. Originally a milk shipping station called Spring Valley, established by the Chicago and North Western Railroad in the early 1880s. The nearby Milwaukee Road station was Dumser, named for site owner Simon Dumser. About 1885 officials of the post office and the railroads agreed on the name *Almora,* perhaps for Almora, a city in Uttar Pradesh in northern India. As a place name Almora occurs only in Illinois and Minnesota (www.elginhistory.com). Post office established Feb. 28, 1881, as Padell; changed to Spring Valley Feb. 14, 1882; changed to Almora Dec. 16, 1885.

ALORTON. St. Clair. Village (1944) south of East St. Louis. Formerly known as Alcoa, the trade name of the Aluminum Company of America, a major local employer. Alorton is probably a shortening of "Aluminum Ore Town." This is the only Alorton in the United States (Fitzgerald, "Centreville Pushes for Alorton Annexation"; *Illinois Gazetteer*).

ALPHA. Henry. Village (1894) twelve miles southwest of Cambridge. Formerly known as Oxford, named by settlers from Oxford, Chenango County, N.Y. In

1869 the station on the Galva and Keithsburg Railroad was named Anson in honor of site owner Anson Calkins, and the community was known informally as Calkinsville until it was formally organized as Alpha in the early 1870s. Calkins was a deeply religious man who donated land for both the Baptist and Methodist churches. While at a Baptist revival meeting where the text was Revelation 1:8, "I am Alpha and Omega," he chose the name for the community, not only for its religious significance but also to convey the notion of a new beginning (*Alpha*, 19). Post office established June 28, 1871.

ALSEY [AL zi, AWL si]. Scott. Village (1927) seven miles northwest of Roodhouse. Laid out in 1870 as Smithfield by Alsey R. Smith, the first postmaster. To avoid duplicating the name of an existing post office, Smith changed the name to Alsey (*Scott County Bicentennial Book*, 56). Post office established July 17, 1872.

ALSIP [AWL sip]. Cook. Village (1927). Named for Frank Alsip and his son Charles, who founded the Alsip Brick Company in 1885 (Cates, "Despite Changes").

ALTA [AL tuh, AWL tuh]. Peoria. Three miles north of Peoria. Founded in 1873 as a station on the Peoria and Rock Island Railroad and reportedly named Alta (high) because this was thought to be the highest point between Peoria and Rock Island (*History of Peoria County*, 607). Post office established April 4, 1873, as Medina; changed to Alta April 28, 1873.

ALTAMONT [AL tuh mahnt]. Effingham. City (1872) twelve miles west-southwest of Effingham. Founded in 1870 by J. W. Conologue, site owner and superintendent of the Vandalia Railroad. Because the site was near Blue Mound, presumed to be the highest point on the railroad line between St. Louis and Terre Haute, Conologue combined *alta* (high) with *mont* (from the community of Montville, several miles to the south). With the growth of Altamont, Montville declined and ultimately disappeared (Pulliam, ed., *Towns of Effingham County*, 3). Post office established June 10, 1867, as Mountville; changed to Altamont Dec. 8, 1870.

ALTMAR. LaSalle. Two miles west of Streator. The origin of the name is unknown. Perhaps a transfer from Altmar, Oswego County, N.Y. These are the only Altmars in the United States.

ALTO PASS. Union. Village (1882) eleven miles south-southwest of Carbondale. Established in 1875 as Quetil, a station on the Cairo and St. Louis Railroad, named for Julian Quetil, who purchased land in the area in the early 1870s. The name was changed by the railroad to Alto, presumably because of the relative elevation of the site. The word *Pass* was added in the late 1870s, perhaps to avoid confusion with Alton (Norton and Anderson, *The History of Alto Pass*, 29). Post office established Sept. 7, 1875.

ALTON [AWL tuhn, AWLT n]. Madison. City (1821, 1877). Laid out in 1817 by Rufus Easton, attorney general of Missouri in the 1820s, and named for his son,

Alton Rufus Easton. Present Alton includes the former communities of Salu, Hunterstown, Upper Alton, Buck Inn, Milton, and several others. Marquette and Jolliet passed the site of Alton in June, 1673, where they were struck by the sight of the Piasa petroglyphs (q.v. Piasa) (Norton, ed., *Centennial History of Madison County,* 468; Underwood, "A New Geography of Illinois: Madison County," 28). Post office established July 27, 1819.

ALTONA [al TO nuh]. Knox. Village (1857, 1874) seven miles southwest of Galva. Founded in 1834 as La Pier (or Lapierre) by descendants of John Thompson, regarded as the first permanent settler in the area. By 1863 the name had become Reno, probably in honor of Jesse Reno, a Union general who was killed in a Civil War battle in Maryland in 1862. The post office was called Walnut Grove, and the station on the Central Military Tract Railroad was Altona. Both the post office and village names were changed to Altona in the late 1860s. The name was chosen by officials of the CMT, perhaps for Altona, Clinton County, N.Y., itself named for Altona, Germany, once an independent city, now part of Hamburg (Bateman and Selby, eds., *Historical Encyclopedia of Illinois and Knox County,* 812; Perry, *History of Knox County,* 484). Post office established May 23, 1844, as Walnut Grove; changed to Reno Dec. 4, 1868; changed to Altona Dec. 15, 1868.

ALTORF [AL torf]. Kankakee. Six miles northwest of Kankakee. Founded in 1858 by Isaac Fred Merkle and named after the Swiss village of Altorf (Altdorf), traditionally the site of the William Tell stories (Johnson, comp., "Kankakee County Communities"). Post office established Jan. 22, 1886.

ALVIN. Vermilion. Village (1892) fifteen miles south of Hoopeston. Named for Alvan Gilbert, who was instrumental in securing a railroad station at the site. Both the Illinois Central and the Chicago and Eastern Illinois railroads called the station Alvan, but the post office department insisted on the more conventional spelling *Alvin*. About 1910 the station name was changed to agree with that of the post office. In its early years the area was known as Henpeck (q.v.) (Beckwith, *History of Vermilion County,* 669; Jones, *History of Vermilion County,* 413; Williams, *History of Vermilion County,* 498). Post office established Feb. 12, 1872.

AMBOY [AM boy]. Lee. City (1857, 1888) eleven miles southeast of Dixon. Founded about 1853 by the Illinois Central Railroad. According to one early report the community was named for Perth Amboy, N.J.; according to another, the name of choice was Bath, for Bath Township, itself named for Bath, N.Y., but Lorenzo Wasson, from near Binghamton, N.Y., took it upon himself to meet with the county commissioners and convince them that the name should be Amboy, presumably for Amboy, N.Y., and by still another the name was chosen by Asa B. Searls, also presumably for Amboy, N.Y. Still another possibility is that the name was transferred from Michigan. The Rev. Joseph Farwell moved from Amboy, Mich., to Palestine Grove (now Amboy), Ill., in 1836, where he established the first Congregational Church in the area. Farwell owned the town site at the time the community was established by the IC. A transfer from Perth Amboy, N.J., is most probable. A number of early settlers were from New Jersey, but more telling is the fact that an alternate name for Amboy is Ompoge, which is also an early name for the area around Perth Amboy, N.J., and would have been known to settlers from New Jersey but to few if any others (Ackerman, *Early Illinois Railroads*, 142; Bateman and Selby, eds., *Historical Encyclopedia of Illinois and History of Lee County*, 638; Becker, *The Biography of a Country Town*, 88, 102; Kennedy, *Recollections of the Pioneers of Lee County*, 57; F. Stevens, *History of Lee County*, 273). Post office established Sept. 19, 1853; discontinued Jan. 31, 1855. The Binghampton post office was changed to Amboy March 31, 1855.

AMENIA [uh MEEN ee uh]. Piatt. Four miles west of Monticello. Amenia grew around a grain elevator established by Samuel Allerton (q.v. Allerton). Named for Allerton's birthplace, Amenia, Dutchess County, N.Y. (personal communication from the Piatt County Historical and Genealogical Society).

AMENT CORNERS [ah MENT]. Kendall. Two miles south of Yorkville. Founded about 1831 by early settler Edward Ament and his brothers, Hiram, Anson, Alfred, and Calvin (Farren, ed., *A Bicentennial History*, 103).

AMERICA. Pulaski. Nine miles northeast of Cairo. Laid out about 1817 by Dr. William Alexander, for whom Alexander County is named, acting as agent for a Cincinnati land company, which expected that this would become a major American city and perhaps even the new inland capital of the United States. On the original plat, streets were named for each of the existing states and for famous Americans. America was the seat of Alexander County from 1819 until 1833 when it was moved to Unity (Allen, *Legends and Lore of Southern Illinois*, 350; *Pulaski County*, 9–10). Post office established Aug. 29, 1820.

AMES. Monroe. Eighteen miles west of Sparta. Originally called Yankeetown for the large number of settlers from New England; subsequently named for the Ames family (Klein, ed., *Arrowheads to Aerojets*, 596). Post office established June 23, 1881.

AMITY. Livingston. Township. The community of Amity, now part of Cornell, was laid out by Willard D. Blake about 1871 and named from Amity Township. The name is probably a transfer from an Amity further east, perhaps Amity, Ohio. From Latin "pleasant, agreeable" (*History of Livingston County, Illinois* [1878], 415). Post office established June 30, 1858.

ANCHOR. McLean. Village (1959) twelve miles south of Fairbury. Founded by site owner Daniel B. Stewart in 1880 and named from Anchor Township, which was probably named by George R. Buck, the first township supervisor and a local minister, who likely took the name from a popular hymn of the day, "My Soul Is Anchored in the Cross" (Hoffman, *History of Lawndale*, 49, 62). Post office established March 10, 1880.

ANCONA [an KO nuh]. Livingston. Five miles south-southwest of Streator. Laid out in 1854 by Orson Shackleton and Joseph Gumm as a station on the Air Line Railroad, extended from Terre Haute to Council Bluffs. The name was proposed by miners from Ancona, Italy, who worked the coal mines around Streator. This is the only Ancona in the United States (*History of Livingston County, Illinois* [1991], 14). Post office established July 17, 1856.

ANDALUSIA [an duh LOO zhuh]. Rock Island. Village (1884) seven miles southwest of Rock Island. Founded as Rockport in 1836. The site was purchased at a tax sale in 1845 by Napoleon Bonaparte Buford and renamed Andalusia by Buford's wife for the province in southern Spain (Bateman and Selby, eds., *Historical Encyclopedia of Illinois and History of Rock Island County*, 942). Post office established April 24, 1846.

ANDERSON. Township. Clark. Named for postmaster James B. Anderson. The Anderson post office operated from Dec. 30, 1850 until March 16, 1860 (Adams, comp., *Illinois Place Names*).

ANDOVER. Henry. Village (1895) five miles west of Cambridge. Established about 1835 by the New York Association as the Andover Colony, named for Andover, N.Y. The choice of the name was possibly influenced by one or another of the Andovers in New England. The colony was organized and financed largely by the Rev. Ithamar Pillsbury, a Presbyterian minister who modeled the community on New Haven, Conn., and envisioned it as a western center of learning, religion, and commerce. Pillsbury's Connecticut Association founded Wethersfield (q.v.) near Kewanee at about the same time (*History of Henry County*, 137; Swank, *Historic Henry County*, 11). Post office established May 15, 1837.

ANNA. Union. City (1865, 1872). Laid out in 1853 with construction of the Illinois Central Railroad by site owner Winstead Davie and Col. Lewis T. Ashley, division engineer for the IC. Davie, a county clerk and probate judge from Jonesboro, named the community for his wife, Anna Willard Davie (*One Hundred Years of Progress: The Centennial History of Anna*, 17). Post office established March 14, 1855.

ANNAPOLIS [uh NAP luhs]. Crawford. Nine miles north-northwest of Robinson. Named about 1879 by Silas Howell for his former home, Annapolis, Md. (Bateman and Selby, eds., *Illinois Historical Crawford County Biographical*, 645). Also known as Spencerville. Post office established April 21, 1858.

ANNAWAN [AN uh wahn]. Henry. Town (1869) ten miles north of Kewanee. Several accounts, copied uncritically from one to another, claim that the community was named for a local Winnebago leader named Annawan. The actual source of the name is indeed a Native American leader named Annawan, but he was neither a Winnebago nor a local. The historical Annawan was a leader of the Wampanoag Tribe of Massachusetts around the time of King Philip's War in the 1670s. The name was probably brought to Illinois by Charles Atkinson, from Newburyport, Mass., who founded Annawan about 1853. He was also the founder of Atkinson, five miles northwest of Annawan, and a cofounder of Moline (*History of Henry County,* 528; Kiner, *History of Henry County,* 417; Vogel, *Indian Place Names in Illinois*). Post office established April 25, 1854.

ANTIOCH [AN tee ahk]. Lake. Village (1857, 1892) fifteen miles west of Zion. Founded about 1843 by the Disciples of Christ and named for the city in Asia Minor where the disciples of Jesus were first called Christians. The former communities of Apostleville, Jerico, and the Land of Nod are now part of the village of Antioch (Adams, comp., *Illinois Place Names; Past and Present of Lake County,* 242). Post office established Dec. 9, 1845.

APPALONIA. Morgan. Former community. Laid out in the mid-1830s near Waverly. The name was probably inspired by nearby Apple Creek, often spelled *Appall* Creek in early accounts. The Appalonia School was located about six miles southeast of White Hall (Hageman, comp., *Partial Encyclopedia of Waverly,* 8). Post office established Dec. 19, 1832, as Apple Creek.

APPANOOSE [AP uh noos]. Hancock. Township. The projected town of Appanoose was founded in 1836 by pioneers Edward White and Amzi Doolittle. The community never materialized beyond a town plat, but it did provide a name for the township. Named for Appanoose (Child), a Meskwaki (Fox) leader who lived along the Des Moines River near present Ottumwa, Iowa. Appanoose was considered friendly to European settlers because he remained neutral during the Black Hawk War (Bateman and Selby, eds., *Historical Encyclopedia of Illinois and History of Hancock County,* 1952–53; Vogel, *Iowa Place Names of Indian Origin*). Post office established July 18, 1836.

APPLE RIVER. Jo Daviess. Village (1876) seventeen miles northeast of Galena. Named from Apple River, itself probably a translation of Rivière de la Pomme (River of Apples), named for the local crab apple trees. Possibly named for Henry Apple, a German immigrant reportedly killed by the Sauk in the early days of the Black Hawk War of 1832 (Ackerman, *Early Illinois Railroads,* 139; Bateman and Selby, eds., *Historical Encyclopedia of Illinois and History of Jo Daviess County,* 633). Post office established Dec. 11, 1828.

APTAKISIC [ap tuh KIS ik]. Lake. Four miles south of Libertyville. Aptakisic (Op-ta-gu-shick, literally "Half Sky," taken to mean "Half Day") was a Potawatomi leader whose village was in the area northwest of Chicago in the 1830s. He was perhaps so named because he once performed in half a day a task that normally took a full day (personal communication with Michael McCafferty; Vogel, *Indian Place Names in Illinois*). Post office established July 29, 1889.

ARCADIA. Morgan. Six miles north of Jacksonville. Founded in 1829 as New Lexington by the Rev. Samuel Bristow, a Baptist minister. The community took the name of the Arcadia post office in 1853. Arcadia was a district in ancient Greece that came to be seen as a land of simplicity and purity, a near paradise on earth. Perhaps a transfer; Arcadia is a popular place name in the United States, occurring in about half the states (Bateman and Selby, eds., *Historical Encyclopedia of Illinois and History of Morgan County*, 660). Post office established Oct. 3, 1831.

ARCHER HEIGHTS. Cook. Chicago community. Named from Archer Avenue, itself named for William B. Archer, a commissioner of the Illinois and Michigan Canal in the late 1830s (Kitagawa and Taeuber, eds., *Local Community Fact Book*, 128).

ARCHIE. Vermilion. Eleven miles southwest of Georgetown. Named for Archie McDonald, who donated land for a station on the line of the Chicago and Ohio River Railroad in 1881 (Tuggle, comp., *Stories of Historical Days*, 13; Underwood, "A New Geography of Illinois: Vermilion County," 37). Post office established March 27, 1882.

ARCOLA [ahr KOL uh]. Douglas. City (1865, 1873). Established as Okaw (q.v.) by the Illinois Central Railroad in 1855. The name was soon changed to Arcola to avoid duplicating the Okaw post office in Washington County. The source of the name is uncertain. Several early historians (including Ackerman, who wrote with the archives of the IC at his disposal) claim that the name is a transfer from the village of Arcole in northern Italy, where Napoleon defeated an Austrian army in 1796. Others argue that the name was created on the spot. In the words of an early county history, "Mr. E. Hewitt, the first Illinois Central Railroad agent at this point, after cudgeling his brains to no effect, observing a knot of citizens near, came out of his office at the depot, and . . . asked for suggestions, whereupon James Kearney said 'Arcola'" (*County of Douglas*, 190). There are several dozen Arcolas in the eastern states, and one or more of these may have influenced the naming of Arcola, Ill. It is also possible that the name is a creation of the Illinois Central Railroad, perhaps based upon the name *Tuscola*, established by the IC ten miles north of Arcola at about the same time (Ackerman, *Early Illinois Railroads*, 128; Gresham, comp., *Historical and Biographical Record*, 26; Redlich, *The Postal History of Coles County*, 139). Post office established July 23, 1857.

ARENZVILLE [EHR uns vil]. Cass, Morgan. Village (1893) twelve miles north-northwest of Jacksonville. Founded about 1839 by Francis A. Arenz, an emigrant from Blakenburg, Prussia. Arenz also founded the first newspaper in the area, the *Beardstown Chronicle and Illinois Bounty Land Advertiser,* in 1839 (Bateman and Selby, eds., *Historical Encyclopedia of Illinois and History of Cass County,* 800). Post office established April 24, 1840.

ARGENTA [ahr JEN tuh]. Macon. Village (1891) nine miles northeast of Decatur. Founded in 1874 as a companion town to Oreana (q.v.) and reportedly named by a Mr. Wood and a Mr. Smith, officials of the Illinois Central Railroad, for a Union Pacific station in the West, possibly Argenta, Nev., itself named from Latin *argentum* (silver) (Richmond, *Centennial History of Decatur,* 96). Post office established July 6, 1870, as Newburgh; changed to Argenta Feb. 2, 1874.

ARGYLE [ahr GEYEL]. Boone, Winnebago. Six miles northeast of Rockford. Formerly known as the Kintyre settlement, named by settlers from Kintyre, Argyleshire, Scotland. Formerly established as Argyle, a station on the Kenosha and Rockford Railway, by John Andrew about 1860 (Harvey, *The Argyle Settlement,* 88). Post office established March 22, 1860, as Kintyre; changed to Argyle Sept. 20, 1869.

ARGYLE PARK. Cook. Chicago community. Named by Chicago alderman and land developer James A. Campbell for his ancestor, Archibald Campbell, Marquess and Second Duke of Argyll, Scotland (Karlen, *Chicago's Crabgrass Communities,* 129).

ARISPIE. Bureau. Township. Named from Arizpe, Sonora, Mexico. The name was brought to Illinois by soldiers returning from the Mexican War. Spelled *Arizpe* until about 1890 (Leonard, ed., *Big Bureau,* 74). Post office established April 11, 1848, as Arispe.

ARLINGTON. Bureau. Village (1874) eight miles southwest of Mendota. Founded by Capt. Michael Kennedy with construction of the Chicago, Burlington and Quincy Railroad about 1853 and named for Kennedy's former home, Arlington, Dutchess County, N.Y. Originally the name of several English villages, "Arlington" was transferred to Virginia in the seventeenth century and was the name of Robert E. Lee's estate, part of which is now the site of Arlington National Cemetery. There are more than a hundred Arlingtons in the United States, making this one of the more popular American place names. Historical Arlingtons in Illinois include Arlington Heights in St. Clair County (now part of Fairmont City), Arlington Heights in Winnebago County (now part of Rockford), Arlington Heights in Sangamon County (now part of Springfield), Arlington Place in St. Clair County (now part of East St. Louis), and Arlington Place in Peoria County (now part of Peoria) (Leonard, ed., *Big Bureau,* 67; www.outfitters.com/illinois/bureau/communities_bureau.html). Post office established Aug. 19, 1850.

ARLINGTON HEIGHTS. Cook. Village (1887). Platted in 1854 as Dunton, a station on the Illinois and Wisconsin Railroad, by site owner William H. Dunton. The

Dunton name became something of a liability, thought to diminish the attractiveness of the community, and was changed to Arlington and then to Arlington Heights by popular referendum in 1874. The specific reasons for the choice of Arlington are unknown. Perhaps a transfer. The fact that Arlington National Cemetery was established a few years before may have had an influence as well (Hansen, ed., *Illinois*, 568; Souter, ed., *Chronicle of a Prairie Town*, 229). Post office established Feb. 21, 1854, as West Wheeling; changed to Dunton May 8, 1861; changed to Arlington Heights March 9, 1874.

ARMINGTON. Tazewell. Village (1904) twelve miles north-northeast of Lincoln. Founded in 1855 by Hesekiah Armington, the first supervisor of Hittle township (Bateman and Selby, eds., *Historical Encyclopedia of Illinois and History of Tazewell County*, 857). Post office established Feb. 8, 1849.

ARMSTRONG. Vermilion. Fourteen miles east of Rantoul. Founded about 1876 by Thomas and Henry Armstrong as a station on the line of the Havana, Rantoul and Eastern Railroad (Tuggle, comp., *Stories of Historical Days*, 10). Post office established May 2, 1876.

ARNOLD. Carroll. Six miles northeast of Savanna. Named for pioneer Daniel Arnold, who settled at what became known as Arnold's Grove about 1840 (Thiem, ed., *Carroll County*, 97).

ARNOLD. Morgan. Four miles west of Jacksonville. Established about 1888. Named for the Arnold family. J. W. Arnold was an early settler, and Thomas J. Arnold was an early postmaster (Adams, comp., *Illinois Place Names;* Hutchison, "Old Morgan County Village"). Post office established July 13, 1888.

AROMA PARK [uh ROM uh]. Kankakee. Two miles southeast of Kankakee. Founded in 1852 by Alvin and Slocum Wilbur, who created the word *Aroma* by playing on the name of their friend and associate James L. Romer. Reportedly, possible confusion between Aroma and Aurora led to changing the name to Waldron in 1872. It was changed back to Aroma, and the word *Park* was added about 1915 (Houde and Klasey, *Of the People*, 54). Post office established Feb. 1, 1852, as Aroma; changed to Waldron Nov. 25, 1872; changed to Aroma Park Sept. 22, 1915.

ARRINGTON. Wayne. Township. Named from Arrington Prairie, itself named for early settler Charles Arrington. The community of Arrington is now called Sims (q.v.) (*History of Wayne and Clay Counties*, 262).

ARROWSMITH. McLean. Village (1890) thirteen miles west of Gibson City. Arrowsmith Township was named about 1858 for Ezekiel Arrowsmith, an early settler and first township supervisor. The community of Arrowsmith was founded about 1870 and took its name from the township. The post office was established as Senex; the reason for this unusual name is unknown (Bateman and Selby, eds., *Historical Encyclopedia of Illinois and History of McLean County*, 663, 675;

Townley, *Historic McLean,* 18). Post office established July 29, 1834, as Senex; changed to Arrowsmith Dec. 18, 1872.

ARTHUR. Douglas, Moultrie. Village (1877). Established in 1872 by the Paris and Decatur Railroad as Glasgow. Renamed with submission of the post office application by Robert G. Harvey, president of the P&D, who suggested the name in honor of his brother, Arthur (*Combined History of Shelby and Moultrie Counties,* 288–89; Miller, *History of Arthur,* 6). Post office established Jan. 20, 1873.

ASH GROVE. Iroquois. Township. An original Iroquois County township, organized in 1855. According to Dowling (*History of Iroquois County,* 25), so named "because of a real big, old ash tree that had fallen across the creek."

ASHKUM. Iroquois. Village (1875) fifteen miles south-southwest of Kankakee. Founded in 1856 and named for Ashkum, a Potawatomi leader whose name appears in a number of treaties of the 1820s and 1830s and whose main village was on the Eel River east of Terre Haute. The word *Ashkum* reportedly means "more and more" or "more so" (Edmunds, *The Potawatomis,* 256; Vogel, *Indian Place Names in Illinois*). Post office established June 24, 1856.

ASHLAND [ASH luhnd]. Cass. Village (1869, 1872) sixteen miles northwest of Springfield. Founded in 1857 as a station on the Jacksonville, Petersburg and Tonica Railroad and named for Henry Clay's estate, Ashland, in Lexington, Ky. The consortium of land developers that purchased the site included Richard Yates, a future governor of Illinois (q.v. Yates). Ashland Township was formerly known as Lancaster, probably named for Lancaster, Ky. (Bateman and Selby, eds., *Historical Encyclopedia of Illinois and History of Cass County,* 802). Post office established Oct. 23, 1857.

ASHLEY. Washington. City (1857, 1876) twelve miles south of Centralia. Probably named for L. W. Ashley, a division engineer for the Illinois Central Railroad. The choice of the name may have been influenced by John Ashley, an early settler (Ackerman, *Early Illinois Railroads,* 123; Hansen, ed., *Illinois,* 504–5). Post office established June 26, 1854.

ASHMORE. Coles. Village (1873) eight miles east-northeast of Charleston. Laid out in 1855 by Hezekiah Ashmore and James D. Austin. The Ashmores were early settlers in the area, arriving about 1829. James M. Ashmore was the first postmaster (Perrin, Graham, and Blair, *History of Coles County,* 403; Redlich, *The Postal History of Coles County,* 68). Post office established Nov. 9, 1855.

ASHTON. Lee. Village (1867, 1872) eight miles southwest of Rochelle. Established by the Galena and Chicago Union Railroad in 1855 as Ogle Station, named for Ogle County. The community was redistricted out of Ogle County when Lee County was formed in 1839. The source of the name is unknown. There is little to recommend the suggestion that the village was named Ashton because this was the site where wood-burning locomotives dumped their ashes (Bateman and Selby, eds., *Historical Encyclopedia of Illinois and History of Lee County;* Brass, "Ashton," 13). Post office established July 14, 1855, as Ogle Station; changed to Ashton March 8, 1867.

ASSUMPTION. Christian. City (1876) eight miles north of Pana. Founded in 1852 by the Illinois Central Railroad as Tacusa. In 1856 E. E. Malhiot established a colony alongside Tacusa that was eventually settled by some one hundred French Canadian families. Malhiot, reportedly a Louisiana state senator, named the colony Assumption, possibly for Assumption Parish, La. (Goudy, *History of Christian County,* 256–57, 268). Post office established Nov. 9, 1885, as Tacusa; changed to Assumption March 10, 1858.

ASTORIA. Fulton. Town (1839) fifteen miles southwest of Lewistown. The adjacent communities of Washington, founded in 1836, and Vienna, founded in 1837, merged in 1839 as Astoria, named for John Jacob Astor, whose American Fur Company loaded pelts for transport on the Illinois River from near the site (Hansen, ed., *Illinois,* 663). Post office established Sept. 9, 1836, as Washington; changed to Astoria Sept. 13, 1837.

ATHENS [AY thuhnz]. Menard. City (1875) ten miles north of Springfield. Previously known as Rogers, named for Henry Clay Rogers, who brought his family from Otsego County, N.Y., in the late 1820s. The community was formally laid out as Athens by Harry Riggin and Abner Hall in 1831. The reason for the choice of the name is unclear. It may have been a result of the general fascination for classical names, which was characteristic of American place naming in the first half of the nineteenth century, or Riggin as an individual may have been attracted to classical names. Twelve years earlier, he and his brother founded Troy in Madison County. It is also possible that Riggin simply transferred both names from his home state of Tennessee (Hanford and O'Hara, *Menard County,* 293; *Illustrated Atlas Map of Menard County,* 15; Miller, *Past and Present,* 234). Post office established Jan. 2, 1828, as Rogers; changed to Athens Nov. 4, 1831.

ATHERTON [ATH er tuhn]. Pulaski. Former community. Named for Aaron Atherton, who established the first settlement in what is now Pulaski County in 1816. Atherton, a Baptist minister, organized the Shiloh Baptist Church, claimed to be the second-oldest church in Illinois, in his home in 1817. The church was located about three miles north of Mounds (Moyer, *Moyers' Brief History,* 25; *Pulaski County,* 71).

ATKINSON. Henry. Town (1867) seven miles east-southeast of Geneseo. Founded in 1856 by Charles Atkinson, site owner and first county treasurer. Atkinson was also the founder of Annawan, five miles southeast of Atkinson, and a cofounder of Moline (*History of Henry County,* 530). Post office established Nov. 6, 1855, as Cedar Hill; changed to Atkinson May 31, 1856.

ATLANTA. Logan. City (1855, 1912). Founded in 1853 as Xenia by settlers from Xenia, Ohio. When it was learned that there was an existing Xenia in Illinois, Richard Gill, one of the site owners, suggested changing the name to Atlanta, for Atlanta, Ga., which he had recently visited. For nearly a decade the post office was called Atalanta, the result of either a scribal error or confusion between Atlanta and Atalanta of classical Greek mythology (*History of Atlanta*, 3, 5; Stringer, *History of Logan County*, 601). Post office established Nov. 26, 1847, as New Castle; changed to Atalanta Oct. 20, 1853; changed to Atlanta March 4, 1861.

ATLAS. Pike. Ten miles southwest of Pittsfield. Founded by William Ross and Rufus Brown in 1823. As reported in *The Jess M. Thompson Pike County History*, "The name of Atlas . . . was suggested by one of the Rosses who recalled the day in 1820 when the little party of home-seekers, after weeks of weary travel, beheld before them the beautiful prairie at the foot of the Mississippi bluffs. One of their number [William Ross], as they paused in admiration of the scene, exclaimed 'At last!,' whence the name 'Atlas'" (12). Thompson fully realized that this account had all the trappings of popular etymology, but his extensive research into the origin of the name, which included reports of interviews with many of the pioneers of Atlas, led him to conclude, "I have found no better explanation" (12). Atlas was the seat of Pike County from 1824 until 1833, when it was moved to Pittsfield. Post office established May 6, 1822, as Ross Settlement; changed to Atlas Dec. 23, 1825.

ATTERBERRY. Menard. Five miles northwest of Petersburg. Laid out by site owner Daniel Atterberry in 1872 as a station on the Springfield and Northwestern Railroad (Hanford and O'Hara, *Menard County*, 295). Post office established July 1, 1872, as Atterberry Station; changed to Atterberry May 15, 1883.

ATTILA. Williamson. Eight miles northeast of Marion. Named from the Attila post office, itself named by the first postmaster, William N. Mitchell, an ancient history buff, for Attila, the fifth-century king of the Huns (the "Scourge of God"). The community was informally known as Poor-do, meaning a hard go or a difficult enterprise, in reference to a wholesale tobacco business established by Richard P. Dodds, whose fellow citizens thought this was a poor choice of business at an unpromising location. It was said, "It will be a poor do for them to try and do any business there to any amount" (Hubbs, *Pioneer Folks and Places*). This is the only community named Attila in the United States. Post office established July 9, 1854.

ATWOOD. Douglas, Piatt. Village (1844) nine miles west of Tuscola. The origin of the name is uncertain. It is perhaps the name of an early settler or a transfer from an Atwood in an eastern state. According to an often-repeated story, but undoubtedly a popular etymology, early settlers agreed to meet at a nearby grove, saying "see you at the wood," which became Atwood. Equally implausible is the notion that the name derives from the claim that the early settlement was known as the "one at the wood" (Bateman and Selby, eds., *Historical Encyclopedia of Illinois and History of Piatt County*, 700; *Illinois Guide*). Post office established Jan. 7, 1874.

AUBURN [AW bern]. Ultimately from Auburn in Yorkshire, England. The name was popularized by Oliver Goldsmith's poem "The Deserted Village" (1770), which begins "Sweet Auburn: loveliest village of the plain." In the United States, the name first appeared at the beginning of the nineteenth century in New York. It became popular and quickly spread to other parts of the country. In Illinois, most of the two dozen or so occurrences of Auburn are transfers by settlers from Auburn, Cayuga County, N.Y. Some may be by way of Auburns in Ohio or Indiana.

AUBURN. Sangamon. City (1865, 1872). Old Auburn was founded in 1835 about a mile northwest of the present location by Thomas Eastman and his sons, Asa and George, and named by Eastman's daughter, Hannah, for Auburn, their former home in Androscoggin County, Me. Present Auburn is on the site of Wineman, established for the Alton and Sangamon Railroad by Philip Wineman about 1853. When Old Auburn failed, Asa Eastman bought Wineman and renamed it Auburn (Grubbs, "Origins of Auburn"). Post office established Nov. 29, 1838, as Sugar Creek; changed to Auburn March 22, 1839.

AUDUBON. Montgomery. Township. Audubon Township was named for Audubon, now known as Ohlman (q.v.), which was established as a planned community by colonists from Massachusetts about 1834. Probably named for John James Audubon, at the time a well-known naturalist and ornithologist. In 1843 the Illinois legislature authorized the organization of Audubon County, to be created from parts of Shelby, Montgomery, and Fayette counties, but the proposal was rejected by popular vote (Bateman and Selby, eds., *Historical Encyclopedia of Illinois and History of Montgomery County*, 838; Sublett, *Paper Counties*, 57; Traylor, *Past and Present of Montgomery County*, 714). Post office established Oct. 15, 1839.

AUGSBURG [AWGZ berg]. Fayette. Seven miles southeast of Vandalia. Named about 1898 by storekeeper Gottfried Metzger for Augsburg, Germany, the birthplace of the local pastor, a Rev. Suhren (Hanabarger, "Fayette County Place Names," 43). Post office established Jan. 13, 1898.

AUGUSTA. Hancock. Village (1859, 1879) twenty miles southwest of Macomb. Founded about 1832 by Joel Catlin, William D. Abernethy, and Samuel B. Mead. Named for Augusta, Ga., where Catlin had lived for several years before coming to Illinois (*History of Hancock County*, 173). Post office established March 12, 1834.

AURORA. Clark. Former community north of Darwin. Aurora was established in 1819 as the seat of Clark County; it served in this capacity until 1823, when the seat was moved to Darwin. Aurora has now disappeared, but its name is preserved in Aurora Bend, an area named from a former loop in the Wabash River about seven miles southeast of Marshall. The name may be a transfer from New York, but it is more likely taken directly from Latin *aurora* (dawn) (*History of Marshall, Illinois and Eastern Clark County,* 22).

AURORA [uh ROR uh]. Kane. City (1863, 1887). The area was originally known as the Big Woods for the forest that extended some twenty-five miles along the Fox River. Samuel and Joseph McCarty emigrated from Elmira, N.Y., in the mid-1830s, dammed the river and built a sawmill, giving rise to the name *McCarty's Mills.* When the post office was established in 1837 there was a good deal of sentiment for naming it Waubonsee after the Potawatomi leader whose main village was nearby, but Elias Terry, a cousin of the McCartys, proposed Aurora for his former home, Aurora, Cayuga County, N.Y., itself named from Latin for "morning" or "dawn," which is coincidentally similar in meaning to Waubonsee, reported to mean daybreak, morning light (Burton, *Aurora,* 10; Seits, "The Names of Kane County," 169). Post office established March 2, 1837.

AUSTIN. Cook. Far west Chicago community. Founded in 1866 as Austinville by developer Henry W. Austin (Karlen, *Chicago's Crabgrass Communities,* 287). Post office established April 5, 1867.

AUSTIN. Macon. Township. Named for Benjamin R. Austin, first justice of the peace and first surveyor of Macon County. Austin platted the city of Decatur in 1829 (Richmond, *Centennial History of Decatur,* 95, 428).

AUX SABLE [aw SAY buhl]. Grundy. Four miles northeast of Morris. Named from Aux Sable Creek, itself probably named from French *aux sable* (at the dark or sandy water), but possibly a development from *eau sable* (sandy water) (Brown, ed., *Grundy County,* 47). Post office established May 29, 1841.

AVA [AY vuh]. Jackson. City (1894) eight miles southeast of the intersection of Jackson, Perry, and Randolph counties. The area was first known as Headquarters, named after a local tavern. Platted about 1875 with construction of the Narrow Gauge Railroad. Named for Ava Johnson, the daughter of site owner and postmaster George W. Johnson (*Ava,* 1). Post office established July 15, 1857.

AVENA [uh VEE nuh]. Fayette. Ten miles east-northeast of Vandalia. Laid out in 1870 by J. H. Henry. The source of the name is unknown. Avena is Spanish for "oats," and the namer may have noticed some fields of wild oats nearby. The only other Avena in the United States is in San Joaquin County, Calif., founded several decades after Avena, Ill. (Hanabarger, "Fayette County Place Names," 43). Post office established Feb. 24, 1874.

AVERYVILLE [AYV ree vil]. Peoria. Named for the Avery Manufacturing Company, established by Cyrus M. Avery and his brother, Hanneman Avery, in the 1880s. The company manufactured planters, threshers, and other farm machinery. Now part of Peoria (Gannett, *The Origin of Certain Place Names*).

AVISTON [AY vis tuhn]. Clinton. Village (1874) four miles west of Breese. Laid out in 1860 by J. W. Dugger and named from the Aviston post office, itself named for John Avis, a gunsmith and early entrepreneur (*Aviston Quasquicentennial*, 5). Post office established July 14, 1836.

AVOCA [uh VO kuh]. Livingston. Township and former community six miles southeast of Pontiac. Laid out in 1854 by Woodford G. McDowell (q.v. McDowell) and named from the Avoca post office, itself named by Nicholas Hefner, the first postmaster. Avoca is the name of a valley and river in County Wicklow, Ireland, where the Avonbeg and Avonmore rivers join. The name was popularized by Thomas Moore's poem "The Meeting of the Waters," which contains the lines "Sweet vale of Avoca! How calm could I rest / In thy bosom of shade, with the friends I love best." It is a popular place name in the United States, occurring in about twenty states. Avoca, Ill., is likely a transfer from an Avoca further east, possibly Avoca, Lawrence County, Ind. (*History of Livingston County* [1878], 377). Post office established June 7, 1838.

AVON [AY vahn]. Fulton. Village (1867, 1873) eight miles northeast of Bushnell. Founded about 1852 as Woodville by site owners Ira, Orlando, Jonas, Edwin, and Riverus Woods, settlers from New York. The post office had been established in 1843 as Woodstock. In April 1852 the U.S. postmaster general changed the name of the Woodstock post office to Avon (probably named for Avon, N.Y.); the community's name was changed to Avon shortly thereafter (Fennessy and Woods, comps., *Centennial History of Avon*, 2–3; *History of Fulton County*, 880–81).

AVON. Township. Lake. Named by settlers from Avon, Livingston County, N.Y., itself named for the River Avon in Warwickshire, England. Other names under consideration at the time of township formation in 1849 were Hainesville and Eureka (Dretske, *What's in a Name?*).

AVONDALE. Cook. Chicago community. Named by developer John L. Cochran for Avondale, Pa., near his home in Philadelphia (Karlen, *Chicago's Crabgrass Communities*, 174).

AYERS. Bond. Five miles north-northwest of Greenville. Founded about 1895 and named for Augusta E., John A., and Marshall P. Ayers (Bateman and Selby, eds., *Historical Encyclopedia of Illinois and History of Bond County*, 637). Post office established Aug. 22, 1895.

AZOTUS. Pope. Former community two and a half miles south of Bay City. Named from the Old Azotus Church, organized in the late 1840s and destroyed by a tornado in the early 1880s. The name *Azotus* is the Latin form of *Ashdad*, the biblical city mentioned in Isaiah, First Samuel, and elsewhere, some thirty miles west of Jerusalem. The Azotus community persisted into the late 1950s; the name is preserved by the Azotus Cemetery some twelve miles east-northeast of Metropolis (Allen, *Pope County Notes,* 69). Post office established Aug. 17, 1895.

B

BABYLON. Fulton. Eight miles east-northeast of Bushnell. Founded in 1837 by Philip Aylesworth, one of the founders of Meredosia (q.v.). The immediate source of the name is unknown. Babylon may be named directly for the ancient city now in Iraq, or it may be a transfer, perhaps from Babylon, N.Y. (Irwin, *A to Z Fulton County*). Post office established April 9, 1875.

BADER [BAY der]. Schuyler. Eleven miles north of Beardstown. Founded in 1870 as Osceola. To avoid duplication of post offices, the community was renamed for William Bader, operator of a local grain elevator (*Schuyler County*, 76). Post office established Oct. 8, 1872, as Baders; changed to Bader Dec. 23, 1907.

BAGDAD. Douglas. Former community in Bourbon Township. The source of the name is unknown. Possibly a transfer from Ohio or New York. The Bagdad Cemetery (now called Campbell Cemetery) is about four miles west of Arcola (Bateman and Selby, eds., *Illinois Historical Douglas County Biographical*, 623).

BAILEYVILLE. Ogle. Six miles south-southeast of Freeport. Named for Orville, Samuel, and Ransom Bailey, settlers from Vermont who arrived in the mid-1850s (*Bicentennial History of Ogle County*, 270). Post office established July 19, 1852, as Crane's Grove; changed to Baileyville April 10, 1858.

BAINBRIDGE. Schuyler. Township. Named for William Bainbridge (1774–1833), a naval commander in the War of 1812 and the war with Tripoli. Probably a transfer by settlers from Bainbridge, Putnam County, Ind., itself named for the same William Bainbridge, or from Bainbridge, Ky. (Baker, *From Needmore to Prosperity;* Walker, ed., *Bainbridge Township*, 2).

BAINBRIDGE. Williamson. Named for the first postmaster Allen Bainbridge, his brother, John, or both. Bainbridge was the temporary first seat of Williamson County, serving from February 1839 until Marion was established later that year. The site of Bainbridge is now part of Marion. The name is preserved by the Bainbridge Cemetery west of Marion (Allen, *Legends and Lore of Southern Illinois*, 342; Hubbs, *Pioneer Folks and Places*). Post office established Feb. 16, 1837.

BAKER. LaSalle. Six miles south-southeast of Earlville. Named for Auston Baker Sanderson, a local farmer. Previously known as Munson (Rasmusen, *LaSalle County Lore*, 35). Post office established Nov. 28, 1890.

BAKERS CROSSROADS. Williamson. Nine miles southeast of Carbondale on Devils Kitchen Lake. Named for the three Drs. Baker, Alonzo P., Griffin J., and

Miles D., brothers who practiced medicine in the area until the 1920s (Hubbs, *Pioneer Folks and Places*).

BAKERVILLE. Jefferson. Three miles south of Mount Vernon. Named for John Baker, proprietor of a general store near the line of the Chicago and Eastern Illinois Railroad in the early 1900s. Also known as Cub(b), named from Cubb Prairie (www.genealogytrails.com/ill/jefferson/ghostowns.html). Post office established March 26, 1868, as Cub Prairie.

BALCOM. Union. Three miles southeast of Anna. Named for and probably by S. F. Balcom, an official of the Illinois Central Railroad (Mohlenbrock, "A New Geography of Illinois: Union County," 31). Post office established Feb. 21, 1888.

BALD BLUFF. Henderson. Seven miles northest of Oquawka. Named from Bald Bluff, an elliptical summit claimed to be the highest point in Henderson County, so sparsely vegetated that it appeared to be barren (Bateman and Selby, eds., *Historical Encyclopedia of Illinois and History of Henderson County*, 637). Post office established Oct. 11, 1899.

BALL. Sangamon. Township. Named for James A. Ball, an early settler and a soldier in the Winnebago and Black Hawk wars (Bateman and Selby, eds., *Historical Encyclopedia of Illinois and History of Sangamon County*, 794).

BANDOW. Cook. Named for Peter W. Bandow, the first postmaster. Now part of Chicago (Karlen, *Chicago's Crabgrass Communities*, 192). Post office established Jan. 11, 1884.

BANGS LAKE. Lake. Named for Justus Bangs, believed to be the first permanent settler in Wauconda Township, who arrived about 1836. The lake is now encircled by Wauconda (Dretske, *What's in a Name?*).

BANKLICK. Saline, Williamson. Ten miles northwest of Harrisburg. Named from Bank Lick Creek (now called Prairie Creek), so named for the salt deposits frequented by wild animals (Hubbs, *Pioneer Folks and Places*; Musgrove, "Saline County Gazetteer"). Post office established Oct. 1, 1897.

BANNOCKBURN. Lake. Village (1929) five miles southeast of Libertyville. Founded in 1924 by developer William Atkin. Probably named for Bannockburn, the city in central Scotland where Robert the Bruce defeated the English in 1314 (Adams, comp., *Illinois Place Names*).

BARBERS CORNERS. Will. Northern part of Bolingbrook. Named for Capt. John Barber, an early settler of the 1830s (*"Where There's a Will . . . ,"* 43). Post office established Dec. 21, 1846.

BARCLAY. Sangamon. Village (1904) five miles northeast of Springfield. Founded by the Barclay Coal and Mining Company, which opened a shaft at the site in 1872. The mine was abandoned in 1926. The source of the Barclay name is unknown. It was likely chosen by the mine owner, George N. Black, who was instrumental in the building of the Gilman, Clinton and Springfield Railroad

(Bateman and Selby, eds., *Historical Encyclopedia of Illinois and History of Sangamon County,* 1052–53; Wallace, *Past and Present,* 76). Post office established Jan. 25, 1872.

BARDOLPH [BAHR dawlf]. McDonough. Village (1869, 1876) five miles northeast of Macomb. Founded in 1854 as Randolph, named for founder William H. Randolph. The name was changed shortly thereafter to avoid duplicating the name of an existing post office. The source of "Bardolph" is uncertain. It may have been formed from "Randolph" by replacing the first syllable with part of the name of a family member or business associate (*History of McDonough County,* 999). Post office established July 9, 1856.

BARNETT. DeWitt. Township. Named for Franklin Barnett, who at the time of township formation in 1859 was the oldest living resident (*History of DeWitt County* [1910], 315).

BARNHILL. Wayne. Six miles south of Fairfield. Originally called Fairfield. The name was changed to Douglas in June of 1860 in honor of Sen. Stephen A. Douglas. For unknown reasons, but probably having to do with Douglas's political views, the name was changed in early September of 1860 to Barnhill for the Barnhill family, especially Hardin and George Barnhill, who built the first houses in the town of Fairfield (*History of Wayne and Clay Counties,* 179). Post office established Feb. 10, 1871.

BARR. Macoupin. Six miles west-southwest of Palmyra. Named for Benjamin Barr, storekeeper, postmaster, and one of the first settlers, who arrived in the mid-1830s (*History of Macoupin County,* 157). Post office established Aug. 9, 1850, as Barr's Store; changed to Barr Jan. 30, 1895.

BARREN. Franklin. Township. According to an early county history, the area was "very thinly settled [with] so much brush and waste land that it was named Barren" (Aiken, *Franklin County History,* 73).

BARREVILLE [BEHR uh vil]. McHenry. Four miles south of McHenry. The source of the name is uncertain. By a local account the community was named Barre for an English nobleman, Lord Barre or Barrie ("Barreville"). Post office established May 30, 1849.

BARRINGTON [BEHR ing tuhn]. Cook, Lake. Barrington Township, an original Cook County township established in 1848, and the city of Barrington, laid out in the early 1850s by Robert Campbell, were named by settlers from Great Barrington, Mass., itself named for the second Viscount Barrington (1717–93). In the 1950s Barrington became a fashionable address, and a number of satellite communities were established in order to trade on the positive associations of the Barrington name: Barrington Hills, North Barrington, South Barrington, Lake Barrington, Barrington Center, and Barrington Woods. More than fifty years later, the drawing power of the name is undiminished. In the late 1990s the Village of Hoffman Estates proposed changing its name to East Barrington, and in 2002 the Village of Fox River Valley Gardens voted to change its name to Port Barrington (Bateman and Selby, eds., *Historical Encyclopedia of Illinois Cook County Edition*, 773; Dretske, *What's in a Name?*; Long, "A Mouthful Name"). Post office established Feb. 12, 1845.

BARROW. Greene. Two and a half miles northwest of Roodhouse. Named for Alfred Barrow, who donated land for a station and adjacent stock pens to the Chicago, Burlington and Quincy Railroad in 1871 (Clapp, *History of Greene County*, 428). Post office established Jan. 5, 1871.

BARRY. Pike. City (1859, 1872) sixteen miles east of Hannibal, Mo. Founded about 1835 by Calvin R. Stone as Reedfield. Worcester, probably named for Worcester, Vt., was laid out just east of Reedfield. When Reedfield failed and it was noticed that Worcester would duplicate an existing post office name, D. B. Brown and his wife, Mary, members of the consortium that founded Worcester, suggested the name Barre for their former home, Barre, Vt. The Vermont name is pronounced as though it were spelled *Barry*, and postal officials recorded the name to reflect the pronunciation they were given (Watson, *History of Barry*, 11–12). Post office established Dec. 14, 1839.

BARSTOW. Rock Island. Three miles east of East Moline. Founded in 1869 as Franklin, named for site owner and first postmaster Joel G. Franklin. The name was changed to Barstow in 1878 to agree with the name of the Chicago, Burlington and Quincy station. The source of the name is unknown (*Portrait and Biographical Album of Rock Island County*, 804). Post office established March 4, 1870, as Franklin Crossing; changed to Barstow Aug. 12, 1878.

BARTELSO [bar TEL so, bar TEL zo]. Clinton. Village (1898) six miles south-southeast of Breese. Formerly known as Santa Fe. Formally organized about 1884 as Bartholomaea by Father Bartholomew Bartels, pastor of St. Cecilia's Church. Bartholomaea proved to be an unsatisfactory name because it was long and often misspelled. Bartels then suggested that the name be changed to Bartelso, which he said was the Latin dative form of Bartels (*Commercial History of Clinton County*, 12). Post office established Aug. 21, 1885.

BARTLETT. Cook, DuPage. Village (1891). Founded in 1873 as a station on the Chicago and Pacific Railroad by site owner and first postmaster Luther Bartlett (*see* Ontarioville) (*Illinois Guide*). Post office established Dec. 11, 1873.

BARTONVILLE. Peoria. Village (1903) south Peoria suburb. Founded in 1881 by site owner William Coatsworth Harrison Barton (Harder, *Illustrated Dictionary of Place Names*).

BASCO [BAS ko]. Hancock. Village (1867) six miles south-southwest of Carthage. First platted in 1852 as Sommerset. The site was bought in 1871 and replatted as Basco, a station on the Burlington Railroad, by William S. Woods, who probably took the name from the Basco post office. The source of the name is unknown (*History of Hancock County,* 193). Post office established Sept. 23, 1852, as Summersett [*sic*]; changed to Basco Aug. 18, 1853.

BATAVIA [buh TAY vee uh]. Kane. City (1872). Earlier known as Head of the Big Woods, a name given by Christopher Payne, who built the first cabin in the area in the late 1830s. The name was changed about 1838 at the suggestion of Isaac Wilson, a public official and the first postmaster, for his former home, Batavia, Genesee County, N.Y. Batavia, a name referring to the Netherlands, was brought to New York by Dutch settlers in the early seventeenth century (*Biographical and Historical Record of Kane County,* 969). Post office established Feb. 6, 1841.

BATCHTOWN. Calhoun. Village (1897) seventeen miles southeast of Jerseyville. Originally known as Batcheldersville, named for William Batchelder, a justice of the peace and local merchant. The name was shortened to Batchtown when the post office was established in 1879 (Carpenter, *Calhoun Is My Kingdom,* 20).

BATH. Mason [BATH]. Village (1857, 1876) eight miles southwest of Havana. Founded in the 1830s by site owner John Kerton (for whom Kerton Creek and Kerton Township in Fulton County are named). Abraham Lincoln surveyed the site in November 1836, and, according to a local story, it was Lincoln who was responsible for the name. After a hard day's work, Lincoln is supposed to have looked toward Grand Island in the Illinois River and remarked, "That would be a good place to take a bath." The name, however, is most likely a transfer by settlers from Bath, Ohio, or Bath, N.Y. Ultimately from Bath, England. Bath was the seat of Mason County from 1843 until 1851 (Lynn, *Prelude to Progress,* 287; Parrott, ed., *Village of Bath,* 2). Post office established Sept. 9, 1834.

BATTERY ROCK. Hardin. A cliff on the Ohio River some seven miles northeast of Cave-in-Rock. The origin of the name is uncertain. There is a persistent story that the name comes from a battery of artillery stationed at the site to protect the North from southern advances during the Civil War. This is likely in error, however, because, according to the Griffiths, the cliff was referred to as Battery Rock as early as 1814. If, indeed, the name is from the emplacement of an artillery battery, then it was during the War of 1812 rather than the Civil War (Griffith, *Spotlight on Egypt,* 5; personal communication with Noel E. Hurford).

BAYLIS. Pike. Village (1887) nine miles northwest of Pittsfield. Founded as Pineville by William Pine Jr. in 1869 and subsequently named for the Baylis post office (Adams, comp., *Illinois Place Names; History of Pike County,* 628). Post office established May 24, 1870, as Pineville; changed to Baylis June 5, 1874.

BEAR. As in most states, Illinois has a number of names associated with bears (*ursidae*). Often these began as stream names and then became the names of communities or townships. Most as well began as "incident names" where contact of a remarkable nature between humans and bears took place. Bear

Creek in Christian County was so named because an especially large bear was killed near there; Bear Creek in Hancock County was where an early settler and his sons killed the last bear in the area; and Bear Lake in Clinton County was where Benjamin Allen reportedly killed three bears in the 1820s (Bateman and Selby, eds., *Historical Encyclopedia of Illinois and History of Christian County*, 754; *History of Wayne and Clay Counties*, 242; Hubbs, *Pioneer Folks and Places*).

BEARDSTOWN. Cass. City (1837, 1896). Founded about 1826 by Thomas Beard and Enoch C. March. Beard, the first permanent settler in the area, established Beard's Ferry across the Illinois River in 1819 and became a well-known trader and merchant. Beardstown was the seat of Cass County from 1837 to 1839 and again from 1843 to 1867 (Bateman and Selby, eds., *Historical Encyclopedia of Illinois and History of Cass County*, 804). Post office established Dec. 4, 1830, as Beard's Ferry; changed to Beardstown Aug. 5, 1831.

BEARSDALE. Macon. Northwest of Decatur. Founded about 1872, taking the name of the Peoria, Decatur and Evansville railroad station, itself named for site owner Samuel Bear. The area was previously known as Lickskillet (q.v.), named from the Lickskillet School (Richmond, *Centennial History of Decatur*, 97). Post office established March 22, 1882.

BEASON [BEE suhn]. Logan. Nine miles east of Lincoln. Laid out in 1872 by Silas Beason, a lawyer who was instrumental in securing a station on the Illinois Central Railroad (*History of Logan County* [1886], 824). Post office established June 2, 1873.

BEATY [BAY tee]. Fulton. Ten miles southwest of Havana. Probably named for Isaac Beaty, an early settler from Ohio, who arrived about 1840 (*Fulton County*, 26).

BEAUBIEN. Cook. Forest Preserve. Named for John B. Beaubien, who established a trading post in Chicago about 1817 (Hicks, *History of Kendall County*, 39).

BEAUCOUP. Perry. Former community. Laid out in 1873 about a mile west of Pinckneyville for the Beaucoup Coal Company, itself named from Beaucoup Creek (http://perrycountyillinois.net/sub69.htm).

BEAUCOUP [BUHK oo]. Washington. Four miles east of Nashville. Named from Beaucoup Creek, itself perhaps named by Philip Francois Renault (q.v. Renault), who came to Illinois from France in 1719 in search of mineral wealth. From French *beaucoup* (much) (Coulet du Gard, *Dictionary of French Place Names*). Post office established Jan. 1, 1815.

BECKEMEYER [BEK uh meyer]. Clinton. Village (1905) two miles west of Carlyle. Previously known as Buxton. Formally organized in 1905 by August Beckemeyer (*Commercial History of Clinton County*, 12). Post office established Aug. 2, 1867, as Buxton; changed to Beckemeyer July 27, 1905.

BEDFORD. Wayne. Township. Probably named by settlers from Bedford, Cuyahoga County, Ohio, itself named for Bedford, N.Y. (*History of Wayne and Clay Counties*, 235; Miller, *Ohio Place Names*).

BEDFORD PARK. Cook. Village (1940). West Chicago community near Midway Airport. Established about 1920 by Edward T. Bedford as a company town for employees of the Corn Products Corporation (now CPC International), best known as the maker of Argo Starch (Miller, "This Place Is Known").

BEECHER. Will. Village (1883). First called Center and later known as Washington Center. The community was renamed in 1870 by site owner Timothy L. Miller in honor of preacher and abolitionist Henry Ward Beecher (Berko, "In These Parts"; *Illinois Guide*). Post office established June 17, 1862, as Washington Centre; changed to Beecher June 21, 1870.

BEECHER CITY. Effingham. Village (1895) fourteen miles west-northwest of Effingham. The source of the name is uncertain. Several early histories claim the village was named for Henry Ward Beecher, at the time a popular, indeed famous, clerical orator and social critic. Others say the namesake was Henry L. Beecher, a local businessman and an early postmaster. A more likely candidate, however, is Charles A. Beecher, vice president of the Springfield and Southeastern Railroad, which laid out the community in 1871. The word *City* was added to avoid confusion with Beecher in Will County (Bateman and Selby, eds., *Illinois Historical Effingham County Biographical*, 639; Perrin, ed., *History of Effingham County*, 241; Pulliam, ed., *Towns of Effingham County*, 6). Post office established Aug. 6, 1872.

BELGIUM. Vermilion. Village (1908) five miles south of Danville. Established as a "wet" town in the early 1900s in response to Danville's voting itself "dry." Named for the country of Belgium, the former home of a number of early settlers. Belgium Row is six miles west of Danville (Stapp, *History under Our Feet*, 61; Tuggle, comp., *Stories of Historical Days*, 10).

BELKNAP [BEL nap]. Johnson. Village (1880) seven miles south of Vienna. Laid out on the line of the Big Four Railroad in 1873. According to local accounts, George Morgan and Jim Bell operated sawmills several miles apart on the Cache River. Morgan often sold logs to Bell and floated them downriver to Bell's mill. During dry periods the water level would drop to the point where the logs could no longer be floated, and these slack periods gave Bell the opportunity to doze off or to take "Bell's naps." An engaging story, but the namesake is surely William Worth Belknap, who served as Ulysses S. Grant's Secretary of War from 1869 until 1876 (Mohlenbrock, "A New Geography of Illinois: Johnson County," 24). Post office established April 7, 1873.

BELLAIR. Crawford. Ten miles north of Oblong. Named about 1856. Probably a transfer from Bellaire, Belmont County, Ohio (*History of Crawford County*, 105). Post office established March 7, 1846, as Bell Air; changed to Bellair April 21, 1894.

BELLE PRAIRIE CITY. Hamilton. Town (1869) eight and a half miles north of McLeansboro. Founded in 1862 by Clyde Crouch and Wilson Lewis through the merger of Belle Prairie and Belle City. Ultimately from French *belle* (beautiful) (*History of Gallatin, Saline*, 310).

BELLE RIVE [BEL REYEV, BEL REEV]. Jefferson. Village (1875) ten miles east-southeast of Mount Vernon. Founded in 1871 with construction of the St. Louis and Southeastern Railroad and named for Louie Groston *dit* (also known as) St. Ange *dit* Bellerive, the last commandant of Fort Chartres, who surrendered the Illinois country to the British in 1765. French for "beautiful riverbank" (Coulet du Gard, *Dictionary of French Place Names*; Perrin, ed., *History of Jefferson County*, 258). Post office established Jan. 2, 1872.

BELLEVIEW. Calhoun. Seventeen miles south of Pittsfield. Named from its location at the head of Belleview Hollow, the name of which may be a translation of French *belle vue* (beautiful view) (Underwood, "A New Geography of Calhoun County," 34). Post office established Jan. 2, 1829.

BELLEVILLE. St. Clair. City (1819, 1876). Founded in 1814 by site owner George Blair. According to one historian, "Blair . . . said that he had found a place where he was going to form a settlement which might become one of the most beautiful cities in America, and therefore he named it Belleville, from French for 'beautiful city'" (Nebelsick, *A History of Belleville*, 23). Belleville has been the seat of St. Clair County since 1814. Post office established March 14, 1816.

BELLFLOWER. McLean. Village (1890) eight miles northeast of Farmer City. Probably named by Jesse Richards, the first township supervisor, for the Bellflower apple, of which he was especially fond (Bateman and Selby, eds., *Historical Encyclopedia of Illinois and History of McLean County*, 679). Also known as Prairie. Post office established Jan. 1, 1872, as Belle Flower; changed to Bellflower June 20, 1892.

BELLMONT. Wabash. Village (1833) seven miles west-southwest of Mount Carmel. Named in the early 1870s in honor of county judge Robert S. Bell of Mount Carmel. Bell's name was combined with *mont*, the resulting *Bellmont* suggesting French for "beautiful mountain" (Bateman and Selby, eds., *Illinois Historical Wabash County Biographical*, 644, 652). Post office established Jan. 8, 1874.

BELLTOWN. Greene. Three miles south of White Hall. Laid off in 1867 by John Bell and F. M. Bell. Also known as New Providence (*History of Greene and Jersey Counties*, 428).

BELLWOOD. Cook. Village (1900). Founded in the 1890s by site owners Lucian and Julia Rice. The origin of the name is uncertain. Harder and others have suggested that Bellwood is a contraction of "Bell's Woods" for a land owner named Bell, but an older spelling *Bellewood*, the name of an early subdivision, suggests otherwise. A local story claims that the name derives from the fact that this was a popular area for socializing, and young ladies (belles) and their beaux would drive out from neighboring communities to picnic in the grove, which came to be known as the Belles' Woods. But this explanation is more folklore than fact, and the true source of the name remains a mystery. The change in spelling from Bellewood to Bellwood was apparently the result of a scribal error in the documents of incorporation (Harder, *Illustrated Dictionary of Place Names;* Kerch, "Village"). Post office established Jan. 25, 1893, as Bellewood; changed to Bellwood July 1, 1929.

BELMONT CRAGIN. Cook. Created from the names of Belmont Park and Cragin, adjacent communities, which, along with Galewood and Hanson Park, merged as Belmont Cragin in 1882 (Kitagawa and Taeuber, eds., *Local Community Fact Book,* 52).

BELTREES. Jersey. Eight miles northwest of Alton. Origin unknown. Perhaps named for Beltrees, a hamlet near Renfrew, Scotland; perhaps by relatives of James Semple, whose ancestors were from Renfrew. Beltrees is one mile south of Elsah (q.v.), founded by Semple in the early 1850s. Post office established Jan. 27, 1891, as Haynes; changed to Beltrees May 16, 1898.

BELVIDERE. Boone. City (1852). Founded about 1835 by the Belvidere Company and named by Ebenezer Peck, a Montreal lawyer and a founder of the Belvidere Company, for his former home, Belvidere (Belvédère), on the south side of the city of Sherbrooke, Quebec (Bateman and Selby, eds., *Historical Encyclopedia of Illinois and History of Boone County,* 673; Franck, *Landmarks,* 4). Post office established Feb. 15, 1837.

BEMENT [bee MENT, buh MENT]. Piatt. Village (1874) seven miles south of Monticello. Founded in 1855 and named for Edward Bement, an official of the Chicago Great Western Railroad, who offered to donate a bell for the first church in the community. Unfortunately, Bement died before the bell could be installed (Morgan, ed., *The Good Life,* 70). Post office established Jan. 23, 1856.

BENBOW CITY. Madison. Founded by A. E. Benbow, who also served as first president of the board of trustees. Benbow City was annexed by Wood River in 1917 (Norton, ed., *Centennial History of Madison County,* 615).

BENLD [ben ELD]. Macoupin. City (1904) one mile south of Gillespie. Founded in 1903. From the name of Ben L. Dorsey, an early settler (Stennett, *A History of the Origin,* 43). Post office established March 21, 1904.

BENNINGTON. Edwards. Ten miles northwest of Albion. Founded about 1839 and named for Bennington, Vt., home of a number of early settlers (Harper, ed., *History of Edwards County,* 55). Post office established July 20, 1869.

BENNINGTON. Marshall. Township. Probably named for Bennington, Vt. In the mid-1850s the Vermont Emigration Association sited Rutland (q.v.), named for Rutland, Vt., in what is now Bennington Township. The choice of the name may have been influenced by the Thomas Bennington family, which moved into the area in the early 1830s (Ellsworth, *Records of the Olden Times,* 434; *History of Marshall County* [1983], 32).

BENSENVILLE. Cook, DuPage. Village (1894). Formerly known as Tioga, probably named for Tioga, N.Y. Formally established in 1873 on the line of the Milwaukee Road as Bensenville at the suggestion of Henry Schuette, who said the community reminded him of Benzen, Germany, his former home. Because there was an existing Benson post office, the suffix *ville* was added (Jones, *Bensenville,* 15; Ritzert, "Bensenville," 114). Post office established Nov. 28, 1873.

BENSON. Woodford. Village (1878) nine miles northwest of El Paso. Established in 1874 with construction of the Chicago, Pekin and Southwestern Railroad. Named for S. H. Benson of Streator, the general freight manager of the CP&S (Yates, *The Woodford County History,* 36). Post office established Feb. 5, 1873.

BENTLEY. Hancock. Town (1869) four miles south-southeast of Carthage. Formerly called Sutton, named for John Sutton. The name was changed about 1864 with construction of the Wabash Railroad, for E. Bentley, the site owner (*History of Hancock County,* 336). Post office established Aug. 13, 1863 as Bentley Station; changed to Bentley Aug. 5, 1870.

BENTON. Franklin. City (1841, 1875). Founded in 1840 and named for Thomas Hart Benton (1782–1858), U.S. senator from Missouri (1821–51) and great-uncle of the artist of the same name. Benton has been the seat of Franklin County since 1841. Benton Township in Lake County was named for the same Thomas Hart Benton (Dretske, *What's in a Name?*). Post office established July 1, 1840.

BENTOWN. McLean. Seven miles east of Bloomington. A Quaker community founded as Benjaminville in 1855 by John R. Benjamin. Benjaminville began to decline when the railroad was built south of the settlement through what would become Holder (q.v.) (Quaid, *A Little Square,* 30; Townley, *Historic McLean,* 18). Post office established Jan. 30, 1866, as Benjaminville.

BENVILLE. Brown. Three miles southeast of Siloam Springs State Park. Named for Ben Akright, who kept a general store near the site in the 1850s (*History of Brown County,* 225).

BERDAN [ber DAN]. Greene. Four and a half miles south of White Hall. Established in 1865 by the Chicago and Alton Railroad. Named for James Berdan of Jacksonville, an official of the C&A (Clapp, *History of Greene County,* 430; Miner, *Past and Present,* 186). Post office established March 1, 1860, as New Providence; changed to Berdan April 11, 1869.

BERKELEY [BERK lee]. Cook. Village (1924). Likely named for Berkeley, Calif., either by a returning traveler or by officials of the Chicago, Aurora and Elgin Railroad. According to local tradition, the station name was originally spelled *Berkley,* and the medial *e* was added later to agree with the spelling of Berkeley, Calif. (Johnson, *From Oats to Roses,* 17; Young, "A Quiet Place").

BERLIN [BER luhn]. Sangamon. Ten miles west of Springfield. Laid out in 1826. New Berlin, two miles south of Berlin, was laid out about 1838. Both Berlin and New Berlin were founded by Henry Yates, father of Illinois governor Richard Yates and grandfather of another Illinois governor, also named Richard Yates. Named for Berlin, Germany (Bateman and Selby, eds., *Historical Encyclopedia of Illinois and History of Sangamon County*, 723). Post office established Feb. 27, 1826, as Island Grove; changed to Berlin Oct. 15, 1833.

BERNADOTTE. Fulton. Township and former community. Originally known as Bennington, probably named by settlers from Bennington, Vt. Formally established as Fulton about eight miles west of Lewistown in 1835 by grist mill operator Joseph Coleman and named for Fulton County. Why or even when the name was changed to Bernadotte is unclear. The generally accepted account is that the name was given in honor of Jean Baptiste Jules Bernadotte (1763–1844), one of Napoleon's generals, who later became King Charles XIV of Sweden and the founder of the current Swedish royal house. Bernadotte himself reigned from 1818 until 1844. Bernadotte is reported to have visited relatives near Avon on several occasions, but these alleged visits have not been verified. During World War II the area was taken over by Camp Ellis, named for Sgt. Michael B. Ellis of St. Louis, awarded the Silver Star and Congressional Medal of Honor for valor in World War I (Bordner, *From Cornfields to Marching Feet*, 5; Derry, *Through the Years*, 7; Irwin, *A to Z Fulton County*). Post office established Sept. 20, 1833, as Bennington; changed to Bernadotte March 3, 1837.

BERREMAN. Jo Daviess. Township. Reportedly named by an A. Mahony for a friend in Tennessee. This is the only place name so spelled in the United States (Bateman and Selby, eds., *Historical Encyclopedia of Illinois and History of Jo Daviess County*, 633).

BERRY. Sangamon. Eight miles southeast of Springfield. Named for Robert E. Berry, site owner and postmaster. Previously known as Clarksville, Custer, Mortarsville, and South Fork (Coulet du Gard, *Dictionary of French Place Names*). Post office established March 7, 1863, as Mortarsville, named for postmaster William Mortar; changed to South Fork Aug. 18, 1869; changed to Berry April 1, 1870.

BERRYVILLE. Richland. Twelve miles southeast of Olney. Named for the Berry family. Joseph and John Berry were early postmasters (Adams, comp., *Illinois Place Names*). Post office established Aug. 1, 1884.

BERWYN [BER wuhn]. Cook. City (1901). Named for Berwyn, Pa., a western suburb of Philadelphia, either by developer Wilbur J. Andrews or by P. S. Eustis, general passenger agent for the Chicago, Burlington and Quincy Railroad. The local story is that Andrews selected Berwyn from a Pennsylvania Railroad timetable. The name is ultimately from the Berwyn Mountains of northern Wales (Cutshall, *A Gazetteer;* Hansen, ed., *Illinois*, 666–67). Post office established April 11, 1891.

BESSIE. Franklin. Five miles west of Du Quoin. Founded about 1895 by John A. Whetstone and named for his daughter, Bessie, who reportedly died of tuberculosis in 1896 (*Franklin County*, 12; Sneed, *Ghost Towns*, 11). Post office established July 27, 1896.

BETHALTO [beth AL to]. Madison. Village (1869, 1873). Founded by Joel Starkey in 1854 as Bethel, taking its name from the nearby Bethel Church. To avoid duplicating an existing post office, a new name was created by blending the word *Bethel* with -*alto*, taken either from Alton, the nearest community, or from Latin *altus* (high) (Norton, ed., *Centennial History of Madison County*, 612; *Souvenir History for the Bethalto Centennial*, 2). Post office established May 19, 1854.

BETHANY. Moultrie. Village (1877) seven miles northwest of Sullivan. Originally called Marrowbone (q.v.), named from Marrowbone Creek. The name was changed by missionaries from the Bethany Cumberland Presbyterians of Tennessee, who established a church at the site in the 1830s (*Illinois Guide*). Post office established June 9, 1857, as Marrowbone; changed to Bethany Dec. 13, 1875.

BETHEL. Morgan. Nine miles west-northwest of Jacksonville. Laid out and named by Samuel and Catherine Whitley in 1833. Perhaps named from a local Bethel church (Bateman and Selby, eds., *Historical Encyclopedia of Illinois and History of Morgan County*, 660; Hutchison, "Old Morgan County Village"). Post office established Sept. 27, 1833.

BETHEL. Vermilion. Seven miles southeast of Georgetown. Laid out in 1836 by John Hayworth and others as Munroe. Later renamed for the Bethel Church (Underwood, "A New Geography of Illinois: Vermilion County," 38).

BETHESDA. Pope. Former community about five miles north of Golconda. Named from the Bethesda Church. Informally known as Bushwack, reportedly so named when a Mr. Finney was shot from ambush (McCormick, "The Significance of Pope County Place Names," 28).

BEVAN. Grundy. Former community. Named for Thomas G. Bevan, president of the Elgin, Joliet and Eastern Railroad (Donovan, "Named for Railroad Presidents," 26).

BEVERLY. Adams. Six miles south-southwest of Siloam Springs State Park. Laid out in 1836 by William Raymond and named by his sisters, Eliza and Hanna Raymond, for their former home, Beverly, Mass., northeast of Boston (Genosky, ed., *People's History*, 698). Post office established Dec. 24, 1837.

BIBLE GROVE. Clay. Fifteen miles north of Flora. Founded in the early 1840s. Previously known as Edinburg and Georgetown. The traditional story is that the community takes its name from an incident where hunters found a bible in a grove along Georgetown Creek (*Prairie Echo*, 121). Post office established June 19, 1854.

BIG BAY. Massac. Eleven miles north of Metropolis. Named from Bay Creek, reported to have been named *Gros Baie* (Big Bay) by early French explorers or settlers (Allen, *Pope County Notes,* 63; May, *History of Massac County,* 175). Post office established May 7, 1835.

BIG FOOT PRAIRIE. McHenry. Four miles north of Harvard. Named for Mawgeh-set (Big Foot), a Potawatomi leader of the 1820s and 1830s whose village was near Lake Geneva, Wis. The traditional account is that Big Foot received his name from the large tracks left by his snowshoes as he pursued game around the lake (Edmunds, *The Potawatomis,* 230; Vogel, *Indian Place Names in Illinois*). Post office established May 15, 1848.

BIGGS. Mason. Eight and a half miles southeast of Havana. Named for Paul G. Biggs, who operated a local grain elevator in the 1870s (Lynn, *Prelude to Progress,* 413). Post office established Oct. 3, 1875.

BIGGSVILLE. Henderson. Village (1879) eleven miles west-southwest of Monmouth. Named for John Biggs, who operated a grist mill on South Henderson Creek in the 1840s. The village was platted shortly after the original mill was destroyed by a flood in 1844 (*Biggsville;* Sutton, *Rivers, Railways,* 35). Post office established Feb. 5, 1846, as Grove Farm; changed to Biggsville Jan. 23, 1856.

BIG MOUND. Township. Wayne. From the elevation near Boyleston known as Big Mound, claimed to be the highest point in Wayne County (*History of Wayne and Clay Counties,* 194).

BIG ROCK. Kane. Nine miles west of Aurora. Named from Big Rock Creek, itself possibly the translation of a native name, but the source is unknown (*Past and Present of Kane County, Illinois,* 496). Post office established May 23, 1850.

BILLET. Lawrence. Four miles southeast of Lawrenceville. Named for postmaster John Billet(t) (Adams, comp., *Illinois Place Names*).

BINGHAM [BING uhm]. Fayette. Village (1888) twelve miles northwest of Vandalia. Named for Judge Horatio Bingham (Hanabarger, "Fayette County Place Names," 44). Post office established May 31, 1883.

BINGHAMPTON [BING uhm tuhn]. Lee. Twelve miles southeast of Dixon. Laid out in 1848 and named by the proprietor, Asa B. Searles, for his former home, Binghamton, Broome County, N.Y. The [p] is excrescent; it does not occur in the name of Binghamton, N.Y., and did not appear in the name of Binghamton, Ill., until several years after its founding, probably with the establishment of the post office in 1850. Even then the spelling alternated; well into the twentieth century, county historians wrote both *Binghamton* and *Binghampton* (*History of Lee County* [1881]; Stevens, *History of Lee County,* 271, 276). Post office established April 17, 1844, as Rocky Ford; changed to Shelburn Feb. 20, 1846; changed to Binghampton Feb. 27, 1850.

BINNIE. Madison. Three miles southeast of Staunton. Named for postmaster Walter P. Binney (Adams, comp., *Illinois Place Names*). Post office established Nov. 19, 1898.

BINNIE HILLS. Kane. Five miles northwest of Elgin. Named for the Binnie family. Robert and Agnes Binnie emigrated from Stirlingshire, Scotland, and settled in the Dundee area about 1849 (*Past and Present of Kane County,* 230).

BIRD. Macoupin. Township. Named for land owner Joseph Bird, who emigrated from Butler County, Pa., in the early 1850s (*History of Macoupin County,* 136).

BIRDS. Lawrence. Village (1890) seven miles north of Lawrenceville. Founded about 1878 as Bird's Station by site owner John Bird (*Combined History of Edwards, Lawrence, and Wabash Counties,* 344). Post office established June 6, 1876, as Bird's Station; changed to Birds May 21, 1883.

BIRKBECK. DeWitt. Four miles east-northeast of Clinton. Possibly named for Morris Birkbeck, one of the founders of Albion (q.v.), but more likely the name was coined by William Wilderson, superintendent of the Springfield Division of the Illinois Central Railroad, from the names of two officers of the Iowa and Illinois Division of the IC, a Mr. Birk and a Mr. Beck (*Clinton 1835–1985*). Post office established July 7, 1882, as Suttonville; changed to Birkbeck March 3, 1884.

BIRKS PRAIRIE. Edwards. Named for Jeremiah Birk (or Birks), generally regarded as the first settler in Albion precinct. The Birks Prairie Cemetery is located in the southwest corner of Edwards County, between Camp Creek and Stinking Creek (*Combined History Edwards, Lawrence, and Wabash Counties,* 203).

BIRMINGHAM. Schuyler. Fifteen miles southwest of Macomb. Founded in 1836 by David Graham and David Manlove. Likely named by Graham for Birmingham in his home state of Virginia. It is unlikely that the name is a direct transfer from Birmingham, England, and Birmingham, Ala., and Birmingham, Ky., were not founded until later (*Atlas Map of Schuyler County,* 7). Post office established April 28, 1843.

BISHOP. Effingham. Township. Named from Bishop Creek, itself named for one or more early settlers named Bishop. The names of William Bishop and Samuel Bishop appear in early township records (Pulliam, ed., *Townships of Effingham County,* 3).

BISHOP. Mason. Ten miles east-northeast of Havana. Founded in 1875 as a station on the Peoria, Pekin and Jacksonville Railroad. Named for site owner Henry Bishop (Lynn, *Prelude to Progress,* 326). Post office established Oct. 14, 1869, as Bishop's Station; changed to Bishop May 15, 1883.

BISHOP HILL. Henry. Village (1893) nine miles west-southwest of Kewanee. Laid out in 1861 by Olof Johnson, Jonas Erickson, Swan Swanson, Jonas Olson, Jonas Kronberg, Olof Stenberg, and Jacob Jacobson, the trustees of Bishop Hill. Bishop Hill is perhaps the best known of all Illinois colonies. It was organized in 1846 by a group of Swedish religious dissenters led by Erik Janson ("the prophet") and named for his birthplace, Biskopskulla (Bishop Hill) in Uppland, Sweden. The colony prospered for a time and at one point had a population of more than seven hundred, but it fell into decline beginning with the murder of Janson in 1850. It dissolved in 1862, and the communal property was divided among the remaining members (*Illinois Guide;* Landelius, *Swedish Place-Names*). Post office established June 5, 1848.

BISMARCK [BIZ mahrk]. Vermilion. Village (1998) six miles north of Danville. Founded in 1872 by Joseph E. Young, a contractor for the Chicago, Danville and Vincennes Railroad and named for Otto von Bismarck, chancellor of Germany, in recognition of the support German bondholders had given to the railroad (*Century of a Town,* 16). Post office established Jan. 7, 1858, as Myersville; changed to Bismarck Jan. 9, 1873.

BISSELL. Sangamon. Two miles northeast of Springfield. Probably named for William Harrison Bissell (1811–60), governor of Illinois from 1857 to 1860. Post office established Oct. 8, 1896.

BLACKBERRY. Kane. Township. Named from Blackberry Creek, so called for the local wild blackberries. The area was first known as Lance's Grove for first settler William Lance. The Blackberry Cemetery is eleven miles east-southeast of DeKalb (*Past and Present of Kane County,* 473). Post office established April 8, 1840.

BLACKHAWK. Carroll. Seven miles northeast of Savanna. Also Township in Rock Island County. Black Hawk was a leader of the Sauk (Sac) who led a group of his people back into Illinois in the spring of 1832 from Iowa, where they had been exiled. This was the precipitating act of the Black Hawk War, which effectively destroyed Indian resistance to European settlement east of the Mississippi River. The conflict was brief but notable for the fact that participants included Abraham Lincoln, Jefferson Davis, Zachary Taylor, and a number of others who would make marks for themselves in American history. Black Hawk's name appears in his autobiography as "Mà-ka-tai-me-she-kià-kiak" and in the 1816 Treaty of St. Louis as "Mucketamachekaka, or Black Sparrow Hawk." He died in Iowa in 1838. Black Hawk is the most famous Illinois Indian, and his name has been given to scores of parks, schools, and streets as well as various commercial enterprises, social organizations, and sports teams (Vogel, *Indian Place Names in Illinois*).

BLACKLAND. Macon. Seven miles southwest of Decatur. Named for John Black (Richmond, *Centennial History of Decatur,* 96).

BLACKSTONE. Livingston. Seven miles southeast of Streator. Named for Timothy B. Blackstone, president of the Chicago and Alton Railroad in the 1870s (Donovan, "Named for Railroad Presidents," 26). Post office established April 29, 1870.

BLAINE. Boone. Nine miles west-northwest of Harvard. Probably named for James G. Blaine, secretary of state in Garfield's administration and candidate for president in 1884. Formerly known as Union Corners (Moorhead, ed., *Boone County*, 27). Post office established Jan. 14, 1840, as Amazon; changed to Parks Corners, named for postmaster Samuel Parks May 23, 1850; changed to Blaine April 8, 1881.

BLAIR. Clay. Township. Named at the time of township organization by Henry R. Neff in honor of Josiah, Jesse, and James Blair, settlers in the late 1830s (*History of Wayne and Clay Counties*, 441).

BLAIR. Randolph. Five miles northeast of Dwight. Founded about 1859 as Blairsville. Named for Thomas Blair, the first postmaster and first justice of the peace (*Combined History of Randolph, Monroe, and Perry Counties*, 465). Post office established Oct. 6, 1860.

BLAIRSVILLE. Hamilton. Six miles northeast of McLeansboro. According to a local account, "For some reason, boys passing the house of Adam Cluck about 1890 on the way to school . . . began calling him Blair, to which he responded in a fit of anger. One day soon after, one of the boys lettered a sign with the word 'Blairsville' and nailed it to Cluck's fence. The name stuck" (*Hamilton County*, 41).

BLAIRSVILLE. Williamson. Four miles west of Herrin. Named for Stephen Blair, who operated a mill on Big Muddy River in the 1830s. The nickname of Blairsville was Pull Tight, reportedly so named because the east bank of the Big Muddy was so high and steep that drivers had to fully engage their brakes as they drove down to the river (Hale, comp. and ed., *Williamson County*, 119; Hubbs, *Pioneer Folks and Places*). Post office established April 26, 1856.

BLANDINSVILLE. McDonough. Village (1859, 1872) eleven miles northwest of Macomb. Named for Joseph L. Blandin, proprietor of the first general store. The village was platted in 1842 on part of the tract known as Job's Settlement, named for early settlers William and Ira Job (*History of McDonough County*, 880; Shadwick, *History of McDonough County*, 219). Post office established June 23, 1843.

BLISSVILLE. Jefferson. Township. Named for Augustus Bliss, who laid out a community in the early 1840s, presumably called Blissville, which never materialized. The historical Blissville Polling Place was located about eleven miles west-southwest of Mount Vernon (Perrin, ed., *History of Jefferson County*, 413). The Blissville post office was active from Aug. 4, 1841, until March 15, 1858.

BLODGETT. Will. Four miles east of Channahon. Founded in the 1850s and named for Henry W. Blodgett (1821–1905), general counsel for the Chicago and Milwaukee Railroad and later justice of the U.S. District Court for Northern Illinois (Stennett, *A History of the Origin*, 45).

BLOOD'S POINT. Boone. Named for Arthur Blood, the first settler in Flora Township. The community has now disappeared, but the name is preserved by Blood's Point Road and Blood's Point Cemetery, some five miles south of Belvidere (Moorhead, ed., *Boone County,* 144). Post office established Dec. 8, 1847.

BLOOM. Township. Cook. Named Blu(h)m at the time of township formation in 1849 in honor of Robert Blum, German leftist leader and writer who was executed in 1848 for his political activities (Dionne, *Olympia Fields 1927,* 17).

BLOOMFIELD. Johnson. Three miles north-northeast of Vienna. Laid out by Jonathan Waters in 1873 on the line of the Big Four Railroad. The source of the name is unknown (Mohlenbrock, "A New Geography of Illinois: Johnson County," 25). Post office established July 2, 1875.

BLOOMINGDALE. DuPage. Village (1923). The area was first known as Meacham's Grove, named for the Meacham brothers, Silas, Daniel, Harvey, and Lyman, who emigrated from Rutland, Vt., in the early 1830s. Bloomingdale was formally organized about 1845 by Erasmus Hills, Hilamon Hills, and Hiram Goodwin, who took the name from the Bloomingdale post office, which may have been named from Bloomingdale's Grove, itself perhaps named for an early settler named Bloomingdale. The name reportedly appears on a surveyor's notes of about 1840 just east of Meacham's Grove (Bateman and Selby, eds., *Historical Encyclopedia of Illinois and History of DuPage County,* 666; Perkins and Perkins, "Bloomingdale," 119). Post office established July 20, 1837.

BLOOMINGTON. McLean. City (1839, 1897). Originally known as Keg Grove, so called, according to tradition, because a group of Kickapoo Indians happened across several kegs of whiskey that had been hidden by early settlers. The Indians carried the kegs to their village and from then on referred to the place where they had found them as Keg Grove. In the 1820s Keg Grove acquired the additional name of Blooming Grove, the origin of which is unclear, but several early accounts credit Mrs. William Orendorff, who reportedly remarked to some visitors that Blooming Grove would be an appropriate name because of the foliage and buds on the maple trees each spring. Other sources credit Mrs. Orendorff's brother-in-law, Thomas, with suggesting the name. According to these accounts, Thomas Orendorff and John Rhodes were in the grove writing letters, and Rhodes asked what return address he should use. Orendorff reportedly looked around at the maple trees and replied, "It looks blooming here; I think we had better call it Blooming Grove." Also unclear is how the name *Blooming Grove* came to be replaced by Bloomington. Several early historians suggest that Bloomington evolved naturally from Blooming Grove, but that is highly unlikely because Bloomington was chosen as the name of the county seat by the Illinois legislature in 1830, while the location of the seat was still undetermined. Some sources claim that James Allin, an important political figure in early McLean County, suggested the name, but whatever reasons he may have had are unknown. See Syfert, "The Naming of Bloomington," for a detailed and comprehensive account of the naming of the city. (Ackerman, *Early Illinois Railroads*, 145–46; Hasbrouck, *History of McLean County*, 71, 122; *History of McLean County, Illinois*, 316; Light, *This Blooming Town*, 14). Post office established Jan. 29, 1829, as Blooming Grove; changed to Bloomington May 2, 1831.

BLOUNT [BLUHNT]. Vermilion. Township. Created from Newell and Pilot townships as Fremont, named for western explorer John C. Frémont, the Republican candidate for president in 1856. When Democrats objected to the name, Abraham Blount, an early settler, offered his name as a substitute (Stapp, *History under Our Feet*, 37). Post office established Dec. 15, 1876.

BLUE ISLAND. Cook. City (1843, 1872). The "island" was actually a swampy ridge of higher ground at the foot of Lake Michigan. The name reportedly was chosen for the blue wildflowers that grew along the ridge and from the purple haze that hung over the area in the early mornings and late evenings. Blue Island was platted by Peter Barton about 1837 as Portland, perhaps named for Portland, Maine (Bateman and Selby, eds., *Historical Encyclopedia of Illinois Cook County Edition*, 775; *Illinois Guide*). Post office established Dec. 5, 1839.

BLUE MOUND. Macon. Village (1876). A glacial formation reportedly named by site owner Isaac Goltree for the abundance of blue flowers (Blevins, *Peculiar, Uncertain, and Two Egg*, 95). Post office established June 26, 1861.

BLUE MOUND. McLean. Township. Named from Blue Mound, a summit about ten miles east of Normal. The mound served as a landmark for early travelers. A granite marker placed at the base of Blue Mound by the Cooksville–Blue Mound Township Bicentennial Commission in 1976 reads in part: "Distance gave blue cast to this landmark on early trails across McLean county" (Quaid, *A Little Square*, 2).

BLUE POINT. Effingham. Eight miles west of Effingham. Likely named by Griffin Tipsword, an early traveler who was impressed by the expanse of bluestem prairie grass. (Since 1989 the big bluestem has been the official prairie grass of Illinois.) It has also been reported that the name comes from the frequent blue haze in the vicinity (Feldhake, *Effingham County*, 44). Post office established Dec. 30, 1874.

BLUFF SPRINGS. Cass. Four miles southeast of Beardstown. Established as a station on the Springfield and Illinois Southeastern Railroad in 1871. Named from the Bluff House, a local inn and tavern (Bateman and Selby, eds., *Historical Encyclopedia of Illinois and History of Cass County*, 819; Hutchison, "Old Morgan County Village"). Post office established Feb. 6, 1872.

BLUFFS. Scott. Village (1883). Laid out by Henry Oakes as Bluff City in 1871. Named for the bluffs along the Illinois River (*Scott County Bicentennial Book*, 71; Hutchison, "Old Morgan County Village"). Post office established Nov. 29, 1872.

BLUFORD [BLOO ferd]. Jefferson. Village (1926) seven miles east of Mount Vernon. Established as a station on the Air Line Railroad in the early 1880s. Named for Bluford, son of village promoters Wiley and Minerva Green (*Facts and Folks*, 61). Post office established May 31, 1882, as Tilford, named for Tilford Green, Bluford's brother; changed to Bluford Feb. 6, 1888.

BOAZ [BOZ]. Massac. Eight miles south of Vienna. Named for a local shopkeeper and postmaster named Boaz, whose given name has been recorded as Lynn, Lin, and Linn (*History of Massac County*, 17; May, *History of Massac County*, 175). Post office established April 13, 1891.

BOGOTA [buh GO tuh]. Jasper. Five miles southwest of Newton. Named for Bogota, now the capital of Colombia, South America, but the circumstances surrounding the naming are unclear. The name may have been chosen because of political events that kept Bogota in the news at the time, or it may have been suggested or inspired by James Semple, the founder of Elsah and one of the first national political figures in Illinois. After serving in state government, Semple was minister plenipotentiary to Santa Fe de Bogotá, the capital of what was then known as New Grenada, from 1837 until 1842. Post office established April 27, 1882.

BOGUS HOLLOW. Henderson. Valley near Gladstone. Reportedly where a gang of counterfeiters minted fake half dollars that they put into circulation across the river in Burlington, Iowa (Bateman and Selby, eds., *Historical Encyclopedia of Illinois and History of Henderson County*, 629).

BOIS D'ARC. Township. Montgomery. From French "wood of the bow," referring to the Osage orange, said to make superior bows. The township was named by Lewis H. Thomas, who promoted the planting of Osage orange trees as natural fences to contain livestock (Bateman and Selby, eds., *Historical Encyclopedia of Illinois and History of Montgomery County*, 844).

BOLINGBROOK. Will. Village (1965). Established as the Bolingbrook subdivision by the Dover Construction Company in 1960. Bolingbrook is a developer's promotional name chosen for its presumed association with British elegance and tradition. Advertisements for the subdivision featured a British butler named Mr. Dover (www.bolingbrook.com).

BOLIVIA. Christian. Fifteen miles east southeast of Springfield. Founded about 1905 with completion of the railroad and named from the Bolivia post office. The post office was probably named as a complement to Bolivar, a community laid out in 1833 by Joseph Bondurant and named in honor of Simon Bolivar, the founder of Bolivia, South America. Bolivar, a community that never materialized, was laid out a mile north of Bolivia (*Christian County History*, 49). Post office established Nov. 7, 1879.

BOLO. Township. Washington. Changed from May in March 1883. The source of the name is unknown. Bolo is also an alternate name for Posen (q.v.).

BOND. County. Created from Madison County on January 4, 1817, and named for Shadrach Bond (1773–1832), at the time the Illinois receiver of public funds and later the first governor of the state of Illinois, serving from 1818 to 1822. The seat was originally at Perryville and moved to Greenville in 1821.

BONDVILLE. Champaign. Village (1971) three miles west of Champaign. Named for L. J. Bond, a promoter of the community and an official of the Indianapolis, Bloomington and Western Railroad (*History of Champaign County*, 164). Post office established June 24, 1872.

BONE GAP. Edwards. Village (1891) six miles northwest of Albion. Reportedly named for the large number of animal bones found by settlers in the 1830s (Harper, ed., *History of Edwards County*, 46). Post office established March 11, 1868.

BONFIELD. Kankakee. Village (1888) seven and a half miles west of Bourbonnais. Laid out about 1881 as Verkler by site owner John Verkler. Renamed with construction of the Big Four Railroad for Thomas P. Bonfield, an attorney for the railroad and first president of the village of Kankakee (Taylor, *Salina*, 36). Post office established June 19, 1874, as McDowell Farm; changed to Bonfield Feb. 2, 1882.

BONGARD. Champaign. Nine miles southeast of Tolono. Named for site owner Joseph Bongard, who emigrated from Lorraine, France, about 1857 (Bateman and Selby, eds., *Historical Encyclopedia of Illinois and History of Champaign County*, 326).

BONNIE. Jefferson. Village (1914) seven miles south of Mount Vernon. Probably named for Bonnie Johnson, daughter of Pressley Johnson of St. Elmo, an official of the Chicago and Memphis Railroad. Possibly named for Bonnie Johnston, daughter of Benjamin F. Johnston, for whom Johnston City in Williamson County was named (Roberts, *Glimpses of the Past*, 4). Post office established July 27, 1894.

BONPAS. From French *bon pas* (good walk), the name given by early French explorers and settlers to Bon Pas Prairie, from which Bonpas Creek was named. From the stream, the name radiated to several communities and townships. The pronunciation is usually [BUHM puhs] but has varied considerably as suggested by such recordings as Bum-paw, Bumpus, Bompare, Bompas, and Bonpass (Adams, comp., *Illinois Place Names*; *Combined History Edwards, Lawrence, and Wabash Counties*, 81, 319; Harper, ed., *History of Edwards County*, 57).

BONPAS. Richland. Seven miles north-northeast of West Salem. Laid out by Bradford Birkbeck, son of Morris Birkbeck, one of the founders of Albion (q.v.), and Gilbert T. Pell. Named from Bonpas Creek (*History of White County*, 737). Post office established May 15, 1876.

BONUS. Boone. Township. Named from Bonus Prairie. The source of the name is uncertain. One history of Boone County says the name is from Latin *bono* (good) and refers to the quality of the land in the township; another claims that the area was called "Bono" by local Indians, which settlers turned through popular etymology into the more familiar Bonus (Franck, *Landmarks*, 10; *Past and Present of Boone County*, 307). Post office established May 13, 1851, as Russell's Store, named for postmaster James M. Russell; changed to Bonus Oct. 29, 1851.

BOODY. Macon. Six miles southwest of Decatur. Founded about 1870 and named for Col. William Boody, first president of the Decatur and East St. Louis Railroad (Richmond, *Centennial History of Decatur*, 96). Post office established Nov. 18, 1870.

BOONE. County. Created from Winnebago County on March 4, 1837. The enabling legislation specified that the county was "to be called Boone, in honor of Col. Daniel Boone, the first settler of the state of Kentucky." The seat has always been at Belvidere.

BOOS. Jasper. Four miles southeast of Newton. Named for early settler and grocery store proprietor Joseph Boos (*Jasper County*, 12). Post office established April 16, 1878, as Boos Station.

BORTON. Edgar. Twelve miles west-northwest of Paris. Founded about 1881 and named for Jesse Borton, site owner and postmaster (*Prairie Progress*, 153). Post office established July 24, 1882, as Van Sellar; changed to Borton Feb. 15, 1889.

BOSKYDELL. Jackson. Three miles south of Carbondale. Founded about 1877 and named by the Rev. J. L. Hawkins of Carbondale, who claimed that he was dictionary browsing one day and happened upon the word *bosky* (brushy), which he found pleasing, especially when combined with "dell" (Ackerman, *Early Illinois Railroads*, 135–36). Post office established July 24, 1885.

BOURBON [BER buhn]. Douglas. Six miles southwest of Tuscola. Founded in 1853 by Malden Jones. Named for Bourbon County, Ky., home of a number of early settlers, itself named for the French royal family, Les Bourbons, for their help in the American War for Independence (Bateman and Selby, eds., *Illinois Historical Douglas County Biographical*, 623; Niles, *History of Douglas County*, 65; Rennick, *Kentucky Place Names*). Post office established Aug. 18, 1853.

BOURBONNAIS. Kankakee. Village (1875). François Bourbonnais, a French-Potawatomi trapper and fur trader known to white settlers as Bulbona and Bull Bony, established a trading post at what became known as Bulbona Grove in Bureau

County south and west of present Wyanet in the 1820s or early 1830s. Present Bourbonnais was named for François Bourbonnais or for another member of the Bourbonnais family. The Bourbonnais name has a long history in Illinois; one Jean Jacque Brunet *dit* (also known as) Bourbonnais was reported in southern Illinois at the beginning of the eighteenth century. The pronunciation has long been divided between [ber BO nuhs] and [ber buh NAY]. Early spellings such as *Bullbonus* suggest a development to [ber BO nuhs], while others such as *Bourbonne* suggest a development to [ber buh NAY]. The issue of the "proper" pronunciation of the name is of some concern to village officials. In 1976, for the U.S. Bicentennial, the village board passed a resolution making [ber buh NAY] the "official" pronunciation, but, of course, that action had little effect upon those who said [ber BO nuhs]. In general, [ber BO nuhs] is more likely to be heard from people who live in or near the village. The further one gets from Bourbonnais, the more likely the pronunciation will be [ber buh NAY] (Brown, "French Place Names," 465; Brown, ed., *Grundy County*, 464; Hicks, *History of Kendall County*, 45; *Illinois Gazetteer*). Post office established May 6, 1836, as Kankakee; changed to Bulbona's Grove March 15, 1838; changed to Bourbonnais Grove June 30, 1855; changed to Bourbonnais June 20, 1892.

BOWDRE. Douglas. Township. Named for Benjamin Bowdre, a justice of the peace and one of the first county supervisors (*County of Douglas*, 299).

BOWEN. Hancock. Village (1898) twelve miles south-southeast of Carthage. Platted as Bowensburg by Peter C. Bowen in 1863 (Bateman, *Historical Encyclopedia of Illinois and History of Hancock County*, 1070). Post office established Sept. 16, 1857, as Chili Centre; changed to Bowensburg Oct. 23, 1863; changed to Bowen Aug. 5, 1887.

BOWES. Kane. Five miles southwest of Elgin. Formerly known as East Plato. Renamed for Frank B. Bowes, traffic director for the Illinois Central Railroad in the 1910s (Ghrist, *Plato Center Memories*, 39).

BOWLESVILLE. Gallatin. Township and former community. Named for Joseph Bowles, who established Bowlesville in the mid-1850s about three miles southwest of Shawneetown as a residential community for employees of the Bowlesville coal mine (*History of Gallatin, Saline*, 124). Post office established Sept. 21, 1871.

BOYNTON. Tazewell. Fourteen miles north of Lincoln. Formerly called Boyington; changed to Boynton in 1854. The particular Boyington or Boynton family for which the community was named is unknown (Bateman and Selby, eds., *Historical Encyclopedia of Illinois and History of Tazewell County*, 821; *History of Tazewell County*, 396). Post office established June 28, 1852, as Big Prairie; changed to Boynton March 16, 1857.

BRACEVILLE. Grundy. Village (1880) three miles northeast of Gardner. Founded about 1861 and named by the first township supervisor, B. R. Down (or Dowd), for his former home, Braceville, Trumbull County, Ohio. In several early records the name appears as Braysville, apparently a mishearing of Braceville (Adams, comp., *Illinois Place Names;* Bateman and Selby, eds., *Historical Encyclopedia of Illinois and History of Grundy County,* 696; Ullrich, *This Is Grundy County,* 171). Post office established March 2, 1865.

BRADFORD. Stark. Village (1869, 1873) fifteen miles east-southeast of Kewanee. Founded by Bradford S. Foster in the early 1850s (Leeson, *Documents and Biography,* 577). Post office established Oct. 6, 1853.

BRADFORD. Lee. Township. A transfer from Bradford County, Pa., home of a number of early settlers (*History of Lee County,* 448).

BRADLEY. Jackson. Township and former community. Laid out about 1874 southwest of Campbell Hill and named for William Bradley, the first county judge (*History of Jackson County,* 15). Post office established June 25, 1846.

BRADLEY. Kankakee. Village (1896). Founded by J. Herman Hardebeck in 1892 as North Kankakee. The name was changed in 1895 for David Bradley, president of the Bradley Manufacturing Company, makers of farm implements (Bateman and Selby, eds., *Historical Encyclopedia of Illinois and History of Kankakee County,* 744; Johnson, "Kankakee County Communities"; *Illinois Gazetteer*). Post office established Oct. 26, 1892, as North Kankakee; changed to Bradley Oct. 8, 1895.

BRAIDWOOD. Will. City (1873). Founded about 1865. Named for James Braidwood, a Scottish steamship engineer who emigrated to America in 1863 and was instrumental in developing the coal industry in Will County (*Souvenir of Settlement and Progress,* 441; Stevens, *Past and Present of Will County,* 111). Post office established May 29, 1867.

BRECKENRIDGE. Sangamon. Ten miles southeast of Springfield. Founded in 1870 and named for Preston Breckenridge, a local miller (Bateman and Selby, eds., *Historical Encyclopedia of Illinois and History of Sangamon County,* 711). Post office established April 17, 1865, as New Harmony; changed to Breckenridge Dec. 1, 1875.

BREEDS. Fulton. Four miles east of Canton. Founded as Breeds Station by Calvin G. Breed (Irwin, *A to Z Fulton County*). Post office established June 16, 1873.

BREESE [BREEZ]. Clinton. City (1876). Founded about 1855 and named for former resident Sidney Breese (1800–1878), U.S. senator from 1843 to 1849, justice of the Illinois Supreme Court from 1857 to 1878, and author of *The Early History of Illinois* (*Illinois Gazetteer*). Post office established Oct. 30, 1857, as Shoal Creek Station; changed to Breese Jan. 21, 1881.

BREMEN. The name of several communities and townships. Named for Bremen in northwestern Germany, the embarkation point for many German emigrants. The pronunciation is regularly [BREE muhn].

BREMEN. Randolph. Five miles northeast of Chester. Founded by John Lacy and Michael Harman and known as the Harman Settlement until it was formally laid out by Hiram Chapman about 1840. The name *Bremen* may have been suggested by Isaac Lehnherr, proprietor of the first general store (personal communication with Virginia Mansker; www.randolphcountyillinois.net/sub88 .htm). Post office established May 31, 1856.

BRERETON. Fulton. Two miles north of Canton. Founded about 1901 by the Monmouth Coal Company. Probably named for a local family named Brereton; possibly a transfer from Brereton, England. This is the only Brereton in the United States (Irwin, *A to Z Fulton County*). Post office established Aug. 29, 1903.

BREWERSVILLE. Randolph. The current precinct and former community were named for Thomas Brewer, who laid out Brewersville about 1880 (www .randolphcountyillinois.net/sub88.htm). Post office established Oct. 2, 1868.

BRICKTOWN. Randolph. Named from the brick kilns, including the McClurken kiln, which provided building materials and employment in the last half of the nineteenth century. Now part of Sparta (Eggemeyer, *Bricktown, Illinois,* 15).

BRIDGEPORT. Lawrence. City (1865, 1896) four miles west of Lawrenceville. Established by the Ohio and Mississippi Railroad and named by John Burke, railroad foreman, for the bridge that spanned Indian Creek (*Combined History of Edwards, Lawrence, and Wabash Counties,* 328). Post office established March 30, 1855.

BRIDGEVIEW. Cook. Village (1947). Named about 1938 at the suggestion of Richard Lutticke, who reportedly was inspired by the view from the Harlem Avenue bridge (Betsanes, "Miniature Building Boom").

BRIGHTON. Jersey, Macoupin. Village (1859, 1886). Brighton and Bristol were adjacent communities laid out by Nathan Scarritt's land company about 1837. Both names are transfers from Massachusetts, ultimately from Brighton and Bristol in England. Bristol is now part of Brighton (Bentley, *There the Heart Is,* 8; Walker, *History of Macoupin County,* 412). Post office established March 11, 1837.

BRIGHTON PARK. Cook. Chicago community. Founded in 1840 as Brighton, taking its name from the Brighton race track that operated in what is now McKinley Park (Kitagawa and Taeuber, eds., *Local Community Fact Book,* 130). Post office established Oct. 8, 1872, as Factoryville; changed to Brighton Park June 27, 1873.

BRIMFIELD. Peoria. Village (1843, 1895) twelve miles northwest of Peoria. Founded in 1835 as Charleston by Jacob Showalter and Almon Clark. The name was changed in 1843 by William W. Thompson, an Illinois state senator and member of the constitutional convention of 1847, in honor of his birthplace, Brimfield, Mass. (*History of Peoria County*, 574). Post office established June 8, 1837, as Charleston; changed to Brimfield March 30, 1843.

BRISTOL. Kendall. Two miles northeast of Yorkville. Named for Lyman Bristol, who operated a sawmill near the site in the late 1830s. Bristol was annexed by Yorkville in 1957 (Dickson, "Geographical Features and Place Names").

BROADLANDS. Champaign. Village (1902) fifteen miles northeast of Tuscola. Founded in 1883. Broadlands was the estate of Michael Sullivant, for whom Sullivant Township in Ford County and Sullivan [*sic*] Township in Livingston County are named. Sullivant established large-scale, organized farming on several thousand acres in the 1870s. The operation, although on a grand scale, was from all reports remarkably unsuccessful (Bateman and Selby, eds., *Historical Encyclopedia and History of Champaign County*, 803). Post office established Dec. 5, 1877.

BROADMOOR. Marshall, Stark. Fourteen miles east-southeast of Kewanee. Formerly known as Bradford, named for Bradford, Pa. The name was changed when the community was formally organized in 1901. Broadmoor reportedly was chosen for the appearance of the surrounding countryside, which looked, at least to one observer, "like a broad moor" (Stennett, *A History of the Origin*, 47).

BROADWELL. Logan. Village (1869, 1894) six miles south-southwest of Lincoln. Founded in 1856 on the line of the Chicago, Alton and St. Louis Railroad and named for site owner William Broadwell (Stringer, *History of Logan County*, 615). Post office established July 17, 1856.

BROCTON. Edgar. Village (1890) fourteen miles west-northwest of Paris. Named for Brockton, Mass., home of several officials of the Toledo, St. Louis and Western Railroad (*Prairie Progress*, 154). Post office established Feb. 16, 1882.

BROOKFIELD. Cook. Village (1893). Founded in 1889 as Grossdale subdivision by Samuel Eberly Gross. The name *Brookfield* was the winning entry in a contest held in 1905 (*Illinois Guide*). Post office established Oct. 3, 1892, as Grossdale; changed to Brookfield Oct. 1, 1906.

BROOKLYN. There are currently at least four communities in Illinois named Brooklyn: in St. Clair, Schuyler, Grundy, and Lee counties and two townships (in Lee and Schuyler counties). In addition, there have been a number of Brooklyn post offices, historical communities, townships, and voting precincts. Brooklyn Township (McHenry County) is now Nunda, Brooklyn Township (Ogle County) is now Rockvale, and Brooklyn (Will County) is now part of Joliet. Illinois Brooklyns were named for Brooklyn, N.Y., often by way of Brooklyns in Ohio and Indiana. Of particular note is Brooklyn in St. Clair County, now a northern suburb of East St. Louis, which was founded by free African Americans and escaped slaves in 1830 as Lovejoy, named for Elijah P. Lovejoy, the crusading abolitionist newspaper editor. The community was formally laid out as Brooklyn by Thomas Osburn, James P. Morris, Charles Collins, Joseph Tabor, and W. J. Austin in 1837, the year Lovejoy was murdered by a mob in Alton (Cha-Jua, *America's First Black Town*, 31).

BROOKPORT. Massac. City (1888) north of Paducah, Ky. Platted in 1855 as Brooklyn by Charles Pell and a Captain Davis. The word *Brookport* is a blend of "Brooklyn" and "port" (May, *History of Massac County,* 189). Post office established Oct. 18, 1854, as Pellonia, named for Charles Pell; changed to Brookport March 12, 1901.

BROOKS GROVE. McLean. Former community in Allin Township. Named for Miles Brooks, a veteran of the War of 1812. The Brooks Grove Cemetery is twelve miles west-southwest of Bloomington (Townley, *Historic McLean,* 18).

BROUGHTON [BROT uhn]. Livingston. Seven miles north of Eldorado. Named by William Broughton, the first township supervisor and generally acknowledged as the first settler in the area. Originally called Broughtonville (*History of Livingston County* [1878], 287).

BROUILLETTS CREEK. Edgar. Township. Named from Brouilletts Creek, which heads in Edgar County and flows through Vermillion County Ind., before emptying into the Wabash River. Named for Pierre Brouillett or Broullette, a French explorer, trader, and interpreter, who established a trading post at the mouth of the stream about 1801 (*History of Edgar County,* 495).

BROWN. County. Created Feb. 1, 1839 from Schuyler County. Named for Gen. Jacob Jennings Brown (1775–1828), who distinguished himself during the War of 1812, particularly in engagements at Fort Erie, Sacketts Harbor, and Lundy's Lane. The same Jacob Brown founded Brownville, N.Y., near Watertown, in 1802 (Vasiliev, *From Abbotts to Zurich*).

BROWN. Champaign. Township. Named for William Brown, regarded as the second permanent settler in the area (Bateman and Selby, eds., *Historical Encyclopedia and History of Champaign County,* 803).

BROWNFIELD. Pope. Sixteen miles north-northeast of Metropolis. Probably named by Ferris Trovillion for two prominent citizens, John Brown and Lewis Field. Brown ran a hotel and general store at the site, beginning around 1850. In 1857 he added a post office, which he named Wool in honor of Gen. John Elias Wool, who at the time was well known for his service in the War of 1812 and the Mexican War. The early community was informally called Shakerag, reportedly because the stationmaster would wave a piece of cloth to flag coaches on the stage line. With the establishment in 1901 by the Illinois Central Railroad of a new Brownfield a short distance away, most of the buildings were disassembled and moved to the new location along the IC tracks. The few remaining structures became known as Old Brownfield (McCormick, "The Significance of Pope County Place Names," 27; *Pope County,* 24–25). Post office established Aug. 5, 1857, as Wool; changed to Brownfield Aug. 27, 1892.

BROWNING. Franklin. Township. Named for John Browning, an early settler who arrived in the area about 1814 (*History of Gallatin, Saline,* 340).

BROWNING. Schuyler. Village (1882) eight miles north-northeast of Beardstown. Founded in 1848 and named for Orville H. Browning (1810–81), U.S. senator from Illinois from 1861 to 1863, and secretary of the interior under President Andrew Johnson (*Schuyler County,* 241). Post office established April 9, 1850.

BROWNS. Edwards. Village (1892) three miles east of Albion. Originally called Bonpas, named from Bonpas Creek. The name was changed to Frazier in the 1820s for Robert Frazier, the first settler on Frazier's Prairie. An 1892 referendum changed the name to Browns, for John L. Brown, one of the site owners (Harper, ed., *History of Edwards County,* 58; *History of Edwards County,* 15). Post office established May 16, 1881, as Bonpas; changed to Browns Jan. 10, 1882.

BROWNSTOWN. Fayette. Village (1909) eight miles east-northeast of Vandalia. Founded in 1870 by John Brown, the first postmaster (Bateman and Selby, eds., *Historical Encyclopedia of Illinois and History of Fayette County,* 653). Post office established Feb. 25, 1870.

BROWNSVILLE. Jackson. Former community on the Big Muddy River, five miles southwest of Murphysboro. Brownsville was the first seat of Jackson County, serving from 1817 until the courthouse burned in January, 1843, after which the seat was moved to Murphysboro. Brownsville then went into decline and has now disappeared. Likely named for Jacob Brown, a member of the Illinois Territorial Legislature who was instrumental in the formation of Jackson County (Husband, *Old Brownsville Days,* iv; Mohlenbrock, "A New Geography of Illinois: Jackson County," 27). Post office established Nov. 24, 1817.

BRUBAKER. Marion. Five miles northeast of Salem. Founded in 1895 by E. E. Brubaker upon completion of the Chicago, Paducah and Memphis Railroad (Brinkerhoff, *Brinkerhoff's History,* 200). Post office established March 4, 1895.

BRUCE. LaSalle. Township. Probably named for Alexander Bruce, who supervised the building of the locks on the Illinois and Michigan Canal at Marseilles (*Past and Present of LaSalle County,* 329).

BRUCE. Moultrie. Five miles south of Sullivan. Named for John Bruce, one of the first directors of the Wabash, St. Louis and Pacific Railroad (*Combined History of Shelby and Moultrie Counties,* 211). Post office established Feb. 2, 1874.

BRUSH JUNCTION. Williamson. Established near Cambria about 1889. Named for Samuel T. Brush, general manager of the St. Louis and Big Muddy Coal Company (Hubbs, *Pioneer Folks and Places*).

BRUSHY MOUND. Macoupin. Township. Named from Brushy Mound Prairie, itself named for Brushy Mound, a prominent summit near the center of the township (*History of Macoupin County,* 162).

BRUSSELS. Calhoun. Village (1888) twelve miles north of St. Peters, Mo. Named for Brussels, Belgium, the home of the area's first permanent priest, Fr. John Molitor (Underwood, "A New Geography of Calhoun County," 34). Post office established March 14, 1851, as News; changed to Brussels April 7, 1875.

BRYANT. Fulton. Village (1874) six miles southwest of Canton. Named either for Lemuel O'Bryant, a sawmill operator, or for Henry L. Bryant, a director of the Forsyth Mining Company (Irwin, *A to Z Fulton County*). Post office established June 26, 1862.

BUCK. Edgar. Township. Changed from Pilot Grove in May 1857. Probably named for President James Buchanan, called "Buck" in the campaign of 1856 (Bateman and Selby, eds., *Historical Encyclopedia of Illinois and History of Edgar County,* 643).

BUCKEYE. Names with the word *buckeye,* of which there are about two dozen in Illinois, are generally associated with the buckeye oak tree (horse chestnut), itself so named for the resemblance of its nut when it first opens to a buck's eye. In particular, many early schools in Illinois were constructed of logs sawed or hewn from buckeye oaks and called simply the "Buckeye School."

BUCKHEART. Fulton. Township. The traditional account is that one John Pixley, while hunting in a nearby grove, claimed to have shot a deer in the heart, but it escaped. Local citizens derided Pixley for this tall tale and facetiously named the grove Buckheart. The name then spread to Buckheart Creek and from there to the township (Irwin, *A to Z Fulton County*).

BUCKHORN. Brown. Four miles southwest of Mount Sterling. Laid out in 1862 by John L. Briggs. The name was reportedly inspired by an unusually large set of antlers that were on display at the local blacksmith shop (Dearinger, "A New Geography of Brown County," 25). Post office established Dec. 3, 1850.

BUCKINGHAM. Kankakee. Village (1902) sixteen miles southwest of Kankakee. Established in the late 1870s as a station on the Illinois Central Railroad by Ebenezer Buckingham (Bateman and Selby, eds., *Historical Encyclopedia of Illinois and History of Kankakee County,* 761). Post office established Nov. 26, 1878.

BUCKLEY. Iroquois. Village (1872) eleven miles north of Paxton. Founded in 1856 by Ira A. Manly, first station agent for the Illinois Central Railroad. Named by Manly either for a Philadelphia relative named Bulkley (Buckley) or for an employee of the IC (Ackerman, *Early Illinois Railroads,* 125; Dowling, *History of Iroquois County,* 24; *Iroquois County History,* 116). Post office established June 2, 1858, as Bulkley; changed to Buckley Aug. 25, 1865.

BUCKNER. Franklin. Village (1912) five miles west of Benton. Named for Moses Buckner, an early settler. Formerly known as Safronia or Soffrona (Ramsey and Miller, *The Heritage of Franklin County*, 35). Post office established Dec. 30, 1898.

BUDA [BYOO duh]. Bureau. Village (1872) ten miles west-southwest of Princeton. The area was originally known as French Grove, a name it retained until construction of the Chicago, Burlington and Quincy Railroad in 1853–54. Several names were proposed for the CB&Q station, including Concord and Watusa along with Buda. Officials of the CB&Q apparently chose the name for Buda, Hungary (now part of Budapest), which was in the news in the late 1840s because of demonstrations for independence from Austria. LaBuda (a variant name of Golden) in Adams County is unrelated (Arnold, *Buda Our Home Town*, 11–12). Post office established June 19, 1837, as French Grove; changed to Buda Sept. 15, 1855.

BUENA VISTA [BYOO nuh VIS tuh]. Stephenson. Nine miles north of Freeport. Spanish for "good view." Founded in 1852. Named for the battle of Buena Vista, where American forces under the command of Zachary Taylor defeated General Santa Anna during the Mexican War in 1847.

BUFFALO GROVE. Cook, Lake. Village (1958). The area was first known as Muttersholtz (Mother Woods), a name given by early German settlers. Formally established in 1847 and reportedly named for the many buffalo bones found by pioneers (Dretske, *What's in a Name?*). Post office established Sept. 4, 1874.

BUFFALO GROVE. Ogle. One mile west of Polo. Also Buffalo Township. Claimed to be a translation of the Native American word *nanusha* (buffalo). Laid out by Oliver Kellogg and Hugh Stevenson in 1835 as St. Mary's or St. Marion. The name was changed about 1839 to match that of the Buffalo Grove post office. The community prospered until about 1895, when the railroad went through Polo, isolating Buffalo Grove (Bateman and Selby, eds., *Historical Encyclopedia of Illinois and History of Carroll County*, 120; *Bicentennial History of Ogle County*, 208). Post office established Feb. 12, 1833.

BUFFALO HART. Sangamon. Ten miles northeast of Springfield. Named from Buffalo Hart Grove, generally acknowledged as the site of the first permanent settlement in the township; reportedly named for the buffalo and the hart (stag), both of which were plentiful in the area when the first settlers arrived (*History of Sangamon County*, 804). Post office established Feb. 12, 1850.

BUG TUSSLE. Franklin. According to a local story, the community was named when a revival meeting attracted more june bugs than attendees, and the congregation spent most of the evening "tussling with the bugs." Bug Tussell Church (also known as Union Hill Church) is one mile southeast of Christopher (Jurich, *This Is Franklin County*, 19).

BULL CREEK. Lake. Stream. Between Butler Lake and the Des Plaines River; named for early land owner Julius Bull (Dretske, *What's in a Name?*).

BULL FLAT. Effingham. Historical area. Apparently named from Bull Flat Corn Whiskey, "a tablespoonful of which was warranted to kill any human being except the native Bull Flatter, but a half pint of it only made him feel jubilant and a full pint of it put him in good fighting trim" (Perrin, ed., *History of Effingham County,* 148).

BULL VALLEY. McHenry. Village (1977) four miles west-southwest of McHenry. The local story is that sometime in the 1860s William Willis was finding it difficult to plow a particular field with his team of oxen, so he yoked some bulls to the plow with better results. Since then the area has been known as Bull Valley (Young, "One Animal Threatens This Valley").

BULPITT. Christian. Village (1914) seven miles northwest of Taylorville, adjacent to Kincaid. Founded in 1912 by members of the J. C. Bulpit(t) family (Goudy, *History of Christian County,* 288). Post office established Jan. 30, 1824.

BUNCOMBE [BUHNG kuhm] Johnson. Village (1916) five miles northwest of Vienna. According to a local tradition, the name was suggested by Levi Casey for his former home in Buncombe County, N.C. However, W. J. Suit and Thaddeus Q. Proctor, the founders of Buncombe, may have transferred the name from a different Buncombe, perhaps Buncombe, Tenn. (Bucciferro, ed., *Parker's History,* 314; Chapman, *A History of Johnson County,* 286). Post office established June 19, 1871.

BUNGAY. Hamilton. Nine miles northeast of McLeansboro. Formerly known as Needmore because the people who lived there were so poor they "needed more" of everything. The name is probably a transfer from Massachusetts, perhaps influenced by Bungay in Suffolk, England. Related forms include Bungy in Maine and New Hampshire and Bungee in Connecticut. From Algonquian with the general meaning "boundary" or "boundary marker." Bunje, twelve miles northwest of Greenville in Bond County, is likely from the same source (*Hamilton County* 42; Stewart, *American Place-Names*). Post office established Aug. 31, 1893.

BUNKER HILL. Macoupin. City (1857, 1872) fifteen miles northeast of Alton. The town site was purchased by a land company formed in New England in the 1830s. The first settlers, Moses True and John Tilden, arrived at what was then known as Wolf Ridge in 1835, laid out a community in 1836, and named it for Bunker Hill, Mass., site of one of the first battles of the American Revolution (*History of Macoupin County,* 145). Post office established June 22, 1833, as Lincoln; changed to Bunker Hill June 23, 1842.

BURBANK. Cook. City (1970). Earlier known as South Stickney or Burbank Manor. Probably named from the Burbank Manor Fire District, which served the community before its incorporation in 1970; perhaps influenced by the nearby Luther Burbank School (Thompson, "A Town of Regular Joes").

BURDEN CREEK. Pope. Stream. Named for William Burden. Formerly known as Halfway Branch (Allen, *Pope County Notes,* 63).

BUREAU. County. Created Feb. 28, 1837 from Putnam County. Named for Pierre de Bureau, an early French explorer and trapper who established a trading post at the mouth of Bureau Creek in the late eighteenth century. His name has been recorded as Bureo, Beuro, Buero, and Buru, which became Bureau by popular etymology (*Bureau County Centennial,* n.p.; Matson, *Map and Sketches of Bureau County,* 1).

BURGESS. Mercer. Seven miles southeast of Aledo. Named for County Judge H. E. Burgess (Bassett and Goodspeed, *Past and Present of Mercer County,* 482). Post office established Oct. 24, 1911.

BURGESS. Bond. Township. Named for William Burgess, a surveyor who arrived in the area shortly after the end of the War of 1812 (Bateman and Selby, eds., *Historical Encyclopedia of Illinois and History of Bond County,* 637).

BURKSVILLE. Monroe. Four miles south of Waterloo. Founded in 1857 and named for storekeeper John G. Burkhardt (Klein, ed., *Arrowheads to Aerojets,* 579). Post office established Aug. 24, 1857.

BURLINGTON. Kane. Village (1906) three miles south of Hampshire. Named about 1846 by J. W. Hapgood for his former home, Burlington, Vt. (*Biographical and Historical Record of Kane County,* 992). Post office established May 28, 1846.

BURNHAM [BERN uhm]. Cook. Village (1907). Laid out in 1883 and apparently named for Telford Burnham, about whom little is known except that he apparently was not related to Daniel Burnham, the landscape architect who planned and directed much of the development of the Chicago lakefront (Papajohn, "Air Burnham"). Post office established April 16, 1890.

BURNSIDE. Cook. Established in 1862 as a station on the Illinois Central Railroad. Later known as Burnside Crossing, where the tracks of the Chicago, Rock Island and Pacific Railroad crossed those of the IC. Named for Ambrose E. Burnside, treasurer of the IC and a Union general in the Civil War. Probably named by W. W. Jacobs, the principle site owner (Ackerman, *Early Illinois Railroads,* 115; Karlen, *Chicago's Crabgrass Communities,* 93; Kitagawa and Taeuber, eds, *Local Community Fact Book,* 108). Post office established Nov. 23, 1888 as Burnside Crossing.

BURNSIDE. Hancock. Six miles north of Carthage. Platted by J. B. McMillan about 1868; also named for Ambrose E. Burnside (*History of Hancock County,* 451). Post office established April 17, 1868.

BURNT PRAIRIE. White. Village (1928) ten miles southeast of Fairfield. Reportedly named from the fact that this section of the prairie had been thoroughly burned over in the recent past. Formerly known as Liberty (*History of White County*, 622). Post office established Aug. 14, 1828.

BURR RIDGE. Cook, DuPage. Village (1956). Named from Burr Oak Ridge, an elevated area whose primary vegetation was bur [*sic*] oaks. In the late 1950s the village of Harvester, named for the International Harvester Corporation, and two unincorporated subdivisions, Burr Ridge Estates and Woodview Estates, merged as Burr Ridge (Tennison, "Quite a Find").

BURTON. Adams. Six miles east of Quincy. Founded about 1836. The traditional story is that the name was brought to Illinois by settlers from Burton upon Trent, Staffordshire, England (Genosky, ed., *People's History*, 696; www.rootsweb .com/~iladams/places/placenames.htm). Post office established Dec. 7, 1840.

BURTON. McHenry. Township. Formerly known as English Prairie; settled by immigrants from England in the 1830s. The name was subsequently changed to Benton and in 1850 to Burton, for Burton Stevens, the son of Maj. Alfred Stevens, a Revolutionary War veteran and early settler (Nye, ed., *McHenry County Illinois*, 423).

BUSH. Williamson. Village (1905) five miles northwest of Herrin. Founded in 1902 and named for Benjamin Franklin Bush, president of the Western Coal and Mining Company and fuel agent for the Missouri and Pacific Railroad. Bush was later president of the M&P (Hubbs, *Pioneer Folks and Places*). Post office established July 25, 1904.

BUSHNELL [BUSH nuhl]. McDonough. City (1865, 1878). Founded in 1854 and named for Nehemiah Bushnell, president of the Northern Cross Railroad (Donovan, "Named for Railroad Presidents," 26; Shadwick, *History of McDonough County*, 220). Post office established July 25, 1848 as Drowning Fork; changed to Bushnell March 13, 1858.

BUSHTON. Coles. Six miles north-northeast of Charleston. Founded in 1881 by site owners David and John Bush. David Bush was the first postmaster, and John Bush was the third (Redlich, *The Postal History of Coles County*, 107). Post office established Aug. 22, 1881.

BUTLER. Montgomery. Village (1873) three miles northwest of Hillsboro. Laid out in 1855 and named for early settler Butler Seward. The name was perhaps influenced by settlers from Butler County, Ohio (Traylor, *Past and Present of Montgomery County*, 755). Post office established Jan. 29, 1856.

BUTLER. Vermilion. Township. Named in 1864 at the suggestion of the first township supervisor for Gen. Benjamin Franklin Butler, who distinguished himself in the Civil War, especially during the capture of New Orleans in 1862 (Beckwith, *History of Vermilion County*, 313).

BUTTON. Ford. Township. Named for James Porter Button, county treasurer, justice of the peace, and first township supervisor (*Ford County History*, 38). Post office established March 13, 1876.

BYBEE [BEYE bee]. Fulton. Seven miles northwest of Canton. Probably named for David Bybee, who donated land for construction of a station on the Fulton County Narrow Gauge Railway about 1880. Possibly named for Postmaster William Bybee (Irwin, *A to Z Fulton County*). Post office established Sept. 29, 1881.

BYRON. Ogle. City (1878). Founded in 1835 as Fairview by Jared Sanford and named for his former home, Fairview, Conn. For unknown reasons the name was changed to Bloomingville and later to Bloomingdale. To avoid confusion with Bloomington in McLean County, Leonard Andrus suggested Byron for George Gordon, Lord Byron. At the time (about 1838) Byron was quite popular in America, and Andrus admired his poems (*History of Ogle County*, 299; Thompson and Thompson, *Byron Centennial Souvenir Booklet*, 4). Post office established May 26, 1838.

C

CABERY [KAY bree]. Ford, Kankakee. Village (1881) twenty miles southwest of Kankakee. Founded about 1878 with construction of the Bloomington branch of the Kankakee and Southwestern Railroad. Named for John R. Caberry [*sic*], a Chicago merchant and a benefactor of the Masonic lodge in the late 1870s (Majorowiz, comp., *History of Norton Township*, 45). Post office established April 27, 1869.

CABLE. Mercer. Thirteen miles south of Moline. Probably named for Ransom R. Cable, president of the Chicago, Rock Island and Pacific Railroad in the 1870s. Possibly named for Philander Cable, who extended the railroad line from Reynolds to the coal mines at Cable (Bassett and Goodspeed, *Past and Present of Mercer County*, 473; Donovan, "Named for Railroad Presidents," 26). Post office established March 7, 1877.

CACHE [KASH]. French for "hidden" or "hiding place." Most names with the word *Cache* derive from the Cache River. According to local tradition, the Cache, which flows through five southern Illinois counties, was given its name about 1702 by Fr. Jean Mermet. Mermet and a party of French explorers were crossing an area where they could hear but not see running water because of accumulated debris and driftwood. Father Mermet is said to have remarked "ce crique est cache" (this creek [cove] is hidden). Lily Cache in Will County southeast of Plainfield was named from La Cache Creek, now called Lily (or Lilly) Cache Creek, reportedly where an early trader named Cerré secreted bundles of trade goods and supplies while he bargained with Indians (Beadles, *A History of Southernmost Illinois*, 5; Maue, *History of Will County*, 341).

CADIZ [KAY diz, kuh DIZ]]. Hardin. Twenty miles southeast of Harrisburg. Possibly named for Cadiz, the province and port in southwestern Spain, but more likely a transfer from Cadiz, Ky. Post office established June 30, 1905.

CAHOKIA [kuh HO kee uh]. St. Clair. Village (1927). Southern fringe of the St. Louis metropolitan area. Also township in Macoupin County. Cahokia is the oldest permanent European settlement in Illinois. A French missionary post, the Mission of the Holy Family, was established at the site in 1699 by missionaries from the Seminary of Quebec. The name is from the Cahokia, a subtribe of the Illinois, recorded as Kaockhia by LaSalle about 1682. Cahokia was the seat of St. Clair County from its formation in 1790 until 1814, when it was moved to Belleville (*History of St. Clair County,* 67). Post office established April 1, 1802.

CAIRO. Alexander. City (1818, 1873). Chartered in 1818 as the City and Bank of Cairo by John G. Comegys, Shadrach Bond (the first governor of the state of Illinois and the namesake of Bond County), and several others who organized a land company for the purpose of developing the southern tip of Illinois. The enterprise collapsed, and the land lay vacant until 1835, when it was reentered by the Cairo City and Canal Company. According to most sources, Comegys named the community for Cairo, Egypt, because it lies at the confluence of the Ohio and Mississippi rivers, much as Cairo, Egypt, lies along the Nile. This account is certainly plausible. For a number of years before Cairo was founded, the Mississippi River was known as the American Nile, and that may indeed have inspired the original site owners. In 1940, however, Barry Gilbert claimed that his grandfather, Miles Gilbert, one of the incorporators of the Cairo City and Canal Company, told him that "people were mistaken in thinking that it was named Cairo because of the rivers, but that it had been named for a man who was known as 'Dr. Cairo' and who called himself Care-o" ("KI-RO?" 360). Unfortunately, a likely Dr. Cairo has yet to be found. The local pronunciation is regularly [KER o], but outside of southern Illinois one is as likely as not to hear [KAY ro] (*see* Egypt) (*Illinois Guide;* Wade, *The Urban Frontier,* 64). Post office established Nov. 8, 1837, as Mouth of Ohio; changed to Cairo Sept. 16, 1839.

CALEDONIA [kal uh DON yuh]. Boone. Village (1995) seven miles north-northwest of Belvidere. First known as the Scotch Settlement for the large number of immigrants from Aberdeen, Scotland, in the 1840s and 1850s. Caledonia, the Roman name for northern Britain, was suggested by Gavin Ralston, an early settler (Bateman and Selby, eds., *Historical Encyclopedia of Illinois and History of Boone County,* 57; Hadley, *A History of Boone County,* 93). Post office established May 1, 1844, as Precinct; changed to Caledonia Station Dec. 17, 1853; changed to Caledonia May 15, 1883.

CALEDONIA. Pulaski. Former community on the Ohio River near Olmsted. Founded about 1843 by Justus Post and named from the Caledonia post office. Caledonia was the first seat of Pulaski County, serving from 1843 until 1865, when it was moved to Mound City (Moyer, *Moyers' Brief History,* 19). Post office established Jan. 16, 1835.

CALHOUN. County. Created January 10, 1825, from Pike County. Named for John C. Calhoun (1782–1850) of South Carolina, U.S. senator, and secretary of state under President John Tyler. When the county was created, Calhoun was vice president of the United States. The county is sometimes called the "Kingdom of Calhoun," a name that probably originated with John Shaw, an Illinois state representative of the 1830s who often began his speeches with "I am John Shaw, a prince, and Calhoun is my kingdom." The *Encyclopedia of Illinois* is in error when it claims that the county was named for John B. Calhoun, a land commissioner for the Illinois Central Railroad (personal communication with Louis E. Retzer).

CALUMET. The word *calumet* refers to the ceremonial pipe, the "peace pipe" used by Native Americans of the Great Lakes region. The word probably originated in Canadian French through popular etymology where *calumet,* French for "reed, pipe," was substituted for a native word of roughly similar sound. There are about three dozen features in Illinois named Calumet; all but one are in Cook County. The first named was the Calumet River, which was also recorded as Callimink, Calumic, and Kellimock (Avis, *A Dictionary of Canadianisms; Calumet Region Historical Guide,* 8–9; Vogel, *Indian Place Names in Illinois*).

CALVIN. White. Eleven miles northeast of Carmi. Named for the Calvin family, early settlers in what is now Phillips township. A. W. Calvin or Price Calvin (or both) owned the land on which the Wabash, St. Louis and Pacific Railroad was built about 1895. Orville Calvin was an early station agent (*Centennial History of Crossville,* 11). Post office established April 28, 1897.

CAMARGO [kuh MAHR go]. Douglas. Village (1904) six miles east of Tuscola. Isaac Moss founded a community called New Salem in 1836. New Albany was laid out adjacent to New Salem in 1840. The communities merged about 1868 and took the name of the township, Camargo, itself named for Cuidad Camargo, south of Chihuahua, Mexico. The name was suggested by Col. Joseph B. McCown, one of the commissioners appointed to organize the county into townships. McCown may have passed through Ciudad Camargo during his service in the Mexican War (*County of Douglas,* 287, 292). Post office established Feb. 20, 1858.

CAMBRIA [KAM bree uh]. Williamson. Village (1905) four miles west-southwest of Herrin. Formerly known as Reeves, named for farmer Albert P. Reeves, and later known as Lauder, for Hugh Lauder, mayor of Carbondale in the late 1890s. The name was changed to Cambria about 1911. Cambria is the medieval Latin name for Wales and was suggested as the name of the Illinois Central station by Evan and Thomas John, natives of South Wales and part owners of the Carterville and Big Muddy Coal Company (Hale, comp. and ed., *Williamson County,* 117, 119, 128; Hubbs, *Pioneer Folks and Places*). Post office established March 17, 1905, as Reeves; changed to Cambria July 22, 1911.

CAMBRIDGE. Henry. Village (1861, 1874). Founded about 1843 by Joseph Tillson and named for Cambridge, Mass. Tillson was from Wrentham, Mass., southwest of Boston. Cambridge has been the seat of Henry County since 1843 (Kiner, *History of Henry County,* 456). Post office established April 17, 1841, as Strawberry Grove; changed to Cambridge Aug. 24, 1844.

CAMERON. Warren. Seven miles east of Monmouth. Founded in 1854 by Robert Cameron as Cameronville, a station on the Chicago, Burlington and Quincy Railroad (*Past and Present of Warren County,* 172). Post office established April 3, 1837, as Cold Brook; changed to Cameron April 4, 1855.

CAMPBELL. Coles. Five miles south of Charleston. Named for postmaster Eugenia Campbell. Also known as Farmington, named by a Mrs. Adams for her former home, Farmington, Tenn. (Perrin, Graham, and Blair, *History of Coles County,* 429; Redlich, *The Postal History of Coles County,* 38). Post office established Dec. 22, 1838.

CAMPBELL HILL [KAM uhl HIL]. Jackson. Village (1875) fifteen miles east of Chester. Originally called Bradley for Judge William Bradley. The name was changed in honor of Elisha and Lavina Campbell, early settlers who built a log cabin in the area about 1839 (Ruebke, *Do You Remember Campbell Hill?* 2). Post office established June 25, 1846, as Bradley; changed to Campbell Hill May 15, 1876.

CAMPBELL'S ISLAND. Rock Island. Island in the Mississippi River north of Moline. Named for John Campbell, a U.S. Army officer whose troops engaged a force of Indians near the site in July 1814 (*Galena Guide,* 526).

CAMP CREEK. McDonough. Stream. Reportedly so named because William Osborne, the first settler in the township, camped along the creek in the summer of 1829 (Clarke, *History of McDonough County,* 69).

CAMP LOGAN. Lake. Named for Gen. John A. Logan, who raised and commanded a regiment from southern Illinois in the early years of the Civil War. Camp Logan was located in what is now Illinois Beach State Park, northeast of Zion. It was established in 1890 as a rifle range for the Illinois militia and later used as a training camp by the Illinois National Guard (Dretske, *What's in a Name?*). Post office established Oct. 11, 1918.

CAMP POINT. Adams. Village (1857, 1874) eighteen miles northeast of Quincy. Originally known as Garrett's Mill for Peter B. Garrett, who operated a grist and carding mill at the site. Platted by Garrett as Indian Camp Point in 1854, named for a point of timber that extended onto the prairie and was thought to be an Indian campground (Genosky, ed., *People's History,* 680). Post office established May 19, 1848.

CAMPTON. Kane. Township. Originally called Fairfield, named by Timothy Garvin for Fairfield, Vt., and later known as Milo. The name was changed in 1850 at the request of Joseph P. Bartlett, the first township supervisor, for his birthplace,

Campton Township in Grafton County, N.H. (*Biographical and Historical Record of Kane County*, 250; *Past and Present of Kane County*, 468). Post office established Oct. 27, 1851.

CANADA SETTLEMENT. Ogle. Former community west of Mount Morris. Founded by a group of Torontonians in the late 1830s. Canada Road is now the only reminder of the settlement (*Bicentennial History of Ogle County*, 201).

CANAVILLE [KAY nuh vil]. Williamson. Former community about three miles northwest of Creal Springs on Canaville Road. Founded about 1889 and named from the Cana Missionary Baptist Church. The church was originally called the Caney Church, named after the Big and Little Caney (now Cana and Little Cana) Creeks, themselves named for the local canebrakes. Through popular etymology, the name of the church became Cana, for the biblical city of Cana northeast of Nazareth, where, according to the Book of John, Jesus performed his first miracle. The former Caney School was located about seven miles southwest of Creal Springs. Later known as Willeford (Hubbs, *Pioneer Folks and Places;* Sneed, *Ghost Towns of Southern Illinois*, 246). Post office established May 31, 1888.

CANTEEN. St. Clair. Township. Named from Cantine Creek, itself named from La Cantine (the tavern), a trading post established for French soldiers about 1776 near present-day Fairmont City. By popular etymology the word *cantine* became *canteen.* The post was abandoned in the mid-1780s (Walthall and Benchley, *The River L'abbe Mission*, 85).

CANTON [KANT uhn]. Fulton. City (1849, 1892). Founded in 1825 by Isaac Swan and Nathan Jones. Named by Swan for the city of Canton (Guangzhou) in southeastern China. According to Alonzo M. Swan, "Canton received its name . . . from a notion [Isaac Swan] entertained that in its location it was directly the antipodes of its Chinese namesake. Pekin . . . had been laid out a short time previously, and Isaac determined, he said, 'that the two celestial cities should be represented at precisely their opposite pole on the earth's surface'" (*Canton*, 7). It was a general notion in the nineteenth century (and later) that if Americans dug deep enough they would eventually emerge in China (*see* Pekin) (Lewis, *Reflections of Canton*, 4–5). Post office established Aug. 3, 1826.

CANTRALL [KAN truhl]. Sangamon. Village (1894) eight miles north of Springfield. Founded as a station on the Springfield and Northwestern Railroad in 1872 by site owner Joseph Cantrall (Bateman and Selby, eds., *Historical Encyclopedia of Illinois and History of Sangamon County*, 901). Post office established July 24, 1873.

CAPRON [KAY pruhn]. Boone. Village (1873) six miles west-southwest of Harvard. Formerly called Helgasaw (or Halgisaw) for one of the leaders of the group of Scandinavian settlers that arrived in the early 1840s. Renamed about 1859 for

John Capron, a conductor on the Galena and Chicago Union Railroad (Hadley, *A History of Boone County,* 86). Post office established Sept. 27, 1860, as Halgisaw; changed to Capron July 9, 1861.

CARBONDALE. Jackson. City (1869, 1873). Founded in 1852 with construction of the Illinois Central Railroad. The name was suggested by Daniel H. Brush, one of the founders of Carbondale. In his words, "I proposed that inasmuch as the town was in a coal region it should be called Carbondale, which was agreed to, and this name was entered upon the plat" (Mitchell, *Carbondale,* 10). Post office established Feb. 27, 1854.

CARDIFF. Livingston. Seven miles east-southeast of Dwight. Named by Welsh coal miners for the city of Cardiff in southern Wales (Bateman and Selby, eds., *Historical Encyclopedia of Illinois and History of Livingston County,* 824). Post office established Jan. 3, 1899.

CARLIN. Calhoun. Precinct. Formed in 1839. Probably named for Thomas Carlin, elected governor of Illinois the year before (Carpenter, *Calhoun Is My Kingdom,* 28).

CARLINVILLE. Macoupin. City (1837, 1887). Founded in 1829 and named for Thomas Carlin (1789–1852), at the time an Illinois state senator who was instrumental in securing passage of the act that created Macoupin County. Carlin was later governor of Illinois, serving from 1838 to 1842. Carlinville has been the seat of Macoupin County since 1829 (Walker, *History of Macoupin County,* 79). Post office established Feb. 26, 1830.

CARLOCK. McLean. Village (1959) seven miles northwest of Normal. Founded about 1886 with construction of the Lake Erie and Western Railroad by site owner John Franklin Carlock. When the railroad bypassed the nearby community of Oak Grove, most of the buildings there were disassembled and moved to Carlock (*Carlock,* 14; Hasbrouck, *History of McLean County,* 121). Post office established May 14, 1866, as Oak Grove; changed to Carlock Jan 17, 1889.

CARLYLE [kahr LEYEL]. Clinton. City (1837, 1884). Founded about 1815. The traditional story is that the city and later the township were named in honor of Thomas Carlyle (1795–1881), the Scottish historian and philosopher. There are several problems with this account, however. As historian John Allen points out, the name was in use "long before Carlyle had become at all noted" (*Legends,* 49). Furthermore, the post office was established as Carlisle and not Carlyle. Most likely the name is a transfer from Carlisle, Schoharie County, N.Y. (itself named in 1807 for Carlisle Pierce), and perhaps influenced by settlers from Carlisle, Pa., or Carlisle, Ind., itself named for Carlisle, Pa. The spelling was changed from Carlisle to Carlyle in 1830 at the request of postmaster Charles Slade, probably in recognition of Thomas Carlyle, who was then developing a reputation as an author. Slade was born in England and would have been familiar with Carlyle's writings (*Commercial History of Clinton County,* 32; Maxey, ed., *Annals of Carlyle,* 5, 9–10).

CARMAN. Henderson. Four miles southeast of Burlington, Iowa. When the Carthage and Burlington Railroad was completed in 1870, much of Shokokon (q.v.) was physically moved a mile or so southeast to trackside and renamed Carman for site owner Joseph Carman (Sutton, *Rivers, Railways,* 85). Post office established Aug. 26, 1833, as Shokoken; changed to Carman April 24, 1872.

CARMI [KAHR meye]. White. City (1819, 1873). Founded about 1815 by Lowry Hay, Leonard White, and James Ratcliffe. A traditional account is that Carmi was named for the biblical Carmi, the son of Reuben and grandson of Jacob, a name perhaps proposed by the Rev. John C. Slocumb, a Methodist minister, or by Daniel Hay. An early history of Carmi by William D. Hay, grandson of Daniel Hay, offers the following explanation for the choice of this unusual name: "There were several names suggested, but it was desired that it have some significance and be a Bible name and short. So when the name Carmi was mentioned and it was shown that Carmi . . . was a worker in a vineyard and the word itself meant vinedresser, it was at once considered as being very appropriate, as the woods were almost a tangle of wild grape vines" ("A Matter of History," 65). The biblical Carmi was indeed the ultimate source of the name, but the immediate source was probably Carmi Wells, an early settler from Vermont who was named for the biblical Carmi, and his son, also named Carmi. Carmi Wells, father and son, moved into the area about the time the community was formally established. Carmi has been the seat of White County since 1816 (Griffith, "Egyptian Place Names," 30; Hay, "A Matter of History," 3, 65; Pyle, "Judge," n.p.; *Sesquicentennial Carmi,* n.p.). Post office established Feb. 12, 1817.

CAROL STREAM. DuPage. Village (1959). Named by developer Jay Stream, the founder of Streamwood, for Carol Stream, the creek running through the subdivision, which was named for his daughter, Carol (Moore, *Build Your Own Town,* 28).

CARONDELET, East [kuh RAHN duh LET]. St. Clair. Village (1876). Named for its location east of the Carondelet neighborhood of St. Louis, itself named for Francesco Luis Hector de Carondelet, the governor general of Louisiana in the 1790s. Formerly known as Morganville and Henryville (Ramsay, *Our Storehouse of Missouri Place Names,* 48; *Tapestry of Time,* 39). Post office established March 11, 1874, as Henryville; changed to East Carondelet June 1, 1875.

CARPENTERSVILLE. Kane. Village (1887). Charles and Daniel Carpenter, from Uxbridge, Mass., were early settlers who established a sawmill on the Fox River in the late 1830s. The community was founded by Charles's son, Angelo, about 1850. Carpentersville has long been concerned about the "working-class" image the name presents relative to neighboring West Chicago suburbs such as

Barrington and Crystal Lake, and an issue in the mayoral campaign of 1987 was whether or not to change the name to Dundee in order to trade upon the more prestigious associations of nearby East Dundee and West Dundee. The pro-change candidate lost the election, but there is still talk of changing the name in an attempt to create a more upscale, cosmopolitan image for the community (Armstrong, "Carpentersville Looking to 'Dundee'"). Post office established Feb. 4, 1863.

CARR CREEK. Monroe. Stream. Called by the French Grand Risseau (Large Gully). Fort Piggott, erected by James Piggott about 1783, was located along the creek near present Columbia. The particular Carr for whom the stream is named is unknown (*History of Columbia*, 7).

CARRIER MILLS. Saline. Village (1894) six miles southwest of Harrisburg. Founded about 1871 by William H. Carrier, known as "Uncle Wash." Carrier operated several sawmills in the area and was engaged by the Cairo and Vincennes Railroad to supply ties for tracks and timbers for bridges. At one time the community was known as Catskin, which, according to local stories, originated when a trapper tricked the local storekeeper into accepting in trade a "mink pelt" that was in fact a cat's hide (Harris, "Illinois Place-Name Lore," 220; *History of Saline County*, 195). Post office established Oct. 2, 1873.

CARROLL. County. Created from Jo Daviess County on Feb. 22, 1839. Named for Charles Carroll (1737–1832) of Carrollton (Md.), the longest surviving signer of the Declaration of Independence. When the county was created, the honor of choosing its name was given to Isaac Chambers, from Allegheny County, Md., and the oldest living resident. Clayton's *Illinois Fact Book* claims the county was named for John Carroll of Carrollton (1735–1815), an acquaintance of Charles Carroll and the first bishop of the Roman Catholic Church in the United States, but that is in error (Thieme, ed., *Carroll County*, 1).

CARROLL. Vermilion. Township. Probably named for Charles Carroll of Carrollton as well. The name was first applied to Carroll Precinct, named in the late 1820s, about the time Charles Carroll would have been celebrating his ninetieth birthday. The choice of the name may have been influenced by Abraham Carroll, a prominent local figure (*History of Carroll Township, History of Casey, Illinois*, 8; Williams, *History of Vermilion County*, 247).

CARROLLTON. Greene. City (1861, 1883). Also named for Charles Carroll of Carrollton, by site owner Thomas Carlin, for whom Carlinville (q.v.) was named, at the time a state senator and a great admirer of Charles Carroll of Carrollton (Cunningham, *History of the Carrollton, Illinois, Area*, 42). Post office established Oct. 12, 1822.

CARSON. Fayette. Township. Named for W. L. Carson, an agricultural entrepreneur credited with introducing the first purebred livestock to the area (Bateman and Selby, eds., *Historical Encyclopedia of Illinois and History of Fayette County,* 644).

CARTERVILLE. Williamson. City (1892). Founded about 1870 as Georgetown by George McNeill (McNeal). Because there was an existing Georgetown post office, the community was renamed for Laban Carter, who opened the first commercial coal mine in the area about 1872 (Scoby, *The History of Carterville,* 93). Post office established May 28, 1837, as Fredonia; changed to Carterville Dec. 18, 1871.

CARTHAGE [KAHR thij]. Hancock. City (1837, 1883). Founded in 1833 as the seat of Hancock County. Carthage was apparently named by one or more of the commissioners appointed by the state legislature to locate the county seat, William Gilham, Scott Riggs, and John Hardin. In their report they state simply that they called the site Carthage but give no reasons. Some writers attribute the choice to a general interest in exotic names characteristic of the first half of the nineteenth century, and others feel that Carthage was named directly for the city in North Africa noted for its bitter battles with Rome (the Punic Wars). A recent county history claims that two of the three men who sited and named the community were from Carthage, Tenn., and that is likely the direct source of the name (Allen, *Legends and Lore of Southern Illinois,* 47; *History of Hancock County,* 207; Stewart, *American Place-Names;* personal communication with Frank Burkett). Post office established April 27, 1833.

CARTWRIGHT. Sangamon. Township. Named for Peter Cartwright, a pioneer Methodist circuit rider in Indiana, Kentucky, and Illinois. Cartwright made his home in Pleasant Plains in Sangamon Township from 1824 until his death in 1872 (Bateman and Selby, eds., *Historical Encyclopedia of Illinois and History of Sangamon County,* 702; *History of Sangamon County,* 817).

CARY. McHenry. Village (1893). Founded in 1856 by site owner William D. Cary as a station on the Illinois and Wisconsin Railroad (*Illinois Guide*). Post office established April 25, 1856, as Cary Station; changed to Cary on May 15, 1927.

CASEY [KAY si]. Clark. City (1874). Earlier called Cumberland, a trading post and rest stop on the Cumberland or National Road. Formally laid out about 1854 and named from the Casey post office, itself named for Zadoc Casey, at the time a U.S. representative from Illinois (Bateman and Selby, eds., *Historical Encyclopedia of Illinois and History of Clark County,* 662). Post office established March 27, 1838.

CASEYVILLE [KAY si vil]. St. Clair. Village (1869, 1875) eight miles east of St. Louis. Named for Zadoc Casey, former lieutenant governor of Illinois and at the time an official of the Illinois Coal Company, which founded the village in 1849 (*History of St. Clair County,* 247). Post office established Feb. 3, 1853.

CASNER. Jefferson. Township. Named for George Casner, regarded as the first permanent settler, arriving in the early 1820s (Wall, *Wall's History,* 186).

CASPARS. Washington. Fourteen miles west-southwest of Nashville, between Biddleborn and Lively Grove. Named for postmaster Caspar Schaefer (Adams, comp., *Illinois Place Names*). Post office established Feb. 1, 1876.

CASS. County. Created March 3, 1837 from Morgan County. Named for Lewis Cass (1782–1866), governor of Michigan Territory, secretary of war under Andrew Jackson, and secretary of state under James Buchanan. At the time the county was formed, Cass was U.S. ambassador to France.

CASS. Township. Fulton. Also named for Lewis Cass (Irwin, *A to Z Fulton County*).

CASTLE FIN. Clark. Five miles north of Marshall. Founded by Robert Wilson in 1848 and named for Caislean na Finne, his ancestral home in Ireland (*History of Marshall, Illinois, and Eastern Clark County*, 23).

CASTLETON. Stark. Four miles northeast of Wyoming. Founded in 1870 by Dr. Alfred H. Castle (Leeson, *Documents and Biography*, 609). Post office established April 20, 1870.

CATFISH CREEK. Edgar. Stream. Reportedly named for a "monster" catfish caught by Thomas Dohette, an early settler (*History of Edgar County*, 499). Post office established June 15, 1869.

CATLIN [KAT luhn]. Vermilion. Village (1873) six miles southwest of Danville. Originally called Butler's Point for first settler James Butler. Formally laid out in 1856 by Guy Merrill and Josiah Hunt and named for J. M. Catlin, president of the Great Western Railroad (*Illinois Guide*; Tuggle, comp., *Stories of Historical Days*, 10). Post office established Dec. 22, 1854, as Butler's Point; changed to Catlin July 27, 1858.

CAVE. Franklin. Township. Named from the Cave post office, itself named for Cave Johnson, postmaster general of the United States from 1845 to 1849 (Aiken, *Franklin County History*, 97). Post office established Sept. 27, 1847.

CAVE IN ROCK. Hardin. Village (1901) twenty-five miles southeast of Harrisburg. Named from the natural cave in the bluff along the Ohio River, a landmark for boatmen since the seventeenth century. The name was recorded in a French account of about 1729 as Caverne dans Le Roc. Cave in Rock has been an Illinois state park since 1929 (Hansen, ed., *Illinois*, 445–46). Post office established March 13, 1832, as Rock and Cave; changed to Cave-in-Rock Oct. 24, 1849.

CAYUGA. Livingston. Four miles northeast of Pontiac. Transferred by settlers from Cayuga County in western New York state in the 1850s. Cayuga is the name of an Iroquois tribe (Vogel, *Indian Place Names in Illinois*). Post office established May 1, 1857.

CAZENOVIA [ka zuh NO vee uh]. Woodford. Four miles northeast of Metamora. Named by four brothers-in-law: Jeter Foster, Elisha Rice, Thomas Clark, and John Safford, from Cazenovia, Madison County, N.Y., itself named about 1795 for Theophilus Cazenove, the first agent of the Holland Land Company. The area had informally been called Cazanovia for some time before the township was created in 1852. The community of Cazenovia was founded about 1870 and took the name of the township (Adams, comp., *Illinois Place Names;* Perrin and Hill, *Past and Present,* 359; Vasiliev, *From Abbotts to Zurich*). Post office established Jan 30, 1871.

CEDAR. Knox. Township. Reportedly named for a cedar tree that grew from a seedling that early settler Joseph Latimer had carried to Illinois in 1831. The name was changed from Cherry Grove in 1853 (*Annals of Knox County,* 34).

CEDARVILLE. Stephenson. Village (1849, 1884) five miles north of Freeport. Founded in 1840 as Harrison, named for William Henry Harrison, at the time a candidate for president of the United States. Shortly after Harrison was elected, the name was changed to Cedar Creek Mills for the grist mill on the Cedar River (*History of Stephenson County,* 64; *Illinois Guide*). Post office established April 7, 1840, as Cedar Creek Mills; changed to Cedarville May 26, 1853.

CENTERVILLE. Most of the two dozen or so Centervilles in Illinois took their names from the actual or presumed fact that the location was near the center of a particular county or township. Shifting county boundaries often repositioned the site, but the name was usually retained. About half are spelled Centreville, adding a fashionable European touch to the name.

CENTRAL CITY. Marion. Village (1857, 1891). North suburb of Centralia. Named about 1851 by and for the Illinois Central Railroad (Seibel, *My Home Town,* 17). Post office established April 22, 1854.

CENTRALIA. Clinton, Marion. City (1859, 1893). Founded in 1853 by the Illinois Central Railroad. Named for the IC at the suggestion of John W. Merritt, publisher of the *Salem Advocate* newspaper (*Illinois Gazetteer;* Ross, *Centralia, Illinois,* 22). Post office established Sept. 13, 1837, as Crooked Creek; changed to Centralia March 31, 1854.

CEREAL. Livingston. Four miles south of Chatsworth. Originally known as Healey for the Healey Grain Elevator built by local farmers on a spur of the Illinois Central Railroad in the 1850s. The elevator was bought by the Quaker Oats Company, which changed the name to Cereal (*History of Livingston County* [1991], 27).

CERRO GORDO [SEHR uh GOR do, SEHR uh GOR duh, SEHR o GOR duh]. Piatt. Village (1873) eight miles east of Decatur. Formerly known as Griswald, named for the president of the Great Western Railroad, which established a station in the early 1840s. Renamed about 1854 for the Cerro Gordo post office, itself named in commemoration of the Mexican War battle between American and Mexican troops in 1847. The name may have been suggested by John S. Williams, an officer in the Mexican War who was known locally as Cerro

Gordo Williams. Cerro Gordo (Fat Hill) is a mountain pass between Veracruz and Jalapa on the east coast of Mexico (*Cerro Gordo Centennial;* n.p.; Miller, *Life and Times of Cerro Gordo,* 3; Piatt, *History of Piatt County,* 461). Post office established Aug. 19, 1847.

CHADWICK. Carroll. Village (1892) seven miles southeast of Mount Carroll. Established about 1886 by the St. Paul Land Company as a station on the Chicago, Burlington and Northern Railroad, which was extending its line from Aurora to Savanna. The name is probably that of a railroad official (Bateman and Selby, eds., *Historical Encyclopedia of Illinois and History of Carroll County,* 698; Thiem, ed., *Carroll County,* 210). Post office established Aug. 19, 1886.

CHALFIN BRIDGE. Monroe. Three miles south of Monroe City. Named for the Chalfin (or Chaffin) family, early settlers in the 1790s. Family members include Isaac Chalfin and his sons, James and William (Klein, ed., *Arrowheads to Aerojets,* 553). Post office established Jan. 29, 1874.

CHALLACOMBE. Macoupin. Thirteen miles west-southwest of Carlinville. Named for Nicholas Challacombe, the first supervisor of Chesterfield Township, who emigrated from Devonshire, England about 1840 (*History of Macoupin County,* 179). Post office established June 3, 1887.

CHAMNESS. Williamson. Seven miles south-southwest of Marion. Named for the Chamness family. Wiley B. Chamness was one of the first settlers in 1825, and Marshall E. Chamness was the first postmaster (Hubbs, *Pioneer Folks and Places*). Post office established Jan. 24, 1889.

CHAMPAIGN. County, City (1861, 1833). Created Feb. 20, 1833, from Vermilion County. The act creating Champaign County was introduced and seen through the state legislature by Sen. John W. Vance, who chose the names Champaign and Urbana for his former home, Champaign County, Ohio (apparently named directly for the French province of Champagne) and its seat, Urbana. The city of Champaign was platted in 1853 as West Urbana, taking its name from the Illinois Central station in Urbana. The name was changed to Champaign in 1860. From Latin *campagne* (field, plain) (Bateman and Selby, eds., *Historical Encyclopedia of Illinois and History of Champaign County,* 807; Johnson, *Medicine in Champaign County,* 64). Post office established March 2, 1855, as West Urbana; changed to Champaign April 28, 1860.

CHANA [CHAY nuh]. Ogle. Eight miles northwest of Rochelle. Laid out by Phineas Chaney in 1871. The word *Chana* is probably a variant of Chaney, representing a local pronunciation or an alternate spelling (Barge and Caldwell, "Illinois Place Names"; *Bicentennial History of Ogle County,* 600). Post office established July 11, 1872.

CHANDLERVILLE. Cass. Village (1861, 1894) fifteen miles east of Beardstown. Named for Dr. Charles Chandler, a member of a Rhode Island land association organized in the early 1830s for the purpose of establishing a colony in Illinois but deterred by the outbreak of the Black Hawk War. Chandler eventually founded the community in 1848 and hired Abraham Lincoln to survey the town site (*Illinois Gazetteer*; Perrin, ed., *History of Cass County*, 126). Post office established June 29, 1837, as Panther Creek; changed to Chandlerville Aug. 20, 1856.

CHANNAHON [shan uh HAHN, shan uh HON]. Will. Fourteen miles southwest of Joliet. Established by the commissioners of the Illinois and Michigan Canal as Sniften, named for an official of the I&M. The name was changed to Channahon about 1838, apparently through the efforts of a W. B. Peck. Traditionally, the word *Channahon* is taken to be from an Algonquian language with the general meaning "where the waters meet," perhaps referring to the confluence of the DuPage and Des Plaines rivers (*History of Will County*, 597; Maue, *History of Will County*, 175; Vogel, *Indian Place Names in Illinois*). Post office established Sept. 4, 1837, as Dresden; changed to Channahon March 2, 1838.

CHAPIN [CHAY puhn]. Macon. Seven miles east of Decatur. Named for Abraham Chapin, a commissioner of the Macon County court in the 1830s (Richmond, *Centennial History of Decatur*, 31).

CHAPIN. Morgan. Village (1873) seven miles west-northwest of Jacksonville. Founded in 1858 by Lyman and Horace Chapin (*History of Morgan County*, 430). Post office established July 9, 1861.

CHARLES MOUND. Jo Daviess. Summit northeast of Scales Mound. At about 1,230 feet, Charles Mound is the highest point in Illinois. Named for early land owner Elijah Charles, who emigrated from Pennsylvania in the late 1820s (Reardon, "No Frills").

CHARLESTON. Coles. City (1839, 1872). Established by the Illinois legislature as the seat of Coles County in 1831. Named for shopkeeper, miller, and first postmaster Charles Morton, who donated land for the county offices. The traditional account is that the name is a blend of Charles with *-ton* from *Morton* (Perrin, Graham, and Blair, *History of Coles County*, 309–10). Post office established May 22, 1830, as Morton's Store; changed to Coles Courthouse March 31, 1831; changed to Charleston April 29, 1843.

CHARLOTTE. Livingston. Fifteen miles northeast of Fairbury. According to a local story, when Charlotte Township was created from Pleasant Ridge in 1864, the name was suggested by Louis Dart for a woman he had once courted. More likely, it was chosen for Dart's former home, Charlotte, Vt. (Bateman and Selby, eds., *Historical Encyclopedia of Illinois and History of Livingston County*, 639; *History of Livingston County* [1878], 454). Post office established March 8, 1880.

CHARLOTTESVILLE. Lawrence. Former community. Founded in 1837 by Asahel Heath and named for his daughter, Charlotte. The Charlottesville Cemetery is eight miles north-northwest of Lawrenceville (*Combined History of Edwards, Lawrence, and Wabash Counties,* 344).

CHARTER GROVE. DeKalb. Three and a half miles southeast of Genoa. The origin of the name is unknown. Possibly named for an early French settler named Chartres. Post office established May 31, 1889.

CHATHAM [CHAT uhm]. Sangamon. Village (1874). Laid out in 1836 by Luther Ransom and probably named from the Chatham Presbyterian Church, which was organized the year before by William Thornton and the Revs. Dewey Whitney and T. A. Spilman. The church may have been named from the Chatham Presbyterian Church in Pittsylvania County, Va. (www.chathampresbyterian .org). Post office established June 17, 1840, as Lick Creek; changed to Chatham Aug. 9, 1841.

CHATSWORTH. Livingston. Eleven miles east of Fairbury. Founded about 1859. A popular story of the naming of Chatsworth credits county supervisor William H. Jones with suggesting the name, claiming it was taken from a British story he was reading in which a Lord Chatsworth was a major character. More likely, however, the name was proposed by William Osborn, a former president of the Illinois Central Railroad, in honor of the Duke of Devonshire, whose seat was at Chatsworth in Derbyshire, England, and who had a financial interest in the IC. Formerly known as Oliver's Grove, named for first settler Franklin C. Oliver (Bateman and Selby, eds., *Historical Encyclopedia of Illinois and History of Livingston County,* 639; *Chatsworth Area Centennial Celebration,* n.p.; *History of Livingston County* [1878], 287, 388; *History of Livingston County* [1991], 15). Post office established Jan. 29, 1859.

CHATTON. Adams. Seventeen miles south-southeast of Carthage. Named from Chatton, the Chicago, Burlington and Quincy station at Houston, itself named for B. I. Chatten [*sic*] of Quincy (Genosky, ed., *People's History,* 708). Post office established May 4, 1863.

CHAUTAUQUA [shuh TAW kwuh]. Most if not all of the sixteen Chautauquas in Illinois were named for the local Chautauqua grounds, sites of the cultural and entertainment camp meetings called Chautauquas, which originated as religious gatherings in Chautauqua, N.Y., and became popular in the Midwest in the late nineteenth century. By the early 1900s there were at least forty such sites in Illinois, including Chautauqua in Jersey County, which developed from the New Piasa Chautauqua, established in the 1880s (Fabian, *Chautauqua, Illinois*).

CHEBANSE [shuh BANS]. Iroquois, Kankakee. Village (1869, 1874) eight miles south-southwest of Kankakee. Established by the Illinois Central Railroad in 1854 and named for Chebanse (Chebass; Little Duck), a Potawatomi leader of the early nineteenth century whose main village was on the St. Joseph River in northern Indiana. Chebanse was a signatory to the Treaty of Chicago in 1821, which was also signed by Lewis Cass, for whom Cass County is named (Acker-man, *Early Illinois Railroads,* 124; Edmunds, *The Potawatomis,* 202). Post office established June 15, 1855.

CHE-CHU-PIN-QUA WOODS. Cook. Forest Preserve. Named for a Potawatomi leader of the nineteenth century who was known to settlers as Alexander Robinson. The word *che-chu-pin-qua* reportedly means "blinking eyes" and referred to one of Robinson's mannerisms or perhaps to a facial tic (Mann, *Origins of Names,* 14; Vogel, *Indian Place Names in Illinois*).

CHECKROW. Fulton. Six miles east of Bushnell. Several sources suggest that the name may be a shortening of "checker row," a venue where the game of checkers was often played. It is also possible that the name refers to a field or fields where corn was planted in "check rows," forming a checkerboard pattern, which allowed the crop to be cultivated from east to west on one occasion and from north to south the next (Irwin, *A to Z Fulton County*).

CHEMUNG [shuh MUHNG]. McHenry. Two miles west of Harvard. Founded about 1844 by William Seward and other settlers from Chemung, N.Y., near Elmira. The name is from Delaware (Algonquian) and means "big horn," probably referring to the site where a prominent big horn was found, perhaps the tusk of a mastodon (Nye, ed., *McHenry County, Illinois,* 437; Vogel, *Indian Place Names in Illinois*). Post office established Dec. 9, 1845.

CHENEYS GROVE. McLean. Township. Named for one of the first settlers, Jonathan Cheney, who emigrated from Ohio about 1825 (*History of McLean County, Illinois,* 536).

CHENEYVILLE [CHAY nee vil]. Vermilion. Four miles west of Hoopeston. Founded in 1871 and named for J. H. Cheney, vice president of the Lake Erie and Western Railroad (Underwood, "A New Geography of Illinois: Vermilion County," 38). Post office established June 7, 1880, as Cheneysville; changed to Cheneyville Feb. 27, 1892.

CHENOA. McLean. City (1865, 1872) ten miles southwest of Pontiac. Founded as Chenowa by Matthew T. Scott in 1856 where the proposed Peoria and Oquawka Railroad would cross the line of the Chicago and Alton. Scott maintained that Chenowa was a native name for his home state of Kentucky. He claimed that postal officials took down the name incorrectly as Chenoa and that spelling persisted in spite of his efforts to have it corrected. The Kentucky Historical Society, however, has no record that Chenowa or Chenoa was ever a name for all or part of that state (Bateman and Selby, eds., *Historical Encyclopedia of Illinois and History of McLean County,* 690; personal communication with the Kentucky Historical Society). Post office established May 31, 1856.

CHERRY. Bureau. Village (1905) eight miles southwest of Mendota. Named from the Cherry Coal Mine established about 1905 by James Cherry of the St. Paul

Coal Company. In 1909 the mine caught fire, and more than 250 miners lost their lives in the worst disaster in Illinois coal mining history (Fliege, *Tales and Trails of Illinois,* 166). Post office established March 20, 1906.

CHERRY VALLEY. Winnebago. Village (1857, 1896). Named for Cherry Valley, Otsego County, N.Y., probably by site owner Edward Fletcher, possibly by Mrs. Joseph Butler, both of whom had previously lived in Cherry Valley, N.Y. For unknown reasons, in its early years the community was known informally as Grabtown and Graball (Nelson, comp., *Sinnissippi Saga,* 27; Stennett, *A History of the Origin,* 55). Post office established June 13, 1839, as Long Prairie; changed to Cleveland June 25, 1840; changed to Newburgh June 28, 1847; changed to Cherry Valley Aug. 29, 1849.

CHESTER. Randolph. City (1835, 1873). Founded as Smith's Landing by Samuel Smith, who operated a ferry across the Mississippi River near the site. About 1830 Smith's wife, Jane, suggested that the name be changed in honor of her former home, Chester, in Cheshire, England. Chester has been the seat of Randolph County since 1847 (Pirtle, *Where Illinois Began,* 29; *Randolph County,* 11). Post office established July 11, 1832.

CHESTERFIELD. Macoupin. Village (1881) eight miles west of Carlinville. Laid out by site owners Jesse Peebles and Aaron Tilly in 1836. Probably named by settlers from Chesterfield, Derbyshire, England (*History of Macoupin County,* 179–80). Post office established May 9, 1838.

CHESTLINE. Adams. Three miles south of Siloam Springs State Park. Supposedly named for a nearby line of chestnut trees (Genosky, ed., *People's History,* 699). Post office established May 4, 1882.

CHESTNUT. Logan. Six miles northeast of Mount Pulaski. Laid out by David W. Clark in 1872. Named for Logan B. Chestnut, a director of the Gilman, Clinton and Springfield Railroad (www.outfitters.com/illinois/logan/communities_logan.html). Post office established May 30, 1856, as Laenna; changed to Allenville Jan. 29, 1872; changed to Chestnut June 7, 1873.

CHICAGO [shi KAW go, shi KAH go]. Cook. City (1835, 1875). At least thirteen meanings have been proposed for the word *Chicago,* from "something great" to "cracked corn makers" to "standing by a tree," and the name has been recorded in at least forty spellings. It was recorded by LaSalle in 1680 as Checagou. Two years later LaSalle applied the name to the Des Plaines River, which continued to be called the Chicago River into the 1790s. Origins in Fox and Ojibwa have been suggested, but it is clear that "Chicago" derives from *sikaakwa,* the Miami-Illinois word for the striped skunk. (The initial character represents the sound *sh,* as in *ship,* which was spelled *ch* in French; thus the current spelling *Chicago* rather than *Shicago.*) In Miami-Illinois, sikaakwa was homophonous with the word for the ramp or wild leek, thus the meaning "onion field" as well as "place of the skunk." Carl Sandburg weaves both meanings into his poem "The Windy City": "Early the red men gave a name to the river, / the place of the skunk / the river of the wild onion smell / Shee-caw-go."

Although Michael McCafferty is surely correct in claiming a Miami-Illinois source for Chicago, the name continues to invite speculation and discussion. For a spirited exchange of views see Weber ("A Critique") and McCafferty ("Revisiting Chicago"). Chicago's nickname, "the Windy City," is usually attributed to an editorial by Charles A. Dana in the *New York Sun,* written in 1889 or 1890 when Chicago and New York were competing to host the 1893 World's Columbian Exposition. Dana reportedly took Chicago's blustering politicians to task for boasting about the merits of their city. But this story, however often repeated, is a myth.

Etymologist Barry Popik was the first to show that "Windy City" as a sobriquet for Chicago predated the alleged editorial by many years. Popik traced the origin of the term to 1876 in Cincinnati, where a story in the *Cincinnati Enquirer* for May of that year reported on the Cincinnati Red Stockings' trip to Chicago to play baseball in the "Windy City." Since Popik's first reports, Fred Shapiro has provided even earlier citations. The *Daily Cleveland Herald* of June 4, 1870, reported "CLEVELAND vs. CHICAGO. The Great Game between the Forest City and Chicago Clubs—the Windy City Wins by a Score of 15 to 9—a Hotly Contested Game." A decade earlier, in its July 4, 1860, issue, the *Milwaukee Daily Sentinel* contained the following: "We are pround of Milwaukee because she is not overrun with a lazy police force as is Chicago—because her morals are better, he [*sic*] criminals fewer, her credit better, and her taxes lighter in proportion to her valuation than Chicago, the windy city of the West" (Bright, *Native American Placenames;* McCafferty, "A Fresh Look at the Place Name Chicago"; Popik, "Coinage of 'The Windy City'"; Shapiro on ADS-L@listserv. uga.edu [discussion list of the American Dialect Society], Nov. 6, 2006; Swenson, "Chicagoua/Chicago"; Vogel, *Indian Place Names in Illinois*). Post office established March 31, 1831.

CHILI [CHEYE leye]. Hancock. Thirteen miles south of Carthage. The local account is that the Worrell brothers were planning to go to South America, and in 1836 Elisha and Elijah Worrell were in Quincy waiting for their brother Joseph to join them. Elisha Worrell took a liking to the area and decided to stay. He bought a farm and laid out a town, which he named after the country of Chili, which was to have been their destination (*History of Hancock County,* 259). Post office established March 27, 1837, as Woodville; changed to Chili Jan. 3, 1838.

CHILLICOTHE [chil uh KAH thi, chil uh KAW thi]. Peoria. City (1861, 1873). Laid out in 1834 by Samuel T. McKean and resurveyed in 1836 by Harrison H. Jameson and Joseph Hart, who named the community for their former home, Chillicothe,

Ross County, Ohio. The word *Chillicothe* designated one of the four major divisions of the Shawnee people (Bradley, *History of Chillicothe,* 58; Bright, *Native American Placenames*). Post office established Feb. 13, 1841.

CHINA. Lee. Township. Formerly known as Fremont. The name was changed to China in 1850 at the request of George Russell Lynn (Linn), a landholder from China Township, Kennebec County, Maine. In April 2003 the Lee County Board voted to change the name to Franklin Grove, the name of the largest community in the township (Markel, "Township"; Markel, "Township Residents"). Post office established July 16, 1849, as Theoika; changed to China Dec. 12, 1850.

CHIPPEWA. Kane. Four miles southwest of Elgin. Named for the Chippewa (Ojibwa) tribe of the Great Lakes region. The name is derived from a word meaning "puckered," referring to stitching moccasins in such a way that the edges appear crinkled or plaited (Bright, *Native American Placenames*).

CHITTYVILLE. Williamson. Named for early settler Benjamin Chitty. Chittyville is now the northern part of Herrin (Hale, comp. and ed., *Williamson County,* 118; Mohlenbrock, "A New Geography of Williamson County," 31).

CHOAT. Massac. Four and a half miles northwest of Metropolis. Named for Isaac M. Choat, James M. Choat, or both. Isaac Choat owned the local general store and was postmaster in the 1890s. James Choat was a banker and general manager of the Massac Iron Company. The Chicago, Burlington and Quincy station was named Choate in 1910, taking the name of the post office. In its early years the community was known as Forktown for the Forktown store operated by Jack Smith (*History of Massac County,* 23; May, *Massac Pilgrimage,* 90). Post office established April 27, 1896.

CHOUTEAU. Madison. Township. Named from Chouteau Island, a large island in the Mississippi River between St. Louis, Missouri, and Granite City, Illinois. The island was named for Pierre Chouteau, an early nineteenth century St. Louis trader and manager for John Jacob Astor's American Fur Company (Coulet du Gard *Dictionary of French Place Names; History of Madison County,* 472).

CHRISTIAN. County. Created as Dane County, Feb. 15, 1839, from parts of Montgomery, Sangamon, and Shelby counties. Named for Nathan Dane (1752–1835), a member of Congress and author of the Northwest Ordinance of 1787 (and for whom Dane County, Wis., is named). For political reasons Daniel C. Goode and others began to circulate petitions calling for a change in the name of the county, and in 1840, likely at the suggestion of Thomas P. Bond, it was renamed for Christian County, Ky., itself named for Col. William Christian (1743–86), a Revolutionary War officer who was killed in Kentucky while leading a raid against Indians (Goudy, *History of Christian County,* 40; McBride, *Past and Present of Christian County,* 33–34; Rennick, *Kentucky Place Names*).

CHRISTOPHER. Franklin. City (1903) eleven miles north of Herrin. Sydney Harrison and F. O. Harrison, who laid out the site in 1835, said it was named for their father, Christopher Harrison, an early settler who claimed to be a relative of William Henry Harrison (Aiken, *Franklin County History,* 79; *Franklin County,* 13). Post office established Feb. 9, 1880.

CHRISTY. Lawrence. Township. Named for William Christy, state representative from Lawrence County from 1853 to 1855 (Bateman and Selby, eds., *Illinois Historical Lawrence County Biographcal,* 631).

CHURCHILL. DuPage. Forest Preserve and former community northwest of Lombard. Named for Winslow Churchill and his son, Seth, early settlers in 1834 (Knoblauch, ed., *DuPage County,* 190).

CICERO [SIS uh ro]. Cook. Town (1867). Founded in 1857 by Augustus Porter and named for his former home, Cicero, Onondaga County, N.Y. That city, named for the Roman statesman and orator, Marcus Tullius Cicero, has one of the classical names fashionable in western New York state in the late eighteenth century. Near Cicero, N.Y., are Syracuse, Cato, Pompey, and Euclid. An earlier Cicero was laid out by Archibald E. Constant in 1836 in Sangamon County, but it never materialized beyond a town plat (*History of Sangamon County,* 1047; Spelman, *Town of Cicero*). Post office established May 15, 1867, as Hyman; changed to Hawthorne April 17, 1900; changed to Cicero Jan. 28, 1910.

CIMIC. Sangamon. Four miles west of Pawnee. An acronym formed from the names of the Chicago and Illinois Midland, and Illinois Central railroads. Formerly known as Pawnee Junction (Adams, comp., *Illinois Place Names*).

CINCINNATI. Tazewell. Township and former community. Laid out about 1826 by site owner Jonathan Tharp and named for Cincinnati, Ohio. About 1829 Pekin was laid out beside Cincinnati, which it later absorbed (*History of Tazewell County,* 416).

CIPSCO PARK. Jackson. An acronym created from the Central Illinois Public Service Company. Established in the 1930s north of Grand Tower (Adams, comp., *Illinois Place Names*).

CISCO [SIS ko]. Piatt. Village (1896) seven miles west of Monticello. Some historians claim that Cisco is a railroad name, transferred from a station in one of the western states or named for a railroad official. (John J. Cisco, a railroad promoter of the 1860s, was the namesake of Ciscos in California and Texas.) Others say it derives from *cisco,* a French Canadian borrowing from Ojibwa for a kind of whitefish, which is the source of the names of Cisco Bay in Wisconsin and Cisco Lake in Michigan. It is certain, however, that the village was named for Francisco Dallas, the mother of Erastus F. Dallas, the first station agent at Cisco and one of the site owners (Bateman and Selby, eds., *Historical Encyclopedia of*

Illinois and History of Piatt County, 701; Bright, *Native American Placenames;* Miller, *Life and Times of Cerro Gordo,* 26; Morgan, ed., *The Good Life,* 114). Post office established June 11, 1874.

CISNE [SIS nee]. Wayne. Village (1898) ten miles south of Flora. Founded by Levi Cisne in 1870 with construction of the Ohio and Mississippi Railroad (*History of Wayne and Clay Counties,* 237). Post office established Jan. 6, 1871.

CISSNA PARK [SIS nuh PAHRK]. Iroquois. Village (1891) twelve miles northwest of Hoopeston. Founded about 1881 by William Cissna as a station on the Chicago and Eastern Illinois Railroad (*Cissna Park,* 3). Post office established April 6, 1882.

CLANK. Alexander. Former community about three miles southwest of Tamms. Named for A. L. Klank, station agent for the Chicago and Eastern Illinois Railroad. The spelling was changed through popular etymology when the post office was renamed (personal communication with Louise Ogg). Post office established Feb. 23, 1890, as Dunning; changed to Clank May 4, 1901.

CLARENDON HILLS. DuPage. Village (1924). Named by Robert Harris, president of the Chicago, Burlington and Quincy Railroad in the late 1870s, for his birthplace in the Clarendon Hills section of Boston. The name of the post office has alternated between Clarendon and Clarendon Hills since it was established in 1874 (Knoblauch, ed., *DuPage County,* 208).

CLARK. County. Created March 23, 1819 from Crawford County. Named for George Rogers Clark (1752–1818), a hero of the Revolutionary War on the western frontier. In 1778 Clark and a small group of volunteers captured Kaskaskia, Cahokia, and Vincennes, ensuring that the Illinois Country would not fall into British hands.

CLARKSDALE. Christian. Five miles southwest of Taylorville. Laid out by Young B. Clark in 1871. Probably named for himself; possibly named for Walter Clark, regarded as the first settler, or postmaster Charles S. Clark (Goudy, *History of Christian County,* 129–30). Post office established Dec. 11, 1871.

CLAY. County. Created Dec. 23, 1824, from parts of Fayette, Crawford, and Wayne counties. Named for Henry Clay (1777–1852). Clay, U.S. representative and senator from Kentucky, presidential candidate in 1824, secretary of state under John Quincy Adams, and perhaps best known for his support of the Compromise of 1850, was an esteemed figure in Illinois, particularly in the southern part of the state, where many settlers had emigrated from Kentucky. The seat was established at Maysville and moved to Louisville in 1841.

CLAY CITY. Clay. Village (1869, 1874) six miles east of Flora. Laid out by Daniel May as Hubbardsville. The name was changed to Maysville for Daniel May by the Clay County commissioners in 1825 when it was designated the seat of Clay County. An adjacent community was laid out in the mid-1850s by J. D. Per-key and named Clay City for Clay County. Clay City absorbed Maysville with construction of the Ohio and Mississippi Railroad in 1855 (*History of Wayne and Clay Counties*, 401; *Illinois Guide*). Post office established June 13, 1825, as Maysville; changed to Clay City Jan. 29, 1858.

CLAYS PRAIRIE. Edgar. Eight miles east-northeast of Paris. Named for Henry Clay, who reportedly owned several thousand acres in Hunter Township. Clay's son was overseer of the property (Colson, *Souvenir History of Edgar County*, 68). Post office established July 27, 1870.

CLAYSVILLE. Sangamon. Eleven miles northwest of Springfield. Founded by John Broadwell, who owned and operated a kiln and tannery near the site. Named by Broadwell in honor of Henry Clay (Hochstetter, ed., *Guide to Illinois' Historical Markers*).

CLAYTON. Adams. Village (1837, 1880) ten miles west-northwest of Mount Sterling. Founded in the mid-1830s by Charles McCoy and named for Henry Clay, whom McCoy greatly admired (*History of Adams County*, 517). Post office established March 26, 1833, as Daviston; changed to Clayton Feb. 7, 1837.

CLAYTON. Woodford. Township. When townships were organized in Woodford County in the mid-1850s, Clayton and Linn were alternate names for the same township, there being insufficient population for two townships but anticipating a division at a later date. Separation came in 1859 (Yates, *The Woodford County History*, 36).

CLEARING. Cook. West of Midway Airport. Originally a switchyard for clearing freight trains, established by A. B. Stickney (q.v. Stickney), president of the Chicago Great Western Railroad in the early 1900s. The yard was later incorporated into the Chicago Transfer Clearing Company. Clearing was annexed to Chicago in 1915 (Karlen, *Chicago's Crabgrass Communities*, 332–33). Post office established July 1, 1902.

CLEONE. Clark. Nine miles north-northeast of Casey. Laid out by Burns Harlan in 1846 as Centerville and informally known as Knawbone. The source of the name is unknown. The only other community named Cleone is in Mendocino County, Calif. (*History of Westfield, Illinois*, 17). Post office established March 4, 1886.

CLIFFORD. Williamson. Northwest of Herrin. Named for Clifford Garrison, son of O. L. Garrison, president of the Big Muddy Coal and Iron Company. Laid out about 1902 (Hubbs, *Pioneer Folks and Places*). Post office established Jan. 26, 1905.

CLIFTON. Iroquois. Village (1867, 1874) twelve miles south-southwest of Kankakee. Named by William A. Veech (or Viets) with construction of the Illinois Central Railroad in 1854. Veech was the owner of the site, which he named for the Clifton House, a Chicago hotel where he boarded (Ackerman, *Early Illinois Railroads*, 124). Post office established Aug. 24, 1857.

CLINTON. County. Created Dec. 27, 1824, from parts of Washington, Bond, and Fayette counties. Named for DeWitt Clinton (1769–1828), U.S. senator, mayor of New York City, and governor of New York in the 1820s. Many Illinoisians admired Clinton because he supported the Erie Canal, which, when it officially opened in 1825, provided an all-water route from the Northeast through the Great Lakes to Chicago.

CLINTON. DeKalb. Township. Named for Clinton, N.Y., itself named for George Clinton (1739–1812), the first governor of New York, vice president of the United States under Thomas Jefferson and James Madison, and uncle of DeWitt Clinton. DeKalb County was heavily populated by New Yorkers, so much so that at the time of township formation, voters in four of the original thirteen townships chose the name Clinton. The current Clinton Township was awarded the name by lot (Boies, *History of DeKalb County*, 500).

CLINTON. DeWitt. City (1855, 1882). Laid out about 1836 by James Allen and James Fell and named for DeWitt Clinton, of whom Allen was a great admirer. Clinton has been the seat of DeWitt County since its formation in 1839 (*History of DeWitt County* [1882], 151). Post office established Feb. 13, 1836.

CLINTONIA. DeWitt. Township. Named from the city of Clinton, which was the name of the township until it was changed to Clintonia in 1859.

CLIOLA [kleye OL uh]. Adams. Founded as a station on the Chicago, Burlington and Quincy Railroad. The source of the name is unknown; perhaps from a female given name. This is the only Cliola in the United States. The Cliola post office was about five miles northeast of Quincy (Genosky, ed., *People's History*, 677). Post office established Aug. 1, 1868.

CLYDE. Whiteside. Township. Originally known as Watertown, probably named for Watertown, N.Y. The name was changed to agree with that of the Clyde post office about 1851. Clyde is ultimately from the Clyde River in Scotland and may be a direct transfer because many English and Scots settled in the area. It may also be a transfer from Clyde, Wayne County, N.Y., and/or the city of Clyde in Sandusky County, Ohio (Bastian, *A History of Whiteside County*, 159). Post office established April 22, 1851.

COAL CITY. Grundy. Village (1881). Founded in 1875 by the Wilmington Coal Company. Named for the local bituminous coal mines (Bateman and Selby, eds., *Historical Encyclopedia of Illinois and History of Grundy County*, 696). Post office established Feb. 2, 1875.

COAL VALLEY. Henry, Rock Island. Village (1876) three miles south of Moline. Established in 1856 by the Coal Valley Mining Company (*Portrait and Biographical Album of Rock Island County*, 789). Post office established April 28, 1857.

COALTON. Montgomery. Village (1916) southeast of Nokomis. Also Coalton in Vermilion County four miles southeast of Hoopeston. Both named for local coal mines.

COATSBURG. Adams. Village (1869, 1879) twelve miles northeast of Quincy. Named for Richard P. Coates, who surveyed the site in 1855 (Hansen, ed., *Illinois*, 664). Post office established April 1, 1856, as Coatsburgh; changed to Coatsburg June 19, 1893.

COBDEN [KAHB duhn]. Union. Village (1875) twelve miles south of Carbondale. Formerly known as South Pass. The name was changed about 1860 by George B. McClellan, vice president of the Illinois Central Railroad, in honor of the visit of Sir Richard Cobden, a member of the British Parliament and a shareholder in the IC (Ackerman, *Early Illinois Railroads*, 136; *Illinois Guide*). Post office established Feb. 8, 1858, as South Pass; changed to Cobden June 5, 1873.

COE. Rock Island. Township. Organized as Fremont and named for famed western explorer John C. Frémont, a presidential candidate in 1856. For unknown reasons, but probably having to do with national politics, in October 1857 at the first meeting of the board of supervisors the name was changed to Penn and changed again a few months later, in January 1858, to Coe, for A. S. Coe, the first county commissioner (Bateman and Selby, eds., *Historical Encyclopedia of Illinois and History of Rock Island County*, 960). Post office established March 23, 1898.

COELLO [ko EL o, ko EL uh]. Franklin. Eight miles west of Benton. Originally called North City. Pete Coello, the incoming postmaster, offered local officials $50 if they would name the post office after him. They apparently accepted the offer (*Franklin County*, 13). Post office established June 3, 1918.

COFFEE. Wabash. Precinct. Also Coffee Island and Coffee Creek. The traditional story is that a keelboat loaded with coffee was proceeding up the Wabash River and took shelter for the night at the mouth of what is now Coffee Creek, about seven miles below Mount Carmel. In the morning, the boat was found capsized, and the cargo of coffee was lost (Bateman and Selby, eds., *Illinois Historical Wabash County Biographical*, 644).

COFFEEN [kaw FEEN]. Montgomery. City (1889) six miles southeast of Hillsboro. Established about 1880 by the Toledo, St. Louis and Kansas City Railroad on a site owned by Gustavus "Gus" Coffeen, an Illinois state representative of the 1860s and part owner of the Coffeen Coal and Copper Company (Traylor, *Past and Present of Montgomery County*, 739). Post office established June 23, 1883.

COLBERT. Gallatin. South of Equality. Jean Baptiste Colbert (1619–83), Louis XIV's minister of finance, has been suggested as the source of the name, but more likely it derives from a local Colbert family, probably that of Samuel Colbert, who was postmaster in the 1880s (Adams, comp., *Illinois Place Names;* Coulet du Gard, *Dictionary of French Place Names; History and Families of Gallatin County*, 62). Post office established Nov. 13, 1886.

COLCHESTER [KAHL ches ter, KOL ches ter]. McDonough. City (1887, 1884) six miles west-southwest of Macomb. Founded about 1855 by the Northern Cross

Railroad. Several writers have suggested that the name was transferred from Colchester, England, or from Chester, England, with prefixed *col,* generally explained as a form of "coal." However, in an 1890 letter quoted by Moon, Lewis H. Little wrote, "[I] laid out the original town and named it after Steven Chester of New York" (*"Multum in Parvo,"* 21). The source of the prefix remains a mystery (Chenoweth and Semonis, comps., *The History of McDonough County,* 54; Clarke, *History of McDonough County,* 677; *History of McDonough County,* 598). Post office established April 1, 1856.

COLEHOUR. Cook. Founded by Charles Colehour, a Chicago lawyer, and his brother William, who subdivided part of Hyde Park Township for a residential community in the early 1870s. Now part of Chicago (Karlen, *Chicago's Crabgrass Communities,* 58). Post office established July 9, 1875.

COLES. County. Created Dec. 25, 1830, from Clark County and named for Edward Coles (1786–1868), second governor of the state of Illinois, serving from 1822 to 1826.

COLETA [ko LEE tuh]. Whiteside. Village (1914) seven miles northwest of Sterling. Originally known as Crum's Store for proprietor John Thompson Crum and later called Clayton. According to local accounts, the community was named Coleta about 1868 at the suggestion of Nora Porter for a character in a book she was reading (Bent, ed., *History of Whiteside County,* 230). Post office established June 8, 1844, as Genesee Grove; changed to Coleta Nov. 12, 1868.

COLFAX. Champaign. Township. Created from Tolono Township in 1868 and named for Schuyler Colfax, vice president of the United States at the time (Bateman and Selby, eds., *Historical Encyclopedia and History of Champaign County,* 808).

COLFAX. McLean. Village (1883) nineteen miles east-northeast of Normal. Founded about 1880 by William G. Anderson and James E. Wood and named from the Colfax post office, itself named for Schuyler Colfax (Hoffman, *History of Lawndale,* 25). Post office established Jan. 8, 1880.

COLLINSVILLE. Madison, St. Clair. City (1855, 1872). Named from the Collinsville post office, itself named for the Collins brothers, Anson, Augustus, Frederick, Michael, and William, who emigrated from Litchfield, Conn., in 1817. Formally laid out about 1837 by William Collins, the only brother to remain in the area (Norton, ed., *Centennial History of Madison County,* 493–95; Stehman, *Collinsville, Illinois,* 22). Post office established Nov. 20, 1819, as Downing's Station; changed to Unionville in 1822; changed to Collinsville Dec. 13, 1825.

COLLISON [KAH luh suhn]. Vermilion. Ten miles northwest of Danville. Named for the Collison family. Absolom Collison was an early settler, and Thomas A. Collison was the site owner (Stapp, *History under Our Feet,* 35; Williams, *History of Vermilion County,* 292). Post office established May 24, 1880, as Bixby; changed to Collison Jan. 30, 1894.

COLMAR [KAHL mer]. McDonough. Thirteen miles southwest of Macomb. Founded in 1857 by settlers from Colmar (Kolmar), Alsace, now Haut-Rhin in northeastern France (Coulet du Gard, *Dictionary of French Place Names; History of McDonough County,* 663). Post office established July 27, 1858.

COLOMA. Whiteside. Township. Probably brought to Illinois by a traveler or prospector returning from the California gold fields, where Coloma is the name of a community in El Dorado County and the site of Sutter's Mill, where gold was discovered in 1848 (Bent, ed., *History of Whiteside County,* 129). Post office established July 18, 1853.

COLONA [kuh LO nuh]. Henry. Village (1903) seven miles east of Moline. Laid out in 1855 by Marcus Warren. The source of the name is unknown. Perhaps a variant of "Coloma"; perhaps a railroad name from Colona, Colo.; or perhaps from a personal name (*History of Henry County,* 540). Post office established May 19, 1855, as Colona Station; changed to Colona April 14, 1906.

COLP [KUHLP]. Williamson. Village (1913) two miles west of Herrin. Founded about 1910 as Colpville, named from the John Colp Coal Company (Hale, comp. and ed., *Williamson County,* 131). Post office established March 25, 1915.

COLUMBIA. This Latinized form of Columbus, after the Italian seaman who brought Europe and the Americas into contact in 1492, became popular as a place name after the American Revolution and continued to increase in popularity throughout the nineteenth century. It was especially attractive as a name for the new settlements then being founded in the Midwest. There are currently more than 120 communities in the United States named Columbia and another fifty named Columbus. In Illinois there have been at least fourteen communities or post offices named Columbia and at least eight named Columbus. Some of these are transfers, especially from Indiana or Ohio, but many were independently given in honor of Christopher Columbus. A number have merged with or been absorbed by larger communities. Columbia, Boone County, is now part of Belvidere; Columbia, Madison County, is now part of Troy; Columbia, Marshall County, is now Lacon; Columbia Heights, Knox County, is now part of Galesburg; Columbia Park, McHenry County, is now part of Johnsburg; and Columbia Place, Rock Island County, is now part of Moline.

COLUMBIAN CORNERS. Ogle. Former community. Named for the Chicago Columbian Exposition of 1893. The Columbian School was near Grand Detour (*Bicentennial History of Ogle County,* 398).

COLUMBIANA. Greene. Former community one mile south of Kampsville. Destroyed by a flood in February 1883 (Cunningham, *History of the Carrollton, Illinois, Area,* 33).

COLUSA [kuh LOO suh]. Hancock. Ten miles north of Carthage. Founded about 1870. Formally laid out about 1894 on the line of the Chicago, Burlington and Quincy Railroad. Apparently the site owners, Iris (or Eleanor) Bailey and B. J.

Johnson, each expected naming rights, and an impasse developed. Evan J. Kidson, who had recently returned from a trip to the West, suggested Colusa Station, for Colusa, Calif. (*History of Hancock County,* 282). Post office established Nov. 30, 1870.

COMMANCHE VILLAGE. Sangamon. One mile west of Pawnee. A variant of Comanche, the name of a Native American tribe of the southern plains.

COMO. Whiteside. Three miles west of Rock Falls. Named from a wide spot in the Rock River that reportedly reminded the namer of Como, the lake in northern Italy (Bent, ed., *History of Whiteside County,* 250). Post office established June 7, 1840.

COMPROMISE. Champaign. Township. Created in 1869 from Kerr and Rantoul townships. The local story is that the exact boundaries of the new township were the result of give and take; thus its final form was a compromise. It is also possible (even likely) that the township was named by supporters of Henry Clay for his part in securing passage of the Omnibus Bill of 1850, known as the Compromise of 1850, which among other things admitted California to the Union as a free state. Many in Illinois held Clay in high regard (Bateman and Selby, eds., *Historical Encyclopedia and History of Champaign County,* 809). Post office established Aug. 14, 1871.

COMPTON. Lee. Village (1875) ten miles north of Mendota. Founded in 1873 with construction of the Kenyon Railroad by site owner Joel Compton (Stevens, *History of Lee County,* 40). Post office established May 18, 1841, as Melugin Grove, named for first settler Zachariah Melugin; changed to Compton July 16, 1873.

COMPTON. Wabash. Precinct. Organized in 1899 and named for Levi Compton, who, along with Joshua Jordan, established the first American settlement in Wabash County in 1802 (Bateman and Selby, eds., *Illinois Historical Wabash County Biographical,* 646).

CONCORD [KAHNGK erd]. Bureau. Township. Named by settlers from Concord, N.H. Concord, a community four miles north of Princeton, was founded in March 1836 by Joseph Brigham and vacated in Feb. 1837 (Leonard, ed., *Big Bureau,* 72; www.genealogytrails.com/ill/bureau/Concord.html).

CONCORD. Morgan. Eight miles northwest of Jacksonville. Named from the Concord Congregational Church, established in 1844, itself named by Mrs. Samuel French for Concord, N.H. (Bateman and Selby, eds., *Historical Encyclopedia of Illinois and History of Morgan County,* 660). Post office established July 17, 1849.

CONCORD. White. Ten miles east of Norris City near Emma. Laid out in 1869 as Elsinor by Charles and Stephen Slocumb. The circumstances surrounding the name change to Concord are unknown (*History of White County,* 674). Post office established March 2, 1827.

CONDIT. Champaign. Township. Named for A. B. Condit, an early township supervisor (*History Champaign,* 810).

CONGERVILLE [KAHNG ger vil]. Woodford. Village (1959) twelve miles north-west of Normal. Originally a siding on the Lake Erie and Western Railroad known as Schrock for its location on the Joseph Schrock farm. The name was changed to honor Ben Conger, an early settler. Because Conger was at times confused with Cruger, the suffix *ville* was added in 1888 (Yates, *The Woodford County History,* 119). Post office established Feb. 27, 1888, as Conger; changed to Congerville July 31, 1888.

COOK. County. Created Jan. 15, 1831, from Putnam County and named for Daniel Pope Cook (1794–1827), nephew of Nathaniel Pope, for whom Pope County is named. Cook was a delegate to Congress from the Illinois Territory from 1816 to 1818 and U.S. representative from the state of Illinois from 1819 to 1827.

COOKSVILLE. McLean. Village (1901) thirteen miles east-northeast of Normal. Founded in 1882 as Kochville by site owner Frederick W. Koch. The word *Kochville* was anglicized to Cooksville later that year (Quaid, *A Little Square,* 17). Post office established Dec. 31, 1882.

COOPER. Sangamon. Township. Named for the Rev. John W. Cooper, a Methodist minister, justice of the peace, and county commissioner in the 1850s (Bateman and Selby, eds., *Historical Encyclopedia of Illinois and History of Sangamon County,* 710).

COOPER LAKE. Hancock. Named for Hugh L. Cooper, chief engineer of the Ke-okuk dam project of 1910–13 (Hansen, ed., *Illinois,* 533).

COOPERS DEFEAT CREEK. Stream. Stark, Bureau. Named for Jerry Cooper, an agent for the American Fur Company hired to trade with the Indians. Cooper, along with several companions, was caught in a sudden, fierce snowstorm and froze to death on the prairie in the winter of 1831–32 (Leeson, *Documents and Biography,* 603).

COOPERSTOWN [KUP erz town, KOOP erz town]. Brown. Eight miles east of Mount Sterling. Several accounts claim that because barrelmaking was an im-portant industry, many coopers were employed. Even so, it is likely that the name was influenced by, if not directly transferred from, an existing Coopers-town, the city of that name in Logan County, Ky., being a likely candidate (Dearinger, "A New Geography of Brown County," 26). Post office established Jan. 10, 1852.

COPLEY. Knox. Township. Originally called Prince Albert Precinct, adjoining Victo-ria Precinct. The name was changed in 1853 at the time of township formation for Isaac Copley, who was instrumental in the organization of the township (*Annals of Knox County,* 184; *Portrait and Biographical Album of Knox County,* 1066).

CORA. Jackson, Randolph. Nine miles southeast of Chester. Founded by Charles Brown in 1903 with construction of the St. Louis Valley Railroad and named for his daughter, Cora (Allen, *Jackson County Notes,* 9). Post office established April 23, 1903.

CORDOVA [kor DO vuh]. Rock Island. Village (1877) fifteen miles northeast of Moline. Laid out about 1837 by site owners John Marshall, Archie Allen, and Dr. Thomas Baker. Named by Baker, probably for Cordova, Spain. Baker reportedly took an interest in southern Spain after reading the Spanish-inspired works of Washington Irving, whose *Tales of the Alhambra* was published in 1832 (Marshall, "The History of Cordova"). Post office established May 9, 1839.

CORINTH [kor INTH]. Williamson. Nine miles northeast of Marion. Formerly known as Roberts Settlement for the first settler, John Sutton Roberts. Named Corinth with establishment of the post office by William Augustus Stewart, the first postmaster, for his former home, Corinth, Tenn., and also in recognition of the Civil War siege of Corinth, Miss., in 1862 in which the Twenty-ninth Illinois Infantry took part (Hale, comp. and ed., *Williamson County*, 118; Hubbs, *Pioneer Folks and Places*). Post office established June 18, 1864.

CORNELL. Livingston. Village (1873) nine miles north-northwest of Pontiac. Laid out by Walter B. Cornell with construction of the Chicago and Paducah Railroad in 1871 (*History of Livingston County* [1991], 17). Post office established April 22, 1864, as Oak Dale; changed to Cornell July 13, 1871.

CORNWALL. Township. Henry. Surveyed by Elijah Benedict about 1855 and named for his former home, Cornwall, Addison County, Vt. (Colby, "Historic Spots in Henry County," 165). The Cornwall post office operated intermittently from May 28, 1879, until Sept. 26, 1894.

CORTLAND [KORT luhnd]. DeKalb. Town (1865) three miles east of DeKalb. Previously known as Luce's Corners. The name was changed to Courtland at the request of S. L. Porter, for his former home, Cortland, N.Y. (itself named for Pierre Van Cortlandt). Cortland Township was first known as Richland and later as Pampas, a name suggested by J. R. Crosslett, who presumably saw a resemblance between the Illinois prairie and the grasslands of South America. The spelling *Courtland* continued well into the twentieth century, long after the name of the post office had been changed to Cortland (Boies, *History of DeKalb County*, 484). Post office established Sept. 11, 1849, as Lost Grove; changed to Courtland Station March 7, 1854; changed to Courtland May 15, 1883; changed to Cortland June 20, 1892.

COULTERVILLE. Randolph. Village (1869, 1874) six miles northeast of Sparta. Founded about 1825 by James B. Coulter as Grand Cote, taking its name from Grand Cote Prairie, itself named from French *Grand Côte* (Big Hill). Platted as Coultersville about 1850 (*Illinois Guide;* Allen, *Randolph County Notes,* 4). Post office established April 4, 1854, as Coultersville; changed to Coulterville June 20, 1892.

COUNCIL HILL. Jo Daviess. Five miles northeast of Galena. Founded about 1853 and named from the local tradition that Indian councils were held near the site. The early mines in the area were known as the Council Hill diggings. The township name was changed from Scales in 1853 (*History of Jo Daviess County,* 595). Post office established July 1, 1840.

COUNTRY CLUB HILLS. Cook. City (1958). South Chicago suburb. Known as Cooper's Grove until the mid-1950s when it was subdivided and given a promotional name by developer Joseph E. Merrion, the founder of Merrionette Park and Hometown (*Illinois Guide*).

COVELL. McLean. Five miles southwest of Bloomington. Founded by Merritt L. Covell, a commander in the Black Hawk War and co-founder of Le Roy (Townley, *Historic McLean,* 19, 23). Post office established Jan. 28, 1868.

COWDEN [KOW duhn]. Shelby. Village (1875) eleven miles south of Shelbyville. Founded in 1872 by H. M. Cowden (Bateman and Selby, eds., *Historical Encyclopedia of Illinois and History of Shelby County,* 651). Post office established April 4, 1872.

COWLING [KO ling, KOW ling]. Wabash. Eleven miles southeast of Mount Carmel. Founded in 1875 by former sheriff Francis M. Cowling (Bateman and Selby, eds., *Illinois Historical Wabash County Biographical,* 652). Post office established Nov. 13, 1872, as Logansburg; changed to Cowling May 15, 1876.

CRAB ORCHARD. Williamson. Six miles east of Marion. Founded about 1851. Named from Crab Orchard Creek, which meanders through that part of Williamson County known as the Crab Orchard, named for the wild crab apple trees. Crab Orchard was once known as "steal easy," and several stories are told to explain the name. According to one, the first mill had no doors, and some people soon learned that after the miller had left for the day it was easy to pick up a sack or two of cornmeal or flour without paying. According to another, the miller wore a shirt with oversized cuffs and had developed a technique of pouring grain or meal so that after it was weighed much of it found its way into his cuffs rather than into the customers' sacks. It was said that the miller could steal easier with his shirt than he could with a gun (Brewer, *Steal Easy,* 3; Hale, comp. and ed., *Williamson County,* 127, 129; Hubbs, *Pioneer Folks and Places*). Post office established Aug. 18, 1853.

CRAGIN. Cook. Named for William P. and Edward F. Cragin, whose Cragin Manufacturing Company produced tin and metal products in the mid-nineteenth century. Now part of Belmont-Cragin (q.v.) (Karlen, *Chicago's Crabgrass Communities,* 182). Post office established Sept. 12, 1882.

CRAIN. Jackson. Nine miles west of Murphysboro. Founded in the 1890s and named for John R. Crain (Allen, *Jackson County Notes,* 19; Mohlenbrock, "A New Geography of Illinois: Jackson County," 28). Post office established Feb. 13, 1894.

CRAINVILLE. Williamson. Village (1881). Established as a station on the Carbondale and Shawneetown Railroad and named for early settler and site owner

Jasper "Uncle Jep" Crain. Now a suburb of Carterville (Hale, comp. and ed., *Williamson County,* 132; Hubbs, *Pioneer Folks and Places*). Post office established Sept. 26, 1888.

CRAMER. Peoria. Three miles east of Farmington. Founded about 1882 as Cramer Crossing, a station on the Iowa Central Railroad. Named for site owner William Cramer (Bateman and Selby, eds., *Historical Encyclopedia of Illinois and History of Peoria County,* 837). Post office established Oct. 28, 1840, as Rockvale; changed to Brunswick Jan. 11, 1844; changed to Cramer May 29, 1882.

CRANE CREEK. Mason. Township and former community. Named from Crane Creek, itself so named either for Amzy C. Crane, an early settler, or from the sandhill cranes often seen in the area (Lynn, *Prelude to Progress,* 301). The Crane Creek post office operated intermittently from July 8, 1842, until June 14, 1870.

CRATER. Calhoun. Precinct. Named for the first known settler, Jacob Crater (or Crader) (Carpenter, *Calhoun Is My Kingdom,* 98).

CRAWFORD. County. Created Dec. 31, 1816, from Edwards County. Probably named for William Harris Crawford (1772–1834), U.S. senator from Georgia and secretary of war and secretary of the treasury under James Madison. At the time the county was created, Crawford was a leading candidate for the presidency (Perrin, ed., *History of Crawford and Clark Counties,* 39).

CREAL SPRINGS. Williamson. City (1883) nine miles southeast of Marion. The mineral waters in the area were known to Native Americans and to the French, who reportedly called the springs *eau minéral* (mineral water). The community was founded about 1883 by Edward G. Creal, who developed the springs into a spa and resort (Hale, comp. and ed., *Williamson County,* 133; Hubbs, *Pioneer Folks and Places*). Post office established Sept. 22, 1846, as Sulphur Springs; changed to Creal Springs Feb. 8, 1883.

CREEK. DeWitt. Township. Probably named for Salt Creek (*History of DeWitt County* [1910], 418).

CRESCENT CITY. Iroquois. Village (1884) five miles west of Watseka. Also Crescent Township. Named about 1860 by Hiram Dunn for the semicircular shape of the stand of timber along Spring Creek and the Iroquois River. The township was created as Logan in 1868; the name was changed to Grenard in 1869 for first township supervisor Elisha Grenard and to Crescent in 1871 (Beckwith, *History of Iroquois County,* 404; Dowling, *History of Iroquois County,* 51). Post office established April 23, 1860.

CREST HILL. Will. City. (1960). North Joliet suburb. Created in 1960 through a merger of Idylside, Ingalls Park, Raynor Park, Ridgewood, Rockdale Junction, and Lidice.

CRESTON. Ogle. Village (1869, 1872) four miles east of Rochelle. Founded about 1854 as Dement Station, named for John Dement, Illinois state treasurer in the 1830s and mayor of Dixon in the 1870s. The name was changed in 1869 to Creston because this was thought to be the highest point on the Chicago and North Western railroad line between Chicago and the Mississippi River (*see* Dement) (*Bicentennial History of Ogle County,* 234; Stennett, *A History of the Origin,* 61). Post office established Sept. 23, 1852, as Brawdie's Grove; changed to Dement Station April 7, 1854; changed to Creston Aug. 11, 1869.

CRETE. Will. Village (1880). Originally known as Wood's Corners, named for first settler Willard I. Wood, who emigrated from Vermont in the mid-1830s. The name *Crete* was chosen when the post office was established in 1838. By one account, Wood leafed through his bible, looking for a name and happened upon "Crete," which struck him favorably. By another, Wood was visited by a minister on his circuit, who asked Wood the name of the place. Wood responded that it had none but a name was needed if there were ever to be a post office. The minister then thumbed through his bible, offered several possibilities, and said, "How's Crete?" Wood liked the name because it was short, easy to pronounce, and not likely to duplicate an existing post office (James, "Southern Isle"; Lazaros and Monks, *Crete,* 10). Post office established Feb. 13, 1838.

CREVE COEUR [KREEV KOR]. Tazewell. Village (1921) four miles south of Peoria. Named from Fort Crève Coeur, erected by LaSalle and Tonti in 1680. Most writers take the name literally, "Broken Heart," and claim that it was given by LaSalle because of his great disappointment in having to leave the fort and because of his general despair at the failure of his expedition. There are several more likely sources for the name, however. Crève Coeur was the name of a site near the village of Bois le Duc in the Netherlands that the French army had captured in 1672 through an action in which Tonti probably had taken part. Crèvecoeur was a reasonably common French surname, and the fort may well have been named for a member of the expedition or for one of its underwriters; LaSalle gave such honorary names on a number of occasions (Balesi, *The Time of the French,* 63; Coulet du Gard, *Dictionary of French Place Names;* Franke, *French Peoria,* 73; *Illinois Guide*).

CRITTENDEN. Champaign. Township. Created from Philo Township in 1863 with the expectation that it would be named Morgan for Woodson Morgan, who was instrumental in the township's organization. Morgan, however, asked that it be named instead for John J. Crittenden (1787–1864), governor of Kentucky from 1848–50 and U.S. senator, recognized at the time for his efforts to preserve the federal union and avoid civil war (Bateman and Selby, eds., *Historical Encyclopedia and History of Champaign County,* 811).

CROPSEY. McLean. Nine miles south of Fairbury and Township. Named for Andrew J. Cropsey, a member of the Illinois legislature in the early 1860s (*History of McLean County, Illinois,* 739). Post office established March 2, 1880.

CROW CREEK. Marshall. Stream. Named for White Crow, a Potawatomi leader of the early nineteenth century (Vogel, *Indian Place Names in Illinois*).

CRUGER. Woodford. One mile west of Eureka. Founded in 1856 as Cruger Station, named for William H. Cruger, then superintendent of the Toledo, Peoria and Western Railroad (Yates, *The Woodford County History*, 47). Post office established June 21, 1855, as Mount Zion; changed to Cruger Dec. 30, 1856.

CRYSTAL LAKE. McHenry. City (1914). Named from Crystal Lake, the small lake described about 1835 by early settler Zeba Beardsley as having water "clear as crystal." North Crystal Lake, formerly known as Nunda, was annexed by Crystal Lake in 1914 (Heisler, Riegler, and Smith, eds., *Crystal Lake, Illinois*, 10). Post office established May 27, 1837, as Chrystal Lake; changed to Crystal Lake ca. June 30, 1857.

CUBA. Fulton. City (1853, 1895) seven miles north of Lewistown. In 1836 Centerville and Middleton were laid out side by side, both named for their location near the center of Fulton County. When they decided to merge the following year neither would accept the name of the other, but for unknown reasons the name *Cuba* provided an acceptable alternative. Some writers have suggested that the inspiration came from Havana, some fifteen miles to the southeast; others that the name is for the Caribbean island nation of Cuba (*History of Fulton County*, 866; Irwin, *A to Z Fulton County*). Post office established Dec. 2, 1837.

CUBA. Lake. Three miles north of the junction of Cook, Lake, and McHenry counties. Established as Troy, probably named for Troy, N.Y. The name was changed in 1851 at the suggestion of township supervisor Philetus Beverly for the island of Cuba, which was in the news at the time. Especially newsworthy was the expedition led by Narciso Lopez, which left New Orleans in 1850 with the intention of freeing Cuba from Spanish rule. The expedition was a failure, but it inspired the naming of several Cubas in the United States (*Past and Present of Lake County*, 258).

CULLOM. Livingston. Village (1882) eighteen miles east of Pontiac. Founded in 1878 as a station on the Illinois Central Railroad by site owner Frederick Hack, who sought to name the station Jeffrey for the roadmaster of the IC. Jeffrey, however, wanted to call it Hack. The compromise was Cullom, for Shelby M. Cullom (1829–1914), then governor of Illinois (*History of Livingston County* [1991], 17). Post office established Dec. 2, 1878.

CUMBERLAND. County. Created March 2, 1843, from Coles County. Named for the Cumberland, or National, Road, the first great commercial artery linking the developed east with the developing west. The road originated in Cumberland, Md., and was eventually extended to Vandalia, Ill., by the late 1830s. Modern Interstate I-70 roughly follows the route of the original road. The county seat was established at Greenup and moved to Toledo (then called Prairie City) in 1855.

CUMMINGS. Cook. First known as Irondale for the rolling mills of the Joseph H. Brown Iron and Steel Company. The name was changed in 1882 upon establishment of a station on the Nickel Plate Railroad. Named for Columbus R. Cummings, first president of the Nickel Plate. Now part of Chicago (Karlen, *Chicago's Crabgrass Communities,* 63). Post office established May 9, 1878, as Brown's Mill; changed to Cummings June 7, 1882.

CUSTER. Township. Will. Created from Clinton Township in 1886. Likely named for George Armstrong Custer, whose Seventh Cavalry had been destroyed at the Little Big Horn in Montana a decade earlier (Stevens, *Past and Present of Will County,* 74).

CUTLER. Perry. Village (1907) five miles east-northeast of Steeleville. Named for Cutler Dawson, construction supervisor for the Tamaroa, Chester and Western Railroad (*Perry County,* 7, 9). Post office established July 2, 1872, as Cutler Station; changed to Cutler May 15, 1883.

CUYLER. Cook. Named for Edward J. Cuyler, an official of the Chicago and North Western Railroad. Formerly known as Belle Plaine. Now part of Chicago (Stennett, *A History of the Origin,* 62).

D

DAHINDA [dah HIN duh]. Knox. Twelve miles west of Galesburg. Laid out in 1888 on the site of a former Indian village by the Santa Fe Town and Land Company, acting for the Santa Fe Railroad. The name was taken from Henry Wadsworth Longfellow's *The Song of Hiawatha,* in which Dahinda is the Ojibwa name of the bullfrog (Bateman and Selby, eds., *Historical Encyclopedia of Illinois and Knox County,* 881; Vogel, *Indian Place Names in Illinois*). Post office established Feb. 14, 1888.

DAHLGREN [DAL gruhn]. Hamilton. Village (1887) ten miles northwest of McLeansboro. Established as a station on the Louisville and Nashville Railroad in 1870. Named by an official of the L&N for Adm. John Adolphus Bernard Dahlgren (1809–70), prominent during the Civil War. Dahlgren, a mathematician, wrote several books on the construction and use of ordnance and is best known for his design of cannons with interiors that curved inward from breech to muzzle, called Dahlgrens (Landelius, *Swedish Place-Names*). Post office established Dec. 18, 1871, as Dahlgreen; changed to Dahlgren Jan. 1, 1880.

DAKOTA. Stephenson. Town (1869) eight miles northeast of Freeport. Founded in 1857 with construction of the Western Union Railroad by Ludwig Stanton and S. J. Davis. The name was reportedly chosen by Robinson Baird or Benjamin Dornblazer, perhaps for the Dakota Sioux, who at one time were resident in the Midwest, but more likely for Dakota, that part of the Upper Midwest that would become Dakota Territory and later the states of North and South Dakota. From *dakhota* (friendly) (Tilden, comp., *History of Stephenson County,* 496). Post office established Feb. 11, 1857.

DALE. Hamilton. Seven miles southeast of McLeansboro. Founded about 1871 with construction of the railroad and named for early settler Reuben Dale, who entered land in 1818, and his son, John. The station was known as Dales (*Hamilton County,* 29; Munsell, "A History of Hamilton County," 30). Post office established May 10, 1882.

DALLAS CITY. Hancock, Henderson. City (1859, 1905) six miles east of Fort Madison, Iowa. Founded in 1848 by John M. Finch and William H. Rolloson, proprietors of the local general store. Named for George Mifflin Dallas (1792–1864), at the time vice president of the United States under James K. Polk. Finch reportedly noticed that a nearby island in the Mississippi River was called Polk Island and decided that the vice president should be honored as well as the president. George M. Dallas was a popular politician of the mid-nineteenth century, serving as U.S. senator and minister to Britain as well as vice president. A number of communities in the United States are named for him, including the city in Texas (*History of Mercer and Henderson Counties,* 1204; Sutton, *Rivers, Railways,* 35). Post office established April 27, 1840, as Camp Creek; changed to Dallas City April 15, 1850.

DALLASANIA. Saline. Former community near Carrier Mills. Named for William J. Dallas, the first postmaster (*History of Saline County,* 223). Post office established July 25, 1899.

DALZELL [dal ZEL]. Bureau. Village (1903) two miles northwest of Peru. Named for Samuel M. Dalzell, general manager of the Spring Valley Coal Company (Leonard, ed., *Big Bureau,* 70). Post office established Jan. 15, 1902.

DAMASCUS. Stephenson. Five miles north northwest of Freeport. Founded and named in 1837 by Norman Phillips, the first postmaster. The source of the name is unknown. Possibly a transfer from Damascus, Broome County, N.Y. (Fulwider, *History of Stephenson County,* 378). Post office established Oct. 18, 1854.

DAMIANSVILLE. Clinton. Village (1977) four miles east-southeast of New Baden. Settled in the late 1830s, largely by German Catholics, as Dempter, named for Dempter (now Deventer) in the Netherlands. In the 1860s Bishop Damian Junker of Alton obtained twenty acres of land on which the St. Damian's Catholic Church was built. The community and post office were named from the church (*History of Marion and Clinton Counties,* 260; www.papadocs.com/villages/damiansville/dvilhist.htm). Post office established June 7, 1862.

DAMON. Brown. Seven miles northwest of Mount Sterling. Origin unknown. A recent county history says only, "No record is available as to when Damon originated, nor how it was named" (*History of Brown County,* 608). Post office established July 24, 1894.

DANA. LaSalle. Village (1875) five miles northeast of Minonk. Founded as Martin, named for John M. Martin, one of the site owners, and subsequently called Conklin. The name was changed to Dana about 1873, for Thomas Dana, superintendent of the Chicago, Pekin and Southwestern Railroad (*History of La-Salle County,* 300; Rasmusen, *LaSalle County Lore,* 254). Post office established March 5, 1873.

DANFORTH [DAN ferth]. Iroquois. Village (1878) twenty-one miles southwest of Kankakee. Founded in 1872 with construction of the Illinois Central Railroad by site owners George W. and A. H. Danforth (Ackerman, *Early Illinois Railroads,* 125). Post office established Jan. 11, 1866, as Danforth Station; changed to Danforth May 21, 1883.

DANVERS. McLean. Village (1878) nine miles west-northwest of Bloomington. Founded in 1836 by site owners Israel Hall and Matthew Robb as Concord, named for Concord, N.H. Renamed in 1861 for Danvers, Mass., Hall's former home northwest of Boston (*Danvers, Illinois,* 9, 11). Post office established Feb. 3, 1848, as Stout's Grove; changed to Danvers Feb. 19, 1862.

DANVILLE. Vermilion. City (1839, 1874). The area was originally known as the Salt Works for the local salt springs. Platted in 1827 and named for Dan Beckwith, who, along with Guy Smith, donated land for the county seat. Danville has been the seat of Vermilion County since 1827 (*Illinois Guide*). Post office established March 27, 1826, as Vermilion Courthouse; changed to Danville May 3, 1827.

DANWAY. LaSalle. Eight miles northeast of Ottawa. Named for early settler Daniel Way (Rasmusen, *LaSalle County Lore,* 123). Post office established Oct. 18, 1872.

DAREVILLE. Jefferson. Eight miles south-southwest of Mount Vernon. Founded by Hubbard (or Herbert) Dare in the early 1840s and named for the Dare family. Dareville is now part of Nason (*Facts and Folks,* 128).

DARIEN. DuPage. City (1969). A settlement called Cass, named from the Cass post office, was established by Thomas Andrus on the site of present Darien about 1834. Another community was founded about twenty years later just north of Cass and, by tradition, was named Lace when a local merchant, when asked for a name, looked around his store, eyed a bolt of lace, and decided that would be a good name for the post office. Rather, the Lace post office was named by John Keig in honor of his grandmother, Mrs. Tom Lace. Neither Cass nor Lace prospered, and they were absorbed by growing subdivisions. Modern Darien was created by a merger of the Marion Hills, Brookhaven, Clairfield, and Hinsbrook subdivisions in 1969 and named by Sam Kelley, one of the city's founders and several times its acting mayor, after a visit to Darien, Conn. (Elbe et al., "Darien," 141–42).

DARMSTADT. St. Clair. Thirteen miles north of Sparta. Founded in 1855 by Isaac Rainey and named for Darmstadt in southern Germany, the former home of a number of early settlers (*History of St. Clair County,* 368). Post office established Aug. 9, 1864.

DARWIN. Clark. Eight miles south-southeast of Marshall. Formerly known as McClure's Bluff for early settler Samuel McClure. Founded in the early 1820s and named by Septer Patrick, probably for physician Robert Darwin, the son of physician and naturalist Erasmus Darwin and father of naturalist Charles Darwin. Patrick was a prominent physician in his own right, having practiced in both New York state and Terre Haute, Ind., before coming to Illinois, and would have been familiar with both Erasmus and Robert Darwin. Darwin was the seat of Clark County from 1823 until 1838, when it was moved to Marshall (personal communication with L. K. Ortman; Perrin, ed., *History of Crawford and Clark Counties,* 240, 359). Post office established Aug. 17, 1820, as Clark Courthouse; changed to Darwin Nov. 8, 1836.

DAUM [DOWM]. Greene. Fives miles north-northeast of Carrollton. Named for Postmaster Christian Daum (Adams, comp., *Illinois Place Names*) Post office established July 1, 1884.

DAVIS. Stephenson. Village (1873) fourteen miles northeast of Freeport. Laid out about 1856 by site owners John and Samuel Davis on the line of the Racine and Southwestern Railroad (Tilden, comp., *History of Stephenson County,* 488). Post office established Feb. 3, 1858.

DAVIS JUNCTION. Ogle. Village (1977) nine miles south of Rockford. Founded about 1875 by Jeremiah Davis and others as a station on the Pacific railroad (*Bicentennial History of Ogle County,* 427). Post office established July 9, 1875.

DAWSON. Sangamon. Village (1867, 1883) ten miles east-northeast of Springfield. Founded in 1854 on the line of the Wabash Railroad. Named for John Dawson, an early settler and member of the Illinois General Assembly from 1830 to 1846 (Bateman and Selby, eds., *Historical Encyclopedia of Illinois and History of Sangamon County,* 728). Post office established Feb. 12, 1850, as Buffalo Hart; changed to Dawson Nov. 15, 1854.

DAWSON. McLean. Township and former community. The post office and railroad station were established as Padua in the early 1850s. The township, originally formed as Lee, was renamed Padua in 1858. The community was formally named about 1890 for John Wells Dawson, generally recognized as the first permanent settler in the area. The Dawson Cemetery is six miles northeast of Le Roy (Bateman and Selby, eds., *Historical Encyclopedia of Illinois and History of McLean County,* 697).

DAYSVILLE. Ogle. Two miles southeast of Oregon. Founded by Col. Jehiel Day, an early settler (Barge and Caldwell, "Illinois Place-Names"). Post office established Feb. 22, 1839.

DAYTON. Henry. Eight miles east of Moline. Laid out in 1836 by site owners Mark M. Atkinson and George Brandenburg, proprietor of the Brandenburg Tavern. Probably named for Dayton, Ohio (*Portrait and Biographical Album of Henry County,* 700; Swank, *Historic Henry County,* 1).

DAYTON. LaSalle. Northeast of Ottawa. Founded by settlers from Dayton, Ohio (*History of LaSalle County,* 84). Post office established May 10, 1837.

DEADMAN'S GROVE. Coles. A former area in Lafayette Township along Kickapoo Creek. Named from the fact that an early settler named Coffman was found frozen to death in the grove in 1826. Reportedly, he was found sitting at the base of a tree with a horse's bridle on his shoulder (Dole, "Pioneer Days," 112).

DECATUR. Macon. City (1839, 1881). Established as the seat of Macon County in 1829 and named for Stephen Decatur (1779–1820), the popular naval commander of the War of 1812 and the second war against the Barbary pirates in 1815 (*Illinois Gazetteer*). Post office established Oct. 6, 1831.

DECKER. Richland. Township. Named for Thomas J. Decker, an early settler and the first district tax collector. Changed from Jackson in 1859 (*Counties of Cumberland, Jasper, and Richland,* 624).

DECORRA. Henderson. Eight miles southeast of Burlington, Iowa. Established on the line of the Santa Fe Railroad about 1888. Probably a transfer from Decorah, Iowa. The name derives from Sabrevoir de Carrie, a French officer who, with his Winnebago wife, were the progenitors of a line of Winnebago leaders, all called Decorah, the better known of which include One-eye Decorah, signatory to a number of Winnebago treaties from the late 1820s to the early 1850s, and Waukon Decorah, for whom Decorah, Iowa, was named (Bateman and Selby, eds., *Historical Encyclopedia of Illinois and History of Henderson County,* 704; Vogel, *Iowa Place Names of Indian Origin*). Post office established Oct. 23, 1888.

DEERFIELD. Lake. Village (1903). The area was first known as Cadwell's Corner; Jacob Cadwell was an early settler in 1835, and his son, Caleb, was the first postmaster. Later called Le Clair. The present community was named from Deerfield Township, whose name was chosen about 1850 by public referendum in which Deerfield received seventeen votes and Erin received thirteen. The name was proposed by John Millen for his former home, Deerfield, Conn. (*Past and Present of Lake County,* 259; Reichelt, *History of Deerfield,* 10). Post office established May 4, 1850.

DEERING, South. Cook. Named about 1903 for William Deering, proprietor of the Deering Harvester Company, which manufactured farm equipment (Stennett, *A History of the Origin,* 63).

DEER PARK. LaSalle. Township. Named from Deer Park grotto, a canyon near the Vermilion River. Now part of Matthiessen State Park (*History of LaSalle County,* 102).

DEERS. Champaign. Five miles southeast of Urbana. Originally called Deer Station. Named for early settler Thomas Deer (Bateman and Selby, eds., *Historical Encyclopedia of Illinois and History of Champaign County,* 679). Post office established Dec. 22, 1887.

DEGOGNIA [duh GON yuh]. Jackson. Nine miles east-southeast of Chester. Named from Degognia Creek, itself named for Phillipe (or Gregore, early reports differ) Degognia (or DeGognie), a part French Canadian, part Indian army officer, who was a member of William Boon's company of rangers, organized to protect settlers on the frontier from Indian attacks during the War of 1812. At the end of the war, Degognia built a small fort near Rockwood in what is now Randolph County, near the Jackson County line (Allen, *Jackson County Notes*, 5; Mohlenbrock, "A New Geography of Illinois: Jackson County," 17; *Randolph County*, 36). Post office established Oct. 2, 1886, as Degognia; changed to Degonia June 23, 1892; changed back to Degognia July 13, 1892.

DEKALB. Cumberland. Former community. Probably named for Johann DeKalb. Formerly known as Sconce's Bend, named for Thomas Sconce. DeKalb vied with Greenup and several other towns for the seat of Cumberland County through much of the 1840s (*Counties of Cumberland, Jasper, and Richland*, 128–29).

DEKALB [di KALB]. DeKalb County was created from Kane County on March 4, 1837, and named for Johann DeKalb, born Johann Kalb in Germany in 1721. Kalb called himself Jean de Kalb when he served in the French infantry and later presented himself as Baron de Kalb. A natural soldier of fortune, DeKalb was drawn to the American Revolution, where he served with George Washington at Valley Forge. He was killed during a gallant but foolish charge into Cornwallis's troops at Camden, S.C., in 1780. The present city of DeKalb, incorporated 1861 and 1873, was originally known as Huntley's Grove, named for early settler Russell Huntley, and later as Buena Vista, named for the Mexican War battle of Buena Vista. It was formally platted in 1853 as DeKalb Centre (Bigolin, "Landmarks of Barb City"). Post office established Feb. 8, 1849, as DeKalb Centre; changed to DeKalb May 24, 1883.

DELAFIELD. Hamilton. Four miles northwest of McLeansboro. Laid out on the line of the St. Louis and Southeastern Railroad in 1872. Named for John Delafield (*Hamilton County*, 42). Post office established May 17, 1872.

DELAVAN [DEL uh vuhn]. Tazewell. City (1888) sixteen miles north-northeast of Lincoln. Named for the Delavan Association, founded in 1836 in Providence, R.I., by the Rev. Jonas R. Gale for the purpose of establishing a colony in the Midwest. The association was named for Edward Cornelius Delavan of Albany, N.Y., a land speculator and the primary financial backer of the enterprise (*History of Tazewell County*, 433–34). Post office established Jan. 7, 1840.

DELHI [DEL heye]. Jersey. Six miles southeast of Jerseyville. Founded by Nelson R. Lurton, Sarah A. Lurton, and others and named from the Delhi post office (which itself may have been named by the Lurtons). Likely a transfer, but the source and circumstances are unknown (*History of Greene and Jersey Counties*, 334; personal communication with Lois Lock). Post office established July 5, 1833, as Lurton's; changed to Delhi July 27, 1836.

DELL'ERA [del EHR uh]. Williamson. Former community. Named for Louis Dell'Era from Milan, Italy, who, along with Paul D. Herrin, established several stations on the line of the Chicago, Burlington, and Quincy Railroad. Dell'era is now part of Freeman Spur (Hale, comp. and ed., *Williamson County*, 118; Hubbs, *Pioneer Folks and Places*).

DE LONG. Knox. Fourteen miles east of Urbana. Founded in 1882 by S. H. Malory and named for George Washington De Long, naval officer and Arctic explorer, who, along with his crew, perished from exposure when their ship was crushed by ice in the Pacific Ocean north of Siberia in 1881 (*Annals of Knox County*, 144). Post office established May 28, 1883.

DEL REY. Iroquois. Fifteen miles north-northeast of Paxton. Named for the 1847 Mexican War battle of Molino del Rey (the King's Mill). Post office established June 13, 1854.

DEMENT. Ogle. Township. Created from Flagg Township in 1856. Named for John Dement of Dixon, receiver at the Dixon land office of the Illinois Central Railroad. Dement was Illinois state treasurer in the 1830s and commander of a spy (scout) company in the Black Hawk War (Bateman and Selby, eds., *Historical Encyclopedia of Illinois and History of Ogle County*, 756). Post office established Sept. 23, 1852, as Brawdie's Grove; changed to Dement Station April 7, 1854.

DENISON. Lawrence. Township. Named for William Den(n)ison, local land owner and justice of the peace (*Combined History of Edwards, Lawrence, and Wabash Counties*, 286).

DENMARK. Perry. Eight miles east of Steeleville. Laid out in 1860 as John's Town by John D. Rees and familiarly known as Jack Town. The generally accepted account is that the name was changed by postmaster Chris Wittmac, a native of Denmark, about 1897. Another Denmark, in Vermilion County, is now part of Danville (*Perry County*, 10). Post office established Dec. 18, 1865.

DENVER. Hancock. Eight miles south of Carthage. Founded in 1863 and named by Sanford C. Seybold in recognition of his trip to Colorado several years before. Previously known as Rough and Ready (*History of Hancock County*, 339). Post office established July 30, 1863.

DEPUE [di PYOO]. Bureau. Village (1867, 1888) eight miles east-southeast of Princeton. First known as Newport Steamboat Landing. Formally established as Trenton by Benjamin Newell in 1853. About 1865 the name was changed to Sherman and in 1867 to DuPu, named from DuPu Lake. The spelling was changed to Depue shortly thereafter. The origin of the name is uncertain. Most likely it recalls an early French explorer or trader named Dupuis or Dupuy (Coulet du Gard, *Dictionary of French Place Names*; Leonard, ed., *Big Bureau*, 71). Post office established March 31, 1854, as Selby Station; changed to De Pue May 6, 1867; changed to DePue July 14, 1894.

DERINDA. Jo Daviess. Township. Named in the early 1850s. When a referendum to choose a name for the township resulted in a tie between "New Germany" and "Rush," the presiding officer, David Barr, suggested the name of his wife, Derinda (*History of Jo Daviess County,* 597). The Derinda post office operated intermittently from April 3, 1852, until July 9, 1895. The Derinda Center post office operated from Jan. 2, 1873, until Sept. 30, 1905.

DESELM. Kankakee. Seven miles west of Kankakee. Founded about 1867; named for postmaster John B. Deselm (Adams, comp., *Illinois Place Names*). Post office established March 7, 1867.

DE SOTO. Jackson. Village (1895) eleven miles west of Herrin. Established in the mid-1850s by the Illinois Central Railroad and named for the Spanish explorer Hernando De Soto, the first European to see the Mississippi River (Ackerman, *Early Illinois Railroads,* 134). Post office established April 6, 1855.

DES PLAINES [DEZ PLAYNZ, de SPLAYNZ]. Cook. City (1869, 1873). Laid out about 1859 as Rand, named for Socrates Rand, an early settler and flour mill proprietor. The name was changed at the time of incorporation to match that of the Chicago and North Western station, itself named for the Des Plaines River. The Des Plaines was generally known as the Chicago River in the late seventeenth century and as the Illinois River until the 1770s, when it appears as Plein on Thomas Hutchins's map. The 1829 Treaty of Prairie du Chien granted to Claude Laframboise one section of land on the Riviere aux Pleins. The name is from American French *plaine* (maple tree). Likely a translation of a Potawatomi word for the sugar maple. (Smith, *The Des Plaines River,* 26–28; Vogel, *Indian Place Names in Illinois*). Post office established March 21, 1837.

DETROIT. Pike. Village (1903) seven miles east of Pittsfield. Founded in 1837 by Peter H. Lucas and named after the post office, itself named for Detroit, Mich. French for "strait, narrow passage" (*History of Pike County,* 427). Post office established Sept. 13, 1837, as Newburgh; changed to Detroit Dec. 13, 1845.

DEWITT [dee WIT]. County and Village (1879). The village of DeWitt was established in 1832 by Benjamin S. Day, James Morrison, James McCord, Z. G. Cantrell, and James Hutchison and platted as Marion in 1836. The name was changed to DeWitt the following year when it was reorganized by James Allen (Allin) and James M. Fell. DeWitt County was created March 1, 1839, from parts of Macon, McLean, Piatt, and Logan counties and took the name of the village. The township, also originally known as Marion, took the name of the county in 1859. All were named in honor of DeWitt Clinton (1769–1828), governor of New York, perhaps best known for his promotion of the Erie Canal. The name was probably suggested by James Allen, an admirer of DeWitt Clinton (*see* Clinton) (*Clinton 1835–1985,* 77). Post office established Jan. 9, 1840, as Lemon for the Lemon (or Leming or Lemen) Settlement; changed to DeWitt March 7, 1844.

DEWMAINE. Williamson. Two miles southwest of Herrin. Founded as a residential community for African American strikebreakers by the St. Louis and Big Muddy Coal Company in 1898. The name is a blend of the words *Dew* for Adm. George Dewey, who destroyed a Spanish fleet in Manila Bay in 1898, and *Maine* for the American battleship that was sunk in Havana Harbor, also in 1898, precipitating the Spanish-American War (Hale, comp. and ed., *Williamson County*, 118). Post office established March 6, 1901.

DEXTER. Effingham. Seven miles southwest of Effingham. Named for early settler Josia Lufkin Dexter (Feldhake, *Effingham County*, 41). Post office established Feb. 11, 1837, as Benton; changed to Freemanton March 12, 1840; changed to Dexter July 31, 1876.

DIAMOND. Grundy. Village (1895) east of Coal City. Located in a major coal-producing area and named from a synonym for coal, "black diamonds," specifically from the Diamond Mine of the Wilmington Coal Mining and Manufacturing Company. (Hochstetter, ed., *Guide to Illinois' Historical Markers*). Post office established Feb. 7, 1872.

DICKEYS. Kankakee. Nine miles southwest of Kankakee. Founded about 1870 and named for local farmer Sylvester Dickey. Formerly known as Dickey's Siding (Bateman and Selby, eds., *Historical Encyclopedia of Illinois and History of Kankakee County*, 909).

DIETERICH [DEE drik]. Effingham. Village (1893) ten miles east-southeast of Effingham. Founded in 1880 by Michael Dieterich as Dieterichsburg, a station on the Springfield, Effingham and Southeastern Railroad (Banbury, comp., *The Sesquicentennial of Effingham County*, 626). Post office established March 28, 1881.

DILLON. Tazewell. Six miles southeast of Pekin. Founded in 1836 and named for Nathan Dillon, an early settler and first township supervisor. Originally called Liberty (Bates, *Souvenir of Early and Notable Events*, 24). Post office established Oct. 5, 1826, as Mackinaw Settlement; changed to Dillon July 21, 1828.

DIMMICK [DIM ik]. LaSalle. Six miles north of LaSalle. Named for the Dimmick (Dimick) family. Daniel Dimmick was one of the first settlers in 1833, and a J. Dimmick was an early justice of the peace. Formerly known as Homer. The name was changed to Dimmick with construction of the Illinois Central Railroad about 1875 (Ackerman, *Early Illinois Railroads*, 143; *History of LaSalle County*, 132; Stennett, *A History of the Origin*, 63). Post office established July 16, 1850.

DIONA. Coles, Cumberland. Six miles south of Charleston. This is the only Diona in the United States, and the origin of the name is unknown. Informally known as Dogtown. According to local legend, when a dog fight broke out in front of the blacksmith shop, "Uncle Johnny" Stallings stuck his head in the door and shouted, "Hurray for Dogtown!" The community's nickname comes from that remark—or so the story goes (*Cumberland County History*, 13). Post office established Oct. 25, 1872.

DIVERNON [deye VER nuhn]. Sangamon. Village (1900) thirteen miles south of Springfield. Named about 1887 by H. C. Barnes for Diana Vernon, known as Di Vernon, the heroine of Sir Walter Scott's novel *Rob Roy* (Brady, *Divernon*, 20). Post office established Feb. 23, 1887.

DIVIDE. Jefferson. Ten miles north-northeast of Mount Vernon. Reportedly named for the ridge dividing the watersheds of Casey Fork and Horse Creek (www .genealogytrails.com/ill/jefferson/ghostowns.html). Post office established Oct. 27, 1879.

DIX. Jefferson. Village (1873) eight miles north of Mount Vernon. Originally called Rome by settlers from Rome, N.Y. The name was changed about 1865 to honor John Adams Dix (1798–1879), secretary of the treasury, U.S. senator, and later governor of New York. Dix Township in Ford County is named for the same John Dix (*see* Drummer) (Gardner, *History of Ford County*, 117; Perrin, ed., *History of Jefferson County*, 364). Post office established July 20, 1835, as Jordan's Prairie; changed to Rome Feb. 24, 1852; changed to Dix April 17, 1865.

DIXMOOR. Cook. Village (1922). Founded in 1922 by the first village president, Charles Special, and known as Specialville. The name was changed later in 1922, when the village incorporated as Dixmoor, taking the name of an adjacent unincorporated subdivision (Zimmerman, "History of Incorporated Municipalities," 3).

DIXON. Lee. City (1853, 1904). First known as Ogee's Ferry, named for Joseph Ogee, who operated a ferry across the Rock River in the late 1820s. John Dixon bought the ferry from Ogee in 1830. Dixon was a revered local figure known as Father Dixon. Dixon has been the Lee County seat since 1839. Dixon precinct in Edwards County is named for a different John Dixon (*see* Nachusa) (Bateman and Selby, eds., *Historical Encyclopedia of Illinois and History of Lee County*, 647; Harper, ed., *History of Edwards County*, 48). Post office established May 25, 1829, as Ogee's Ferry; changed to Dixon's Ferry Feb. 23, 1833; changed to Dixon Jan 3, 1842.

DIXON SPRINGS. Pope. Ten miles west of Golconda. Named for the mineral springs owned and developed by William and Caroline Dixon. Local Native Americans, aware of the medicinal properties of the waters, reportedly called the springs Kitche-Mus-Ke-Be, from Potawatomi for "big medicine" (personal communication with Michael McCafferty; *Pope County*, 26). Post office established Feb. 1, 1896, as Resort; changed to Dixon Springs Feb. 11, 1905.

DODDS. Jefferson. Township. Named for the first known settler, James Dodds (Perrin, ed., *History of Jefferson County*, 406).

DODDSVILLE. McDonough, Schuyler. Twelve miles south of Macomb. Founded by Samuel Dodds and Paris Wheeler about 1836. Dodds built the first house in the community and established the first general store (Chenoweth and Semonis, comps., *The History of McDonough County,* 80; *Combined History of Schuyler and Brown Counties,* 241, 313). Post office established Jan. 31, 1833, as Brattleville; changed to Doddsville March 14, 1839.

DODGE GROVE. Coles. Two miles north of Mattoon. According to local accounts, a family living near the grove had a racing mare named the Dodge Filly. She was used to secure a bet during a race at Springfield but lost. Her owners, not wanting to give her up, hid her in the grove until the sheriff called off the search (Dole, "Pioneer Days," 112).

DOG HOLLOW. Pope. Valley twelve miles south of Harrisburg. The traditional story is told by John W. Allen: "Two young men had seen their girls safely home from a church service. They were returning at a late hour through the hollow. By their story they were pursued by a headless dog. Thus the hollow received its name and has ever since been called Dog Hollow" (Allen, *Pope County Notes,* 65).

DOGTOOTH. Alexander. Island. Named from Dogtooth Bend, the sharp east, then north, then northwest bend in the Mississippi River that forms the extreme southwestern tip of Illinois. The Dogtooth post office was active from Feb. 13, 1854, until Dec. 2, 1863.

DOG WALK. Williamson. One mile north of Marion. Established for employees of a local coal company. The traditional story is that most families owned several dogs that constantly ran up and down the roads or paraded on the paths to and from the mines. These paths became known as dog walks (Harris, "Illinois Place-Name Lore," 218–19).

DOLTON. Cook. Village (1892). Previously known as Calumet Junction for its location on the Little Calumet River. Named for the Dolton family. George Dolton arrived about 1835, followed shortly by his brothers Henry, Charles, and Andrew. George Dolton was the first postmaster (Huizenga, *Dolton,* 3; *Illinois Guide;* Karlen, *Chicago's Crabgrass Communities,* 50). Post office established Jan. 7, 1854.

DONGOLA [dahn GOL uh]. Union. Village (1883) eight miles southeast of Anna. Founded in 1857 by site owner Ebeni Leavenworth, an engineer for the Illinois Central Railroad. Probably named for Dongola in the Sudan. Dongola (Dunqulah) and the Sudanese struggle for independence were in the news at the time (Ackerman, *Early Illinois Railroads,* 137; Leonard, *History of Union County,* 59). Post office established Nov. 9, 1855, as Unionville; changed to Dongola April 16, 1857.

DONICA. Coles. Former settlement several miles southeast of Oakland. Named from Donica Creek, itself named for early settlers Hiram and Samuel Donica. Also known as Donica's Point (Perrin, Graham, and Blair, *History of Coles County,* 448).

DONKVILLE. Madison. Two miles north of Collinsville. Named for Emile Donk and his brother, operating as the Donk Brothers Coal and Coke Company. Their first mine opened about 1902. The community is now known as Maryville (q.v.). Post office established Jan. 20, 1901.

DONNELLSON [DAHN uhl suhn]. Montgomery, Bond. Village (1897) eight miles south of Hillsboro. Founded about 1858. Named for Thomas Carson Donnell, a veteran of the Black Hawk War (Bateman and Selby, eds., *Historical Encyclopedia of Illinois and History of Montgomery County*, 874). Post office established Nov. 13, 1850, as Bear Creek; changed to Donnellson July 9, 1861.

DONOVAN. Iroquois. Village (1901) nine miles northwest of Watseka. Founded in 1872 by John L. Donovan, who said he named the village for his father, Joseph Donovan, keeper of the Buckhorn Tavern (Beckwith, *History of Iroquois County*, 512; Dowling, *History of Iroquois County*, 29). Post office established June 30, 1858.

DORANS. Coles. Nine miles west-northwest of Charleston. Named from the Illinois Central station, built in 1878 on land owned by Samuel A. Doran (Perrin, Graham, and Blair, *History of Coles County*, 323). Post office established May 16, 1898.

DORR. McHenry. Township. Named for Thomas Wilson Dorr (1805–54), who at the time the township was named was in active revolt against the government of Rhode Island in what was known as Dorr's Rebellion. Dorr attempted to replace the colonial charter under which Rhode Island was governed with a "people's constitution" and to seize the arsenal at Providence, an action for which he was convicted of treason and sentenced to life in prison. He served one year (Nye, ed., *McHenry County Illinois*, 543). Post office established March 13, 1845.

DORRIS HEIGHTS. Saline. A subdivision established in 1923 on land owned by W. S. and Bertha Dorris. Annexed by Harrisburg in 1979 (*History of Saline County*, 61).

DORRISVILLE. Saline. Named for John and Hugh Dorris. Annexed by Harrisburg in 1923 (*History of Saline County*, 34). Post office established Aug. 14, 1905.

DORSEY. Madison. Four miles north of Bethalto. Named for early settler Samuel L. Dorsey (Underwood, "A New Geography of Illinois: Madison County," 29).

DOTY. Coles. Former community. Founded about 1885 on the line of the Toledo, Cincinnati and St. Louis Railroad and named for the Doty family, early settlers. James Ira Doty was the first and only postmaster. The Doty cemetery is about five miles southwest of Charleston (Redlich, *The Postal History of Coles County*, 118). Post office established Oct. 22, 1885.

DOUGLAS. A county; several communities; townships in Clark, Iroquois, and Effingham counties; and scores of streets, schools, and parks are named for Stephen Arnold Douglas, apart from Abraham Lincoln arguably the best known and most influential national political figure of the nineteenth century from Illinois. Douglas (1813–61) held several state offices, was U.S. representative from 1843 to 1847, and U.S. senator from 1847 to 1861. He defeated Lincoln after the famous series of debates in the senatorial campaign of 1858 and was in turn defeated by Lincoln for the presidency in 1860. Douglas, an ardent supporter of westward expansion and economic development of the western states, was largely responsible for passage of the legislation that led to the creation of the Illinois Central Railroad in 1850.

DOUGLAS. Cook. Also named for Stephen A. Douglas, who purchased land in the area in 1852; part of his lakefront estate, Oakenwald, was later donated to the University of Chicago (Kitagawa and Taeuber, eds., *Local Community Fact Book*, 84).

DOUGLAS. County. Created in February 1859 from Coles County. Two names for the new county were initially considered: Watson, for W. D. Watson, a state senator from Camargo (which was to be the first county seat), and Richman, for John Richman, the first permanent settler in the area. For reasons that are unclear but likely political, the state legislature found both names unacceptable and went so far as to make it a condition for approval of its creation that the county be named for Sen. Stephen A. Douglas (*County of Douglas*, 8; Gresham, *Historical and Biographical Record*, 27).

DOVER. Bureau. Village (1873) five miles northeast of Princeton. Laid out by Sylvester Brigham in 1833 and named after his hometown of Dover, N.H. An adjacent area was platted in 1837 by Eli Lapsley as Livingston, named for U.S. Secretary of State Edward Livingston, for whom Livingston County was named. The communities merged as Dover with establishment of the post office in 1839 (Leonard, ed., *A Pioneer Tour of Bureau County*, 39).

DOW [DOW]. Jersey. Seven miles south of Jerseyville. Founded in 1883 by John and Medora McDow as a station on the Wabash, St. Louis and Pacific Railroad (*History of Greene and Jersey Counties*, 456). Post office established Jan. 29, 1829, as Eminence; changed to Newbern Aug. 24, 1834; changed to Dow June 3, 1896.

DOWELL [DOW uhl]. Jackson. Village (1919) three miles south of Du Quoin. Named for George Dowell, legal advisor for the Progressive Miners of America (Hansen, ed., *Illinois*, 505). Post office established Dec. 12, 1918.

DOWNERS GROVE. DuPage. Village (1873). Founded about 1835 by Pierce Downer, who emigrated from New York about 1832 (*Illinois Guide*). Post office established Sept. 11, 1839.

DOWNS. McLean. Village (1917) eight miles southeast of Bloomington. Named for Lawson Downs, a local farmer and veteran of the Black Hawk War. The township name was changed from Savanna in 1858 (*History of McLean County*, 703).

DOZAVILLE. Randolph. Six miles west of Chester. Established on the site of Pujol (q.v.) about 1872 by William Doza, possibly a descendant of Alexis (Elexe) Doza, one of a number of French Canadians who settled in the Kaskaskia area toward the end of the seventeenth century. Much of Dozaville was destroyed by a flood in 1973 (Allen, *Randolph County Notes*, 5; *Randolph County*, 80).

DRESDEN. Grundy. Dresden, named for Dresden, Germany, was laid out in 1835 by Salmon Rutherford on the stagecoach line between Chicago and Peoria. The community never prospered and has now disappeared. The name is perpetuated by the Dresden Cemetery about three miles west-southwest of Channahon, the Dresden nuclear power plant, and Dresden Heights, a hundred-foot-high summit, part of the Kankakee Bluffs at the confluence of the Kankakee and Des Plaines rivers (Brown, ed., *Grundy County*, 50). Post office established Feb. 17, 1842. A Dresden post office was active in Will County from Sept. 4, 1837, until March 2, 1838, when it was relocated to Channahon.

DRESSOR. Fayette. Former community fourteen miles south of Pana. Named for site owner Nathaniel Dressor of Greenville (Hanabarger, "Fayette County Place Names," 45). Post office established March 21, 1888.

DRIVERS. Jefferson. Four miles west-northwest of Mount Vernon. Founded about 1887 and named for postmaster James R. Driver (Adams, comp., *Illinois Place Names*; Sneed, *Ghost Towns of Southern Illinois*, 93). Post office established Jan. 9, 1888.

DROWNING FORK. McDonough. Stream. Reportedly named for three soldiers who were returning to the fort near Industry after taking part in skirmishes with Indians. Two of them drowned while attempting to cross the stream, which was swollen from recent heavy rains. The incident is said to have occurred in 1827 (Clarke, *History of McDonough County*, 129; Frazer and Frazer, "Place Name Patterns," 23). The Drowning Fork post office was active from July 25, 1848, until March 12, 1858, when it was relocated to Bushnell.

DRUCE LAKE. Lake and community five miles north of Waukegan in Lake County. Named from Druce Lake, itself named for Alexander Druce (Halsey, ed., *A History of Lake County*, 397).

DRUM HILL BRANCH. St. Clair. Stream. Named from Drum Hill, near New Athens, where an early settler named Carr is said to have beat a drum each morning and evening, apparently to call farmers to and from the fields (*History of St. Clair County*, 270).

DRUMMER. Ford. Township. Named in honor of a noted hunting dog named Drummer. According to a local story, Drummer (supposedly so named because he was good at drumming up game) became exhausted while chasing a deer and died. He was buried among the nearby trees in what became known as Drummer Grove. Drummer Grove Township was organized in 1858, and the name was changed to Dix (q.v.) for John Adams Dix by local referendum in

1864. Drummer township was subsequently formed from Dix in 1869, thereby, as Gardner so aptly puts it, "dividing the honors of the territory equally between General Dix and the dog" (*History of Ford County*, 117).

DRURY. Rock Island. Township. Named for Miles, Reynolds, Isiah, Silas, James, and Eli Drury, the earliest settlers in the township, who arrived in the mid-1830s (Bateman and Selby, eds., *Historical Encyclopedia of Illinois and History of Rock Island County*, 964). Post office established July 5, 1848, as Drury's Landing; changed to Walnut Valley Sept. 10, 1850.

DRY GROVE. McLean. Township. Named from the tract of timber known as Dry Grove, itself probably so named because the grove was on high ground rather than by a stream, where most groves were found (*History of McLean County*, 686). Post office established April 21, 1858.

DRY HILL. Jackson. Eleven miles west-northwest of Murphysboro. Named from nearby Dry Hill. The local story is that the hill was so named because it was hard to find water there. It may have been named, however, for local resident Samuel Dry (Allen, *Jackson County Notes*, 12). Post office established June 23, 1871.

DU BOIS [doo BOYZ]. Washington. Village (1869, 1896) twelve miles southeast of Nashville. Formerly known as Coloma. Renamed in 1868 for Jesse K. Du Bois, auditor for the Illinois Central Railroad (Ackerman, *Early Illinois Railroads*, 133). Post office established July 18, 1856.

DUBOIS HILLS. Lawrence. Former community in Allison Township. Named for the Toussaint Dubois family. Dubois, for whom Dubois County, Ind., is named, fought at Tippecanoe with William Henry Harrison (Baker, *From Needmore to Prosperity*; Coulet du Gard, *Dictionary of French Place Names*).

DUDLEYVILLE. Bond. Four miles south of Greenville. Founded in 1857 by John Dudley, site owner and keeper of the local grocery store (Bateman and Selby, eds., *Historical Encyclopedia of Illinois and History of Bond County*, 635).

DUNCAN. Mercer. Township. Named for first settler Buford Duncan, who emigrated from Indiana about 1836 (Bassett and Goodspeed, *Past and Present of Mercer County*, 517).

DUNCAN. Stark. Founded about 1870 by Alfred H. Castle and named for James Henry Duncan, U.S. representative from Massachusetts from 1849 to 1853 (Gannett, *The Origin of Certain Place Names*). Post office established Sept. 19, 1853, as Slack Water; changed to Duncan May 12, 1870.

DUNCAN MILLS. Fulton. Four miles south-southwest of Lewistown. Named from the mills operated by George Duncan (Irwin, *A to Z Fulton County*). Post office established April 21, 1858.

DUNDEE, East and West [duhn DEE]. Kane. Also Dundee Township. East Dundee and West Dundee lie on opposite sides of the Fox River just north of Elgin. Dundee is the post office for both. An early Scots immigrant, Alexander Gardiner, is usually credited with naming the communities for Dundee, Scotland, in the late 1830s. A number of early settlers, however, were from the area around Dundee in western New York state (itself named for Dundee, Scotland), and that may be the direct source of the name. James T. Gifford claims credit for naming Dundee, N.Y. in 1833, and also for naming Elgin, Ill. (q.v.). Referenda to unite East and West Dundee into Dundee failed in 1956 and 1962 (*Biographical and Historical Record of Kane County*, 1008; Dupre, Braden, and Bullinger, *Dundee Township*, 17–18; *Past and Present of Kane County*, 370). Post office established April 13, 1837, as McClure's Grove; changed to Dundee Sept. 3, 1841.

DUNFERMLINE. Fulton. Village (1947) four miles south of Canton. Named by early settlers from Dunfermline, Scotland (Irwin, *A to Z Fulton County*). Post office established Dec. 24, 1887.

DUNHAM. Township. McHenry. Solomon J. Dunham, a local justice of the peace, was asked to choose a name for the township, and he obliged by offering his own (Nye, ed., *McHenry County Illinois*, 591). Post office established Jan. 28, 1846.

DUNKEL. Christian. Five miles north of Pana. Founded in 1876 by J. M. Dunkel, shopkeeper and postmaster. Named for himself or for Elias Dunkel, station agent for the Illinois Central Railroad (Ackerman, *Early Illinois Railroads*, 149; *Christian County History*, 35). Post office established April 5, 1877.

DUNLAP. Peoria. Village (1951) six miles north of Peoria. Founded by site owner Alva Dunlap in 1871 (*History of Peoria County*, 614). Post office established Sept. 29, 1871.

DUNLEITH. Jo Daviess. Township. Named for the community of Dunleith (now East Dubuque). Founded about 1854 by a consortium of land speculators operating as the proprietors of the town of Dunleith, named for Dunleith, Scotland (*History of Jo Daviess County*, 543). Post office established Aug. 1, 1854.

DUNNING. Cook. Established as a station on the Chicago, Milwaukee and St. Paul Railroad in 1882 and named for the Dunning family. David Dunning emigrated from Canada in 1836. The community was formally laid out by site owner Andrew Dunning in the late 1860s. Now part of Chicago. (Karlen, *Chicago's Crabgrass Communities*, 186). Post office established May 11, 1838, as Monroe; changed to Maine May 30, 1850; changed to Leyden Centre July 6, 1853; changed to Dunning June 11, 1883.

DU PAGE. County. Created in 1839 from Cook County. Named from the DuPage River, itself named for a French or French Indian explorer and trapper whose name is reported in the early histories as DuPazhe and about whom little is known except that he set up a trading post on the river in the late eighteenth century. The name of the county has been spelled in a number of ways. In 1994 the county board adopted as official the spelling DuPage, or, when spelled with all capital letters, as it is on the county seal, DU PAGE. The county seat was established at Naperville in 1839 and moved to Wheaton in 1867 (Bateman and Selby, eds., *Historical Encyclopedia of Illinois and History of DuPage County*, 618; Grady, "County No Longer Has Space").

DUPAGE. Will. Established by the Illinois and Michigan Canal Commission at the junction of the canal and the DuPage River. Laid out about 1845 by Mirvin Benjamin and named from the DuPage post office. Now part of Channahon (Chavez, "Nothing but a Memory"; *History of Will County*, 597).

DUPO [DOO po]. St. Clair. Village (1907) six miles east of East St. Louis. Established about 1905 with the location of the Missouri Pacific (Mopac) shops and switching yards, replacing Prairie du Pont, a much earlier settlement located a short distance to the north. The original French Prairie du Pont (Prairie of the Bridge) was progressively shortened to Dupont and then to Dupo about 1906 at the suggestion of Louis J. Dyroff, chair of the committee charged with incorporating the village. The original name is retained in Prairie du Pont Creek (q.v.). In 1997 Dupo considered changing its name back to Prairie du Pont in an effort to change the village's "aging industrial image." Supporters argued that changing the name would allow the community to capitalize on its French heritage and aid in attracting tourists (Beal and Trost, *Portrait of Yesterday*, 20, 155; *Illinois Guide*; "Town of Dupo"; Walton, *Centennial, McKendree College, with St. Clair County History*, 511). Post office established Feb. 19, 1906.

DU QUOIN [doo KOYN]. Perry. City (1861, 1873). Founded in 1844 by Avery Chapman. The site is now known as Old Du Quoin. Present Du Quoin, two miles northwest of Old Du Quoin, was laid out for the Illinois Central Railroad by Chester Keys and Isaac Metcalf. With the establishment of the IC station in 1853 many of the buildings in Old Du Quoin were disassembled and moved to trackside. Named for Jean Baptiste (John) Ducoigne, the son of a French Canadian father and a Kaskaskia mother, who became a Kaskaskia leader of the late eighteenth and early nineteenth centuries. The Marquis de Lafayette is reported to have given Ducoigne a letter of commendation for his service to the American cause during the Revolutionary War, noting in particular his assistance to George Rogers Clark in capturing Kaskaskia (Coulet du Gard, *Dictionary of French Place Names*; Neville, comp., *Student's History*, 21; Vogel, *Indian Place Names in Illinois*). Post office established Dec. 28, 1844, as Duquoin.

DURAND [du RAND]. Winnebago. Village (1869, 1872) thirteen miles northwest of Rockford. Founded about 1857 by J. R. Herring and named for Henry S. Durand, president of the Racine and Mississippi Railroad (Nelson, comp., *Sinnissippi Saga*, 28). Post office established Jan. 24, 1850, as Medina; changed to Durand Station April 30, 1858.

DURHAM. Hancock. Five miles west of La Harpe. Founded in 1839 and named by Lyman Wilcox and other settlers from Durham, Middlesex County, Conn.;

itself named for Durham, England (*History of Hancock County*, 285). Post office established Nov. 28, 1850.

DURLEY. Bond. Four miles northeast of Greenville. Founded about 1884 and named for Horatio Durley, an early settler (Peterson, "Place Names of Bond County," 39). Post office established May 3, 1888.

DUTCH CHURCH CREEK. Pike. Stream. Reportedly named "after a rocky bluff near its bank which is supposed to resemble an old Dutch church in the city of Albany, N.Y." (Massie, *Past and Present of Pike County*, 49).

DUTCH HILL. St. Clair. Former community. Laid out by Fred (or Frank) Griebel and named from Dutch Hill, a summit near the St. Clair–Monroe county line, itself probably named for the large number of German settlers, primarily from Saxony (*Tapestry of Time*, 139). Post office established April 24, 1839, as Lively; changed to Lenzburg June 16, 1853; changed to Dutch Hill Jan. 7, 1868.

DUTTON. Pike. Four miles north of Pittsfield. Named for David Dutton, an early county commissioner. Also called Dutton's Mineral Spring (Thompson, *The Jess M. Thompson Pike County History*, 62).

DWIGHT. Livingston. Village (1869, 1872). Founded about 1853 by the Chicago and Mississippi Railroad. Named by Richard P. Morgan Jr., then an engineer and later general superintendent of the C&M, for Henry A. Dwight of New York, who financed much of the construction of the railroad from Bloomington to Joliet. This proved a financial disaster for Dwight, who years later complained that his fortune "lay buried beneath the tracks of the railroad" (*Dwight Centennial*, 13; *History of Livingston County* [1878], 287, 486).

E

EARLVILLE. LaSalle. City (1869, 1877) ten miles east-northeast of Mendota. Also Earl Township. Earlville was founded in the late 1840s by members of the Boston Colony; early settlers were largely from Massachusetts and New York. Several early writers claim that the name was transferred from Earlville, Madison County, N.Y., by Charles H. Sutphen, the first postmaster at Earlville and one of the site owners. By his own account, however, Sutphen named the community for his nephew Earl at the request of his wife (Stennett, *A History of the Origin*, 66; genealogytrails.com/ill/lasalle/Earlville.html). Post office established Aug. 24, 1844.

EAST BEND. Champaign. Township. Named for the southeast-to-southwest bend in the Sangamon River near Greenwood Lake. The area was earlier known as Sodom, named from the Sodom post office, itself presumably named for the biblical city of Sodom (Bateman and Selby, eds., *Historical Encyclopedia of Illinois and History of Champaign County*, 812). Post office established Sept. 19, 1853, as Sodom; changed to East Bend Jan. 20, 1857.

EASTBURN. Iroquois. Four miles east of Watseka. Named for postmaster Allen M. Eastburn (Adams, comp., *Illinois Place Names*). Post office established June 17, 1891.

EAST CAPE GIRARDEAU [KAYP juh RAHR do]. Alexander. Village (1975). Founded about 1890. Named for its location across the Mississippi River from Cape Girardeau, Mo., itself named for the Sieur Girardeau (or Girardat), who was stationed at Fort Kaskaskia in the early years of the century and later became a prosperous trader and merchant (Ramsay, *Our Storehouse of Missouri Place Names*, 48). Post office established July 9, 1874.

EAST DUBUQUE [duh BYOOK]. Jo Daviess. City (1857). Previously known as Dunleith, named for Dunleith, Scotland. Renamed for its location opposite Dubuque, Iowa, itself named for founder Julian Dubuque, regarded as the first European settler in Iowa (Ackerman, *Early Illinois Railroads*, 138). Post office established Aug. 1, 1854, as Dunleith; changed to East Dubuque June 9, 1879.

EAST HANNIBAL. Pike. On the east bank of the Mississippi River, opposite Hannibal, Mo., from which it takes its name.

EAST LYNNE. Vermilion. Six miles west of Hoopeston. Founded about 1872. The name was probably taken from the novel *East Lynne Tonight* by the nineteenth-century American author Anna S. Stephens (Beckwith, *History of Vermilion County*, 1001). Post office established Jan. 18, 1869, as Luddenville for postmaster Benjamin M. Ludden; changed to East Lynn Dec. 18, 1872.

EAST OAKLAND. Township. Coles. Originally called Oakland. "East" was added in 1860 "because some geographer present said there was an Oakland Township in some other county to the west," possibly referring to Oakland Township in Schuyler County (Bateman and Selby, eds., *Historical Encyclopedia of Illinois and History of Coles County*, 703).

EASTON. Mason. Village (1896) seven miles west-northwest of Mason City. Founded as Shermanville in 1872. The site was purchased in 1873 and renamed by Oliver C. Easton, the postmaster at Havana (Lynn, *Prelude to Progress*, 414). Post office established May 8, 1873.

EAST ST. LOUIS. St. Clair. City (1865, 1878). Named for its location east of St. Louis, Mo., itself named for Louis IX (1214–70), canonized in 1297. The first settlement at the site of current East St. Louis was Cahokia, founded by French-Canadian missionaries in 1799. The name was changed to Illinoistown about 1818, when ferry service was established across the Mississippi River, and to East St. Louis with the arrival of railroads (*Illinois Gazetteer;* Ramsay, *Our Storehouse of Missouri Place Names*, 103). Post office established March 31, 1824, as Illinoistown; changed to Wiggins Ferry Aug. 7, 1826; changed to East St. Louis April 22, 1864.

EBERLE. Effingham. Fourteen miles southeast of Effingham. According to an early account, the community was founded and named by a Dr. Z. Allen in honor of "Dr. Eberle, one of his favorite authors." This may be Dr. John Eberly (1787–1838),

American physician and author (Banbury, comp., *The Sesquecentennial of Effingham County,* 633). Post office established Dec. 8, 1870.

EDDYVILLE. Pope. Village (1883) fifteen miles south of Harrisburg. Founded in 1866 and named for site owner Edward Fulghum. The post office was established as Book, reportedly because no one could propose an acceptable name and there were many books in the house in which the meeting was taking place. As McCormick notes, however, a John Book appears on the 1866 tax roll, and he or a relative may have been the source of the name ("The Significance of Pope County Place Names," 26; *Pope County,* 27). Post office established Jan. 26, 1861, as Book; discontinued Aug. 24, 1869; reestablished as Eddyville Oct. 18, 1869.

EDELSTEIN [ED uhl steen]. Peoria. Seven miles west-northwest of Chillicothe. Named for John Edelstein, an official of the Atchison, Topeka, and Santa Fe Railroad (Marshall, *Santa Fe,* 354). Post office established April 9, 1888.

EDEN. Peoria. Eight miles west of Peoria. Laid out as Milo in the early 1880s on the line of the Iowa Central Railroad by Milo M. Long. Because Milo duplicated an existing post office in Bureau County, the name was changed to Eden, reportedly because of the rich soil and abundant water (Bateman and Selby, eds., *Historical Encyclopedia of Illinois and History of Peoria County,* 744–45). Post office established April 7, 1882.

EDEN. Randolph. One mile east of Sparta. Founded in the 1820s by the Rev. Samuel Wylie, who reportedly chose the name because "it was the closest type of Eden of any spot in Illinois" (Montague, *Directory,* 179).

EDGAR. County. Created Jan. 3, 1823, from Clark County. Named for John Edgar, a Kaskaskia merchant and land speculator who was instrumental in the formation of the county. Edgar was a British army officer who married an American, resigned his commission, and moved to Kaskaskia. He became a major general in the Illinois militia and reportedly was at one time the wealthiest man in the state. When the Illinois General Assembly approved the creation of the county, Mrs. Edgar was asked to name it. She supposedly said, "My husband gave this name to me; it is mine, and I give it to this new county—I name it Edgar" (Bateman and Selby, eds., *Historical Encyclopedia of Illinois and History of Edgar County,* 624).

EDGEWOOD. Effingham. Village (1882) fifteen miles southeast of Effingham. Established in 1857 by A. J. Galloway for the Illinois Central Railroad. Probably named for an Edgewood in one of the eastern states, of which there are about 100 (Pulliam, ed., *Townships of Effingham County,* 9). Post office established March 23, 1858.

EDGINGTON. Rock Island. Eleven miles southwest of Rock Island. Named for Daniel and John Edgington, early settlers who emigrated from Steubenville, OH, in the mid-1830s (*Past and Present of Rock Island County,* 223). Post office established Oct. 31, 1839, as Lower Rock Island; changed to Edgington Oct. 14, 1847.

EDINBURG [ED in berg]. Christian. Village (1874) eight miles northeast of Taylorville. Created in 1870 through the merger of Blueville and Blue Point, two communities that had grown up around the Greenwood mines. The source of the name is unclear; likely a transfer, perhaps from an Edinburg in New York, Indiana, or Ohio (*Christian County History,* 39). Post office established April 19, 1855, as Blueville; changed to Edinburgh July 18, 1870; changed to Edinburg July 14, 1893.

EDISON PARK. Cook. First called Canfield, a station on the Illinois and Wisconsin Railroad, probably named for an early settler named Canfield, and later known as Roseneath, which Stennett calls "a fanciful manufactured name that was supposed to assert the place was buried in roses" (*A History of the Origin,* 67). The name is surely a transfer from Roseneath, Scotland. It was changed about 1890 in honor of Thomas A. Edison's inventions and also to promote the fact that this was the first community on Chicago's Northwest Side to use electricity, or in the parlance of the day "to be electrified" (Karlen, *Chicago's Crabgrass Communities,* 207; Kitagawa and Taeuber, eds., *Local Community Fact Book,* 32). Post office established Oct. 6, 1890.

EDWARDS. County. Created Nov. 28, 1814, from parts of Madison and Gallatin counties. Named for Ninian Edwards (1775–1833), governor of Illinois Territory (1809–18), the first U.S. senator from Illinois (1818–24), and third governor of Illinois (1826–30).

EDWARDS. Peoria. Five miles west of Peoria. Founded as Edwards Station, a stop on the Chicago, Burlington and Quincy Railroad. Named for E. D. Edwards, who opened the first general store in the early 1850s (Rice, *Peoria City and County,* 295). Post office established April 16, 1856, as Edwards Station; changed to Edwards May 15, 1883.

EDWARDSVILLE. Madison. City (1819, 1872). Founded in 1812 and named for Ninian Edwards, at the time governor of Illinois Territory (*see* Edwards County) (Norton, ed., *Centennial History of Madison County,* 499). Edwardsville has been the seat of Madison County since its formation in 1812. Post office established Nov. 21, 1822.

EFFINGHAM. County. Created Feb. 15, 1831, from Crawford and Fayette counties. The city of Effingham was founded in 1853 by David B. Alexander and Samuel W. Little as Broughton, probably named for John Brough in an effort to attract a station on the proposed Mississippi and Atlantic Railroad, of which Brough was president. Andrew J. Galloway, acting for the Western Land Company, laid out Effingham, named for Effingham County, adjacent to Broughton in 1855. The communities merged as Effingham in 1859. The county was named for Lord Thomas Howard (1746–91), Third Earl of Effingham, who resigned his commission in the British Army in 1775 rather than fight against the American colonists. Effingham's resignation speech in Parliament made him extremely popular in the Colonies, and several communities in the United States and at least two ships were named in his honor. The name was likely suggested by W. L. D. Ewing, who introduced the legislation creating the county and for whom the first county seat, Ewington (q.v.), was named (Feldhake, *The Lords Effingham; Fiftieth Anniversary Souvenir of Effingham,* 7–8)

EGYPT. An area whose boundaries are not sharply defined but which includes at least the southernmost eleven counties of Illinois and as many as the southernmost twenty-eight counties. The traditional explanation is that the name derives from a time when there was an extended crop failure in central Illinois, when cold weather delayed planting and an early frost left little to harvest. Many people drove their wagons into southern Illinois, where crops had been bountiful, and returned with grain and seed corn. Some of them, remembering the Bible story in which the Israelites, after suffering similar crop failures, journeyed to Egypt for food and in answer to greetings along the way replied, "We are the sons of Jacob, going into Egypt to buy corn." This account, however, appears to be more folklore than fact. Of the forty or so Egypts in the United States, those whose stories are known all have remarkably similar naming legends with similar motifs: poor growing seasons and the journey to a neighboring land to procure food. It has also been suggested that "Egyptian" place names in the area inspired the name, but other than Cairo, the rest, such as Karnak, New Memphis, and Thebes, were all established well after the name *Egypt* had come into general use. The source of the name may lie in a nickname for the Mississippi River. From at least the late eighteenth century, the Mississippi was known as the "American Nile." In 1811 the lawyer and journalist Henry Marie Brackenridge wrote in the *Missouri Gazette* that St. Louis was destined to become "the Memphis of the American Nile" (Wade, *The Urban Frontier,* 64). Association of the Mississippi with the Nile may have inspired John Comegys or one of the other founders to call their new city Cairo in 1818. That name, and the name *Egypt* itself, may have provided models for the Egyptian place names that followed. Many social, cultural, and educational institutions in southern Illinois have adopted and extended the Egyptian theme. The Southern Illinois University (Carbondale) mascot is the saluki, a hunting dog of ancient Egypt, and the Benton High School yearbook (once called the *Egyptian Star*) is now the *Scarab* (Allen, *Legends and Lore,* 40–42; Halpert, "'Egypt'"; Ramsey and Miller, *The Heritage of Franklin County,* 12).

EICHORN. Hardin. Five miles north-northwest of Rosiclare. Named for Martin Eichorn, who emigrated from Bavaria about 1870 (*Hardin County,* 97). Post office established Oct. 5, 1893.

ELA. Lake. Township. Named for George Ela, the first postmaster and a state representative from Lake County in the late 1840s (Halsey, ed., *A History of Lake*

County, 427; *Past and Present of Lake County*, 269), Post office established March 23, 1846, as Serryse; changed to Ela Feb. 16, 1852.

ELBA. Gallatin. Six miles east of Eldorado. Laid out about 1866. Most likely a transfer, possibly from Elba, Ky., or Elba, Tenn. (*History and Families of Gallatin County*, 11). Post office established March 6, 1857, as Buffalo; changed to Elba March 13, 1866.

ELBA CENTER. Knox. Eighteen miles north of Canton. Also Elba Township. Probably named by settlers from Elba, Genesee County, N.Y., itself named in 1820 for the island of Elba in the Mediterranean Sea to which Napoleon was exiled in 1814. The township was organized as Liberty and the name changed to Elba in 1853 (Perry, *History of Knox County*, 442). Post office established Feb. 27, 1872, as Spoon River; changed to Elba Center Oct. 29, 1877.

ELBRIDGE. Edgar. Nine miles southeast of Paris. Laid out in 1836 by site owner James Ray and named from the Elbridge post office, itself named by the Rev. John B. Campbell, a Presbyterian minister, in honor of Elbridge G. Howe, an itinerant purveyor of books, tracts, and other religious fare (*History of Edgar County*, 406). Post office established Dec. 4, 1827.

ELBURN. Kane. Village (1883) seven miles west of Geneva. Laid out in 1854 by Jacob Johnson as Blackberry, a station on the Galena and Chicago Union Railroad, taking its name from Blackberry Creek. In 1886 the name was changed to Elburn at the request of the railroad. The first choice was apparently Melbourne, perhaps for Melbourne, Australia, but for unknown reasons the Post Office Department rejected that name. Although several authors claim that Elburn is a made-up name, "manufactured for the place" (Stennett, *A History of the Origin*, 67), it seems to be a shortened and Americanized form of "Melbourne" (Martin, "An Elburn History"; Robinson, *Sidewalks of Elburn*, 9, 91). Post office established May 24, 1854, as Blackberry Station; changed to Elburn Feb. 26, 1886.

ELCO. Alexander. Eleven miles south of Anna. Originally known as Hazelwood for first settler Felix Hazelwood, and later as Toledo. The traditional story is that some townspeople were discussing possible names in front of the E. Levenworth and Company General Store. Several names had been proposed and rejected when someone noticed that the boxes piled in front of the store were stenciled "E. L. Co" and suggested the name Elco (*Alexander County*, 13). Post office established Sept. 30, 1870, as Hazelwood; changed to Toledo Jan. 21, 1874; changed to Elco Sept. 11, 1878.

EL DARA [el DEHR uh]. Pike. Village (1881) nine miles west of Pittsfield. Founded in 1836 as Washington by Nathaniel Winters. The origin of the name is uncertain. The traditional story is that a Pike County official named Underwood, while serving in the Mexican War, passed through "a picturesque town" named Eldora, from which he posted a letter home to Washington, which was in process of changing the name of its post office. Town officials noted the postmark on Underwood's letter and decided to adopt that name. The postmark was slightly smeared, however, and the *o* was mistaken for an *a*. The problem with this account is that there is no record of a Mexican town named Eldora or El Dora. Rather, the name is either a shortening of Eldorado, a name popularized by the California gold rush, or a transfer from an existing Eldora, a name that occurs in about a dozen states and is a shortening of Eldorado. In either case, an indistinct *o* may indeed have been taken for *a*. This is the only El Dara in the United States (*History of Pike County*, 757; Stewart, *American Place-Names*). Post office established July 14, 1849.

ELDENA [el DEE nuh]. Lee. Five miles southeast of Dixon. Named for Mrs. Eldena Van Epps, wife of a local land owner (Ackerman, *Early Illinois Railroads*, 142). Post office established March 14, 1864.

ELDERVILLE. Hancock. Six miles southeast of Keokuk, Iowa. Originally called Kingston, named for shopkeeper J. W. King, whose store was purchased by Hugh M. Elder about 1875 (*History of Hancock County*, 613). Post office established April 25, 1873.

ELDORADO [el duh RAY do]. Saline. City (1873). Also East Eldorado Township. Founded in 1856 by Samuel Elder and his son, William, and Joseph Reed and his son, also named William. The name was proposed by William H. Parish, who claimed, "I was called on to suggest a name for the new town and replied that it should be called Elder-Reado in honor of the two men who had furnished the land on which it was to stand." Subsequently, according to a local tradition, a sign painter for the railroad took the station name *Elderedo* as a misspelling of *Eldorado* and corrected it accordingly (Miller-Mathis, *History of Eldorado*, 7). Post office established Dec. 8, 1858.

ELEROY [EL roy]. Stephenson. Six miles northwest of Freeport. Established on the line of the Illinois Central Railroad in 1853 and named by Hiram S. Jones for his son Leroy, known as Eleroy. Jones was proprietor of the Eleroy House, at the time the only hotel in the area (Ackerman, *Early Illinois Railroads*, 140; Johnston, *Sketches of the History of Stephenson County*, 297). Post office established July 1, 1847.

ELGIN. Kane, Cook. City (1854, 1880). Founded about 1836 and named by one of the first settlers, James T. Gifford, for the Scots hymn "Elgin." Gifford explained that he "had been a great admirer of that tune from boyhood" and it was his intention to call his former home in N.Y. Elgin, "but finding a post office was established in that state of that name, I had substituted Dundee and kept Elgin in reserve." Gifford made clear that the pronunciation was to be [EL jin] rather than British [EL gin] ("James T. Gifford," 69–70). Post office established July 19, 1837.

ELIZABETH. Jo Daviess. Village (1887) Twelve miles east-southeast of Galena. According to an Illinois state historical marker, in June 1832, at the height of the Black Hawk War, a group of Sauk warriors threatened Apple River Fort. With many of the men away hunting, Mrs. Elizabeth Armstrong rallied the women, and they put up such stiff resistance that the Indians withdrew. The settlement was named in her honor. Another account claims that three Elizabeths were among the women defending the fort, and the community was named for them collectively. The village was laid out about 1839 by site owner John Winters, whose wife was also named Elizabeth. Whether Elizabeth Winters was one of the Elizabeths who defended Apple River Fort is unknown (Bateman and Selby, eds., *Historical Encyclopedia of Illinois and History of Jo Daviess County*, 633; *Illinois Guide; Past to Present: Elizabeth*, n.p.). Post office established Dec. 11, 1828, as Apple River; changed to Elizabeth Nov. 25, 1842.

ELIZABETHTOWN. Hardin. Village (1857, 1873) two miles northeast of Rosiclare. Founded about 1812. Probably a transfer by settlers from Elizabethtown, Hardin County, Ky. Likely influenced by (and possibly named for) Elizabeth McFarland, wife of James McFarland, who kept a tavern and operated a ferry across the Ohio River to Kentucky (Hansen, ed., *Illinois*, 446; *Hardin County*, 8, 13). Post office established May 8, 1840.

ELK GROVE VILLAGE. Cook. Village (1956). Named from Elk Grove, settled about 1834. In 1934 the William Busse family brought ten elk from Wyoming and released them into what is now the Ned Brown Cook County Forest Preserve (McCarthy, *Elk Grove*, 37).

ELK PRAIRIE. Township. Jefferson. Formerly known as Anderson. The name was changed in 1870 for Elk Prairie, itself reportedly named for the large number of elk bones and antlers found by early settlers (Perrin, ed., *History of Jefferson Couunty*, 377).

ELKHART CITY. Logan. Village (1861) ten miles south-southwest of Lincoln. Laid out in 1855 by John Shockey. Named from Elkhart Hill, at 771 feet claimed to be the highest point in Logan County. According to tradition, Elkhart Hill was so named by a band of Illinois Indians whose totem was the elk heart. White Blossom, the daughter of an Illinois chief, had two suitors, one Shawnee and one Illinois, who demanded that she choose between them. An elk wandered by, and White Blossom said she would choose the warrior who shot an arrow closer to the elk's heart. They both shot their arrows, and the arrow of the Illinois warrior pierced the elk's heart. He and White Blossom were married, and their descendants took the elk heart as their totem (*Village of Elkhart City* 3, 6). Post office established Feb. 29, 1856, as Elkhart City; changed to Elkhart May 21, 1883.

ELKHORN POINT. Washington. Claimed to be a translation of French *corne de cerf* (horn of the deer) (Brinkman, ed., *This Is Washington County*, 35).

ELLERY [EL ree]. Edwards, Wayne. Twelve miles east of Fairfield. Reportedly named for a Mr. Ellery, who surveyed the community and the railroad right of way in 1880 (Harper, ed., *History of Edwards County,* 59). Post office established May 15, 1882.

ELLINGTON. Adams. Township. Named for Ellington, Tolland County, Conn., former home of Erastus W. Chapman, the first township clerk (Genosky, ed., *People's History,* 674). The Ellington post office operated from Jan. 15, 1883, until Oct. 15, 1900.

ELLIOTT [EL yuht]. Ford. Village (1903) five miles east of Gibson City. Named for site owner Samuel Elliott (Gardner, *History of Ford County,* 162). Post office established Nov. 7, 1872.

ELLIOTTSTOWN. Effingham. Nine miles southeast of Effingham. Founded about 1853. Named for site owner Smith Elliott (Feldhake, *Effingham County,* 51). Post office established Oct. 16, 1855.

ELLIS. Vermilion. Fifteen miles east-northeast of Rantoul. Founded in 1902 by site owner Albert Ellis (Underwood, "A New Geography of Illinois: Vermilion County," 39). Post office established June 2, 1908.

ELLIS GROVE. Randolph. Village (1894) eight miles northwest of Chester. Founded about 1852. Named for George Ellis, shopkeeper and first postmaster. For a time, the community was informally known as Dryburg because of its lack of taverns (*Combined History of Randolph, Monroe, and Perry Counties,* 34; *Illustrated Historical Atlas Map of Randolph County,* 27). Post office established Aug. 18, 1853.

ELLIS MOUND. Hamilton. Former community. Named for an Ellis family who reportedly passed through the area in the mid-1880s and buried one of their young children beside the trail near the site. The Ellis Mound Church is ten miles southwest of Fairfield (*Hamilton County,* 43). Post office established April 2, 1873.

ELLISON. Warren. Township and former community south of Smithshire. Founded about 1836. Reportedly named for a stranger named Ellison who was found dead nearby (*History of Mercer and Henderson Counties,* 1025; Rowley, *The History of Kirkwood, Illinois,* 26). Post office established Aug. 19, 1843.

ELLISVILLE. Fulton. Village (1872) eleven miles east-northeast of Bushnell. Founded about 1830 and named for Levi G. Ellis, who established a mill near the site in the late 1820s. Formerly known as Sorghum City, named for the cereal grass (*Historic Fulton County,* 615, 725). Post office established July 6, 1838.

ELLSWORTH. McLean. Village (1925) thirteen miles east of Bloomington. Founded in 1871 by site owners Oliver Ellsworth, A. B. Ives, and Jonathan Cheney. About 1837 Ellsworth emigrated from Ellington, Conn., to Bloomington, where he was employed as a blacksmith, specializing in the manufacture of plows (Evans,

Ellsworth's Hundredth Year, n.p.). Post office established May 13, 1852, as Padua; changed to Ellsworth March 25, 1872.

ELMHURST. DuPage. City (1888). Present Elmhurst dates from about 1843, when Darius Hovey and Gerry Bates established the Hill Cottage Tavern and Hotel, named for Hill Cottage, their former home in Painesville, Ohio. The Post Office Department transposed the name in 1845, and the community was known as Cottage Hill until the late 1860s. The name *Elmhurst* was proposed by Thomas B. Bryan about 1869 for the elm trees he and Jedediah Lathrop had planted in the late 1850s, "hurst" being the English cognate of German *hoorst* (grove), an appropriate choice given that the community was largely bilingual in English and German at the time (Berens, *Elmhurst,* 65–66, 85–86; *Illinois Guide*). Post office established Dec. 9, 1845, as Cottage Hill; changed to Elmhurst Nov. 20, 1868.

ELMIRA. Stark. Five miles southeast of Kewanee. Named for Elmira, Chemung County, N.Y., by Oliver Whitaker, the first postmaster (*Elmira, Illinois, Centennial,* 11). Post office established Sept. 12, 1840.

ELMWOOD. Peoria. City (1867, 1892) fifteen miles north of Canton. Founded in 1854. Elmwood was the name of the estate of William J. Phelps, who arrived about 1834 and was one of the area's first settlers. Phelps was later a justice of the peace, a Peoria County commissioner, and state legislator in the early 1840s (*History of Peoria County,* 583). Post office established May 15, 1884.

ELMWOOD PARK. Cook. Village (1914). Known as Orrison, probably for early settlers of that name, from about 1850 to 1905 and later as Ellsworth and Marwood Park, named for one of the first families to settle in the area. Merritt Marwood was the first village president. Developers chose the name *Elmwood Park* to attract potential buyers and promote the community (Borcover, "Not Much Happens Here").

EL PASO. Woodford. Village (1861, 1891). Founded in the early 1850s by George Gibson and James Wathen. George Bestor, president of the Peoria and Oquawka Railroad, offered Gibson and Wathen $250 if they would name the community Bestor. They refused Bestor's offer but could not agree on a name themselves; Gibson would not accept Wathen, and Wathen would not accept Gibson City. To break the deadlock they drew straws with the understanding that the winner would not name the town after himself. Gibson drew the long straw and chose the name *El Paso,* which he remembered from his return trip from California through Texas several years before. Gibson would probably have been referring to the name of the mountain pass in west Texas or to the newly created El Paso County because the city of El Paso, Tex., was not founded until 1858, several years after the naming of El Paso, Ill. The choice of the name may have been influenced by El Paso Gap, a break in the El Paso Ridge in southeastern New Mexico near the Texas border, through which Gibson may also have passed.

From Spanish for "the pass" (Ackerman, *Early Illinois Railroads*, 144; *El Paso Story*, 50, 56; Yates, *The Woodford County History*, 52–53). Post office established March 21, 1857.

ELSAH [EL suh, EL zuh]. Jersey. Village (1873) nine miles northeast of Alton. Formerly known as Askew Hollow, named for Joseph Askew, an early settler in 1819, and later as Jersey Landing, a fueling station for steamboats on the Mississippi River. Elsah was laid out by James Semple about 1853 and named Ailsah [*sic*] for Ailsa Craig, a rocky island at the mouth of the Firth of Clyde in southwestern Scotland near the home of Semple's ancestors. The name was apparently heard as Elsa and was so recorded. The spelling was changed to Elsah when the post office was established in 1859 (Hosmer and Williams, *Elsah*, 6). Post office established April 8, 1852, as Jersey Landing; changed to Elsah Dec. 21, 1859.

ELVA. DeKalb. Four miles south of DeKalb. Named by site owner Joseph F. Glidden, one of the inventors of barbed wire, in honor of his daughter, Elva (Gross, *Past and Present of DeKalb County*, 142).

ELVASTON. Hancock. Village (1869) six miles west of Carthage. Founded about 1858. An adaptation of Elva Stone, the name of a young girl who died near the site while traveling west with her family (*History of Hancock County*, 484). Post office established Feb. 16, 1857.

ELVIRA. Johnson. Eleven miles east-northeast of Anna. Elvira was established in 1812 as the first seat of Johnson County. Named for Elvira Edwards, wife of then Illinois territorial governor Ninian Edwards, for whom Edwards County is named (Mohlenbrock, "A New Geography of Illinois: Johnson County," 28; *Johnson County*, 33). Post office established March 2, 1869.

ELWIN. Macon. Three miles south of Decatur. A blend of the surnames of the founders, Daniel Elwood and William Martin (Richmond, *Centennial History of Decatur*, 133). Post office established July 26, 1860, as South Wheatland; changed to Elwin March 19, 1863.

ELWOOD. Vermilion. Township. Named from the Elwood Meeting House, itself named for Thomas Elwood, an honored figure among early Quakers. The name was probably suggested by John Haworth, an organizer of the Quaker community in Vermilion County (Beckwith, *History of Vermilion County*, 561).

ELWOOD. Will. Village (1869, 1873) nine miles south-southeast of Joliet. Laid out in 1854 for the Chicago and Alton Railroad and named for N. C. Elwood, mayor of Joliet in the mid-1850s (*Souvenir of Settlement and Progress*, 258). Post office established May 28, 1846, as Reed's Grove; changed to Elwood Aug. 27, 1855.

EMBARRASS [AM braw]. Coles. Five miles east-northeast of Charleston. Named from the Embarras River. From early American French, *embarras* meant an obstruction in a waterway created by uprooted trees and accumulated debris that hindered navigation and posed a danger to boatmen. The river is spelled

Embarras; the community in Coles County and township in Edgar County are spelled *Embarrass* (McDermott, *A Glossary of Mississippi Valley French*).

EMDEN. Logan. Ten miles northwest of Lincoln. Established in 1871 as a station on the Peoria, Lincoln and Decatur Railroad and named for Emden, Germany, the home of a number of area settlers. The name may have been suggested by blacksmith Teis Smith (*History of Logan County* [1886], 847; Stringer, *History of Logan County,* 618). Post office established Aug. 7, 1871.

EMERSON CITY. Jefferson. Three miles north of Sesser. Named for Louis L. Emmerson [*sic*] (1863–1941), governor of Illinois from 1929 to 1933 (Wall, *Wall's History,* 245).

EMERY. Macon. Seven miles north of Decatur. Named for Charles F. Emery, a member of the Macon County board of supervisors (*History of Macon County,* 170). Post office established March 27, 1879.

EMMINGTON. Livingston. Village (1883) fifteen miles northeast of Pontiac. Founded about 1880 on William Marvin's farm and known briefly as Marvin. Emmington is a blend of the words *Emma,* the name of Marvin's wife, and *Livingston* (*History of Livingston County* [1991], 19). Post office established March 24, 1880.

EMPIRE. McLean. Four miles southeast of Le Roy. The origin of the name is unclear. "Empire" reportedly was suggested by S. A. Moore, a local justice of the peace. According to an early history of McLean County, the name was "proudly and eagerly accepted by the people, for to them it seemed really an empire" (*History of McLean County,* 515). Post office established Aug. 2, 1876, as Empire Station; changed to Empire May 15, 1883.

ENERGY. Williamson. Village (1907) one mile south of Herrin. Founded about 1904 as Fordville by Wiley Ford of Herrin. The Taylor Coal Company commenced operations in Fordville in 1909 and in 1913 requested that the name be changed to Energy, the company's trademark, so that Energy coal could be shipped from Energy, Illinois (Hale, comp. and ed., *Williamson County,* 138; Hubbs, *Pioneer Folks and Places*). Post office established Jan. 9, 1905, as Fordville; changed to Energy April 2, 1913.

ENFIELD. White. Village (1869, 1875) nine miles west of Carmi. Founded in the early 1850s. By one account the name *Enfield* derives from its location ("Well, it's at the end of a field, so let's call it Enfield"). By another, the name was proposed by a Colonel Enfield, about whom nothing seems to be known except that he may have had the site surveyed. Rather, the community was founded by Dr. Martin Johnson, who apparently wanted to name it after himself, but because there was an existing Johnsonville he chose Enfield, reportedly a name he remembered from a story in one of McGuffey's Readers (Land, comp., *History of Enfield,* 4). Post office established Aug. 1, 1840, as Northfield; changed to Enfield June 10, 1850.

ENGELMANN. St. Clair. Township. Named for Theodore, George, and Adolph Engelmann, who settled in the Shiloh Valley in the early 1830s (*Tapestry of Time*, 121).

ENGLEWOOD. Cook. Originally called Junction Grove, where the Wabash and Fort Wayne railroads crossed. The name was changed to Englewood in 1868, largely through the efforts of developer Henry B. Lewis, formerly of Englewood, New Jersey. Now part of Chicago (Karlen, *Chicago's Crabgrass Communities*, 219; Kitagawa and Taeuber, eds., *Local Community Fact Book*, 150). Post office established Dec. 2, 1861, as Junction Grove; changed to Englewood Sept. 29, 1868.

ENGLISH. Jersey. Township. Probably named for the first county sheriff, John Nelson English, although Revel W. English has also been suggested as the source of the name (Adams, comp., *Illinois Place Names; History of Greene and Jersey Counties*, 348, 471).

ENION [EE nuhn, EN ee uhn]. Fulton. Six miles west of Havana. The origin of the name is uncertain. Possibly a form of "Enon" and named from the Enon post office (Irwin, *A to Z Fulton County*). Post office established June 5, 1890.

ENON. A variant of Aenon, mentioned once in the Bible (John 3: 23). Enon or Aenon is a popular name for churches and cemeteries, especially in the southeastern United States, where there are several hundred. The Enon Church in Coles County is seven miles east of Charleston. An Enon post office was active in Bureau County from June 15, 1849, until June 12, 1872; another, in Fulton County, was active from Oct. 6, 1870, until June 12, 1872.

EOLA [ee OL uh]. DuPage. Two miles east of Aurora. Formerly known as Belt City. The Chicago, Burlington and Quincy station was established as Lund's Crossing in 1860. The name was changed about 1871 to Eola at the suggestion of George S. Bangs, former postmaster at Aurora and an official of the Burlington mail service. Why Bangs chose the name is unknown. It may be a form of Aeolus, the god of winds in classical mythology ("Eola"; Seits, "The Names of Kane County," 170). Post office established June 13, 1871.

EPPARDS POINT. Livingston. Township. Named for John Eppard, one of the first settlers (Bateman and Selby, eds., *Historical Encyclopedia of Illinois and History of Livingston County*, 639).

EPPLEYANNA. Stephenson. Twelve miles northeast of Freeport. Founded about 1839. Created by mill owner Conrad Epley by reversing the names of Anna Epley, the wife of his brother, John (Fulwider, *History of Stephenson County*, 383, 390).

EPWORTH. White. Three miles east-southeast of Carmi. Named by the predominately Methodist settlers for Epworth, Lincolnshire, England, the birthplace of John Wesley, the founder of Methodism (*Times*, 223). Post office established Dec. 6, 1872, as Hawthorne; changed to Epworth Sept. 2, 1892.

EQUALITY. Gallatin. Village (1851, 1872) ten miles east of Harrisburg. Founded about 1827 by Willis Hargrave, John Black, and Thornton Cum(m)ings. Formerly known as the Gallatin Salines, a tract of some hundred thousand acres set aside for the federal government's salt works. The name is attributed to a French historian, Etienne Volney, who visited the salines in the winter of 1797 and suggested the name *Equality* as a reflection of one of the main principles of the American and French revolutions (Lawler, *Gallatin County,* 81; Miller, "Building Towns," 53). Post office established May 24, 1812, as United States Saline; changed to Equality July 20, 1827.

ERIE. Whiteside. Village (1872) twelve miles southwest of Morrison. Founded about 1850 by Samuel Carr, M. G. Wonser, James McMillen, and George Marks. A transfer from Erie County, N.Y., the former home of a number of early settlers. The name of Mount Erie in Wayne County is probably from a different source, possibly a variant of Mount Airy (Bent, ed., *History of Whiteside County,* 147; Davis, *History of Whiteside County,* 130). Post office established May 23, 1840, as Crandall's Ferry for ferry operator Lewis D. Crandall; changed to Erie Jan. 9, 1850.

ERIENNA. Grundy. Township. Several writers have suggested that Erienna is a variant of Erina, an ancient name for Ireland, and several others that it is a variant of Ariana, a port of the ancient Persian Empire and the current name of a city in Tunisia. The most likely source, however, is suggested by Virginia S. Brown, who notes that a large number of the people who built the Erie Canal in New York also worked on the Illinois and Michigan Canal, and many of them settled in the Will–Grundy–LaSalle area after work on the I&M was completed in the 1840s. The township was probably named for the Erie Canal suffixed with *-enna.* An earlier spelling, *Arianna,* was an accurate representation of a local pronunciation of Erienna, where orthographic <er> was often pronounced [ahr] (Bateman and Selby, eds., *Historic Encyclopedia of Illinois and History of Grundy County,* 639; Brown, ed., *Grundy County,* 9, 48).

ERIN. Stephenson. Township. Named in the mid-1800s for the large number of Irish settlers. Erin is a poetic name for Ireland (*History of Stephenson County,* 78).

ERWIN. Schuyler. Seven miles west of Rushville. Laid out by Columbus Meeks in 1860 and named for Lewis D. Erwin, who served in the Illinois legislature in the 1850s (Bateman and Selby, eds., *Historic Encyclopedia of Illinois and History of Schuyler County,* 700). Post office established Feb. 5, 1858.

ESMEN. Livingston. Township. Named by Billings P. Babcock, who took the name from the first-person plural form of the Greek verb "to be." Babcock's reason for choosing this particular name is unknown. This is the only Esmen in the United States (Bateman and and Selby, eds., *Historic Encyclopedia of Illinois and History of Livingston County,* 639).

ESSEX. Kankakee. Village (1885) fifteen miles west-northwest of Kankakee. Founded about 1880 and named from Essex Township. The name was probably suggested by Gardner Royce for his former home in Essex County, N.Y. (Bateman and Selby, eds., *Historic Encyclopedia of Illinois and History of Kankakee County*, 735). Post office established May 4, 1854.

ESSEX. Stark. Township. Named in the 1850s, when the county was divided into townships, for Isaac Essex, an early settler from Virginia (Leeson, *Documents and Biography*, 493).

ETHERTON. Jackson. Five miles southwest of Carbondale. Founded about 1892 and named for the first postmaster, Thomas Etherton (Mohlenbrock, "A New Geography of Illinois: Jackson County," 13). Post office established May 28, 1892.

ETNA. Coles. Six miles south-southwest of Mattoon. Established in the late 1850s by the Illinois Central Railroad. The name was probably chosen by E. B. McClure, roadmaster of the IC, or by Robert S. Mills, the first station agent and also the first postmaster. The original spelling was *Aetna*, possibly suggested by Mt. Etna (Aetna), a volcano in Sicily that had erupted spectacularly a few years earlier (Ladd and Kimball, *History of Coles County*, 427; Redlich, *The Postal History of Coles County*, 73). Post office established Dec. 31, 1859.

EUREKA [yoo REE kuh]. Woodford. City (1859, 1880). Formerly known as Walnut Grove, named from a stand of timber along Walnut Creek. A Christian school called the Walnut Grove Academy (now Eureka College) was established in 1848. The community that grew around the academy was laid out as Walnut Grove by John Darst with construction of the Peoria and Oquawka Railroad in 1855. When the petition for a post office was denied because of an existing Walnut Grove, *Eureka*, from Greek for "I have found [it]," was substituted. There have been a number of suggestions as to who proposed the name. Several sources credit it to John Lindsay, an evangelist and teacher at the academy, who would have been familiar with Classical Greek. Susan Jones Grant, however, claims that her father, John T. Jones, chose the name. Jones was a founder and the first president of Walnut Grove Academy, and he was undoubtedly familiar with Classical Greek as well. Jones may have selected the name on his own, or maybe it was suggested to him, perhaps by Lindsay. Another influence may have been Eureka, Calif. By 1850 Eureka was not only the name of a California community but also the state motto, and the California gold rush was prominent in the news of the day (Dickinson, *History of Eureka, Illinois*, 14; *History of Eureka College*, 223–24; Yates, *The Woodford County History*, 122). Post office established Feb. 27, 1852.

EVANSTON. Cook. City (1857, 1872). Named for Dr. John Evans, an obstetrician on the faculty of Rush Medical College in Chicago. Evans and eight others founded Northwestern University in 1851 as an institution of "sanctified learning" under the sponsorship of the Methodist Episcopal Church. Evans was president of the

Northwestern board of trustees and reportedly wanted to name the community after the renowned preacher Matthew Simpson, who had converted Evans to Methodism several years earlier, but his wife, Margaret, suggested the name *Evanston.* In 1864 Evans was appointed governor of the Colorado Territory by President Abraham Lincoln (*Illinois Guide;* Perkins, *Evanstonia,* 22). Post office established Dec. 28, 1846, as Gross Point; changed to Ridgeville April 26, 1850; changed to Evanston Aug. 27, 1855.

EVANSVILLE. Randolph. Village (1869, 1885) twelve miles west of Sparta. Laid out about 1834 by gristmill owner Caldwell Evans (*Combined History of Randolph, Monroe, and Perry Counties,* 416). Post office established July 14, 1849.

EWING [YOO ing]. Franklin. Village (1891) six miles northeast of Benton. Named for John Ewing, a decorated veteran of the Black Hawk and Mexican wars (*Franklin County,* 13). Post office established July 19, 1850.

EWINGTON. Effingham. Three miles southwest of Effingham. Founded about 1834 and named for William Lee D. Ewing (1795–1846), a Vandalia lawyer who as state representative was instrumental in the creation of Effingham County. Ewing had the distinction of serving as governor of Illinois for the shortest time, fifteen days, in late 1834. Ewington was the seat of Effingham County from 1831 until 1859 (Perrin, ed., *History of Effingham County,* 177). Post office established Jan. 23, 1832.

EXERMONT. St. Clair. Southwest of Collinsville. Likely named for Exermont, France, although details are unknown. This is the only Exermont in the United States.

EXETER. Scott. Village (1876). Laid out in 1825 by Enoch March, from Salisbury, Essex County, Mass. March probably named the village for one of the Exeters in New England. Exeter was laid out in typical New England fashion, organized around a central village green. March was also one of the proprietors of Naples, and he and Thomas Beard laid out Beardstown in 1829 (*Scott County Bicentennial Book,* 137). Post office established Feb. 26, 1826.

EXLINE. Kankakee. Four miles northeast of Kankakee. Named for early settler Samuel Exline (Bateman and Selby, eds., *Historic Encyclopedia of Illinois and History of Kankakee County,* 754). Post office established July 7, 1882.

F

FAIRDALE. DeKalb. Twelve miles west of Genoa. Formerly known as Fielding, named for Albert Fielding. Formally established by Henry A. Koch. The source of the name is unknown (www.rootsweb.com/~ildekalb/places.htm). Post office established Sept. 30, 1875, as Wallace, named for Wallace Koch, son of Henry Koch; changed to Fairdale Nov. 14, 1895.

FAIRFIELD. Wayne. City (1840, 1884). Laid out about 1819. Although early county histories claim that the name is fitting because, in the words of one, "the site is not excelled by that of any town in the State [and] no fairer field could certainly be found," the name is probably a transfer from a Fairfield in an eastern state. Fairfield is a popular place name; there are more than a hundred Fairfields in the United States. Fairfield has been the seat of Wayne County since its formation in 1819 (*History of Wayne and Clay Counties,* 179). Post office established Jan. 29, 1820, as Wayne Courthouse; changed to Fairfield May 25, 1820.

FAIRGRANGE. Coles. Six miles north of Charleston. Named from the Fair Grange post office, itself named for the National Grange, the farmers' fraternal organization founded in 1867 to promote the social and educational interests of rural Americans (Bateman and Selby, eds., *Historical Encyclopedia of Illinois and History of Coles County,* 752). Post office established May 4, 1883, as Arena; changed to Fair Grange June 15, 1883.

FAIRMONT CITY. St. Clair. Village (1914) five miles northeast of East St. Louis. Founded in 1910 with construction of a roundhouse for the Pennsylvania Railroad. Formerly known as Willow Town (*Illinois Gazetteer*).

FAIRMOUNT. Vermilion. Village (1894) ten miles southwest of Danville. Founded about 1850 on the line of the Great Northern Railroad as Salina by site owner Josiah Hunt. Because Salina was similar to several existing Salines, the name *Fairmount* was suggested by Francis Dougherty, possibly for a Fairmount further east (Stapp, *History under Our Feet,* 34). Post office established June 23, 1857.

FAIRVIEW. Fulton. Village (1859, 1900) eight miles northwest of Canton. Founded in 1837 as Utica, named for Utica, N.Y. The name *Utica* was changed to *Fairview* the following year to avoid duplication of post offices. The name is almost certainly a transfer and may have been suggested by Richard Foster, who had previously lived in Fairview, Ohio (*History of Fulton County,* 424; Irwin, *A to Z Fulton County*). Post office established May 9, 1838.

FAIRVIEW HEIGHTS. St. Clair. City (1969). Originally an unorganized area known as Fairview or Fairview Station. Named about 1906 by a real estate developer named Fairbrother. In February 1965 the St. Clair County Board of Supervisors changed the name to Lincoln Heights at the request of the Lincoln Heights Civic Association. That name met with considerable opposition, and four months later it was changed by public referendum to Fairview Heights (*Highlights of Fairview Heights,* 29).

FAITHORN. Will. One mile southeast of Crete. Likely named for John N. Faithorn, a Chicago railroad magnate of the 1890s.

FALL CREEK. Adams. Six miles north-northeast of Hannibal, Mo. Named from Fall Creek, itself so named for a prominent waterfall (*History of Adams County,* 528). Post office established March 25, 1872.

FALLING SPRING. St. Clair. Two miles south of Cahokia. Named from Falling Spring, a waterfall with a drop of some seventy feet, reportedly called by the French *l'eau tomb* (falling water) (*History of St. Clair County*, 31).

FALL RIVER. LaSalle. Township. Created in 1862 from Grand Rapids Township. Both Grand Rapids and Fall River townships were named for the rapids in the Illinois River, now largely controlled by the Marseilles lock and dam (O'Byrne, *History of LaSalle*, 397).

FALMOUTH. Jasper. Four miles north of Newton. Laid out in 1881 by Tom Wycoff and Amaziah Hunt, the first postmaster. Possibly a transfer from Falmouth, Ind. Post office established April 15, 1878.

FANCHER. Shelby. Nine miles south of Shelbyville. Named for land owner William Fancher (Bateman and Selby, eds., *Historical Encyclopedia of Illinois and History of Shelby County*, 865). Post office established April 23, 1883.

FANCY CREEK. Township. Sangamon. Named from Fancy Creek. The origin of the name is unknown. Formerly called Power, named for George Power, a prominent local citizen (Wallace, *Past and Present*, 32).

FANCY PRAIRIE. Menard. Twelve miles north of Springfield. Previously known as Scratch Prairie. According to a local story, during a meeting to choose a more dignified name, one particular suggestion caused someone in the audience to exclaim, "Well fancy that" (*Menard County*, 295). Post office established Feb. 8, 1875.

FARGO. Brown. Village (1875) four miles west of Mount Sterling. Previously known as Mt. Pleasant and later as Raymond, for S. C. Raymond, who kept the local general store. The source of the name is uncertain; it may be from the personal name of a prominent citizen, or a transfer, possibly from Fargo, Ohio (*History of Brown County*, 349). Post office established Jan. 30, 1888.

FARINA [fuh REYE nuh]. Fayette. Village (1875) seventeen miles north-northeast of Salem. Founded about 1857 and named from the Illinois Central railroad station, itself so named because of its location in a wheat-growing area. From Latin for "flour" (Ackerman, *Early Illinois Railroads*, 130). Post office established Sept. 22, 1858.

FARMER CITY. DeWitt. City (1869, 1872). Formerly known as Hurley's Grove, named for first settler Dennis Hurley. By 1869 the community was known as Mount Pleasant and also as Santa Anna, apparently named for Antonio Lopez de Santa Anna, president of Mexico and best known for his defeat of Texians at the Alamo in 1836. According to a local story, at a meeting to decide on a single name, someone said, "The majority of the people here tonight are farmers and the room is heated with burning corn . . . , fuel which is produced by the farmer. I move that we change the name of Mount Pleasant to Farmer City." The new name was accepted by acclamation (*Six Score and Five*, 7). Post office established Jan. 9, 1840, as Santa Anna; changed to Farmer City April 14, 1869.

FARMINGTON. Fulton. City (1887). Founded about 1834 and named by Joseph Cone, an early settler, for his former home, Farmington, Conn., itself named for Farmington in Gloucestershire, England (Bordner, *From Cornfields to Marching Feet*, 78; Irwin, *A to Z Fulton County*). Post office established Jan. 6, 1836.

FARNISVILLE. Woodford. Former community on the Mackinaw River. Named for Christian and Peter Farni, site owners and grist mill proprietors. Also known as Farneyville, Faneyville, and Fannyville. (Adams, comp., *Illinois Place Names;* R. Moore, 186; Yates, 119). Post office established July 6, 1857.

FARRINGTON. Jefferson. Township and former community. Surveyed in 1856 by A. M. Grant and Jehu J. Maxey. The historical Farrington school was eight miles northeast of Mount Vernon, near Harmony. The particular Farrington or Farrington family for which the township was named is unknown (www .genealogytrails.com/ill/jefferson/ghostowns.html).

FAYETTE. County. Created Feb. 14, 1821, from parts of Bond, Crawford, and Clark counties. Named for the Marquis de Lafayette (1757–1834), the French noble who served with great distinction during the American Revolution. Lafayette became a national hero and was honored by scores of place names, especially in the Midwest. Some two hundred U.S. communities or civil divisions are named for Lafayette, and another three dozen or so are named for his estate in France, La Grange (q.v.). After the Revolution, Lafayette returned to the United States on several occasions, the last in 1824–25, when his triumphal tour included visits to Vandalia and Shawneetown. Fayette in Greene County, Fayetteville in St. Clair County, and Lafayette in Ogle County were also named for the Marquis de Lafayette.

FAYETTE. Livingston. Township. Formed from Belle Prairie in 1870. Named by Philander Morgan for Fayette County, Pa., the birthplace of his father, Rees Morgan, the first permanent settler in Fayette County, Ill. (*History of Livingston County* [1991], 24).

FAYVILLE. Alexander. Eleven miles southeast of Cape Girardeau, Mo. Formerly called Santa Fe. The community and the nearby Santa Fe Hills were probably named for Santa Fe, N.M. The name was changed to Fayville, an adaptation of "Santa Fe," about 1900. (*Alexander County*, 13; Fults, Chisholm, and Novella, *Promised Land in Southern Illinois*, 99; Griffith, "Egyptian Place-Names," 30). Post office established July 24, 1838, as Santa Fe; changed to Fayville July 12, 1906.

FEAKEYVILLE. Hamilton. Former community near Broughton. Named for Felix Gross, proprietor of the local general store and first postmaster, who was popularly known as Feakey (Sneed, *Ghost Towns of Southern Illinois*, 50). Post office established April 11, 1895, as Felix.

FELIX. Grundy. Township. Organized in 1854 and named for Felix Grundy, the namesake of Grundy County (q.v.) (Ullrich, *This Is Grundy County*, 180).

FENTON. Whiteside. Seven miles southwest of Morrison. Named for Joseph Fenton, regarded as the first permanent settler, who arrived about 1835. Eden Precinct was renamed Fenton at the time of township formation in 1852 (Bastian, *A History of Whiteside County,* 213; Davis, *History of Whiteside County,* 145, 623). Post office established May 15, 1862.

FERGESTOWN. Williamson. Four miles east of Herrin. Named for the Ferges family. Informally known as Fudgetown (Hale, comp. and ed., *Williamson County,* 118).

FERRELL. Edgar. Ten miles southeast of Paris. Established about 1873 as a grain siding on the Illinois Midland Railroad. Formally organized in 1874 by I. C. Ferrell, site owner and postmaster (*History of Edgar County,* 409). Post office established Dec. 4, 1827, as Elbridge; changed to Ferrell Feb. 27, 1874.

FERRIS. Hancock. Village (1882) four miles north-northwest of Carthage. Founded in 1869 by Hiram G. Ferris and Charles Gilchrist on the line of the Chicago, Burlington and Quincy Railroad (Bateman and Selby, eds., *Historical Encyclopedia of Illinois and History of Hancock County,* 1096; *History of Hancock County,* 493). Post office established Dec. 26, 1869.

FEVER RIVER. *See* Galena.

FIATT [FEYE uht, FEYE at]. Fulton. Seven miles northwest of Canton. Named in 1843 by Royal C. Kimes. According to local accounts, Kimes was studying medicine at the time the post office was established and suggested the name *Fiatt,* which he took from his medical texts, slightly altered. From Latin *fiat* (let it be done) (Irwin, *A to Z Fulton County*). Post office established July 17, 1843.

FICKLIN. Douglas. Three miles west of Tuscola. Named for Orlando Bell Ficklin (1808–86), U.S. representative from Illinois in the 1840s and 1850s. The name was changed from Howe at the time of Ficklin's death in 1886. Post office established Aug. 1, 1881, as Howe; changed to Ficklin June 14, 1886.

FIDELITY. Jersey. Village (1882) nine miles south-southeast of Jerseyville. Founded about 1850. According to a local story, a party from Tennessee was exploring the area, looking for homestead sites, when one of their horses broke down. A companion volunteered his horse so the group could continue. The beneficiary of the gift horse reportedly remarked, "This is true fidelity," from which the community supposedly took its name (Postlewait, ed., *History of Jersey County,* 49). Post office established May 11, 1850, as Phill's Creek; changed to Fidelity May 26, 1851.

FIELD. Jefferson. Township. Named for the Field family. Early settlers included Nathan, James, and Henry Field, who arrived about 1830 (Perrin, ed., *History of Jefferson County,* 397).

FILLMORE. Montgomery. Village (1890) twelve miles east-southeast of Hillsboro. Founded about 1881 with construction of the Clover Leaf Railroad and named from the Fillmore post office, itself named for Millard Fillmore, president of the United States from 1850 to 1852 (Bateman and Selby, eds., *Historical Encyclopedia of Illinois and History of Montgomery County*, 870). Post office established April 26, 1850.

FINDLAY [FIN lee]. Shelby. Village (1892) five miles northeast of Shelbyville. Named by the first postmaster, George Mauzey, for Findlay, Ohio, the former home of Michael Bare, Enoch Fritter, and other early settlers. (Cruitt and Coventry, comps., *Findlay, Illinois*, 1). Post office established Dec. 18, 1884.

FISHER. Champaign. Village (1894) ten miles west of Rantoul. Founded in 1876 by Robert Fisher, a contractor for the Illinois Central Railroad (*Illinois Guide*). Post office established Jan. 8, 1859, as Newcomb; changed to Fisher Feb. 3, 1876.

FITHIAN. Vermilion. Village (1896) twelve miles west of Danville. Founded in 1870 and named for Dr. William Fithian of Danville, who was instrumental in securing a station on the Indiana, Bloomington and Western Railroad. Fithian served in the Illinois legislature with Abraham Lincoln in the 1830s (Underwood, "A New Geography of Illinois: Vermilion County," 39; Stapp, *History under Our Feet*, 32). Post office established April 18, 1870.

FITZGERRELL. Jefferson. Former community. Founded in the early 1850s about twelve miles south-southwest of Mount Vernon by site owner J. J. Fitzgerrell. Also known as Winfield (www.genealogytrails.com/ill/jefferson/ghostowns .html). Post office established July 3, 1874.

FLAGG. Ogle. Four miles southwest of Rochelle. Also Flagg Center two miles northwest of Rochelle. Named for the Flagg family, especially early settlers Willard P. and Richard P. Flagg (*History of Ogle County*, 299). Post office established March 6, 1866, as Flag Station; changed to Flag May 15, 1883; changed to Flagg Feb. 25, 1884.

FLANAGAN. Livingston. Village (1882) eleven miles west of Pontiac. Founded about 1880 on the line of the Illinois Central Railroad by the Flanagan brothers, Patrick, Edward, and Peter (Bateman and Selby, eds., *Historical Encyclopedia of Illinois and History of Livingston County*, 789). Post office established Sept. 26, 1876, as Yorkville; changed to Nebraska March 12, 1879; changed to Flanagan Feb. 20, 1882.

FLETCHER. McLean. Ten miles east of Normal. The area was known as Pleasant View until construction of the Illinois Central Railroad, which named its station for site owner John Fletcher (Quaid, *A Little Square*, 23). Post office established Nov. 7, 1883.

FLINT. Pike. Township. Named from Flint Creek, itself named for the local flint deposits. Perhaps a translation of French *pierre à la flèche* (arrow stone), named for the flint chipped into arrow and spear points by Native Americans. (Brown, "French Place Names in Illinois," 464; McDermott, *A Glossary of Mississippi Valley French*).

FLINT CREEK. Lake. Stream. Named for first settler Amos Flint. (*Past and Present of Lake County,* 255). Post office established July 1, 1839.

FLORA. Boone. Township. Perhaps the name of the wife or daughter of an early settler or township official, or perhaps, in the words of the 1877 Boone County history, "The name of this township is derived from the primitive beauty of the landscape. Originally, it was an open, . . . undulating prairie. In spring time it was bedecked and bespangled with myriads of flowers of every conceivable hue and color." Formerly known as Fairfield and later as Benton. (*Past and Present of Boone County,* 314).

FLORA. Clay. City (1876, 1884). Named for Flora Whittleby, the daughter of a member of the firm of Songer, Camp, and Company, which surveyed the site for the Ohio and Mississippi Railroad about 1854 (Hansen, ed., *Illinois,* 483; *History of Wayne and Clay Counties,* 357). Post office established May 10, 1854, as Moore's; changed to Flora Sept. 4, 1855.

FLORENCE. Pike. Village (1925) ten miles east of Pittsfield. Formerly known as Augusta. Florence was established in 1836 as a landing site on the Illinois River by a consortium of Pittsfield business executives organized as the Florence Company. The source of the name is unknown (*History of Pike County,* 428). Post office established April 6, 1837, as Clear Lake; changed to Florence Jan. 7, 1840.

FLORID. Putnam. Thirteen miles southeast of Princeton. Founded about 1835 by William M. Stewart and Aaron Thompson. The source of the name is unknown (Ford, *A History of Putnam and Marshall Counties,* 95). Post office established June 25, 1849.

FLOSSMOOR. Cook. Village (1924) south of Chicago. The name was the winning entry in a naming contest held in the late 1890s and sponsored by the Illinois Central Railroad. Residents claim the name is derived from Scots *floss* (dew on the flowers) and *moor* (gently rolling countryside). Early streets such as Braeburn, Argyle, and Wallace maintained the Scottish theme. This is the only Flossmoor in the United States (Adair and Sandberg, *Indian Trails to Tollways,* 61, 63; Kabbes and GiaQuinta, *Flossmoor, Illinois,* 8). Post office established Feb. 29, 1904.

FLOUR CREEK. Hancock, Schuyler. Stream. According to an early county history, the name derives from an incident in which a settler was attempting to cross the stream with his ox team and a wagon loaded with provisions when the current swept away a large sack of flour. Also called Flower Creek (Gregg, *History of Hancock County,* 512).

FONDULAC. Tazewell. Township. Laid out in 1855. French for "lower part of the lake," a reference to the southern part of Peoria Lake. Now part of East Peoria (Bates, *Souvenir of Early and Notable Events,* 20). Post office established March 26, 1872.

FOOSLAND [FOOS luhnd]. Champaign. Village (1959) seven miles southwest of Gibson City. Founded in 1874 and named for William Foos, an absentee landlord who owned some 3,500 acres in Champaign county in the 1840s (Bateman and Selby, eds., *Historical Encyclopedia of Illinois and History of Champaign County*, 685). Post office established June 19, 1874.

FORD. County. Created Feb. 17, 1859. Named for Thomas Ford (1800–1850), eighth governor of Illinois, serving from 1842 to 1846. Ford was the author of *A History of Illinois* (1854), one of the first histories of the state.

FORD HEIGHTS. Cook. Village (1949). In 1987 the village of East Chicago Heights renamed itself Ford Heights in an effort to attract the Ford Motor Company stamping plant that was planning to relocate from an unincorporated area of Cook County. As the mayor explained, "We thought Ford might have a tender thing in their heart for us because we changed the community over to their name." Ford, however, chose to relocate in Chicago Heights (Millenson, "Rich in Hope").

FOREST PARK. Cook. Village (1907). In 1836 the Chicago and Galena Union Railroad built a roundhouse in what is now the village of River Forest. Henry Quick from New York City built a hotel nearby, which he called the Harlem House. The community that took the name of the Harlem House was subsequently founded by Ferdinand Haase. The name was changed to Forest Park, a developers' promotional name, in 1907 (*Illinois Guide;* Van, "It's Keeping Alive Small-Town Feeling"). Post office established June 29, 1922.

FOREST VIEW. Cook. Village (1924). Reportedly so named because of the woods visible across Harlem Avenue in Lyons (Villarosa, "The Whole Town Is a Neighborhood").

FOREVILLE. Williamson. Former community west of Marion. Named for Samuel T. Russell, known as "Big Fore" or "Pate Fore" because of his prominent forehead. The site was flooded when Crab Orchard Lake was created in the 1930s (Hubbs, *Pioneer Folks and Places;* Mohlenbrock, "A New Geography of Williamson County," 36).

FORMAN. Johnson. Eighteen miles east-southeast of Vienna. Previously known as Shoo Fly and later as Collinsburg and Ridenhower. About 1911 the Marshall family donated land a short distance from Ridenhower to be used as a railroad construction camp. Several businesses in Ridenhower moved to the new site, and the settlement became known as Forman. Several years later, the Chicago, Burlington and Quincy Railroad laid tracks through the original site of Ridenhower, and most businesses that had moved to Forman moved back to Ridenhower and brought the name Forman with them. Probably named for an individual named Foreman or for a Foreman family (personal communication with Gary Hacker). Post office established Jan. 20, 1873 as Forman; discontinued Jan. 17, 1884; reestablished Nov. 19, 1895, as Ridenhower; changed to Forman Aug. 21, 1911.

FORREST. Livingston. Village (1874) five miles east of Fairbury. Founded about

1866. Reportedly named by a Mr. Frost, an official of the Toledo, Peoria and Western Railroad, for his former partner, a Mr. Forrest of New York (*History of Livingston County* [1991], 287, 529). Post office established March 1, 1860, as Forest Station; changed to Forest Jan. 21, 1868; changed to Forrest July 30, 1890.

FORRESTON. Ogle. Village (1869, 1888) eleven miles south of Freeport. Laid out in 1854, probably for David A. Neal, vice president of the Illinois Central Railroad. The source of the name is unknown. Originally Foreston (Boss, *Sketches of the History of Ogle County*, 73). Post office established Feb. 28, 1855, as Foreston; changed to Forreston June 1878.

FORSYTH [FOR seyeth]. Macon. Village (1958) three miles north of Decatur. Established about 1864 by the Illinois Central Railroad and named for Robert Forsyth, first general freight agent of the IC (Richmond, *Centennial History of Decatur,* 97). Post office established July 17, 1865, as Forsythe; changed to Forsyth May 5, 1886.

FORT CHARTRES. Former community in northwestern Randolph County. Established in 1719 by French settlers and militia under the leadership of Commandant Pierre Dugué Boisbriant and named by him for Louis, duc de Chartres, son of the French regent, Philippe d'Orléans. Fort Chartres Village grew around the stockade and reportedly housed some forty families in the 1760s. The location is now the Fort de Chartres State Historic Site (Balesi, *The Time of the French*, 145; Ekberg, *French Roots*, 35).

FORT RUSSELL. Madison. Township. Named from Fort Russell near Edwardsville, established about 1812 by Gov. Ninian Edwards to house military stores and munitions. Named for Col. William Russell, who commanded ten companies of rangers formed to protect the American population from British and Indian attacks (*History of Madison County*, 475).

FOSTER. Marion. Township. Also Fosterburg, former community. Laid out in 1854 by Hardy Foster, the first permanent settler, a member of the state legislature from 1839 to 1841, and a county judge (Brinkerhoff, *Brinkerhoff's History,* 157; *History of Marion and Clinton Counties*, 251).

FOSTERBURG. Madison. Five miles north of Wood River. Founded about 1857 by Oliver P. Foster. Named for him and for his father, also Oliver Foster. The elder Foster operated the Foster Inn, a relay station on the Alton-Springfield stage line, in the 1820s and 1830s (Norton, ed., *Centennial History of Madison County,* 512–13; Underwood, "A New Geography of Illinois: Madison County," 29). Post office established Feb. 3, 1858, as Harris; changed to Fosterburgh July 15, 1858; changed to Fosterburg July 21, 1893.

FOUNTAIN. Monroe. Seven miles west-northwest of Waterloo. Named from its location on Fountain Creek, itself formerly called *l'Aigle* (Eagle) *Creek* by early French settlers (Klein, ed., *Arrowheads to Aerojets*, 570).

FOUR MILE. Wayne. Township. Named from Four Mile Creek. The reason for the name is unknown. (*History of Wayne and Clay Counties*, 247).

FOWLER. Adams. Seven miles northeast of Quincy. Founded about 1856 by site owner Edward Fowler of Mendon (Genosky, ed., *People's History*, 705; Underwood, "A New Geography of Illinois: Adams County," 37). Post office established Oct. 7, 1859, as Fowler's Station; changed to Fowler Dec. 7, 1869.

FOX. Township. Jasper. The original township report called for the name Union, probably in honor of the federal union. Renamed for the Fox River (Robins, *Historical Development*, 17).

FOX LAKE. Lake. Village (1906). Named from Fox Lake, itself named for the Fox River, itself a translation of French *renard* (fox), probably a clan name for a subgroup of the Fox Tribe.

FOX RIVER GROVE. McHenry. Village (1919). Named for the grove of oak trees at the bend in the Fox River near the Lake–McHenry County line. The name was probably the creation of Eman Opatrny, who developed the grove as a picnic and entertainment center in the early 1900s. In 1958 there was an attempt to change the name from Fox River Grove to Castle for the village's most notable landmark, Castle Vianden, a faux medieval structure overlooking the village. The castle itself was built by Ted Bettendorf over several decades beginning in the 1930s and named for the castle in Vianden, Luxemburg (Nye, ed., *McHenry County Illinois*, 401; Roop, *History of Fox River Grove*, 53). Post office established Sept. 30, 1920.

FOX RIVER VALLEY GARDENS. Lake, McHenry. Village (1969) three miles southwest of Wauconda. Named for its location on the Fox River by developer Tyra Due Nielsen in the 1920s. In September, 2002 the village trustees voted to change the name to Port Barrington in order to trade on the prestige of the Barrington name and at the same time rid themselves of a long and cumbersome name (Long, "'Mouthful Name Gets a Makeover'"; McRoberts, "Where Residents Take Life One Improvement at a Time").

FOXVILLE. Marion. Thirteen miles east of Centralia. Laid out by T. M. Haines, whose nickname was Fox. Formerly known as Fox and Foxtown (*History of Marion and Clinton Counties*, 277). Post office established Sept. 9, 1872.

FRANCIS. Saline. Five miles north of Eldorado. Named for postmaster Nelson J. Francis. Formerly known as Francis Mills (Adams, comp., *Illinois Place Names*). Post office established Aug. 26, 1893.

FRANKFORT [FRANGK fert]. Will. Village (1879). Frankfort Township was named in the early 1850s by a Mr. Cappell (or Coppell) for his birthplace, Frankfurt-am-Main, Germany. The village of Frankfort was laid out about 1855 with construction of the Joliet and Northern Indiana Railroad and named for the township by site owner Sherman W. Bowen (*Frankfort Centennial*, 6; *History of Will County*, 512; Rice, "Tradition Still Calls This Home"). Post office established Feb. 1, 1838, as Chelsea; changed to Frankfort Station April 29, 1868; changed to Frankfort June 12, 1905.

FRANKFORT. Franklin. Township. Also West Frankfort. City (1901). Named from the stockade built by Frank Jordan near the present Franklin–Williamson County line about 1810 and known as Frank Jordan's Fort, or Frank's Fort. The stockade was abandoned about 1817, but the name continued as Frankfort. West Frankfort was founded about 1895, when the Chicago and Eastern Illinois Railroad was built a mile or so west of Frankfort (Jurich, *This Is Franklin County*, 2). Post office established June 22, 1818, as Franklin Courthouse; changed to Frankfort Dec. 1, 1821; changed to West Frankfort Sept. 16, 1904.

FRANKLIN. Morgan. Village (1837, 1887) twelve miles southeast of Jacksonville. Founded in 1832 by William Woods, John Wyatt, and Walter Butler as Simpson, named for their former home, Simpson County, Ky. Later in 1832 the name was changed for Franklin, the seat of Simpson County. (Bateman and Selby, eds., *Historical Encyclopedia of Illinois and History of Morgan County*, 977; Hutchison, "Old Morgan County Village"). Post office established Jan. 31, 1831.

FRANKLIN. County. Created Jan. 2, 1818, from parts of St. Clair, White, Johnson, and Gallatin counties. Named for Benjamin Franklin (1706–90), one of the outstanding figures of colonial America. Franklin was a member of the Continental Congress; a signer of the Declaration of Independence; and an ambassador, author, and inventor.

FRANKLIN GROVE. Lee. Village (1865, 1872) eight miles east of Dixon. Probably named for Franklin Dixon, a son of John Dixon, for whom the city of Dixon is named. Possibly named for James R. Franklin, an early settler (Bateman and Selby, eds., *Historical Encyclopedia of Illinois and History of Lee County*, 644; Stennett, *A History of the Origin*, 74). Post office established Feb. 29, 1848.

FRANKLIN PARK. Cook. Village (1892). Founded in the early 1890s and named for himself by Lesser Franklin, a Chicago real estate developer (Hermann, "Town Thrives on Industry"). Post office established Feb. 27, 1891.

FRANKLINVILLE. McHenry. Four miles southwest of Woodstock. Named for land owner Franklin Stringer. Previously known as Snarltown, for George Albrow, called Snarl Albrow because of his quick temper and generally unpleasant disposition (*History of McHenry County* [1885], 933–34; Nye, ed., *McHenry County Illinois*, 862).

FRANKS. DeKalb. Five miles northwest of Sandwich. Named from the Franks post office, established at Frank Richey's creamery in 1891 (www.rootsweb.com/~ildekalb/places.htm). Post office established Nov. 6, 1891.

FREDERICK. Schuyler. Four miles north of Beardstown. Founded about 1836 as Fredericksville by George Frederick Jonte and Frederick Merchant (*Schuyler County*, 110). Post office established Sept. 22, 1837, as Wilcoxville; changed to Fredericksville April 17, 1846; changed to Frederick July 21, 1887.

FREDONIA. Williamson. Four miles southwest of Herrin. Named from the Fredonia post office, itself named by first postmaster, William T. Ryburn, for his daughter, Fredonia. Now part of Cambria. Coincidentally, the name echoes the early French traders' name for the prairie, *fredonner* (hum, buzz), referring to the swarms of bees that hovered over prairie flowers in summer (Hubbs, *Pioneer Folks and Places*). Post office established May 28, 1837.

FREEBURG. St. Clair. Village (1859, 1875). Founded about 1836 as Urbana by John Lemen and named for Lemen's former home, Urbana, Champaign County, Ohio. The name was changed in the late 1850s by German settlers, most likely for Freiburg, Germany, or Freiburg (Fribourg), Switzerland (Davis, comp., *Freeburg's Centennial*, n.p.; Walton, *Centennial, McKendree College, with St. Clair County History*, 508–9). Post office established June 28, 1840, as Twelve Mile Prairie; changed to Chowning Jan. 15, 1853; changed to Freeburgh Feb. 19, 1857; changed to Freeburg Oct. 2, 1893.

FREEMAN SPUR. Franklin, Williamson. Village (1913) three miles northeast of Herrin. When the Possum Ridge Mine opened about 1908, Freeman, Franklin, Dillard, and Dell'era provided homes for the miners. In 1913 these communities merged as Freeman Spur, named for James R. Freeman, who owned the land on which the main mining property was located (*Franklin County*, 14; Hale, comp. and ed., *Williamson County*, 118; Hubbs, *Pioneer Folks and Places*). Post office established Oct. 12, 1821.

FREEMANTON. Effingham. Former community. Founded about 1834 and named for William and John Freeman, early businessmen. Also known as Fremington. The Fremington Cemetery is about seven miles southwest of Effingham (Feldhake, *Effingham County*, 30). Post office established Feb. 11, 1837, as Benton; changed to Freemanton March 2, 1840.

FREEPORT. Stephenson. City (1855, 1882). Previously known as Winneshiek (q.v.). Formally laid out about 1835. Apparently, the name came about in the following manner: William Baker and his wife operated a well-known hotel and tavern patronized by travelers on their way to and from the lead mines around Galena. Baker was never one to keep exact books and in fact often invited guests into his wife's kitchen for meals at no charge. Mrs. Baker eventually grew tired of her husband's generosity and exclaimed, "This place is getting to be a free port for everybody coming on the trail, so we will just call it Freeport." Freeport has been the seat of Stephenson County since 1837 (Tilden, comp., *History of Stephenson County*, 370). Post office established June 20, 1837.

FREMONT CENTER. Lake. Four miles northeast of Wauconda. At the time of township formation about 1849, several names were suggested, including Hale, Fort Hill, Seneca, Tickleville, Gilmer (for Thomas W. Gilmer, President John Tyler's secretary of the navy), and Haddam (for Haddam, Conn., home of several early settlers). None of these received a majority of votes, and Fremont, for John C. Frémont, the well-known western explorer, was then proposed and accepted (*Past and Present of Lake County*, 280). Post office established Dec. 27, 1853, as Fremont Centre.

FRIELINGS [FREE lingz]. Kankakee. Thirteen miles west-northwest of Kankakee. Named for the Frieling family. Diedrick Frieling emigrated from Hanover, Germany, in 1869. (Bateman and Selby, eds., *Historical Encyclopedia of Illinois and History of Kankakee County*, 943).

FRIENDS CREEK. Macon. Township. Named from the stream called Friend's Creek, which was named for George W. Friend, reported to be the first settler in the area, arriving from Ohio in 1822 (Richmond, *Centennial History of Decatur*, 94).

FRIENDSVILLE. Wabash. Six miles north of Mount Carmel. Founded about 1839 and named for Friendsville, Susquehanna County, Penn., the home of a number of early settlers (Bateman and Selby, eds., *Historical Encyclopedia of Illinois and History of Wabash County*, 653). Post office established April 3, 1840.

FRISCO. Franklin. Ten miles northeast of Benton. Named from the Frisco post office, located in the Frisco General Store. By tradition the store was named from a customer's remark, "Why, this is a little San Francisco," apparently referring to the wealth of merchandise available (Goss, *A History of Northern Township*, 363; Sneed, *Ghost Towns of Southern Illinois*, 17). Post office established May 8, 1893.

FRUIT. Madison. Four miles northeast of Edwardsville. Established in the 1880s as a station on the Clover Leaf Railroad and named for station agent and postmaster John A. Fruit (Underwood, "A New Geography of Illinois: Madison County," 30). Post office established Jan. 27, 1886.

FULLER. Coles, Moultrie. Seven miles east of Sullivan. Named from the Fuller's Point post office, established in 1849 in the home of postmaster Henry Fuller (Bateman and Selby, eds., *Historical Encyclopedia of Illinois and History of Coles County*, 740). Post office established Sept. 18, 1849, as Fuller's Point.

FULLER PARK. Cook. Chicago community. Named for Melville Fuller (1833–1910), a Chicago attorney and chief justice of the Supreme Court from 1888 to 1910 (www.dreamtown.com/neighborhoods/canaryville_fullerpark.html).

FULLERSBURG. Cook, DuPage. Founded about 1850 by Benjamin Fuller and named for the Fuller family. Jacob Fuller was an early settler in 1835. Fullersburg was annexed by Hinsdale in 1923 (Hansen, ed., *Illinois*, 615). Post office established March 10, 1835, as Brush Hill; changed to Fullersburg Feb. 3, 1859.

FULLERTON. DeWitt. Six miles southwest of Farmer City. Formerly known as Fullerton Station, named for site owner David Fuller (*History of DeWitt County* [1882], 288).

FULLS. Champaign. Five miles east of Urbana. Founded by site owner Nicodemus Full (*Portrait and Biographical Album of Champaign County*, 742).

FULTON. County. Created Jan. 28, 1823, from Pike County. Named for Robert Fulton (1765–1815), inventor of the submarine and the first commercially successful steamboat in 1807. The name was proposed by Ossian M. Ross, the founder of Lewistown (Irwin, *A to Z Fulton County*).

FULTON. Whiteside. City (1859, 1899) north-northeast of Clinton, Iowa. Founded about 1838 and named for Robert Fulton by ferry owner R. J. Jenks. Formerly known as Bakers Ferry (Bastian, *A History of Whiteside County*, 218). Post office established March 6, 1838.

FULTS. Monroe. Village (1937) twelve miles south of Waterloo. Originally known as Brownsburg. Renamed with establishment of the post office for Jacob Fultz, a soldier in the War of 1812 (*Combined History of Randolph, Monroe, and Perry Counties*, 383; Klein, ed., *Arrowheads to Aerojets*, 596–97). Post office established Sept. 2, 1903.

FUNKHOUSER. Effingham. Four miles southwest of Effingham. Founded in 1869 by John and Wilson Funkhouser (Feldhake, *Effingham County*, 39). Post office established Dec. 9, 1869.

FUNKS GROVE. McLean. Nine miles southwest of Bloomington. Named for Isaac Funk, cattle baron, state representative, and Illinois state senator in the 1840s (*History of McLean County*, 618).

FUTURE CITY. Alexander. One mile north of Cairo. Laid out about 1876 as Futrell City by Richard Futrell. Through popular etymology the word *Futrell* became *Future* (Havighurst, "The Way to Future City," 225).

G

GAGES LAKE. Lake. Six miles north of Mundelein. Named from Gages Lake, itself named for early settlers Leonard and George Gage (Halsey, ed., *A History of Lake County*, 397).

GALATIA [guh LAY shuh]. Saline. Village (1861, 1875) nine miles west of Eldorado. Founded in 1836 by David Upchurch and William I. Gatewood. The site was then in Gallatin County. The name was apparently to have been Gallatin, named for Gallatin County, but the final *n* was either smeared or mistaken for an *a* by a postal agent or county official. The word *Gallatia* was then changed to *Galatia* by someone familiar with the biblical references to Galatia, the country in Asia Minor (*History of Saline County,* 99; Stewart, *American Place-Names*). Post office established Feb. 3, 1837, as Gallatia; changed to Galatia June 20, 1892.

GALENA. Jo Daviess. City (1835, 1882). Laid out in 1822 by James Johnson. Several names for the community were considered, including Jackson for Andrew Jackson and Harrison for William Henry Harrison. Richard Chandler proposed Galena (Latin for "lead ore") because lead mining was the principle occupation. The area around Galena was previously known as Fever River, a name of uncertain derivation. "Fever" may be simply a popular etymology of *La Fevre,* perhaps the name of an early miner or explorer; it may also be a partial translation (perhaps through French *fièvre*) of the native *mah-cau-bee,* reported in early accounts to mean "the fever that blisters" (smallpox), given at a time when a smallpox epidemic destroyed much of the local Native American population. It is noteworthy that Smallpox Creek flows into Lake Galena about four miles east of the city. It is also possible that the word is a popular etymology from the French *Rivière à Fèves* (Bean River), probably named for the beanlike pods of the honey locust tree. Galena has been the seat of Jo Daviess County since the county's formation in 1827 (Hobbs, *Glamorous Galena,* 22; McDermott, *A Glossary of Mississippi Valley French*). Post office established June 4, 1825, as Fever River; changed to Galena Jan. 5, 1826.

GALESBURG. Knox. City (1841, 1876). Founded in 1836 by the Rev. George Washington Gale, a Presbyterian minister from Whitesboro, N.Y. Galesburg was planned as a "thrifty, moral" community to be built around a college to prepare young men for the frontier ministry. To this end, the Knox Manual Labor College (now Knox College) was established and chartered by the state of Illinois in 1837. Galesburg has been the seat of Knox County since 1872 (Hansen, ed., *Illinois,* 624–25). Post office established Sept. 20, 1837, as Galesburgh; changed to Galesburg April 20, 1893.

GALESVILLE. Piatt. Eight miles north of Monticello. Laid out about 1877 on the line of the Chicago and Paducah Railroad as Calef's Station by site owner Rufus Calef. The name was subsequently changed to honor Calef's mother, whose maiden name was Gale (Morgan, ed., *The Good Life,* 109). Post office established July 13, 1877, as Calef's Station; changed to Galesville July 26, 1877.

GALLAGHER. Richland. Seven miles southwest of Olney. Named for postmaster James M. Gallagher (Adams, comp., *Illinois Place Names*). Post office established June 2, 1888.

GALLATIN. County. Created Sept. 14, 1812, from Randolph County. Named in honor of Abraham Alfonse Albert Gallatin (1761–1849), a Swiss-born public official and diplomat who at the time was secretary of the treasury under President James Madison. The name was suggested by John Bradolette, registrar at the Vincennes land office, a fellow Swiss and an admirer of Gallatin. The county seat was established at Shawneetown in 1812, moved to Equality in 1827, and back to Shawneetown in 1848 (*History of Gallatin, Saline*, 41).

GALT. Whiteside. Two miles west of Sterling. Named for Robert A. Galt, proprietor of the Galt Cheese Manufacturing Company, or for John Galt, a local property owner. Originally called Como, presumably after Lake Como in Italy (Bent, ed., *History of Whiteside County*, 250; Stennett, *A History of the Origin*, 75). Post office established Jan. 6, 1851, as Empire; changed to Galt Oct. 5, 1865.

GALTON. Douglas. Four miles south of Tuscola. Named for Douglas Galton, an English actuary who visited Illinois on several occasions to examine the books of the Illinois Central Railroad on behalf of British and Dutch investors (Ackerman, *Early Illinois Railroads*, 128). Post office established Feb. 8, 1883.

GALVA [GAL vuh]. Henry. City (1867, 1879) six miles southwest of Kewanee. Founded as a satellite of Bishop Hill (q.v.) on the line of the Central Military Tract Railroad by William L. and James W. Wiley in 1854. Named by Olof Johnson for Gävle, the largest city in Norrland, Sweden. Galva, Ill., and Gävle, Sweden, became sister cities in the late 1940s (Landelius, *Swedish Place-Names*). Post office established Feb. 5, 1855.

GANEER. Kankakee. Township. Named for the Potawatomi wife of Isadore Momence. Her name appears as Ge-neir in the 1832 Treaty of Tippecanoe, which granted her a reservation of one section of land (Vogel, *Indian Place Names in Illinois*).

GANNTOWN. Johnson. Fourteen miles north of Metropolis. Founded in 1887 and named for Dr. John Gann, a physician from Massachusetts, or for William Gann, a local farmer and property owner (Chapman, *A History of Johnson County*, 294). Post office established Sept. 27, 1889.

GANO. Cook. Named for Howell Gano, the first site owner. Now part of Chicago (Karlen, *Chicago's Crabgrass Communities*, 278). Post office established Dec. 14, 1887.

GARDEN PLAIN. Whiteside. Four miles southeast of Clinton, Iowa. Presumably named for the richness and productivity of the soil. As an 1877 county history put it, "The name of Garden Plain was rightfully and properly given to this township. Nature and man have . . . made it a garden, and he who owns a portion of its fertile acres can congratulate himself upon being one of the favored few whose heritage is in a goodly land." The choice of the name is generally attributed to Col. Samuel M. Kilgore (Bent, ed., *History of Whiteside County*, 204). Post office established March 12, 1846.

GARDEN PRAIRIE. Boone. Five miles east of Belvidere. Founded for the Chicago and North Western Railroad about 1851 by David Sackett as Amesville, named from the Amesville post office, itself named for first postmaster William Ames. The name was changed to Garden Prairie, a "hopeful" name, in 1853 (Hadley, *A History of Boone County,* 99).

GARDNER. Grundy. Village (1869, 1914) seven miles south of Coal City. Named for Henry A. Gardner, chief engineer for the Chicago and Alton Railroad and owner of the site on which the station was built in 1854 (*History of Grundy County,* 275). Post office established March 14, 1855.

GARDNER. Sangamon. Township. Organized in 1861 and named for John Gardner, one of the three commissioners appointed to organize the county into townships (Wallace, *Past and Present,* 33).

GARDS POINT. Wabash. Eight miles northwest of Mount Carmel. Named for Seth Gard, a member of the Illinois territorial legislature and a delegate to the first Illinois constitutional convention. Gard emigrated from Hamilton County, Ohio, and settled at what is now Gards Point about 1815 (Bateman and Selby, eds., *Illinois Historical Wabash County Biographical,* 718). Post office established April 25, 1826, as Centreville; changed to Gard's Point Nov. 5, 1852.

GARFIELD. LaSalle. Seven miles southwest of Streator. Founded in the late 1860s and named for James A. Garfield (1831–81), at the time a U.S. representative from Ohio and later president of the United States (Gannett, *The Origin of Certain Place Names*). Post office established March 30, 1868, as Soho; changed to Garfield Dec. 18, 1868.

GARRETT. Douglas. Village (1903) seven miles west of Tuscola. Named for the Garrett family. Isom Garrett and his sons Caleb and Nathan were early settlers (Niles, *History of Douglas County,* 58). Post office established Aug. 20, 1885.

GARRISON. Hamilton. Ten miles north of McLeansboro. Named for the Garrison family. David Garrison, along with his son, Andrew, established a general store at the site about 1892. Andrew Garrison was the first postmaster (*Hamilton County,* 47). Post office established Nov. 15, 1893.

GARTSIDE. St. Clair. Three miles northwest of Belleville. Named for postmaster Mary Gartside (Adams, comp., *Illinois Place Names*). Post office established Feb. 24, 1868.

GASKINS CITY. Saline. Laid out by site owner George Gaskins. Now part of Harrisburg (*History of Saline County,* 49).

GATHON. Bond. Former community. An acronym formed from the names of the founders: Gallager, Adams, Tremblay, and Herzog. Apparently, a postal official who was displeased by the name *Gath* decided to add -*on* (Peterson, "Place Names of Bond County," 3). Post office established Aug. 22, 1895.

GAYS. Moultrie. Village (1905) five miles west-southwest of Mattoon. Established in 1860 by the Indianapolis and St. Louis Railroad as Summit Station, presumed to be the highest point on the route between Terre Haute and St. Louis. Renamed for Edward F. Gay, president of the Oil Creek and Allegheny Railroad in the 1860s (*Combined History of Shelby and Moultrie Counties,* 210). Post office established May 14, 1847, as Whitley's Point; changed to Gays Jan. 5, 1882.

GEBHARD WOODS STATE PARK. Grundy. West of Morris. Established by the Grundy County Rod and Gun Club on land purchased from Mrs. William Gebhard and her son, F. W. Gebhard, in 1934 (Brown, ed., *Grundy County,* 7).

GEFF [JEF]. Wayne. Four miles north-northwest of Fairfield. A familiar form of *Jefferson.* Jeffersonville was the name of the community until the 1850s, and the cemetery is still called Jeffersonville. Post office established May 8, 1857, as Jeffersonville; changed to Geff Aug. 11, 1917.

GENESEE [JEN uh see]. Whiteside. Township. Transferred by settlers from Genesee County in northwestern New York state. Ultimately from a Seneca (Iroquoian) word meaning "pleasant valley" (Bright, *Native American Placenames*). The Genesee Grove post office operated from June 8, 1844, until Nov. 12, 1868, when it was changed to Coleta. The New Gennessee [*sic*] post office was established May 23, 1854, and was discontinued May 14, 1894.

GENESEO [JEN uh SEE o]. Henry. City (1855). A variant of "Genesee." Geneseo was organized as a religious colony in 1836 by the Rev. Jarius Wilcox and others associated with the First Congregational Church of Bergen, N.Y. The community was formally laid out in 1838 by John D. Ward, Roderick R. Stewart, and Cromwell K. Bartlett and named by Stewart for Geneseo, Livingston County, N.Y. (Colby, "Historic Spots in Henry County," 172; Swank, *Historic Henry County,* 33). Post office established Feb. 1, 1838, as Richmond; changed to Geneseo Aug. 19, 1840.

GENEVA [juh NEE vuh]. Kane. City (1867, 1887). The area was formerly known as Herrington's Ford, named for early settler and first postmaster James Herrington. Geneva was founded in 1832 and named at the suggestion of Charles Volney Dyer, a Chicago lawyer and noted abolitionist, for his former home in western New York state, itself named for Geneva, the city and lake in Switzerland. Geneva has been the seat of Kane County since its formation in 1836 (Joslyn and Joslyn, *History of Kane County,* 819; *Past and Present of Kane County,* 321). Post office established March 12, 1836, as La Fox; changed to Geneva April 9, 1850.

GENOA [juh NO uh]. DeKalb. City (1876). Founded about 1836 and named for Genoa, Cayuga County, N.Y., by Thomas Madison (or Matteson), the first postmaster and a justice of the peace (Boies, *History of DeKalb County,* 453). Post office established May 5, 1837.

GEORGES CREEK. Massac, Johnson. Stream. By tradition, the stream takes its name from Chief George, a Native American leader whose village was nearby (May, *History of Massac County,* 176). Post office established Aug. 10, 1846.

GEORGETOWN. Vermilion. City (1869, 1909). Founded in 1827 by site owner James Haworth and named for his son, George. Several early county histories erroneously claim that Haworth named the community for George Beckwith, brother of Dan Beckwith, the founder of Danville. (Beckwith, *History of Vermilion County,* 513; *Illinois Guide;* Stark and Brown, 4). Post office established May 27, 1831.

GERLAW [GER law]. Warren. Five miles north-northeast of Monmouth. Founded by Robert W. Gerlaw about 1871 (*Portrait and Biographical Album of Warren County,* 873). Post office established July 6, 1871.

GERMAN VALLEY. Stephenson. Village (1907) eight miles southeast of Freeport. Named for (and probably by) settlers from Germany. Due to anti-German sentiment during World War I, the name was changed to Meekin and then changed back to German Valley after the war (Rennick, "On the Success of Efforts," 28). Post office established April 17, 1884, as Wieman, named for postmaster Anko H. Wieman; changed to Ballton March 28, 1887; changed to German Valley May 16, 1887; changed to Meekin March 19, 1919; changed back to German Valley April 19, 1922.

GERMANTOWN. Clinton. Village (1874). three miles south of Breese. Named for the many German settlers in the area. Formerly known as Hanover, for Hanover, Germany. Post office established Jan. 1, 1846.

GERMANVILLE. Livingston. Township. Changed from Germantown in 1879. Also named for the large number of German settlers. The Germanville cemetery is six miles south of Chatsworth (*History of Livingston County,* 287).

GIBRALTAR. Kendall. Former community nine miles east of LaSalle. Laid out about 1836 by Benjamin Thurston on Buffalo Rock, so named because it was believed that Indians killed buffalo by stampeding them over the precipice. The outline of Buffalo Rock reportedly reminded Thurston of the Rock of Gibraltar (Hicks, *History of Kendall County,* 162).

GIBSON CITY. Ford. City (1894). Founded in 1870 as Gibson by Jonathan B. Lott and named for the family of his wife, Margaret Gibson Lott. The word *City* was added by the post office department to avoid confusion with the Gilson post office in Knox County (*Ford County History,* 48). Post office established May 15, 1871.

GIBSONIA. Gallatin. Sixteen miles east-southeast of Harrisburg. Established in the early 1900s. The particular Gibson or Gibson family for whom Gibsonia is named is unknown (*History and Families of Gallatin County,* 13). Post office established March 3, 1903.

GIFFORD. Champaign. Village (1954) six miles east of Rantoul. Founded by Benjamin F. Gifford and Harvey E. Bullock in 1875 (*History of Champaign County,* 166). Post office established June 1, 1876.

GILA. Jasper. Fourteen miles east of Effingham. Founded about 1874 and probably named for the Gila River in Arizona. The name was likely brought to Illinois by returning prospectors or travelers (Vogel, *Indian Place Names in Illinois*). Post office established June 28, 1882.

GILBERTS. Kane. Village (1890) four miles northwest of Elgin. Established as Gilbert's Station by the Galena and Chicago Union Railroad. Named for Amasa Gilbert, an early settler. Formerly known as Rutlandville, named for Rutland, Vt. (Stennett, *A History of the Origin*, 77). Post office established Jan. 7, 1854, as Rutland; changed to Gilberts Aug. 26, 1870.

GILBIRDS. Brown. Five miles southeast of Mount Sterling. Originally called Gilbirds Port, a flag station on the Wabash Railroad. Named for Charles H. Gilbirds, a railroad employee (*History of Brown County*, 326).

GILCHRIST. Mercer. Six miles east of Aledo. Named for Hugh Gilchrist, who was instrumental in developing the local coal mines. Gilchrist was the founder of Wanlock, north of Gilchrist (Bateman and Selby, eds., *Historical Encyclopedia of Illinois and History of Mercer County*, 643). Post office established Feb. 26, 1886.

GILEAD. Calhoun. Seventeen miles west of Jerseyville. Commissioners George Allen and Gershom Flagg selected Coles Grove (named for Governor Edward Coles) to be the seat of Calhoun County. Giving no reasons, they recommended that the name be changed to Gilead. The name was probably taken from the biblical mountain and district now in Jordan or from a nearby Gilead Church. In 1825, when the community was formally laid out, Gilead was a popular name for churches and cemeteries (there are currently about a dozen in Illinois) but rare as a community name. Gilead was the seat of Calhoun County from 1825 until 1847, when it was moved to Hardin (Carpenter, *Calhoun Is My Kingdom*, 16; Carpenter, *—and They Changed the Name to Gilead*, n.p.; Underwood, "A New Geography of Illinois: Calhoun County," 34). Post office established Jan. 15, 1822, as Coles Grove; changed to Gilead Oct. 25, 1825.

GILLESPIE [guh LIS pee]. Macoupin. Village (1859, 1883). Named in the early 1850s by officials of the Indianapolis and St. Louis Railroad for Joseph Gillespie, a jurist and Illinois state legislator of the 1840s and 1850s (Walker, *History of Macoupin County*, 387). Post office established March 31, 1852, as Prairie Farm; changed to Gillespie Feb. 13, 1854.

GILLUM [GIL uhm]. McLean. Six miles southeast of Bloomington. Named for Mary Gillum (Gillam) Condon (Townley, *Historic McLean*, 19). Post office established June 27, 1874.

GILMAN. Iroquois. City (1867, 1874) thirteen miles west of Watseka. Named for Samuel Gilman of New York, a partner in the firm of Cruger, Secor and Gilman, which oversaw construction of the Peoria and Oquawka Railroad between Gilman and El Paso (Ackerman, *Early Illinois Railroads*, 125; *Gilman Centen-*

nial, n.p.). Post office established March 2, 1858, as Douglas City; changed to Gilman July 13, 1858.

GILMER. Adams. Township. Organized as Dover. Renamed in 1850 in honor of Dr. John Thornton Gilmer, the first local physician (Genosky, ed., *People's History,* 705).

GILMER. Lake. Five miles southeast of Wauconda. Named for Thomas Walker Gilmer (1802–44), secretary of the navy, following his accidental death in 1844. According to local sources, the name of the post office was to have been Wentworth for U.S. representative John Wentworth. Before presenting the petition to postal officials, however, Wentworth changed the name to Gilmer (Dretske, *What's in a Name?*). Post office established May 15, 1844.

GILMORE. Effingham. Fourteen miles southwest of Effingham. Named for William or James Gilmore, both early county commissioners. William Gilmore was also the first supervisor of West Township. Formerly known as Welton, named for W. S. and Lucy Welton (Bateman and Selby, eds., *Illinois Historical Effingham County Biographical,* 647, 762; Feldhake, *Effingham County,* 42). Post office established Jan. 2, 1872.

GILSON. Knox. Nine miles southeast of Galesburg. Founded in 1857 by James Gilson and Linneus Richmond (Perry, *History of Knox County,* 442). Post office established March 6, 1857.

GINGLE CORNERS. Mercer. Four miles north of Aledo. Named for James Gingles, the first postmaster. Also known as Gingle's Corner (Bateman and Selby, eds., *Historical Encyclopedia of Illinois and History of Mercer County,* 657).

GIRARD [juh RAHRD]. Macoupin. City twelve miles north-northeast of Carlinville. Laid out by Barnabas Boggess and Charles H. Fink in the early 1850s. Probably named for Stephen Girard of Philadelphia, reported to be the richest person in the United States (and also probably a substantial stockholder in the Chicago and North Western Railroad). The name, however, may have been taken from Girard's Mills, established by a settler named Girard in the early 1830s (*History of Girard,* 1; *Illinois Guide;* Stennett, *A History of the Origin,* 77; Walker, *History of Macoupin County,* 368). Post office established July 20, 1848, as Pleasant Grove; changed to Girard Jan. 20, 1855.

GLADSTONE. Henderson. Village (1881) five miles northeast of Burlington, Iowa. Founded about 1856 as Sagetown, named for Gideon Sage, an early settler. The name was changed to Gladstone in 1881, probably for William Gladstone, at the time prime minister of Britain (Sutton, *Rivers, Railways,* 85).

GLASFORD [GLAS ferd]. Peoria. Village (1889) eight miles west of Pekin. Named for Samuel A. Glasford, who owned the site on which the Toledo, Peoria and Western station was built in 1868. Formerly known as Glascoe (*Illinois Guide*).

Post office established June 25, 1846, as Timber; changed to Glasford Jan. 7, 1869.

GLASGOW [GLAS ko]. Scott. Village (1867) eight miles northwest of Roodhouse. Founded in 1836 and named by James McEvers for Glasgow, Scotland (*Atlas, History and Plat-Book of Scott County,* 78). Post office established Dec. 3, 1845.

GLASGOW CITY. Monroe. Laid out by James Glasgow in 1860. Now part of Renault (*Combined History of Randolph, Monroe, and Perry Counties,* 383).

GLENBURN. Vermilion. Six miles west of Danville. Named by C. M. Swallow for Glenburn, Lackawanna County, Pa., Swallow opened a coal mine at the site about 1885 (Underwood, "A New Geography of Illinois: Vermilion County," 39). Post office established Feb. 3, 1886.

GLEN CARBON. Madison. Village (1892). Named about 1892 by James Harry Lister, originally from England, one of the first village trustees and a specialist in opening mines and installing mining equipment. Lister named the community Carbon Glen (i.e., Coal Valley). Reportedly, his daughter said that it sounded better to reverse the words to Glen Carbon (Cedeck and Foster, eds., *A History of Glen Carbon,* 38). Post office established Jan. 6, 1892.

GLENCOE. Cook. Village (1869). Formerly known as Taylorsport, named for early settlers Anson and Lisa Taylor. Glencoe was the name of the estate of Walter S. Gurnee (q.v. Gurnee). It is either a direct transfer from Glencoe, Scotland, or created from the words *glen* (small valley) and *coe* (the maiden name of Gurnee's wife). Upon incorporation in 1869 the village adopted a great seal modeled on that of Glencoe, Scotland (Handley, "Old Not Stuffy;" Stennett, *A History of the Origin,* 78). Post office established Sept. 26, 1857.

GLENDALE. Pope. Twenty miles north of Metropolis. Founded about 1860 by site owner and postmaster George Waters. Named for Glen Wright, an early settler (*Pope County,* 28). Post office established June 13, 1849, as Broad Oaks; changed to Glendale Feb. 19, 1861.

GLENDALE HEIGHTS. DuPage. Village (1959). Originally a small subdivision called Glen Ellyn Countryside. Formally organized in 1959 as Glendale, named for its location between Glen Ellyn and Bloomingdale. The word *Heights* was added in 1960 (Crisler, "Glendale Heights," 84).

GLEN ELLYN. DuPage. Village (1892). Formerly called Babcock's Grove, named for early settlers Ralph, Morgan, and Anson Babcock, and subsequently known as DuPage Center; Stacy's Corners; Milton, named by Winslow Churchill for Milton, Mass., the location of the Churchill family estate; Newton's Station; Danby, named by David Kelly, first station agent for the Galena and Chicago Union Railroad, for his former home, Danbury, Vt.; and Prospect Park. The name *Glen Ellyn* was coined by Philo Stacy and village president Thomas E. Hill. About 1885,

Stacy created Glen Ellyn Lake as the center of a public park and recreation area. The word *Ellyn,* a variant of *Ellen,* is in honor of Ellen Hill, the wife of Thomas Hill (Bateman and Selby, eds., *Historical Encyclopedia of Illinois and History of DuPage County,* 689–90; Harmon, *The Story of an Old Town,* 76; Knoblauch, ed., *DuPage County,* 68). Post office established Jan. 15, 1852, as Danby; changed to Prospect Park Jan. 26, 1874; changed to Glen Ellyn July 10, 1891.

GLENN. Jackson. Eighteen miles southeast of Steeleville. Named for either Walter J. Glenn, the first postmaster, or for the family of Robin Glenn, who settled along Kinkaid Creek in the mid-1820s (Adams, comp., *Illinois Place Names;* Allen, *Jackson County Notes,* 18; Mohlenbrock, "A New Geography of Illinois: Jackson County," 31). Post office established Feb. 26, 1892.

GLENWOOD. Cook. Village (1903). Founded as Hickory Bend by Job Campbell and O. P. Axtell and settled largely by Irish and German immigrants in the late 1830s. For unknown reasons the name was changed to Glenwood about 1871 (Simon, "Being Dull"). Post office established March 5, 1875.

GLOVER. Champaign. Nine miles east of Urbana. Named for John A. Glover, mayor of Urbana from 1901 to 1905.

GODFREY. Madison. Village (1991) two miles north of Alton. Founded by Benjamin Godfrey, a retired sea captain from Cape Cod, Mass. Godfrey founded the Monticello Female Seminary (now Lewis and Clark College) about 1838 (Norton, ed., *Centennial History of Madison County,* 121). Post office established Aug. 25, 1841.

GOESELVILLE. Cook. Three miles north of Tinley Park. Named for postmaster George C. Goesel (Adams, comp., *Illinois Place Names*). Post office established May 19, 1884.

GOLCONDA [gahl KAHN duh]. Pope. City (1845, 1923) twenty-four miles south of Harrisburg. Previously known as Sarahville (or Sarahsville), named for the wife of site owner Thomas Ferguson. Apparently, Sarahville was to have been renamed Corinth, but in 1817, at the request of the proprietors, the name was changed to Golconda instead. The reasons for the choice of the name are unknown. Golconda is a ruined fortress and city in south central India (Allen, "Golconda Got Its Name"; Allen, *Pope County Notes,* 29, 75). Post office established June 28, 1820.

GOLDEN. Adams. Village (1873) twenty-two miles northeast of Quincy. Earlier known as LaBuda, probably for a local family. Formally laid out as Keokuk Junction in 1866, named for Keokuk, Iowa. The name was changed in the early 1880s for the Golden family, proprietors of the Golden Hotel (*One Hundred Golden Years,* 3, 5). Post office established June 12, 1863, as Keokuk Junction; changed to Golden Oct. 18, 1880.

GOLDEN GATE. Wayne. Village (1896) eight miles east of Fairfield. Founded about 1881. The origin of the name is uncertain. One local story claims that the name arose when land owner Ethan Fowler built a fence across the proposed route of the Louisville, Evansville and St. Louis Railroad and padlocked the gate. After some negotiations the railroad agreed to buy the property from Fowler, but he insisted upon being paid in gold; thus the gate that led to the favorable financial settlement was "golden." According to another story, the name was from a yellow gate near the Little Wabash River. The actual source of the name, however, may be California's Golden Gate, the entrance to San Francisco Bay. In the late nineteenth century this part of southern Illinois was known as Lower California, and those who lived there were called Californians. The Golden Gate in California was named before 1850, so there was plenty of time for a returning prospector or traveler to bring the name to Illinois by the time Golden Gate was founded in the early 1880s (Allison, *History of Leech Township*, 127; Blevins, *Peculiar, Uncertain, and Two Egg*). Post office established July 3, 1886, as Beech Bluff; changed to Golden Gate Oct. 18, 1888.

GOLD HILL. Gallatin. Township. Named from Gold Hill Ridge, which runs from east to west through the township. The ridge was named for early settler Calvin Gold, a clerk of the county commissioners court (*History of Gallatin, Saline*, 65).

GOLF. Cook. Village (1928). Named for the game of golf. The local story is that Albert J. Erling, president of the Milwaukee Road, would have the train stopped at this point so that he and his friends could play a round at the Glen View Golf Club (Reich, "The Suburb That Growth Forgot"). Post office established Aug. 30, 1898.

GOODE. Franklin. Township. Named for Benjamin Goode, the first permanent settler (Ramsey and Miller, *The Heritage of Franklin County*, 16).

GOODENOW [GUD now]. Will. Three miles south of Crete. Founded about 1869 by shopkeeper George W. Goodenow upon the construction of the Chicago and Eastern Illinois Railroad (*History of Will County*, 567; *Souvenir of Settlement and Progress*, 391). Post office established Dec. 19, 1870.

GOODFIELD. Woodford. Village (1957) six miles south of Eureka. Originally called Guthville, for John Guth of Washington, Ill. Apparently, the name evolved from Guthville through Goodville to Goodfield (Moore, *History of Woodford County*, 230). Post office established Feb. 18, 1889, as Goodville; changed to Goodfield June 28, 1889.

GOOD HOPE. McDonough. Village (1869, 1875) six miles north of Macomb. Three adjacent communities had been established near the line of the Toledo, Peoria and Western Railroad by the time it was completed in the mid-1860s: Good Hope, Sheridan, and Milan. It was said that the railroad sold tickets to Sheridan, the conductors called out "Milan," and letters were delivered to Good Hope. By 1870 the name *Good Hope* had replaced both Sheridan and Milan. The source of the name is unknown (Shadwick, *History of McDonough County,* 228). Post office established April 21, 1858, as Goodhope.

GOODWINE. Iroquois. Seven miles northwest of Hoopeston. Named for William Goodwine, site owner and township officer in the 1880s (Dowling, *History of Iroquois County,* 60). Post office established Feb. 28, 1876, as Seemly; changed to Goodwine April 7, 1882.

GOOFY RIDGE. Mason. Nine miles northeast of Havana. The origin of the name is unknown. According to a local story, the name dates from the Prohibition era of the 1920s, when moonshine whiskey flowed freely in the area. As the story goes, one day several people with nothing better to do were sitting around drinking when one, inebriated, of course, bet he could shoot a walnut off someone's head with a rifle. Another, equally inebriated, accepted the bet and placed a walnut on his head. When the rifle cracked, the walnut flew—through better luck than skill. Both parties withdrew, presumably to celebrate with another round, leading one witness to exclaim, "This is sure a goofy place!" According to another story, a man was chasing a naked woman through the woods in earlier times (what her being naked had to do with the story is unknown). Those who saw them said, "That's a pretty goofy thing to do" (Orr, "Goofy Ridge").

GOOSE CREEK. Piatt. Township. Named from Goose Creek. Reportedly so named because some geese were permanent residents and nested along the stream for many years (Bateman and Selby, eds., *Historical Encyclopedia of Illinois and History of Piatt County,* 690).

GOOSE LAKE. Grundy. Township. Formed from Felix Township in 1897 with the proposed name of Jugtown. In the middle decades of the nineteenth century Jugtown was a thriving community, its economy based on pottery and drain tiles made from the rich clay deposits in the area—thus the name. For reasons probably having to do with the association of "jug" with liquor, Goose Lake, named from Goose Lake Prairie, was substituted for Jugtown. The historical Jugtown school was about five miles southeast of Morris (Bateman and Selby, eds., *Historical Encyclopedia of Illinois and History of Grundy County,* 700, 708; Ullrich, *This Is Grundy County,* 286).

GORDON. Crawford. Two miles east of Robinson. Named for postmasters Charles A. and George E. Gordon (Adams, comp., *Illinois Place Names*). Post office established Aug. 13, 1882.

GOREVILLE. Johnson. Village (1900) eleven miles northwest of Vienna. Named for the Gore family. John Gore was an early settler, arriving about 1809, and Wesley Gore was an early postmaster (Adams, comp., *Illinois Place Names;*

Mohlenbrock, "A New Geography of Illinois: Johnson County," 41). Post office established June 15, 1866.

GOSHEN. Stark. Township. Probably a transfer from an eastern state, perhaps brought to Illinois by settlers from Goshen, Ohio, or Goshen, Ind. Goshen is a biblical name, the land where Jacob's descendants lived until the Exodus. There have been at least four other Goshens in Illinois, in Cook, Madison, Randolph, and Stark counties, along with numerous Goshen churches, cemeteries, and schools (Cedeck and Foster, eds., *A History of Glen Carbon*, 1). The Goshen post office was active from Nov. 18, 1834, when it was changed from Spoon River, until Jan. 24, 1835, when it was changed back to Spoon River.

GOSSETT. White. Eight miles north-northeast of Eldorado. Laid out in 1873 by site owner John D. Gossett (Oliver, *Norris City and Indian Creek Township*, 4). Post office established Oct. 9, 1871, as Young's Station, named for postmaster Milton P. Young.

GOUGARS. Will. Named for the Gougar family. John Gougar was an early settler who emigrated from Indiana about 1830. Now a suburb of Joliet (*History of Will County*, 495).

GOWINS [GO uhnz]. Pope. Twenty miles south-southeast of Harrisburg. Named for the Gowins family. The first settler in the area was William McGowen (or McGowan), from Edinburgh, Scotland. His son, William G. Gowan, settled near Golconda. By 1900 the name had become Goin or Goins, with several variations; the name of the first postmaster has been reported as Samuel Goin, Samuel Goins, and Samuel Gowin (Adams, comp., *Illinois Place Names*; Allen, *Pope County Notes*, 77; *Pope County*, 28). Post office established April 7, 1900.

GRAFTON. Jersey. City (1837, 1907) twelve miles west-northwest of Alton. Situated at the confluence of the Illinois and Mississippi rivers. Marquette and Jolliet passed this point twice in 1673; on their return trip they became the first Europeans to enter the Illinois River. The site is marked by several plaques and monuments commemorating the event, and Pere Marquette State Park is nearby. Grafton was settled about 1832 by James Mason and named in 1836 for Mason's former home, Grafton, Mass. (*Illinois Guide*; Postlewait, ed., *History of Jersey County*, 112). Post office established April 15, 1834.

GRAFTON. McHenry. Township. Named by Prescott Wittemore for one of the Graftons in New England, probably Grafton, Mass., near his birthplace (*History of McHenry County* [1922], 397; Nye, ed., *McHenry County Illinois*, 607).

GRAND CHAIN. Pulaski. Eighteen miles northeast of Cairo. The name is a translation and shortening of French Le Grand Chain à la Rocher (The Great Chain of Rocks), named for the six-mile-long procession of rocks that cuts through the area and formerly extended into the Ohio River. The rocks are now below water level as a result of dams built by the U.S. Army Corps of Engineers in the 1920s. New Grand Chain, founded just south of Grand Chain in 1872 by Joseph W. Gaunt, Warner K. Bartleson, and David Porter, has replaced the original Grand Chain (Beadles, *A History of Southernmost Illinois*, 11; Moyer, *Moyers' Brief History*, 2, 69).

GRAND CROSSING. Cook. Laid out in 1871 as Cornell by site owner and land developer Paul Cornell, the founder of Hyde Park (q.v.). The name was changed for the number of railroad lines that intersected at the site (Ackerman, *Early Illinois Railroads*, 115; Karlen, *Chicago's Crabgrass Communities*, 41).

GRAND DETOUR. Ogle. Named for the horseshoelike bend on the Rock River some five miles northeast of Dixon. In early American French, a *detour* was a bend in a river. Large bends such as this one were known as *grand detours* (McDermott, *A Glossary of Mississippi Valley French*). Post office established May 26, 1838.

GRAND PIERRE [GRAN PIHR]. Pope. Precinct. Named from Grand Pierre Creek. The source of the name is unknown. It may be from an early explorer or settler named Pierre, or it may be from Grandpier, a family name modified to Grand Pierre in an attempt to create an apparent but nonetymological French source meaning "big rock." The name has also been recorded as Grandpear, Grampear, Grampeer, and Grand Pier, each spelling inviting a different popular etymology (Allen, *Pope County Notes*, 63; personal communication with Mildred B. McCormick). Post office established March 30, 1855, as Grand Pier.

GRAND RAPIDS. LaSalle. Township. Named for the rapids in the Illinois River now largely controlled by the Marseilles lock and dam (*History of LaSalle County*, 225, 284).

GRAND RIDGE. LaSalle. Village (1891) eight miles south of Ottawa. Named Grand Ridge about 1871 by officials of the Chicago, Burlington and Quincy Railroad either because it was thought to be the highest point on the line between Streator and Aurora or for its location near the common boundary of Grand Rapids and Farm Ridge townships (*History of LaSalle County*, 233). Post office established March 1, 1871, as Livonia; changed to Grand Ridge May 2, 1873.

GRAND TOWER. Jackson. City (1872) twelve miles southeast of Murphysboro. Founded about 1867. Grand Tower is a translation of La Grand Tour, the name given by early French explorers to Tower Rock, a monolith projecting from the Mississippi River some twenty miles north of Cape Girardeau, Mo. The rock has long been a landmark for travelers and was mentioned in the accounts of both Marquette and LaSalle. The modern city of Grand Tower includes a section once called Red Town, established in 1867 as a company town for employees of the Pilot Knob Ore Company and named from the fact that the houses were all painted with red iron oxide paint (Allen, *Jackson County Notes,* 19; *Illinois Guide;* McDermott, "The French Impress," 233; Sneed, *Ghost Towns of Southern Illinois,* 85). Post office established Feb. 5, 1855.

GRANDVIEW. Edgar. Nine miles southwest of Paris. Founded in 1831 by James Archer. According to an early county history, the community was named for the "grand view" it commanded of the surrounding area from its elevated location (*History of Edgar County,* 338). Post office established Feb. 19, 1830, as Sutherland's; changed to Grand View Sept. 10, 1833.

GRANITE CITY. Madison. City (1896) seven miles north of East St. Louis. Named from the Granite Iron Rolling Mills, which produced graniteware, cookware coated with enamel made with ground granite, a process developed by Frederick and William Niedringhaus, St. Louis tinners, about 1890. The community was established on the site then known as Kinder (q.v.) (Engelke, *Looking Back,* 17, 20). Post office established May 15, 1893, as Granite; changed to Granite City Nov. 17, 1903.

GRANT. Lake. Township. Originally called Goodale for innkeeper Devereaux Goodale. Goodale had promised to donate a meeting hall for the township government but failed to do so, and in 1867 the name was changed to Grant in honor of Ulysses S. Grant, then becoming a prominent figure in the Republican Party (Dretske *What's in a Name?; Past and Present of Lake County,* 286). The Grant post office was active from March 4, 1862, until July 22, 1865.

GRANT. Vermilion. Township. Changed from Lyon in 1862 in honor of Ulysses S. Grant, who had just won a major victory with the surrender of Confederate forces at Fort Donelson, Tenn. This is claimed to be the first honorary use of Grant's name (Beckwith, *History of Vermilion County,* 703; Stapp, *History under Our Feet,* 46). Post office established Aug. 14, 1868.

GRANT PARK. Kankakee. Village (1883) twelve miles northeast of Kankakee. Grant, named for President Ulysses S. Grant, was established by William J. Stratton in the late 1860s, and Judson was established nearby by C. C. Campbell. When the Chicago, Danville and Vincennes Railroad located its station at Grant, the name was changed to Grant Park (Johnson, comp., "Kankakee County Communities"). Post office established July 30, 1862, as East Sumner; changed to Judson Feb. 28, 1870; changed to Yellowhead April 25, 1871; changed to Grant Park March 12, 1875.

GRANTSBURG. Johnson. Fifteen miles north of Metropolis. Founded about 1889 on the line of the St. Louis, Alton and Terre Haute Railroad. Also named in honor of Ulysses S. Grant (*Johnson County,* 40). Post office established May 21, 1857, as Crimea, named for the Crimean War, which had ended the year before; changed to Grantsburg June 2, 1864.

GRANVILLE. Putnam. Village (1861, 1880) six miles southwest of Peru. Founded about 1836. Named by an early settler named Ware for his former home, Granville, Mass., itself named for John Carteret (1690–1763), the Earl of Granville (Ellsworth, *Records of the Olden Times,* 277; Ford, *A History of Putnam and Marshall Counties,* 91; Stewart, *American Place-Names*). Post office established April 29, 1847.

GRAYMONT. Livingston. Eight miles west of Pontiac. Founded by George B. Gray (Bateman and Selby, eds., *Historical Encyclopedia of Illinois and History of Livingston County,* 823). Post office established Sept. 7, 1880, as Huber; changed to Graymont Dec. 13, 1880.

GRAYSLAKE. Lake. Village (1895) and lake. Founded about 1885 and named for William Gray, an early settler who located on the south side of the lake about 1835 (Dretske, *What's in a Name?; Illinois Guide*). Post office established Jan. 26, 1895, as Gray's Lake; changed to Grayslake Feb. 3, 1895.

GRAYVILLE. Edwards, White. City (1851, 1884) fourteen miles northeast of Carmi. Three small settlements, Oxford, Florence, and Bonpas, were established near the point where Bonpas Creek flows into the Wabash River. These grew together and were platted as Grayville by James Gray and/or his brother, Thomas, about 1826 (Harper, ed., *History of Edwards County,* 61; *History of White County,* 737). Post office established March 28, 1819, as Bon Pas; changed to Grayville Jan. 5, 1837.

GREASY CREEK. Coles. Stream. A local story is that hog thieves, in order to prevent identification of stolen animals from their ear markings, would cut off the heads of the pigs they had stolen and throw them into the stream. The action of the current and general decomposition made the water greasy (Gannett, *The Origins of Certain Place Names*).

GREENE. County. Created Jan. 20, 1821, from Madison County. The original legislation called for the county to be named Carroll, for Charles Carroll of Carrollton. In the Illinois senate, however, the bill was amended, and "Carroll" was replaced by "Greene," for Nathanael (Nathaniel) Greene (1742–86). Greene, a hero of the Revolutionary War, served with George Washington in New Jersey and later commanded the Continental Army in the South, where he faced the British Gen. Charles Cornwallis on several occasions (Cunningham, *History of the Carrollton, Illinois, Area,* 13).

GREENE. Mercer. Township. Probably named for Gen. Nathanael Greene, at the suggestion of John Collins (Bassett and Goodspeed, *Past and Present of Mercer County,* 453; *History of Mercer and Henderson Counties,* 660).

GREENFIELD. Grundy. Township. Named for Thomas L. Green, a Chicago land speculator and owner of several large tracts in the area (*History of Grundy County,* 265).

GREEN GARDEN. Will. Township. Probably an optimistic name, given in hopes of fair weather and bountiful harvests, although G. M. Green, an early settler, was from Vermont, the Green Mountain State—either or both of which may have influenced the choice of the name (Stevens, *Past and Present of Will County,* 83). The Green Garden post office was active intermittently from Aug. 1, 1851, until Dec. 13, 1902.

GREEN ROCK. Henry. City (1950). Six miles east of Moline. Named for its location where the Green River flows into the Rock River. Green Rock merged with Colona in 1997 (Harder, *Illustrated Dictionary of Place Names*).

GREEN'S CREEK. Jackson. Stream. Named for Green W. Henson, who settled at Big Hill about 1807 (*History of Jackson County,* 36).

GREENUP. Cumberland. Village (1855, 1872) nine miles southwest of Casey. Founded about 1828 as Rossville and later known as Embarrass, named for the Embarras River (q.v.). The name was changed to Greenup when the community was formally laid out in 1834. Named for William C. Greenup, clerk of the Illinois territorial legislatures of 1812 and 1815, secretary of the state constitutional convention of 1818, and surveyor of the town site for the state capital at Vandalia. Greenup was the nephew of Christopher Greenup, for whom Greenup and Greenup County, Ky., are named. Greenup was the seat of Cumberland County from 1843 until 1855, when it was moved to Prairie City (now Toledo) (*Counties of Cumberland, Jasper, and Richland,* 113; *Cumberland County History,* 20). Post office established Jan. 4, 1833, as Embarrass; changed to Greenup Nov. 5, 1834.

GREEN VALLEY. Tazewell. Village (1916) eleven miles south of Pekin. Laid out in 1872 by Samuel Schureman and named from the Green Valley post office, itself named for the Green Valley Sunday School, which was established in 1853 and reportedly named by settlers from Green Valley, N.J. (Bateman and Selby, eds., *Historical Encyclopedia of Illinois and History of Tazewell County,* 856; *Green Valley,* 1, 20). Post office established June 7, 1866.

GREENVIEW. Menard. Village (1869, 1877) eight miles south of Mason City. Named for William G. Greene, a local banker and farmer who was instrumental in securing a station on the Chicago and Alton Railroad. Greene was also one of the founders of Tallula (*History of Menard and Mason Counties,* 353). Post office established Oct. 7, 1858.

GREENVILLE. Bond. City (1855, 1872). The origin of the name is uncertain. There are several traditional accounts. According to one, at the time of the founding of Greenville about 1816, Thomas White, the oldest living resident, was given the honor of choosing a name. He allegedly responded, "Everything looks so green and nice, we will call it Greenville." According to another, Greenville was named by settlers from Greenville, S.C.; and according to still another, the community was named for Green P. Rice, a prominent Presbyterian minister (or Methodist, depending on the source). Each story may be true in whole or in part, and all may have contributed to the favorable reception of the name (Bateman and Selby, eds., *Historical Encyclopedia of Illinois and History of Bond County,* 639; *Bond County History,* 15; Perrin, ed., *History of Bond and Montgomery Counties,* 78; Peterson, "Place Names of Bond County," 40). Post office established Dec. 2, 1819.

GRIDLEY. McLean. Village (1869, 1905) seven miles east of El Paso. Founded in 1856 by Thomas Carlyle and George Washington Kent on land purchased from Asahel Gridley. Gridley, a prominent local figure, was a veteran of the Black Hawk War and a state senator from McLean County in the early 1850s (Hasbrouck, *History of McLean County,* 104; *Illinois Gazetteer*). Post office established June 15, 1857.

GRIGG. Randolph. Four miles east-southeast of Red Bud. Established as a station on the St. Louis and Cairo Railroad and named for S. E. Grigg, proprietor of the general store and operator of a local grain elevator (http://illtrails.org/randolph/t4r7.htm). Post office established March 23, 1904.

GRINDSTONE CREEK. McDonough. Stream. Originally called Turkey Creek, presumably for the wild turkeys in the area. Renamed for the stone, useful for grindstones, which was quarried near the site (Clarke, *History of McDonough County,* 602). Post office established Sept. 27, 1853.

GRINNELL. Massac. Eleven miles northwest of Metropolis. Several writers have suggested that the name derives from the fish known as the bowfin or grindle (pronounced [GRIN uhl] in southern Illinois). It is also possible that Grinnell is the name of a local family or families, perhaps related to that of J. B. Grinnell, the founder of Grinnell, Iowa (*History of Massac County,* 24). Post office established April 14, 1890.

GRISHAM. Montgomery. Township. Named for Spartan Grisham, reported to be the first permanent settler in the area. Grisham was also an early county commissioner and a justice of the peace. Formerly known as Bear Creek (Bateman and Selby, eds., *Historical Encyclopedia of Illinois and History of Montgomery County,* 872; Perrin, ed., *History of Bond and Montgomery Counties,* 402).

GRIST ISLAND. Grundy. Island in the Illinois River four miles west-southwest of Morris. Originally called Perry's Island for Perry Claypool. Renamed for the Grist family which owned the adjacent mainland (Brown, ed., *Grundy County,* 20).

GRISWOLD. Lawrence. Fourteen miles east of Pontiac. Founded in 1866. Named for William D. Griswold, then general superintendent of the Ohio and Mississippi Railroad. Now part of Lawrenceville (Bateman and Selby, eds., *Illinois Historical Lawrence County Biographical,* 637).

GROSS. Hardin. Seven miles north of Rosiclare. Named for the Gross family. The first post office was established in John Gross's store in 1891 (*Hardin County,* 116). Post office established June 8, 1891, as Grossville; changed to Gross Nov. 9, 1905.

GROSS PARK. Chicago community. Founded by developer Samuel Eberly Gross, also the namesake of Grossdale (now Brookfield). Now part of Chicago (Karlen, *Chicago's Crabgrass Communities,* 130). Post office established Feb. 18, 1886.

GROVELAND. LaSalle. Township. Origin uncertain. Possibly named by John Wadleigh for Groveland, Essex County, Mass.; possibly named for John Grove, an early settler (Burns, *A Link to the Past,* 18; *History of LaSalle County,* 296).

GRUNDY. County. Created Feb. 17, 1841, from LaSalle County. Named for Felix Grundy (1777–1840), a Kentucky and Tennessee lawyer and statesman who served in the U.S. House of Representatives and Senate in the 1830s. The name was proposed by William E. Armstrong, who was instrumental in the organization of the county and admired Grundy. Felix Township is also named for Felix Grundy (Bateman and Selby, eds., *Historical Encyclopedia of Illinois and History of Grundy County,* 639).

GULFPORT. Henderson. Village (1928) east of Burlington, Iowa. Originally a ferry landing called East Burlington. The ferry ceased operations with completion of the Burlington railroad bridge. Laid out in 1855 by Maj. W. A. Armstrong and A. D. Green, a representative of the Chicago, Burlington and Quincy Railroad, which planned a center for stockyards and shipping at the site. The source of the name is unknown (*Illinois Gazetteer;* Sutton, *Rivers, Railways,* 30, 35).

GURNEE [ger NEE]. Lake. Village (1928). Founded about 1873 with construction of the Chicago, Milwaukee and St. Paul Railroad and named for Walter S. Gurnee, a director of the CM&StP and mayor of Chicago from 1852 to 1853. The choice of the name may have been influenced by Louis J. Gurnee, a surveyor for the railroad (*see* Glencoe) (Dretske, *What's in a Name?; Illinois Guide*). Post office established Feb. 23, 1847, as Wentworth; changed to O'Plain Aug. 10, 1870; changed to Gurnee Station June 27, 1874; changed to Gurnee July 27, 1874.

GUTHRIE. Ford. Four miles northeast of Gibson City. Established about 1876 as a station on the Illinois Central Railroad. Named for A. S. Guthrie, a stockholder and director of the IC (*Ford County History,* 44). Post office established May 22, 1876.

H

HADLEY. Pike. Ten miles northwest of Pittsfield. Named from Hadley Creek; itself named for Col. Levi Hadley, an early settler (*History of Pike County,* 240). Post office established July 20, 1870, as Cool Bank; changed to Coolbank July 3, 1895; changed to Hadley Jan. 20, 1899.

HADLEY. Will. Five miles east of Lockport. Founded about 1831 by a colony from New England. Probably named for Hadley, Mass. (Nelson, *The Role of Colonies,* 11). Post office established July 27, 1835.

HAEGERS BEND. McHenry. Two miles northeast of Algonquin. Founded about 1915 and named for site owners Arthur and Mae Haeger (Roop, *History of Fox River Grove*, 138).

HAHNAMAN. Whiteside. Eleven miles south of Sterling. Founded about 1852 and probably named in honor of Christian Friedrich Samuel Hahnemann (1755–1843), the founder of homeopathic medicine. The change in spelling may have been influenced by an early settler named Hahnaman (Stennett, *A History of the Origin*, 81). Post office established Sept. 9, 1872, as Hahneman.

HAINES. Township. Marion. Named for early settler Edmond Haines (*History of Marion and Clinton Counties*, 276).

HAINESVILLE. Lake. Village (1847, 1902) one mile west of Grayslake. Founded about 1846 by site owner Elijah M. Haines, the first postmaster, a state legislator and speaker of the Illinois House of Representatives in the 1870s (Halsey, ed., *A History of Lake County*, 397). Post office established Jan. 20, 1846.

HALDANE. Ogle. Seven miles west of Mount Morris. Founded by Alexander Haldane from Scotland, the first station agent for the Illinois Central Railroad (Ackerman, *Early Illinois Railroads*, 141). Post office established Aug. 29, 1856.

HALF DAY. Lake. Northwest of Lincolnshire. Founded in 1836. Half Day is a translation of Aptakisic (q.v.), the name of a Potawatomi leader of the 1830s and 1840s whose village was nearby. Half Day was annexed by Vernon Hills in 1996 (Vogel, *Indian Place Names in Illinois*). Post office established Aug. 22, 1836.

HALLIDAYBORO. Jackson. Ten miles north of Carbondale. Founded about 1889 as Muddy Valley. Renamed in 1894 for Capt. William P. Halliday of Cairo, part owner of the Muddy Valley Mining and Manufacturing Company (Sneed, *Ghost Towns of Southern Illinois*, 80). Post office established June 26, 1889, as Muddy Valley; changed to Hallidayboro Aug. 11, 1894.

HALLTOWN. Saline. Former community thirteen miles northwest of Harrisburg. Named from Hall Creek, itself named for Alfred Hall, the first postmaster (*History of Saline County*, 118). Post office established Aug. 25, 1862.

HAMBURG. Bond. Seven miles east-southeast of Greenville. Founded by Daniel Sturgis as New Hamburg, named for Hamburg, Germany. Also known as Sorghumtown for the cereal grain grown locally (Peterson, "Place Names of Bond County," 40).

HAMBURG [HAM berg]. Calhoun. Village (1897) sixteen miles west-southwest of Carrollton. Named for Hamburg, Germany (Underwood, "A New Geography of Calhoun County," 35). Post office established Oct. 31, 1829, as Hamburgh; changed to Hamburg Sept. 12, 1893.

HAMEL. Madison. Village (1955) seven miles northeast of Edwardsville. Named for A. J. "Jack" Hamel, who established a steam-powered flour mill at what was then known as Hamel's Corner shortly before 1820 (Norton, ed., *Centennial History of Madison County*, 523). Post office established March 30, 1871.

HAMILTON. County. Created Feb. 8, 1821, from White County. Named for Alexander Hamilton (1757–1804), a major figure in the early United States. Hamilton was an officer in the Revolutionary War and first secretary of the treasury. He died from a gunshot wound suffered in a duel with Aaron Burr in July 1804.

HAMILTON. Lee. Township. Probably named for the youngest son of Alexander Hamilton, William Stephen Hamilton, who established a lead mining operation near Galena in the late 1820s and later participated in the Black Hawk War. Hamilton reportedly was a frequent visitor to Dixon's Ferry (Stevens, *History of Lee County*, 43).

HAMLET. Mercer. Eight miles north of Aledo. Founded in 1868. Named for Hamlet Cooper, an early English settler (*History of Mercer and Henderson Counties*, 317). Post office established Oct. 18, 1854.

HAMLETSBURG. Pope. Village (1897) seventeen miles east of Metropolis on the Ohio River opposite Smithland, Ky. Founded by Hamlet Ferguson and his brother, Richard, in the 1820s. Formally organized in 1859. Hamlet Ferguson was instrumental in the organization of Pope and Johnson counties and was the first sheriff of Pope County (Ferguson, "'He Acted Well His Part'"). Post office established Feb. 2, 1885, as Hamletsburgh; changed to Hamletsburg Aug. 5, 1893.

HAMMOND. Moultrie, Piatt. Village (1890) thirteen miles north of Sullivan. The area was first known as Shumway and later as Unity. Hammond was laid out in 1873 where the Chicago and Paducah Railroad crossed the line of the Indianapolis, Decatur and Springfield. Named for Charles Goodrich Hammond, president of the ID&S (Morgan, ed., *The Good Life in Piatt County*, 12). Post office established Oct. 3, 1873.

HAMPSHIRE. Kane. Village (1876). Founded in the late 1830s and moved about three miles southwest to its present location with construction of the Chicago and Pacific Railroad about 1875. The generally accepted account is that Hampshire was named by its first mayor, Samuel Rowell, for his home state of New Hampshire. Formerly known as Henpeck (q.v.) (Dell'Angela, "Nothing but a Memory"; Van Matre, "Its Rural Feeling"; *Word and Picture Story*, 10, 14). Post office established Feb. 27, 1841.

HAMPTON. Rock Island. Village (1849, 1876). Founded in 1837 as Milan. The village and township were subsequently named for the Hampton post office. The source of the name is unknown (*Historic Rock Island County*, 101). Post office established Feb. 1, 1838.

HANAFORD. Franklin. Village (1909) five miles southeast of Du Quoin. Formerly known as Smothersville. The name was changed to Hanaford about 1908 for John P. Hanaford, a local real estate developer. In 1916 the name was apparently changed to Logan after the John A. Logan Coal Company, which operated the Black Star Coal Mine. The current status of the name is unclear. The Illinois secretary of state's list of incorporated municipalities has an entry for both Hanaford and Logan with a notation at Logan that the village was incorporated as Hanaford (*Franklin County*, 17; Ramsey and Miller, *The Heritage of Franklin County*, 34). Post office established Nov. 24, 1879, as Smothersville; changed to Hanaford Dec. 28, 1908.

HANCOCK. County. Created Jan. 13, 1825. Named for John Hancock (1737–93), president of the Continental Congress and governor of Massachusetts. His signature appears first on the Declaration of Independence. The county seat has been at Carthage since 1833.

HANNA. Henry. Township. Named for early settlers Philip, Washington, Luke, and Wesley Hanna, who arrived about 1835. Philip Hanna was one of the first local clergymen (Kiner, *History of Henry County*, 516).

HANNA CITY. Peoria. Village (1903) six miles west of Peoria. Laid out as Summerville by Robert G. McCullough. The site was purchased in 1882 by L. K. Gooding and J. I. Runkle and renamed Hanna City. The source of the name is unknown. Post office established Oct. 3, 1855, as Leo; changed to Summerville April 14, 1856; changed to Hanna City Jan. 23, 1883.

HANOVER. Cook. Township. The area was originally known as Independence Grove and later as Hoosier Grove. Named by German Protestant settlers from Hanover, Lower Saxony, Germany about 1850 (Bateman and Selby, eds., *Historical Encyclopedia of Illinois Cook County Edition*, 782).

HANOVER. Jo Daviess. Village (1849, 1877) thirteen miles southeast of Galena. Founded in the late 1820s by Daniel Fowler and Charles Ames. About 1836 James Craig purchased the site, which he named Wapello for a leader of the Meskwaki (Fox) tribe. At the suggestion of James W. White, the community was renamed Hanover in the early 1840s for White's former home, Hanover, Grafton County, N.H. (*see* Wapella) (Bateman and Selby, eds., *Historical Encyclopedia of Illinois and History of Jo Daviess County*, 634; *Illinois Guide*; Miller, *Hanover*, 11–12). Post office established July 14, 1836.

HARCO. Saline. Six miles northwest of Harrisburg. An acronym derived from the Harrisburg Colliery Company, which established the first coal mine in the area about 1917 (*History of Saline County*, 7). Post office established Nov. 21, 1917.

HARDIN. County. Created March 2, 1839, from Pope County. Several writers claim that Hardin county was named for the same Col. John J. Hardin for whom the village of Hardin in Calhoun County was named. In early 1839, however, when Hardin County was formed, John J. Hardin was an obscure army officer. He was, in fact, largely unknown until the Mexican War, when he led a charge of the First Illinois Volunteers at Buena Vista in 1847. The county was named for

Hardin County, Ky., home of a number of early settlers. The county in Kentucky was itself named for a different Col. John Hardin (and therein lies much of the confusion), a surveyor and veteran of the Revolutionary War. This John Hardin was killed by Indians in Ohio in 1792. The seat of Hardin County, Ill., is Elizabethtown, as is the seat of Hardin County, Ky. (Griffith, "Egyptian Place-Names," 30; Rennick, *Kentucky Place Names*).

HARDIN. Calhoun. Village (1880) fifteen miles west of Jerseyville. Known as Terry's Landing for Dr. William Terry until 1835, when Terry sold out to Benjamin Childs. Child's Landing was renamed Hardin in 1847 when the county seat was moved from Gilead. Hardin has been the seat of Calhoun County since that time. The name was chosen to honor Col. John J. Hardin, who was killed in the Mexican War (Carpenter, *Calhoun Is My Kingdom*, 26; *Illinois Gazetteer*). Post office established Feb. 21, 1848.

HARDIN. Township. Pike. Named for Jacob Henry Hardin, an early settler from Warren County, Ky. (*History of Pike County*, 593).

HARDING. LaSalle. Fourteen miles east of Mendota. Founded about 1845 and named for the Rev. Charles Harding, first pastor of the first Baptist church in the area (O'Byrne, *History of LaSalle*, 400). Post office established Oct. 30, 1844, as Munson; changed to Harding July 23, 1847.

HARDINVILLE. Crawford. Seven miles southwest of Robinson. Laid out about 1847 by Abel Prior and Daniel Martin, for whom Martin Township is named. The source of the name is unknown (*History of Crawford County*, 135). Post office established Sept. 27, 1853, as Hardinsville; changed to Hardinville Feb. 8, 1895.

HARGRAVE PRAIRIE. Wayne. Near Johnsonville. Named for Capt. Willis Hargrave, who came through the area toward the end of the War of 1812 (*History of Wayne and Clay Counties*, 204).

HARLEM. Cook. Named about 1856 by J. H. Quick for his birthplace, Harlem N.Y., itself named for Haarlem in the Netherlands by Peter Stuyvesant, governor of the Dutch colony of New Netherland (New York) (Bateman and Selby, eds., *Historical Encyclopedia of Illinois Cook County Edition*, 791).

HARLEM. Winnebago. Two miles east-southeast of Machesney Park. According to Stennett, the name was chosen "for the curious reason that Harlem was six miles from New York city and this [site] is six miles from Rockford, Ill." (*A History of the Origin*, 81). Post office established July 9, 1839.

HARMON. Lee. Village (1900) eight miles east-southeast of Rock Falls. Named for Dr. Harmon Wasson, a prominent local physician (Barge and Caldwell, "Illinois Place-Names"). Post office established April 29, 1872.

HARNESS. Logan. Six miles northeast of Mason City. Founded in 1900 for the Chicago and Alton Railroad by Daniel R. Harness (Stringer, *History of Logan County*, 622). Post office established Nov. 16, 1898.

HARP. DeWitt. Township. Named for early settlers Joseph and Tyre Harp (*History of DeWitt County, 1839–1968,* 432). Post office established Feb. 10, 1870.

HARRIS. Fulton. Township. Named for first settler John Harris, who emigrated from Ohio about 1825 (*History of Fulton County,* 615).

HARRISBURG. Saline. City (1861, 1888). Founded in 1853 and named for James A. Harris, one of the site owners. Harris emigrated from Tennessee and established a sawmill in what would become Harrisburg in the 1820s. Harrisburg has been the Saline County seat since 1859, when it was moved from Raleigh (*Saline County,* 11). Post office established April 25, 1846, as Bankton; changed to Harrisburg Feb. 28, 1856.

HARRISON. Winnebago. Nine miles northeast of Machesney Park. Founded in 1840 and named for William Henry Harrison, recently elected president of the United States (Nelson, comp., *Sinnissippi Saga,* 32). Post office established Jan. 20, 1846.

HARRISONVILLE. Bond. Former community eleven miles south-southwest of Hillsboro, east of Sorento. Founded in the 1830s by Andrew Finley and named for William Henry Harrison, defeated for president in 1836 and elected in 1840 (Peterson, "Place Names of Bond County," 40).

HARRISONVILLE. Monroe. Founded in July 1816 as Carthage. The name was changed later in 1816 in honor of William Henry Harrison, former governor of Indiana Territory and at the time a U.S. representative from Ohio (*Combined History of Randolph, Monroe, and Perry Counties,* 140, 413). Post office established Oct. 1, 1810.

HARRISTOWN. Macon. Village (1869) five miles west of Decatur. Formerly called Summit because it was thought to be the highest point between Indianapolis and Springfield. At the urging of Macon County veterans, the name was changed to honor Maj. Thomas Harris, commander of the Fourth Illinois Regiment during the Mexican War (Nelson, *City of Decatur,* 382; *Past and Present of the City of Decatur,* 70). Post office established March 2, 1858.

HARTER. Clay. Township. Created about 1860 and named for the Harter family, early settlers. George Harter was the first stationmaster at Flora (*History of Wayne and Clay Counties,* 361, 366).

HARTFORD. Madison. Village (1920), south suburb of Wood River. The source of the name is unknown. Founded in 1890 as Factory Town by the International Shoe Company of St. Louis. Also known as Saint Marie. Post office established Sept. 27, 1820.

HARTLAND [HAHRT luhnd]. McHenry. Three miles northwest of Woodstock. During discussions to choose a name for the community, a large number of immigrants from Ireland argued for Antrim, but an even larger number argued for their former home, Hartland, Niagara County, N.Y., itself named for

Hartland, Vt. (Nye, ed., *McHenry County Illinois,* 643, Vasiliev, *From Abbotts to Zurich*). Post office established Oct. 15, 1839.

HARTSBURG. Logan. Village (1886) seven miles northwest of Lincoln. Founded in 1871 by David H. Harts of Lincoln (Stringer, *History of Logan County,* 618). Post office established Oct. 19, 1871, as Hartsburgh; changed to Hartsburg Jan. 4, 1893.

HARTSVILLE. Pope. Named for the Hart family. John Byron Hart kept a general store in the 1880s (*Pope County,* 231). Post office established April 17, 1882.

HARVARD. McHenry. City (1867, 1891). In 1856 Elbridge Gerry Ayer, a justice of the peace and hotel keeper, donated land to secure a station on the Chicago and North Western Railroad. Ayer, from Haverhill, Mass., named the community for Harvard, Mass., some thirty miles northwest of Boston (and coincidentally very close to the town of Ayer) (*Biographical Directory of the Tax-Payers and Voters of McHenry County,* 157; Nye, ed., *McHenry County Illinois,* 441). Post office established Jan. 28, 1846, as Dunham; changed to Harvard Jan. 9, 1857.

HARVEL. Christian, Montgomery. Village (1873) fifteen miles northeast of Litchfield. Founded in 1869 by John Harvel as a station on the Wabash Railroad (Bateman and Selby, eds., *Historical Encyclopedia of Illinois and History of Montgomery County,* 881). Post office established June 13, 1871.

HARVEY. Cook. City (1891). The area was first known as South Lawn, and its first industry was the Hopkins Mower Works, established in 1880 by Harvey L. Hopkins. By 1891 Turlington Harvey had made major land purchases in the area that he conveyed to his umbrella organization, the Harvey Land Association, presumably named for himself. Harvey made it clear that he wanted the community to be named Turlington, but that met with unexpected opposition. Postmaster William H. Pease suggested Harvey, which, consciously or not, honored both Turlington Harvey and Harvey Hopkins. The name change from South Lawn became official in 1890 (*City of Harvey,* 16). Post office established Dec. 13, 1875, as South Lawn; changed to Harvey March 4, 1890.

HARWOOD. Champaign. Township. Originally called Sheldon; later changed to Shuck and to Harwood in 1870. Named for Abel Harwood of Champaign, a member of the county's board of supervisors and a delegate to the Illinois Constitutional Convention of 1870 (Bateman and Selby, eds., *Historical Encyclopedia of Illinois and History of Champaign County,* 813). Post office established May 5, 1876.

HARWOOD HEIGHTS. Cook. Village (1947). The generally accepted account is that the word *Harwood* blends the names of Harlem Avenue, a major village thoroughfare, and Norwood Park, the township in which Harwood Heights is located. It is also possible that the name derives from a contractor named Harwood who reportedly built part of the community (Fegelman, "It's Not Chicago"; *Illinois Guide*).

HAVANA. Mason. City (1853, 1872). Founded in the 1820s and formally laid out in 1835 by site owner Ossian M. Ross, the founder of Lewistown. According to local sources, the Island of Canton (Bell Rose Island) north of the mouth of Spoon River is generally shaped like the island of Cuba. The resemblance reportedly suggested the name *Havana*. The city is situated, however, among a number of other communities that have exotic names, including Bath, Matanzas, Liverpool, and Moscow, and the name may have been chosen simply for its foreign flavor. Cuba, named several years later, is some fifteen miles north northwest of Havana, which has been the seat of Mason County since 1851, when it was moved from Bath (Cochran, *Centennial History of Mason County*; Lynn, *Prelude to Progress,* 199). Post office established April 23, 1829.

HAWTHORN WOODS. Lake. Village (1958). Established as a residential subdivision in 1953. Reportedly named for the local hawthorn trees (Dretske, *What's in a Name?*).

HAYES. Douglas. Four miles north of Tuscola. Named about 1877 for Samuel Jarvis Hayes, superintendent of machinery for the Illinois Central Railroad (Ackerman, *Early Illinois Railroads,* 127). Post office established July 26, 1877.

HAYPRESS. Greene. Seven miles northwest of Carrollton. The name was changed from Bluffdale when the first hay press (forerunner of the hay baler) was brought to the area (Cunningham, *History of the Carrollton, Illinois, Area,* 21).

HAZEL CREST. Cook. Village (1911). Founded about 1891 as South Harvey by William McClintock, a newspaper publisher from Ohio. The name was changed about 1900, presumably for the local hazel bushes. Neighboring East Hazel Crest, in an attempt to establish its own identity, has considered changing its name on several occasions. In the 1940s the owner of Washington Park Racetrack offered the village a number of incentives if it would annex the track and change its name to Washington Park, but this, like all referenda to date, was defeated by East Hazel Crest voters (*Illinois Guide*; Lonngren, "Glacial Lake Spawns Town"; Schoon, *Calumet Beginnings,* 121; Smith, "But There's No Shortage of Good Neighbors"). Post office established Feb. 8, 1892, as South Harvey; changed to Hazel Crest Aug. 22, 1906.

HAZEL DELL. Cumberland. Seven miles south-southwest of Casey. Founded about 1845 and formally laid out in 1866. A local story is that the community was named for a popular song of the day, "Hazel Dell," by George F. Root. The Hazledell post office, however, was established several years before the song was published. The popularity of the song may have influenced the change in spelling from Hazledell to Hazel Dell (*Cumberland County History,* 357). Post office established Aug. 1, 1851, as Hazledell.

HEATHSVILLE. Crawford. Fifteen miles northeast of Lawrenceville. Named from the Heath Inn, a roadhouse on the stagecoach line from Vincennes operated by Renick Heath (*History of Crawford County,* 146). Post office established Nov. 12, 1874.

HEBRON [HEE bruhn]. McHenry. Village (1895) nine miles east-northeast of Harvard. Named by Harriet Tryon, wife of the first postmaster of Hebron. The Tryons frequently held songfests at their home, which were attended by large numbers of the area's bachelors. At one of these events, following the singing of the hymn "Hebron," Mrs. Tryon is said to have remarked, "That is my choice of all tunes and I think the name Hebron would make a good name for our township." The name was accepted "enthusiastically." The village of Hebron was originally called Mead Station, named for Henry W. Mead, who donated land to the Chicago and North Western Railroad and in return was appointed the first station agent (*History of McHenry County* [1885], 707, 727). Post office established July 1, 1839.

HECKER. Monroe. Village (1895) six miles north of Red Bud. Formerly known as Freedom. The name was changed in the mid-1860s to honor Friedrich Karl Franz Hecker, the political activist who attempted to establish a German republic in 1848. Hecker fled to the United States the same year. He served in the Union Army during the Civil War and later settled in St. Clair County (Klein, ed., *Arrowheads to Aerojets,* 588). Post office established Feb. 13, 1854.

HEGELER. Vermilion. Three miles south of Danville. Named for Herman and Julius Hegeler, who established a zinc plant at the site in 1906 (Underwood, "A New Geography of Illinois: Vermilion County," 39).

HEGEWISCH. Cook. Two miles north of Calumet City. A planned residential and industrial community founded in 1883 by Achilles Hegewisch, president of the United States Rolling Stock Company (later the United States Steel and Supply Company) (Kitagawa and Taeuber, eds., *Local Community Fact Book,* 124). Post office established July 28, 1884.

HELMAR. Kendall. Seven miles south-southwest of Yorkville. Laid out about 1899 and named for an early Norwegian settler, Hjalmar Anderson. Formerly known as North Prairie (Dickson, "Geographical Features and Place Names"). Post office established June 13, 1894.

HELVETIA. Madison. Township. In 1831 Dr. Kaspar Koepfli of Sursee, Lucerne, Switzerland, led a group of Swiss colonists to Looking Glass Prairie, where they established a community called Highland about 1837. Because of a post office conflict, the name was changed to Helvetia, the Latin name for Switzerland, in 1840. When the name of the existing Highland post office was changed in 1843, Helvetia and the Helvetia post office were renamed Highland. The name of Highland Precinct was changed to Helvetia at the time of township organization in 1875 (Coats and Spahn, *The Swiss on Looking Glass Prairie,* 50; Norton, ed., *Centennial History of Madison County,* 527). Post office established Jan. 23, 1840.

HEMAN. Macon. Nine miles northwest of Decatur. Originally called Bullardsville, named for Warner Bullard, a local grain elevator operator. The name was changed by the Illinois Central Railroad, possibly for an employee named Heman (Richmond, *Centennial History of Decatur,* 97).

HENDERSON. Henderson County, the communities of Henderson and Henderson Grove, Henderson Township in Knox County, the village of North Henderson, and North Henderson Township in Mercer County all take their name from Henderson Creek, which heads in Knox County and flows through Mercer, Warren, and Henderson counties before emptying into the Mississippi River near Gladstone. The source of the stream name is unknown. It derives either from a local Henderson family or is a transfer.

HENDRIX. McLean. Three miles south of Bloomington. Named for John Hendrix, generally regarded as the first permanent settler in McLean County, arriving about 1822 (Ackerman, *Early Illinois Railroads,* 164). Post office established July 18, 1876.

HENLINE CREEK. McLean. Stream. Named for John Henline, who, along with his brothers George and William, emigrated from Boone County, Ky., about 1828 (*History of McLean County,* 639).

HENNEPIN [HEN uh puhn]. Putnam. Village (1839, 1872) eight miles northeast of Henry. Named for Fr. Jean Louis Hennepin, the Franciscan Recollect friar who accompanied LaSalle on his expedition to the Mississippi River in 1679 (Hansen, ed., *Illinois,* 724). Post office established Oct. 31, 1831.

HENNING. Vermilion. Village (1904) eleven miles south of Hoopeston. Founded as a station on the Havana, Rantoul and Eastern Illinois Railroad by site owner John Putnam. By one account, "John Putnam asked for a suggestion for a name. Someone replied 'Call it Henning after my wife. Her name is Henning. I liked the name in courting days and I would like my wife to gain some distinction from marrying me'" (Stapp, *History under Our Feet,* 49). Another account claims that Putnam named the station for his wife's family, saying that her maiden name was Henning (Underwood, "A New Geography of Illinois: Vermilion County," 39). Post office established Feb. 19, 1878.

HENPECK. Kane. Henpeck is located at the junction of Big Timber Road and U.S. 20, about three miles northeast of Hampshire. The origin of this curious and intriguing name is unknown. By the 1830s Henpeck was a celebrated rest stop, camp ground, and tavern catering to teamsters and travelers on the Chicago-Galena road. As the 1878 history of Kane County describes the scene, "It was no uncommon occurrence for fifty and sixty wagons to camp over night at the old village of Hampshire, known familiarly by . . . the sobriquet of 'Hen Peck.' It was then that there was kept at Hen Peck a kind of summer bar room, for the accommodation of thirsty travelers" (465). The name invites popular etymologies. William Schmidt, a former mayor of Hampshire, maintains, "There was a mill out there, with a lot of hens pecking at the grain, and that is one explanation of the name Henpeck. . . . Another explanation is that the postmaster there was henpecked by his wife. Lore has it that he finally went just up the road—presumably without his wife—and started another little settlement called Harmony" (Van Matre, "Its Rural Feeling"). Laurence Seits has suggested that the origin of the name may lie with a tavern keeper or local merchant named Henry Peck, known familiarly as Hen Peck. Several Peck families were prominent in the area in the 1830s, but I have been unable to locate a likely Henry Peck. There have been at least three other Hen Pecks in Illinois. Oblong in Crawford County was once known by that name (and there its source is very likely a Henry Peck); Hen Peck is another name for Rossville in Vermilion County; and Alvin, five miles southeast of Rossville, is claimed to have been known "far and near" as Henpeck. The name has also been reported in Kentucky, Missouri, and Ohio (Bateman and Selby, eds., *Historical Encyclopedia of Illinois and History of Kane County*, 713; *Past and Present of Kane County*, 465; Seits, "The Names of Kane County," 171).

HENRIETTA. DeKalb. Former community southwest of Genoa. Named for Henrietta Hesing, wife of Washington Hesing, publisher of the German-language *Illinois Staats Zeitung*, a Chicago newspaper that began publication in the 1840s. Hesing offered to donate a bell for the Henrietta town hall, but it is unknown if the bell was ever installed (Stennett, *A History of the Origin*, 83).

HENRY. Marshall. City (1854, 1879). Founded about 1833 and named for Gen. James D. Henry, commander of Illinois volunteers during the Black Hawk War of 1832. The name was likely suggested by Hooper Warren, a friend of Henry's and clerk of the court in Hennepin. Henry, located on the Illinois River, promotes itself as the "best town in Illinois by a dam site" (*History of Marshall County*, 37). Post office established Nov. 18, 1836.

HENRY. County. Created January 13, 1825. Named for Patrick Henry (1736–99), Revolutionary War–era statesman and orator, member of the Continental Congress, and governor of Virginia.

HENSLEY. Champaign. Township. Organized in 1867 and named for Archibald P. Hensley, the first township supervisor (*History of Champaign County*, 118).

HENTON. Shelby. Seven miles northwest of Shelbyville. Named for Isiah Henton, shopkeeper and first postmaster (Gordon, *Here and There in Shelby County*, 94). Post office established Sept. 3, 1884.

HERALDS PRAIRIE. White. Township. From the prairie named for a Mr. Herald, about whom little is known. As an early history of White County laconically puts it, "After squatting on the prairie for a time, Herald . . . moved West" (*History of White County*, 821).

HERBERT. Boone. Five miles northwest of Genoa. Named by Daniel D. Bathrick, an official of the Chicago and North Western Railroad, for his son, Herbert (Stennett, *A History of the Origin,* 83). Post office established March 17, 1880, as Will; changed to Herbert Oct. 11, 1886.

HEROD. Pope. Northwest corner of Pope County. Originally known as Herod Springs, named for the Herod family. David W. Herod Sr., David W. Herod Jr., John A. L. Herod, and Thomas G. S. Herod were early postmasters (Adams, comp., *Illinois Place Names;* Allen Collection). Post office established April 19, 1888, as Herod Springs; changed to Herod July 26, 1895.

HERR GOTT'S ECK. Monroe. A strip of land in the extreme eastern part of the county, between Richland Creek and the Okaw and Kaskaskia rivers. German for "Mr. Gott's Corner," perhaps named for a land owner named Gott (Klein, ed., *Arrowheads to Aerojets,* 587).

HERRICK. Fayette, Shelby. Village (1890) twelve miles southeast of Pana. Originally known as Beck's Creek for early settler Guy Beck. Herrick was formally laid out in 1881 as New London by William T. Hadley. The name was changed to honor Jacob T. Herrick in appreciation for his efforts in securing a railroad station in 1883 (Bateman and Selby, eds., *Historical Encyclopedia of Illinois and History of Shelby County,* 656; http://herrickil.com). Post office established Sept. 5, 1848, as Beck's Creek; changed to London March 29, 1882; changed to Herrick Aug. 16, 1883.

HERRIN. Williamson. City (1898). Named from Herrin's Prairie, itself named for Isaac Herring, generally regarded as the first permanent settler, who entered a claim at Shawneetown in 1816. Over time Herring's name (informally pronounced [HEHR uhn] or [HEHR in]) came to be written *Herrin.* Ephraim S. Herrin and David R. Harrison, grandsons of Isaac Herring, are credited with the founding of Herrin in 1896. Ephraim Herrin was also instrumental in developing the local coal industry (Hale, comp. and ed., *Williamson County,* 180; Hubbs, *Pioneer Folks and Places*). Post office established May 26, 1864, as Herrin's Prairie; changed to Herrin May 8, 1896.

HERSCHER. Kankakee. Village (1882) twelve miles southwest of Kankakee. Founded in 1878 by site owner John Herscher, who later served as the first village president (Bateman and Selby, eds., *Historical Encyclopedia of Illinois and History of Kankakee County,* 759). Post office established July 11, 1870, as Pilot Centre; changed to Herscher March 24, 1879.

HERSMAN [HERZ muhn, HERS muhn]. Brown. Two miles southeast of Mount Sterling. Named for George Hersman, a mill operator of the 1860s, or for William T. Hersman, an early postmaster (Adams, comp., *Illinois Place Names; Combined History of Schuyler and Brown Counties,* 253). Post office established June 21, 1861, as Hersmans; changed to Hersman June 1, 1865.

HERVEY CITY. Macon. Five miles southeast of Decatur. Founded about 1872 on land owned by P. S. Outten and named for Robert G. Hervey, president of the Paris and Decatur Railroad (Richmond, *Centennial History of Decatur*, 96). Post office established Jan. 20, 1879, as Henry City (a likely misreading or mishearing of Hervey).

HEYWORTH. McLean. Village (1869, 1901). Founded about 1855 by the Illinois Central Railroad and named for Laurence Heyworth, an IC stockholder and former member of the British parliament (Ackerman, *Early Illinois Railroads*, 146; *Illinois Guide*). Post office established April 29, 1847, as Short's Point; changed to Independence May 22, 1850; changed to Heyworth March 29, 1858.

HIAWATHA. Although Hiawatha was an Iroquois leader of the mid-fifteenth century, most occurrences of the name are from Henry Wadsworth Longfellow's popular narrative poem *The Song of Hiawatha* (1855). There are more than a hundred Hiawathas in the United States, most being the names of schools, parks, or campgrounds. In Illinois, three schools and one park are named Hiawatha.

HICKORY. Although most of the several dozen Hickories in Illinois are named for the American tree, Hickory Township in Schuyler County is probably named for Andrew Jackson, known as "Old Hickory" (*Combined History of Schuyler and Brown Counties*, 241, 269).

HICKS. Hardin. Four miles south of the Garden of the Gods State Park. Founded about 1890 by Vol Ferrell, who opened a general store and established the first post office on land he bought from Charles Hicks (*Hardin County*, 16). Post office established Aug. 7, 1891.

HIDALGO [heye DAL go]. Jasper. Village (1900) twelve miles north of Newton. Laid out in 1878 as Briggs Station on the line of the Peoria, Decatur and Evansville Railroad by George D. Briggs. Renamed later in 1878, taking the name of the Hidalgo post office, which may have been named for the Treaty of Guadalupe Hidalgo, which formally ended the Mexican War in 1848 (*Jasper County*, 14). Post office established April 4, 1854.

HIGGINSVILLE. Vermilion. Seven miles northwest of Danville. Laid out about 1836 as Vermilion Rapids by Amando D. Higgins and Marcus C. Stearnes, who anticipated a station on the Chicago and Eastern Illinois Railroad. Unfortunately for Vermilion Rapids, the railroad came through Jamesburg instead (Williams, *History of Vermilion County*, 497). Post office established June 28, 1851.

HIGHLAND [HEYE luhnd]. Madison. City (1863, 1884). Settled largely by immigrants from Sursee, Switzerland. Founded about 1837 with the support and assistance of James Semple, then speaker of the Illinois House of Representatives, with the expectation that the railroad from Alton to Mount Carmel would pass near the site. The founders, Joseph Suppiger and Kaspar Koepfli, favored a name such as Helvetia or New Switzerland. Semple, however, thought a more appropriate name would be Highland, which sounded less foreign than Helvetia yet suggested the landscape of Switzerland. Unfortunately for Highland, poor economic conditions and general mismanagement postponed the building of the railroad for thirty years (*see* Helvetia) (Spencer, *Centennial History of Highland,* 26, 146). Post office established Jan. 23, 1840, as Helvetia; changed to Highland Dec. 15, 1843.

HIGHLAND PARK. Lake. City (1869, 1875). Modern Highland Park has its origins in two small settlements on the shore of Lake Michigan: Port Clinton and St. John. About 1854, with construction of the Chicago and Milwaukee Railroad, the site was purchased by Walter Gurnee, who named the station Highland Park, perhaps for its associations with the highlands of Scotland, his ancestral home. Highmoor, a confected faux Scottish name, is northwest of Highland Park (*see* Glencoe and Gurnee) (*Past and Present of Lake County,* 262). Post office established Jan. 13, 1849, as St. John; changed to Port Clinton March 19, 1850; changed to Highland Park Dec. 14, 1861.

HIGHWOOD. Lake. City (1886). Founded about 1868 by E. Ashley Mears and the Rev. William Wallace Everts. Named Highwood because the site was presumed to be the highest point between Chicago and Milwaukee (Wittelle, *Twenty-eight Miles North,* 25). Post office established May 6, 1872.

HILLERMAN. Massac. Ten miles west-northwest of Metropolis. Named for L. D. Hillerman, who purchased the site in the mid-1830s. The original Hillerman, about one mile south of the present community, was washed away by the Ohio River. According to a local story, one of Hillerman's best-known residents was a woman named Culpepper who spent her time going from house to house and gossipping with her neighbors, earning her the nickname *Gabby;* the community's nickname thus became Gabbtown (*History of Massac County,* 25; May, *History of Massac County,* 174). Post office established Sept. 8, 1843.

HILLSBORO. Montgomery. City (1855, 1882). When Montgomery County was organized in 1821, the commissioners appointed to locate the county seat chose a site about three miles southwest of present Hillsboro and called it Hamilton. For reasons that are unclear, there was a great deal of dissatisfaction with that name, and it was changed to Hillsboro in 1823. The source of the name is unknown. It has been attributed to undulations in the prairie (the "hills"); to settlers from Hillsboro, Ky.; and to Hillsborough, N.C., the former home of John Nussman, reported to be the area's first permanent settler (Bliss and Bliss, *Hillsboro,* 4; *Hillsboro Guide,* 9, 12, 13). Post office established July 7, 1821, as Hamilton; changed to Hillsboro Dec. 30, 1823.

HILLSDALE. Rock Island. Village (1950) seventeen miles northeast of Moline. Probably named by the founder, James Hill, an English immigrant and early postmaster (Bateman and Selby, eds., *Historical Encyclopedia of Illinois and*

History of Rock Island County, 941, 958). Post office established Feb. 1, 1870, as Hill's Station; changed to Hillsdale Feb. 28, 1871.

HILLYARD. Macoupin. Township. Named for the Hilyard family. John M. Hilyard emigrated from Virginia in 1831. Through popular etymology "Hilyard" became "Hillyard" (*History of Macoupin County,* 248).

HIMROD. Vermilion. Five miles south-southeast of Danville. Founded about 1850 and named for the Himrod Coal Company. Joseph B. Himrod was an early postmaster (Adams, comp., *Illinois Place Names;* Tuggle, comp., *Stories of Historical Days,* 16). Post office established Jan. 20, 1900.

HINCKLEY. DeKalb. Village (1877) eight miles north of Sandwich. Established in 1872 and named for Francis E. Hinckley, president of the Chicago and Iowa Railroad (*Illinois Guide*). Post office established Jan. 27, 1853, as Squaw Grove; changed to Hinckley Aug. 12, 1872.

HINDSBORO. Douglas. Village (1889) nine miles east of Arcola. Laid out in 1873 by the Paris and Decatur Railroad as Hinesborough and named for the Hines brothers, the site owners (Gresham, comp., *Historical and Biographical Record,* 79). Post office established April 2, 1873, as Hinesborough; changed to Hindsboro May 16, 1892.

HINSDALE. Cook, DuPage. Village (1897). The temporary station established by the Burlington Railroad in the early 1860s was called Brush Hill. When the permanent facility was being constructed under the direction of Charles G. Hammond, Isaac S. Bush, Hammond's friend who was active in real estate, suggested the name *Hinsdale,* for Bush's birthplace, Hinsdale, N.Y. Hammond then suggested the name to William Robbins, who was developing the community, and also to railroad officials. Hammond was favorably disposed to the name because of his friend and business associate Henry W. Hinsdale, a leading figure in Chicago's business and civic community in the 1860s and a member of the Chicago Board of Trade. For many years both Bush and Hinsdale claimed to have provided the "true" source of the name. The one person who might have set the record straight, Charles Hammond, died while shopping at Marshall Field's in Chicago in 1884 (Bakken, *Hinsdale,* 11–13; Dugan, *Villages on the County Line,* 48, 62). Post office established May 6, 1867.

HIRE. McDonough. Township. Changed from Rock Creek in 1857. Named for George W. Hire, a veteran of the War of 1812 and an Illinois state legislator in the 1850s (*History of McDonough County,* 629).

HITTLE. Tazewell. Twelve miles north of Lincoln. Named for George Hittle, who along with his son, Jonas, emigrated from Ohio in 1825. Hittle Township was created as Union early in 1850; the name was changed to Armington in May 1850 and to Hittle in August 1850 (Bateman and Selby, eds., *Historical Encyclopedia of Illinois and History of Tazewell County,* 813).

HODGES PARK. Alexander. Eleven miles northwest of Cairo. Founded about 1876 by A. C. Atherton and Alexander C. Hodges, a circuit judge of Alexander County (Fults, Chisholm and Novella, *Promised Land in Southern Illinois,* 81). Post office established March 1, 1834, as Unity; changed to Hodges Park May 8, 1876.

HODGEVILLE. Pope. Fifteen miles northeast of Metropolis. Named for the Hodge family. George Hodge was an early settler; John Hodge and Della Hodge were early postmasters (Page, *History of Massac County,* 271). Post office established Jan. 19, 1899.

HODGKINS. Cook. Village (1896). Italian immigrants who worked on the Chicago Sanitary and Ship Canal in the 1890s called the community Gary, perhaps a shortening of Garabaldi, for Giuseppe Garabaldi, who united Italy in the 1860s. When the village was formally laid out it was named for Jefferson Hodgkins, president of the Kimball and Cobb Stone Company, the major employer in the area. There have been several attempts in recent years to change the name in order to disassociate the community from any perceived connections with Hodgkin's Disease, but to date they have come to nothing (Zorn, "Small-Town").

HOFFMAN ESTATES. Cook. Village (1959). Named for Sam Hoffman and his son, Jack, who together built the first subdivision in the area in 1955. In the late 1990s the village considered changing its name to East Barrington in order to trade on the fashionable connotations of the name *Barrington,* but the referendum was defeated by a margin of eleven to one (Christian, "Living Here").

HOLCOMB [HOL kuhm]. Ogle. Nine miles north of Rochelle. Founded about 1876. Named for William H. Holcomb, an officer of the Chicago and Iowa Railroad and superintendent of transportation at the Columbian Exposition of 1893 in Chicago (Bateman and Selby, eds., *Historical Encyclopedia of Illinois and History of Ogle County,* 822). Post office established Dec. 27, 1875.

HOLDER. McLean. Seven miles east of Bloomington. Founded in 1871 by Charles W. Holder, a director of the Lafayette and Bloomington Railroad (Hasbrouck, *History of McLean County,* 96; Quaid, *A Little Square,* 42). Post office established Sept. 23, 1872.

HOLIDAY HILLS. McHenry. Village (1976) five miles southeast of McHenry. A developer's promotional name. Holiday Hills originated as a residential subdivision developed by Riverview Homes in the 1950s. The community was organized around fairy-tale themes; early home models included the Cinderella and the Hansel and Gretel (Lavin, "Water, Water Everywhere").

HOLLIDAY. Fayette, Shelby. Twelve miles south of Shelbyville. Founded about 1873 by Thomas or Matthew Holliday (Hanabarger, "Fayette County Place Names," 47). Post office established April 4, 1872.

HOLLIS. Peoria. Two miles northwest of Pekin. Named for Denzil Hollis, an early settler from England (*History of Peoria County*, 595). Post office established Feb. 4, 1850.

HOLLOWAYVILLE. Bureau. Village (1893) eight miles east of Princeton. Known as the Hassler Settlement, named for John Hassler from Munich, Bavaria, until the 1850s when the community was formally laid out and named for himself by Dr. S. S. Holloway (*Bureau County Centennial*, n.p.; *Voters and Tax-Payers*, 162). Post office established Jan. 24, 1848, as Selby; changed to Hollowayville June 28, 1852.

HOLSTEIN. Kane. Former community in the northwestern corner of Rutland Township. Named for the Holstein Cheese Factory (Adams, comp., *Illinois Place Names; Biographical and Historical Record of Kane County*, 1068). Post office established July 6, 1876.

HOMBERG. Pope. Fifteen miles northeast of Metropolis. Established by the Illinois Central Railroad about 1902 on land donated by the family of J. F. "Fritz" Hombirg, a German immigrant. The name was errantly recorded as Homberg (*Pope County*, 31).

HOMER. Champaign. Village (1872) thirteen miles east-southeast of Urbana. Old Homer was established in the mid-1830s a mile or so north of present Homer. The traditional story is that M. D. Coffeen and Samuel Groendyke, shopkeepers and owners of the town site, were discussing the advantages of establishing a community to help their business. Groendyke supposedly said, "That would be more homer [i.e., homelike] to me." Coffeen replied, "Then Homer it will be." When the Wabash Railroad established a station some distance away, many of the buildings of Old Homer were loaded onto sleds and moved to trackside (Bateman and Selby, eds., *Historical Encyclopedia of Illinois and History of Champaign County*, 683; *History of Champaign County*, 150; *Illinois Guide;* Johnson, *Medicine in Champaign County*, 66). Post office established March 15, 1830, as Union; changed to Homer Oct. 19, 1841.

HOMER. Will. Township. Named by Alanson Granger for his former home, Homer, Cortland County, N.Y. (*History of Will County*, 525).

HOMETOWN. Cook. City (1953). Established about 1948 as a residential community for returning World War II veterans by entrepreneur Joseph E. Merrion, the founder of Merrionette Park (q.v.) (Johnson, "For Its Residents").

HOMEWOOD. Cook. City (1893). Originally called Hartford, named for James Hart who laid out the site in 1852. The stop on the Illinois Central Railroad was established in 1853 as Thornton Station. Confusion of Thornton Station with several other Thorntons in the area led to the change to Homewood in 1869. The name was suggested by Mrs. J. C. Howe after Homewood, Pa., near Pittsburgh (Ackerman, *Early Illinois Railroads*, 119; Adair and Sandberg, *Indian Trails to Tollways*, 22–25). Post office established Oct. 3, 1853, as Thornton Station; changed to Homewood Nov. 15, 1869.

HONONEGAH [hah nuh NEE guh]. Winnebago. Forest preserve. Named for Hononegah, the Winnebago wife of Stephen Mack, who established a trading post near Grand Detour in the 1820s. Mack is regarded as the first permanent settler in Winnebago County. The name reportedly means "dear little one" and was customarily given to the first girl born into a Winnebago family (Vogel, *Indian Place Names in Illinois*).

HOODVILLE. Hamilton. Three miles south of McLeansboro. Founded about 1866 and named for John D. Hood, an early settler (Harrelson, *Hoodville*, 3). Post office established April 12, 1871.

HOOKDALE. Bond. Seven miles southeast of Greenville. Laid out about 1883 as Lehnsville, named for site owner Louis Lehn, and changed to Hookdale in 1887. The name is probably that of a local Hook family or a promoter of the Jacksonville and Southeastern Railroad named Hook (Bateman and Selby, eds., *Historical Encyclopedia of Illinois and History of Bond County*, 632; Peterson, "Place Names of Bond County," 41). Post office established March 8, 1884, as Lehnsville; changed to Hookdale April 6, 1887.

HOOPESTON [HUP stuhn]. Vermilion. City (1877). Modern Hoopeston is the result of an early 1870s merger of three communities: Hoopeston, laid out by Thomas Hoopes and Joseph Satterwhaite; North Hoopeston, laid out by Alba Honeywell; and Leeds, established by the Chicago, Danville and Vincennes Railroad. Railroad officials proposed to name the station after Honeywell, who declined and in turn suggested Hoopeston, for Thomas Hoopes (Cox, comp., *A History of Hoopeston*, 1–2). Post office established Oct. 25, 1871.

HOOPPOLE [HOOP pol]. Henry. Village (1917) twenty miles southwest of Rock Falls. Apparently named by coopers from Rock Island who found that the hickory saplings in the area made excellent bands for their barrels (Kiner, *History of Henry County*, 661). Post office established July 12, 1880.

HOPEDALE. Tazewell. Village (1872) seventeen miles north of Lincoln. The township was known as Highland until 1850, when, for unknown reasons, the name was changed to Hopedale at the suggestion of Moses Meeker. The village of Hopedale was founded as Osceola, but when it was learned that there were several other Osceolas in Illinois the name was changed to agree with that of the township (Bateman and Selby, eds., *Historical Encyclopedia of Illinois and History of Tazewell County*, 821; *History of Tazewell County*, 494). Post office established Aug. 12, 1853.

HOPKINS. Whiteside. Township. Named for Jason Hopkins in recognition of his service in a cavalry regiment during the Black Hawk War (Davis, *History of Whiteside County*, 90). The Hopkins post office was active from March 7, 1882, until June 12, 1895.

HOPKINS PARK. Kankakee. Village (1970) six miles south-southeast of Kankakee. Named for Carey M. Hopkins. Formerly known as Pembroke (Bateman and

Selby, eds., *Historical Encyclopedia of Illinois and History of Kankakee County,* 751). Post office established June 6, 1889.

HOPPER. Henderson. Three miles east of Burlington, Iowa. Founded in 1838 by Lambert Hopper as Warren, possibly named for Warren, N.Y. (Sutton, *Rivers, Railways,* 30, 33). Post office established Aug. 17, 1839, as Hopper's Mills; changed to Hopper May 16, 1894.

HORACE. Edgar. Three miles north of Paris. Founded in 1876 by storekeeper and postmaster Horace Johnson (*History of Edgar County,* 537). Post office established Jan. 20, 1873.

HORD. Clay. Named for George Hord. Originally called Jordan for site owner William Jordan (*Prairie Echo,* 121). Post office established Nov. 10, 1858.

HOUSTON. [HYOO stuhn]. Adams. Township. Named for Sam Houston, president of the Republic of Texas in the late 1830s and early 1840s. A community called Houston was laid out in 1839 but never materialized (*History of Adams County,* 533; www.rootsweb.com/~iladams/places/placenames.htm). The Houston post office was active from Oct. 22, 1838, until Dec. 12, 1864.

HOUSTON Randolph. Five miles northwest of Sparta. Founded in 1868 with the establishment of the first blacksmith shop and the first general store by William Houston (*Randolph County,* 100). Post office established July 7, 1874.

HOWARD. Fulton. Ten miles west of Havana. Named for the Howard family. Samuel Howard was a local merchant and an early county sheriff (*Fulton County Heritage,* 177).

HOYLETON. Washington. Village (1881) nine miles northeast of Nashville. Established about 1857 by a group of Congregational ministers under the leadership of the Rev. J. A. Bent and known as Yankeetown for the many settlers from New England. When the community was formally laid out it was named for Henry Hoyle, who donated a bell for the seminary (Brinkman, ed., *This Is Washington County,* 22). Post office established Dec. 17, 1857.

HUDGENS. Williamson. Four miles south of Marion. Established in the early 1900s as a station on the Chicago and Eastern Illinois Railroad on land owned by Zachariah Hudgens (Hale, comp. and ed., *Williamson County,* 118). Post office established May 18, 1900.

HUDSON. McLean. Village (1888) six miles north of Normal. Founded in the late 1830s. Named for Hudson, N.Y., home of several founding members of the Illinois Land Association, which was organized for the purpose of establishing a colony in Illinois. Each member of the colony was to receive a quarter section of land, four lots in the proposed village of Hudson, and a portion of the overall profits of the enterprise. After a number of setbacks, some twenty shareholders eventually settled in the area (Bateman and Selby, eds., *Historical*

Encyclopedia of Illinois and History of McLean County, 710; *History of McLean County*, 603–4). Post office established Oct. 5, 1836.

HUFFMANVILLE. Edgar. Seven miles east-northeast of Paris. Probably named for Daniel Huffman, site owner, storekeeper, and postmaster. Possibly named for Oscar Huffman, also a postmaster (Adams, comp., *Illinois Place Names; History of Edgar County*, 389). Post office established April 17, 1872.

HULL. Pike. Village (1892) eight miles east of Hannibal, Mo. Founded about 1871 as Hull's by postmaster David Hull (Adams, comp., *Illinois Place Names*). Post office established Nov. 20, 1871.

HUMBOLDT. Coles. Village (1878) five miles south of Arcola. Humboldt Township was first called Milton, named for local businessman J. Milton True. The name was changed to Humbolt in 1860 at the suggestion of postmaster Arick A. Sutherland, an admirer of the German traveler and naturalist Friederich Heinrich Alexander von Humboldt, who had died the year before. The community was platted about 1859, also as Milton, but in spite of a name change to Milton Station it was frequently confused with Milton in Pike County. This led to the change to Humbolt in 1875. Official Illinois documents retained the spelling *Humbolt* until at least 1902, a decade after the name of the post office had been changed to Humboldt. Von Humboldt is also the namesake of the Chicago community of Humboldt Park (Bateman and Selby, eds., *Historical Encyclopedia of Illinois and History of Coles County*, 711; *History of Coles County* [1976], 316; Perrin, Graham, and Blair, *History of Coles County*, 470, 477–78). Post office established March 16, 1858, as Milton Station; changed to Humbolt June 25, 1875; changed to Humboldt June 20, 1892.

HUME. Edgar. Village (1881) fifteen miles northwest of Paris. Founded in 1873 on land owned by postmaster Elizipahn W. S. Hume and others (*History of Edgar County*, 523). Post office established Feb. 2, 1874.

HUMM WYE. Hardin. Twenty-two miles south-southeast of Harrisburg. Named for the "Y" intersection (viewed from the north) of Illinois routes 34 and 146, constructed on the farm owned by Frederick "Fritz" Humm (*Hardin County*, 16; personal communication with Noel E. Hurford).

HUNT CITY. Jasper. Eight miles northeast of Newton. Named for John A. Hunt, who established the first general store in the area and was instrumental in procuring the post office in 1874 (*Counties of Cumberland, Jasper, and Richland*, 490). Post office established July 6, 1874, as Hunts City.

HUNTER. Edgar. Township. Named for John Hunter, who was instrumental in the creation of the township from Stratton and Brouilletts townships in 1851 (*Our First 150 Years*, 9; *Souvenir History of Edgar County*, 68).

HUNTLEY. McHenry. Village (1872). Founded in 1851 as a station on the Chicago and North Western Railroad by site owner Thomas Stillwell Huntley. Huntley built the first house in the area and kept the first general store (Nye, ed., *McHenry County Illinois,* 608). Post office established June 19, 1851, as Huntley Grove; changed to Huntley March 15, 1886.

HUNTSVILLE. Schuyler. Three miles southeast of Weinberg-King State Park. Founded in 1836 and named by George H. Brisco, one of the site owners, for his brother's home, Huntsville, Ala. (*Combined History of Schuyler and Brown Counties,* 241, 365). Post office established July 18, 1836.

HURLBUT. Logan. Township. Named for one or more members of the Hurlbut family. A William Hurlbut lived in Elkhart, an E. P. Hurlbut lived in Lincoln, and at least one Hurlbut served with the Forty-first Illinois during the Civil War (personal communication with the Logan County Genealogical and Historical Society).

HURRICANE. Fayette. Township. Named from Hurricane Creek, itself apparently named for an especially severe storm in the early 1800s (Bateman and Selby, eds., *Historical Encyclopedia of Illinois and History of Fayette County,* 645).

HURST. Williamson. City (1905) five miles northwest of Herrin. Founded about 1903. Named for William Charles Hurst, president of the Chicago, Peoria and St. Louis Railroad in the 1920s (Donovan, "Named for Railway Presidents," 26). Post office established Jan. 24, 1905.

HUTSONVILLE. Crawford. Village (1853, 1875) eight miles northeast of Robinson. Founded in 1832 and named for the Hutson family, a mother and six children who were killed in an Indian raid during the War of 1812 (Perrin, ed., *History of Crawford and Clark Counties,* iv, 29). Post office established Jan. 2, 1833.

HUTTON. Coles. Five miles southeast of Charleston. Founded about 1837 as Stewart by John Hulin and George K. Harris. The name was changed about 1850 to Ashby in honor of pioneer John Ashby, the town's first blacksmith. The confusion of Ashby with Ashley in Washington County led to the change to Hutton about 1861, named from Hutton Township, itself named for John Hutton, one of the commissioners who divided the county into townships. For a time the community was also known as Salisbury, a name chosen by John Hulin for his birthplace, Salisbury, N.C. (Bateman and Selby, eds., *Historical Encyclopedia of Illinois and History of Coles County,* 717; Perrin, Graham, and Blair, *History of Coles County,* 442–43). Post office established April 9, 1850, as Ashby; changed to Hutton Dec. 5, 1861.

HYDE PARK. Cook. Founded about 1856 and named for Hyde Park, Dutchess County, N.Y., by Paul Cornell, a New York lawyer and agent for the Hyde Park Company. Now part of Chicago (Ackerman, *Early Illinois Railroads,* 114). Post office established March 23, 1860.

ILES. Sangamon. Formerly known as Iles Junction, named either for early set-tler Washington Iles or Elijah Iles, the postmaster at Springfield. Now part of Springfield. Post office established June 16, 1873.

ILLIANA. Vermilion. Five miles northeast of Danville on the Illinois-Indiana state line. Founded in 1857 by Robert Casement as State Line City, a name suggested by A. P. Andrews. The name was soon changed to Illiana, a blend of the words *Illinois* and *Indiana* (Jones, *History of Vermilion County,* 415).

ILLINOIS. State. The name is from the Illinois, a group of loosely organized but independent tribes—often described as a confederation—which spoke a com-mon language and shared a number of historical and cultural traditions. The number of tribes composing the Illinois is variously reported but include the Kaskaskia, Cahokia, Tamaroa, Peoria, and Michigamea. The language of the Illinois was nearly identical with that of the Miami and is usually referred to as Miami-Illinois. Illinois is not the name the Illinois people called themselves; rather, they were the Inoca, a name of unknown origin and meaning. The name from which Illinois is derived apparently originated in the Miami dialect of Miami-Illinois and was taken into Ojibwa, where it was modified to fit Ojibwa morphology and phonology. It was recorded in 1640 as Eriniouai, in 1656 as Liniouek, in 1657 as Aliniouek, and about 1666 as Iliniouek (pronouned ap-proximately [ilinoowek]). The name was subsequently taken into French, where the Ojibwa plural suffix *-wek* was changed to French *-ois* (The pronounciation at this time was approximately [ilinway].) By the early 1670s the name began to appear in its current form. (For an extended—albeit technical—discussion of the etymology of *Illinois,* see Costa, "Illinois.") As far as can be determined, the first to offer a meaning for the name was Marquette, who wrote, "When one speaks the word 'Illinois' it is as if one said in their language 'the men,'—As if the other Savages were looked upon by them merely as animals." This interpretation was extended and embellished over the years, and the word has been claimed to mean "excellent people," "superior people," or "perfect and accomplished people." Costa finds these interpretations to be little more than popular etymologies and offers the translation "I speak in the regular way" or "I speak my language." At least one ingenious popular etymology of Illinois has been reported (apparently seriously) by no less an authority than a governor of Illinois. In his *Pioneer History of Illinois,* John Reynolds offered a second etymology: that the name was an English adaptation of French Îsle aux Nois [*sic*] (Island of Nuts), a name early French explorers gave to an island in the Mississippi River that abounded in black walnut groves. There is no evidence to support this claim other than the fact that the French did bestow that name on a number of occasions (there are four Îles aux Noix in Quebec alone). Illinois was admitted to the union as the twenty-first state on Dec. 3, 1818. The northern boundary was to have been near the foot of Lake Michigan, at the approximate latitude of the current northern boundary of Indiana. Through the efforts of Nathaniel Pope (for whom Pope County is named and the territorial representative in Congress), the boundary was moved some fifty miles north (Bright, *Native American Placenames;* Costa, "Illinois," 46–47; Reynolds, *The Pioneer History of Illinois,* 24).

ILLIOPOLIS [il ee AHP luhs]. Sangamon. Village (1867, 1883) thirteen miles west of Decatur. A blend of "Illinois" and the Greek *polis* (city). Platted about 1856 as Wilson, for William Wilson, one of the site owners. The station on the Illinois Central Railroad and the post office were established as Illiopolis in the late 1850s, and the community's name was changed to agree in 1869. At one time Illiopolis was promoted as the natural site for the state capital, being that it is near the geographic center of Illinois (Bateman and Selby, eds., *Historical Encyclopedia of Illinois and History of Sangamon County,* 720; *History of Sangamon County,* 921). Post office established Sept. 23, 1858, as Illiopolis Station.

INA. Jefferson. Village (1898) ten miles north of Benton. Probably named by Pressley Johnson for Ina Brown, the granddaughter of site owner C. M. Brown (Griffith and Griffith, *Spotlight on Egypt,* 32). Post office established Dec. 4, 1894.

INDIAN. Names that include the word *Indian* are generally derived from the natural features with which Indians were associated (or were thought to have been); where they were presumed to have lived, camped, or traveled; where Indian artifacts were found; or where various interactions between Indians and Europeans took place. The names were usually given by whites, often long after actual Indian presence or influence had ceased. There are more than one hundred names with the word in Illinois; the most popular is Indian Creek, of which there are about thirty.

INDIAN CREEK. Cass, Morgan. Stream. The site of a massacre of Indians in 1814 by Illinois volunteers under the command of Samuel Whiteside, for whom Whiteside County was later named.

INDIAN CREEK. DeKalb, LaSalle. Stream. Reportedly the site of a massacre during the Black Hawk War in which a band of Potawatomi killed fifteen white settlers and abducted several girls (Vogel, *Indian Place Names in Illinois*).

INDIAN CREEK. Kane. Stream. A tributary of the Fox River. So named because it was the location of the main village of Waubonsee (q.v.).

INDIAN CREEK. Lake. Stream. So named because the area was frequented by the Potawatomi leader Aptakisic (q.v.) and his band (Vogel, *Indian Place Names in Illinois*).

INDIAN GROVE. Livingston. Township. Created as the Township of Worth in November 1857; six months later the name was changed to Indian Grove. This was the location of a large Kickapoo village, said to number more than six hundred persons in the 1820s (Bateman and Selby, eds., *Historical Encyclopedia of Illinois and History of Livingston County*, 639; Vogel, *Indian Place Names in Illinois*). Post office established Feb. 19, 1846.

INDIAN OAKS. Kankakee. Four miles north of Kankakee. Likely named from the fact that it adjoins the land granted to the Potawatomi woman known as Mawteno or Manteno (q.v.).

INDIANOLA. Vermilion. Village (1882) six miles southwest of Georgetown. Founded as Chillicothe, named for Chillicothe, Ohio, the former home of surveyor William Swank. The post office was established as Dallas, named for Vice President George Mifflin Dallas (*see* Dallas City). The postmaster at Dallas, a Mr. Culbertson, upon learning of the existence of the Dallas City post office in Henderson County, and without local consent, petitioned the Post Office Department in Washington, D.C., for a change to Indianola, a blend of *Indiana* with a presumed Latin suffix, a name apparently of his own devising. There are several other Indianolas in the United States (Beckwith, *History of Vermilion County*, 781; *History of Carroll Township, History of Casey, Illinois*, 33, 34). Post office established Dec. 2, 1844, as Dallas; changed to Indianola Nov. 13, 1850.

INDIANTOWN. Bureau. Township. Named from Indiantown, once the site of a Potawatomi village. Indiantown is now part of Tiskilwa (Vogel, *Indian Place Names in Illinois*). Post office established Aug. 5, 1835, as Indian Town.

INDUSTRY. McDonough. Village (1867, 1873) nine miles southeast of Macomb. Laid out in 1846 by Johnson Downen, who, according to the traditional account, offered to build a blacksmith shop for John Price if Price would set an example of "industrious activity" for the community, which he apparently did. Also known as Pinhook (q.v.) (Shadwick, *History of McDonough County*, 225). Post office established May 30, 1849, as Hickory Point; changed to Industry Oct. 19, 1852.

INGLESIDE. Lake. Northeast of Round Lake Beach. Named from the Ingleside Club, one of the first hunting and fishing reserves in the Chain-of-Lakes area (Dretske, *What's in a Name?*). Post office established March 20, 1885, as Dighton; changed to Ingleside Nov. 12, 1901.

INGRAHAM [ING gruh ham]. Clay. Thirteen miles southwest of Olney. Originally known as Ingraham Prairie, named for Philo and William Ingraham, early settlers in the 1830s. "Prairie" was dropped from the name in the early 1860s (*Prairie Echo*, 121). Post office established Oct. 19, 1852, as Ingraham Prairie; changed to Ingraham May 28, 1862.

INLET. Lee. Five miles east-northeast of Amboy. Named from its location at the margin of Inlet Swamp, which was reported to cover some thirty thousand acres in the early nineteenth century (Bateman and Selby, eds., *Historical Encyclopedia of Illinois and History of Lee County*, 627). Post office established April 1, 1836.

INMAN. Gallatin. Fifteen miles west of Eldorado. Founded in 1878 as Gwaltney, named for Benjamin K. Gwaltney, who donated the acre of land upon which the Gwaltney School was built. The name of the school and community were changed to Inman in 1885, named from the Inman store kept by William Inman (*History and Families of Gallatin County*, 14). Post office established Sept. 24, 1885, as Gwaltney; changed to Inman Nov. 3, 1885.

INVERNESS. Cook. Village (1962) three miles southeast of Barrington. Platted by Arthur McIntosh in the 1930s and named for Inverness, Scotland (Hansen, ed., *Illinois*, 570).

IOLA [eye OL uh]. Clay. Thirteen miles northwest of Flora. The origin of the name is unknown. Possibly from a female given name or perhaps a transfer. Iola occurs as a place name in about a dozen states. Post office established Jan. 31, 1850, as Larkinsburg; changed to Iola March 24, 1874.

IOWA JUNCTION. Henderson. One mile northeast of Lomax. Named for the state of Iowa.

IPAVA [eye PAY vuh]. Fulton. Village (1853, 1872) nine miles west-southwest of Lewistown. Platted for John Easley as Easleyburg in 1846 and apparently replatted as Pleasantville later that same year. A post office was established, also as Pleasantville, on Sept. 13, 1847, and renamed Ipava on Dec. 1, 1852. Beyond these few facts, little is certain; the namer of Ipava, the source of the name, and the circumstances surrounding the naming are unknown, although there has been no dearth of speculation. Wayne Azbell, in his *History of Ipava,* has the most complete account of the suggestions that have been offered to explain the name. First, that it is an adaptation of the name of Henry Pavey, who operated a hardware store in Ipava (this story persists even though Pavey did not arrive until 1869, at least seventeen years after the name had become established). Second, that it is derived from the name of the proprietor of a junkyard near the Chicago, Burlington and Quincy tracks that was announced by a sign reading "Isaac Pava." Railroad employees supposedly said they were going to "I. Pava." Third, that community officials sought a more distinctive name than Pleasantville and found Ipava, the name of a remote island, in a world gazetteer (unfortunately, that account does not say where the island is to be found). And, fourth, that the name was suggested by a Dr. Johnson, a world traveler who was visiting relatives in Pleasantville. He is said to have remarked, "I will give you a name that will not be found in North America" and offered Ipava, alleging it to be the name of a lake in South America. The source of the name may lie in a personal name. "Pava" is an uncommon surname, but at present there are about one hundred residential telephone listings in the United States under that name. The name may have a more exotic origin. Azbell notes that a small native community in Brazil, called Igarapava, may have been visited by the mysterious Dr. Johnson and may, in a shortened form, have provided the model for Ipava, Ill. Irwin has uncovered the variant spelling "Ipavia" in the 1871 *Atlas of Fulton County*, and although it is likely a transcription error, given that the post office was established earlier as Ipava, more than five hundred U.S. telephone subscribers have the surname *Pavia*. The source of this intriguing name remains a mystery (Azbell, *A History of Ipava;* Irwin, *A to Z Fulton County*).

IRENE. Boone. Six miles south-southwest of Belvidere. Named for Irene McGuire, whose father donated land for a station on the Chicago, Madison and Northern Railroad in the mid-1880s (Moorhead, ed., *Boone County,* 150). Post office established Dec. 24, 1888.

IROQUOIS. Iroquois. Village (1881). Platted by Henry Moore in 1836 and named for Iroquois County. The present village of Iroquois is the successor to Concord, founded about 1834, and Montgomery, founded in 1835 by site owner Richard Montgomery. The competition between the communities was settled in 1871 when the station on the Big Four Railroad was established as Iroquois (Dowling, *History of Iroquois County,* 49; Ely, *A Centennial History of the Villages*). Post office established March 2, 1833.

IROQUOIS. County. Created Feb. 26, 1833. Named from the Iroquois River, itself named for the Iroquois tribe, in particular for an encounter or series of encounters between the Iroquois and the Illinois in the last decades of the seventeenth century. Charlevoix recorded "River of the Iroquois" in his journal in 1721. Although their homeland was further east, the Iroquois frequently raided tribes living around Lake Michigan.

IRVING. Montgomery. Village (1869, 1873) six miles northeast of Hillsboro. Laid out in 1868. Possibly named for Washington Irving, a popular author of the 1830s and 1840s, or for a land owner named Irving, prominent in the affairs of the community (Bateman and Selby, eds., *Historical Encyclopedia of Illinois and History of Montgomery County,* 909). Post office established July 9, 1856.

IRVING PARK. Cook. Originally known as Irvington. Probably named for Irvington, Westchester County, N.Y., itself named for the Irving family, of which author Washington Irving was a well-known member (Karlen, *Chicago's Crabgrass Communities,* 152). Post office established April 16, 1872.

IRVINGTON. Washington. Village (1881) six miles southwest of Centralia. Established in 1855 as a station on the Illinois Central Railroad. Probably named by N. W. Way, the first IC agent, for his father, Irving Way, and his in-laws, the Irving family. Ackerman (*Early Illinois Railroads,* 132) claims, however, that writer Washington Irving was the source of the name (Griffith, "Egyptian Place-Names," 32; *Washington County,* 30). Post office established May 23, 1862.

ISABEL [IZ uh bel]. Edgar. Fifteen miles north-northwest of Paris. Founded in 1872 as a station on the Paris and Decatur Railroad by John Corzine and named for his wife, Isabel. Isabel includes the former community of New Athens (*History* *of Edgar County,* 511). Post office established June 15, 1859, as Catfish; changed to Isabel July 17, 1872.

ISABEL. Fulton. Township. Named for Point Isabel, a shipping station opposite Havana on the Illinois River. The source of the name is unknown (Irwin, *A to Z Fulton County*).

ISLAND LAKE. Lake, McHenry. Village (1950). So named for its location on Island Lake, a small lake created about 1930 by damming Mutton Creek (Dretske, *What's in a Name?*).

ITASCA [eye TAS kuh]. DuPage. Village (1890). Founded in 1873 with construction of the Chicago and Pacific Railroad by Dr. Elijah J. Smith, one of the site owners, who named the community after Lake Itasca in northwestern Minnesota, where he had vacationed several years before. Itasca is a manufactured name, coined by William T. Boutwell and Henry Rowe Schoolcraft, who thought they had located the source of the Mississippi River in a lake in Clearwater County, Minn., southwest of Bemidji. Over the years Schoolcraft gave several different (and conflicting) accounts of the creation of the name; the most likely is that Boutwell coined the pseudo-Latin *veritas caput,* referring to the "true head" of the Mississippi. Schoolcraft then created the word *Itasca* from the last two syllables of *veritas* and the first syllable of *caput* (Greenblatt, *History of Itasca,* 21; Vogel, *Indian Place Names in Illinois*). Post office established July 29, 1846, as Bremen, named for Bremen, Germany; changed to Pierce May 30, 1850, for Smith D. Pierce, an early postmaster; changed to Sagone Aug. 26, 1850; changed to Ithica [*sic*] Sept. 24, 1873; changed to Itasca Oct. 21, 1873.

IUKA [eye YOO kuh]. Marion. Village (1867, 1882) eight miles east of Salem. Originally called Middleton, named for Thomas L. Middleton, a preacher, physician, and progressive agriculturist of the 1840s. The name was changed in 1867 by an act of the state legislature at the request of Illinois soldiers who had fought in the Civil War battles of Iuka in Mississippi in 1862 and 1863 (*History of Marion and Clinton Counties,* 263). Post office established Feb. 15, 1858, as New Middleton; changed to Iuka Sept. 2, 1867.

IVANHOE. Lake. One mile northwest of Mundelein. Formerly known as Dean's Corners, named for Edwin D. Dean, the first postmaster. The community developed from a subdivision, the Village of Ivanhoe, established in 1879 and named for the popular novel by Sir Walter Scott (Dretske, *What's in a Name?; Past and Present of Lake County,* 282). Post office established Aug. 10, 1861, as Dean's corners; changed to Ivanhoe May 22, 1876.

IVESDALE. Champaign, Piatt. Village (1872) eight miles southeast of Monticello. Founded in the mid-1860s by W. H. Johnson. The station on the Great Western Railroad was established as Norey, named for Johnson's daughter, Nora. The village was formally laid out in 1867 and named for the site owner, Robert Ives, a partner in a Providence, R.I., accounting firm who owned some eighty thousand acres in Illinois (Gates, *The Illinois Central Railroad,* 118; Piatt, *History of Piatt County,* 352). Post office established Feb. 20, 1866.

J

JACKSON. Jackson County, like most of the dozen or so other Jacksons and Jacksonvilles in Illinois, was named for Andrew Jackson (1767–1845), hero of the War of 1812 and later president of the United States. Jackson County was created from Randolph County by the Illinois legislature on January 10, 1816, while the memory of Jackson's greatest victory, the Battle of New Orleans, fought Jan. 8, 1815, was still fresh in memory. The county seat was established at Brownsville and moved to Murphysboro in 1843.

JACKSON. Will. Township. Named from Jackson Creek, itself probably named for Andrew Jackson, reportedly at the suggestion of Wesley Jenkins, an admirer (Stevens, *Past and Present of Will County,* 541).

JACKSONVILLE. Morgan. City (1840, 1887). Laid out by Johnston Shelton in 1825 on land donated for the seat of Morgan County by Isaac Dial and Thomas Arnett. Probably named for Andrew Jackson; a number of early settlers were veterans of the War of 1812. A. W. Jackson, an African American minister, has also been proposed as the source of the name. Jacksonville has been the seat of Morgan County since 1825 (Harder, *Illustrated Dictionary of Place Names;* Hutchison, "Old Morgan County Village"; *Illinois Gazetteer*). Post office established Aug. 15, 1825.

JALAPA. Greene. Six miles north of Jerseyville. Founded in 1867 by Fred Sunkel and others. Named from the Jalapa post office, itself named for Jalapa, the city in Veracruz that American troops occupied in 1847 during the Mexican War. Ultimately from Nahuatl (Aztec) meaning "sandy spring" (Cunningham, *History of the Carrollton, Illinois, Area,* 20). Post office established Feb. 9, 1850.

JAMAICA. Vermilion. Nine miles west-northwest of Georgetown. The settlement was originally known as Kingsley, taking its name from Kingsley Chapel. The name was later changed at the suggestion of W. T. Baird for Jamaica, Queens County, N.Y., itself named for the Jamaica, a small northeastern Algonquian tribe (Stapp, *History under Our Feet,* 22). Post office established March 21, 1894.

JAMESBURG. Vermilion. Nine miles northwest of Danville. Founded in 1894 as a station on the Chicago and Eastern Illinois Railroad and named for James Goodwin (Tuggle, comp., *Stories of Historical Days,* 12). Post office established March 1, 1894.

JAMESTOWN. Clinton. Eight miles north of Breese. Probably named for James M. Massey, who, along with William Lenox, laid out the community in 1850 (*History of Marion and Clinton Counties,* 226). Post office established March 24, 1851.

JAMESTOWN. Perry. Seven miles west-southwest of Pinckneyville. Founded in 1920 and named for James R. Allen, proprietor of the Allen Coal Company (*Perry County*, 15). Post office established May 11, 1923.

JAQUES [JAYK wish, JAYK rish]. Brown. Seven miles south of Mount Sterling. Formerly known as Jaques Mill. Named for proprietor Hiram Jaques, who emigrated from Schoharie County, N.Y., in 1837. The present pronunciations developed from earlier [JAY kwez] or [JAY kweez], which date from at least the thirteenth century (*History of Brown County*, 317).

JASPER. County. Created Feb. 15, 1831, from parts of Clay and Crawford counties. Named for William Jasper of South Carolina, a noncommissioned officer in the Revolutionary War, serving under Gen. William Moultrie (for whom Moultrie County was named). During the siege of Charleston Harbor in 1776, Jasper, at great personal risk, retrieved a U.S. flag the British shot from its staff. Then Jasper attached it to a ramrod used to load cannons and remounted it on the wall of Fort Sullivan. For this heroic action he reportedly was offered a commission, which he refused. He was later killed in the fighting around Savannah, Ga. Jasper's name has long been linked with that of a Sergeant Newton, and several states have both Jasper and Newton counties or communities (in Illinois, Newton is the seat of Jasper County). Jasper's and Newton's names were furnished to the public not through actual reports of their military service but through a fictional account first published in 1809 by Parson Mason L. Weems, author of the now-discredited story of George Washington and the cherry tree. In *The Life of Francis Marion*, Weems tells a highly romanticized and largely fictitious story of how Jasper and Newton—alone, of course—pursued and subdued a squad of British soldiers who were marching a group of Americans to Savannah to be hanged. The account, which became more embellished with each revision, went through numerous editions and made Francis Marion, Sergeant Jasper, and Sergeant Newton heroes of the American Revolution and especially attractive to the communities being created in the Midwest (Allen, *Legends and Lore*, 45; Chapin, "Newton and Jasper"; *Counties of Cumberland, Jasper, and Richland*, 370–71).

JASPER. Wayne. Township. Also named for Sergeant Jasper.

JEFFERSON. County. Created March 26, 1819, from parts of Edwards and White counties. Named for Thomas Jefferson (1743–1826), author of the Declaration of Independence and president of the United States from 1801 to 1809.

JEFFERSON CITY. Jefferson. Former community eight miles northwest of Mount Vernon. Founded in 1854 and named for Jefferson County.

JEFFERSONVILLE. Wayne. *See* Geff.

JEISEYVILLE. Christian. Village (1914) six miles northwest of Taylorville. Founded as a residential and support community for employees of the Peabody Coal

Mine on land formerly owned by the Jeisey family (Goudy, *History of Christian County*, 299).

JERSEY. County. Created from Greene County, Feb. 28, 1839. Several names were suggested for the new county of Jersey, including South Greene and Lafayette. Jersey is a shortening of Jerseyville (q.v.), which had been established several years earlier and then as now was the most important community in the county.

JERSEYVILLE. Jersey. City. (1855, 1883). Settled about 1827 by James Faulkner from Pennsylvania and first called Hickory Grove. The name was changed to Jerseyville, for the state of New Jersey, when the post office was established in 1835. The story of the selection of the name is delightfully told by Marshall Cooper: "Maj. Patterson proposed that it be called Livingston. Carpenter, an old soldier, wished it to be called Liberty. Richards, a New Hampshire man, wished to immortalize the memory of that decaying state, by christening this promising town with the insignificant name, New Hampshire. Cheney proposed that the proprietors should give it whatever name they pleased. This proposition seeming to meet the views of the majority of the meeting, Dr. Lott, a native of New Jersey, was called on for a name. He arose and thanked the people, and with a characteristic expletive, and in genuine Jersey dialect, cried out, 'I'd like to have it called Jerseywille.' The doctor . . . did not obtain the full accomplishment of his wishes, for the meeting voted to call the place Jerseyville, not Jerseywille" (*History of Jerseyville*, 6). Post office established March 20, 1835.

JEWETT [JYOO it]. Cumberland. Village (1872, 1901) fifteen miles west-southwest of Casey. Formerly known as Pleasantville. Laid out about 1870 and named for one or more members of a Jewett family, perhaps for Judge Thomas L. Jewett or for T. M. Jewett, an officer of the Pittsburgh, Cincinnati and St. Louis Railroad, or it may be a transfer from Jewett, Harrison County, Ohio (*Cumberland County History*, 29; Miller, *Ohio Place Names*). Post office established May 18, 1835, as Woodbury; changed to Ogden Aug. 22, 1849; changed back to Woodbury May 1, 1850; changed to Jewett Jan. 25, 1871.

JO DAVIESS. County. Created Feb. 17, 1827. The original bill establishing the county called for the name *Ludlow*, for Augustus C. Ludlow, a naval officer of the War of 1812 who was killed in an engagement with British warships off Nova Scotia in 1813. While still in the legislature, however, the bill was amended and adopted with the wording "to perpetuate the memory of Colonel Joseph Hamilton Daviess, who fell in the battle of Tippecanoe, gallantly charging upon the enemy at the head of his corps, the said county shall be called Jo Daviess." Daveiss [*sic*] (1774–1811) was the U.S. attorney for Kentucky who prosecuted Aaron Burr for treason in 1806. When Daviess County, Ky., was created in 1815, Daveiss's name was misspelled Daviess, and the error was never corrected. The repeated "misspelling" in

Illinois suggests that the county may not have been named directly for Daveiss but rather that the name was transferred from Daviess County, Ky. Outside the county the name is more often than not mispronounced [DAY veez]; the local pronunciation is regularly [DAY vis], as it is in Kentucky. John Reynolds, then in the state legislature and later governor of Illinois, claims to have proposed the name (*History of Jo Daviess County,* 295; Rennick, *Kentucky Place Names*).

JOE'S CREEK. Macoupin. Stream. Named for early explorers Joseph Elliott and Joseph Hodges, who reportedly killed a bear in the vicinity (*History of Macoupin County,* 157).

JOETTA. Hancock. Thirteen miles west of Macomb. Named Joettabo by James Martin, the first postmaster, for his son-in-law and daughter, Joel and Marietta Booz. Subsequently shortened to Joetta. Formerly known as Uniontown (*History of Hancock County,* 318). Post office established July 2, 1869.

JOHNSBURG. McHenry. Village (1956) three miles north-northeast of McHenry. Founded as Miller's Settlement about 1840, probably named for early settler John Baptiste Mueller. The origin of the name *Johnsburg* (originally Johnsburgh) is unclear. It may be in honor of Mueller; it may be in honor of John Frett, a relative of Nicholas Frett, one of the earliest settlers; or it may have been taken from St. John the Baptist Catholic Church, the oldest existing structure in the village, organized in the early 1840s. Johnsburg merged with Sunnyside in 1991 (*History of McHenry County* [1885], 789; Johnson, "The Real Name Here Is 'Change'"). Post office established July 3, 1863.

JOHNSON. County. Created Sept. 14, 1812, from Randolph County. Named for Col. Richard M. Johnson (1780–1850), a hero of the War of 1812 and rumored to have killed the Shawnee leader Tecumseh at the Battle of the Thames in Ontario in 1813. At the time of county formation, Johnson was a U.S. representative from Kentucky and a friend of Ninian Edwards, then governor of Illinois Territory. The seat was established in the home of John Bradshaw in 1813, moved to Elvira in 1814, and to Vienna in 1818 (Aiken, *Franklin County History,* 18; Chapman, *A History of Johnson County,* 19).

JOHNSTON CITY. Williamson. City (1896) five miles east of Herrin. Founded about 1893 by the Chicago, Paducah and Memphis Railroad. Named for railroad contractors Benjamin F. and P. M. Johnston (Roberts, *Glimpses of the Past,* 4). Post office established Dec. 10, 1852, as Lake Creek; changed to Johnston City Dec. 30, 1903.

JOHNSTOWN. Cumberland. Ten miles southwest of Charleston. Founded about 1838 as Sheffield by Bob Dixon and Walter Patterson. Sheffield never prospered, and the town site was purchased in 1846 by Alfred Alexander, whose son, John, revived the faltering community and renamed it after himself. Noteworthy but probably coincidentally, Janesville is two and a half miles northeast of Johnstown (*Counties of Cumberland, Jasper, and Richland,* 211; Misenheimer, *The Johnstown Story,* 17). Post office established March 30, 1855.

JOLIET. Will. City (1845, 1876). Laid out as Juliet by James B. Campbell, treasurer of the board of commissioners of the Illinois and Michigan Canal. Several sources of that name have been proposed: that Juliet was the name of Campbell's wife or daughter; that the name was taken from Shakespeare's *Romeo and Juliet;* that it was given as a complement to the community of Romeo (now Romeoville, six miles north of Joliet); and that it was given in honor of Louis Jolliet, who reportedly camped nearby in 1673. The community does take its name from Jolliet, but, indirectly, through Mount Joliet, once a sixty-foot-high ridge along the Des Plaines River but leveled by quarrying in the nineteenth century. The 1674 map attributed to Jolliet identifies the ridge as Mont Joliet. As eighteenth-century spellings such as *Juliette* suggest, the early pronunciation was [JOO lee et]. Through popular etymology the spelling became Juliet, which appears on Thomas Hutchins's map of 1778. Juliet was probably the name of the general area when Campbell laid out the community in 1834. An association between Juliet and Jolliet developed in the late eighteenth and early nineteenth centuries where the spellings *Juliet* and *Joliet* are both found, often with the former being the name of the community and the latter the name of the mound. This discrepancy was apparently pointed out by President Martin Van Buren and his secretary of the navy, James Paulding, on their tour of the West in 1842, which prompted S. W. Bowen and others to petition the legislature to change the name to Joliet, which was done in 1845. The pronunciation has long been divided between [JO lee et] and [JAH lee et]. As early as the 1830s, community officials became involved and declared that "the only official correct and proper pronunciation . . . shall be Jo-li-et: the accent on the first syllable, with the 'o' . . . pronounced in its long sound, as in the words 'so,' 'no,' 'foe,' and that any other pronunciation be disowned and discouraged." Early-nineteenth-century spellings such as Jolliette suggest that the pronunciation [JAH lee et] has a long history and shows no signs of receding, much less disappearing (Adams, comp., *Illinois Place Names;* Mitchell, *Historical Fragments,* 122; Sterling, *Joliet,* 11, 14–15). Post office established June 29, 1883, as Juliet; changed to Joliet May 24, 1845.

JONATHAN CREEK. Moultrie. Township. Named from Jonathan's Creek, itself named for Jonathan Anderson, an early settler (*Combined History of Shelby and Moultrie Counties,* 273).

JONESBORO. Union. City (1857) one mile southwest of Anna. Founded about 1817 and probably named for Col. Michael Jones, receiver at the U.S. Land Office at Kaskaskia. Jonesboro has been the seat of Union County since its formation in 1818 (Condon, *Pioneer Sketches,* 89). Post office established May 12, 1818, as Union Courthouse; changed to Jonesboro June 5, 1823.

JONESVILLE. LaSalle. North of Oglesby. Named for O. L. Jones, owner of the La-Salle County Carbon Coal Company, which opened a mine in the early 1860s (*Oglesby*, 210).

JOPPA. Massac. Village (1901) seven miles northwest of Metropolis. Founded in the 1870s and named by A. J. Kuykendall, probably for the biblical seaport of Joppa (now part of Tel Aviv–Jaffa). George May, a Massac County historian, claims that Kuykendall proposed the name *Joppa*, "likening the hauling of timber out of the country to the river bank to build the town, to the hauling of cedars for the building of . . . Joppa of Biblical times" (May, *History of Massac County*, 193). Post office established Jan. 5, 1874.

JOSHUA. Fulton. Township. Named for Joshua Moore, generally recognized as the first settler in the area (*History of Fulton County*, 724). Post office established Dec. 14, 1892.

JOSLIN. Rock Island. Twelve miles east-northeast of Moline. Laid out by Benjamin B. Joslin in the late 1860s. Benjamin Joslin's son, Nahum, was the first postmaster (*Historic Rock Island County*, 99). Post office established March 10, 1870, as Joslyn; changed to Joslin March 25, 1878.

JOY. Mercer. Village (1901) six miles west of Aledo. Named for James F. Joy, who organized the Chicago, Burlington and Quincy Railroad about 1850 (Donovan, "Named for Railway Presidents," 26). Post office established May 10, 1849, as High Point; changed to Monroe Aug. 8, 1856; changed back to High Point May 21, 1858; changed to Joy Sept. 26, 1873.

JUBILEE. Peoria. Township. Named from Jubilee College, founded in the late 1830s by Philander Chase of the Protestant Episcopal Church. Chase called the first school building the Robin's Nest because it was "built of mud and sticks and filled with young ones." The original campus is now an Illinois state park and historic site (*History of Peoria County*, 597). Post office established Feb. 18, 1873, as Robin's Nest; changed to Jubilee June 25, 1883.

JUDD. Cook. Named for S. Corning Judd, candidate for lieutenant governor of Illinois in 1864 and Chicago postmaster in the 1880s. Now part of Chicago (Karlen, *Chicago's Crabgrass Communities*, 88). Post office established Oct. 29, 1885.

JUDY CREEK. Madison. Stream. An Anglicization of the name of the first settler, Samuel Tschdui, a Swiss immigrant (Cedeck and Foster, eds., *A History of Glen Carbon*, 5).

JUNCTION. Gallatin. Village (1909) sixteen miles east of Harrisburg. Named from the junction of the Louisville and Nashville and Baltimore and Ohio railroads (*History and Families of Gallatin County*, 14). Post office established June 18, 1884, as Cypress Junction; changed to Junction City May 1, 1888; changed to Junction Dec. 27, 1894.

JUNKERVILLE. Clinton. Named for Bishop Damian Junker. Now part of Bartelso (*see* Damiansville).

JUSTICE. Cook. Village (1911). All the known accounts regarding the naming of Justice are pure folklore. Justice was founded on land deeded by the Illinois and Michigan Canal Corporation to William Cronin Jr. By one story, when signing the papers of incorporation Cronin proclaimed, "Finally, we have justice in this town." A second account claims that when the commissioners of the I&M were meeting to choose a name, an aggrieved (and tipsy) citizen staggered into the meeting room from a nearby saloon and shouted, "Justice! I want some justice!" The commissioners looked around and agreed that Justice would make a good name for the community (Johnson, "Village's Friendliness").

K

KAMPSVILLE. Calhoun. Village (1887) twelve miles west of Carrollton. Formerly known as Beeman's Landing for James L. Beeman, who operated a ferry across the Illinois River in the 1840s. Later called Farrowtown, named for Stephen Farrow, who purchased the ferry from Beeman. Formally laid out in 1872 and named for Michael A. Kamp, a former postmaster at Silver Creek and an early president of the village board (Carpenter, *Calhoun Is My Kingdom,* 28). Post office established March 12, 1857, as Vedder; changed to Kampsville March 6, 1872.

KANE. County. Created Jan. 16, 1836. Named for Elias Kent Kane (1794–1835) of Kaskaskia, an Illinois territorial judge, the first Illinois secretary of state (1818–22), a member of the Illinois legislature, and U.S. senator from Illinois from 1825 to 1835. Kane's name was probably suggested by his friend, James Herrington, one of the founders of Geneva.

KANE. Greene. Four miles north of Jerseyville. Laid out by Thomas Boyd in 1866. The source of the name is unknown. Kane includes the former community of Hollidaysburg, laid out by Tobias Holliday in 1865. Old Kane, or Homer, platted in 1837, is just west of Kane (Cunningham, *History of the Carrollton, Illinois, Area,* 34; Miner, *Past and Present,* 179). Post office established Oct. 25, 1827.

KANEVILLE. Kane. Nine miles northwest of Aurora. Laid out in 1861 by Thaddeus Hoyt and named from the Kaneville post office. The generally accepted account is that the post office application called for the name *Royalton* and was forwarded to the postmaster general by U.S. Rep. John Wentworth. When informed that this would duplicate an existing post office, Wentworth changed the name to Kaneville, presumably named for Kane County. Several writers, however, including Gannett and Russ, claim that the source of the name is Gen. Thomas Kane of Philadelphia. When the Kaneville post office was established in 1848, Thomas Leiper Kane (1822–83) was a nationally known (indeed, famous in many quarters) lawyer, philanthropist, and staunch abolitionist who would certainly have been familiar to and perhaps personally known by John Wentworth. Thomas Kane gave his name to Kane County, Utah, and Kane, Iowa (now Council Bluffs) (*Biographical and Historical Record of Kane County,* 1057; Gannett, *The Origin of Certain Place Names;* Russ, "The Export of Pennsylvania Place Names," 210). Post office established Aug. 10, 1848.

KANGLEY [KANG lee]. LaSalle. Village (1888) one mile northwest of Streator. Originally known as Ripley. The name was changed to Kangley about 1889 for John Kangley, owner of the Star Coal Company (Rasmusen, *LaSalle County Lore,* 259). Post office established Jan. 21, 1888.

KANKAKEE [KANG kuh kee]. County. Created Feb. 11, 1853, from parts of Iroquois and Will counties and named from the Kankakee River. The source and meaning of the name have been disputed. Stewart and others argue for the meaning "wolf" or "wolf-land" based on Charlevoix's statement in 1721 that the Kankakee River was so named "because the [Mohicans], who are likewise called the wolves, had formerly taken refuge on its banks," whereas Vogel and others claim that a more likely origin lies in a Potawatomi word meaning "swampy ground." More recently, however, McCafferty argues convincingly for a Miami-Illinois source, reconstructed as *teeyaahkiki* (open country; exposed land). Part of the uncertainty surrounding the source and derivation of the name is the result of the number of ways it has been written, beginning with LaSalle, who recorded the name first as Téakiki and later as Teatiki and Théakiki. Other early spellings include Aue-que-que, Ti-ah-ke-kink, and Quin-que-que (McCafferty, "'Kankakee'"; Nichols, *The Kankakee,* 1; Stewart, *American Place-Names;* Vogel, *Indian Place Names in Illinois*). Post office established Oct. 3, 1853, as Kankakee Depot; changed to Kankakee June 7, 1866.

KANSAS. Edgar. Village (1857, 1872) thirteen miles southwest of Paris. Founded by Lovel Wilhoit in 1853 as Midway because the site was thought to be halfway between Paris and Charleston. Given that Midway duplicated an existing post office, the name was changed to Kansas in 1858. The several Kansas place names in Illinois were given in the years immediately following passage of the Kansas-Nebraska Act of 1854, which organized Kansas and Nebraska as territories that could determine for themselves whether to allow slavery. Illinois senator Stephen A. Douglas introduced and vigorously supported this legislation (*Our First Hundred Years,* 7; Yates, *The Woodford County History,* 83). Post office established Feb. 23, 1855.

KAOLIN. Union. Four miles northwest of Anna. Named for kaolin, the fine white powder also known as China clay used in the manufacture of porcelain. Kaolin has been mined in the area since at least the 1850s (Mohlenbrock, "A New Geography of Illinois: Union County," 34). Post office established May 28, 1879.

KAPPA. Woodford. Village (1884) eleven miles north of Normal. Established by the Illinois Central Railroad about 1853. Ackerman (*Early Illinois Railroads,*144–45) claims that the IC station was named Kappa from the tenth letter of the Greek alphabet because this was the tenth station south on the route from Dunleith (now East Dubuque) to Bloomington. Rather, Kappa is a form of "Quapaw," the Native Americans reported in Arkansas in 1687 and by Jedidiah Morse in southern Illinois a decade later. The word *Quapaw* was recorded as "Kapaha" in 1682; Tonti, LaSalle's second in command, wrote of the "village of the Kappas" about 1688 (Yates, *The Woodford County History*, 52, 74). Post office established May 26, 1852, as Roxan; changed to Kappa Dec. 17, 1853.

KARBERS RIDGE. Hardin. Fifteen miles southeast of Harrisburg. Named for Frank C. Karber, who established a blacksmith shop at the site in 1874 (*Hardin County*, 17). Post office established Jan. 20, 1879.

KARNAK. Pulaski. Village (1915) fifteen miles northwest of Metropolis. Founded in 1905 by the Main brothers, proprietors of the Main Bros. Box and Lumber Company. Apparently named after Karnak, Egypt, prompted by the location of the community in that part of Illinois known as Egypt (q.v.) (*Pulaski County*, 13). Post office established March 25, 1905.

KASBEER [KAZ bihr]. Bureau. Ten miles north of Princeton. Platted by Romanus Hodgman for site owners J. S. and Sumner Kasbeer (www.genealogytrails.com/ill/bureau/#Ohio). Post office established Jan. 24, 1889.

KASKASKIA [kas KAS kee uh]. Randolph. Village (1818, 1873) four miles west of Chester. Named from the Kaskaskia, one of the tribes of the Illinois Confederation. The name appears as Kachkaska on Marquette's map of 1673. From Illinois for "katydid" (Bright, *Native American Placenames*). Post office established March 22, 1800.

KAUFMAN. Madison. Ten miles northeast of Edwardsville. Established in the 1880s by the Toledo, St. Louis and Western Railroad and named for site owner Gustav Kaufman (Underwood, "A New Geography of Illinois: Madison County," 31). Post office established Feb. 14, 1884.

KEARSARGE. Warren. Former community near Little York, twelve miles northwest of Monmouth. Kearsarge is the name of a summit in Merrimack County, N.H., from an Algonquian word meaning "pointed mountain." The Illinois name was either transferred from New Hampshire or given in recognition of the *USS Kearsarge*, the Union ship that sank the Confederate cruiser *Alabama* off the coast of Cherbourg, France, in 1864 (Stewart, *American Place-Names*). Post office established June 4, 1900.

KEDRON. Gallatin. Eleven miles southeast of Harrisburg. Possibly a transfer from Kedron, Maury County, Tenn. Possibly the name of a local church named for the biblical Kedron, a stream near Jerusalem (*History and Families of Gallatin County*, 15; Stewart, *American Place-Names*). Post office established April 16, 1883.

KEENE. Adams. Township. According to a local story, at a meeting to choose a name for the township there was no agreement because too many people wanted to name it after themselves. The moderator then reportedly remarked, "If you all weren't so 'keen' on having this township named after yourselves, we might be able to decide on a name." The name *Keene* proved acceptable to a majority of those present (Genosky, *People's History,* 711). The Keene post office was active from May 8, 1857, until May 8, 1866.

KEENSBURG. Wabash. Village (1906) seven miles southwest of Mount Carmel. Founded about 1874 and named for one or more members of the Keen family. Daniel, Ezra, Ornamiel, and William Keen have been suggested as namesakes (Adams, comp., *Illinois Place Names;* Bateman and Selby, eds., *Illinois Historical Wabash County Biographical,* 652; *Combined History of Edwards, Lawrence, and Wabash Counties,* 335). Post office established Dec. 30, 1842, as Rochester Mills; changed to Keensburgh March 23, 1874; changed to Keensburg April 10, 1893.

KEITHSBURG. Mercer. City (1857, 1889) eleven miles southwest of Aledo. Founded in 1837 as Keith's Landing by Robert Keith, from Belfrone, Scotland (Bateman and Selby, eds., *Historical Encyclopedia of Illinois and History of Mercer County,* 661; *History of Mercer and Henderson Counties,* 119). Post office established June 13, 1848, as Keithsburgh; changed to Keithsburg by 1893.

KELLER. Peoria. North Peoria suburb. Originally spelled *Kellar;* named for the Rev. Isaac Kellar, a Presbyterian minister (Rice, *Peoria City and County,* 261).

KELLERVILLE. Adams. Nine miles southwest of Mount Sterling. Named for John Henry Keller, an early settler and land owner. Formerly known as Payton for postmaster George Payton (Genosky, *People's History,* 723; www.rootsweb .com/~iladams/places/placenames.htm). Post office established Dec. 19, 1860, as Peyton's; changed to Kellerville April 9, 1875.

KELLOGG. Randolph. North of Ste. Genevieve, Mo. Established as a loading dock on the Mississippi River by the Kellogg Coal Company (www.iltrails.org/ prairietrails.html).

KEMPER. Jersey. Eleven miles northeast of Jerseyville. Named for the first postmaster, William H. Kemper (Postlewait, ed., *History of Jersey County,* 140). Post office established Feb. 8, 1871.

KEMPTON. Ford. Village (1889) twenty miles southwest of Kankakee. Founded in 1878 by Wright Kemp as a station on the Kankakee and Southwestern Railroad (Gardner, *History of Ford County,* 181). Post office established Oct. 3, 1869, as Sugar Loaf; changed to Kempton Nov. 22, 1878.

KENDALL. County. Created Feb. 19, 1841, from parts of LaSalle and Kane counties. The original petition called for the name *Orange,* proposed by settlers from Orange County, N.Y. The reasons for the name change are obscure, but between the time the petition was presented and the legislature had acted, "Orange" was replaced by "Kendall," for Amos Kendall (1789–1869), a close associate of Henry Clay. Kendall served capably in the administrations of both Andrew Jackson and Martin Van Buren, and when the county was created in 1841 he had just completed a six-year term as U.S. postmaster general.

KENILWORTH. Cook. Village (1896). Founded in the early 1890s as a modern planned suburban community by cottonseed oil executive Joseph Sears. Sears was a great traveler, and supposedly the landscape of Warwickshire reminded him of Sir Walter Scott's idyllic novel *Kenilworth* (Cross, "You Can't Get Past the Wealth"). Post office established April 2, 1891.

KENNEY. DeWitt. Village (1875) seven miles southwest of Clinton. Founded by Moses Kenney in 1871 and named for him and his father, John (*History of De-Witt County, 1839–1968*, 29). Post office established Jan. 25, 1872.

KENT. Stephenson. Twelve miles west of Freeport. Established by the Chicago Great Western Railroad in 1887 and probably named for the Rev. Aratus Kent, a circuit-riding evangelist from Galena (Fulwider, *History of Stephenson County*, 361; Keister, *Kent for a Century*, 3). Post office established July 29, 1850.

KENTUCKY. Edgar. Four miles east-southeast of Paris. Founded in 1854 by settlers from the state of Kentucky. Probably named by site owner Isaiah Welch (*History of Edgar County*, 485; *Our First 150 Years*, 16).

KENWOOD. Cook. Named from the Illinois Central station established in the late 1850s, which took its name from Kenwood, the estate of Dr. John A. Kennicott, itself named after his ancestral home near Edinburgh, Scotland (Ackerman, *Early Illinois Railroads*, 114).

KERR. Champaign. Township. Originally called Middlefork, named from the middle fork of the Vermilion River. The name was changed in 1860 for early settler Samuel Kerr (*History of Champaign County*, 168).

KERTON. Fulton. Township. Named for early settler John Kerton, the founder of Bath (*History of Fulton County*, 748).

KEWANEE [kee WAH nee]. Henry. City (1855, 1872). Founded about 1854 on the line of the Central Military Tract Railroad by Sullivan Howard, known as "the father of Kewanee." The station was to have been named Berrien (or Berien) for the chief engineer of the CMT, but Berrien politely refused the honor and suggested instead that it be called Kewanee, for Kee-waw-nee or Kee-waw-nay, probably meaning "prairie chicken," a Potawatomi leader of the 1820s and 1830s. Kewanna, Ind., and Kewaunee, Wis., are from the same source (*Kewanee Story*, 9; Vogel, *Indian Place Names in Illinois*). Post office established March 2, 1855.

KEYESPORT. Bond, Clinton. Village (1887) twelve miles southeast of Greenville. Founded in 1846 by Thomas Keyes, an early postmaster who also operated a sawmill and meat packing plant at the site (*History of Marion and Clinton Counties*, 276). Post office established June 2, 1847.

KIBBIE. Crawford, Jasper. Eleven miles west-northwest of Robinson. Originally a tent city that grew up around the local oil wells and became known as Pilwig, a name of unknown origin. The post office was established Jan. 5, 1887, as Kibbie, named for Hamilton C. Kibbie, a local doctor (*History of Crawford County*, 161).

KICKAPOO. Peoria. Six miles northwest of Peoria. Founded in 1836 by John Coyle and named from Kickapoo Creek, itself named for the Kickapoo tribe that lived in central Illinois in the eighteenth and nineteenth centuries. The name is generally taken to mean "moves about, first here, then there," in other words, "wanderers" (Bateman and Selby, eds., *Historical Encyclopedia of Illinois and History of Peoria County*, 725; Bright, *Native American Placenames*; Vogel, *Indian Place Names in Illinois*). Post office established April 28, 1847.

KIDD. Monroe. Fifteen miles south of Waterloo. Named for Robert Kidd, a soldier in George Rogers Clark's command, which captured Kaskaskia in 1778 (*Combined History of Randolph, Monroe, and Perry Counties*, 383).

KILBOURNE. Mason. Village (1903) ten miles south-southeast of Havana. Founded about 1870 and named for Edward Kilbourne of Keokuk, Iowa, supervisor of construction for the Springfield and Northwestern Railroad, which came through the township in the 1870s (Lynn, *Prelude to Progress*, 339). Post office established Oct. 15, 1872, as Kilbourn; changed to Kilbourne May 21, 1982.

KILDEER. Lake. Village (1958). Four miles southeast of Lake Zurich. Named from the Kildeer Country Club, established in the 1930s, itself named for the killdeer, the American plover, plentiful at the time but now rare (personal communication with Clayton W. Brown).

KILLBUCK. The name of several streams in northern Illinois. Local stories claim they were so named because a large buck was found dead there or because several bucks were killed nearby. Possibly, but equally possible the names may be transfers. Killbuck was the name of several Delaware Indian leaders and became a Delaware family name. Killbuck, Ohio, and Killbuck Creek, Ind., were both named for members of the Killbuck family, and settlers from one or another of these states may have brought the names to Illinois (Baker and Carmony, *Indiana Place Names*; Stewart, *American Place-Names*).

KINCAID. Christian. Village (1915) six miles northwest of Taylorville. Founded by the Peabody Coal Company in 1913 and named for James R. Kincaid, one of the town planners (*Illinois Gazetteer*). Post office established Oct. 3, 1913.

KINDER (Kinderhook). Madison. A railroad station was established on land owned by Calvin Kinder in 1856. According to a local account, Kinder was later accused of diverting or "hooking" money from the community's education fund. Now part of Granite City (Engelke, *Looking Back*, 12).

KINDERHOOK. Pike. Village (1869, 1896) eleven miles east of Hannibal, Mo. Founded in 1836 by Chester Churchill and Bridge Whitten. Churchill was from

Batavia, N.Y., and may have named the community for Kinderhook, N.Y., but more likely it was named for Martin Van Buren, who was known as "Old Kinderhook" for his birthplace, Kinderhook, N.Y., and who was elected president in 1836. From Dutch *kinder hoeck* (children's point), claimed to have been given by the explorer Henry Hudson to a bend in the river that now bears his name where he saw native children playing (Gannett, *The Origin of Certain Place Names; History of Pike County,* 854). Post office established Dec. 27, 1837.

KINGS. Ogle. Five miles northwest of Rochelle. Laid out in 1875 on the line of the Chicago, Rockford and Northern Railroad by William Henry King and/or John R. King (Adams, comp., *Illinois Place Names; Bicentennial History of Ogle County,* 445). Post office established Dec. 18, 1866, as King; discontinued Jan. 10, 1868; reestablished as Kings Dec. 27, 1875.

KINGSTON. Adams. Nineteen miles southeast of Quincy. Named for one of the founders, James King. Also known as Fair Weather (*History of Adams County,* 503). Post office established Oct. 4, 1836.

KINMUNDY. Marion. City (1867, 1875) ten miles northeast of Salem. Laid out about 1857 on the line of the Illinois Central Railroad by William T. Sprouse and named for the birthplace in Scotland of William Ferguson, a British stockholder in the IC. Ferguson visited Illinois in 1856 (Ackerman, *Early Illinois Railroads,* 130–31; *Kinmundy,* 11). Post office established July 14, 1855.

KINNIKINNICK [kuh NIK uh nik]. Boone, Winnebago. Stream. Named from *kinnikinnick,* the Native American smoking material consisting of bark, leaves, and such other dried plant material as was available, preferably mixed with tobacco. From Algonquian for "mixture."

KINNORWOOD. LaSalle. Former community on the Illinois River near the LaSalle–Putnam County line. Laid out in 1836. The name is a blend of the names of the site owners H. L. *Kin*ney, George H. *Nor*ris, and Robert P. *Wood*worth (www .rootsweb.com/~ilbureau/towns.htm).

KINSMAN. Grundy. Village (1886) ten miles northwest of Dwight. A transfer from Kinsman, Trumbull County, Ohio, itself named for railroad contractor John Kinsman (Miller, *Ohio Place Names;* Ullrich, *This Is Grundy County,* 208). Post office established Aug. 17, 1876.

KIRKLAND. DeKalb. Village (1882) seven miles west of Genoa. Founded about 1876 as Kirkwood, named for William T. Kirk, a pioneer settler at one time reported to be the largest land owner in Franklin Township. The name was changed to Kirkland with establishment of the post office (Gross, *Past and Present of DeKalb County,* 136). Post office established July 26, 1875.

KIRKWOOD. Warren. Village (1872) six miles southwest of Monmouth. Kirkwood was incorporated as Young America in 1865, a name some people thought lacked dignity and did not bring the community the respect it deserved. The name was changed about 1874 to commemorate Samuel J. Kirkwood, governor of Iowa in the 1860s and 1870s (Rowley, *The History of Kirkwood, Illinois,* 14). Post office established Dec. 26, 1855, as Linden; changed to Young America May 19, 1856; changed to Kirkwood June 11, 1874.

KISCH. Cass. Two miles south of Virginia. A shortening of "Jokisch." Founded in 1910 by the Jokisch family, early settlers in Cass County. Charles Gotthelf Jokisch and William Jokisch emigrated from Saxony, Germany, in the mid-1830s (Hutchison, "Old Morgan County Village"; www.rootsweb.com/~ilschuy/BioCassSchuyler/CTJokisch.html).

KISHWAUKEE. Winnebago. Five miles southeast of Rockford. Named from the Kishwaukee River. Several early histories claim that Kishwaukee means "fish eaters" or "clear waters." Rather, it is probably from a Meskwaki (Fox) word for "sycamore tree." Kishwaukee was a Native American name for at least part of the stream; in his autobiography, Black Hawk writes, "The next day, I started with my party to kish-wá-co-kee" (*Black Hawk,* 140). The word *sycamore* (q.v.) is a translation (Bateman and Selby, eds., *Historical Encyclopedia of Illinois and History of Winnebago County,* 628; Bright, *Native American Place Names; History of Winnebago County,* 227; Vogel, *Indian Place Names in Illinois*). Post office established Jan. 26, 1838.

KLONDIKE. Alexander. Four miles northwest of Cairo. Named for the Klondike in Alaska at the time of the gold rush in 1896. Post office established March 5, 1896.

KNOLLWOOD. Lake. East of Lake Bluff. Named from the Knollwood County Club, itself named for Knollwood Farm on which it was established (Dretske, *What's in a Name?*).

KNOX. County. Created Jan. 13, 1825, from Fulton County. Named for Henry Knox (1750–1806), a hero of the Revolutionary War, George Washington's secretary of war, and Washington's friend and confidant.

KNOXVILLE. Knox. City (1832, 1873). Known as Henderson until 1832, when it was renamed for its location in Knox County. Knoxville was the seat of Knox County from 1831 until 1873, when it was moved to Galesburg. Post office established Sept. 10, 1830, as Knox Courthouse; changed to Knoxville Jan. 19, 1844.

L

LACON [LAY kuhn]. Marshall. City (1839, 1873) nine miles northeast of Chillicothe. Previously known as Strawn's Landing. Formally laid out in 1831 as Columbia, a nationalistic name much in vogue in the mid-nineteenth century. The name was changed in 1836 or 1837 to Lacon at the suggestion of D. C. Holbrook. The source of the name is uncertain. Lacon may be a form of Laconia, originally a district of ancient Greece, perhaps transferred and shortened from Laconia,

N.H., or Lacona, N.Y. (Ellsworth, *Records of the Olden Times,* 326, 336; *History of Marshall County,* 45). Post office established Dec. 22, 1835, as Putnam; changed to Lacon March 21, 1837.

LACROSSE. Hancock. Ten miles northeast of Carthage. Founded and named in 1836 by John W. Lionberger, site owner, auctioneer, and first postmaster. Probably a transfer from La Crosse, Wis., itself named from French *la crosse* (the hooked stick), the primary piece of equipment used in the game played by Native Americans of the Great Lakes region (*History of Hancock County,* 305). Post office established March 2, 1868.

LADD. Bureau. Village (1890) five miles northwest of Peru. Founded about 1887 as Osgood, a construction camp for the Chicago, Burlington and Quincy Railroad. The name was changed to Laddville about 1888 and to Ladd shortly thereafter for grain elevator operator George D. Ladd of Peru (*Illinois Guide;* Leonard, ed., *Big Bureau,* 70; Stennett, *A History of the Origin,* 91). Post office established July 12, 1888, as Laddville; changed to Ladd Aug. 29, 1888.

LAFAYETTE. Townships in Coles and Ogle. Named for the Marquis de Lafayette (*see* Fayette).

LAFAYETTE. Stark. Village (1872) nine miles south of Kewanee. Founded about 1836 on a site owned by William Dunbar, who donated land for civic buildings with the understanding that the community would be named for his son LayFette Dunbar, pronounced [lay FET]. The spelling was changed about 1839, undoubtedly influenced by the popularity of the Marquis de Lafayette (http://archiver .rootsweb.ancestry.com/th/read/ILKNOX/2000–08/0966128168). Post office established April 17, 1840, as Fraker's Grove; changed to Lafayette June 14, 1845.

LAFOX. Kane. Five miles west of Geneva. Founded about 1866 and named from the La Fox post office, itself named from the Fox River. Formerly known as Kane or Kane Station, named by the Northwestern Railroad from its location in Kane County (Stennett, *A History of the Origin,* 91). Post office established March 12, 1836.

LAFRAMBOISE WOODS. Cook. Forest. Named for Claude La Framboise, a French-Potawatomi veteran of the Black Hawk War. For his services to the United States he was granted one section of land in 1832. From French for "the raspberry" (Vogel, *Indian Place Names in Illinois*).

LAGRANGE. Cook. Village (1879). Formerly known as Kensington Heights. The site was purchased in 1871 and renamed by site owner Franklin D. Cossitt, the first president of the Village of LaGrange, for his former home, LaGrange, Tenn. LaGrange (the Barn) was the name of the Marquis de Lafayette's estate near Paris (Cromie, Young, and Young, *La Grange Centennial History,* 8). Post office established May 31, 1866, as Hazel Glen; changed to West Lyons Dec. 16, 1868; changed to LaGrange Jan. 21, 1876.

LAGRANGE. Henry. Founded by the LaGrange Colony in Albany, N.Y., in 1836. Now the site of Orion (Nelson, *The Role of Colonies*, 73). Post office established Sept. 10, 1838.

LAHARPE. Hancock. City (1859) seventeen miles northwest of Macomb. Founded about 1836 as Franklin by William Smith and Marvin Tryon (or Tyrone). To avoid duplication of post offices, in 1836 the name was changed to La Harpe, suggested by postmaster Louis R. Chaffin. The source of the name is uncertain. According to several local publications, the community is named for a Berrard (Bénard?) de La Harpe, a member of LaSalle's expedition. De La Harpe was leading a small company of men to join LaSalle at Fort Creve Coeur when they were overtaken by severe weather and forced into a temporary camp just north of the present city of La Harpe. Others suggest the name may honor Jean Baptiste Bénard de La Harpe (1683–1765), a French explorer, soldier, and trader in the lower Mississippi Valley who was appointed commandant of LaSalle's outpost at Saint Bernard Bay (now Matagorda Bay) on the Texas coast in 1720. He may have led a company up the Illinois River as far as the Peoria area in the 1720s. By still another local account, the community was named by Chaffin for Jean Francis La Harpe, identified only as an early French explorer (*Historic Sites*, 177; *History of Hancock County*, 354; *Illinois Guide*; Peyron, *LaHarpe*, 2). Post office established June 11, 1836.

LAHOGUE. Iroquois. Nineteen miles west of Watseka. Organized about 1870. A blend of the names of J. T. Laney and a Mr. Hogue, who owned a hay press (hay baler) that they took from farm to farm to harvest wild hay (Dowling, *History of Iroquois County*, 54; *Iroquois County History*, 92). Post office established Jan. 2, 1872.

LAKE. County. Created March 1, 1839 from McHenry County. Named for its location bordering Lake Michigan and for the many small lakes (more than one hundred) in the county. The county seat was established at Burlington and moved to Little Fort (Waukegan) in 1841.

LAKE BLUFF. Lake. City (1895). Named from the summer religious retreat established in 1877 by the Lake Bluff Camp Meeting Association of the Methodist Episcopal Church, itself named for the bluffs along Lake Michigan (Dretske, *What's in a Name?*; Stennett, *A History of the Origin*, 91). Post office established June 2, 1846, as Dulanty, named for tavern owner Michael Dulanty; changed to Oak Hill March 24, 1848; changed to Rockland, named for the Northwestern station, Sept. 17, 1859; changed to Lake Bluffs Jan. 5, 1882; changed to Lake Bluff April 19, 1882.

LAKE CITY. Moultrie. Ten miles southeast of Decatur. Laid out by Robert G. Harvey, president of the Paris and Decatur Railroad and named for James C. Lake, who donated twenty acres of land for the P&D station (*Combined History of*

Shelby and Moultrie Counties, 235). Post office established Sept. 20, 1869, as Sumter; changed to Lake City July 3, 1873.

LAKE FOREST. Lake. City (1861). Founded about 1856 by the Lake Forest Association, organized by a group of Presbyterian ministers from Chicago under the leadership of the Rev. Robert W. Patterson, which sought to establish an academy (which became Lind University, named for benefactor Sylvester Lind and now Lake Forest College) "where Christian teaching would hold a central place." Presumably, the name was chosen by members of the association for the location of the site in a wooded area on Lake Michigan. There is, however, a local tradition that the community was named for David J. Lake and Joseph Forest. Lake reportedly was prominent in city affairs. The post office was established as Lake Forrest, the spelling of which, if not a scribal error, would suggest a human rather than an arboreal referent (Arpee, *Lake Forest Illinois,* 31; Dretske, *What's in a Name?;* Harder, *Illustrated Dictionary of Place Names;* Schulze, Cowler, and Miller, *Thirty Miles North,* 15). Post office established July 14, 1859, as Lake Forrest; changed to Lake Forest June 1, 1865.

LAKE IN THE HILLS. McHenry. Village (1952). Founded about 1950 and named from the lake of the same name, which was created in the early 1920s when Walter LaBuy, a Chicago attorney, dammed Woods Creek (www.cardunal.com/lake.htm).

LAKE RUN. Kane. Stream. Named for local land owner Zaphna Lake (Seits, "The Names of Kane County," 166).

LAKEVIEW. Madison. Six miles west of Edwardsville. Founded about 1815 as the Pond Settlement, named for the large wetland known as the Cypress Pond. Renamed from the Lakeview school. Lakeview is one of several communities in Illinois settled largely by free African Americans (Cofield, *Memories of Lakeview,* 2; *Saline County,* 62).

LAKE VILLA. Lake. Village (1901). Founded as Lake City about 1883 as a summer retreat from the heat and humidity of Chicago by Ernst J. Lehmann, proprietor of the Fair Department Store. Because of an existing Lake City in Moultrie County, Lehmann, for unknown reasons, renamed the community Stanwood, which was further changed to Lake Villa in the late 1880s (Roberts, "Growth Goes Rural"). Post office established Oct. 23, 1884, as Stanwood; changed to Lake Villa Aug. 21, 1886.

LAKE ZURICH. Lake. Village (1896). Originally known as Cedar Lake, a commune established by Seth Paine, a Chicago dry-goods merchant. The name was changed by Paine about 1836, who likened the natural beauty of the lake to Lake Zurich in Switzerland, which he had recently visited (Loomis, *Pictorial History,* 4). Post office established July 1, 1839, as Flint Creek; changed to Lake Zurich July 13, 1841.

LAMB. Hardin. Five miles northeast of Cave-in-Rock State Park. Named for early settler Edgar Lamb. Over the years the community has been known as Lambs Stockade, Lambs Spring, Lambs Mill, and Lambtown (*Hardin County*, 17). Post office established July 21, 1884.

LAMOILLE [luh MOYL]. Bureau. Village (1867, 1888) eight miles west of Mendota. Laid out in 1836 as Greenfield by Tracy Reeve and John Kendall. The name was changed in 1839 by Kendall for his former home in Vermont, where Lamoille is the name of a county, a river, and several other geographic features (Leonard, ed., *Big Bureau*, 66). Post office established April 15, 1831, as Bureau Grove; changed to Greenfield Aug. 9, 1837; changed to Lamoille July 25, 1840.

LAMOINE. Township. McDonough. Named from the La Moine River, previously known as Crooked Creek. In 1915, at the insistence of State Senator William A. Compton of Macomb, the Illinois legislature changed the name of Crooked Creek to Riviere a la Mine. Why Compton chose that particular name is unknown. By 1920 when road signs were placed by the Illinois Highway Department, Riviere a la Mine had become Lamoine River, probably an adaptation of la Mine, created by analogy with the Des Moines River that empties into the Mississippi less than twenty miles from the La Moine (Chenoweth and Semonis, comps., *The History of McDonough County*, 64; Frazer and Frazer, "Place Name Patterns," 25).

LAMONE VILLAGE. McDonough. North Macomb suburb on the La Moine River. Possibly an adaptation of "LaMoine" (q.v.), but just as likely a transfer from Lamone, Italy.

LAMOTTE. Crawford. Township. Named for an early-nineteenth-century individual or family named LaMotte, possibly descended from John LaMotte, reportedly a member of LaSalle's expedition. There were several LaMotte (or Lamotte) families in the area by the early nineteenth century, including those of Joseph LaMotte, who operated a ferry near Vincennes, Ind., in the 1790s, and William Lamotte, who arrived in the area about 1808 (Bateman and Selby, eds., *Illinois Historical Crawford County Biographical*, 635; *History of Crawford County*, 67).

LANARK [LAHN ahrk]. Carroll. City (1867, 1876) fifteen miles southwest of Freeport. Founded as Glasgow. The name was changed to Lanark in 1859 for Lanark, Scotland, the home of several of the financiers who underwrote construction of the Western Union Railroad (Thiem, ed., *Carroll County*, 180). Post office established July 5, 1836, as Cherry Grove; changed to Lanark Dec. 6, 1861.

LANCASTER. There have been at least a dozen Lancasters in Illinois; most if not all are transfers from a Lancaster in an eastern state. The names of Lancaster Township in Stephenson County and New Lancaster in Warren County are probably transfers from the city and county of Lancaster in southeastern Pennsylvania. The name of Lancaster Precinct in Wabash County is likely from the same source but perhaps influenced by Lancaster, Ky. Ultimately from Lancaster, England (Bateman and Selby, eds., *Illinois Historical Wabash County Biographical*, 647, 652).

LANDES. Crawford. Twelve miles southwest of Robinson. Named for Silas Z. Landes of Mount Carmel, a member of Congress during the 1880s (*History of Crawford County*, 254). Post office established Jan. 5, 1887.

LANE. DeWitt. Six miles east-southeast of Clinton. Laid out in 1873 by site owner Tillman Lane (*History of DeWitt County, 1839–1968*, 29). Post office established July 12, 1873.

LANGLEY. Bureau. Twelve miles west of Princeton. A transfer from Langley, Aiken County, S.C., itself named for Langley, England (Stennett, *A History of the Origin*, 92).

LANGLEYVILLE. Christian. Two miles west-northwest of Taylorville. Founded about 1917. Named for site owner Lydia A. Langley (Goudy, *History of Christian County*, 403). Post office established July 2, 1923.

LANSING. Cook. Village (1893). Founded in 1863 by John Lansing, who with his brothers George and Henry emigrated from New York in 1846. Henry was the first postmaster at Lansing. The Lansings may have been related to another John Lansing, for whom Lansing, N.Y., and Lansing, Mich., are named (*Illinois Guide*). Post office established June 21, 1865.

LAONA [lay ON uh]. Winnebago. Township. The source of the name is unclear. Perhaps a transfer from Laona, Chautauqua County, N.Y., possibly influenced by Laona, Wis. Post office established July 11, 1846, as Redding; changed to Laona Dec. 29, 1848.

LAPLACE. Piatt. Ten miles east-southeast of Decatur. Laid out in 1873 as Stoner by site owner George W. Stoner. Stoner changed the name several years later for unknown reasons. French (or faux French) for "the place" (Bateman and Selby, eds., *Historical Encyclopedia of Illinois and History of Piatt County*, 689). Post office established Feb. 3, 1874.

LAPRAIRIE. Adams. Town (1869) twenty-five miles northeast of Quincy. French (or presumed French) for "the prairie." Established in 1855 as Gibbs, a station on the Chicago, Burlington and Quincy Railroad. Subsequently known as Gibbstown and Pitman. The circumstances surrounding the name change are unknown (www.rootsweb.com/~iladams/places/placenames.htm). Post office established April 1, 1856, as Pitman; changed to La Prairie June 8, 1863.

LARKINSBURG. Township. Clay. Named for Larkin Thrash, an early settler and postmaster (*History of Wayne and Clay Counties*, 457). Post office established Jan. 31, 1850; changed to Iola March 25, 1874.

LAROSE. Marshall. Village (1887) fifteen miles northeast of Chillicothe. Origin unknown. Formerly known as "Romance," perhaps a translation of French *romance* "ballad," and later as Montrose. The name was changed in 1871, possibly for a French settler named LaRose (Coulet du Gard, *Dictionary of French Place Names*). Post office established April 27, 1871, as Romance; changed to La Rose June 23, 1871.

LARUE. Union. Sixteen miles southwest of Carbondale. Possibly named for an early French settler named LaRue (Coulet du Gard, *Dictionary of French Place Names*). Post office established June 3, 1903.

LASALLE. County. Created Jan. 15, 1831, from Putnam County. Named for René Robert Cavelier, Sieur de LaSalle (1643–87), an ardent promoter of French interests and French expansion in North America. In 1680 LaSalle established Fort Creve Coeur near Lake Peoria, and in 1681 he proceeded down the Illinois and Mississippi rivers to the Gulf of Mexico, where he claimed the entire Mississippi watershed for France. LaSalle was killed by a mutinous member of his own company in 1687.

LASALLE. LaSalle. City (1852, 1876). Platted about 1838 for the Illinois and Michigan Canal Commission. The sale of building lots helped finance construction of the I&M (*City of LaSalle*, 1, 8). Post office established Feb. 10, 1836, as Peru; changed to LaSalle Jan. 10, 1838.

LATHAM [LAYTH uhm]. Logan. Village (1884) eleven miles northwest of Decatur. Founded in 1871 and named for Robert B. Latham of Lincoln, a director of the Peoria, Lincoln and Decatur Railroad (Stringer, *History of Logan County*, 616). Post office established Jan. 2, 1872.

LATONA. Jasper. Seven miles west of Newton. Founded in 1869. The source of the name is unknown. Possibly from a female given name. Ultimately from classical mythology where Latona is the mother of Apollo and Artemis. The only other Latonas in the United States are a community near Seattle, Wash., and a township in South Dakota (Sunderland, *New and Complete History*, 80). Post office established Jan. 2, 1887.

LAURA. Peoria. Eighteen miles northwest of Peoria. Laid out about 1888 by first postmaster James M. Kellar and named for the daughter of a contractor for the Santa Fe Railroad (Bateman and Selby, eds., *Historical Encyclopedia of Illinois and History of Peoria County*, 764; Marshall, *Santa Fe*, 355). Post office established May 18, 1888.

LAURETTE. McLean. Eleven miles east of Le Roy. Named for Laura, wife of the first president of the Le Roy Narrow Gauge Railroad (Bateman and Selby, eds., *Historical Encyclopedia of Illinois and History of McLean County*, 679).

LAWLER. Gallatin. Thirteen miles east of Harrisburg. Named for Gen. Michael K. Lawler, who recruited and led the Eighteenth Illinois Volunteers during the Civil War (*History and Families of Gallatin County*, 15).

LAWNDALE. Logan. Five miles east-northeast of Lincoln. Laid out in the early 1850s by Thomas Esten (Eston), site owner and first storekeeper, acting as agent for a Massachusetts company that planned a colony in Illinois. The area around present Lawndale was first known as Kickapoo, named from Kickapoo Creek where Esten had established a sawmill in the late 1840s. The source of the name is unknown (Petro, "Lawndale," 14; Stringer, *History of Logan County,* 616). Post office established May 19, 1855.

LAWNDALE. McLean. Township. Perhaps named for Lawndale, Mich.; perhaps a hopeful descriptive name. It was suggested by John Cassady, the first township supervisor. According to an early history of McLean County, this was a most appropriate and "natural name for one of Nature's most beautiful lawns" (Bateman and Selby, eds., *Historical Encyclopedia of Illinois and History of McLean County,* 712).

LAWN RIDGE. Marshall, Peoria. Six miles northwest of Chillicothe. Named from the Lawn Ridge post office, itself named by the first postmaster, a Mr. Ordway, reportedly for the ridge separating the Illinois and Spoon River watersheds (Burt and Hawthorne, *Past and Present of Marshall and Putnam Counties,* 45; *Deep Are the Roots,* 62). Post office established April 28, 1850.

LAWRENCE. County. Created Jan. 16, 1821, from parts of Edwards and Crawford counties. Named for Capt. James Lawrence (1781–1813), a naval commander who served with Stephen Decatur in the Tripolitan War in the early nineteenth century. Lawrence became a national hero during the War of 1812 when he was mortally wounded during an engagement with the British frigate *Shannon* off Boston Harbor and died uttering the now-famous words, "Don't give up the ship."

LAWRENCE. McHenry. One mile northwest of Harvard. Founded about 1856 and named for Lawrence Bigsby (or Bixby), site owner and proprietor of the first general store. When the Chicago and North Western station was constructed at Harvard, many buildings in Lawrence were dismantled and moved to trackside (*History of McHenry County* [1885], 434). Post office established July 24, 1856.

LAWRENCEVILLE. Lawrence. City (1835, 1879). Named for Capt. James Lawrence (*see* Lawrence County). Post office established July 14, 1820.

LEAF RIVER. Ogle. Village (1882) five miles north-northeast of Mount Morris. Named from Leaf River. The traditional explanation is that the river was named for the colorful leaves that covered its surface each fall (*Bicentennial History of Ogle County,* 291). Post office established March 31, 1841, as Mount Morris; changed to Leaf River March 13, 1844.

LEAMINGTON. Gallatin. Fourteen miles southeast of Harrisburg. Named by Dr. S. R. Cone for his former home, Leamington, England. Leamington (Royal Leamington Spa) is on the Leam River in Warwickshire, near Stratford (*History and Families of Gallatin County,* 16). Post office established Oct. 27, 1879.

LEANDERVILLE. Randolph. Six miles south of Steeleville. The settlement grew around a store and post office established by Jesse Beer and named for his landlord, Leander Johnson (www.iltrails.org/randolph/t7r5.htm). Post office established Feb. 1, 1892.

LE-AQUA-NA. Stephenson. Lake and Illinois state park three miles north of Lena. The name was formed by infixing *aqua* (water) to *Lena* (q.v.).

LEBANON [LEB uh nuhn], [LEB nuhn]. St. Clair. City (1857, 1874). Founded about 1814. Formally laid out in 1825 by Thomas Ray and William Kinney (the third lieutenant governor of Illinois, serving in the late 1820s) and named from the Lebanon post office, itself probably a transfer from a Lebanon further east (*Lebanon, 7*). Post office established Nov. 17, 1819.

LECLAIRE. Madison. Founded in 1890 by Nelson O. Nelson for employees of the Nelson Manufacturing Company. Named for Edme-Jean Leclaire (1801–72), whose notions of social justice and profit sharing Nelson greatly admired. Leclaire was annexed by Edwardsville in the 1930s (Lossau, "Leclaire," 22).

LEDFORD. Saline. Two and a half miles southeast of Harrisburg. Probably named for Solomon Ledford, an early settler (*History of Saline County*, 38). Post office established Sept.30, 1880.

LEE. County. Created Feb. 27, 1839, from Ogle County. Several sources of the name have been proposed: Henry "Light Horse Harry" Lee, a hero of the American Revolution; Richard Henry Lee, a member of the Continental Congress and senator from Virginia; Robert E. Lee, the Confederate general; and another Robert E. Lee, a St. Louis merchant. Part of the confusion is a result of the fact that several early histories conflate the first two Lees and claim that Richard Henry Lee was the "Light Horse Harry" Lee of Revolutionary War fame. Even though a number of authors and even state publications such as the *Illinois Blue Book* state that the county was named for Richard Henry Lee, the evidence points clearly to Henry "Light Horse Harry" Lee as the namesake. The county was named by Frederick R. Dutcher, a Lee County magistrate and an admirer of Henry Lee (Barge, *Early Lee County*, 160; Barge and Caldwell, "Illinois Place-Names").

LEECH. Wayne. Township. Changed from Wabash in 1860. Named for Gen. Samuel Leech, the first Clerk of Wayne County (*History of Wayne and Clay Counties*, 271).

LEEF. Madison. Township. Named for Jacob Leu from Schaffhausen, Switzerland, who emigrated to America in 1834 and changed his name to Jacob Leef (Norton, ed., *Centennial History of Madison County*, 562).

LEEPERTOWN. Bureau. Township. Named for John (or Joseph) Leeper, who operated a grist mill near the site. The township name was first recorded as Liepertown (Bradsby, ed., *History of Bureau County*, 140, 436; Leonard, ed., *Big Bureau*, 74). Post office established March 25, 1851.

LEESBURG. Fulton. Fifteen miles southwest of Havana. Founded in 1880 as Leesburgh by Frank Leese (Irwin, *A to Z Fulton County*).

LEHIGH [LEE heye]. Kankakee. Seven miles west of West Kankakee. A transfer from eastern Pennsylvania, where Lehigh is the name of a river, a county, a university, and a number of other artificial and natural features. From a Delaware (Algonquian) word meaning "forks of a river" (Stewart, *American Place-Names*).

LELAND [LEE luhnd]. LaSalle. Village (1872) nine miles west of Sandwich. Founded about 1853 as Whitfield. At about the same time, the Chicago, Burlington and Quincy railroad station was established as Waverly. By one account, the petition for a post office called for the name *Adams* for postmaster John Leland Adams. Because there was an existing Adams post office, however, the application was withdrawn and resubmitted as Leland, again for postmaster John Leland Adams. By another account, the post office and community were named for Edwin S. Leland, an attorney and circuit court judge of the 1850s and/or his cousin Cyrus Leland, also an attorney. The name *Whitfield* was officially changed to Leland in 1867 (Benson, *Leland "66,"* 1, 5; Gannett, *The Origin of Certain Place Names; History of LaSalle County,* 16). Post office established Feb. 15, 1854, as Waverly Station; changed to Leland Jan. 10, 1857.

LELAND GROVE. Sangamon. City (1950). Named for site owner Jerome Leland. Now a suburb of southwest Springfield (*Illinois Guide*).

LEMENTON [LEM uhn tuhn]. St. Clair. Ten miles southeast of Belleville. Platted in 1874 on the line of the Cairo Short Line Railroad, midway between Freeburg and New Athens, by John T. Lemen and others (*History of St. Clair County,* 271). Post office established June 2, 1871.

LEMONT [luh MAHNT]. Cook. Village (1873). Formerly known as Keepataw, named for a Potawatomi subchief under Yellowhead (q.v.) and later as Athens and Palmyra. Apparently, the name *Lemont,* French for "the mountain," was chosen in 1850 when the township name was changed from Palmyra. Lemont was suggested by postmaster and justice of the peace Lemuel Brown or by his brother, Nathaniel, a contractor for the Illinois and Michigan Canal. Possibly a transfer from Lamont [*sic*], Wyoming County, N.Y.; both Browns were born in western New York state (*Lemont, Illinois,* 3, 25). Post office established March 13, 1840, as Keepatau; changed to Palmyra April 9, 1850; changed to Lemont May 30, 1850.

LENA [LEE nuh]. Stephenson. Village (1869). Ackerman (*Early Illinois Railroads,* 140) claims that the community was named from Ossian's poem "Fingal," where Lena is the site in Ireland of a great battle between the hero, Fingal, and Swaran. Alternatively, Lena may be the name of a female relative of Samuel F. Dodds, who laid out the community for the Illinois Central Railroad about 1854, or a popular etymology from Alida, the name of the first post office (Tilden, comp., *History of Stephenson County,* 522). Post office established Jan. 4, 1849, as Alida; changed to Terre Haute Jan. 6, 1853; changed to Lena July 1, 1853.

LENZBURG. St. Clair. Village (1884) fourteen miles south of Mascoutah. Founded in 1862 by Peter Baumann and named for his birthplace, Lensburgh, Switzerland (*Tapestry of Time,* 140). Post office established Jan. 7, 1868, as Lenzburgh, to Lenzburg Dec. 14, 1894.

L'ERABLE [luh RAB]. Iroquois. Ten miles north-northwest of Watseka. Settled largely by French-Canadians from Quebec and formally organized about 1855. From French *l'érable* (the maples), named for the local maple trees, probably a shortening of *l'érabière* (a grove of maple trees) (Hansen, ed., *Illinois,* 649). Post office established April 4, 1854.

LEROY [luh ROY]. McLean. City (1857, 1874). Settled by John Buckles, a tanner, in the late 1820s and first known as Buckles Grove. Formally laid out about 1835 by Asahel Gridley and Merrit Covell and named for their former home, Le Roy, Genesee County, New York (*Illinois Guide*). Post office established June 11, 1839.

LEROY. Boone. Township. Named for LeRoy "Doc" Chamberlain, a justice of the peace in Blaine. Formerly called Lambertson Precinct for James B. and Jeremiah Lambert, who in 1836 were the first settlers to file a claim in the area (Moorhead, ed., *Boone County,* 21).

LEVEE. Pike. Township. Formerly known as Douglas. Renamed in 1876 for the levee along the Mississippi River at the suggestion of Frank Lyon, the first county supervisor (*History of Pike County,* 868).

LEWISTOWN. Fulton. City (1857, 1882). Founded in 1822 by Ossian M. Ross and named for his son, Lewis. Lewistown has been the seat of Fulton County since its formation in 1823 (*History of Fulton County,* 770). Post office established Jan. 9, 1824, as Fulton Courthouse; changed to Lewistown March 14, 1831.

LEXINGTON. McLean. City (1867, 1890) thirteen miles northeast of Normal. Founded in 1836 by Asahel Gridley and James Brown. Named for Lexington, Mass., and Lexington, Ky. Gridley's father fought in the Revolution at the Battle of Lexington in Massachusetts in 1775, and Brown was from Lexington, Ky., itself named for Lexington, Mass. (Bateman and Selby, eds., *Historical Encyclopedia of Illinois and History of McLean County,* 715; *Lexington Centennial,* 26). Post office established May 10, 1837.

LEYDEN. Cook. Township. Organized in 1850 as Monroe. The name was changed later in 1850 to Leyden, probably a transfer from Leyden, Lewis County, N.Y., itself named for Leiden in the Netherlands (Bateman and Selby, eds., *Historical Encyclopedia of Illinois Cook County Edition,* 784). Post office established Aug. 9, 1837, as Cazenovia, for Cazenovia, N.Y.; changed to Leyden May 30, 1850.

LIBERTYVILLE. Lake. Village (1882). In the late 1830s the area was known as Vardin's Grove for Englishman George Vardin, an early settler who built a cabin in the grove in 1835. The name was changed to Independence Grove at the Independence Day celebration in July 1836. Because an Independence post office already existed, Archimedes B. Wynkoop suggested the name *Libertyville,* which would preserve some of the associations of Independence Grove. When

Libertyville became the seat of Lake County in 1839, the name was changed to Burlington; when the seat was relocated to Little Fort (Waukegan) in 1841, the name was changed back to Libertyville. The township name was chosen by popular vote in 1850 from among Libertyville, Burlington, and Bem, the latter name for Józef Bem, commander of the Army of Transylvania, which defeated the Austrians at Piski the year before. "Libertyville" received thirty-seven votes, and "Bem" received thirty-two (Condor, "A Place Where Old Meets New"; Dretske, *What's in a Name?*; *Past and Present of Lake County,* 294). Post office established April 16, 1838.

LICKING. Crawford. Township. Named by settlers from Licking County, Ohio, itself named from the salt licks along the Licking River (personal communication with Sue Jones).

LICKSKILLET. Lickskillet is a popular (usually informal) place name, occurring at least a hundred times in the United States. The stories told to explain the name are remarkably similar, usually having to do with the fact that the cook for a construction crew prepared such scanty meals that the men had to "lick the skillet" to survive or that local pets cleaned the plates. Both stories are found in Illinois. Bearsdale in Macon County northwest of Decatur was formerly known as Lickskillet, apparently taking its name from the Lickskillet School, subsequently called the Prairie Center School. How the school came by that name is unknown. Officials of the Illinois Central Railroad thought Lickskillet to be an inappropriate name for the station and changed it to Bearsdale, for site owner Sam Bear. Lickskillet, a now-vanished hamlet near a country store a mile or so northeast of Georgetown in Vermilion County, was reportedly given its name by a local doctor named Hawes who saw "how poor the land was around this store and told the folks at Georgetown that the soil was so poor that not enough food could be raised to 'lick a skillet.' Thereafter, whenever Dr. Hawes was called to that area, he would leave word that he was going out to 'Lickskillet'" (Tuggle, comp., *Stories of Historical Days,* 16). Centerville in Piatt County came to be known as Lickskillet reportedly because it was the practice of the local innkeeper to invite neighborhood dogs and cats to clean the plates of diners, a story said to have greatly amused Abraham Lincoln (Richmond, *Centennial History of Decatur,* 97).

LIDICE. Will. Originally known as Stern Park Gardens. The name was changed to Lidice in July 1942 as an expression of sympathy for Lidace, Czechoslovakia, which had been destroyed by the German army the month before. Lidice was one of several communities to merge as Crest Hill, now a northern suburb of Joliet (Rennick, "On the Success of Efforts"; *Will County Places,* 4).

LIGHTSVILLE. Ogle. Four miles north-northwest of Byron. Founded in the 1840s by site owner John Light (*History of Ogle County,* 615).

LILLY. Tazewell. Ten miles southeast of Morton. Founded about 1871 by Edward H. Bacon and named for his father-in-law, Joseph Lilly, an early settler from Frederick County, Md. (Adams, comp., *Illinois Place Names;* Bates, *Souvenir of Early and Notable Events,* 24). Post office established June 26, 1861, as Hamlin; changed to Lilly Nov. 25, 1870.

LILLYVILLE. Cumberland. Six miles northeast of Effingham. Probably named from the Lillyville School, itself likely named by Clem Uptmor of Teutopolis, who taught there. Lillyville became the official name of the community when the post office department rejected the name *Maurice,* proposed in honor of the Rev. P. Mauritius Klosterman (*Lillyville,* n.p.).

LILY CACHE. Will. *See* Cache.

LILY LAKE. Kane. Village (1990) eleven miles east-southeast of Sycamore. Platted in 1887 by Renalwin Outhouse and named from Lily Lake. Formerly known as Campton and also as Canada Corners (Bateman and Selby, eds., *Historical Encyclopedia of Illinois and History of Kane County,* 708). Post office established Oct. 27, 1851, as Campton; changed to Lily Lake June 6, 1887.

LIMA [LEYE muh]. Adams. Village (1847, 1886) sixteen miles north of Quincy. Laid out about 1835 by Joseph and William Orr. The traditional story is that Joseph Orr, the proprietor of the first general store, was searching for a name for the community and sought advice from his houseguest, who was from Peru. The visitor told Orr that in all his travels he had not seen women more beautiful than those in his native country until he came to this part of Illinois. That declaration convinced Orr to name the town Lima, for the capital of Peru and the home of his guest. This makes a good story, but Lima, Ill., is probably a transfer, most likely by settlers from Lima, Ohio (Genosky, *People's History,* 718; *History of Adams County,* 536). Post office established March 12, 1836.

LIMERICK. Bureau. Seven miles north of Princeton. Founded in 1857 and named for site owner and first postmaster George Limerick (D. Leonard, ed., *Big Bureau,* 67). Post office established Oct. 14, 1857.

LIMESTONE. Townships in Peoria and Kankakee counties. Named for the nearby quarries. The limestone deposits were described in early records not only as "abundant" but also "inexhaustible" (*History of Peoria County,* 602; Stennett, *A History of the Origin,* 94). Post office established May 9, 1848.

LINCOLN. Logan. City (1857, 1886). Postville was founded by Russell Post in 1834 and served as the first seat of Logan County, from 1839 until 1847. Lincoln was founded in 1853 about a mile from Postville by John G. Gillett, Robert B. Latham, then sheriff of Logan County, and several others. The documents preliminary to the town plat were drawn up by Abraham Lincoln, then a Springfield lawyer. In later years Latham claimed credit for choosing the name, but Gillett's daughter said it was proposed by her mother, who, after hearing Latham and Gillett arguing over possible "Indian" names, suggested they name it after their lawyer, Abraham Lincoln. According to a local story, Lincoln attended the dedication of the community. At the ceremony he is supposed to have cut a watermelon, collected the juice into a cup, and poured it on the ground with the words "I now christen this town site." Of the hundreds of communities, counties, and townships named for Abraham Lincoln, this is claimed to be the only one named for him before he became president. Lincoln annexed Postville in 1865 (Beaver, *History of Logan County*, 51; Dooley, ed., *The Namesake Town*, 3; Stringer, *History of Logan County*, 567). Post office established March 2, 1838, as Postville; changed to Lincoln Oct. 6, 1854.

LINCOLNSHIRE. Lake. Village (1957). Founded in 1955 as Ladd's Lincolnshire by Chicago builder Roger Ladd. The name was inspired more by Lincolnshire, England, than by Abraham Lincoln; original street names included Essex and Cambridge (Holt, "A Lovely Town for Trees").

LINCOLNWOOD. Cook. Village (1911). Previously called Tessville for early settler Johan Tess. Renamed Lincolnwood in 1936 from its main thoroughfare, Lincoln Avenue, U.S. 41 (McRoberts, "Residents").

LINDENHURST. Lake. Village (1956). Founded in the late 1940s as a community for returning World War II veterans by Chicago developer Morton Engle on the site of Lindenhurst Farm, itself named for the double row of linden trees in the farmhouse yard (Christian, "It's Not Cutting Edge").

LINN. Woodford. Township. Named for early settlers William and Simon (or Simeon) Linn (*see* Clayton) (Perrin and Hill, *Past and Present of Woodford County*, 376).

LINTNER. Piatt. Twelve miles east-southeast of Decatur. Named for William Lintner of Decatur, who manufactured furniture, hay presses, and pumps in the 1860s (Piatt, *History of Piatt County*, 467). Post office established Oct. 18, 1878, as Lintner Station; changed to Lintner May 14, 1883.

LIS. Jasper. Six miles northwest of Newton. Formerly known as Fort List Station, named for site owner Aaron Manfort List. The name *Lis* is a shortening of List Station, where List was informally pronounced [LIS] (Sunderland, *New and Complete History*, 82). Post office established April 14, 1881.

LISBON. Kendall. Village (1894). Founded about 1836 by Levi Hills, John H. Moore, and others. Several early sources claim that Moore chose the name because it was easy to pronounce and remember. In fact, the community was established by a religious colony from New England, and the name is almost certainly a transfer from one of the Lisbons in the northeast, likely Lisbon, St. Lawrence County, N.Y. It is unclear who proposed the name, Moore or Hills, but both were from New York state (Dickson, "Geographical Features and Place Names"; Farren, ed., *A Bicentennial History*, 110; Hicks, *History of Kendall County*, 146).

Post office established April 4, 1834, as Holderman's Grove; changed to Lisbon Sept. 17, 1836.

LISLE [LEYEL]. DuPage. Village (1956). Previously known as DuPage. The name was changed to Lisle about 1850. Although several accounts claim that Lisle was named in honor of Samuel Lisle Smith, a prominent Chicago attorney of the early nineteenth century, it is rather a transfer from Lisle, Broome County, N.Y. The name was suggested by Alonzo B. Chatfield, who emigrated from New York about 1835 (Carroll, "In the Name of"; Cawiezel, "Lisle," 186; Richmond and Vallette, *A History of the County of DuPage,* 131). Post office established Dec. 22, 1854.

LITCHFIELD. Montgomery. City (1859, 1896). Founded about 1853 by the Litchfield Town Company, a consortium of executives organized for the purpose of attracting the Terre Haute and Alton Railroad. Electus Bachus Litchfield, originally from Brooklyn, N.Y., was a member of the consortium and later its sole owner (*Centennial History of Litchfield,* 12, 16). Post office established July 27, 1850, as Hardinsburg; changed to Litchfield March 23, 1855.

LITERBERRY [LEYE ter behr ee]. Morgan. Six miles north of Jacksonville. Founded in 1869 and named for postmaster Jonas Liter (Adams, comp., *Illinois Place Names;* Bateman and Selby, eds., *Historical Encyclopedia of Illinois and History of Morgan County,* 661; Hutchison, "Old Morgan County Village"). Post office established July 20, 1869, as Liter; changed to Literberry Sept. 29, 1886.

LITHIA. Shelby. Five miles northeast of Shelbyville. Named from the local mineral springs, which, according to a 1901 advertisement, "contain Lithium and other properties, making the water equal to any mineral water in the world for good health and the cure of many ills" (*Historic Sketch Shelby,* 100). Post office established July 14, 1898.

LITTLE AMERICA. Fulton. Seven miles northeast of Lewistown. Founded about 1935. By local tradition the name is credited to a tavern keeper who commuted from Canton, about ten miles away. As he left for work each morning he would take his leave by saying, "Well, I'd better get started for Little America." The choice of the name was likely influenced by Little America, the base camp established in Antarctica by Adm. Richard E. Byrd in 1929 (Blevins, *Peculiar, Uncertain, and Two Egg*).

LITTLE INDIAN. Cass. Ten miles north-northeast of Jacksonville. Named from Little Indian Creek, itself so named because of its size in relation to nearby Indian Creek. Post office established Feb. 1, 1870.

LITTLE ROCK. Kendall. Three miles north-northwest of Plano. Founded in 1845 and named from Little Rock Creek. Post office established March 21, 1837.

LITTLETON. Schuyler. Village (1911) eight miles north-northwest of Rushville. Founded about 1849. Named at the request of Dr. W. H. Window for his father-in-law James Little (Bateman and Selby, eds., *Historical Encyclopedia of Illinois and History of Schuyler County,* 704). Post office established July 14, 1849.

LIVELY GROVE. Washington. Fourteen miles north-northeast of Sparta. Named for the John Lively family, killed by Indians in 1813 (Brinkman, ed., *This Is Washington County,* 52). Post office established Feb. 25, 1861.

LIVINGSTON. County. Created Feb. 27, 1837 from parts of LaSalle and McLean counties. Named for Edward Livingston of New York (1764–1836), who held a number of offices in the early years of the United States and was a highly regarded statesman and diplomat. He was mayor of New York, U.S. representative and senator, a member of Andrew Jackson's staff at the Battle of New Orleans, Jackson's secretary of state, and minister to France.

LIVINGSTON. Madison. Village (1905) three miles south of Staunton. Probably named for David G. Livingston, first president of the village board, serving from 1905 until 1911 (Norton, ed., *Centennial History of Madison County,* 587). Post office established Dec. 23, 1904.

LOAMI [lo AM ee, lo AM uh]. Sangamon. Village (1875) seven miles west of Chatham. The origin of the name is unknown. A local story, told tongue-in-cheek, claims that the name comes from a remark made by William Colburn after his mill burned: "Low am I." This is the only Loami in the United States (Campbell, *The Sangamon Saga,* 11). Post office established Dec. 21, 1843, as Lick Creek; changed to Loami April 30, 1855.

LOCKHAVEN. Jersey. Seven miles northwest of Alton. Founded about 1856 by site owner John Locke (Hamilton, *History of Jersey County,* 368).

LOCKPORT. Will. City (1853, 1890). Laid out as Runyontown by Armstead Runyon. Lockport was formally organized about 1837 by the Illinois and Michigan Canal Commission and named for the first of the series of locks on the I&M between Chicago and Peru (*Lockport Has a Birthday,* n.p.; *Souvenir of Settlement and Progress,* 419). Post office established March 21, 1837.

LODA. Iroquois. Village (1869, 1873) four miles north-northeast of Paxton. Established by the Illinois Central Railroad in 1855. The origin of the name is unknown. Several sources have been proposed: that Loda, meaning "light of the woods," was the name of an Indian woman; that Loda was the name of the wife of an employee of the IC; and that Loda was taken from the poem "Cath-loda" by the legendary Irish hero and poet Ossian. In that work Loda is the equivalent of Odin, the Scandinavian chief of the gods. It may be, however, merely a variant of Lodi (q.v.). The only other Lodas in the United States are in Michigan and West Virginia (Ackerman, *Early Illinois Railroads,* 125; Dowling, *History of Iroquois County,* 65; Peterson, *Story of Loda,* 2). Post office established Nov. 9, 1855, as Mixville; changed to Oakalla Dec. 21, 1855; changed to Loda March 10, 1880.

LODEMIA. Livingston. Four miles northwest of Fairbury. Formerly known as Lodemia Station, a stop on the Chicago and Paducah Railroad. The source of the name is unknown. This is the only Lodemia in the United States (*History of Livingston County* [1878], 385). Post office established July 13, 1877.

LODI. The name of several former communities. The Lodi in Clark County (post office established Oct. 14, 1842) is now Clark Center; the Lodi in Kane County (post office established March 31, 1854) is now Maple Park; and the Lodi in Kendall County (post office established Jan. 24, 1837) is now Oswego. Lodi is a popular place name in the United States; the Geographic Names Information System lists forty-four Lodi communities, townships, or post offices. One of these, perhaps in Indiana or New York, may have been transferred to Illinois. Ultimately from Lodi in northern Italy, where Napoleon defeated an Austrian army in 1796.

LOGAN. County. Created Feb. 15, 1839, from Sangamon County. Several sources of the name have been proposed, among them Logan County, Ky.; a Judge Logan; a Native American leader named Logan; and Stephen T. Logan, Abraham Lincoln's law partner. The county is almost certainly named, however, for Dr. John Logan (1786–1853), a pioneer physician and the father of Gen. John A. Logan. The senior Logan served with Lincoln in the Illinois legislature. In spite of their political differences, the two men became good friends, and by one account it was Lincoln who suggested to the legislature that the new county be called Logan (Barge, "Illinois County Names"; Cutshall, *A Gazetteer; History of Logan County* [1878], 227; Stringer, *History of Logan County,* 149–50).

LOGANSPORT. Hamilton. Former community about six miles east of McLeansboro. Founded about 1857 by William Logan Malone (or Marlow, sources differ) (*Hamilton County,* 42; *History Gallatin, Saline,* 310; Rowley, *The History of Kirkwood, Illinois,* 53). Post office established Jan. 19, 1858.

LOMAX. Henderson. Village (1913) eight miles south-southeast of Burlington, Iowa. Laid out in 1853 by Robert Lomax (*History of Mercer and Henderson Counties,* 894). Post office established March 1, 1870.

LOMBARD. DuPage. Village (1869, 1903). First known as Babcock's Grove for early settlers Ralph and Morgan Babcock. Formally laid out in 1868 by Benjamin Sweet, Silas Janes, and Josiah L. Lombard, a Chicago developer and banker who provided his services gratis, asking in return that the community be named Lombard (Dunning, *The Story of Lombard,* 13; Vann, "Entrepreneurial Spirit Blooms"). Post office established May 14, 1844, as Babcock's Grove; changed to Lombard April 7, 1868.

LOMBARDVILLE. Stark. Thirteen miles east of Kewanee. Founded about 1870. Platted for Julia A. Lombard and Alfred H. Castle (Leeson, *Documents and Biography,* 587). Post office established April 29, 1870.

LONDON MILLS. Fulton, Knox. Village (1883) ten miles northwest of Henry. Originally called London Mill, named by James Eggers from London, England, who established a grist mill on Spoon River in 1846 (Boden, *History of the Town of Young Hickory*, 4). Post office established Feb. 3, 1875.

LONE TREE CORNERS. Bureau. About eight miles northwest of Henry. Named from a large and solitary oak tree that was a landmark for early travelers and hunters. It was reportedly blown down in a storm in the mid-1860s (Bradsby, ed., *History of Bureau County*, 11).

LONG CREEK. Township. Macon. Named from Long Creek, itself named either for its perceived length or for a local family named Long (Richmond, *Centennial History of Decatur*, 95). Post office established April 5, 1875.

LONG GROVE. Lake. Village (1956). This part of Lake County was known to German settlers of the 1830s and 1840s as Muttersholtz (Mother Forest). By the late 1840s the name *Long Grove* had became widespread and was from a stand of timber that extended into Cook County (Dretske, *What's in a Name?*). Post office established March 8, 1847, as Muttersholtz; changed to Long Grove June 28, 1847.

LONG POINT. Livingston. Village (1899) eight miles south-southwest of Streator. Named from Long Point Creek, itself named for a stand of timber that jutted onto the prairie (*History of Livingston County* [1878], 287). Post office established Nov. 2, 1847.

LONG PRAIRIE. Clay. Named for Rosmond Long, who settled on the prairie between Raccoon Creek and Elm Creek east-southeast of Flora. The former Long Prairie School was located about five miles east of Flora (*Prairie Echo*, 120).

LONGVIEW. Champaign. Village (1903) thirteen miles northeast of Tuscola. Laid out about 1888 as Prairieview, a stop on the Chicago and Eastern Illinois Railroad about 1888. Longview is likely a descriptive name derived from Prairieview. Post office established April 6, 1879, as Orizaba (q.v.); changed to Longview Aug. 3, 1889.

LOOGOOTEE [LO guh TEE]. Fayette. Four miles east-southeast of Vandalia. Surveyed in 1873. Local folklore claims that the name derives from a tall tree used in early pioneer times as an observation post and known as the Look Out Tree, which over time became Loogootee. Rather, the name is a transfer from Loogootee, Martin County, Ind., where it was formed from the name of the founder, Thomas N. Gootee, prefixed by part of another personal name, perhaps that of Gootee's wife, reported as Lucinda, or possibly from the name of a Mr. Lowe, the engineer who drove the first train through the town in the 1850s. These are the only Loogootees in the United States (Baker, *From Needmore to Prosperity*; Hanabarger, "Fayette County Place Names," 49). Post office established April 21, 1836, as Hickory Creek; changed to Loogootee Aug. 5, 1878.

LORAINE. Adams. Village (1881) eighteen miles northeast of Quincy. Founded about 1870 as a station on the Chicago, Burlington and Quincy Railroad. Named for Loraine Laramore, daughter of CB&Q president William Laramore (Genosky, *People's History*, 711). Post office established May 15, 1871.

LORAINE. Henry. Township. Likely named by settlers from Lorraine, France (Kiner, *History of Henry County*, 594).

LORAN. Stephenson. Fourteen miles west southwest of Freeport. Laid out in 1854 by land owner George Lashell. The origin of the name is unknown (Fulwider, *History of Stephenson County*, 411). Post office established May 20, 1854.

LOSTANT [LAWS tuhnt]. LaSalle. Village (1865, 1873) twelve miles west of Streator. Founded in 1861 by John M. Richey as Ellsworth after a Civil War veteran, but that name duplicated the name of an extant post office. Late in 1861 the president of the Illinois Central Railroad was entertaining European dignitaries in his private car and a name for the community was discussed. One guest, Baron Mercier, the French ambassador to the United States, suggested the name of his wife, Cecile Elizabeth Philbert de L'Ostende, Countess of Ostende, an estate in northwestern Belgium. L'Ostende became L'Ostant—Lostant with the establishment of the post office (Ackerman, *Early Illinois Railroads*, 144; O'Byrne, *History of LaSalle*, 402; Rasmusen, *LaSalle County Lore*, 236). Post office established Oct. 16, 1861.

LOST GROVE. DeKalb. Near Cortland. Perhaps named from the fact that this copse was isolated from the main stand of timber. Post office established June 11, 1849.

LOST NATION. Ogle. Seven miles northeast of Dixon. The origin of the name is unknown although a number of explanations have been offered. Three in particular have persisted but are probably more folklore than fact. The first claims the name came about because some who lived in the area never attended church and thus were lost souls who must perforce live in a lost nation. The second concerns an early settler who lived some distance from the main road. He became lost because the highway commission would not maintain the long lane to his property, and his farm became a lost nation. According to the third, the roads further into the countryside were narrow and overgrown with brush and vines, making homesteads more difficult to find and the area a lost nation. The name also occurs in New Hampshire and Vermont, two states that provided a large number of settlers to this part of Illinois, and some may have brought the name with them (*Bicentennial History of Ogle County*, 439).

LOUIS. Pope. Former community. Earlier known as Stalions, named for postmaster William Riley Stalions. The name of the post office was changed to Louis in 1884, perhaps a misreading of Louisa, the name of Stalions's wife (*Pope County*, 355). Post office established June 30, 1884, as Stalion [*sic*]; changed to Louis Oct. 27, 1884.

LOUISVILLE [LOO uhs vil]. Clay. Village (1867, 1882) seven miles north of Flora. Founded in the late 1830s as Lewisville by site owner Crawford Lewis, who, along with his brothers, William, Robert, John, and David, emigrated from Indiana about 1830. When the plat was filed the spelling was changed to Louisville, either by the surveyor, a Mr. Blackburn, or by an official in the recorder's office (*History of Wayne and Clay Counties,* 375; *Prairie Echo,* 64). Post office established July 1, 1839.

LOURDES. Woodford. Former community. The area west of Metamora was known as Black Partridge, and the post office was established under that name in 1836. Black Partridge came to be known, at least informally, as Lords, for several local leaders known as the "lords" of the area. Priests at the Catholic church picked up the name and changed its spelling, first to Lourds and then to Lourdes, either believing that the name was from Lourdes, France, or (more likely) in order to associate it with Lourdes, one of the major shrines of Europe. The name *Black Partridge* is partially retained in Partridge Creek and Partridge Township (*see* Partridge). The Lourdes church is five miles west of Metamora (Wiltz, "History of Black Partridge"). Post office established Dec. 31, 1883.

LOVE. Vermilion. Township. Named for county Judge I. A. Love of Danville (Jones, *History of Vermilion County,* 436).

LOVES PARK. Winnebago. City (1947). Northeastern Rockford suburb. Named for Malcolm Love, a Rockford industrialist and alderman who laid out the community on his farm about 1909.

LOVILLA. Hamilton. Eight miles northwest of McLeansboro. Founded in 1854 and named by Simon McCoy, probably for Lovilla McLean, the daughter of a county judge. The community never prospered. In the words of an early county history, "Lovilla was killed by the railroad avoiding it" (*History of Gallatin, Saline,* 310). Post office established June 29, 1857.

LOVINGTON. Moultrie. Village (1873) seven miles north of Sullivan. Named for early settler and first postmaster Andrew Love (*Combined History of Shelby and Moultrie Counties,* 224). Post office established Dec. 30, 1839.

LOWDER [LOW der]. Sangamon. Five miles northwest of Virden. Founded by George W. Lowder as a station on the Jacksonville and Southeastern Railroad (Bateman and Selby, eds., *Historical Encyclopedia of Illinois and History of Sangamon County,* 737). Post office established March 17, 1872.

LOWELL. LaSalle. Seven miles southeast of LaSalle. Laid out in 1830 by William Seeley. Perhaps a transfer from Lowell, Mass. (Rasmusen, *LaSalle County Lore,* 223). Post office established March 9, 1835, as Vermillionville; changed to Lowell Jan. 31, 1850.

LOW POINT. Woodford. Ten miles north of Eureka. Founded about 1871 and apparently named for a point of timber in a low-lying area along the south branch of Richland Creek (Moore, *History of Woodford County,* 226). Post office established Dec. 10, 1849.

LOXA. Coles. Seven miles west of Charleston. Founded about 1862 as Stockton by a Capt. B. F. Jones. Stockton duplicated an existing post office, and postal authorities changed the name to Loxa, giving no source. Loxa may be named for Loxa (now Loja) in Granada, Spain, or it may be a transfer with shortening from Loxahatchee, Fla. (Seminole for "turtle river"). This is the only Loxa in the United States (Bateman and Selby, eds. *Historical Encyclopedia of Illinois and History of Coles County,* 720; Stewart, *American Place-Names*). Post office established July 22, 1862.

LUDA. Ogle. The origin of the name is unknown; possibly a female given name. The historical Luda School was located about six miles north of Rochelle. The Luda post office was active from Jan. 6, 1859, until Jan. 2, 1874.

LUDLOW. Champaign. Village (1876) five miles north of Rantoul. Known as Pera or Pera Station, a stop on the Illinois Central Railroad, until 1867, when the name was changed for Thomas W. Ludlow of New York, a major shareholder in the IC (Ackerman, *Early Illinois Railroads,* 125). Post office established Dec. 22, 1854, as Para Station; changed to Ludlow March 8, 1867.

LUKIN. Lawrence. Township. Named for Joel Lukin, an early settler (*Combined History of Edwards, Lawrence, and Wabash Counties,* 302). The Lukin post office was active from Feb. 25, 1895, until July 3, 1895.

LUMAGHI HEIGHTS. Madison. East of Collinsville. Named for the Lumaghi family. Dr. Octavius Lumaghi emigrated from Italy in the 1840s and opened the Lumaghi mines in 1871 (Turner, "The Lumaghi Family's Impact," 20).

LUSK. Pope. Eighteen miles south of Harrisburg. Founded about 1860 and named by the first postmaster, James Floyd, for James V. and Sarah Lusk. Lusk, a veteran of the Revolutionary War, operated a ferry across the Ohio River from Kentucky to what is now Golconda in the late 1790s (McCormick, "The Significance of Pope County Place Names," 26; *Pope County,* 11). Post office established Nov. 14, 1860.

LYMAN. Ford. Township. Named for Samuel Lyman, the first of a colony of settlers from Connecticut in 1856 (*Ford County History,* 70).

LYNCHBURG. Jefferson. Former community about two miles north of Opdyke. Laid out about 1853 by W. H. Lynch (Dearinger, "A New Geography of Illinois: Jefferson County," 25; Perrin, ed., *History of Jefferson County,* 357).

LYNCHBURG. Mason. Township. Probably named for Lynchburg, Va., home of early settlers George and Pleasant May (*History of Menard and Mason Counties,* 657).

LYNDON. Whiteside. Village (1874) twelve miles southwest of Sterling. Founded about 1835 as a religious colony by settlers from New England. Named for Lyndon, N.Y. (Nelson, *The Role of Colonies,* 11). Post office established June 18, 1838.

LYONS. Cook. Village (1888). Likely a transfer by settlers from Lyons, Wayne County, N.Y.; perhaps influenced by Lyon, France (Benedetti and Bulat, *Portage, Pioneers,* 14; Cutshall, *A Gazetteer;* Mitchell, *Historical Fragments,* 24). Post office established Feb. 29, 1848.

M

MABEL. Schuyler. Seven miles south-southeast of Georgetown. Named for Mabel Calvert, about whom little is known (*Schuyler County,* 107) Post office established Nov. 14, 1900.

MACEDONIA [mas uh DON yuh, mas uh DON ee]. Franklin, Hamilton. Village (1894) eleven miles east-northeast of Benton. Founded in 1858 as Johnsonville by site owner Robert H. Johnson and changed to Macedonia by the Rev. Tom Reed. The name *Macedonia* is probably a transfer; there are more than fifty communities so named in the United States, largely in the Southeast (Allen Collection; *Franklin County,* 17). Post office established Sept. 15, 1851, as Hall; changed to Macedonia Aug. 27, 1861.

MACHESNEY PARK. Winnebago. Village (1981). Formerly called Harlem, probably named for Harlem, N.Y. The village took the name of the Machesney Airport, established in 1927 by early aviator and barnstormer Fred Machesney. Machesney was Rockford's municipal airport until the 1950s (www.machesney -park.il.us).

MACKINAW. Tazewell. Village (1840, 1897) seven miles southeast of Morton. Founded about 1827 by George W. Minier, the founder of Minier, Charles E. Boyer, and others. Named from the Mackinaw River. Mackinaw, Ojibwa for "snapping turtle," was first recorded as Michilimakinak, the name of an island in Lake Huron between the peninsulas of Michigan. The name was probably brought to Illinois by early explorers and fur traders. Several Kickapoo leaders took their names from the river, including Machina, whose village was near the Mackinaw River in the 1820s. Mackinaw was the first seat of Tazewell County, serving from 1827 until 1831. Mokena (q.v.) is probably a variant (Vogel, *Indian Place Names in Illinois*). Post office established April 14, 1827.

MACOMB [muh KOM]. McDonough. City (1841, 1882). Named for Alexander Macomb, a career military officer who distinguished himself in the War of 1812, especially in 1814 when he defended Plattsburgh, N.Y., against a superior British force. At about the same time, an American fleet commanded by Thomas McDonough (for whom McDonough County is named) decisively defeated a British fleet on Lake Champlain.

MACON. County. Created Jan. 19, 1829, from parts of DeWitt, Moultrie, and Piatt counties. Named for Nathaniel Macon (1758–1837) of North Carolina, speaker of the U.S. House of Representatives and, at the time Macon County was created, a recently retired U.S. senator. It apparently made little difference to Illinoisans that Macon frequently argued against many programs and policies they valued. He opposed providing funds for the construction of roads and canals and was outspoken in defense of slavery.

MACOUPIN [muh KOO puhn]. County. Created Jan. 17, 1829, from Madison County. Named from Macoupin Creek, itself named from an Algonquian word referring to the cow lily or spadderdock, the edible aquatic roots that grew locally, called "white potatoes" or "white yams" in early reports. Macopin, N.J., is from the same source (personal communication with Michael McCafferty; Walker, *History of Macoupin County*, 75).

MADISON. County. Created Sept. 14, 1812, from parts of Randolph and St. Clair counties. Named for James Madison (1751–1836), president of the United States from 1809 to 1817. One of Madison's first acts as president was to appoint Ninian Edwards governor of Illinois Territory. In return, when the new county was created, Edwards proposed that it be named for President Madison. The seat has always been at Edwardsville, named for Ninian Edwards, as is Edwards County (q.v.).

MADISON. Madison. City (1891). Founded in the 1890s by the Madison Land Syndicate, a group of St. Louis industrialists seeking a cheap, direct route for transporting coal from southern Illinois to St. Louis. Named for Madison County (Stern, *A Centennial History of Madison*, 9).

MADONNAVILLE. Monroe. Seven miles southwest of Waterloo. Laid out by Joseph Ruebsam in the early 1840s. The source of the name is unknown. Perhaps a transfer of a Madonna from an eastern state. This is the only Madonnaville in the United States (Klein, ed., *Arrowheads to Aerojets*, 525). Post office established Oct. 24, 1865.

MAEYSTOWN [MAYZ town]. Monroe. Village (1904) eight miles southwest of Waterloo. Founded in 1856 as Maeysville by Jacob Maeys. The name was changed to Maeystown upon establishment of the post office (Klein, ed., *Arrowheads to Aerojets*, 560). Post office established June 1, 1860.

MAGNOLIA. Putnam. Village (1859, 1875) eight miles east of Henry. Founded in 1836 by Thomas Patterson and likely transferred from a Magnolia in an eastern state, perhaps Magnolia, Pa. (Alleman and Immel, *A Putnam County History*, 23). Post office established Nov. 23, 1836.

MAHOMET [muh HAH muht]. Champaign. Village (1872). Laid out about 1832 by Daniel Porter as Middletown because it was thought to be halfway between Danville and Bloomington. The post office was established as Mahomet in 1840, and Mahomet had become the name of the community, at least informally, by the mid-1840s. The name was not formally changed until about 1871 at the urging of T. M. Brown, an official of the Indiana, Bloomington and Western Railroad, who felt it was a nuisance to have different names for the community and the post office. Mahomet is a form of Muhammad, the prophet of Islam. It was also the name of an early-eighteenth-century Mohican leader in Connecticut, a descendant of Owaneco (q.v.) and was probably brought to Illinois by settlers from New England. As a place name, Mahomet occurs only in Illinois and Texas (Bright, *Native American Placenames;* Purnell, *An Unofficial History,* 16; Vogel, *Indian Place Names in Illinois*). Post office established Jan. 31, 1840.

MAINE. Grundy. Township. Created from Braceville Township in March 1898. Named for the battleship *Maine,* which had blown up in Havana Harbor the previous month, precipitating the Spanish-American War (*see* Dewmaine).

MAKANDA [muh KAN duh]. Jackson. Village (1888) seven miles south of Carbondale. The source of the name is unknown. Makanda was named in the early 1850s, almost certainly by officials of the Illinois Central Railroad who perhaps adapted the name from a native language or created it from presumed parts of one or more native languages. Ackerman, an executive of the IC, states confidently that the station was named for "the chief of the last tribe of Indians who inhabited the section of country about here" (*Early Illinois Railroads,* 136), but no local Native American with this or a similar name has been identified. Vogel's suggestion that the name may be derived from Wauconda (q.v.) is possible but unsubstantiated. The derivation of the name is confounded by the fact that the post office was established as Markanda, and in the early 1870s the village name was spelled *Makauda.* Whether these are variants, earlier forms, or transcription errors is unknown (Brieschke, *Notes on Makanda,* 27, 31; Hatton, "Once It Was a Thriving Produce Center"; Vogel, *Indian Place Names in Illinois*). Post office established March 11, 1857, as Markanda; changed to Makanda Jan. 11, 1870.

MALDEN. Bureau. Village (1869, 1882) six miles northeast of Princeton. Founded in 1855 by B. L. Smith as Wiona, possibly a variant of Winona (q.v. Wenona). The name was changed about 1855 by settlers from Malden, Mass., itself named for Malden, England (Leonard, ed., *Big Bureau,* 67). Post office established Nov. 6, 1855, as Wiona; changed to Malden Feb. 19, 1857.

MALTA. DeKalb. Village (1869, 1913) five miles west of DeKalb. Malta Township was created as Etna in 1856, probably named for Mt. Etna in Sicily, which had erupted spectacularly several years before. The name was changed about 1858 with construction of the Galena Railroad, which named its station Malta, presumably for the Mediterranean island of Malta (Boies, *History of DeKalb County,* 492; Stennett, *A History of the Origin,* 95). Post office established Feb. 16, 1857.

MANCHESTER. Scott. Village (1861, 1904) thirteen miles south-southwest of Jacksonville. First known as Elk Horn Point. The name was changed about 1832 by settlers from Manchester, England (*Scott County Bicentennial Book,* 168). Post office established May 30, 1832.

MANHATTAN. Will. Village (1886). Established in 1880 by the Wabash Railroad. Named for Manhattan, N.Y., itself named from the Native Americans who inhabited the island at the time of Dutch settlement. The name was possibly suggested by John Young, who emigrated from New York City in 1849 and became the first Will County supervisor (*Illinois Gazetteer*). Post office established Sept. 10, 1880.

MANITO [MAN uh to]. Mason. Village (1876) fifteen miles southwest of Pekin. Founded about 1858 as a station on the Chicago and Illinois Midland Railroad. Manito, usually spelled *Manitou,* is a general Algonquian word for "spirit, deity." Melish's 1819 map shows the "Manitou R" as a southern tributary of the "Sanguemon River." Manitou became popular as a place name following the publication of Henry Wadsworth Longfellow's *The Song of Hiawatha* in 1855 (*History of Menard and Mason Counties,* 603). Post office established Feb. 12, 1858, as Egypt; changed to Manito Nov. 4, 1861.

MANLEY. Fulton. Four-and-a-half miles east-northeast of Bushnell. Named for the Manley or Manly family. Allen Manly emigrated from Ohio about 1843 (*Fulton County Heritage,* 228). Post office established Jan. 14, 1884, as Luna; changed to Manley Dec. 12, 1884.

MANLIUS. Bureau. Village (1905) eleven miles northwest of Princeton. Founded about 1845 by the Chicago and North Western Railroad and named by Allen S. Lathrop for his former home, Manlius, Onondaga County, N.Y., itself named for one or another of the ancient Romans called Manlius (Leonard, ed., *Big Bureau,* 68; Stewart, *American Place-Names*). Post office established May 22, 1871.

MANNON. Mercer. Eleven miles west of Aledo. Named for Col. James M. Mannon, a Civil War veteran and local farmer (Bateman and Selby, eds., *Historical Encyclopedia of Illinois and History of Mercer County,* 739). Post office established Nov. 15, 1883.

MANSFIELD. Piatt. Village (1876) five miles northwest of Mahomet. Founded about 1870. Possibly named directly for Jared Mansfield (1759–1830), surveyor general of the United States in the early nineteenth century, but more likely a transfer from Mansfield, Ohio, itself named for Jared Mansfield. J. L. Mansfield, a local philanthropist, has also been suggested as the source of the name (McIntosh, ed., *Past and Present,* 53; Piatt, *History of Piatt County,* 596). Post office established July 27, 1870.

MANTENO [man TEE no]. Kankakee. Village (1878) ten miles north of Kankakee. Established by the Illinois Central Railroad as Manteno Station in 1856. Although several writers claim that Manteno is either a scribal error for, or a mishearing of Manitou, the village is almost certainly named for a Potawatomi woman, a daughter or granddaughter of François Bourbonnais, whose name appears as Maw-te-no in the 1832 Treaty of Tippecanoe (Ackerman, *Early Illi-*

nois Railroads, 123; Johnson, comp., "Kankakee County Communities"; Vogel, *Indian Place Names in Illinois*). Post office established April 25, 1854.

MANVILLE. Livingston. Five miles southeast of Streator. Named for Chester R. Manley, first station agent of the Chicago and Paducah Railroad (Bateman and Selby, eds., *Historical Encyclopedia of Illinois and History of Livingston County,* 793). Post office established Jan. 9, 1872, as Collins; changed to Manville Jan. 7, 1883.

MAPLE PARK. Kane. Village (1871) eight miles east of DeKalb. Founded about 1847 as Line, named for its location on the DeKalb–Kane county line. The name was changed to Lodi in 1854 with construction of the Chicago and North Western Railroad. The direct source of the name is unknown. It may be a transfer from Lodi in northern Italy, site of a victory by Napoleon over Austrian armies in 1796. Lodi is a rather common place name in the United States, however, and this may be a transfer, perhaps from Lodi, N.Y., or Lodi, Ohio, two states that contributed a number of settlers to this part of Illinois. Confusion with Loda in Iroquois County led to the change to Maple Park in 1880 (Stennett, *A History of the Origin,* 98). Post office established Jan. 15, 1847, as Line; changed to Lodi Station March 31, 1854; changed to Maple Park Feb. 18, 1880.

MAPLETON. Peoria. Village (1959) five miles west of Pekin. Laid out in 1868 by William T. Maple (*History of Peoria County,* 596). Post office established July 17, 1872.

MAQUON [muh KWAHN]. Knox. Village (1873) nine miles southeast of Knoxville. Laid out about 1837 by Pernach Owen and Elisha Thurman as Bennington, probably named for Bennington, Vt. In 1858 the name was changed to Maquon, probably from a general Algonquian word recorded as A-ma-quon-sip-pi (Squash River), perhaps with the secondary meaning "Mussel Shell River." This was translated into English as "Spoon River," gourds and mussel shells being used as spoons or ladles by some Native Americans (*see* Spoon River) (*History of Maquon and Vicinity,* 45; Perry, *History of Knox County,* 44; personal communication with Michael McCafferty; Stewart, *American Place-Names;* Vogel, *Indian Place Names in Illinois*). Post office established May 5, 1837.

MARAMECH HILL. Summit. Kendall. About five miles west of Yorkville. From a Miami-Illinois word meaning "catfish." Although a Chief Catfish was reported to have a village on the Fox River near the hill, the direct source of the name is probably a mound in the shape of a catfish. Europeans were using the name by the end of the seventeenth century; one Nicholas Perrot was charged with building a fort and trading post at "Marameg" in the 1690s. The word *Merrimac* (q.v.) is a variant (Balesi, *The Time of the French,* 107; Vogel, *Indian Place Names in Illinois*).

MARBLEHEAD. Adams. Five miles south of Quincy. Laid out in 1835. Probably a transfer from Marblehead, Ohio, itself probably a transfer from Marblehead,

Mass. (www.rootsweb.com/~iladams/places/placenames.htm). Post office established July 10, 1878.

MARBLETOWN. Fulton. Eleven miles southwest of Havana. Named from the Marbletown sawmill operated by Hiram Marble and his son in the 1860s (Irwin, *A to Z Fulton County*). Post office established Oct. 3, 1870.

MARCELLINE. Adams. Twelve miles north of Quincy. Laid out by S. M. Jenkins about 1842. Possibly a blend of the names of female members of Jenkins's household, of which Martha and Celesta Iowa were listed in the census of 1850 (Genosky, ed., *People's History*, 738; personal communication with Jean Kay). Post office established Jan. 6, 1843.

MARDEN. Brown. Former community. Named for Mark Marden, proprietor of the area's first general store. The Marden Cemetery is six miles south-southwest of Mount Sterling (*History of Brown County*, 311). Post office established May 21, 1896.

MARENGO. McHenry. City (1857, 1893). Founded in the late 1830s by Calvin Spencer. The name is ultimately from Marengo, Italy, where Napoleon's troops defeated an Austrian army in 1800. Some two dozen communities in the United States are named Marengo and Marengo, Ill., was probably named from a Marengo further east, perhaps in Ohio, Indiana, or New York. Post office established Jan. 22, 1844.

MARIETTA. Fulton. Village (1909) seven miles southeast of Bushnell. Founded in 1837 by Lorenzo Bevans and Benjamin Hoyt. A local story claims that the name *Marietta* is a blend of the names of Marie and Etta Smith, reported to be daughters of an early settler. It is more likely, however, that the community was named by settlers from Marietta, Ohio, itself named for Marie Antoinette (Havens, *Marietta, Illinois*, 1; Irwin, *A to Z Fulton County*). Post office established March 8, 1838; changed to Vanopolis March 10, 1840; changed back to Marietta Jan. 3, 1842.

MARINE. Madison. Village (1867, 1888) nine miles east of Edwardsville. Founded as Madison by Isaac Ferguson and John Warwick in 1813. By about 1820 the community had became known as the Marine Settlement, named for a group of New England sea captains who retired to the area, beginning with Curtis Blakeman and George Allen in 1817 (Loos, *A Walk through Marine*, 6). Post office established April 27, 1835, as Marine Settlement; changed to Marine Sept. 15, 1851.

MARION. County. Created Jan. 24, 1823, from parts of Fayette and Jefferson counties. Named for Francis Marion (ca. 1732–95), the guerrilla commander who operated in the Southeast during the Revolutionary War. His actions were fictionalized, romanticized, and popularized by Mason L. Weems, whose *Life of Gen. Francis Marion*, first published in 1809, brought Marion to the attention of Americans and made him a national hero. The name of the county was suggested by Zadoc Casey, for whom Casey and Caseyville were named and whose father reportedly served under Marion in the Carolinas (*see* Jasper).

MARION. Ogle. Township. Named for Francis Marion by J. C. Rounds. In the middle years of the nineteenth century, Rounds was involved in establishing a number of townships, four of which he named for Francis Marion, first in Michigan, then in Illinois and Wisconsin, and finally in Iowa (Read, "The Recognition of Patterning," 248).

MARION. Williamson. City (1841, 1874). Founded in 1839 as the seat of Williamson County. Probably named for Francis Marion. According to Hubbs, "No record was made of the reason for naming the town, but Francis Marion, the swamp fox, was one of the Revolutionary heroes whose exploits were still common talk" (Hubbs, *Pioneer Folks and Places*). Post office established Jan. 30, 1840.

MARISSA [muh RIS uh]. St. Clair. Village (1882). Founded about 1867 by James Stewart. The generally accepted account is that the name *Marissa* is derived from Marisa, the Greek form of Mareshah, mentioned in the Old Testament, and was chosen by James Wilson, the first postmaster, from his reading of Josephus' *History of the Jews*. The Marissa Public Library has an early-nineteenth-century edition of that volume claimed to be Wilson's personal copy. As a place name, Marissa occurs only in Illinois (*History of St. Clair County*, 246; *Marissa*, 7). Post office established March 31, 1846.

MARKHAM. Cook. City (1925). Named for Charles H. Markham, president of the Illinois Central Railroad in the 1910s and 1920s (Harder, *Illustrated Dictionary of Place Names*).

MARKHAM. Morgan. Three miles west of Jacksonville. Named for Edward Markham, an early settler (Hutchison, "Old Morgan County Village"). Post office established Feb. 28, 1887.

MARLEY. Edgar. Eight miles south-southeast of Paris. Established about 1874 as a station on the Paris and Terre Haute Railroad and named for the Marley family. W. D. Marley was an early grain merchant (*History of Edgar County*, 409).

MARLOW. Jefferson. Five miles east of Mount Vernon. Laid out in the late 1880s by site owner and first postmaster Abraham Marlow (*Facts and Folks*, 233). Post office established April 24, 1882.

MAROA [muh RO uh]. Macon. City (1867, 1889) eight miles south of Clinton. Founded in 1854 by the Associated Land Company and the Illinois Central Railroad. The name is a shortening of Tamaroa (q.v.), one of the tribes of the Illinois Confederacy. According to a local story, the word *Maroa* was created by officials of the IC who drew letters from a hat and rearranged them until a short but grammatical word was formed. This fiction persists in spite of the fact that "Maroa" appears as a tribal name on Marquette's map, and LaSalle refers to the "Tamaroas, or Maroas." This is the only Maroa in the United States (Ackerman,

Early Illinois Railroads, 147; Richmond, *Centennial History of Decatur*, 96–97). Post office established March 30, 1855.

MARQUETTE. Bureau. Ten miles west of Peru. Founded in the 1870s as Loceyville by George Locey of LaSalle. The town site was later sold to Charles Devlin, who changed the name to honor Fr. Jacques Marquette, the French Jesuit missionary who along with Louis Jolliet explored the Mississippi and Illinois river valleys in 1673. The post office was established as Luceyville, apparently a scribal error or a mishearing of Locey. A Marquette County, to be created from the eastern third of Adams County, was authorized by the Illinois legislature in 1840. Because of political infighting, however, it was never formally organized (Leonard, ed., *Big Bureau*, 70; Sublett, *Paper Counties*, 77–88). Post office established Aug. 23, 1883, as Luceyville; changed to Marquette Dec. 31, 1894.

MARROWBONE. Moultrie. Township. Named from Marrowbone Creek. The traditional story is that two hunters, Jacob McCune and Jones Daniels, camped for the night and made their evening meal, venison roasted over the campfire. After eating the meat, they broke the long bones and ate the marrow. The next morning as they were breaking camp, Daniels asked, "What shall we call this place?" McCune looked around at the broken bones and remembering the previous night's meal, replied, 'We will call it Marrowbone'" (*Combined History of Shelby and Moultrie Counties*, 241). Post office established June 19, 1875.

MARSEILLES [mahr SAYLZ]. LaSalle. City (1861, 1884). Laid out about 1835 by Lovell Kimball, founder and director of the Marseilles Manufacturing Company. The traditional story is that Kimball chose the name for Marseilles, France, which he saw as a model for the industrial and manufacturing center he hoped to develop in Illinois. It is possible, however, that Kimball may simply have been attracted to the exotic. His original plat included streets named Valdivia and Valencia, so Marseilles may have been chosen primarily for its foreign flavor (O'Byrne, *History of LaSalle*, 368; *Story of Marseilles*, 12). Post office established Nov. 9, 1835.

MARSHALL. County. Created Jan. 19, 1839, from Putnam County. Named for John Marshall (1755–1835), U.S. secretary of state under John Adams and chief justice of the U.S. Supreme Court, serving from 1801 until 1835.

MARSHALL. Clark. City (1853, 1872). Founded about 1835 by William B. Archer and Joseph Duncan. Named by Archer for John Marshall, chief justice of the U.S. Supreme Court. Marshall has been the seat of Clark County since 1838, when it was changed from Darwin (*History of Marshall, Illinois*, 3). Post office established Aug. 31, 1837.

MARTIN. McLean. Township. Named for Dr. Eleazer Martin of Bloomington, who reportedly owned several thousand acres in the township (*History of McLean County*, 754).

MARTINSVILLE. Clark. City (1875) six miles east of Casey. Founded in 1833 by Joseph Martin. Post office established April 14, 1834.

MARTINTON. Iroquois. Village (1875) ten miles north of Watseka. Founded by Peter Martin, a pioneer from Vermont, who arrived about 1871 (Beckwith, *History of Iroquois County,* 496). Post office established Sept. 8, 1873.

MARYLAND. Ogle. Five miles west-northwest of Mount Morris. Founded in the early 1870s on the line of the Chicago and Iowa Railroad by A. Quinby Allen, a teacher who accompanied a group of colonists from western Maryland (*History of Ogle County,* 468). Post office established July 22, 1874.

MARYVILLE. Madison. Village (1902) two miles north of Collinsville. Named for Mary Lange, who, along with her husband, Charles William Frederick Lange, donated land for the municipal site in 1900. Formerly known as Donkville (q.v.) (www.vil.maryville.il.us/maryville%20 history.html). Post office established June 19, 1903.

MASCOUTAH [mas KOO tuh]. St. Clair. City (1839, 1883). Founded about 1837 as Mechanicsburg by Theodore J. Krafft and John Flanagan. According to local folklore, the name arose among German settlers who welcomed new arrivals with *"machs gut da"* (it's good here). The phrase became a popular expression and eventually the name of the community. In fact, however, the name is from Mascouten (Prairie People), the name of an Algonquian tribe affiliated with the Kickapoo. John Hay, clerk of the circuit court of St. Clair County, is generally credited with suggesting the name in 1839. Muscotten Bay, in Cass County and Mascouten, a Cook County forest preserve, are variants (Bright, *Native American Placenames;* Harris, "Illinois Place-Name Lore," 217; Lill, *An Early History of Mascoutah,* 53). Post office established Sept. 28, 1836, as Mechanicsberg; changed to Mascoutah Aug. 6, 1838.

MASON. County. Created Jan. 20, 1841, from parts of Menard and Tazewell counties. Probably named for Mason County, Ky., itself named for George Mason (1725–92), author of the Virginia Declaration of Rights and delegate to the Constitutional Convention of 1787. Possibly named directly for George Mason.

MASON. Effingham. Town (1865) twelve miles south-southwest of Effingham. First known as Bristol and later as Clio. When the Illinois Central Railroad was completed in 1853, much of Bristol was physically moved about one mile north to trackside. The station was named for Col. Roswell B. Mason, chief engineer for the IC. The post office was established as Ione, a name of uncertain origin; perhaps from a female given name or a railroad name brought to Illinois from California or Nevada (Feldhake, *Effingham County,* 34–35; Pulliam, ed., *Towns of Effingham County, Illinois,* 18). Post office established March 31, 1852, as Ione; changed to Mason Aug. 5, 1857.

MASSAC [MAS ik]. County. Created Feb. 8 and March 3, 1843, from parts of Johnson and Pope counties. Named from Fort Massac east of Metropolis, built by the French about 1757 on the site of a former trading post and mission called Assumption. Some accounts attribute the name to a Lieutenant Massac (or

Marsiac), claimed to be the superintendent in charge of building the fort or having a command there. Rather, the source of the name is the Marquis de Massiac, minister of marine during the French and Indian War. The site is now an Illinois state park (Fortier, "New Light on Fort Massac," 63; *History of Massac County*, 29).

MASSILLON. Wayne. Township and former community. Ebenezer was established some ten miles east-northeast of Fairfield in the 1810s. The site was purchased by William Borah and William Farmer and formally laid out as New Massillon about 1843, named by settlers from Massillon, Stark County, Ohio, itself named for Jean Baptiste Massillon (1663–1742), Bishop of Clermont, France, during the reign of Louis XIV. By 1860 most of the buildings and businesses of New Massillon had been moved to Mount Erie (Coulet du Gard, *Dictionary of French Place Names;* Miller, *Ohio Place Names;* Puckett, *Mount Erie*). Post office established Oct. 18, 1854.

MATANZAS BEACH. Mason. Four miles southeast of Havana. Probably a transfer from the city of Matanzas, east of Havana, Cuba, which was in the news at the time. The choice of the name may have been influenced by Havana, four miles north-northeast, and Cuba, sixteen miles north-northwest. Because the name was in use by 1858, it is not from the Spanish-American War, and there is no evidence to suggest that it was transferred from Matanzas, California, Florida, or Kentucky. From Spanish *matanzas* (slaughter). Post office established Oct. 9, 1858.

MATHERVILLE [MATH er vil]. Mercer. Village (1911) eight miles northeast of Aledo. Named for George Mather, a sales representative for a New York railroad supply firm. The local story is that Mather offered a substantial discount to the builders of the Rock Island Southern Railroad if they would name a station after him (Anderson, *Matherville History*, 8). Post office established Jan. 15, 1910, as Mathersville; changed to Matherville Nov. 28, 1911.

MATTESON. Cook. Village (1889). Founded about 1855 and named for Joel Aldrich Matteson (1808–73), governor of Illinois from 1853 to 1857. By the 1970s the pronunciation [MAT suhn] had become so common that village officials distributed cards with the "correct" pronunciation [MAT uh suhn] to local residents and businesses (Koziol, "Two Syllables or Three"). Post office established Oct. 3, 1853, as Rich; changed to Matteson Nov. 29, 1856.

MATTOON [MA TOON]. Coles. City (1859, 1879). Founded about 1854. Named for William B. Mattoon, a partner in the firm of Barnes, Phelps and Mattoon, of Springfield, Mass., which held the contract for grading this section of the Alton and Terre Haute Railroad. Mattoon reportedly won the right to name the community in a card game (Ackerman, *Early Illinois Railroads*, 128; Redlich, *The Postal History of Coles County*, 59). Post office established July 14, 1855.

MAUD. Wabash. Five miles west of Mount Carmel. Named for Maud Bell, daughter of attorney and county judge Robert S. Bell (Barge and Caldwell, "Illinois Place Names"). Post office established July 11, 1882.

MAUNIE [MAW NEE]. White. Village (1901). Seven miles southeast of Carmi. Although reported to be a variant of Monee (q.v.), Maunie is a blend of the names of Maude Sheridan and Jennie Pumphrey, wives or daughters of early settlers (Ackerman, *Early Illinois Railroads*, 120; *Times*). Post office established June 27, 1872, as Marshall's Ferry; changed to Maunie July 17, 1893.

MAY. Townships in Christian and Lee counties. Named for Capt. Charles A. May, breveted colonel for his leadership at the Battle of Resaca de la Palma during the Mexican War. May was killed at the battle of Palo Alto in 1846 (Goudy, *History of Christian County*, 299; *History of Lee County*, 468).

MAYBERRY. Hamilton. Township. Named for Frederick Mayberry, a local land owner of the 1830s (*History of Gallatin, Saline*, 243).

MAYFAIR. Cook. The name was reportedly taken from a novel named *Mayfair,* set in the Mayfair section of London. Now part of Chicago (Stennett, *A History of the Origin*, 100). Post office established June 2, 1882.

MAYFIELD. DeKalb. Township. Organized early in 1850 as Liberty, possibly so named because the organizers were active in the Underground Railroad. The name was changed later in 1850 at the request of the first township supervisor, Mulford Nickerson, whose daughter, Eunice, thought Mayfield would be more appropriate because of the exuberance of wild flowers there each spring (Boies, *History of DeKalb County*, 465; Gross, *Past and Present of DeKalb County*, 152).

MAYSVILLE. Clay. Laid out about 1824 by Daniel May as Hubbardsville, named for Adolphus F. Hubbard, lieutenant governor of Illinois from 1822 to 1826. The name was changed to Maysville, for Daniel May, by the County Commissioners Court in 1825. Maysville was the first seat of Clay County, serving from 1825 until 1841, when it was moved to Louisville. Now part of Clay City (Hansen, ed., *Illinois*, 702; *History of Wayne and Clay Counties*, 322–23). Post office established June 13, 1825.

MAYWOOD. Cook. Village (1881). Established in 1869 as a planned residential community by William T. Nichols and a group of New England entrepreneurs organized as the Maywood Land Company. Named by Nichols for his daughter, May (Kitagawa and Taeuber, eds., *Local Community Fact Book*, 194). Post office established Arpil 29, 1870.

MAZEPPA [muh ZEP uh]. Sangamon. Former community in Ball Township. Founded by George R. Spottswood in 1837 and probably named for *Mazeppa*, the poem by Lord Byron (*History of Sangamon County*, 792).

MAZON [muh ZAHN]. Grundy. Village (1895) eight miles south of Morris. From an Algonquian word for the nettle or wild hemp plant, the fibers of which

Native Americans braided into rope. Mazonia, eight miles east-southeast of Mazon, is a variant (Brown, ed., *Grundy County*, 23; Vogel, *Indian Place Names in Illinois*).

MCCLELLAN. Jefferson. Township. Originally called Allen. The name was changed in 1870 for Simon McClellan, an early settler who arrived in the 1820s (Perrin, ed., *History of Jefferson County*, 792).

MCCLURE. Alexander. Five miles east of Cape Girardeau, Mo. Originally called Wheatland. The name was changed about 1894 for J. T. McClure (*Alexander County*, 15). Post office established Dec. 4, 1836, as Clear Creek Landing; changed to Wheatland March 15, 1887; changed to McClure April 10, 1895.

MCCONNELL. Stephenson. Ten miles north-northwest of Freeport. In 1838 John Dennison and John Van Zant sold the town site to Robert McConnell, from whom both the formal name and nickname, "Bobtown," derive (*History of Stephenson County*, 207). Post office established June 19, 1849, as McConnell's Grove; changed to McConnell May 14, 1883.

MCCOOK. Cook. Village (1926) two miles south of Brookfield. Named for John J. McCook, general counsel for the Santa Fe Railroad in the 1890s (Stephenson, "Many Towns Named," 55).

MCCORMICK. Pope. Fourteen miles southwest of Harrisburg. Founded in 1889 by Christian L. McCormick, the first postmaster (*Pope County*, 33). Post office established Sept. 16, 1889.

MCCULLOM LAKE. McHenry. Village (1955) northeast of McHenry. Named from McCullom Lake, itself named for early settler William McCullom and his brothers, David and John (Leptich, "President Enjoys a Real-Life Mayberry").

MCDONOUGH [mik DUHN uh]. County. Created Jan. 25, 1826. Named for Thomas McDonough (Macdonough) (1783–1825), a naval commander during the War of 1812 whose victory over the British fleet at Plattsburgh Bay on Lake Champlain in 1814 kept New York and Vermont from British occupation.

MCDOWELL. Livingston. Four miles southeast of Pontiac. Laid out in 1873 by county judge and site owner Woodford G. McDowell (*History of Livingston County* [1878], 385, 387). Post office established Jan. 15, 1872.

MCHENRY. County. Created Jan. 16, 1836, from Cook County. Named for William McHenry (1771–1835). McHenry fought beside Anthony Wayne at the Battle of Fallen Timbers in Ohio in 1794 and in 1811 was appointed captain in the Illinois territorial militia by Gov. Ninian Edwards. McHenry also served in the War of 1812 and the Black Hawk War of 1832 (www.iltrails.org/mchenry/majormchenry.htm).

MCHENRY. McHenry. City (1855, 1872). Named for its location in McHenry County. West McHenry, now part of McHenry, was first known as Gagetown, named for

George Gage, the first state senator from McHenry and a member of the family that gave its name to Gage's Lake. McHenry served as the seat of McHenry County from 1837 until 1843, when it was moved to Centreville (Woodstock). Post office established June 27, 1837.

MCKEE. Adams. Township. Named from McKee Creek, itself named for John McKee (or McGee), who surveyed the area about 1815. The Melish map of 1819 labels the stream "R. Mauvaise Terre or McKees Cr." (Dearinger, "A New Geography of Brown County," 28; *History of Brown County,* 309).

MCLEAN [muh KLAYN]. County. Created Dec. 25, 1830, from Tazewell County. The first name suggested for the new county was Hendricks in honor of William Hendricks, at the time a U.S. senator from Indiana. When it was agreed that the county should not be named for a living person, William L. D. Ewing (for whom Ewington is named) proposed McLean in honor of John McLean (1791–1830) of Shawneetown, recently deceased. McLean was the first U.S. representative from the state of Illinois, serving from 1818 to 1819, and then a U.S. senator from 1824 to 1825 and 1829 to 1830.

MCLEANSBORO [muh KLAYNZ ber o, muh KLAYNZ ber uh]. Hamilton. City (1840, 1874). Named for Dr. William B. McLean, who sold land to Hamilton County on which to establish the county offices. McLeansboro has been the seat of Hamilton County since 1821 (Kinnear, *Brief History,* 1). Post office established Jan. 29, 1822.

MCNABB. Putnam. Village (1959) eleven miles southwest of Peru. Founded in 1900 by site owners John M. and James A. McNabb (Alleman and Immel, *A Putnam County History,* 42). Post office established June 26, 1874, as Whittaker; changed to Clear Creek Dec. 21, 1875; changed to McNabb Sept. 6, 1900.

MCNULTA. McLean. Eight miles southwest of Gibson City. Founded about 1865 and named for Col. John McNulta of the Ninety-fourth Illinois Regiment, a Civil War veteran and U.S. representative from Illinois from 1873 to 1875 (Bateman and Selby, eds., *Historical Encyclopedia of Illinois and History of McLean County,* 67).

MCQUEEN. Kane. Three miles west of Elgin. Named for postmaster John A. McQueen (Adams, comp., *Illinois Place Names*). Post office established March 9, 1885.

MECHANICSBURG. Sangamon. Village (1869, 1907). Laid out by William S. Pickrell in 1832, who offered a free building lot to any mechanic (craftsman) who would establish a business in the community (*Mechanicsburg Sesquicentennial,* 5). Post office established Sept. 29, 1830, as Clear Creek; changed to Mechanicksburg July 15, 1839; changed to Mechanicsburg May 7, 1886.

MEDIA [muh DEE uh]. Henderson. Village (1902) thirteen miles southwest of Monmouth. Founded in 1887 with construction of the Santa Fe Railroad by site owner Nathan Weaver. Media, Latin for "middle," was likely chosen because the site was midway between Chicago and Kansas City on the Santa Fe line (Blevins, *Peculiar, Uncertain, and Two Egg;* Sutton, *Rivers, Railways,* 84). Post office established June 13, 1888.

MEDINA [muh DEYE nuh]. Peoria. Township. The origin of the name is uncertain. Medina in Saudi Arabia is the second-holiest city of Islam and the burial site of the Prophet Muhammad. It is unlikely, however, that this is the direct source of the township name. It is more likely a transfer from one of the several dozen Medinas in the eastern states, perhaps Medina, N.Y or Medina, Ohio. Akron and Chillicothe, both transfers from Ohio, are nearby. The Medina post office was in service for three weeks, from April 4 until April 28, 1873, when it was changed to Alta.

MEDINAH [muh DEYE nuh]. DuPage. Five miles northwest of Addison. Named from the Medinah Country Club, a golf course established by Shriners from the Medina Temple in Chicago in the early 1920s in an area of north DuPage County then known as Meacham (www.medinahcc.org). Post office established Jan. 29, 1874, as Meacham; changed to Medinah March 7, 1924.

MEDORA [muh DOR uh]. Jersey, Macoupin. Village (1874) ten miles east of Jerseyville. Formerly known as Rhoades Point for the six Rhoades brothers: John, Henry, Samuel, Jesse, Jacob, and Josiah. Formally laid out by site owner Thomas B. Rice in 1859. Medora may be from a female personal name, but most likely it was taken from *The Corsair,* a narrative poem by Lord Byron in which Medora is the name of the romantic heroine (*History of Macoupin County* [1879], 179, 180). Post office established April 1, 1837, as Delaware; changed to Rhoades Point June 30, 1851; changed to Trumbull Feb. 16, 1863; changed to Medora July 9, 1866.

MEISENHEIMER. Union. Precinct. Named for the Meisenheimer family. Moses Meisenheimer was an early settler from North Carolina in 1816 (Perrin, ed., *History of Alexander, Union, and Pulaski Counties,* 405).

MELLONSVILLE. Hamilton. Former community six miles south of McLeansboro. Named for a family named Mellon. Previously known as Knight's Prairie and Cracker's Neck. The latter name was derived, some say, by the "sporting" practice of hanging a goose over the main street by its feet. Contestants on horseback would ride under the goose and try to "crack" its neck (*Hamilton County,* 44).

MELROSE. Ultimately from the town and ruined abbey in southeastern Scotland, the setting of Sir Walter Scott's *The Abbey* and *The Monastery.* Melrose townships in Adams and Clark counties were probably named for Melrose, Mass. Melrose Park in Cook County was laid out as Melrose about 1873 by the Melrose Land Company, itself perhaps named for Melrose, Scotland, perhaps for Melrose, Mass., or Melrose, N.Y. (Bateman and Selby, eds., *Historical Encyclopedia of Illinois Cook County Edition,* 791). Post office established May 2, 1888, as Ovington; changed to Melrose Park Jan. 28, 1893.

MENARD [muh NAHRD]. County. Created Feb. 15, 1839, from Sangamon County. Named for Pierre Menard (1766–1844), a French-Canadian trader and entrepreneur who settled in Kaskaskia about 1790 and became an important political figure in early Illinois. Menard was president of the Illinois Territorial Legislative Council in the 1810s and was the state's first lieutenant governor, serving under Shadrack Bond (for whom Bond County is named) from 1818 until 1822.

MENDON. Adams. Village (1839, 1891) thirteen miles northeast of Quincy. Laid out in 1833 as Fairfield, named for Fairfield, Conn., by John B. Chittendon, who organized the first Congregational Church in Illinois. The name was changed to Mendon in 1839 for one of the New England Mendons, likely Mendon, Mass., itself named for Mendon in Suffolk, England (Genosky, ed., *People's History*, 730; *History of Payson*, 3). Post office established May 5, 1837.

MENDOTA [men DO tuh]. LaSalle. City (1859–83). Ultimately from a Dakota (Siouan) word referring to the mouth of a river or the point where one stream flows into another. Mendota was established by the Illinois Central Railroad about 1853, and the name may have been transferred from Mendota, Minn. Alternatively, the name may have been proposed by O. N. Adams, owner of the Mendota Furnace, an ore processing facility near Galena (Ackerman, *Early Illinois Railroads*, 142; Bright, *Native American Placenames*; *History of LaSalle County*, 661). Post office established Dec. 10, 1853.

MENOMINEE. Jo Daviess. Village (1935) seven miles northwest of Galena. Named from the Menominee tribe, now resident in Wisconsin. The name itself is from an Ojibwa word meaning "wild rice people," referring to a major food source of the Menominee. The name was suggested by James Finley, the first township supervisor, in the early 1850s, probably for Menominee, Wis. (Bateman and Selby, eds., *Historical Encyclopedia of Illinois and History of Jo Daviess County*, 633; Bright, *Native American Placenames*). Post office established July 12, 1861, as Excelsior Mills; changed to Menominee Aug. 24, 1885.

MEPPEN [MEP uhn]. Calhoun. Sixteen miles southwest of Jerseyville. Named by settlers from Meppen, Hanover, Germany (Carpenter, *Calhoun Is My Kingdom*, 31). Post office established Sept. 29, 1876.

MERCER. County. Created Jan. 13, 1825. Named for Hugh Mercer (1725–77), an officer in the Revolutionary War killed at the Battle of Princeton, N.J.

MEREDITH. Kane. Ten miles east of DeKalb. Named for the Meredith family. Thomas Meredith Jr. was Kane County clerk in the 1880s (Joslyn and Joslyn, *History of Kane County*, 824).

MEREDOSIA [mehr uh DO shuh]. Morgan. Village (1867, 1906) sixteen miles northwest of Jacksonville. Founded about 1816 by site owners J. E. Waldo and Philip Aylesworth. Platted about 1832 by Thomas January. Named from Meredosia Lake, but the source of the name is uncertain. By one account, it derives from French *mer* (sea) plus *osia* (or *d'osia*) for Fr. Antoine D'Osia, a French priest associated with a mission just north of present Meredosia in the 1810s. By another account, the name is from French *marais* (swamp; lake) plus the same *osia* (or *d'osia*). By a third account, it is from *marais* plus *d'osia* (of the reeds)—in other words, a lake of reeds or willows. This suggestion is supported by the fact that in Mississippi Valley French the word *marais* referred not so much to a marsh as to a shallow lake, particularly an oxbow lake, which could refer to present Meredosia Lake. A fourth possibility is suggested by an alternate name for Meredosia, Marais d'Ogee (Ogee's Lake). The Ogee in question may have been a relative of Joseph Ogee, who operated a ferry across the Rock River at Dixon (Coulet du Gard, *Dictionary of French Place Names; History of Morgan County*, 413; McDermott, "The French Impress on Place Names," 227; *Meredosia Bicentennial Book*, 4; Stewart, *American Place-Names*). Post office established Jan. 19, 1832.

MERIDEN [MEHR uh duhn]. LaSalle. Four miles east-northeast of Mendota. Founded in 1863 by Samuel Wiley as Job's Station. The name was changed later that year by Nathaniel Cook for his former home, Meriden Conn., itself named for Meriden, a village in the West Midlands of England (*Past and Present of LaSalle County*, 352; Rasmusen, *LaSalle County Lore*, 18, 21). Post office established Feb. 16, 1863.

MERIDIAN. Clinton. Township. Named from the third principle meridian, which forms the boundary between Clinton and Marion counties. The third principle meridian was established by the Land Ordinance of 1785 to aid surveyors in laying out townships in the Northwest Territory (*History of Marion and Clinton Counties*, 249).

MERMET. Massac. Ten miles northwest of Metropolis. Named for Fr. Jean Mermet, who established a mission called Assumption near Fort Massac about 1700 (*History of Massac County*, 27; May, *Massac Pilgrimage*, 25). Post office established July 12, 1916.

MERNA. McLean. Six miles east of Normal. Named for the Merna family. William Merna was an early postmaster (Adams, comp., *Illinois Place Names;* Townley, *Historic McLean*, 19). Post office established Aug. 5, 1883.

MERRIMAC. Monroe. Ten miles west-northwest of Waterloo, opposite the mouth of the Meramec River south of St. Louis, Mo., and named for that river. The change in spelling to Merrimac is due to the influence of the more familiar Merrimack River in New Hampshire and Massachusetts. The names *Meramec, Merrimack,* and *Maramech* are from the same Algonquian word that came to mean "deep place" in New England and "catfish" in the Midwest, as in Maramech Hill (q.v.) (Bright, *Native American Placenames;* Stewart, *American Place-Names*). Post office established Aug. 13, 1861, as Merrimack Point; changed to Merrimac Point June 1878; changed to Merrimac May 28, 1895.

MERRIONETTE PARK. Cook. Village (1947). Founded in 1947 and named for himself by developer Joseph E. Merrion, also the founder of Country Club Hills and Hometown (Rhodes, "So Little Space").

MERRITT. Scott. Eight miles west of Jacksonville. Laid out in 1870 by Mary Ann Sharown as the community of Mary Ann. About 1876 the name was changed to Merritt, named for a railroad executive (*Scott County Bicentennial Book*, 181). Post office established Feb. 2, 1870.

MESO. Jefferson. Former community in Bald Hill Township. Named for Cornelius Meso or Mezo, a Civil War veteran and the oldest resident when the community was established (www.genealogytrails.com/ill/jefferson/ghostowns.html). Post office established March 9, 1900.

METAMORA [met uh MOR uh]. Woodford. Village (1845, 1875). Founded in 1836 as Hanover, named for Hanover, N.H., by the Hanover Company, a consortium of land speculators that owned some twelve thousand acres in the area. The name was changed in the mid-1840s at the suggestion of Mrs. Peter H. Willard, who had lived in Vermont and was familiar with a popular play first performed in 1829, *Metamora; or, The Last of the Wampanoags* by John Augustus Stone. Metamora was a literary name for Metacomet, a seventeenth-century Wampanoag leader better known as King Philip (Bright, *Native American Placenames;* Moore, *History of Woodford County,* 179; Smith, *Metamora,* 8–10, 15; Yates, *The Woodford County History,* 289). Post office established Feb. 4, 1836, as Black Partridge; changed to Partridge Point June 7, 1837; changed to Metamora Aug. 23, 1845.

METCALF. Edgar. Village (1855) fourteen miles north-northwest of Paris. Founded in 1874 by site owner John A. Metcalf (*History of Edgar County,* 524). Post office established Dec. 15, 1874.

METROPOLIS [muh TRAHP luhs]. Massac. City (1859, 1873). Founded in 1839 by merchant William A. McBane and site owner James Hendrix Gaines Wilcox, who both saw the location as an ideal spot for a railroad bridge across the Ohio River, linking north and south. They envisioned a commercial and industrial center rivaling and eventually surpassing the established cities of the East, thus the name *Metropolis,* Greek for "great city." Adjacent Massac City merged with Metropolis in 1892 (Hansen, ed., *Illinois,* 489; Page, *History of Massac County,* 128). Post office established Dec. 13, 1837, as Wilcox's Ferry; changed to Metropolis City Feb. 25, 1840; changed to Metropolis Dec. 12, 1904.

METTAWA. Lake. Village (1960) four miles southeast of Libertyville. Named for Mettawa, a Potawatomi leader whose village was just south of the present community in the 1830s. The name was proposed by James Getz, a community official and president of the Lake County Historical Society. From an Ojibwa word perhaps meaning "meeting of waters" (Dretske, *What's in a Name?;* Vogel, *Indian Place Names in Illinois*).

MEYER. Adams. One mile northeast of Canton, Mo. Named for C. Henry Meyer, business manager of the *Quincy Journal* (Genosky, ed., *People's History,* 718). Post office established Jan. 11, 1895.

MIAMI. Cook. Forest preserve. From the name of the Miami tribe, probably meaning "downstream people." Europeans first encountered the Miami in Wisconsin, and they subsequently located in Michigan, Indiana, and Ohio, where a number of place names attest to their presence. The name of Miami, Fla., is apparently unrelated (Bright, *Native American Placenames*).

MIDLAND CITY. DeWitt. Nine miles west of Clinton. Founded early in 1875 as Dunham. The name was changed later that year to Midland for the Illinois Midland Railroad (*History of DeWitt County, 1839–1968,* 29). Post office established Aug. 5, 1875.

MIDLOTHIAN [mid LOTH ee uhn]. Cook. Village (1927). The community grew around the Midlothian Golf Course, established in 1898 by a group of Chicago executives that included George R. Thorne, president of Montgomery Ward. The club's name was influenced by the Scottish origins of golf, possibly by the former county of Midlothian in southeastern Scotland, and by Sir Walter Scott's *The Heart of Midlothian* (Stevens, "High Pride"). Post office established March 10, 1922.

MIDWAY. Massac. Eight miles northeast of Metropolis. Founded about 1900. Reportedly so named because it was thought to be midway between Metropolis and Golconda (*History of Massac County,* 35).

MILAM. Macon. Township. Named for the Milam apple. The name was suggested by J. B. Gleason, the first township supervisor, presumably because the Milam apple grew well in the area (Nelson, *City of Decatur,* 413).

MILAN [MEYE luhn]. Rock Island. Village (1865, 1893) south of Rock Island–Moline. Founded in 1843 by William Dickson as Camden, perhaps named for Camden, N.Y., or Camden, Pa. The name was changed to Camden Mills in 1848 and to Milan in 1870. According to one source, "A man by the name of Sullivan came to Camden Mills with patents for a new type of watch which he said was so wonderfully accurate and yet so simply designed that it would put all other watch factories out of business. Local men bought the patent, built the factory and changed the name of the town to Milan at the gentleman's suggestion as he said that Camden Mills would not look well on a gold watch. The machinery, when it arrived, was not suitable for manufacturing watches and the venture failed" (Scott and Anderson, *Travels in Time,* 184). Post office established Jan. 24, 1845, as Camden Mills; changed to Milan Dec. 21, 1870.

MILAN. DeKalb. Township. Probably a transfer from Milan, Dutchess County, N.Y. The name was perhaps suggested by Lewis McEwen, acknowledged as the first settler, who arrived from New York in 1852 (Gross, *Past and Present of DeKalb County,* 124).

MILES STATION. Macoupin. Named for postmaster Jonathan R. Miles (Adams, comp., *Illinois Place Names*). Post office established March 14, 1856.

MILFORD. Iroquois. Village (1874) twelve miles north of Hoopeston. Formerly known as Pickerell's Mill for miller William Pickerell. Formally established as a Quaker colony by settlers from Ohio. Named Milford about 1836, perhaps for Pickerell's mill but more likely a transfer, perhaps from Milford, Clermont County, Ohio (*Illinois Gazetteer*). Post office established Oct. 15, 1833, as Driftwood; changed to Milford March 13, 1840.

MILKS GROVE. Iroquois. Township. Named for Lemuel Milk, a farmer who raised stock and was proprietor of the Waldron Ice Company (Dowling, *History of Iroquois County*, 87). Post office established March 15, 1876.

MILLBURN. Lake. One mile northeast of Lindenhurst. Settled largely by immigrants from Scotland. The name *Millburn* is said to be a Scots form of Mill Creek, derived from Scots *burn* (creek) (*Past and Present of Lake County*, 242). Post office established Jan. 24, 1848.

MILLEDGEVILLE. Carroll. Village (1887) twelve miles north-northwest of Sterling. The traditional story is that an early settler operated a sawmill on the outskirts of town, this being literally the mill at the edge of the village. More likely, however, this is a transfer from an existing Milledgeville, perhaps Milledgeville, Ga. (Thiem, ed., *Carroll County*, 195). Post office established Feb. 22, 1844.

MILLER CITY. Alexander. Southwest of the Horseshoe Lake Conservation Area. Named for Jesse, Eugene, and Sidney Miller, who had extensive land holdings in the area (*Alexander County*, 16). Post office established Jan. 11, 1890, as Willard; changed to Miller City Oct. 27, 1911.

MILLER GROVE. Pope. Former community. Founded in the 1830s by Harrison and Lucinda Miller, freed slaves from Tennessee. The community was formally organized in the early 1840s and named for the Millers' son, Bedford. The Miller Grove School was about four miles northeast of Glendale (*Pope County*, 33).

MILLERSBURG. Bond. Named for the first mill in the area, built and operated— appropriately—by Charles Miller. Now part of Pierron (Perrin, ed., *History of Bond and Montgomery Counties*, 144).

MILLERSBURG. Mercer. Four miles northwest of Aledo. Founded about 1835 and named for site owner John Miller. Millersburg was the seat of Mercer County from 1837 until 1847, when it was changed to Keithsburg (*History of Mercer and Henderson Counties*, 211). Post office established April 5, 1838, as Millersburgh; changed to Millersburg Nov. 21, 1894.

MILLERSVILLE. Christian. Five miles northwest of Pana. Laid out in 1873 as a railroad station midway between Pana and Owaneco. Named for site owner Thomas Miller (*Christian County History*, 44). Post office established Dec. 14, 1872.

MILLINGTON. Kendall. Village (1893) six miles south of Sandwich. Founded in 1838 as Millford. The name was apparently changed from Millford to Mellington with establishment of the post office in 1861 and then to Millington in 1872. The source of the name is unknown (Hicks, *History of Kendall County*, 192). Post office established July 9, 1861, as Mellington; changed to Millington May 28, 1872.

MILLS. Bond. Township. Named for the Mills family. A. G. Mills was an early settler, followed by Andrew and Joseph Mills (Bateman and Selby, eds., *Historical Encyclopedia of Illinois and History of Bond County*, 635).

MILL SHOALS. White. Village (1896) nine miles south of Fairfield. Founded in the early 1830s by settlers from New York as Waccababa, likely named for Waccabuc, the village and river in Westchester County, N.Y. William Weed established a mill at the site about 1855. The community was formally laid out in 1869 by a Judge Boggs, who took the name from the Mill Shoals post office, itself named from Weed's mill (*Times*, 226, 229). Post office established Sept. 16, 1857.

MILLSTADT. St. Clair. Village (1878). Laid out about 1836 by Joseph Abend as Centerville, named for its location between Belleville and Columbia on the Cahokia-Kaskaskia stagecoach line. When the petition for a post office was denied because of an existing Centerville, settlers from Saxony translated "Centerville" into German *Mittelstadt* (Middle Town), which reportedly was altered by postal officials to the more familiar Millstadt. The community of Mittelstadt was renamed for the Millstadt post office about 1878 (*Illinois Guide; Tapestry of Time*, 154). Post office established June 7, 1843.

MILMINE. Piatt. Fourteen miles east-northeast of Decatur. Laid out about 1853 as Farnsworth by Amos (or Enos) Farnsworth, claimed to be a friend of Abraham Lincoln, who owned much of the land between present Milmine and Cerro Gordo. Farnsworth subsequently sold the site to George and Emma Milmine, who renamed the community after themselves (Piatt, *History of Piatt County*, 467; West, *A Heritage Reborn*, 27). Post office established June 17, 1862.

MILO. Bureau. Thirteen miles northwest of Henry. According to local accounts, someone at a meeting to choose a name for the community noticed that on the county map the township of Wheatland resembled a person with half an arm and said it looked like the Venus de Milo. Even with half an arm, someone else remarked, the Venus de Milo still looked good. Thus the name *Milo*. More likely, however, the name is a transfer, perhaps from Milo, Yates County, N.Y. (Leonard, ed., *Big Bureau*, 75). Post office established May 30, 1850.

MINDALE. Schuyler. Eleven miles northeast of Mount Sterling. Named from the general store known as Mindale, derived from the names of the proprietors, Minnie and Dale Gallaher (*Schuyler County*, 122).

MINDALE. Tazewell. Twenty miles west-southwest of Bloomington. Created by the Illinois Traction Interurban Railroad from the names of two of its stations, Minier and Hopedale (personal communication with the Tazewell County Genealogical and Historical Society).

MINEOLA BAY. Lake. Bay in Fox Lake. Named from the Mineola Hotel, established in 1884 by members of the Chicago Board of Trade. The hotel was probably named for Mineola, Nassau County, N.Y. (Dretske, *What's in a Name?*).

MINERAL. Bureau. Village (1899) ten miles north-northeast of Kewanee. Laid out by William Riley in 1857. Presumably named for the underlying coal deposits (Matson, *Map and Sketches of Bureau County*, 94). Post office established Aug. 5, 1856.

MINIER [meye NIHR, mi NIHR, MEYE nihr]. Tazewell. Village (1872) fourteen miles west of Bloomington. Founded about 1867 by George Washington Minier and several others where the tracks of the Chicago and Alton Railroad crossed those of the Illinois Midland. Minier was also one of the founders of Mackinaw (Bateman and Selby, eds., *Historical Encyclopedia of Illinois and History of Tazewell County*, 854; *History of Tazewell County*, 521). Post office established Feb. 9, 1866, as Broadway; changed to Minier Nov. 26, 1867.

MINONK. Woodford. City (1867, 1872) eleven miles north of El Paso. Established by the Illinois Central Railroad in 1854 and named by David A. Neal, vice president of the IC. From Ojibwa for "good place." Minong, Wis., is a variant (Bright, *Native American Placenames*; Yates, *The Woodford County History*, 106, 112). Post office established Dec. 22, 1854.

MINOOKA [mi NOO kuh]. Grundy. Village (1869). Laid out in 1852 by Ransom Gardner in an attempt to attract a station on the Rock Island Railroad. Named by Dolly Smith, whose husband, Leander, was president of the first village board. Smith reportedly adapted the name *Minooka* from an Algonquian word meaning "good land" or "high land." Minocqua in Oneida County, Wis., is probably a variant. The name also occurs in Pennsylvania and Kansas (Handley, "Boomtown"; Ullrich, *This Is Grundy County*, 159). Post office established Feb. 21, 1854.

MINT CREEK. Jasper. Stream. Empties into the Embarrass River near Newton. Reportedly named for the site where Cornelius Taylor ran a counterfeiting operation in the early 1820s. When the "mint" was discovered, it contained molds and printing apparatus for producing bogus coins and paper currency (Misenheimer, *The Johnstown Story*, 20)

MISSION. LaSalle. Township. Named from Mission Creek, itself named for the mission of the Methodist Episcopal Church established by Jesse Walker at the head of the stream about 1826 to "convert the Indians and educate their children." The Sauk burned the mission in 1832 (*History of LaSalle County*, 424; O'Byrne, *History of LaSalle*, 408).

MISSISSIPPI. Jersey. Township. Named from the Mississippi River, itself named from an Algonquian word meaning "big river." The river appears on Marquette's map of about 1673 as R. de la Conception (River of the Immaculate Conception) and on the map attributed to Jolliet (about 1674) as the Rivière Buade in honor of Louis de Buade, Comte de Frontenac, the governor of New France in the late seventeenth century. By the mid-1680s the name was appearing as *Messipi*. (Stewart, *American Place-Names*).

MISSOURI [mi ZOO ri, mi ZOO ruh]. Brown. Township. Probably named from Missouri Creek, which empties into the LaMoine River some seven miles southwest of Rushville. From an Illinois word meaning "big boat" or "wooden boat," referring to the Missouri, the "big boat people" or "people with boats made of wood," a Siouan tribe living near the mouth of the Missouri River (McCafferty, "On the Birthday and Etymology of the Placename 'Missouri'"; McCafferty, "Correction"; Vogel, *Indian Place Names in Illinois*).

MITCHELL. Madison. Two miles northeast of Granite City. Founded about 1864. Named for John J. Mitchell, an official of the Alton and St. Louis Railroad (Underwood, "A New Geography of Illinois: Madison County," 31). Post office established Feb. 24, 1869, as Long Lake; changed to Mitchell March 10, 1892.

MITCHELLSVILLE. Saline. Five miles south of Harrisburg. Laid out about 1847 as Independence by Stephen E. Mitchell. The name was changed to Mitchellsville in 1848 (*History of Saline County*, 181). Post office established Dec. 22, 1854.

MITCHIE. Monroe. Thirteen miles southwest of Waterloo. A shortening of Michigamea, one of the native people composing the Illinois. A "Metchigamea" village appears on Marquette's map west of the Mississippi River near present Memphis, Tenn. The Michigamea were subsequently forced north into Illinois where they allied themselves with the Kaskaskia. Bellin's map of the mid-1750s shows a "Metchigamia" village just south of present Mitchie (*Combined History of Randolph, Monroe, and Perry Counties*, 395). Post office established March 10, 1857, as Hardscrabble; changed to Mitchie Jan. 18, 1859.

MOAHWAY. Kendall. Originally a tract of 180 acres granted to Mo-Ah-Way, a Potawatomi leader, by the Treaty of Prairie du Chien in 1829. Mo-Ah-Way sold the land to European settlers several years later. Such grants were called reservations, and the Moahway reservation was located near present Reservation Road, south of Aurora. From Potawatomi *moah* (wolf) (Dickson, "Geographical Features and Place Names").

MOCCASIN. Effingham. Ten miles west of Effingham. Named from Moccasin Creek, itself probably named by pioneer Griffin Tipsword, either for some moccasin prints he saw along its banks or for the presence of the snakes known as water moccasins (Bateman and Selby, eds., *Illinois Historical Effingham County Biographical*, 641; Perrin, ed., *History of Effingham County*, 271). Post office established Nov. 17, 1862, as Mocasin; changed to Moccasin June 1865.

MODE. Shelby. Ten miles south of Shelbyville. Laid out in 1866 as Smithville by Jacob Smith. Subsequently renamed for the Mode post office. The source of the name is unknown. This is the only community in the United States named

Mode (*Combined History of Shelby and Moultrie Counties,* 295). Post office established Oct. 18, 1854.

MODENA. Stark. Eleven miles southeast of Kewanee. Founded about 1853 by Williston K. and Miles A. Fuller. Probably a transfer from Modina, Chester County, Pa., itself named for Modena in northern Italy (Leeson, *Documents and Biography,* 257). Post office established Dec. 24, 1849, as Gallatin; changed to Dorrance July 8, 1850; changed to Modena Nov. 13, 1861.

MODESTO [mo DES to]. Macoupin. Village (1896) fourteen miles northwest of Carlinville. Named by I. B. Vancil, one of the site owners, for Modesto, Calif., which he had recently visited (*Modesto Centennial Book,* 2). Post office established March 6, 1882.

MODOC [MO dahk]. Randolph. Eleven miles south of Red Bud. Named for the Modoc War of 1872–73, during which the Modoc leader Kintpuash, better known as Captain Jack, held off U.S. Army troops for months, fighting in the lava beds of northern California. The Modoc War was widely reported in the Midwest. Post office established Oct. 2, 1868, as Brewerville; changed to Modoc June 5, 1882.

MOHAWK. DuPage. Probably a transfer from the Mohawk River and Valley in New York, themselves named for the Mohawk Nation. Now part of Bensenville.

MOKENA [mo KEE nuh]. Will. Village (1880). Laid out in 1852 for the Chicago and Rock Island Railroad by Allen Denny. Although an early account claims that the village was named for Mokanna (al-Moqanna), a major character in Thomas Moore's epic poem *Lalla Rookh,* the name is most likely an adaptation of Algonquian *makina* "turtle" (*see* Mackinaw). This is the only Mokena in the United States (Maue, *History of Will County,* 211; Pitman, *Story of Mokena,* 4; Stewart, *American Place-Names*). Post office established Feb. 10, 1853.

MOLINE [mo LEEN]. Rock Island. City (1855, 1872). Founded about 1841 by David B. Sears, Charles Atkinson, and others as Rock Island Mills, named for the sawmills and grist mills operating along the Rock and Mississippi rivers. The surveyor drew up two plats, one with the name *Hesperia,* the other with *Moline.* When he explained that *hesperia* meant "star of the west" and *moline* meant "mill," Atkinson reportedly said, "Then Moline it will be." From Spanish *molino* (mill) (Tweet, *Quad Cities,* 20). Post office established March 13, 1844.

MOMENCE [mo MENS]. Kankakee. City (1874). Founded about 1845 and named for Isidore Momence (whose name was also recorded as Momenza and Moness), the French-Potawatomi spouse of Ganeer (q.v.) (Harder, *Illustrated Dictionary of Place Names;* Houde and Klasey, *Of the People,* 30). Post office established Sept. 7, 1839, as Lorain, named for Lorain Beebe, sister-in-law of the first postmaster, A. S. Vail; changed to Momence March 29, 1849.

MONA. Ford. Township. Formed in March 1870 as Delhi. The name was changed three months later to Mona, the Latin name of the Isle of Man, presumably brought to Illinois by Manx settlers. Monaville, a former community at the intersection of Monaville and Fairfield roads in Lake County, is probably from the same source (Dretske, *What's in a Name?*).

MONEE [mo NEE]. Will. Village (1874) four miles south of Park Forest. Founded about 1853 by Augustus Herbert and named for Marie Lefevre, the Ottawa (or perhaps Potawatomi) wife of Joseph Bailly (Bailey), a French trader. She is listed as Mo-nee in the 1832 Treaty of Tippecanoe, by which she was awarded a tract of land in what is now Monee Township (Ackerman, *Early Illinois Railroads*, 121; Milne, *Our Roots Are Deep*, 33; Vogel, *Indian Place Names in Illinois*). Post office established Oct. 3, 1853.

MONEY CREEK. McLean. Township. From the stream named Money Creek. By one local account, an early settler who decided to have some fun with his fellow citizens told them he had buried money along the creek but not where it was. He died suddenly and took the secret of the location with him. By another local story, a group of Indians found some coins along the creek and gave it the name (*History of McLean County*, 701). Post office established June 7, 1843.

MONICA [MAHN uh kuh, muh NEE kuh]. Peoria. Fifteen miles northwest of Peoria. Laid out in 1873 as Cornwell by Solomon S. Cornwell. The name was subsequently changed to Moneka to agree with the name of the post office, probably at the suggestion of William J. Phelps, founder of Elmwood (q.v.). The origin of the name is uncertain. Possibly it is from a female personal name, but more likely it is an intentional variant of Mokena. The post office was established as Moneka, which was re-spelled Monica by popular etymology (*Township Histories*, 17). Post office established Nov. 10, 1871, as Moneka; changed to Monica March 12, 1872.

MONMOUTH [MAHN muhth]. Warren. City (1852, 1882). The traditional story is that three names—Isabella, Kosciusko, and Monmouth—were put into a hat and Kosciusko was drawn. The township commissioners, however, claimed that most people would never be able to spell that name correctly, discarded it, and drew again, this time choosing Monmouth. The name was suggested by John McNeil for his former home, Monmouth, N.J., itself named for Monmouth, on the border between England and Wales. Monmouth has been the seat of Warren County since 1831 (Bateman and Selby, eds., *Historical Encyclopedia of Illinois and History of Warren County*, 735). Post office established Dec. 13, 1830, as Warren Courthouse; changed to Monmouth July 20, 1841.

MONROE. County. Created Jan. 6, 1816, from parts of St. Clair and Randolph counties. Named for James Monroe (1758–1831), the fifth president of the United States, serving from 1817 to 1825. When the county was created, Monroe was secretary of state under President James Madison. The seat was established at Harrisonville in 1816 and moved to Waterloo in 1825.

MONROE. Cass. Former community. Founded about 1836 and named for President James Monroe, who signed the bill creating the state of Illinois in 1818. The Monroe Cemetery is about twelve miles north-northwest of Jacksonville (Hutchison "Old Morgan County Village").

MONROE CITY. Monroe. Seven miles southwest of Waterloo. The area was first known as James's Mill for miller and first postmaster Thomas James. Laid out as Monroe City by J. B. Harlow in 1867 and named for Monroe County (Klein, ed., *Arrowheads to Aerojets*, 522–23). Post office established May 16, 1827, as James's Mills; changed to Monroe City Jan. 21, 1856.

MONTEBELLO. Hancock. Township and former community. Probably coined from Romance language roots meaning "beautiful mountain." The community was laid out about two miles north of Hamilton by Luther Whitley and William Vance in 1832 and apparently took the name of the Montebello post office (Bateman and Selby, eds., *Historical Encyclopedia of Illinois and History of Hancock County*, 1084). Post office established Aug. 17, 1830.

MONTEREY. Fulton. Four miles east-southwest of Canton. Platted in 1850 by Jacob Weaver, Philemon Markley, and David Farr. Named in honor of the capture of Monterey, Mexico, by U.S. forces in 1846 during the Mexican War (*Atlas Map of Fulton County*, 54; Irwin, *A to Z Fulton County*). Post office established May 28, 1883.

MONTEZUMA. Pike. Twelve miles east-southeast of Pittsfield. Named from "Montezuma Land," the informal designation of a part of Pike County where, according to legend, Daniel Boone buried treasure at several of his campsites. The area itself was probably named as a result of the general association of the Aztec emperor Montezuma with wealth and opulence. The community was laid out as a landing on the Illinois River by the Alton firm of Riley and Rider, but river traffic declined after the coming of the railroads and Montezuma never prospered (*History of Pike County*, 450, 798; Thompson, *The Jess M. Thompson Pike County History*, 101). Post office established May 15, 1833, as Meacham's Ferry; changed to Montezuma July 30, 1833.

MONTGOMERY. County. Created Feb. 21, 1821, from parts of Bond and Madison counties. Named for Gen. Richard Montgomery (1738–75), who served in the French and Indian War and later with Philip Schuyler (for whom Schuyler County is named) during the capture of Montreal. He was killed at the Battle of Quebec in 1775. Hamilton was designated as the county seat but never formally established. Hillsboro has been the seat since 1823.

MONTGOMERY. Crawford. Township. Named for Andrew Montgomery, prominent in early township affairs (*History of Crawford County*, 144).

MONTGOMERY. Kane, Kendall. Village (1858, 1894). Earlier known as Pierce Crossing for early settler Elijah Pierce and later as Graytown for Daniel Gray.

Formally laid out about 1852 by Daniel Gray and named for his former home, Montgomery County, N.Y., itself named for Gen. Richard Montgomery (*Biographical and Historical Record of Kane County,* 931; Seits, "The Names of Kane County," 166). Post office established Jan. 20, 1848.

MONTGOMERY. Woodford. Township. At the time of township organization about 1855, John Wells wrote to the county supervisor asking that the township be named Montgomery. Why Wells chose this name is not known (Perrin and Hill, *Past and Present,* 457).

MONTICELLO [MAHN ti SEL o]. Piatt. City (1841, 1872). About 1837 Abraham Marquiss, William Barnes, and Maj. James McReynolds formed a stock company and purchased the site of Monticello from James A. Piatt. The name was chosen for Thomas Jefferson's estate in Virginia by McReynolds, who greatly admired Jefferson. Jefferson was known as the Sage of Monticello, and the Monticello High School athletic teams are called the Sages. From Italian for "little mountain," Monticello has been the seat of Piatt County since its formation in 1841 (Bateman and Selby, eds., *Historical Encyclopedia of Illinois and History of Piatt County,* 692; *Illinois Guide;* Morgan, ed., *The Good Life in Piatt County,* 28). Post office established Dec. 18, 1837.

MONT STATION. Madison. Two miles south of Edwardsville. Shortened from Montgomery Station, established on land owned by Nelson Montgomery. Also called Mont (Underwood, "A New Geography of Illinois: Madison County," 31). Post office established May 28, 1896.

MOONSHINE. Clark. Nine miles southeast of Casey. The local story is that the name was conferred about 1840 by settlers who were struck by the dew glistening on the prairie grass in the moonlight (*History of Carroll Township, History of Casey, Illinois,* 27). Post office established Oct. 6, 1871.

MOORES PRAIRIE. Jefferson. Township. Named for Andrew Moore, regarded as the first settler, who arrived in 1810 (Perrin, ed., *History of Jefferson County,* 122, 353). The Moores Prairie post office operated intermittently from April 22, 1825, until Jan. 25, 1894.

MOOSEHEART. Kane. Three miles south of Batavia. Mooseheart is a home and school owned and operated by the Loyal Order of Moose, originally established for dependents of deceased members. Founded in 1913 by James J. Davis, former senator from Pennsylvania and named by Ohio Congressman John Lentz, who created the name from the LOM slogan "where the Moose fraternity will pour out its heart . . . to children of its members in need" (*Illinois Guide*). Post office established Feb. 10, 1914.

MORAINE. Township. Lake. Named for the local moraines, the drifts of accumulated rocks, sand, and gravel left by retreating glaciers.

MOREA. Crawford. Former community seven miles southeast of Robinson near Marco. Probably named by Alexander and Hugh McHatton, United Presbyterian ministers who could read the Bible in Greek. Morea is an alternate name for the Peloponnese, the peninsula forming the southern part of Greece. Why the McHattons chose the name is unknown (*History of Crawford County*, 148). Post office established July 16, 1873.

MOREDOCK. Monroe. Lake. Named for John Casper Moredock. As a youth, Moredock watched as his mother, six brothers, and two sisters were slaughtered by a band of Shawnee. Moredock swore vengeance on all Indians and proceeded to kill as many as possible, often shooting those who were unarmed from ambush, earning him the title John Moredock, Indian Slayer (*Combined History of Randolph, Monroe, and Perry Counties*, 333; Fliege, *Tales and Trails of Illinois*, 21–23; Klein, ed., *Arrowheads to Aerojets*, 568).

MORELAND. Cook. Southwest of Humboldt Park. There are two popular stories of how Moreland got its name. In one, the area was low-lying and under water so often that H. H. Porter, one of the site owners, remarked, "More land and less water is needed here." In the other, one of the owners put up a sign reading "More Land for Sale." It is more likely, however, that Moreland is a transfer or from the surname of an individual yet to be identified (Karlen, *Chicago's Crabgrass Communities*, 299; Stennett, *A History of the Origin*, 105). Post office established Nov. 27, 1882.

MORGAN. County. Created Jan. 31, 1823, from Sangamon County. Named for Gen. Daniel Morgan (1736–1802), a hero of the Revolutionary War who served with distinction in the Carolinas. The county seat was established at Olmstead's Mounds in 1823 and moved to Jacksonville in 1825.

MORGAN. Township. Coles. Named for David Morgan, who emigrated from Kentucky and settled near Greasy Point on Greasy Creek about ten miles north northeast of Charleston in 1834 (Perrin, Graham, and Blair, *History of Coles County*, 458).

MORGAN CITY. Morgan. Former community. Laid out in 1839 by Charles Collins and Myron Leslie with the expectation that it would become the seat of Morgan County. Not only did Morgan City not become the county seat, but it has now disappeared. The Morgan City Cemetery is just west of Chapin, about eight miles west-northwest of Jacksonville (Hutchison "Old Morgan County Village").

MORGAN PARK. Cook. Named for site owner Thomas Morgan, who bought much of the area in the late 1840s after emigrating from Surry, England. Formerly known as Horse Thief Hollow (Bateman and Selby, eds., *Historical Encyclopedia of Illinois Cook County Edition*, 776; Kitagawa and Taeuber, eds., *Local Community Fact Book*, 164). Post office established Oct. 17, 1878.

MORGANVILLE. Jefferson. Former community south of Mount Vernon. Named for Isaac Morgan, an early settler from Cumberland County, Tenn. (*Facts and Folks*, 253).

MORO [MOR o]. Madison. Two miles northeast of Bethalto. Established about 1853. Named for David Morrow, construction engineer for the New York Central Railroad. A local story claims that Morrow was changed to Moro because of confusion with "tomorrow." When passengers said they were going "to Morrow," this was sometimes taken as meaning the next day rather than the destination. The name, however, is simply a local pronunciation of Morrow, which was accurately captured by the spelling (Bandy, comp., *Moro*). Post office established Oct. 21, 1856.

MORO [MOR o]. Randolph. Island and low-lying land between the Kaskaskia and Mississippi rivers east of Ste. Genevieve, Mo. The name *Moro* is a anglicized form of Morreau. Island No. 14 in the Mississippi River (Moro Island) was owned jointly by Pierre Morreau and L. C. Menard (Brown, "French Place Names in Illinois," 463; personal communication with Virginia Mansker).

MORONTS [mor AHNTS]. Putnam. Eleven miles southeast of Princeton. A local story claims the community was named for a Moore and a Chonts, construction workers on the Toluca and Eastern Railroad (*Putnam Past Times,* n.p.)

MORRELVILLE. Brown. Six miles southeast of Siloam Springs State Park. Named for site owner William Morrel(l) (*History of Brown County,* 310). Post office established April 24, 1888.

MORRIS. Grundy. City (1853, 1877). Platted in 1842 as a port on the Illinois and Michigan Canal and named for canal commissioner Isaac N. Morris. The preferred name was Morrisville, which Morris thought sounded "provincial." Because a Morristown already existed, Morris was the logical choice. It has been the seat of Grundy County since 1842 (*Illinois Guide;* Ullrich, *This Is Grundy County,* 221). Post office established Sept. 6, 1842.

MORRISON. Whiteside. City (1867, 1872). Founded in 1855 with construction of the Galena and Chicago Union Railroad. Named by site owners Lyman Johnson and W. H. Van Epps in honor of their friend and benefactor Charles Morrison of New York City. Morrison has been the seat of Whiteside County since 1857, when it was moved from Sterling (Bastian, *A History of Whiteside County,* 311; Stennett, *A History of the Origin,* 104). Post office established Feb. 12, 1840, as Union Grove; changed to Morrison June 5, 1857.

MORRISONVILLE. Christian. Village (1872) thirteen miles southwest of Taylorville. Laid out in 1869 for the Decatur and East St. Louis Railroad by Col. James Lowery Donaldson Morrison, the founder of Addieville. Morrison was a Mexican War veteran and the son-in-law of Thomas A. Carlin, the site owner and former governor of Illinois (*Centennial History of Morrisonville,* 6). Post office established Oct. 19, 1870.

MORRISTOWN. Henry. Ten miles southeast of Moline. Founded in 1835 in New York City by the New York Colony, which purchased some twenty thousand acres in northwestern Henry County. Named for a Colonel Morris of New Jersey, one of the officers of the colony. Morristown was the seat of Henry County from 1840 until 1843, when it was moved to Cambridge (Swank, *Historic Henry County,* 4). Post office established Nov. 26, 1840.

MORRISTOWN. Winnebago. Village (1955) four miles south of Rockford. Founded by William V. Morris as a trailer park for travelers, it later became a permanent trailer village (Nelson, comp., *Sinnissippi Saga,* 34).

MORSE. Stark. Fourteen miles east of Kewanee. Named for W. E. Morse, an official of the Chicago and North Western Railroad (Stennett, *A History of the Origin,* 105).

MORTON. Tazewell. Village (1877). Laid out in 1850 by James M. and Harvey Campbell, whose family had emigrated from Ohio in the 1830s. Some accounts claim that one of the Campbells named the community for Marcus Morton, governor of Massachusetts in the 1840s, while others say that it was named for a Mrs. Webb, an English immigrant who often served homecooked meals to local bachelors and whose maiden name was said to be Morton. In either case the name may have been influenced by Morton, N.Y. and/or Morton, Ohio (Conibear, *Morton Illinois Centennial,* 5; *History of Tazewell County,* 534–35; Roth and Roth, *Morton,* 13). Post office established July 8, 1842, as Mooberry's Mill; changed to Morton Nov. 2, 1842.

MORTON ARBORETUM. DuPage. Park. Established in 1912 by Joy Morton (1855–1934), son of J. Sterling Morton, the originator of Arbor Day and secretary of agriculture under President Grover Cleveland. The arboretum consists of 775 acres of partially wooded land and is devoted to scientific research in horticulture and arbor culture (Knoblauch, ed., *DuPage County,* 205).

MORTON GROVE. Cook. Village (1895). Named for Levi Parsons Morton, an official of the Chicago, Milwaukee and St. Paul Railroad and later vice president of the United States under Benjamin Harrison, serving from 1889 until 1893. The village was originally called Morton. The word *Grove* was added by developers to attract home buyers (*Illinois Guide*). Post office established July 2, 1874.

MOSQUITO. Christian. Township. Named from Mosquito Creek, itself presumably named for an abundance of mosquitos (Bateman and Selby, eds., *Historical Encyclopedia of Illinois and History of Christian County,* 775).

MOSSVILLE. Peoria. Four miles north of Peoria. Named for site owner William S. Moss (*History of Peoria County,* 607). Post office established April 19, 1855.

MOULTRIE. County. Created Feb. 16, 1843, from parts of Macon and Shelby counties. The original petition requesting county formation, presented to the state legislature in 1841, called for organizing parts of Macon and Shelby counties into the new county of Okaw. The referendum failed in Shelby County, and the petition was withdrawn until the following year when it was resubmitted with different boundary lines and with the name *Fleming* for John Fleming, a county organizer. Fleming, however, withdrew his name from consideration, and a Mr. Williamson, the Shelby county representative, proposed Moultrie in honor of colonel and later general William Moultrie. Moultrie (1730–1805) served with distinction during the Revolutionary War, especially at Sullivan's Island in the Charleston, S.C., harbor, which he defended against heavy British bombardment in June 1776. He was later governor of South Carolina and became well known through his war memoirs. The traditional story is that the name of the county seat, Sullivan, was chosen for Sullivan's Island to complement Moultrie. The seat was established at East Nelson in 1844 and moved to Sullivan in 1845 (*Combined History of Shelby and Moultrie Counties,* 67, 182).

MOUND. Township. McDonough. Named from a ridge of high ground known as Dyer's Mound about two miles southeast of Bushnell (Shadwick, *History of McDonough County,* 226).

MOUND CITY. Pulaski. City (1857, 1873) five miles north of Cairo. Founded in the early 1860s as the seat of Pulaski County by Gen. Moses M. Rawlings and named from nearby Indian mounds. The state legislature approved moving the county seat to Mound City, but after no action had been taken for several years a group of citizens formed a posse comitatus, stole the records from the courthouse at Caledonia (now Olmstead), and brought them to Mound City. Emporium City, founded in 1855 by the Emporium Real Estate and Manufacturing Company of Cincinnati, Ohio, merged with Mound City in 1857. Mound City has been the seat of Pulaski County since 1865 (*Illinois Guide;* Moyer, *Moyers' Brief History,* 53–54). Post office established May 31, 1856.

MOUNDS. Pulaski. City (1904) seven miles north of Cairo. Founded about 1889 as Beechwood by N. B. Thistlewood as a company town for employees of the Illinois Central Railroad. The IC station was established as Mound City Junction, named for Mound City, and changed to Mounds about 1906 (*Illinois Guide;* Moyer, *Moyers' Brief History,* 67). Post office established March 1, 1865, as Junction; changed to Mounds Junction Aug. 28, 1886; changed to Beechwood Aug. 16, 1892; changed to Mounds Oct. 15, 1903.

MOUNT CARMEL [mownt KAHR muhl]. Wabash. City (1825, 1877). In 1817 in Chillicothe, Ohio, Methodist ministers Thomas S. Hinde, William McDowell, and William Beauchamp drafted the "Articles of Association for the City of Mount Carmel." Later that year, Hinde and Beauchamp laid out Mount Carmel several miles south of Palmyra. It was to be a "moral, temperate and industrious" community built upon a strict code of personal and social conduct. No gambling, profanity, or drunkenness would be tolerated, nor would any theaters be allowed within the city limits. Perhaps a transfer, perhaps named directly for the bibical Mount Carmel near present Haifa, Israel (Bateman and Selby, eds., *Illinois Historical Wabash County Biographical,* 649; *Illinois Guide*). Post office established May 1819.

MOUNT CARROLL. Carroll. City (1867, 1913) eight miles east of Savanna. Named for Carroll County. Mount Carroll has been the seat of Carroll County since 1843. Post office established Jan. 20, 1845.

MOUNT ERIE. Wayne. Village (1895) eleven miles northeast of Fairfield. Founded about 1853 with the proposed name of Ramsey for site owner Alexander Ramsey. Ramsey, however, said he preferred "Mount Airie," which was heard as "Erie" and so recorded (*History of Wayne and Clay Counties,* 260). Post office established Oct. 18, 1854.

MOUNT HOPE. McLean. Township. Mount Hope had its origins in Rhode Island in 1835 with the organization of the Providence Farmers' and Mechanics' Emigrating Society, which was formed for the purpose of transferring to the west a New England community, complete with its educational, governmental, and religious institutions. Each shareholder was to receive a half section of land and four lots in the proposed community of Mount Hope. A few families from Rhode Island and Massachusetts eventually emigrated, but the town, although surveyed, never materialized. The name was probably taken from Mount Hope, a summit in Bristol County, R.I., reinforced by the positive associations of "mount" and "hope." The Mount Hope Cemetery is northwest of McLean (Bateman and Selby, eds., *Historical Encyclopedia of Illinois and History of McLean County,* 580; *History of McLean County,* 721). Post office established July 19, 1848.

MOUNT MORRIS. Ogle. Village (1857, 1875). The community that became Mount Morris developed around the Rock River Seminary, established by the Illinois Conference of the Methodist Episcopal Church in 1839. The name *Mount Morris* was suggested by both Horace Miller of Kishwaukee, Ill., for his former home, Mount Morris, in Livingston County, N.Y., and by seminarians for Thomas A. Morris, a Methodist bishop then in Cincinnati and active in establishing Methodist ministries in the western states. Morris may have visited the Rock River Seminary in its early years. Miller, one of the seminary's first trustees, was no doubt familiar with Bishop Morris (Bateman and Selby, eds., *Historical Encyclopedia of Illinois and History of Ogle County,* 795; *History of Ogle County,* 296; Kable and Kable, *Mount Morris,* 32). Post office established March 31, 1841.

MOUNT OLIVE. Macoupin. City (1874). Formerly known as Rising Sun and also as Niemann's Settlement, named for John C. Niemann, an early settler and city official who emigrated from Germany with his brothers Fred and Henry. The Niemanns named the community Oelburg, German for the bibical Mount of Olives, and the name was later translated as Mount Olive (*"One Hundred Years of Progress,"* 4).

MOUNT PROSPECT. Cook. Village (1917). Named by Chicago real estate agent and site owner Ezra C. Eggleston about 1874. Eggleston probably chose the name for its promotional value, trading on the positive associations of "mount" and "prospect" (Murphy and Wajer, *Mount Prospect,* 37–38). Post office established Dec. 31, 1885.

MOUNT PULASKI. Logan. City (1872) ten miles south of Lincoln. Formerly known as Scroggin for an early settler of that name. The site was platted in 1836 for a land company headed by Jabez Capps, Barton Robinson, and George W. Turley and named Pulaski for Casimir Pulaski. The word *Mount* was added later that year to distinguish this from several other Pulaskis in Illinois. Mount Pulaski was the seat of Logan County from 1847 until 1853, when it was moved to Lincoln (*see* Pulaski) (Stringer, *History of Logan County,* 590). Post office established March 27, 1837, as Scroggin; changed to Mount Pulaski March 2, 1838.

MOUNT STERLING. Brown. City (1837, 1875). The local story is that the community was named by Robert N. Curry for commendatory reasons, with "Mount" suggesting height and "Sterling" suggesting tradition and value. Alexander Curry, an early settler (relationship to Robert unknown), was from Mount Sterling, Ky., however, and this is more likely the direct source of the name. Mount Sterling has been the seat of Brown County since its formation in 1839 (Dearinger, "A New Geography of Brown County," 30; Hansen, ed., *Illinois,* 663). Post office established March 26, 1833.

MOUNT VERNON. Jefferson. City (1837, 1872). Founded in 1819 as the seat of Jefferson County. The first name proposed was Mount Pleasant, but the founders, Zadoc Casey, Joseph Jordan, and Fleming Greenwood, admired George Washington and chose Mount Vernon for Washington's Virginia estate. Washington's half-brother, Lawrence, named that estate in honor of Edward Vernon, an admiral in the British navy under whom Lawrence Washington had served in the Caribbean. Because Mount Vernon voted itself dry, East Mount Vernon was established in the 1870s to create a venue where liquor could legally be sold and lasted until about 1880 (Wall, *Wall's History,* 37; www.genealogytrails.com/ill/jefferson/ghostowns.html). Post office established Oct. 17, 1820, as Jefferson Courthouse; changed to Mount Vernon March 29, 1827.

MOUNT ZION. Macon. Village (1881). Laid out by S. K. Smith about 1860 and named from the Mount Zion Cumberland Presbyterian Church, organized about 1830 (*Past and Present of the City of Decatur,* 70; Richmond, *Centennial History of Decatur,* 130). Post office established Feb. 23, 1858, as Wilson; changed to Mount Zion Nov. 2, 1866.

MOWEAQUA [mo WEEK wuh]. Christian, Shelby. Village (1877) sixteen miles south-southwest of Decatur. Laid out in 1852 for the Illinois Central Railroad by Michael Snyder and named by Mattie Wells, the daughter of an IC employee awarded two city lots for submitting the winning entry in a naming contest. The source of the name is uncertain. It may be from Potawatomi, but the derivation and meaning are unclear. Several interpretations have been proposed, including "weeping woman," "wolf woman," and "muddy water" (Ackerman, *Early Illinois Railroads,* 148, *Moweaqua Remembers,* 10; Vogel, *Indian Place Names in Illinois*). Post office established Oct. 6, 1853.

MOZIER [MO zher, mo ZIHR]. Calhoun. Eighteen miles west of Carrollton. Named for Jean (John) Mozier, an early French settler. Formerly known as Mozier Landing (Underwood, "A New Geography of Calhoun County," 37). Post office established March 17, 1880.

MT. PALATINE. LaSalle, Putnam. Ten miles south of Peru. Laid out in the 1840s by Christopher Winters. Likely named for the German Palatinate but possibly named for the Palatine Hill, one of the seven hills upon which ancient Rome was built (Alleman and Immel, *A Putnam County History,* 37). Post office established June 19, 1849.

MT. PLEASANT. Township. Whiteside. The name was suggested by A. C. Jackson when the township was organized in the early 1850s. Named from the Mount Pleasant School, a small schoolhouse near Morrison (Bent, ed., *History of Whiteside County,* 291; Davis, *History of Whiteside County,* 296–97).

MUDDY RIVER, Big and Little. Streams that wind across much of southern Illinois. Muddy River is a translation of French *Rivière aux Vase* (River of Mud), from *vase* (morass, swamp), a name given by early French explorers to a shallow, slow-moving stream with a particularly soft bottom (Hubbs, *Pioneer Folks and Places;* McDermott, *A Glossary of Mississippi Valley French*).

MUDDY. Saline. Village (1955) two miles northeast of Harrisburg. Named from the mine sunk in 1903 by the Big Muddy Coal Company of Harrisburg (*History of Saline County,* 56). Post office established Sept. 22, 1908.

MULBERRY GROVE. Bond. Village (1857, 1881) seven miles east of Greenville. Laid out in 1841 by site owners Francis Gill and Asahel Enloe as Houston, probably named for a local family of that name. Samuel Houston, claimed to be a friend of Gill's, was Bond County sheriff in the 1820s. The name was changed at the suggestion of postmaster James B. Woolard to agree with that of the post office, the first of which, his cabin, reportedly was surrounded by mulberry trees. Formerly known as Shakerag because local women would shake debris from dust rags and table cloths from their porches (Bateman and Selby, eds., *Historical Encyclopedia of Illinois and History of Bond County,* 623; *Mulberry Grove;* Perrin, ed., *History of Bond and Montgomery Counties,* 137; Peterson, "Place Names of Bond County," 42).

MULKEYTOWN. Franklin. Ten miles west of Benton. Founded about 1820. Named for the Mulkey family, especially the Rev. John Mulkey, who established the

Christian Church in 1818 (*Franklin County,* 17). Post office established Nov. 28, 1831, as Little Muddy; changed to Mulkeytown June 15, 1869.

MUNCIE. Vermilion. Village (1898) twelve miles west of Danville. Platted in 1875 by Alexander Bowman and Edward Corbley. The name is probably a transfer from Muncie, Delaware County, Ind., itself named for the Muncie or Munsee, a subtribe of the Delaware (Bright, *Native American Placenames;* Tuggle, comp., *Stories of Historical Days,* 12). Post office established Feb. 21, 1876.

MUNDELEIN [MUHN duh leyen]. Lake. Village (1909). First called Mechanics Grove and subsequently known as Holcomb for John Holcomb, who donated a portion of his farm for a railroad station in the 1880s; as Rockefeller, for John D. Rockefeller in recognition of his philanthropic contributions to the University of Chicago; and as Area, a name derived from the motto of the Sheldon School of Business Administration: "Ability, Reliability, Endurance, and Action." The school failed, and the Archdiocese of Chicago purchased its site in 1922. Under the leadership of George William, Cardinal Mundelein, the property was converted into St. Mary's of the Lake Seminary. The name of the village was changed from Area in honor of Mundelein in 1925 (Dretske, *What's in a Name?;* Stokes, "Ask Anyone"). Post office established Feb. 12, 1887, as Rockefeller; changed to Area Aug. 27, 1913; changed to Mundelein May 1, 1925.

MUNGER. DuPage. Southwest of Bartlett. Established in 1888 by the Illinois Central Railroad as North Wayne. Renamed for station agent O. H. Munger (Blatchford, *An Honorable Heritage,* 481).

MUNSON. Henry. Township. Changed from Centre in 1857. Named for Merritt Munson, an early settler. The Munson post office operated from Oct. 14, 1857, until Dec. 11, 1865 (Kiner, *History of Henry County,* 601).

MURDOCK. Douglas. Eleven miles east of Tuscola. Founded about 1881 by John D. Murdock, operator of a local grain elevator (Hansen, ed., *Illinois,* 687). Post office established July 17, 1872, as Gurney City, named for Hiram Gurnea; changed to Murdock March 16, 1874.

MURPHYSBORO. Jackson. City (1867, 1875). After a fire destroyed the courthouse at Brownsville in 1873, the Illinois General Assembly appointed commissioners to locate a new seat near the center of Jackson County. After a site was selected, the name was chosen by placing the names of the commissioners, Samuel T. Russell, John Cochran, and William C. Murphy, in a hat. For several decades after Murphy's name was drawn the spelling oscillated between Murphysborough and Murphysboro. The post office department made "Murphysboro" official in 1893 (Fishback, *A History of Murphysboro,* 3–4). Post office established Dec. 23, 1843.

MURRAYVILLE. Morgan. Village (1867 1914) nine miles south of Jacksonville. Laid out about 1857 by Justice of the Peace Samuel Murray (*History of Morgan County,* 427). Post office established June 29, 1860, as Iatan; changed to Murrayville Feb. 16, 1863.

N

NAAUSAY [nay AW say]. Kendall. Township. The name *Naausay* was chosen by popular vote over Orange, Salem, and several others suggested at the time of township formation about 1850. The township was named from the Native American village of Na-Au-Say located on Aux Sable Creek, itself named for a Potawatomi leader whose name appears as Nay-o-say in the 1833 Treaty of Chicago (Bateman and Selby, eds., *Historical Encyclopedia of Illinois and History of Kendall County,* 656, 707; Farren, ed., *A Bicentennial History,* 106; Vogel, *Indian Place Names in Illinois*). Post office established May 30, 1850.

NACHUSA [nuh CHOO suh]. Lee. Five miles east of Dixon. From Winnebago meaning "white haired." Nachusa was the name given to John Dixon for his long, white hair, reportedly given at the time he was made an honorary member of the Winnebago Tribe (*see* Dixon) (Bateman and Selby, eds., *Historical Encyclopedia of Illinois and History of Lee County,* 652, 684; *History of Lee County,* 35; Vogel, *Indian Place Names in Illinois*). Post office established Nov. 23, 1855.

NAMEOKI [NAM ee O kee]. Madison. Township. Established as a station on the Indianapolis and St. Louis Railroad about 1875. The name is most likely a transfer from Nameoke, Nassau County, N.Y. It was given currency by John Augustus Stone's popular 1829 drama *Metamora; or, The Last of the Wampanoags,* in which Nahmeokee is the wife of Metamora (King Philip). Stone probably based the name on a New England Algonquian word meaning "fishing place." The site of the former I&StL station is now part of Granite City (*see* Metamora) (Bright, *Native American Placenames; History of Madison County,* 500; Vogel, *Indian Place Names in Illinois*). Post office established June 23, 1876.

NAMEQUA CREEK. Rock Island. Stream. Probably named for Namequa, a daughter of Black Hawk who looked after him during his later years in Iowa. The name is said to mean "fish woman" (Vogel, *Indian Place Names in Illinois*).

NAPERVILLE [NAY per vil]. DuPage. City (1857). The Naper brothers, John and Joseph, left Ashtabula County, Ohio, in the summer of 1831 and established a trading post and sawmill at what became known as the Naper Settlement. Formally laid out as Naperville by Joseph Naper in 1842. Naperville was the seat of DuPage County from 1839 until 1867, when it was moved to Wheaton (Bateman and Selby, eds., *Historical Encyclopedia of Illinois and History of DuPage County*). Post office established March 1, 1836.

NAPLATE [NAY playt]. LaSalle. Village (1947). West Ottawa suburb. An acronym created from the National Plate Glass Company, now Libby-Owens-Ford (Adams, comp., *Illinois Place Names*).

NAPLES. Scott. Town (1839) fifteen miles northeast of Pittsfield. Laid out about 1825 by William S. Hamilton, Thomas Cox, and Enoch March, one of the founders of Exeter (*Scott County Bicentennial Book,* 188). Post office established Sept. 15, 1830.

NASHUA [NASH wuh]. Ogle. Township. A transfer from New England. Probably named for Nashua, N.H., or for the Nashua River in New Hampshire and Massachusetts, a tributary of the Merrimack. From New England Algonquian meaning "between" (Bright, *Native American Placenames*). Post office established March 31, 1852.

NASHVILLE. Washington. City (1853, 1872). Founded in 1830 as New Nashville by county commissioners David White, Joseph Wittenberg, and Livesay Carter and named for their former home, Nashville, Tenn., itself named for Gen. Francis Nash, a commander in the Revolutionary War who was mortally wounded at Germantown, Pa., in 1777 (Brinkman, ed., *This Is Washington County*, 30; *History of Washington County*, 43; personal communication with Wanda Groennert). Post office established Oct. 31, 1831.

NASON [NAY suhn]. Jefferson. City (1924) nine miles south-southwest of Mount Vernon. Founded about 1922. Named for Albert J. Nason, president of the Nason Coal Company (www.iltrails.org/jefferson). Post office established Sept. 8, 1823.

NATRONA [nuh TRO nuh]. Mason. Six miles northeast of Mason City. Founded about 1857 as Altoona. To avoid confusion with Altona, the name was changed to Natrona, a blend of *natron* (hydrated sodium carbonate) and *Altoona*. (*History of Menard and Mason Counties*, 614). Post office established Feb. 24, 1868.

NAUVOO [nah VOO, naw VOO]. Hancock. City (1841, 1899) six miles south of Fort Madison, Iowa. The area around modern Nauvoo was known as Quashquema, named for a minor Sauk leader of the late eighteenth and early nineteenth centuries. Quashquema (Jumping Fish) was coerced or tricked by William Henry Harrison into signing over a large tract of northwestern Illinois to the United States in 1804. The community was established as Venus in the 1820s by early settler James White and was later known as Commerce. When the Mormons were expelled from Missouri in 1839, they crossed the Mississippi River and established Nauvoo on the site. Joseph Smith, the founder and prophet of the Mormon Church, created the name, claiming that he had derived it from the Hebrew root *nawa* (na-va) and that it meant "beautiful place" (Bateman and Selby, eds., *Historical Encyclopedia of Illinois and History of Hancock County*, 834, 1089; Hagan, *The Sac and Fox Indians*, 25; *History of Hancock County*, 394). Post office established March 13, 1830, as Venus; changed to Commerce Oct. 11, 1834; changed to Nauvoo April 21, 1840.

NEAL. Cumberland. Twelve miles south of Mattoon. Reportedly named for a Dr. Neal. The community grew around a Baptist church called Hardscrabble, founded in the late 1870s (Misenheimer, *The Johnstown Story*, 108). Post office established Feb. 15, 1892.

NEELYS. Morgan. Twelve miles west of Jacksonville. Founded in 1865 by James and Jonathan Neely. Also known as Neeleyville (Bateman and Selby, eds., *Historical Encyclopedia of Illinois and History of Morgan County*, 663).

NEILSON. Williamson. Six miles south of Marion. Named for Alexander C. Neilson, who owned the site where the tracks of the Chicago and Eastern Illinois Railroad crossed those of the Herrin and Southern (Hale, comp. and ed., *Williamson County*, 119; Mohlenbrock, "A New Geography of Williamson County," 39).

NEKOMA. Henry. Eight miles west of Galva. Founded in 1869 by Maxwell Z. V. Woodhull, the founder of Woodhull. Probably an adaptation of Nokomis (q.v.) (Swank, *Historic Henry County*, 49–50). Post office established July 20, 1869.

NELSON. Lee. Village (1923) six miles southwest of Dixon. Platted in 1862 and named for site owner Samuel Nelson (Snively, comp. and ed., *Lee County Historical Yearbook*, 36). Post office established Jan. 8, 1858.

NEOGA [nee O guh]. Cumberland. City (1869, 1881) eleven miles south-southwest of Mattoon. Established and named by the Illinois Central Railroad about 1854. The source of the name is uncertain. Ackerman, president of the IC, claims that Neoga was created from Iroquois *neo* (deity) and *oga* (place) (*Early Illinois Railroads*, 128–29). A more recent suggestion is that the name derives from a Seneca (also Iroquoian) word for "deer" (Bright, *Native American Placenames*). Post office established May 7, 1852, as Long Point Grove; changed to Neoga Jan. 7, 1857.

NEPONSET [nuh PAHN set] Bureau. Village (1869, 1882) seven miles northeast of Kewanee. Laid out about 1855 by Edward Ferris and others. Named Brawby by William and Ann Studley for their former home in North Yorkshire, England. The name was changed to Neponset about 1866 at the suggestion of Myron Lee, the first station agent for the Central Military Tract Railroad, for his former home, Neponset, Mass. (now part of Boston). Likely from an Algonquian language; the meaning "place of the small summer" has been suggested (Bright, *Native American Placenames*; Harrington, *Past and Present of Bureau County*, 124; *Neponset's Hundred Years*, 3). Post office established June 15, 1855.

NETTLE CREEK. Grundy. Nine miles northwest of Morris. Named from Nettle Creek, itself a translation of *mazon* (nettles) (*see* Mazon) (Bateman and Selby, eds., *Historical Encyclopedia of Illinois and History of Grundy County*, 740). Post office established March 30, 1875.

NEUNERT [NOO nert]. Jackson. Twelve miles west-southwest of Murphysboro. Founded about 1892 and named for Charles F. Neunert, the first postmaster (Allen, *Jackson County Notes*, 26). Post office established Feb. 15, 1892.

NEVADA. Livingston. Six miles west of Dwight. Named in 1858 at the time of township formation by Stephen Kyle, the first township supervisor, who had lived for a time in what is now the state of Nevada (*History of Livingston County* [1878], 429). Post office established April 29, 1870.

NEVINS. Edgar. Six miles southeast of Paris. Established as a station on the Paris and Terre Haute Railroad about 1874. Named for Robert N. Nevins of Paris (*History of Edgar County*, 408). Post office established Feb. 24, 1874.

NEWARK. Kendall. Village (1843, 1875) seven miles south of Sandwich. Founded as Georgetown by George B. Hollenback about 1833. The name was changed in 1842 to avoid duplication of post offices. Possibly named directly for Newark, N.J., but more likely for Newark, Ohio, itself named for Newark, N.J. (Farren, ed., *A Bicentennial History*, 99, 107). Post office established Aug. 9, 1837.

NEW ATHENS. St. Clair. Village (1869, 1881) thirteen miles southeast of Belleville. Laid out as Athens by Narcisse Pensoneau adjacent to the general store he established in 1836. The word *New* was added to avoid confusion with Athens in Menard County (*History of St. Clair County*, 263). Post office established March 12, 1857, as Lively; changed to New Athens April 10, 1866.

NEW BADEN [BAYD n]. Clinton, St. Clair. Village (1867, 1884) fifteen miles east of Belleville. Laid out in the mid-1850s and named for Baden (Baden-Baden), the resort city in southern Germany. Originally called Baden, the name was changed to New Baden upon incorporation in 1867. Baden Baden in Bond County, ten miles southwest of Greenville, is named for the same German city (*Centennial Celebration New Baden*, 8). Post office established March 7, 1846, as Looking Glass; changed to New Baden March 26, 1867.

NEW BEDFORD. Bureau. Village (1950) eight miles south of Tampico. Previously known as Winnebago. Formally laid out and named by settlers from New Bedford, Mass. (Leonard, ed., *Big Bureau*, 67; www.outfitters.com/illinois/bureau/communities_bureau.html). Post office established June 12, 1844, as Winnebago; changed to New Bedford July 31, 1855.

NEW BERLIN. Bond. Founded in 1850 by Charles Plog and named for Berlin, Germany (Bateman and Selby, eds., *Historical Encyclopedia of Illinois and History of Bond County*, 646).

NEW BOSTON. Mercer. City (1859) thirteen miles west of Aledo. Formerly known as Dennison's Landing and later as Upper Yellow Banks. Formally established about 1834 and named by Edward Burrall, one of the site owners, for his former home, Boston, Mass. (Bassett and Goodspeed, *Past and Present of Mercer County*, 428). Post office established Aug. 27, 1835.

NEW BURNSIDE. Village (1879) fifteen miles southwest of Harrisburg. Founded in 1872 by James Heaton, Capt. Mark Whitaker, and J. F. Gray. Named for Ambrose E. Burnside, president of the Indianapolis and Vincennes Railroad at the time (Bucciferro, ed., *Parker's History*, 27; Donovan, "Named for Railroad Presidents," 26). Post office established Dec. 16, 1872, as Morrell; changed to New Burnside Jan. 22, 1873.

NEWBURG. Macon. Ten miles northeast of Decatur. Laid out in 1854 by William Dickey and likely named for Newburg, Franklin County, Ala., home of the Dickey family (*History of Macon County*, 202; Richmond, *Centennial History of Decatur*, 131). Post office established July 6, 1870.

NEWBURG. Pike. Township. Named for Newburg, Wyoming County, N.Y., the former home of early settler Peter K. Stringham, who arrived in 1833 (*History of Pike County*, 573).

NEW CANTON. Pike. Town (1869). Founded in 1835 by Charles T. Brester, Hiram Smith, and Jesse Titsworth. Probably named for Canton, St. Lawrence County, N.Y., itself named for Canton (Guangzhou), China (Massie, *Past and Present*, 88). Post office established April 26, 1827, as Pleasant Vale; changed to New Canton Feb. 12, 1872.

NEWCOMB. Champaign. Township. Named for Ethan Newcom, who established a crossing on the Sangamon River known as Newcom's Ford. The *b* was added when the township was established in 1860 (Bateman and Selby, eds., *Historical Encyclopedia of Illinois and History of Champaign County*, 661). Post office established Jan. 8, 1859.

NEW DENNISON. Williamson. Five miles southeast of Marion. Named for Charles H. Denison, who donated land for a station on the Chicago, St. Louis and Paducah Railroad about 1887. Denison was a financier and multiterm mayor of Marion (Hale, comp. and ed., *Williamson County*, 119; Hubbs, *Pioneer Folks and Places*). Post office established Feb. 28, 1888.

NEW DESIGN. Monroe. Precinct and former community. Founded about 1786 by James Lemen Sr., a Baptist minister and judge of the Monroe County court, whose intent was to bring a "new design," specifically an antislavery design, to Illinois. The New Design Cemetery is about three miles south of Waterloo (*Combined History of Randolph, Monroe, and Perry Counties*, 330; Klein, ed., *Arrowheads to Aerojets*, 575). Post office established July 2, 1874.

NEW DOUGLAS. Madison. Village (1874) fourteen miles northwest of Greenville. Laid out about 1860 and named for Stephen A. Douglas by Alonzo Foster, son of Oliver Foster, the founder of Fosterburg (q.v.) (Norton, ed., *Centennial History of Madison County*, 583). Post office established Dec. 27, 1861.

NEWELL. Vermilion. Two miles northeast of Danville. Named for James Newell, first justice of the peace (Beckwith, *History of Vermilion County*, 943; Williams, *History of Vermilion County*, 286). Post office established Nov. 10, 1854.

NEW HAVEN. Gallatin. Village (1839, 1873) sixteen miles east-southeast of Eldorado. The site was first settled by Jonathan Boone about 1812. Named about 1818 for New Haven, Conn., either by William Robinson and Darius North or by Roswell H. Grant and Paddy Robinson, who purchased the mill established by Boone. All four men were storekeepers (*History and Families of Gallatin County*, 16; Lawler, *Gallatin County*, 109; Miller, "Building Towns," 50–51). Post office established Jan. 25, 1819.

NEW HANOVER. Monroe. Five miles northwest of Waterloo and Precinct. Founded about 1860 by Henry B. Stehr from Hanover, Germany (*Combined*

History of Randolph, Monroe, and Perry Counties, 447–48). Post office established March 5, 1875.

NEW HARTFORD. Pike. Five miles southwest of Pittsfield. Founded by Isaac Hoskins, Abner Clark, John Shinn, and Nathan Brown. Named by Hoskins for his former home, Hartford County, Conn., itself named for Hartford (Hertford), England (*History of Pike County,* 716). Post office established March 20, 1838.

NEW HEBRON. Crawford. Three miles south of Robinson. Laid out about 1840 by Dr. Nelson Hawley and likely named by settlers from Hebron, Licking County, Ohio (Bateman and Selby, eds., *Illinois Historical Crawford County Biographical,* 646; personal communication with Sue Jones). Post office established April 1, 1851.

NEW HOLLAND. Logan. Village (1897) six miles east of Mason City. Founded by Oliver Wiley Holland in 1875 on the line of the Indiana, Bloomington and Western Railroad (*History of Logan County* [1886], 868). Post office established June 1, 1875.

NEW LENOX. Will. Village (1946) five miles east of Joliet. New Lenox Township was originally known as Vernon, probably named for Vernon, N.Y. The name was changed in June 1850 to Lenox, for Lenox, Madison County, N.Y., at the suggestion of John Van Duser (or Van Dusen), the first township supervisor. The village of New Lenox was platted about 1858 as Tracy, named for J. B. Tracy, general superintendent of the Rock Island Railroad, and changed about 1863 at Tracy's request to match the name of the township (*History of Will County,* 504; Maue, *History of Will County,* 308; Stevens, *Past and Present of Will County,* 104). Post office established June 8, 1846, as Young Hickory; changed to New Lenox Oct. 21, 1851.

NEWMAN. Douglas. City (1872) fifteen miles east of Tuscola. Laid out in 1857 and named for one of the site owners, the Rev. B. F. Newman, son-in-law of Peter Cartwright, one of the best known Methodist circuit riders of the 1830s and 1840s (*County of Douglas,* 229, 236; Hansen, ed., *Illinois,* 687). Post office established June 8, 1861.

NEWMANSVILLE. Cass. Nine miles west of Petersburg. Founded in 1858 by the Rev. Wingate Newman (Bateman and Selby, eds., *Historical Encyclopedia of Illinois and History of Cass County,* 821). Post office established Jan. 9, 1850, as Nancemont, named for postmaster Otway P. Nance; changed to Hagley March 8, 1852; changed to Newmansville Feb. 9, 1860.

NEW MILFORD. Winnebago. Village (1955) two miles south of Rockford. Formerly known as Morristown. The name was changed in 1851, probably at the suggestion of Philip Wells Marsh, for his former home, Milford, Conn. (Baxter, *Yesterday, Today,* 10). Post office established May 18, 1850.

NEW MINDEN. Washington. Village (1877) six miles north of Nashville. Named for Minden in northwestern Germany, the home of a number of early settlers (*Washington County,* 31). Post office established July 28, 1868.

NEW PALESTINE. Randolph. Five miles north of Chester. Originally known as the Harmon Settlement, named for Michael Harmon, who emigrated from Tennessee about 1811. The community took its name from the Palestine Methodist Episcopal Church, organized about 1835 (*Randolph County*, 100; Sneed, *Ghost Towns of Southern Illinois*, 179). Post office established April 5, 1888.

NEWPORT. Lake. Township. The name *Newport* was chosen by popular vote at the time of township formation about 1850. Other names receiving votes at the time were Mortimer and Verona, probably for Mortimer and Verona, N.Y. The source of the name is uncertain, but it is likely a transfer, probably from New York or Rhode Island (*Past and Present of Lake County*, 300). Post office established Sept. 13, 1847, as Mortimer; changed to Newport April 1, 1851.

NEW SALEM. McDonough. Township. Probably named for Salem Woods, who bought a tract of land in what is now New Salem Township in 1827 (*History of McDonough County*, 902).

NEWTON. Jasper. City (1831, 1885). *See* Jasper.

NEWTON CORNERS. Whiteside. Nine miles west-southwest of Morrison. Named by settlers from Newton, Luzerne County, Pa. (Bent, ed., *History of Whiteside County*, 333).

NEWTOWN. Vermilion. Seven miles northwest of Danville. Laid out by Benjamin Coddington in 1838 as New Town (Stapp, *History under Our Feet*, 32).

NEW TRIER. Township. Cook. Named for the city of Trier in southwestern Germany, the home of a number of early settlers. Post office established July 19, 1850.

NEW VIRGINIA. Williamson. Former community. Established about 1901 as a company town for employees of the New Virginia Coal Company, which operated until 1906 (Hale, comp. and ed., *Williamson County*, 119).

NIANTIC [neye AN tik]. Macon. Village (1894) ten miles west of Decatur. Founded about 1852 as Long Point, taking its name from Long Point Slough. The post office was established in 1855 as Lockhart, and the Wabash station was called Prairie City. "Niantic," the name of a New England Algonquian tribe, was proposed by settlers from Niantic, New London County, Conn., and was in general use as the name of the village, post office, and railroad station by the late 1850s (Bright, *Native American Placenames;* Nelson, *City of Decatur*, 397; Richmond, *Centennial History of Decatur*, 95, 445). Post office established Jan. 17, 1855, as Lockhart, named for postmaster Calvin Lockhart; changed to Niantic June 19, 1858.

NILES. Cook. Village (1899). First known as Dutchman's Point for the large number of German settlers and later as Lyttleton's Point. The name *Niles* was apparently chosen by community leaders shortly before 1850, when the township was organized. The name is ultimately from the *Niles Register,* a weekly publication of political and commercial news founded in Baltimore by Hezekiah Niles in 1811. It continued as an influential publication of news and opinion until 1849. Niles, Ohio, was named for the *Register* and Niles, Mich., was named directly for Hezekiah Niles. Either of these (or both), as well as Niles, N.Y. (named for Robert Niles, probably unrelated to Hezekiah), may have influenced the naming of Niles, Ill. The Michigan connection is especially strong. Postal service was established between Niles, Ill. (Dutchman's Point) and Niles, Mich., in the early 1830s, and regular stagecoach service between the two began in 1834 (Andreas, *History of Cook County,* 471; *Illinois Guide; Niles Centennial History,* 27; Stennett, *A History of the Origin,* 107). Post office established May 15, 1838, as Dutchman's Point; changed to Niles May 23, 1850.

NIOTA [neye O tuh]. Hancock. East of Fort Madison, Iowa. The origin of the name is unknown. Perhaps from a native language or confected from native or presumed native elements by Europeans. Related names may be Min(n)eota, which appears several times in Minnesota, and Neota, which occurs in several Colorado place names. The only other Niota in the United States is in Tennessee, where the name was reportedly suggested by postmaster John Boggess for Chief Niota, a character in a book he had read (Miller, *Tennessee Place Names;* Stewart, *American Place-Names;* Vogel, *Indian Place Names in Illinois*). Post office established July 18, 1836, as Appanoose; changed to Niota Oct. 24, 1887.

NIPPERSINK. Stream in McHenry County; lake in Lake County. Nippersink Lake is southernmost of the series of lakes that includes Grass Lake, Fox Lake, and Pistakee Lake. From Miami-Illinois for "at the lake." Variants include Nepessing Lake, Mich.; Nipissing, Ontario; and, by popular etymology, Neversink, Sullivan County, N.Y. (Dretske, *What's in a Name?;* personal communication with Michael McCafferty). Post office established July 1, 1830, as Nepasink; reestablished as Nippersink June 7, 1880.

NIXON. DeWitt. Township. Organized in 1859 and named for the Nixons, George, William, and Morris, prominent local farmers who emigrated from Ohio about 1850 (*History of DeWitt County* [1910], 410). Post office established Sept. 3, 1867.

NOBLE. Richland. Village (1869 1873) eight miles south-southwest of Olney. Probably named for a yet to be identified employee of the Ohio and Midland Railroad (Griffith, "Egyptian Place-Names," 32). Post office established Feb. 13, 1854.

NOKOMIS [nuh KOM is]. Montgomery. City (1867, 1893). Founded by T. C. Huggins and Samuel Ryder in 1856 with construction of the Alton and Terre Haute Railroad. Named from Henry Wadsworth Longfellow's *The Song of Hiawatha,* in which Nokomis is Hiawatha's grandmother. From Ojibwa for "my grandmother." The name was suggested by Mrs. Anasa Barry of Alton (Bateman and Selby, eds., *Historical Encyclopedia of Illinois and History of Montgomery County,* 915; Bright, *Native American Placenames*). Post office established July 25, 1856.

NOLTINGS. Washington. Three miles southwest of Centralia. Formerly Nolting, named for Peter W. Nolting, who established the first general store and served as the first postmaster (Adams, comp., *Illinois Place Names; Washington County,* 23). Post office established Aug. 7, 1893.

NORA. Jo Daviess. Village (1883) twenty miles northwest of Freeport. Named by Roswell B. Mason, chief engineer of the Illinois Central Railroad, at the request of site owner John M. Douglas, who reportedly suggested the name *Nora* because this was a very small place that should have, in his opinion, a very small name. Perhaps, however, Nora was the name of the wife or daughter of a railroad official or prominent citizen (Ackerman, *Early Illinois Railroads,* 140; Bateman and Selby, eds., *Historical Encyclopedia of Illinois and History of Jo Daviess County,* 633). Post office established Dec. 21, 1852.

NORMAL. McLean. Town (1867). Originally called North Bloomington or "The Junction," where the tracks of the Illinois Central Railroad crossed those of the Chicago and Alton. The name was changed shortly after the founding of the Illinois State Normal University (now Illinois State University) in 1857 (*History of McLean County,* 425, 428). Post office established June 27, 1861.

NORMAL PARK. Cook. Established as Normalville, site of the Cook County Normal School after it was moved from Blue Island. Now part of Chicago (Karlen, *Chicago's Crabgrass Communities,* 230). Post office established Nov. 13, 1887, as Normalville; changed to Wooster March 3, 1884; changed to Normal Park March 20, 1884.

NORMAN. Grundy. Township. Named for Thomas J. Norman, the first township supervisor (Ullrich, *This Is Grundy County,* 247).

NORMANDY. Bureau. Seventeen miles northwest of Princeton. Named for the Norman family, site owners. The form of the name was likely influenced by the French province of Normandy (Stennett, *A History of the Origin,* 108). Post office established April 7, 1902.

NORMANTOWN. Will. Three miles northwest of Plainfield. Named for Norman Williams, president of the Elgin, Joliet and Eastern Railroad (Donovan, "Named for Railroad Presidents," 26). Post office established May 8, 1843.

NORRIDGE. Cook. Village (1948). Established in the 1940s as a community for returning veterans of World War II. The name is a blend of Norwood Park, the township in which the village is located, and Park Ridge, immediately north of Norridge (Harder, *Illustrated Dictionary of Place Names*).

NORRIS CITY. White. Village (1901) eleven miles southwest of Carmi. Named for early settlers William and Emaline Norris. The name was perhaps suggested by a railroad official and friend of the Norrises (Oliver, *Norris City and Indian Creek Township,* 31). Post office established May 15, 1871.

NORTHBROOK. Cook. Village (1923). Formerly known as Shermerville, named for farmer Frederick Shermer, who donated land for a station on the Chicago, Milwaukee and St. Paul Railroad. Shermerville became known primarily for its brothels and taverns, and some thought a new name would bring a new image. By popular vote in 1923, at the suggestion of Edward D. Landwehr, the name was changed to Northbrook, which was taken from the community's location in Northfield Township near the North Branch of the Chicago River (Coates, "Rollicking Roots"). Post office established July 18, 1840, as Sherman; changed to Northfield June 30, 1853; changed to East Northfield Dec. 2, 1867; changed to Shermerville Nov. 6, 1885; changed to Northbrook Feb. 1, 1923.

NORTHFIELD. Cook. Village (1926). Founded by Samuel Insull about 1926. As the result of a contest sponsored by Insull, the station on the Skokie Valley line of the North Shore Railroad was named Wau-bun, from a Potawatomi word meaning "daybreak" or "early light" and popularized by Juliette Kinzie's *Wau-Bun: The Early Day in the Northwest,* a reminiscence of her life in Chicago in the 1830s. The name was changed for Northfield, Mass., about 1927, probably by Insull (*Illinois Guide*).

NORTH HAMPTON. Peoria. Two miles west-northwest of Chillicothe. Founded in 1836 by Reuben Hamlin and named for his former home, Northampton, Hampton County, Mass. (*History of Peoria County,* 593).

NORTHLAKE. Cook. City (1949). South of O'Hare Airport. Named for its location at the intersection of North Avenue (Route 64) and Lake Street (Hansen, ed., *Illinois,* 581).

NORTONVILLE. Morgan. Twelve miles southeast of Jacksonville. Laid out in 1893 by Charles S. and Sarah M. Norton (Hutchison "Old Morgan County Village"). Post office established Feb. 1, 1876, as Youngblood; changed to Nortonville May 16, 1894.

NORWAY. LaSalle. Twelve miles northeast of Ottawa. Settled in 1834 by Norwegians from Oswego, N.Y., led by Cleng Peerson. An Illinois state historical marker identifies this site as the first permanent Norwegian settlement in the United States. Stavenger, another Norwegian settlement, is five miles southeast of Norway (Burns, *A Link to the Past,* 23; Hansen, ed., *Illinois,* 649). Post office established March 15, 1843, as Mount Knickerbocker, named for postmaster Nelson Knickerbocker; changed to Norway Dec. 2, 1848.

NORWOOD PARK. Cook. Three miles east of O'Hare International Airport. Founded about 1869 by the Norwood Land and Building Association as a summer resort and vacation retreat from the heat and humidity of Chicago. Norwood Park was modeled on and named for the community described in *Norwood; or, Village Life in New England* (1868) by Henry Ward Beecher (Kitagawa and Taeuber, eds., *Local Community Fact Book,* 34). Post office established Jan. 3, 1870.

NUNDA [NUHN day]. McHenry. Township and former community. Known as Dearborn in the 1850s and later as North Crystal Lake. Nunda was formally annexed by Crystal Lake in 1914. Nunda Township was originally called Brooklyn, likely for Brooklyn, N.Y., and renamed in 1850 at the suggestion of William Huffman for his birthplace, Nunda, Livingston County, N.Y. Ultimately from an Iroquoian word probably meaning "hilly" (Nye, ed., *McHenry County Illinois,* 733, 781, 783; Stewart, *American Place-Names*). Post office established Jan. 20, 1857, as Dearborn; changed to Nunda Oct. 7, 1868.

O

OAK BROOK. DuPage. Village (1958). Founded in the 1920s as a planned community by developer Paul Butler. "Oak Brook" is a developer's promotional name, perhaps influenced by the presence of a stream and the odd oak tree or two (Harder, *Illustrated Dictionary of Place Names*).

OAKFORD. Menard. Village (1892) eight miles northwest of Petersburg. Named for William Oakford, site owner and proprietor of the first grocery store, which he established about 1872 (Onstot, *Pioneers of Menard,* 242). Post office established July 17, 1872.

OAKLAND. Coles. City (1855, 1896) thirteen miles northeast of Charleston. Founded in 1835 as Independence by site owner Gideon Madison Ashmore, who also laid out the communities of Ashmore, eight miles south of Oakland, and Liberty, a companion town to Independence that never materialized beyond a town plat. The name was changed from Independence to agree with that of the Oakland post office upon incorporation in 1855. Oakland was also known as Pinhook (q.v.) (Bateman and Selby, eds., *Historical Encyclopedia of Illinois and History of Coles County,* 704; Redlich, *The Postal History of Coles County,* 31). Post office established July 26, 1833.

OAKLAND. Cook. Formerly called Cleaverville, named for Charles Cleaver, who operated a soap factory and rendering plant in the 1850s. The Illinois Central station was established about 1871 as Oakland, named for Oakwood Avenue, itself named for Cleaver's estate, Oakwood Hall (Kitagawa and Taeuber, eds., *Local Community Fact Book,* 68).

OAKLEY. Macon. Seven miles east of Decatur. Laid out in 1856 by William Rea and named from the Oakley post office. The source of the name is unclear. It may be from a prominent local family named Oakley, or it may be a transfer, possibly by settlers from Oakley, Hamilton County, Ohio (Richmond, *Centennial History of Decatur,* 95, 447). Post office established Aug. 5, 1850.

OAK PARK. Cook. Village (1901). Previously known as Kettlestring's Grove for early settler Joseph Kettlestrings, who emigrated from Yorkshire, England, about 1833, and later called Oak Ridge. About 1866 the community and post office names were changed to Oak Park, a developer's promotional name. The Northwestern station was established in 1848 as Harlem, probably named for Harlem, N.Y. (Stennett, *A History of the Origin,* 109). Post office established Aug. 10, 1846, as Noyesville; changed to Oak Park March 6, 1866; changed to East Harlem March 15, 1871; changed to Oak Park April 18, 1871.

OAKWOOD. Vermilion. Village (1903) eight miles west of Danville. Named for Henry Oakwood, justice of the peace, township clerk, and Illinois state legislator in the 1870s (Stapp and Sullenberger, *Footprints in the Sands,* 48; Williams, *History of Vermilion County,* 320). Post office established May 9, 1870.

OBLONG. Crawford. Village (1883) nine miles west of Robinson. Named from Oblong Prairie, itself so called by early settlers for its elliptical shape. The community was first known as Henpeck, for the general store owned by Henry Peck, a name that survived until the post office was established as Oblong in 1852. This is the only community in the United States named Oblong although several geographic features in other states bear the name (Johnston, comp., *Our Crawford County,* 244; Perrin, ed., *History of Crawford and Clark Counties,* 173). Post office established Sept. 23, 1852.

OCONEE [o KO nee, OK uh nee]. Shelby. Village (1867, 1906) seven miles south of Pana. Platted in 1855 for Morris Ketchum. Probably named by the Illinois Central Railroad from one of the "Starved Rock legends," mixtures of history, lore, and imagination popular in the mid-nineteenth century. In one of these stories, Ulah, daughter of the Illinois chief Nepowra, is in love with Oconee, son of Shabbona, whom a member of Ulah's tribe has killed. When her family refuses to bless the union, she and Oconee elope and make their way to the top of Starved Rock, where they are set upon by Illinois warriors and perish together. The creator of this tale may have taken the name *Oconee* from the southeastern United States, perhaps from Georgia, where the word is from a Muskogee place name, or from South Carolina, where it was the name of a Cherokee village. The name *Ulah* (q.v.) is from the same story (*Atlas of Shelby County,* 7; Bright, *Native American Placenames;* Vogel, *Indian Place Names in Illinois*). Post office established May 15, 1854, as Luro; changed to Oconee Station March 30, 1855; changed to Oconee Jan. 29, 1872.

OCOYA. Livingston. Six miles south-southwest of Pontiac. Laid out in 1854 by Jonathan Duff and A. W. Cowan, bankers from Pontiac. Probably derived from a Miami-Illinois word for "whippoorwill," although several other sources have been suggested, including Illinois *apacoya,* reportedly referring to the reed mats and other material used for covering the sapling frames of houses. The name has generated a number of popular etymologies discussed by Vogel in "Some Illinois Place-Name Legends" (Bright, *Native American Placenames;* Vogel, *Indian Place Names in Illinois*). Post office established March 1, 1860.

ODELL. Livingston. Village (1869, 1872) eight miles southwest of Dwight. Founded in 1856 and named by developer S. S. Morgan for William H. Odell, chief engineer for the Chicago and Mississippi Railroad (Bateman and Selby, eds., *Historical Encyclopedia of Illinois and History of Livingston County,* 639; *History of Livingston County* [1878], 287). Post office established Nov. 9, 1855.

ODIN [OD uhn]. Marion. Village (1865, 1874) seven miles northeast of Centralia. Founded in 1856 and named by the Illinois Central Railroad for Odin, in Germanic mythology the chief of the gods and god of war, learning, and poetry. The area had a large number of Germanic, especially Scandinavian, settlers (Ackerman, *Early Illinois Railroads,* 132). Post office established Feb. 15, 1858.

O'FALLON. St. Clair. City (1865, 1874). Established in 1854 by the Ohio and Mississippi Railroad as O'Fallon Depot, named for John O'Fallon, first president of the O&M and a St. Louis merchant with operations on both sides of the Mississippi River. O'Fallon, Mo., west of St. Louis, is named for the same John O'Fallon (*History of St. Clair County,* 284; *Tapestry of Time,* 161). Post office established March 20, 1821, as Cherry Grove; changed to Rock Spring July 12, 1827; changed to Shiloh May 15, 1850; changed to O'Fallon Depot Dec. 22, 1854; changed to O'Fallon March 22, 1888.

OGDEN. Champaign. Village (1883) twelve miles east of Urbana. Founded in 1870 by John W. Leney and named for an Ogden family, whose farm was just south of the site (*History of Champaign County,* 170). Post office established April 18, 1870.

OGLE. County. Created Jan. 16, 1836, from Jo Daviess County. Named for Joseph Ogle (1741–1821), who commanded a company of Virginia troops during the Revolutionary War and later served in the Illinois territorial legislature. Unlike many others for whom communities and counties in Illinois were named, Ogle lived in the state for much of his life. Shortly after the Revolution he moved to Monroe County to join James Lemen at New Design and then to St. Clair County, where he lived until his death in 1821. The county was named for Ogle at the request of Thomas Ford, then a judge of the circuit court and later governor of Illinois and the namesake of Ford County.

OGLE [O guhl]. Mercer. Nine miles southwest of Aledo. Named for Jasper Ogle, who emigrated from Ohio about 1853 (Bateman and Selby, eds., *Historical Encyclopedia of Illinois and History of Mercer County,* 773). Post office established Aug. 23, 1890.

OGLES. St. Clair. Three miles northwest of Belleville. Named for Jacob Ogle, justice of the peace and son of Joseph Ogle, for whom Ogle County was named (*History of St. Clair County,* 76, 281).

OGLESBY [O guhlz bee]. LaSalle. City (1902). Founded in the 1860s by T. T. Bent as Kenosha, named for Bent's former home, Kenosha, Wis. When Kenosha was rejected as a name for the post office, Bent renamed the community for Richard

J. Oglesby (1824–99), then governor of Illinois. In the late 1890s the Chicago Portland Cement Company began operations at the site, and in 1902 part of present Oglesby was incorporated as Portland. The corporate name was changed to Oglesby in 1913 (*Oglesby*, 4, 5). Post office established Aug. 4, 1866.

OHIO. Bureau. Village (1876) twelve miles north of Princeton. Laid out as Albrecht, a station on the Chicago, Burlington and Quincy Railroad, by site owner Jacob Albrecht in 1871. Renamed for the Ohio post office, itself named for the state of Ohio (www.genealogytrails.com.ill/bureau/#Ohio). Post office established March 7, 1854.

OHIO GROVE. Township. Mercer. Named by settlers from Ohio (*History of Mercer and Henderson Counties*, 428).

OHLMAN. Montgomery. Village (1957) seven miles southwest of Pana. Founded about 1885 and named for Michael Ohlman, a retired steamboat captain (Bateman and Selby, eds., *Historical Encyclopedia of Illinois and History of Montgomery County*, 839). Post office established July 11, 1876.

OKAW [O kaw, O kah]. Shelby. Township. Named from the Okaw (Kaskaskia) River, itself named for the Kaskaskia, one of the tribes of the Illinois Confederacy. "Okaw" is an adaptation of *Au Kaskaskies*, Mississippi Valley French for "at the village of the Kaskaskias," which was commonly abbreviated *Aux Kas* or *Au Kas* [O kah]. In 1803, before leaving for the Pacific Ocean with Meriwether Lewis, William Clark recorded his location at the "Kaskaskies River Commonly Called Aucau Creek." An Okaw County was authorized by the Illinois legislature in 1841, but its organization was rejected by public referendum. Essentially the same territory was reauthorized and approved in 1843 as Moultrie County (McDermott, "William Clark's Struggle," 140; Sublett, *Paper Counties*, 51–55).

OKAWVILLE [OK uh vil]. Washington. Village (1894) 10 m nw of Nashville. Founded as Bridgeport by H. P. H. Morgan in the early 1850s and formally laid out by James Garvin and James Davis in 1856. The name was changed to Okawville, named for the Okaw (Kaskaskia) River about 1871. Okawville Township was named from the community in the early 1880s (Brinkman, ed., *This Is Washington County*, 46; Deason et al., eds., *Okawville*, n.p.). Post office established March 1, 1836, as Okaw; changed to Okawville Jan. 22, 1872.

OKLAHOMA. Named for the state of Oklahoma, whose name was coined in 1866 by Allen Wright from Choctaw *oklah* (people) and *homa* (red). Oklahoma Hill is a summit in St. Clair County near Bixby. Little Oklahoma, a former community in Whiteside County, is now part of Fulton (Bright, *Native American Placenames*).

OLDENBURG. Madison. Five miles south of Wood River. Named by settlers from Oldenburg, Lower Saxony, Germany. Post office established July 29, 1892, as Edwardsville Crossing; changed to Oldenburg July 21, 1893.

OLD MILL CREEK. Lake. Village (1958). Three miles east-northeast of Lindenhurst. Founded about 1839. Reportedly named Millburn by Scots immigrants. The name may be a partial translation of Scots *burn* (creek) (Zorn, "Ode to a Spot").

OLD RIPLEY. Bond. Village (1906) eight miles west of Greenville. Founded in 1850 by Charles Plog and Mathias Brown as New Berlin, named for Berlin, Germany. Renamed Old Ripley with reestablishment of the post office in 1850. The source of the name is unknown (Peterson, "Place Names of Bond County," 42). Post office established Nov. 1, 1850.

OLDTOWN. McLean. Township. Named for Indian Old Town, an Indian village in the northern part of the township (*History of McLean County,* 628).

OLENA. Henderson. Sixteen miles southwest of Monmouth. Founded in 1838 by Wilson Kendall and named for his former home, Olena, Huron County, Ohio (Sutton, *Rivers, Railways,* 30, 34). Post office established July 14, 1836, as Ellison Creek; changed to Olena Jan. 23, 1840.

OLGA. Hamilton. Near Tuckers Corners, southwest of McLeansboro. Named by store owner Napoleon Vaughan for Olga, one of his favorite young customers (*Hamilton County,* 40). Post office established July 19, 1886.

OLIVE. Madison. Township. Named for Abel, Joel, and James Olive, early settlers in the 1830s (Norton, ed., *Centennial History of Madison County,* 587).

OLIVE BRANCH. Alexander. Fifteen miles northwest of Cairo. Named from the Olive Branch Methodist Episcopal Church, itself named in the 1880s by Elias Glasgow, reportedly for the olive branch brought back to the ark by the dove released by Noah (Fults, Chisholm, and Novella, *Promised Land in Southern Illinois,* 114). Post office established May 12, 1876.

OLIVER. Edgar. Six miles north of Marshall. Founded in 1857 as Big Siding, on the line of the Paris and Danville Railroad. The name was changed about 1876 to honor Oliver Davis, a circuit judge of the 1860s (*History of Edgar County,* 471). Post office established Sept. 11, 1876.

OLIVET [ahl uh VET]. Vermilion. Two miles south of Georgetown. In 1912 the Church of the Nazarene purchased Illinois Holiness University and renamed it Olivet Nazarene College, from which the community took its name. From the biblical Mount of Olives, in the New Testament called Olivet (Stapp, *History under Our Feet,* 27). Post office established Aug. 28, 1912.

OLMSTED [AHM sted]. Pulaski. Village (1888) thirteen miles northeast of Cairo. Founded about 1872 with construction of the New York Central Railroad. Laid out by Edward Bigelow Olmstead, a Civil War chaplain and Presbyterian minister (*Pulaski County,* 17). Post office established Jan. 16, 1835, as Caledonia; changed to Olmsted June 30, 1876.

OLNEY [AHL nee]. Richland. City (1841, 1911). Probably named by Judge Aaron Shaw, an early settler; for John Olney, a local lawyer; or for Nathan Olney, a

Lawrenceville banker. Olney has been the seat of Richland County since its formation in 1841 (Hansen, ed., *Illinois,* 702; Michels, *History of Olney,* 15). Post office established Nov. 2, 1841.

OLYMPIA FIELDS. Cook. Village (1927) north of Park Forest. Founded about 1915 as the Olympia Fields Country Club by Charles Beach, who later served as the first village president. The name was suggested by Amos Alonzo Stagg, football coach at the University of Chicago and first president of the Olympia Fields Country Club. The village of Olympia Fields was organized about 1926 and maintained the classical Greek theme with such streets as Hellenic Drive, Troy Circle, and Ithaca Road (Blades, "Fields of Dreams"; Dionne, *Olympia Fields,* 7, 9). Post office established Aug. 29, 1918.

OMAHA. Gallatin. Village (1888) nine miles northeast of Eldorado. Founded in 1871 by Henry Pearce, the first baggage master on the St. Louis and Southeastern Railroad. Pearce named the community for Omaha, Neb., where he was previously baggage master (*History and Families of Gallatin County,* 17). Post office established Feb. 17, 1871.

OMEGA. Marion. Ten miles northeast of Salem. Founded in 1856 by Timothy Baldwin, who took the name from the Omega post office. Why the post office should have been given the name of the last letter of the Greek alphabet is not known (*History of Marion and Clinton Counties,* 289). Post office established June 27, 1855.

OMPHGHENT. Township. Madison. Named from the Omph-Ghent Church, organized by a Presbyterian congregation about 1848. The name probably combines an acronym from Our Mother of Perpetual Help (the Virgin Mary) with Ghent, the Belgian city in which the congregation originated. The historical Omphghent School was six miles east-northeast of Bethalto (Adams, comp., *Illinois Place Names; History of Madison County,* 538). Post office established April 23, 1838, as Paddock's Grove, named for postmaster Gaius Paddock; changed to Omph Ghent [*sic*] June 11, 1858.

ONARGA [o NAHR guh]. Iroquois. Village (1867, 1876) eighteen miles north-northeast of Paxton. Also a park in Cook County. Laid out in 1854 by David A. Neal, vice president of the Illinois Central Railroad. The origin of the name is unknown. While this appears to be an Indian name, or a pseudo-Indian name cobbled together from pieces of real or presumed native words, no etyma can be reliably identified. This is the only Onarga in the United States (Dowling, *History of Iroquois County,* 89). Post office established March 24, 1854, as Onargo; changed to Onarga Dec. 31, 1869.

ONECO. Stephenson. Thirteen miles north of Freeport. Founded in 1840 by John K. Brewster. Probably a transfer by settlers from Oneco, Windham County, Conn. Oneco is a variant of Owaneco (q.v.), the name of a Mohican leader of the seventeenth century (Bright, *Native American Placenames;* Johnston, *Sketches of the History,* 305). Post office established March 3, 1840.

ONEIDA [o NEYE duh, o NEE duh]. Knox. City (1869) eleven miles northeast of Galesburg. Platted by Charles F. Camp in 1854. Probably a transfer by settlers from Oneida County, N.Y. Ultimately from the tribal name meaning "people of the standing stone" (Bright, *Native American Placenames;* Bateman and Selby, eds., *Historical Encyclopedia of Illinois and Knox County,* 800). Post office established March 2, 1855.

ONTARIO. Knox. Nine miles north of Galesburg. A transfer by settlers from the area around Lake Ontario, especially the community of Ontario in Wayne County, N.Y., east of Rochester (Perry, *History of Knox County,* 426). Post office established Feb. 5, 1850.

ONTARIOVILLE. DuPage. Three miles southwest of Schaumburg. Edwin and Luther Bartlett each established stations named Bartlett on the line of the Chicago and Pacific Railroad in the 1870s. To avoid confusion, in 1873 Edwin Bartlett renamed his station Ontario, taking the name from a legend that the site was on an Indian trail leading from Lake Ontario to Green Bay, Wis. In 1958 the part of Ontarioville lying in Cook County incorporated as Hanover Park, taking the name of Hanover Township at the suggestion of Emil Rinne (Feeley, *From Camelot to Metropolis,* n.p.). Post office established Dec. 10, 1873.

OPDYKE. Jefferson. Seven miles southeast of Mount Vernon. Laid out in 1871 for the St. Louis and Southeastern Railroad. Named for George Opdyke, a New York banker, railroad investor, and political strategist instrumental in securing Abraham Lincoln's presidential nomination in 1860 (*Facts and Folks,* 263; Perrin, ed., *History of Jefferson County,* 259). Post office established Nov. 12, 1871.

OPHIEM [o FEEM]. Henry. Seventeen miles south-southeast of Moline. Founded about 1850 by Johannes and Carl Johan Samuelson, who named the community for their family farm, Opphem, in Tjärstan, Östergötland, Sweden. The name was recorded as *Ophiem* by a county official or postal agent (Landelius, *Swedish Place-Names;* Swank, *Historic Henry County,* 53). Post office established June 19, 1871.

OPHIR [O fer]. LaSalle. Township. Probably a transfer from Ophir, Placer County, Calif. The name was changed from Frémont, named for western explorer John C. Frémont, to Ophir in May 1850. Ophir is mentioned in the Bible in First Kings as a land of splendor and wealth. Ophir, Calif., was so named during the early gold rush days in hope that it would become famous as well. The name may have been brought back from the California gold fields by an Illinois miner (Stewart, *American Place-Names*). Post office established March 22, 1851.

OQUAWKA [o KWAW kuh]. Henderson. Village (1857, 1880) sixteen miles west of Monmouth. Founded about 1836 by Alexis and Stephen Phelps. The source of the name is uncertain. Traditionally "Oquawka" is assumed to be a translation of the Sauk words *a-saw-we-kee* or *oquawkiek*, reported to mean "yellow earth" or "yellow banks" for the sandy bluffs along the Mississippi River. Several other interpretations have been offered as well: that the name is derived from a Fox leader named Aquoqua (Kettle), a signatory to an 1815 treaty; that it is a transfer from Oquaga, Broome County, N.Y.; and that it was given in honor of the wife of Shabbona, reportedly named Wionex Oquawka Shabbona. None of these, unfortunately, can be substantiated at this time (Bright, *Native American Placenames*; Hicks, *History of Kendall County*, 293; *History of Mercer and Henderson Counties*, 920–21; Sutton, *Rivers, Railways*, 31; Vogel, *Indian Place Names in Illinois*). Post office established Aug. 26, 1833, as Yellow Banks; changed to Oquawka Aug. 5, 1836.

ORANGE. Knox. Township. Named about 1853, probably for Orange County, N.Y., by Asa Haynes, the first township supervisor (Bateman and Selby, eds., *Historical Encyclopedia of Illinois and Knox County*, 909).

ORANGEVILLE. Stephenson. Village (1867, 1873) eleven miles north of Freeport. Originally called Bowersville for John Bowers, who purchased the site in 1846. Renamed by settlers from an Orangeville in one of the eastern states, possibly Orangeville, Columbia County, Pa., or Orangeville, Wyoming County, N.Y. (*Recollections Illustrated, Orangeville*, n.p.; Tilden, comp., *History of Stephenson County*, 554). Post office established Feb. 16, 1854.

ORAVILLE. Jackson. Seven miles north-northwest of Murphysboro. Also Ora Township. Formerly known as Gillsburgh. According to a local account, the name was changed to Ora "because someone had a daughter by that name." Perhaps to distinguish Ora from Ava, six miles to the west, "ville" was added in the 1890s (Arimond, "Oraville"). Post office established May 14, 1875; changed to Ora on Oct. 27, 1879; changed to Oraville June 20, 1892.

OREANA [OR ee AN uh, AHR ee AN uh]. Macon. Village (1952) six miles northeast of Decatur. Founded about 1872 by site owner Henry C. Bower and named by officials of the Illinois Central Railroad. Likely named for Oreana, Nev., a station on the Union Pacific Railroad. The name is derived from "ore," influenced by Spanish *oro* (gold) (*Oreana*, 6; *Past and Present of the City of Decatur*, 68). Post office established Jan. 12, 1874.

OREGON. Ogle. City (1843 1873). Founded about 1835 by the Phelps brothers, John, Benjamin, and George, as Oregon City. Named by John Phelps's daughter, Sarah, for the Oregon country of the Pacific Northwest, which was in the news at the time. An Oregon County was authorized by the Illinois legislature about 1850, to be created from present southwestern Morgan County, southeastern Sangamon County, and northern Macoupin County, but a public referendum defeated its organization. Oregon has been the seat of Ogle County since 1838

(*Bicentennial History of Ogle County,* 376; *Story of Oregon,* 26; Sublett, *Paper Counties,* 97–105). Post office established May 15, 1837, as Oregon City; changed to Oregon Nov. 16, 1843.

ORIENT. Franklin. City (1917) three miles west-northwest of West Frankfort. Named about 1912 for the Orient Number One coal mine, which the Chicago, Wilmington and Vermilion (later the Chicago, Wilmington and Franklin) Coal Company operated in the area known as Heelstring. The sources of both "Orient" and "Heelstring" are unknown (Jurich, *This Is Franklin County,* 26), Post office established May 29, 1913.

ORION [OR ee uhn]. Henry. Village (1873) ten miles southeast of Moline. Founded about 1836 as the LaGrange Colony by a New York land development consortium that purchased some eighteen thousand acres in the area. The planned colony never materialized beyond the LaGrange public house and several scattered structures. The site was purchased and formally platted in 1853 as Deanington by Charles W. Dean. The name was changed to Orion in 1867 to match that of the Orion post office, itself named by Charles T. Trego, the first postmaster. The source of the name is unclear; it may be for local land owner Orion E. Page, who founded Osco five miles east of Orion (Anderson and Norcross, *A History of Orion,* 8; *History of Henry County,* 521, 534). Post office established Sept. 10, 1838, as LaGrange; discontinued May 16, 1845; reestablished as Orion Feb. 29, 1848.

ORION [OR ee uhn]. Township. Fulton. Named by Jonas Rawalt, reportedly for the constellation Orion (Clark, ed., *A History of Fulton County,* 209; Irwin, *A to Z Fulton County*).

ORIZABA. Champaign. Former community in Raymond Township north of Longview. Named by John Southworth, likely for Orizaba, Calif.; possibly for Orizaba, Miss. Orizaba is the name of a city and mountain in Veracruz, Mexico. When the railroad was established, much of Orizaba was disassembled and moved to trackside at Longview (personal communication with Nancy Reed). Post office established April 6, 1879.

ORLAND. Cook. Township. Also Orland Park and Orland Hills. Probably named for Orland, Maine. Orland Park was laid out by Col. Fawcett Plum as Sedgewick, a station on the Wabash, St. Louis and Pacific Railroad, and renamed for its location in Orland Township in 1881. Orland Hills, previously incorporated as the village of Westhaven, was renamed for its proximity to Orland Park in 1986 (Hayes, "For Village"; *Orland Story,* 287). Post office established Jan. 11, 1851, as Orland; changed to Orland Park March 15, 1927.

ORMONDE. Warren. Four miles southeast of Monmouth. Platted in 1888. Probably named for a family or individual named Ormonde, a variant of Ormond (Rowley, *The History of Kirkwood, Illinois,* 27). Post office established July 24,

1889, as Zulu, probably named for the Zulu Wars of the 1880s in South Africa; changed to Ormonde May 23, 1895.

OSAGE. LaSalle. Township. Probably named for the Osage hedge, better known as Osage orange, that farmers planted to serve as natural fencing for livestock. Ultimately from the name of the Osage Tribe, members of which were living in the Lower Missouri Valley when first contacted by Europeans (*History of LaSalle County*, 513). Post office established March 6, 1856.

OSBERNVILLE. Christian. Eleven miles southwest of Decatur. Named for site owner Charles W. Osbern (Adams, comp., *Illinois Place Names;* Bateman and Selby, eds., *Historical Encyclopedia of Illinois and History of Christian County*, 777). Post office established Jan. 5, 1887, as Morgansville, named for postmaster William Morgan; changed to Osbernville Feb. 24, 1903.

OSBORN. Rock Island. Nine miles east-northeast of Moline. Named for Frederick Osborn, site owner and first postmaster (Adams, comp., *Illinois Place Names; Historic Rock Island County*, 99). Post office established Jan. 3, 1870.

OSCEOLA. Stark. Eight miles east-southeast of Kewanee. Laid out about 1836 by Maj. Robert Moore. Named for Osceola, who fought against U.S. forces in the Seminole Wars of the 1830s in Florida. A number of communities in the United States were named for Osceola, especially those founded about the time of his imprisonment in 1835 and death in 1838. Former Osceolas in Illinois include those in Henry County (now Algonquin), Schuyler County (now Bader), and Tazewell County (now Hopedale) (Adams, comp., *Illinois Place Names;* Leeson, *Documents and Biography*, 571). Post office established Oct. 27, 1852, as Oceola; changed to Osceola Dec. 31, 1878.

OSCO [AHS ko]. Henry. Fifteen miles southeast of Moline. Founded about 1836. Although Polson suggests that the community may have been named for an O. S. Coe, who kept the local general store, the name is probably a transfer by settlers from Osco, Cayuga County, N.Y., itself named from an Onandaga (Iroquian) word meaning "bridge." Formally laid out in 1870 by site owner Orion E. Page (Kiner, *History of Henry County*, 606; Polson, *Corn, Commerce, and Country Living*, 85; Vogel, *Indian Place Names in Illinois*). Post office established Nov. 26, 1840, as Morristown; changed to Osco Dec. 1, 1871.

OSKALOOSA. Clay. Eleven miles northwest of Flora. Founded in 1853 by Henry Smith and named for his former home, Oskaloosa, the seat of Mahaska County, Iowa. Oskaloosa, Choctaw for "black reed," is often claimed to have been the name of one of the wives of Osceola (Bright, *Native American Placenames; History of Wayne and Clay Counties*, 425). Post office established June 13, 1851, as Sutton's Point; changed to Oskaloosa May 6, 1867.

OSMAN [AHZ muhn]. McLean. Seven miles north of Mahomet. Named for Moses Osman (1822–93), an official of the Chicago and Paduca Railroad and part owner of the *Ottawa Free Trader* newspaper (Townley, *Historic McLean,* 20). Post office established June 19, 1874.

OSPUR. DeWitt. Four miles south of Clinton. The origin of the name is unknown. This is the only Ospur in the United States. Post office established Oct. 11, 1889.

OSWEGO [ahs WEE go]. Kendall. Village (1857, 1881). Founded in 1835 as Hudson by settlers from Hudson, N.Y. Renamed in 1838 for Oswego, the city and county on Lake Ontario northwest of Syracuse, N.Y., the point of embarkation for many settlers on their passage through the Great Lakes to Chicago. Oswego is the Onandaga and Oneida name for Lake Ontario, with the general meaning "flowing out." Oswego was the seat of Kendall County from 1845, when it was moved from Yorkville, until 1864, when it was moved back to Yorkville (Farren, ed., *A Bicentennial History,* 97; Hicks, *History of Kendall County,* 137). Post office established Jan. 24, 1837, as Lodi; changed to Oswego July 31, 1838.

OTEGO. Fayette. Township. The township was to have been named Otsego, probably for Otsego, N.Y., but possibly for Otsego, Ind., or Otsego, Ohio, themselves named for Otsego, N.Y. Through clerical error the name was recorded as Otego (Bateman and Selby, eds., *Historical Encyclopedia of Illinois and History of Fayette County,* 651), Post office established June 20, 1899.

OTSEGO. Lake. Former community. A transfer from Otsego County, N.Y. Previously known as York House, or New York House, from the tavern kept by Jeremiah Porter. The York House Church is about one mile south of the Waukegan Regional Airport (Dretske, *What's in a Name?*). Post office established July 27, 1837.

OTTAWA [AHT uh wuh]. LaSalle. City (1837, 1882). From the name of an Algonquian tribe of the Great Lakes region. The name was probably brought to Illinois by one Passerat de la Chapelle, who led a contingent of soldiers from Canada along the Illinois River to what is now Buffalo Rock, where in December 1760 he established Fort Ottawa, which he probably named for the Ottawa River in Canada. The present city of Ottawa was established as the western terminus of the Illinois and Michigan Canal in 1831. Burns suggests that the name *Ottawa* may not be a transfer but rather a shortening of Potawatomi. Other than superficial phonetic similarity, however, I know of no evidence to support this claim. Ottawa has been the LaSalle county seat since 1831. Formerly known as Carbonia, named for the local coal deposits (Burns, *A Link to the Past,* 22; Carr, *Belleville, Ottawa, and Galesburg,* 6; Tisler, *Story of Ottawa,* 7). Post office established Dec. 20, 1832.

OTTO. Kankakee. Five miles south-southwest of Kankakee. Otto Township was formed as Carthage in 1855. The name was changed in 1857 at the suggestion of township supervisor Luther Gubtail, who argued that because there was an Aroma Township there ought to be an Otto (or Otter) township as well. [AHT er] was a local pronunciation of attar, the perfumed oil extracted from flowers, especially rose petals. Gubtail was especially taken by the acres of wildflowers that covered the prairie each spring. Otter became Otto through mistranscription or popular etymology. Aroma and Otto townships are adjacent in south central Kankakee County (Bateman and Selby, eds., *Historical Encyclopedia of Illinois and History of Kankakee County*, 757).

OTTVILLE. Bureau. Seven miles west of Peru. Named for postmaster William Ott (Adams, comp., *Illinois Place Names*). Post office established Sept. 13, 1865.

OWANECO [o WAHN uh ko]. Christian. Village (1902) eight miles northwest of Pana. Named for Owaneco, a Mohican leader in New England in the late seventeenth century, also known as Oneco. Owaneco was founded in 1869 and took its name from the Owaneco post office, itself named by Horatio M. Vandeveer, an Illinois state legislator, circuit judge, and postmaster at Taylorville in the 1840s. This is the only Owaneco in the United States (*Christian County History*, 44; Vogel, *Indian Place Names in Illinois*). Post office established Feb. 29, 1856.

OWEGO. Livingston. Township. Transferred by settlers from Owego, Tioga County, N.Y. From an Iroquois word, perhaps meaning "where the valley widens" (Bateman and Selby, eds., *Historical Encyclopedia of Illinois and History of Livingston County*, 639; Stewart, *American Place-Names*).

OXFORD. Henry. Township and former community fourteen miles southwest of Cambridge. Oxford, near New Windsor, was laid out in 1858 by Daniel and James Briggs but disappeared in the early 1880s. Probably named for Oxford, N.Y. (Polson, *Corn, Commerce, and Country Living*, 77). Post office established July 11, 1840.

P

PACIFIC. Cook. Established as Pacific Junction, named by the Chicago and Pacific Railroad about 1877. Now part of Chicago (Karlen, *Chicago's Crabgrass Communities*, 167). Post office established Sept. 25, 1877, as Pacific Junction; changed to Pacific May 14, 1883.

PADERBORN. St. Clair. Ten miles south-southwest of Belleville. Laid out by Valentine Berg and named for Paderborn in west central Germany, the home of a number of settlers and several local priests (*Commercial History of Clinton County*, 75). Post office established Sept. 8, 1882.

PADUA [PAD yoo uh]. McLean. Ten miles east of Bloomington. Laid out in 1873 by Charles R. Coe and named from the Padua post office. The reason for the name is unknown. Padua, ultimately from the city in northeastern Italy, is rare as a community name in the United States, occurring only in Illinois, Minnesota, and Ohio (Evans, *Ellsworth's Hundredth Year*, n.p.). Post office established May 13, 1852.

PALATINE. Cook. Village (1869, 1887). Palatine was an original Cook County township, named at the suggestion of Harrison Cook (formerly Koch) for his previous home, Palatine Bridge in Montgomery County, N.Y. The name obviously resonated with the large number of settlers who had emigrated from the Rhine (Lower) Palatinate in Germany. The village of Palatine was founded in 1855 and named for the township (Paddock, *Palatine Centennial Book,* 21). Post office established July 16, 1842, as Wickliffe; changed to Palatine May 30, 1850.

PALERMO [puh LAHR mo]. Edgar. Fifteen miles southwest of Georgetown. Named from the Palermo post office, itself named by postmaster C. L. C. Bradfield. Bradfield reportedly took the name from a story he was reading that was set in a western town called Palermo. He would, however, also have been familiar with Palermo, Ohio, near Columbiana, where he was born and raised, and this may be the true source of the name. Ultimately from Palermo, Sicily (*History of Edgar County,* 524; personal communication with Nancy Reed). Post office established April 8, 1864.

PALESTINE. Crawford. Town (1855) six miles east of Robinson. The name is usually credited to Jean (John) LaMotte, said to be a member of LaSalle's expedition, who supposedly likened the area to the biblical land of milk and honey. About 1812 American settlers built Fort LaMotte for protection from Indian raids. The fort provided the nucleus for Palestine, which was formally laid out, apparently as Mount Pleasant, in 1818 by Edward N. Cullom, Joseph Kitchell, and David Porter. Palestine was the first community to be platted in Crawford County and served as the county seat from 1818 until 1843, when the county seat was moved to Robinson (*History of Crawford County,* 68; *Illinois Guide;* Perrin, ed., *History of Crawford and Clark Counties,* 139; personal communication with Sue Jones). Post office established May 21, 1818.

PALESTINE. Woodford. Township. Named from Palestine Prairie between Panther Creek and the Mackinaw River. The circumstances surrounding the naming of the prairie are unknown (Perrin and Hill, *Past and Present,* 445).

PALMER. Christian. Village (1871, 1873) eight miles southwest of Taylorville. Founded in 1869 by J. H. Boyd and J. M. Simpson. Named for John M. Palmer (1817–1900), Civil War general and governor of Illinois from 1869 to 1873 (*Christian County History,* 38). Post office established Jan. 10, 1871.

PALMYRA [pal MEYE ruh]. Former community previously in Edwards County, now in Wabash County. Named as the seat of Edwards County in 1814. The community was established in 1815 by Seth Gard, Peter Keen, Gervase Hazleton, Levi Compton, and John Waggoner, operating as Seth Gard and Company, near the falls of the Wabash River north of present Mount Carmel. The name is most likely a transfer from Palmyra, Wayne County, N.Y., itself named for the biblical city now in Syria. Palmyra fell into decline when the county seat was moved to Albion in 1821 and was deserted by the late 1820s (Allen, *Legends and Lore*, 349; *Combined History of Edwards, Lawrence, and Wabash Counties*, 81; Harper, ed., *History of Edwards County*, 63; Vasiliev, *From Abbotts to Zurich*). Post office established Oct. 11, 1815, as Edwards Courthouse; changed to Wabash Courthouse March 21, 1825.

PALMYRA. Lee. Four miles west of Dixon. Settled in the early 1840s by what became known as the New York Colony, a group of settlers from New England, primarily New York. Fred Coe is usually credited for proposing the name, for Palmyra, Wayne County, N.Y. (Bateman and Selby, eds., *Historical Encyclopedia of Illinois and History of Lee County*, 686; Kennedy, *Recollections of the Pioneers*, 492).

PALOMA [puh LO muh]. Adams. Twelve miles northeast of Quincy. Originally known as Pickle Landing, or Pickleville for the pickles loaded from the Chicago, Burlington and Quincy platform. The wife of one of the CB&Q conductors thought the name *Pickleville* lacked dignity and suggested Paloma, reportedly in honor of a small band of Indians (Wilkey, *The Story of a Little Town*, 35–36). Post office established April 1, 1856.

PALOS [PAY luhs]. Cook. Communities in southwestern suburban Chicago: the city of Palos Heights (1959), established by developer Robert Bartlett in 1938 as a residential subdivision named Harlem Heights, and the villages of Palos Park (1914) and Palos Hills (1959). All take their name from Palos Township. The area was formerly known as Trenton, named by settlers from Trenton, N.J. The name *Palos* was apparently suggested by postmaster Medanchon A. Powell for Palos de la Frontera, literally the "sticks along the frontier," a former seaport in southwestern Spain. Powell claimed that one of his ancestors had sailed from Palos with Columbus in 1492 (Harder, *Illustrated Dictionary of Place Names; Illinois Guide*; Johnson, "Where You Can Visit the Country"). Post office established March 7, 1846, as Orange; changed to Trenton Feb. 28, 1850; changed to Palos May 30, 1850.

PALWAUKEE. Cook. A blend of the names of the community's major thoroughfares, Palatine Road and Milwaukee Avenue (Vogel, *Indian Place Names in Illinois*).

PALZO. Williamson. Twelve miles southwest of Harrisburg. The name apparently originated in popular greetings of the 1890s, "Hi, old palzo" and "Hi there, palzo" (Hale, comp. and ed., *Williamson County*, 119). Post office established April 9, 1894.

PANA [PAY nuh]. Christian. City (1857, 1877). Platted about 1854 for David A. Neal, vice president of the Illinois Central Railroad. The name has been claimed to derive from a Cahokia leader named Pana, whose name appears on several French documents of the 1750s, but most likely it is from Pani or Panis, a French form of the tribal name *Pawnee*. The name *Pana* appears on Marquette's map as the name of a Native American tribe west of the Mississippi River (Ackerman, *Early*

Illinois Railroads, 149; Allen, *Legends and Lore,* 46; Goudy, *History of Christian County,* 195; Vogel, *Indian Place Names in Illinois).* Post office established Sept. 19, 1853, as Stone Coal; changed to Pana Feb. 22, 1855.

PANAMA. Bond, Montgomery. Village (1906) eight miles south of Hillsboro. Founded in 1905 as a company town for employees of the Shoal Creek Coal Company. Named for Panama in Central America, which was in the news at the time. Panama had declared independence from Colombia in 1903 and was preparing for construction of the Panama Canal (Bateman and Selby, eds., *Historical Encyclopedia of Illinois and History of Bond County,* 647; Peterson, "Place Names of Bond County," 42). Post office established June 18, 1906.

PANKEYVILLE. Saline. South of Harrisburg. Named for John Pankey, one of the proprietors of the site of Harrisburg, for shopkeeper Andrew Pankey, or both (*History of Gallatin, Saline,* 203; *History of Saline County,* 44).

PANOLA [puh NO luh]. Woodford. Village (1867, 1875) nineteen miles north of Normal. Founded about 1854 by the Illinois Central Railroad. Ackerman claims the name was created by John B. Calhoun, a land commissioner for the IC, "by placing the vowels a, o, a, and filling in with the consonants p, n, l" (*Early Illinois Railroads,* 144). More likely, however, the name is a transfer from the Southeast, where *panola,* Choctaw for "cotton," occurs in a number of place names, especially in Alabama and Mississippi (Bright, *Native American Placenames*). Post office established Aug. 18, 1836, as Josephine; changed to Panola Station Feb. 13, 1854; changed to Panola June 20, 1892.

PAPINEAU [PAP uh naw]. Iroquois. Village (1874) fourteen miles southeast of Kankakee. Formerly known as Weygandt, named for a Weygandt family. The name was changed by Canadian settlers in the early 1860s to honor Louis Joseph Papineau (1786–1871), a French-Canadian violently opposed to the union of Lower and Upper Canada. He was one of the delegates at the St. Charles convention, which decided on rebellion in 1837. Charged with high treason, he fled to the United States. By virtue of a general amnesty he returned to Canada, where he served in the lower house of parliament (Dowling, *History of Iroquois County,* 93). Post office established April 11, 1871.

PARADISE. Coles. Five miles south-southwest of Mattoon. Founded about 1837 by Joseph Fowler and named from the Paradise post office, established in 1830 and apparently named by George M. Hanson, who was instrumental in the creation of Coles County, for his former home, Paradise, Va. (now in W.Va.) (Bateman and Selby, eds., *Historical Encyclopedia of Illinois and History of Coles County,* 743; Perrin, Graham, and Blair, *History of Coles County,* 507; Redlich, *The Postal History of Coles County,* 9). Post office established Feb. 18, 1830.

PARADISE. Perry. Precinct. Named from Paradise Prairie. According to a local story, early settlers were walking across the prairie one fine day when one of the party, a Mr. Wells, remarked, "This is as near Paradise as I ever expect to get."

From that comment the prairie and the precinct supposedly took their names (*Combined History of Randolph, Monroe, and Perry Counties*, 367).

PARIS. Edgar. City (1853, 1873). Samuel Vance donated twenty-five acres of land for the Edgar County seat in 1823. In consideration he was given the right to choose the name, and he proposed Paris, perhaps for Paris, Va., near his former home. Several other sources, if not direct namesakes of Paris, likely contributed to its favorable reception. A number of settlers were from Paris, Ky., and most nineteenth-century Americans held highly favorable attitudes toward Paris, France, due in large part to the immense popularity of the Marquis de La Fayette. Paris has been the seat of Edgar County since 1823 (Bateman and Selby, eds., *Historical Encyclopedia of Illinois and History of Edgar County,* 622; *History of Edgar County,* 319). Post office established 1823 as Edgar Courthouse; changed to Paris Jan. 11, 1826.

PARK CITY. Lake. City (1958). Established by Joseph Koempstedt, Francis Murphy, Gene Palmieri, and Gus Teske, owners of mobile home parks that merged as Park City in 1958 in order to avoid annexation by Waukegan (Crawford, "'The City on Wheels'").

PARK FOREST. Cook, Will. Founded in 1946 as a residential community for returning veterans of World War II by Carroll F. Sweet and American Community Builders. The name was coined by Sweet, who, although recognizing that Forest Park was an existing Chicago suburb, reportedly remarked, "Just because there's already a Forest Park doesn't mean there can't be a Park Forest." The name was to have been temporary and used primarily for administrative purposes. In 1948, when a permanent name was discussed, suggestions included Westlyn, Brynhurst, Sauk Park, and Indianwood, the name of the golf course on which the community was built. Park Forest was the overwhelming choice, and the name was made permanent by a formal vote in 1950 (Randall, *America's Original GI Town,* 87–88, 116).

PARK RIDGE. Cook. City (1873). Formerly known as Pennyville, named for George Penny, who operated a brick kiln and lumber yard at the site. At Penny's request the name was changed to Brickton in the mid-1850s. By the 1870s the brick industry had largely disappeared, and Brickton was seen as an inappropriate name for a progressive community. Park Ridge was chosen because of its location "on a ridge and in a park-like setting," according to one local account. The name was probably suggested by George B. Carpenter, the first village president (Hansen, ed., *Illinois,* 565; *History of Park Ridge,* 17–18; www.park-ridge.il.us). Post office established June 8, 1857, as Brickton; changed to Park Ridge June 9, 1871.

PARKER. Township. Clark. Named for George Parker and his sons, Samuel, Daniel, Jeptha, and William, early settlers in the late 1820s (Bateman and Selby, eds., *Historical Encyclopedia of Illinois and History of Clark County,* 655; Perrin, ed., *History of Crawford and Clark Counties,* 454). Post office established Aug. 30, 1856.

PARKERSBURG. Richland. Village (1927) nine miles south of Olney. Laid out in 1859 by John D. Parker as a station on the Peoria, Decatur and Evansville Railroad (*Counties of Cumberland, Jasper, and Richland,* 722). Post office established Feb. 8, 1837, as Little Prairie; changed to Parkersburgh Dec. 18, 1837; changed to Parkersburg Aug. 17, 1893.

PARKVILLE. Champaign. Seven miles northwest of Tuscola. Parkville replaced a community called Soonover, so named, according to a local story, because the town quickly failed and the founder's efforts were soon over. The particular Park individual or family for whom the community is named is unknown (*History of Champaign County,* 122). Post office established Jan. 13, 1875.

PARNELL. DeWitt. Five miles southwest of Farmer City. Founded by James Porter in 1880. Named by Porter for Charles Stewart Parnell (1846–91), the Irish nationalist and leader of the Irish home rule movement. Parnell was widely known in the United States at the time (*History of DeWitt County* [1882], 288). Post office established April 26, 1880.

PARRISH. Franklin. Six miles southeast of Benton. Formerly known as Charlieville, named for Charlie Eubanks, regarded as the first permanent settler. Renamed with establishment of the Benton and Eastern Railroad station for the Parrish post office, itself named for the Rev. Braxton Parrish, a well-known Methodist minister. Informally known as Sneakout (q.v.) (*Franklin County,* 18; Ramsey and Miller, *The Heritage of Franklin County,* 34; Sneed, *Ghost Towns of Southern Illinois,* 26). Post office established Nov. 10, 1856.

PARTRIDGE. Woodford. Township. Named from Partridge Creek, itself named for a Potawatomi leader whose name appears as Mucketeypokee (Black Partridge) in the 1816 Treaty of St. Louis. Black Partridge warned settlers of impending Indian attacks on several occasions; nevertheless, his village at the head of Peoria Lake was destroyed in 1812 by a contingent of Illinois militia commanded by Ninian Edwards, for whom Edwards County is named and governor of Illinois Territory at the time (Vogel, *Indian Place Names in Illinois*). Post office established Feb. 4, 1836, as Black Partridge.

PATIERDALE. Alexander. Named for site owner Charles O. Patier. Now part of Cairo (*Alexander County,* 17).

PATOKA [puh TO kuh]. Marion. Village (1869, 1885) eleven miles northwest of Salem. Established in 1854 as a station on the Illinois Central Railroad. The name is either a transfer from Patoka, Ind., or was chosen by the IC for one or more Native American leaders named Patoka. Ackerman (*Early Illinois Railroads,* 152) suggests a Chief Patoka, whose main village was located at the nearby mineral springs, and Vogel has identified a Cahokia leader named Patoka who was mentioned in Kaskaskia court records of the 1770s. From French Padouca, itself from a Siouan word that referred to the Comanche and other plains tribes whose members the Illinois and the Miami often kept as slaves. Paducah, Ky., is from the same source (Bright, *Native American Placenames;* Vogel, *Indian Place Names in Illinois*). Post office established Oct. 18, 1854.

PATTERSON. Greene. Five miles northwest of White Hall. Known as Wilmington in the 1830s, later as Breese for Sidney Breese (q.v. Breese), and finally as Patterson for site owner L. J. Patterson (*History of Greene and Jersey Counties,* 970, 972). Post office established Nov. 6, 1846, as Breese; changed to Patterson March 29, 1880.

PATTON. Ford. Township. Named for David H. Patton, first township supervisor and first county judge. Changed from Prairie City about 1857 (Gardner, *History of Ford County,* 107).

PATTON. Wabash. Four miles north of Mount Carmel. Platted in 1877 for Albert B. Keene and named in honor of a Dr. Patton of Vincennes (*Combined History of Edwards, Lawrence, and Wabash Counties,* 295). Post office established June 22, 1874, as Paton; changed to Patton March 29, 1880.

PATTONSBURG. Marshall. Sixteen miles northwest of El Paso. Founded in 1856 by early settler Nathan Patton, known as Father Patton (Ford, *History of Putnam and Marshall Counties,* 121).

PAWNEE. Sangamon. Village (1891). Previously known as Horse Creek Trading Post, named from Horse Creek. The petition for a post office, submitted about 1858, called for the name *Horse Creek.* For unspecified reasons, the Post Office Department found this unacceptable and the postmaster general of the United States wrote to James W. Keyes, then postmaster at Springfield, asking for another name. Keyes suggested Pawnee; presumably for the Pawnee Tribe (*History of Sangamon County,* 977). Post office established Sept. 22, 1858.

PAW PAW. Lee. Village (1882) twelve miles northeast of Mendota. Also DeKalb County township. Named for the local paw paw trees that provided fruit for Native Americans and early settlers. Although the word *paw paw* is an adaptation of Spanish *papaya,* the scientific name of the tree, *asimina triloba,* is derived in part from *asimina,* the native word for its fruit. Paw Paw Grove is a translation of Potawatomi *as-sim-in-eh-kon* (Vogel, *Indian Place Names in Illinois*). Post office established Nov. 18, 1836, as Pawpaw Grove; changed to Paw Paw May 21, 1823; changed to Pawpaw Oct. 28, 1893.

PAXTON. Ford. City (1865, 1872). Originally called Prairie City and platted as Prospect City in 1858. The name was changed to Paxton in 1859, either by William H. Pells, the founder of Pellville, or by James Mix of Kankakee in an attempt to attract a colony planned by the noted English architect and horticulturalist Sir Joseph Paxton. The colony never materialized, but the name remained (Gardner, *History of Ford County,* 81; Harder, *Illustrated Dictionary of Place Names*). Post office established Oct. 6, 1854, as Ten Mile Grove; changed to Prospect City Jan. 14, 1857; changed to Paxton Sept. 15, 1859.

PAYNES POINT. Ogle. Nine miles west-northwest of Rochelle. Named for Aaron Payne (Paine), reportedly the first settler, who arrived in 1835 (*Bicentennial History of Ogle County,* 400). Post office established March 24, 1848, as Paines Point.

PAYSON. ADAMS. Village (1869, 1903) ten miles southeast of Quincy. Founded about 1834 as Paysonville, named by Deacon Albigence Scarborough in honor of the Rev. Dr. Edward Payson, whom Scarborough greatly admired. Payson was a Congregational minister of Portland, Maine, during the 1810s and 1820s (Genosky, ed., *People's History,* 752; *History of Adams County,* 552). Post office established March 11, 1837.

PEACH ORCHARD. Ford. Township. Named for the peach trees (reportedly more than a thousand) brought from southern Illinois by Joshua P. Nicholson and his brothers in 1855 and planted near Melvin. Most of the trees died and were never replaced, but the name endured (*Ford County History,* 124).

PEA RIDGE. Brown. Township. The name was proposed by Henry Pell, probably for the wild peas that grew in the northern part of the township. Several sources claim that the township was named for the March 1862 Civil War battle of Pea Ridge, Ark., but Pea Ridge Township was organized more than a decade earlier (Dearinger, "A New Geography of Brown County," 32; Drury, *This Is Brown County,* 21).

PEARL. Pike. Village (1881) twelve miles west of White Hall. Named for the buttons manufactured from mollusk shells dredged from the Mississippi River. At least five button factories were reported to be operating along the river in the 1880s (www.outfitters.com/illinois/pike/communities_pike.html). Post office established May 19, 1855.

PECAN ISLAND. Fayette. Island in the Kaskaskia River four miles south of Vandalia. Named for the local pecan trees. The word *pecan* is of local origin, having entered English through American French *pacane,* itself a translation of a Miami-Illinois word for "nut" (McDermott, *A Glossary of Mississippi Valley French;* Vogel, *Indian Place Names in Illinois*).

PECATONICA [pek uh TAHN i kuh]. Winnebago. Village (1869, 1881) eleven miles west of Rockford. Formerly known as Lysander, probably named for Lysander, N.Y. Laid out in 1852 by T. D. Robertson and John A. Holland as a station on the Galena and Chicago Union Railroad and named from the Pecatonica River, itself probably named from a Miami-Illinois word claimed to mean "muddy." The first known recording of the name is by Marquette, who labeled the Missouri River the Pekitanoui on his map of about 1673. A related form, Pickotolica, was recorded by an early traveler as the name of a kind of fish, perhaps the mud sucker, reported to be quite flavorful. For many years the Plum River in northwestern Illinois was called the Pecatolikee (Bright, *Native American Placenames;*

History of Winnebago County, 227, 440; Stewart, *American Place-Names;* Thiem, ed., *Carroll County,* 24, 125; Vogel, *Indian Place Names in Illinois*). Post office established Dec. 26, 1838.

PECUMSAUGAN CREEK [PEK uhm SAG un]. LaSalle. Stream. Empties into Split Rock Lake east of LaSalle. Possibly from Potawatomi *pikumisagusin,* said to mean "hatchets." An early county history (Baldwin, *History of LaSalle County,* 15) refers to the *percomsoggin,* which is glossed as "Indian for little axe." Tomahawk Creek, perhaps a translation, is nearby (Bright, *Native American Placenames;* Vogel, *Indian Place Names in Illinois*).

PEKIN. Tazewell. City (1839, 1874). Laid out as Cincinnati about 1826, named for Cincinnati, Ohio. The projected community never materialized and was re-organized and platted as Pekin in 1829. The name was chosen by Ann Eliza Cromwell for Peking (Beijing) China. It was assumed that much of Illinois lay on the opposite side of the world from China. One early settler remarked that the Illinois earth "is fertile and black and loamy down to the bottom of China." One unfortunate consequence of the name and the Chinese motif adopted by the city was that Pekin High School's athletic teams were known as the Chinks, a nickname changed to the Dragons in the early 1980s. Pekin became the seat of Tazewell County in 1849 after years of contending with Tremont (Bates, *Souvenir of Early and Notable Events,* 12; Hansen, ed., *Illinois,* 660; *History of Tazewell County,* 565; *Pekin Sesquicentennial,* 6). Post office established Feb. 20, 1832.

PELLVILLE. Vermilion. Eight miles east of Paxton. Founded as Pellsville by William H. Pells of New York, at the time a member of the board of directors of the Lake Erie and Western Railroad. Pells also founded Pellston, Mich. (Stapp, *History under Our Feet,* 41). Post office established July 7, 1868, as Sugar Creek; changed to Rankin July 25, 1872; changed to Pellsville Sept. 14, 1872.

PEMBROKE. Kankakee, Township. Created from St. Anne and Momence townships in 1877. Probably named by Hiram Whittemore for Pembroke, N.H. (Johnson, comp., "Kankakee County Communities").

PENDLETON. Jefferson. Township. Named for George H. Pendleton of Ohio, vice-presidential candidate on George B. McClellan's Democratic ticket in the election of 1864 (Perrin, ed., *History of Jefferson County,* 356).

PENFIELD. Champaign. Ten miles east of Rantoul. Founded in 1876 by S. H. Busey and named for Guy Penfield, vice president of the Havana, Rantoul and Eastern Railroad (*History of Champaign County,* 166). Post office established May 2, 1876.

PENN. Shelby. Township. A shortening of "Pennsylvania." The name was probably suggested by G. M. or H. B. Thompson (Bateman and Selby, eds., *Historical Encyclopedia of Illinois and History of Shelby County,* 664).

PENNINGTON POINT. McDonough. Eight miles southeast of Macomb. Named for the Pennington family. Riggs Pennington is generally acknowledged as the first permanent settler in present McDonough County. He, along with William Pennington and Stewart Pennington, arrived in the 1820s (Chenoweth and Semonis, comps., *The History of McDonough County,* 108). Post office established May 6, 1847, as Johnson; changed to Pennington Point July 26, 1865.

PENNSYLVANIA. Mason. Township. Formerly known as the Pennsylvania Settlement for the large number of settlers from Pennsylvania (Lynn, *Prelude to Progress,* 400).

PEORIA. County. Created Jan. 13, 1825, from Fulton County. Named for the Peoria, one of the tribes of the Illinois Confederacy. In the seventeenth and eighteenth centuries the tribal name appears in more than fifty different spellings. It was recorded by Marquette in 1673 as *Peoüarea* and also as *Pe8erea* (the 8 representing an [oo] or [w] sound) and later as *Pianrea, Prouaria,* and *Peola.* Marquette gave no translation, but over the years there have been at least seven meanings proposed: "runaways or seceders," "carriers or packers," "he comes carrying a pack on his back," "a place where there are fat beasts," "prairie fire," "turkey," and the personal name of a Native American leader. After a comprehensive account of the proposed sources and interpretations of the name Scheetz concluded, "The meaning of Peoria is an unsolved, and perhaps unsolvable, mystery" ("Peoria," 52). McCafferty, however, has recently suggested that the name derives from a proto-Algonquian verb meaning "to dream with the help of a manitou" ("Peoria," 13). (Gannett, *The Origin of Certain Place Names;* Vogel, *Indian Place Names in Illinois*).

PEOTONE [PEE uh ton]. Will. Village (1869, 1879). Established by the Illinois Central Railroad in 1856. By one account the village was named for a Native American leader named Peotone; by another, officials of the IC combined random consonants and vowels until an acceptable combination was obtained. Perhaps from Potawatomi, where the general meaning "come here" or "bring it here" has been suggested (Ackerman, *Early Illinois Railroads,* 123; Bright, *Native American Placenames; Peotone on Parade,* 7, 45; Vogel, *Indian Place Names in Illinois*). Post office established June 10, 1857.

PERCY. Randolph. Village (1887) eight miles southeast of Sparta. Established by the Cairo and St. Louis Railroad in 1863 on land donated by John T. Short. The namesake is probably Percy Kampen, son of the superintendent of the Kampenville Mine, although local tradition claims the community was named for the engineer who drove the first train through the town (*Towns and Families,* 136). Post office established Feb. 19, 1873.

PERDUEVILLE. Ford. Four miles west of Paxton. Established as Henderson Station, a stop on the Lake Erie and Western Railroad, named for Charles E. Henderson, stationmaster and postmaster. The change to Perdue was probably for a local Perdue family. In the early 1900s, *-ville* was added to avoid confusion with Purdue University because the train also stopped in Lafayette, Ind. (*Ford*

County History, 81). Post office established June 23, 1873, as Henderson Station; changed to Perdue Feb. 15, 1895; changed to Perdueville Feb. 23, 1904.

PERKS. Pulaski. Thirteen miles southeast of Anna. Laid out in 1900 and named for William J. Perks of Mound City, who established one of the first sawmills in the area about 1818 (*Pulaski County,* 17). Post office established April 24, 1900.

PERRY. County. Created Jan. 29, 1827, from parts of Jackson and Randolph counties. Named for Oliver Hazard Perry (1785–1819), naval commander during the War of 1812 and hero of the Battle of Lake Erie. Perry is best known for his dispatch announcing the victory: "We have met the enemy and they are ours."

PERRY. Pike. Village (1855, 1899) twelve miles north-northeast of Pittsfield. Founded about 1834 as Booneville by Edward Boone Scholl(e), reportedly a great nephew of Daniel Boone. Formally laid out by Joseph S. King about 1836 and named Perry at the suggestion of David Callis in honor of Oliver Hazard Perry (*History of Pike County,* 475; Thompson, *The Jess M. Thompson Pike County History,* 309). Post office established April 1, 1837.

PERRYTON. Mercer. Township. Named for the Perry family. Alfred Perry was an early settler in 1837 (Bassett and Goodspeed, *Past and Present of Mercer County,* 512). Post office established March 16, 1848.

PERRYVILLE. Fayette. Former community. Perryville was established near the mouth of Hurricane Creek about 1817 and served as the first permanent seat of Bond County. The source of the name is unknown. With the division of Bond County in 1821, Perryville was redistricted into Fayette County. It disappeared shortly thereafter (Adams, comp., *Illinois Place Names;* Perrin, ed., *History of Bond and Montgomery Counties,* 30). Post office established March 16, 1848.

PERSHING. Franklin. One mile southwest of West Frankfort. Founded in 1918 around the Old Ben Mine Number 15 and named for Gen. John J. Pershing, commander of the American Expeditionary Force in Europe during World War I, from which he returned a national hero. The post office was established in 1920 as Ezra, reportedly drawn from a hat containing a number of biblical names (*Franklin County,* 19).

PERSIFER. Knox. Township. Named from the Persifer post office, itself named for Gen. John Persifer Frazer Smith, who served with distinction in the Mexican War. The name was chosen by informal vote when residents were invited to send suggestions to postal authorities in Knoxville (*Annals of Knox County,* 145; Perry, *History of Knox County,* 437). Post office established Jan. 27, 1849.

PERU. LaSalle. City (1845, 1890). Established by the commissioners of the Illinois and Michigan Canal in 1835. The source of the name is uncertain; several writers claim it was derived from "an Indian word" meaning "plenty of everything, wealth." Others say the name was taken directly from the country in South America, which had gained independence from Spain in 1824 and was there-

fore looked upon sympathetically by many Americans. A more likely immediate source, however, is Peru in Clinton County, N.Y., near Plattsburgh. The
Illinois and Michigan Canal, when it was begun in the mid-1830s, attracted a
large number of engineers, executives, and laborers who had worked on the
Erie Canal in New York and brought a number of New York place names with
them, including Utica and Seneca, which were laid out along the path of the
I&M. Peru may have been another. Peru Township was organized about 1850
as Salisbury, named by Theron D. Brewster, the first mayor of Peru, for his for-
mer home, Salisbury, Conn. (Hansen, ed., *Illinois,* 494; Gannett, *The Origin of
Certain Place Names;* Rasmusen, *LaSalle County Lore,* 197; Vogel, *Indian Place
Names in Illinois*). Post office established Feb. 10, 1836.

PESOTUM [puh SO tuhm]. Champaign. Village (1906) eight miles north of Tuscola.
Established by the Illinois Central Railroad in 1854. Named by the IC for Pesotum, a Potawatomi leader whose main village was near Lake Michigan. By
some accounts it was Pesotum who killed Capt. William Wells, the namesake
of Wells Street in Chicago, at Fort Dearborn in 1812 (Ackerman, *Early Illinois
Railroads,* 127; Bateman and Selby, eds., *Historical Encyclopedia of Illinois and
History of Champaign County,* 821; Vogel, *Indian Place Names in Illinois*). Post
office established June 24, 1856.

PETERSBURG. Menard. City (1841, 1882). Laid out about 1832 by site owners George
Warburton and Peter Lukins, who disagreed on whether the community should
be called Georgetown for Warburton or Petersburg for Lukins. They agreed to
decide the issue by playing a game of "seven up" or "old sledge" (a card game
also known as "all fours") (*History of Menard and Mason Counties,* 293). Post
office established May 30, 1836.

PETERS CREEK. Hardin. Four miles west-northwest of Cave-in-Rock State Park.
Named from Peters Creek, itself named for Peter Holland, an early land owner
(personal communication with the Hardin County Historical Society). Post
office established Jan. 27, 1891.

PETERVILLE. Mason. Six miles southeast of Havana. Laid out by Peter Thornburg
in 1868 (Lynn, *Prelude to Progress,* 199).

PETTY. Lawrence. Township and former community. Named for postmaster Josiah
(or Joseph) Petty. The Petty School was located about seven miles northwest
of Lawrenceville (Adams, comp., *Illinois Place Names; Combined History of
Edwards, Lawrence, and Wabash Counties,* 318). Post office established April
9, 1850, as Petty's.

PHARAOHS GARDENS. Johnson. East of Lake of Egypt. A continuation of the
Egyptian theme associated with southern Illinois. Pharaohs Gardens began as
a subdivision on the Lake of Egypt when the lake was developed in the early
1960s (*see* Egypt) (personal communication with Gary Hacker).

PHELPS. Warren. Six miles southeast of Monmouth. Founded as a station on the Burlington, Monmouth and Illinois River Road railroad and named for Delos Phelps, a director of the railroad in the late 1870s. Post office established May 17, 1883.

PHILADELPHIA. Cass. Fifteen miles northeast of Jacksonville. Laid out about 1837 by John Dutch, a retired sea captain who ran the Half Way House, a tavern approximately midway between Springfield and Beardstown. Named for Philadelphia, Pa. Also known as Lancaster, for Lancaster, Pa. (Hutchison "Old Morgan County Village"). Post office established June 7, 1837, as Lancaster; changed to Philadelphia April 28, 1882.

PHILLIPSTOWN. White. Village (1840, 1874) eight miles east-northeast of Carmi. Also Phillips Township. Laid out in 1837 as Victoria in honor of the newly coronated queen of Great Britain. Because the name *Victoria* would have duplicated an existing post office, it was changed in 1840 for Alexander Phillips, then a representative to the Illinois General Assembly from White County (*Centennial History of Crossville,* 3). Post office established Feb. 12, 1835, as Fox River; changed to Philipstown Nov. 19, 1839; changed to Phillipstown in 1865.

PHILO. Champaign. Village (1875) five miles south-southeast of Urbana. Established as a station on the Great Western Railway about 1858. Formally laid out as Hale by E. B. Hale; later renamed for his father, Philo Hale, the first local land owner (Bateman and Selby, eds., *Historical Encyclopedia of Illinois and History of Champaign County,* 823; *History of Champaign County,* 108–9). Post office established April 17, 1860.

PHOENIX. Cook. Village (1900). Founded in 1900s as a "wet" community in response to the neighboring towns of Harvey and South Holland, which had voted themselves "dry." Named by William H. McLatchy, one of the incorporators, for Phoenix, Ariz., which he had recently visited and found enjoyable. The village symbol is the phoenix, the mythological bird that immolates itself and then rises from its ashes (Lyon, "A Town Poised to Rise"; Zimmerman, "History of Incorporated Municipalities," 30).

PIASA [peye AZ uh, PEYE uh saw]. Macoupin. Eleven miles east of Jerseyville. Named from Piasa Creek, itself named for what has become known as the Piasa "bird." In 1673 Marquette and Jolliet passed by two petroglyphs painted on the bluffs on the east side of the Mississippi River, described in Marquette's journal as "two painted monsters. . . . They are as large As a calf; they have horns on their heads Like those of a deer, a horrible look, red eyes, a beard Like a tiger's, a face somewhat like a man's, a body Covered with scales, and so Long A tail that it winds all around the Body, passing above the head and going back between the legs, ending in a Fish's tail." According to legend, the Piasa lived in a cave along the cliffs and existed on human flesh. It was ultimately killed by a group of Illinois warriors using poisoned arrows and protected by invisible shields. The name is from Miami-Illinois for "legendary dwarf" (Bright, *Native American Placenames*).

PIATT. County. Created Jan. 27, 1841, from parts of Macon and DeWitt counties. Named for one or more members of the Piatt family, perhaps for Benjamin Piatt, attorney general of Illinois Territory from 1810 to 1813, or for James Andrew Piatt, who arrived from Indiana about 1829 and is generally regarded as the first permanent settler.

PICKAWAY. Shelby. Township. Also Pickaway Creek, a stream in Boone County. Pickaway is a variant of Piqua, the name of a division of the Shawnee Tribe. The names in Illinois are probably transfers from Pickaway County in southern Ohio (Bright, *Native American Placenames;* Vogel, *Indian Place Names in Illinois*).

PIERCE. DeKalb. Township. Named for Franklin Pierce. When the township was organized in 1854, Pierce was the newly inaugurated president of the United States. The name was suggested by George W. Kretsinger (Gross, *Past and Present of DeKalb County,* 96; www.rootsweb.com/~ildekalb/places/htm).

PIERCEBURG. Crawford. Ten miles west-southwest of Robinson. Named for an as yet unidentified local figure or official named Pierce. The post office was established in 1893 as Reprah (Harper spelled backward), named for George Harper, editor and publisher of the *Robinson Argus* newspaper, which he founded in 1863 (personal communication with Sue Jones). Post office established Aug. 7, 1893, as Reprah; changed to Pierceburg April 5, 1895.

PIERRON [puh RAHN, pee EHR uhn]. Bond, Madison. Five miles northeast of Highland. Founded in 1868 by Jacques Pierron, proprietor of the first general store. August Pierron was the first postmaster (Bateman and Selby, eds., *Historical Encyclopedia of Illinois and History of Bond County,* 638). Post office established Jan. 25, 1870.

PIERSON. Piatt. Eighteen miles east of Decatur. Originally a switch on the Indianapolis, Decatur and Springfield Railroad, established in 1876 on land owned by A. D. Pierson. The community was formally laid out in 1881 (Morgan, ed., *The Good Life in Piatt County,* 113). Post office established Feb. 8, 1887, as Dry Ridge; changed to Pierson Station Dec. 18, 1877.

PIGEON GROVE. Iroquois. Township. Formed in 1875 and named for Pigeon Grove Farm, the estate of Stephen Cissna and later that of William Cissna, the founder of Cissna Park (q.v.). The farm took its name from Pigeon Creek (*Cissna Park,* 3).

PIKE. County. Created Jan. 31, 1821 from parts of Madison, Bond, and Clark counties. Named for Zebulon Montgomery Pike (1779–1813), who explored the headwaters of the Mississippi River and much of the Southwest and for whom Pikes Peak in Colorado is named. Pike was killed in battle in Ontario, Canada, in

1813. The county seat was established at Coles Grove (Gilead) and then moved to Atlas in 1824 and then Pittsfield in 1833.

PILES FORK. Jackson. Stream. Named for the Pyle family; early settlers were Abner and John Pyle, who may have named the stream for their father, Dr. John Pyle. Also known as Piles Fork Creek (Wright, "A History of Early Carbondale," 4).

PILOT. Kankakee. Township. Named from Pilot Hill (Pilot Knob), a summit about ten miles southwest of Kankakee, a navigational landmark for early travelers and reported to be the highest elevation in southwestern Kankakee County (V. Johnson, comp., "Kankakee County Communities").

PILOT. Vermilion. Township. Named from the Pilot post office, itself named for Pilot Grove, an area of timbered, relatively high ground about six miles south of Georgetown that served as a landmark (Williams, *History of Vermilion County*, 291). Post office established June 8, 1844.

PILOT GROVE. Hancock. Township. Named from Pilot Grove, about nine miles northeast of Carthage, a strip of timber along the Rock Island Indian trail that provided a reference point for early travelers (Bateman and Selby, eds., *Historical Encyclopedia of Illinois and History of Hancock County*, 1091). Post office established May 4, 1850.

PINCKNEYVILLE. Perry. City (1861, 1872). Established in 1827 as the seat of Perry County. Probably named for Charles Cotesworth Pinckney (1746–1825), a recently deceased Revolutionary War veteran, delegate to the Constitutional Convention of 1787, and U.S. minister to France who is now remembered primarily for his involvement in the XYZ Affair (*Perry County*, 16). Post office established July 6, 1827.

PINGREE GROVE [PING gree GROV]. Kane. Village (1907) five miles west of Elgin. Laid out in 1882 by Daniel and Hannah Pingree. Named from Pingree Grove and the Pingree Grove post office, themselves named for the Pingree family. Daniel, Straw, Francis, and Andrew Pingree emigrated from New Hampshire in the late 1830s. The Rev. Andrew Pingree was a Universalist clergyman and the first postmaster (Joslyn and Joslyn, *History of Kane County*, 849, 862; Seits, "The Names of Kane County," 166). Post office established March 6, 1848.

PINHOOK. At least eight features in Illinois have been named Pinhook: communities in Coles (now Oakland), McDonough (now Industry), and Fayette counties; a cemetery in Edwards County; a stream in Hardin County; and schools in Greene and Lawrence counties. For such an undistinguished word, Pinhook is a remarkably common place-name; the Geographic Names Information System lists more than a hundred Pinhooks in the United States. The origins of the names differ. Some are transfers. Others derive from the activities of "pinhookers," speculators who bought vegetables and other foodstuffs directly from farmers and hoped for a quick and profitable resale to distributors, a practice called *pinhooking*. A third origin may come from the practice of using a bent pin as a fishhook. "Pinhook" also describes the practice of circumventing the laws prohibiting liquor sales by serving a customer an alcoholic drink with a bent pin hooked over the edge of the glass. The merchant could then claim to be selling the pin and throwing in the liquor for free.

PINKSTAFF. Lawrence. Four miles north of Lawrenceville. Named for the Pinkstaff family. Andrew Pinkstaff was one of the first permanent settlers, arriving in 1818. The community was formally laid out by Owen Pinkstaff as Pinkstaff Station in 1877 (*Combined History of Edwards, Lawrence, and Wabash Counties,* 344). Post office established Dec. 12, 1877.

PIOPOLIS [peye AHP lis]. Hamilton. Six miles north of McLeansboro. A blend of *pius* and *polis* (city) with linking vowel. Formerly known as the Dutch Settlement, named for German Catholic settlers from Baden, many of whom arrived in the 1840s. Piopolis was founded about 1877 and named by the Rev. I. N. Enzlberger in honor of Pope Pius IX (1792–1878) on the fiftieth anniversary of his appointment as Archbishop of Spoleto in 1827. The community is also known as Saint Francis Xavier (*Hamilton County,* 33; Munsell, "A History of Hamilton County," 32; Sneed, *Ghost Towns of Southern Illinois,* 56). Post office established Sept. 25, 1877.

PIPER CITY. Ford. Village (1869, 1876) seventeen miles east of Fairbury. Founded in 1867 by Dr. William A. Piper, a physician from Philadelphia, and Samuel Cross of Chicago (*Ford County History,* 29). Post office established Jan. 5, 1865, as Brenton; changed to New Brenton Nov. 20, 1865; changed to Piper City Jan. 28, 1868.

PISCASAW [PIS kuh saw]. Boone, McHenry. Stream. The source of the name is uncertain. It may be from an Algonquian word having the general meaning "stream" or "fork" and related to Piscataway and similar place names in New England. A possible origin in Potawatomi, *pesheka* (buffalo), has also been suggested (Bright, *Native American Placenames;* Vogel, *Indian Place Names in Illinois*).

PISGAH. Morgan. Six miles southeast of Jacksonville. Named from the Pisgah Presbyterian Church, established about 1839, itself named for Mt. Pisgah (also known as Mt. Nebo), the summit from which Moses saw the promised land (Bateman and Selby, eds., *Historical Encyclopedia of Illinois and History of Morgan County,* 663). Post office established Feb. 12, 1872.

PISTAKEE HIGHLANDS [pis TAY kee]. McHenry. Five miles north of McHenry. Possibly from a Native American word for buffalo. In the summer of 1673, at a site near present Rock Island, Marquette wrote, "We found Turkeys had taken the place of game; and the pisikious, or wild cattle, That of the other animals." The reference is to the bison, which Marquette describes in great detail. Pisiki may be a local adaptation of a general Algonquian word for buffalo, which appears as *bizhiki* in Ojibwa (Bright, *Native American Placenames*). Post office established June 21, 1899.

PITCHERVILLE. Jo Daviess. Former community about four miles west of Stockton. Named for first postmaster Lester Pitcher (Teeman, *Postal Saga of Jo Daviess,* 57). Post office established Jan. 7,1868.

PITCHIN. Iroquois. Four miles northeast of Cissna Park. The local story is that a man named Stockwell was suing a Mr. Bratton for $5 in back wages. While the jury was deliberating, a Mr. Hann, Stockwell's brother-in-law, began arguing with Bratton. Bratton removed his jacket, rolled up his sleeves, and admonished Hann, "Pitch in, if you are ready." Some bystanders thought the town had been without a name long enough, and Pitchin was as good as any other. Also known as Glenwood and Ash Grove (Beckwith, *History of Iroquois County,* 658).

PITMAN. Montgomery. Township. Named for Joseph H. Pitman, a county supervisor who was instrumental in the organization of the township (Bateman and Selby, eds., *Historical Encyclopedia of Illinois and History of Montgomery County,* 950).

PITTSBURG. Fayette. Eight miles southwest of Vandalia. Named for Postmaster William J. Pitt (Adams, comp., *Illinois Place Names*). Post office established June 17, 1889, as Pittsburgh; changed to Pittsburg April 10, 1893.

PITTSBURG. Williamson. Village (1909) four-and-a-half miles northeast of Marion. Founded in 1906 by John Colp, president of the John Colp Coal Company, who named the community Pittsburg in the hope that it would become an important industrial city like Pittsburgh, Pa. On the original plat the streets were given such Pennsylvania names as Scranton and Lehigh Valley (Hale, comp. and ed., *Williamson County,* 142; Hubbs, *Pioneer Folks and Places*). Post office established March 1, 1907.

PITTSFIELD. Pike. City (1869, 1893). Founded about 1820 by the four sons of Micah Ross. Formally laid out in 1833 as the seat of Pike County by commissioners George W. Hinman, Hawkins Judd, and Benjamin Barney. Col. William Ross chose the name for Pittsfield, Mass., the previous home of the Ross family, itself named for William Pitt the Elder (1708–78), the British statesman noted for his defense of the rights of American colonists (*History of Pike County,* 650, 780; Thompson, "Pike County Settled," 73, 75). Post office established June 29, 1829.

PITTWOOD. Iroquois. Six miles north of Watseka. Founded in 1881 with construction of the Chicago, Danville and Vincennes Railroad. Named for pioneer physician Dr. L. N. Pittwood (*Iroquois County History,* 71). Post office established April 7, 1873.

PIXLEY. Clay. Township. Named for Osman Pixley, an early settler from Posey County, Ind. (*History of Wayne and Clay Counties,* 470).

PLAINFIELD. Will. Village (1869, 1877). Previously known as Walker's Grove, named for James Walker, who established a sawmill near the site about 1830, and his uncle, Jesse Walker, a Methodist circuit rider and missionary. Formally laid out in 1834 by Chester Ingersoll. The name was perhaps chosen for its suggestions of level land and distant horizons (*History of Will County*, 478, 487; *History of Plainfield*, 5–7). Post office established Jan. 6, 1834.

PLAINVIEW. Macoupin. Ten miles southwest of Carlinville. Founded about 1853. According to an early county history, Plainview "took its name from the fact that it stands on an eminence, commanding a good view of the surrounding district." (Walker, *History of Macoupin County*, 359). Post office established June 8, 1846.

PLAINVILLE. Adams. Village (1896) fourteen miles southeast of Quincy. Originally called Stone's Prairie for early settler Sam Stone and informally known as Shakerag. In 1889 the names of the post office and community were changed to Plainville, for founder John Delaplain (Underwood, "A New Geography of Illinois: Adams County," 39). Post office established Jan. 29, 1856, as Stone's Prairie; changed to Plainville July 23, 1889.

PLANO [PLAY no]. Kendall. City (1865, 1883). Established in 1853 as a station on the Chicago and Aurora Railroad. The name *Plano* was suggested by John T. Hollister, but the reason is unknown. Perhaps a transfer, or perhaps a borrowing from Spanish *plano* "plain, level land" (Farren, *Bicentennial History*, 93). Post office established Jan. 27, 1853.

PLATO. Iroquois. Organized in the 1830s by the Plato Company, a land development consortium that advertised and sold lots in New York, Boston, and other eastern cities. Plato was laid out in 1836 by James Smith but never prospered, due in part to the depression of 1837. The enterprise is recalled by the Plato Bridge across the Iroquois River some eight miles northwest of Watseka and the Plato post office, which operated from July 1849 through November 1902. Both the Plato Company and the projected town of Plato were named for Plato, Cattaraugus County, N.Y., itself named for the ancient Greek philosopher (Dowling, *History of Iroquois County*, 62; *Illustrated Atlas Map of Iroquois County*, 16).

PLATO. Kane. Township. First organized as Homer Precinct. The name was changed to Plato at the time of township formation in 1850, not to maintain a classical connection as some have claimed but to honor William B. Plato, a lawyer, justice of the peace, and Illinois state senator of the 1850s. Plato Center, seven miles west-southwest of Elgin, was founded some two miles east of its present location and moved to the Illinois Central tracks about 1890 (Bateman and Selby, eds., *Historical Encyclopedia of Illinois and History of Kane County*, 630; Ghrist, *Plato Center Memories*, 46). Post office established May 18, 1879, as Plato Centre; changed to Plato Center ca. July 1, 1893.

PLATTVILLE. Kendall. Eight miles south of Yorkville. Founded by Daniel Platt, whose ancestors were the founders and namesakes of Plattsburgh, N.Y. (Hicks, *History of Kendall County*, 116). Post office established Nov. 4, 1847.

PLEASANT GROVE. Coles. Township. Possibly named for Pleasant Hart, who built and occupied a rough shelter in the area during the winter of 1836 (Perrin, Graham, and Blair, *History of Coles County,* 425).

PLEASANT HILL. McLean. Fifteen miles northeast of Normal. Founded about 1840 by Isaac Smalley, a local teacher, preacher, and farmer. The name was suggested by Mrs. Milton Smith, who, as the story goes, "found it odd to date a letter from nowhere." She called her place Poverty Hill and the one next door Pleasant Hill because "it was a fairer one to look on" (*History of McLean County,* 497).

PLUM CREEK. Randolph. Stream. Possibly a translation of French *prune* (plum), named for the local wild plums. The name of the stream was earlier recorded as Plumb Creek, however, suggesting that "plum" may be a popular etymology from *plumb* (lead) (Brown, "French Place Names in Illinois," 463).

PLUM RIVER. Jo Daviess. Formerly written *Plumb River,* referring to the lead mines around Galena. By popular etymology "plumb," Latin for "lead," became "plum." On several early maps the river was labeled the Pecatolikee, a form of Pecatonica (q.v.) (Thiem, ed., *Carroll County,* 125). Post office established July 14, 1849.

POCAHONTAS. Bond. Village (1847, 1882) seven miles west-southwest of Green-ville. Founded in 1838 as Amity by site owner Benjamin Johnson. The name was changed about ten years later, apparently for Pocahontas, the daughter of Chief Powhatan of Virginia. According to legend, Pocahontas saved the life of Capt. John Smith by placing her head on the chopping block upon which he was to lose his. She married John Rolf in 1614, charmed English society, and died of smallpox in 1617 (Bateman and Selby, eds., *Historical Encyclopedia of Illinois and History of Bond County,* 637). Post office established Feb. 22, 1831, as Hickory Grove; changed to Pocohontas Jan. 14, 1850.

POLECAT CREEK. Stream. Coles, Edgar. According to a local account, "A new comer in the neighborhood had an encounter with a certain kind of cat which lived in great numbers along this creek and this man was so overwhelmed with the success of the little animal's defence that he buried his clothes on the battle ground and christened the creek by the name of the Pole Cat." Also called Cat Creek (Dole, "Pioneer Days in Coles County," 111).

POLO. Ogle. Founded about 1853 as the Town of Polo on the line of the Illinois Central Railroad by site owner Zenas Applington, a plowmaker from Broome County, N.Y. Applington apparently named the community for Marco Polo, the thirteenth-century Venetian traveler. Why Applington chose this name is unknown. The community has adopted the Marco Polo motif, and Polo High School athletic teams are called the Marcos (*Bicentennial History of Ogle County,* 212; Boss, *Sketches of the History of Ogle County,* 67). Post office established Feb. 12, 1833, as Buffalo Grove; changed to Polo Jan. 30, 1856.

POLSGROVE. Carroll. Eight-and-a-half miles northeast of Savanna. Founded about

1856 and named for Abraham Polsgrove, a sawmill operator of the mid-1850s (Adams, comp., *Illinois Place Names*). Post office established July 6, 1856.

POMONA [puh MO nuh]. Jackson. Eight miles southwest of Carbondale. Named for Pomona, the Roman goddess of orchards and gardens, probably by the classically educated Urbane E. Robinson, the first postmaster (personal communication with Kay Rippelmeyer-Tippy). Post office established May 24, 1875.

POND. Johnson. Four miles northeast of Vienna. Named for the large sinkhole that appeared suddenly in the early 1890s and quickly filled with water (Sneed, *Ghost Towns of Southern Illinois*, 116). Post office established Sept. 22, 1893.

PONEMAH. Warren. Seven miles southwest of Monmouth. Named from Henry Wadsworth Longfellow's *The Song of Hiawatha,* where Ponemah is the home of departed souls. Probably from Ojibwa for "later," used by Longfellow to mean "the hereafter" (Bright, *Native American Placenames;* Vogel, *Indian Place Names in Illinois*). Post office established Feb. 14, 1889.

PONTIAC. Livingston. City (1872). Founded about 1837. Probably named for Pontiac, Mich., and also for Pontiac, great chief of the Ottawas for whom Pontiac, Mich., was named. Jesse Fell, from Pontiac, Mich., and one of the first settlers, claims he named the post office Pontiac, "that being the name of a distinguished Indian chief." Another Pontiac, in St. Clair County and now part of East St. Louis, was founded near the site where Chief Pontiac was killed by an Illinois Indian in 1769 (Bateman and Selby, eds., *Historical Encyclopedia of Illinois and History of Livingston County,* 639; Vogel, *Indian Place Names in Illinois*).

PONTOOSUC. Hancock. Village (1879) five miles east of Fort Madison, Iowa. Founded about 1837 by Hezekiah Spillman, an early settler from Massachusetts. Spillman transferred the name from Berkshire County, Mass., where Pontoosuc is the name of a community and a lake. Ultimately from an eastern Algonquian language likely meaning "the falls on the river" (Bright, *Native American Placenames;* Bateman and Selby, eds., *Historical Encyclopedia of Illinois and History of Hancock County,* 1093). Post office established July 14, 1836, as East Bend; changed to Pontoosuc Oct. 2, 1849.

POPE. County. Created Jan. 10, 1816, from parts of Gallatin and Johnson counties. Named for Nathaniel Pope (1784–1850), cousin of Ninian Edwards, for whom Edwards County is named, and delegate to the U.S. Congress from Illinois Territory. Pope was instrumental in securing the admission of Illinois as the twenty-first state of the federal union in 1818. It was through his efforts that the boundary line between Illinois and Wisconsin was shifted about fifty miles north from the foot of Lake Michigan to its present location.

POPE. Township. Fayette. Formed from Kaskaskia Township in 1877. Also named for Nathaniel Pope (Bateman and Selby, eds., *Historical Encyclopedia of Illinois and History of Fayette County,* 653).

PORTAGE PARK. Cook. Site of the portage from the Chicago River to the Des Plaines River. Now part of Chicago (Kitagawa and Taeuber, eds., *Local Community Fact Book*, 44).

PORT BARRINGTON. *See* Fox River Valley Gardens.

PORT BYRON. Rock Island. Village (1876) eight miles northeast of Moline. Laid out in 1836 by Samuel Allen, Nathaniel Belcher, Moses Bailey, and Dr. Patrick Gregg. Named by Belcher, who admired the English poet George Gordon, Lord Byron (*Past and Present of Rock Island County*, 212). Post office established Dec. 30, 1833, as Canaan; changed to Port Byron March 11, 1837.

PORTERVILLE. Crawford. Six miles north-northwest of Robinson. Formerly known as East Berlin. Renamed for Richard Porter, who established a blacksmith shop at the site in the early 1850s. Porterville is also known as Eaton, named from the Eaton post office, itself named for first postmaster John Eaton (*History of Crawford County*, 192). Post office established May 13, 1852 as Eaton.

PORT JACKSON. Crawford. Nine miles south of Robinson. Laid out in 1855 by Samuel Hanes. Probably named for Andrew Jackson. From this site small flat-bottom boats were loaded with tobacco, which was transported down the Embarras River to the Wabash, then to the Ohio and destinations in Kentucky (*History of Crawford County*, 20; personal communication with Sue Jones). Post office established Aug. 16, 1862.

PORTUGUESE HILL. Morgan. Northwest Jacksonville suburb. Established in the late 1840s as a refuge for Portuguese Presbyterians, primarily from Madeira (Poage, "The Coming of the Portuguese").

POSEN [PO suhn]. Cook. Village (1900). Settled by Polish immigrants in the 1890s and named for Poznan, Poland, at the time a part of Prussia. "Posen" is the German form of "Poznan" (*Illinois Guide*). Post office established July 25, 1931.

POSEN. Washington. Five miles southeast of Nashville. Also named for Poznan, Poland. The community grew around the Catholic Church of Our Lady of Perpetual Help. Also known as Bolo, a name of unknown origin (*Washington County*, 22).

POSEY [PO zee]. Clinton. Four-and-a-half miles south of Carlyle. Named for postmaster Bennett M. Posey (Adams, comp., *Illinois Place Names*). Post office established June 30, 1890.

POSTVILLE. Logan. Former community. Laid out by Russell Post in 1835. Postville, later known as Camden, was the first seat of Logan County, serving from 1839 until 1847, when the county seat was moved to Mount Pulaski. The name is preserved by the Postville Courthouse State Historic Site, and Postville Park, both in Lincoln (q.v.) (*History of Logan County* [1878], 262). Post office established March 2, 1838.

POTATO HILL. Summit. Pope. Twelve miles south-southeast of Harrisburg. Named either by early settlers who reportedly likened the appearance of the hill to the piles of potatoes heaped by early farmers for winter storage or because of the large crops of potatoes grown locally (Allen, *Pope County Notes,* 66).

POTAWATOMI. Cook. Park and Lake. From the name of the Algonquian tribe encountered by early explorers and settlers around Lake Michigan. Traditionally, the name is taken to mean "people of the fire" or "keepers of the fire" (Vogel, *Indian Place Names in Illinois*).

POTOMAC [puh TO mik]. Vermilion. Village (1905) fourteen miles north-north-west of Danville. Founded about 1840 by Isaac Meneley and John Smith as Marysville, named for their wives, both named Mary. The post office was established as Potomac in 1871, probably named by settlers from the Potomac River area of Maryland and Virginia. The name of the community was subsequently changed to agree with that of the post office (Jones, *History of Vermilion County,* 409; Tuggle, comp., *Stories of Historical Days,* 12). Post office established May 13, 1871.

POTOSI. McLean. Former community. Probably a transfer, but the origin is uncertain. Perhaps transferred from San Luis Potosi in Mexico; from Potosi, the city in southern Bolivia; or from one of the Potosi mining operations in the West. The historical Potosi post office in Livingston County at the McLean County line was nine miles south of Fairbury, near Cropsey (Dotterer, "Potosi," 12; Stewart, *American Place-Names*). Post office established Feb. 18, 1868.

POTTSTOWN. Peoria. Founded as a company town for employees of the brick manufacturing plant owned by Samuel Potts. Now a west Peoria suburb (*History of Peoria County,* 601). Post office established June 8, 1888.

POVERTY RIDGE. Fulton. Eleven miles northwest of Lewistown. Named from Poverty Ridge, a string of elevations south of Seville. The origin of the name is unknown (Irwin, *A to Z Fulton County*).

POWELLTON. Hancock. Seven miles south-southeast of Fort Madison, Iowa. Formerly known as Rosseter Corners. Renamed in 1882 for Dr. John E. Powell (*History of Hancock County,* 558). Post office established Aug. 10, 1882.

POWERTON. Tazewell. Named for the substation that distributed electric power. Now a southwest Pekin suburb (Adams, comp., *Illinois Place Names*).

PRAIRIE. Randolph. Three-and-a-half miles southeast of Red Bud. Laid out about 1795 as Washington by Johnson J. Whiteside. Renamed Horse Prairie Town for its location on Horse Prairie and subsequently shortened to Prairie (www .iltrails.com/randolph). Post office established May 7, 1892.

PRAIRIE CITY. McDonough, Warren. Village (1873) five miles northeast of Bush-nell. According to an early county history, the name was created on the spot by Alonzo Barnes, who was asked where he wanted a shipment of goods delivered. Barnes, who knew the site and also knew it was nameless, replied, "Ship it to Prairie City." The shipment arrived, and the name became permanent. Formally laid out on the line of the Northern Cross Railroad in 1854 by Ezra Cadwallader,

Anson Smith, Ezra Smith, and Edwin Reed (*History of McDonough County,* 764). Post office established May 19, 1844.

PRAIRIE DU PONT CREEK. St. Clair. Stream. French for "prairie of the bridge." Named by early French settlers for the log bridge that spanned the stream and divided two land grants in the eighteenth century (*History of St. Clair County,* 296; *Tapestry of Time,* 35).

PRAIRIE DU ROCHER [PREHR ee duh RO sher, PREHR ee duh RO cher]. Randolph. Village (1873) ten miles southwest of Red Bud. Founded as a French settlement near Fort de Chartres in the early 1720s. From French "meadow of the rock," named for the plain extending from the hundred-foot-high limestone bluffs along the Mississippi River (*Illinois Gazetteer;* Suess, *Glimpses of Prairie du Rocher,* 5). Post office established Nov. 14, 1821.

PRATT. Whiteside. Former community eight miles south of Morrison. Laid out in 1869 by James M. Pratt as a station on the Rockford, Rock Island and St. Louis railroad. Pratt was the first station agent and postmaster (Bastian, *A History of Whiteside County,* 214). Post office established May 6, 1870.

PREEMPTION. Mercer. Ten miles south of Rock Island. Named for the preemption laws passed by the U.S. Congress in the nineteenth century that gave squatters the right to "enter" (register) their land with the government and purchase it later when the tract became legally available for sale. The preemption laws protected settlers from claim jumpers and from having to bid against speculators at open auction. Post office established June 7, 1843.

PRENTICE. Morgan. Thirteen miles northeast of Jacksonville. Laid out in 1857 by Patterson Hall and James G. Cox. The source of the name is unknown (Bateman and Selby, eds., *Historical Encyclopedia of Illinois and History of Morgan County,* 663; Hutchison "Old Morgan County Village"). Post office established May 12, 1852, as Emerald Point; changed to Prentice April 9, 1861.

PRINCETON. Bureau. City (1849, 1884). Established in 1831 by the Hampshire Colony Congregational Church of Northampton, Mass., as Greenfield, probably named for Greenfield, Mass. The generally accepted account is that each member of the committee charged with formally siting the community, Roland Moseley, John Musgrove, and John P. Blake, proposed a different name. The impasse was broken when each wrote his choice on a piece of paper and tossed it into a hat. A bystander then drew the slip with the name *Princeton* on it; Musgrove had submitted the name, probably for Princeton in his home state of New Jersey (Smith, *A History of Princeton,* 3). Post office established Dec. 20, 1832, as Greenfield; changed to Princeton Feb. 12, 1833.

PRINCEVILLE. Peoria. Village (1869, 1884) thirteen miles north-northwest of Peoria. Founded about 1837 by William C. Stevens and named for Daniel Prince, one of the first settlers and a philanthropist who donated land for a number of secular and religious purposes (Rice, *Peoria City and County,* 309–10). Post office established June 26, 1840.

PROCTOR. Ford. Three miles south-southwest of Gibson City. Named for post-master Willard E. Proctor (Adams, comp., *Illinois Place Names*). Post office established April 10, 1888.

PROPHETSTOWN. Whiteside. City (1859, 1884) fourteen miles southwest of Rock Falls. Founded about 1838 on the site of the village of Wabokieshiek or Wa-pe-she-ka (White Cloud), better known as The Prophet, a Sauk-Winnebago leader and advisor to Black Hawk. In one of the first acts of hostility of the Black Hawk War, in May 1832 a company of Illinois volunteers under the command of Samuel Whiteside (for whom Whiteside County is named) destroyed his village because he had allegedly conspired with Black Hawk (Bastian, *A History of Whiteside County,* 354; Vogel, *Indian Place Names in Illinois*). Post office established Nov. 27, 1835, as Prophets Town.

PROVIDENCE. Bureau. Nine miles southwest of Princeton. Founded about 1836 by the Providence Colony, a collective formed in Providence, R.I. Several dozen families emigrated from the northeastern states in the late 1830s (Leonard, *A Pioneer Tour,* 18). Post office established March 24, 1837.

PROVISO. Cook. Township. Named about 1850 for the Wilmot Proviso, a bill introduced in the U.S. House of Representatives in 1846 by Rep. David Wilmot of Pennsylvania, which prohibited slavery in any territory acquired as a result of the Mexican War. This is the only Proviso in the United States (Goodspeed and Healy, eds., *History of Cook County,* 300). Post office established May 5, 1851.

PUJOL. Randolph. Six miles west of Chester. Named for Louis Philippe Pujol, a French merchant of Kaskaskia. Dozaville (q.v.) was built on the site of Pujol in the early 1870s (Coulet du Gard, *Dictionary of French Place Names;* Sneed, *Ghost Towns of Southern Illinois,* 181). Post office established Jan. 25, 1886.

PULASKI. County. Created March 3, 1843, from parts of Alexander and Johnson counties. Named for Kazimierz (Casimir) Pulaski, born in Poland about 1747. Pulaski, a hero of the American Revolution, served with George Washington at Brandywine and Valley Forge and commanded the Continental cavalry. He died in a courageous but ill-advised charge into the British lines at Savannah, Ga., in 1779. Some fifty communities or townships in the United States are named in his honor.

PULASKI. Hancock. Eighteen miles southeast of Carthage. Founded about 1836 by Alexander Oliver, William McCready, and Benjamin Bacon. Also named for Casimir Pulaski (*History of Hancock County,* 172). Post office established Feb. 11, 1839.

PULASKI. Pulaski. Village (1898). Founded in 1852 as a construction camp, "Camp in Pulaski," for the Illinois Central Railroad. The name was subsequently shortened to Camp Pulaski and then to Pulaski (Moyer, *Moyers' Brief History,* 70; *Pulaski County,* 18). Post office established May 27, 1856, as Walbridge; changed to Pulaski Dec. 10, 1872.

PULLMAN. Cook. Founded as a model community in 1881 by George M. Pullman to house his employees, serve as headquarters for the Pullman Palace Car Company, and provide facilities for producing Pullman sleeping cars. According to an Illinois state historical marker, this was the first planned industrial community in America. Annexed to Chicago in 1907 (Donovan, "Named for Railroad Presidents," 26; Hochstetter, *Guide to Illinois' Historical Markers,* 17; Karlen, *Chicago's Crabgrass Communities,* 68). Post office established Feb. 24, 1881.

PULLY'S MILL. Williamson. Eight miles south-southwest of Marion. Named for the steam mill on Little Saline Creek built by Barton and Daniel Pully in 1854. Barton Pully was later postmaster (Mohlenbrock, "A New Geography of Williamson County," 40). Post office established Oct. 28, 1864.

PUTMAN. Township. Fulton. Named for the first settler, Reading Putman, who located in the area about 1823 (*History of Fulton County,* 865).

PUTNAM. County. Created Jan. 13, 1825. Named for Israel Putnam (1718–90), a general in the Revolutionary War. Although Putnam's later military career was less than distinguished and even less than honorable (he was brought before a court of inquiry on at least one occasion), he is remembered as the hero of Bunker Hill.

PYATTS. Perry. Five miles south of Pinckneyville. Named either for postmaster and stationmaster James M. Pyatt or for early settler Samuel Pyatt (Dearinger, "A New Geography of Perry County," 26; Sneed, *Ghost Towns of Southern Illinois,* 143). Post office established March 9, 1868, as Four Mile Prairie; changed to Pennyville Feb. 20, 1877; changed to Four Mile Feb. 2, 1881; changed to Pyatt Nov. 15, 1882.

Q

QUARREL CREEK. Pope. Stream. According to one local story, the name derives from an old couple who lived along the creek and quarreled continually. According to another, the stream contains many rapids and its bed is so filled with rocks that it becomes noisy after a heavy rain, giving the impression of people quarrelling. These are nice stories, but the source of the name is unknown. It is likely from an English (possibly French) surname (Allen, *Pope County Notes,* 63).

QUARRY. Township. Jersey. Named for the local limestone quarries. The name was changed from Grafton in 1880 (*History of Greene and Jersey Counties,* 301).

QUATOGA BLUFF. Madison. Four miles northwest of Alton. Named for Quatoga, the legendary slayer of the Piasa (q.v.).

QUEEN ANNE PRAIRIE. McHenry. Named for Ann McQuinn, sister-in-law of Henry Weston. He is believed to be the first permanent settler and she the first European woman in Greenwood Township. The Queen Anne School was located about three miles northeast of Woodstock (*History of McHenry County* [1885], 671).

QUENTIN CORNER(S). Lake. Three miles south of Lake Zurich. Named for Charles Quentin (Quinten). Also known as Ela (q.v.).

QUINCY [KWIN si]. Adams. City (1839, 1895). Founded in 1825 and named for John Quincy Adams, recently elected president of the United States. The name was probably proposed by John Wood, a future governor of Illinois and influential in the creation of Adams County (*see* Adams County). Quincy has been the seat of Adams County since 1825 (*History of Adams County*, 262). Post office established March 15, 1826.

QUIVER. Mason. Township. Also Quiver Beach. Two miles north of Havana. Named from Quiver Creek, which flows into the Illinois River near the Chautauqua National Wildlife Refuge south of Buzzville. According to local accounts, Quiver Creek was so named because early explorers, when they stood near the stream and rocked their bodies back and forth, saw the land around them quivering. The name, however, is a popular etymology from Cuivre (Copper) Creek, an earlier French name for the stream. Copper was mined in the area from at least the early eighteenth century. Delisle's map of about 1718 shows a "mine de Cuivre" south of Peoria (Lynn, *Prelude to Progress,* 403). Post office established Sept. 11, 1849.

R

RADDLE. Jackson. Fourteen miles west of Murphysboro. Named for postmaster Frank J. Raddle (Adams, comp., *Illinois Place Names*). Post office established Dec. 9, 1889, as Raddleville; changed to Raddle Oct. 2, 1903.

RADFORD. Christian. Twelve miles north of Pana. Established by the Illinois Central Railroad about 1874 and named for site owner George Radford (Ackerman, *Early Illinois Railroads,* 148). Post office established March 24, 1875.

RADNOR. Peoria. Township. Named by Evan Evans, the first township supervisor, for Radnor in Delaware County, Pa., and also for Radnor, the former county in Wales and the home of Evans's ancestors (*History of Peoria County,* 613). Post office established Sept. 29, 1881.

RADOM [RAY duhm]. Washington. Village (1929) fourteen miles west of Mount Vernon. Named by Gen. John Basil Turchin in 1873 for Radom, the city then in Russian Poland. Turchin, a Russian by birth and an employee of the Illinois Central Railroad, founded the Agencyja Polskiej Kolonizacyi to promote emigration of Poles to Illinois (Ackerman, *Early Illinois Railroads,* 133; Gates, *The Illinois Central Railroad,* 318). Post office established June 16, 1874.

RALEIGH [RAH lee]. Saline. Village (1865, 1876) five miles west of Eldorado. Named about 1847, either by David Upchurch or members of the Musgrave family, for their former home, Raleigh, N.C., itself named for Sir Walter Raleigh. Raleigh was the seat of Saline County from 1847 until 1859 when it was moved to Harrisburg (James, *History of Raleigh*, 14; *History of Saline County*, 4). Post office established Sept. 23, 1828, as Curran; changed to Raleigh Oct. 27, 1847.

RAMSEY [RAM zi]. Fayette. Village (1877) twelve miles north of Vandalia. Founded about 1855. Named by the Illinois Central Railroad, probably for Alexander Ramsey, mayor of St. Paul, Minn., at the time. Ramsey was later governor of Minnesota and the namesake of Ramsey County, Minn. The name, however, may have been taken from Ramsey Creek, reportedly named for William Ramsey, an early settler (Ackerman, *Early Illinois Railroads*, 149–50; Bateman and Selby, eds., *Historical Encyclopedia of Illinois and History of Fayette County*, 655; Hanabarger, "Fayette County Place Names," 51). Post office established June 15, 1855.

RANDOLPH. County. Created Oct. 5, 1795 from St. Clair County by order of Arthur St. Clair, governor of the Northwest Territory. The name was chosen by St. Clair, probably for Edmund Jennings Randolph (1753–1813), former governor of Virginia and at the time U.S. secretary of state under George Washington. Some historians, however, feel that the namesake was Beverly Randolph, governor of Virginia at the time. St. Clair would have been familiar with Edmund and Beverly Randolph and may have selected the name to honor them both. The seat was established at Kaskaskia and moved to Chester in 1847.

RANDOLPH. McLean. Seven miles south of Bloomington. Originally known as Randolph's Grove, named for Gardner Randolph, generally acknowledged as the first settler, arriving in the early 1820s (*History of McLean County*, 459). Post office established May 7, 1862.

RANKIN. Vermilion. Village (1886) ten miles east of Paxton. Founded about 1872 as a station on the Lake Erie and Western Railroad by site owner David Rankin and his cousin, William A. Rankin (Stapp and Sullenberger, *Footprints in the Sands*, 42; Tuggle, comp., *Stories of Historical Days*, 12). Post office established July 7, 1868, as Sugar Creek; changed to Rankin July 25, 1872.

RANSOM. LaSalle. Village (1885) nine miles east of Streator. Named for Thomas Edwin Greenfield Ransom, an agent for the Illinois Central Railroad and a Union general in the Civil War (Rasmusen, *LaSalle County Lore*, 283). Post office established July 13, 1866, as Allen; changed to Ransom July 18, 1876.

RANTOUL [ran TOOL]. Champaign. Village (1869, 1890). Laid out in 1854 by John Penfield for the Illinois Central Railroad. Named for Robert Rantoul Jr., a stockholder and at the time a director of the IC. Rantoul was a U.S. representative from Massachusetts and had filled part of the unexpired term of Daniel Webster in the U.S. Senate. The area was formerly known as Mink Grove (*History of Champaign County*, 146). Post office established Aug. 1, 1856, as Rantoul Station; changed to Rantoul May 9, 1862.

RAPATEE [RAP uh TEE]. Knox. Eighteen miles southeast of Galesburg. Laid out in 1883 by Benjamin Adams as a station on the Iowa Central Railroad. First known as Wallace; renamed for the Rapalee family. Minor (or Miner) Rapalee is generally regarded as the first settler, arriving from New York in the early 1830s. On the documents changing the name from Wallace, Rapalee was mistakenly written Rapatee (*History of Maquon and Vicinity*, 199). Post office established March 8, 1883.

RAPIDS CITY. Rock Island. Village (1875) seven miles northeast of Moline. Laid out about 1838 and named for the rapids in the Mississippi River, now largely controlled by Lock and Dam No. 14 (Bateman and Selby, eds., *Historical Encyclopedia of Illinois and History of Rock Island County*, 972). Post office established March 12, 1857.

RARDIN. Coles. Eight miles north-northeast of Charleston. Named for the Rardin family. J. L. Rardin emigrated from Kentucky about 1842, Samuel Rardin was the first postmaster, and John H. Rardin was the site owner when the community was platted in 1881 (Bateman and Selby, eds., *Historical Encyclopedia of Illinois and History of Coles County*, 738; Perrin, Graham, and Blair, *History of Coles County*, 790). Post office established March 30, 1875.

RARITAN [REHR uh tan]. Henderson. Village (1959) sixteen miles southwest of Monmouth. Founded in 1856 by members of the Dutch Reformed Church from Raritan, Somerset County, N.J. Ultimately from an Algonquian tribal name (Sutton, *Rivers, Railways*, 36). Post office established Aug. 5, 1856.

RAUM [RAWM]. Pope. Eighteen miles south of Harrisburg. Named either for Green Berry Raum (1829–1909), brigadier general in the Union Army, U.S. representative from Illinois in the late 1860s, and first president of the Cairo and Vincennes Railroad; for his father, John Raum, clerk of the Pope County court and Illinois state senator in the 1830s; or for both (Adams, comp., *Illinois Place Names*; McCormick, "The Country Store," 6; *Pope County*, 35). Post office established March 13, 1883.

RAVEN. Edgar. Thirteen miles southeast of Georgetown. Formerly known as Red Raven. The source of the name is unknown (*Prairie Progress*, 252). Post office established Feb. 16, 1874, as Illiana; changed to Raven May 23, 1892.

RAVENSWOOD. Cook. Chicago community. Named from the Ravenswood Land Company, a development consortium organized in 1868. The company itself was likely named for Ravenswood, Jackson County, W.Va., the home of at least one of its members (Karlen, *Chicago's Crabgrass Communities*, 117). Post office established April 27, 1869.

RAVINIA [ruh VIN ee uh]. Lake. Originally known as South Highland for its location south of Highland Park. Formally organized about 1872. The name *Ravinia* is derived from "ravine" by the addition of a pseudo-Latin suffix. The choice of the name may have been influenced by Ravena, N.Y., or Ravenna, Italy (*Past and Present of Lake County*, 268). Post office established July 1, 1874.

RAWALTS. Fulton. Two miles southeast of Canton. Named for Jonas Rawalt, an early county supervisor and one of the commissioners appointed to locate the seat of Henry County in 1837 (*History of Fulton County*, 899).

RAY. Schuyler. Six miles northeast of Rushville. Laid out as Oakland by William Seachrist. For unknown reasons the name was changed to Ray by officials of the Chicago, Burlington and Quincy Railroad in the 1870s (Bateman and Selby, eds., *Historical Encyclopedia of Illinois and History of Schuyler County*, 706). Post office established Oct. 27, 1870, as Oak Valley; changed to Ray Jan. 8, 1874.

RAYMOND. Champaign. Township. Named for Nathaniel Raymond, the first township supervisor (*History of Champaign County*, 145). The Raymond post office operated from April 6, 1870, until Nov. 13, 1874.

RAYMOND. Montgomery. Village (1873) twelve miles north of Litchfield. Laid out in 1870 for the Wabash Railroad by Ishmael McGowan and Nimrod McElroy. Named for Thomas Raymond, vice president of the St. Louis division of the Wabash (Bateman and Selby, eds., *Historical Encyclopedia of Illinois and History of Montgomery County*, 955; *Raymond Centennial*, 6; Traylor, *Past and Present of Montgomery County*, 747). Post office established Dec. 20, 1870, as Lula; changed to Raymond Dec. 24, 1874.

RAYVILLE. Vermilion. Ten miles north of Danville. Named for site owner R. R. Ray (Beckwith, *History of Vermilion County*, 670). Post office established March 27, 1882.

READER. Macoupin. Eight miles west of Carlinville. Named for postmaster George W. Reader (Adams, comp., *Illinois Place Names*). Post office established April 3, 1888.

READING. Livingston. Three miles south-southwest of Streator. Probably a transfer from a Reading further east, perhaps Reading, Pa., Reading, Ohio, or Reading, Mich. The community was platted in 1851 by Caleb Mathis from Ohio and David Boyle (Bateman and Selby, eds., *Historical Encyclopedia of Illinois and History of Livingston County*, 639; *History of Livingston County* [1878], 287). Post office established Nov. 2, 1847, as Moon's Point; changed to Reading Nov. 28, 1850.

RECTOR. Saline. Township. Named from Rector Creek, itself named for John Rector whom the federal government employed to survey part of the Northwest Territory. About 1805 Rector was killed by a party of Shawnee near the stream that bears his name. The former Rectorville in Hamilton County, now known as Broughton, was founded by site owners Hugh Gregg, James Douglass, Samuel

Wilson, and Hezekiah Gregg in 1852 and also named from Rector Creek (*Hamilton County*, 33; *Saline County*, 131). Post office established Sept. 21, 1893.

RED BUD. Randolph. City (1867, 1875). Founded about 1847 on Horse Prairie by William Simmons and others. Named by Richard D. Durfee, an early settler, for the local red bud trees. In the words of an early history, "Where the city now stands was a jungle, composed of black haws, grape-vines and red bud" (*Combined History of Randolph, Monroe, and Perry Counties*, 400; Montague, *Directory*, 185). Post office established May 1, 1837, as Prairieville; changed to Red Bud May 14, 1847.

REDDICK. Kankakee, Livingston. Village (1890) nine miles east of Dwight. Reportedly named for the person who directed the building of the Indiana, Illinois and Iowa Railroad in the late 1880s. His name is not recorded in the early county histories, but they note that because of his red hair he was known as "Red" Dick, from which came the name Reddick (Johnson, comp., "Kankakee County Communities"; Majorowiz, comp., *History of Norton Township*, 55). Post office established March 30, 1880, as Ben-Moe; changed to Reddick Sept. 10, 1880.

REDDISH. Jersey. Twelve miles west of Jerseyville. Named for the Reddish family. Zeddock Reddish emigrated from Kentucky to what is now Richwoods Township about 1820 (*History of Greene and Jersey Counties*, 386–87).

REDMON. Edgar. Village (1899) nine miles west-northwest of Paris. Founded in 1872 and named for Joseph Redmon (*History of Edgar County*, 508). Post office established Aug. 1, 1872.

RED OAK. Stephenson. Six miles north of Freeport. Named about 1887, reportedly for a prominent red oak tree that stood along the right of way of the Illinois Central Railroad. Earlier known as Cedarville Junction (*History of Stephenson County*, 61). Post office established June 8, 1888.

RED TOP. Edwards. One mile east of Albion. Named for the red top clover introduced to the area by Charles Crackel (Harper, ed., *History of Edwards County*, 59).

REES. Morgan. Nine miles southeast of Jacksonville. Named for the Rees family. John and Georgiana Rees emigrated from Clark Co., Ky., in the 1810s (Bateman and Selby, eds., *Historical Encyclopedia of Illinois and History of Morgan County*, 919).

REEVESVILLE. Johnson. Twelve miles north of Metropolis. Originally known as Wellington. The name was changed to Reevesville about 1890 for W. and A. Reeves, who opened a dry goods store about 1888 (Chapman, *A History of Johnson County*, 292). Post office established Jan. 29, 1890.

RENAULT [REE nawlt]. Monroe. Nine miles southwest of Red Bud. Named for Philippe François Renault, director of mining operations for the Mississippi Company, organized in France around 1717 to exploit the mineral resources of the Mississippi Valley. When Renault arrived at Fort Chartres in the early

1720s he was accompanied by several hundred miners and a number of slaves. Shortly after the founding of the community as St. Philippe du Grand Marais, named for St. Philippe, Renault's patron saint, the enterprise collapsed (Brown and Dean, *The Village of Chartre*, vi; Klein, ed., *Arrowheads to Aerojets*, 591–92). Post office established Jan. 13, 1839.

REND CITY. Franklin. Three miles west-northwest of Benton. Founded about 1907 by William P. Rend for employees of the Rend Coal Company. Rend City is just south of Rend Lake, which was constructed by the Army Corps of Engineers in the 1960s (Fliege, *Tales and Trails of Illinois*, 161, 163; *Franklin County*, 20). Post office established March 16, 1910 as Rend.

RENO. Bond. Eight miles northwest of Greenville. First known as Cottonwood Grove and later as Augusta. Formally established in 1883 with construction of the Jacksonville and Southeastern Railroad. The origin of the name is unknown. It may be an adaptation of the French name *Renault*; it may be a railroad name transferred from Reno, Nev.; or it may be from a personal name. Several Renos in the United States, including Reno, Nev., were named for Jesse L. Reno, a Union Army general killed at the battle of South Mountain in the Blue Ridge range near Frederick, Md., in 1862 (Bateman and Selby, eds., *Historical Encyclopedia of Illinois and History of Bond County*, 467). Post office established Jan 13, 1851, as Cottonwood Grove; changed to Reno April 19, 1883.

RENSHAW. Pope. Fifteen miles north of Metropolis. Founded about 1902 by Rachel Renshaw and her husband, the Rev. Elmer E. Renshaw. Both Renshaws were early postmasters (*Pope County*, 35). Post office established Dec. 27, 1902.

RENTCHLER. St. Clair. Three miles west of Mascoutah. Named for postmaster Daniel Rentchler (Adams, comp., *Illinois Place Names*). Post office established Aug. 13, 1872.

REYNOLDS. Mercer, Rock Island. Village (1994) eleven miles southwest of Rock Island. Founded about 1876 by Rufus Walker and probably named for Elisha P. Reynolds, a contractor for the Rock Island Railroad. Possibly named for John Reynolds, governor of Illinois from 1830 to 1834 (Adams, comp., *Illinois Place Names;* Bateman and Selby, eds., *Historical Encyclopedia of Illinois and History of Rock Island County*, 969; *Historic Rock Island County*, 109). Post office established March 7, 1877.

REYNOLDS. Lee. Township. Named for Sewell Reynolds, the first settler in what is now Reynolds Township (Stevens, *History of Lee County*, 446).

REYNOLDSBURG. Johnson. Eighteen miles southwest of Harrisburg. Named for Wesley Reynolds, site owner and postmaster (Chapman, *A History of Johnson County*, 284). Post office established March. 15, 1851, as Cross Roads; changed to Reynoldsburgh July 6, 1860.

RICE. Jo Daviess. Six miles south-southeast of Galena. Rice Township was created from East Galena Township as Washington, named for George Washington, in

February 1859. In June of the same year the name was changed to honor Henry A. Rice, one of the first settlers, who arrived in 1821 (Bateman and Selby, eds., *Historical Encyclopedia of Illinois and History of Jo Daviess County,* 633).

RICHARDS. LaSalle. Three miles north of Streator. Named for Frederick Richards, site owner and postmaster (Rasmusen, *LaSalle County Lore,* 264). Post office established July 12, 1897.

RICHLAND. County. Created Feb. 24, 1841, from parts of Clay and Lawrence counties. Named for his former home in Richland County, Ohio, by the Rev. Joseph H. Reed, a Methodist minister and Illinois state representative in the late 1840s who was instrumental in the formation of the county (*Counties of Cumberland, Jasper and Richland,* 588, 622).

RICHLAND. Marshall. Township. Named at the suggestion of John Strawn, for his former home, Richland, Ohio (Ellsworth, *Records of the Olden Times,* 464).

RICHMOND. Livingston. Fourteen miles north of Lincoln. Founded about 1850 by Henry Loveless and named for Richmond, his former home in Jefferson County, Ohio (*History of Livingston County* [1878], 326).

RICHMOND. McHenry. Village (1865, 1872) nine miles north of McHenry. Founded about 1840 by Charles Cotting and John Purdy as Montalona, named for a district in New Hampshire that is now part of Dunbarton. The name was changed about 1844, probably at the suggestion of Cotting, for his former home, Richmond, Chittenden County, Vt. (*History of McHenry County* [1885], 887; Stennett, *A History of the Origin,* 118). Post office established July 22, 1840, as Montatona (probably a scribal error for Montalona); changed to Richmond April 7, 1847.

RICHVIEW. Washington. Village (1855, 1873) twelve miles east-northeast of Nashville. Laid out in 1839 as Richmond by W. H. Livesay. The Illinois Central station was established in 1852 as Richview, named, according to Ackerman, "on account of the elevated site of what is now called Old Town, or Old Richview, about half a mile from the station, and the very beautiful view of the surrounding country in all directions" (*Early Illinois Railroads,* 132–33; *Washington County,* 26). Post office established March 6, 1848.

RICKS. Christian. Township. Named for the pioneer Ricks family, especially William Ricks, an early county sheriff instrumental in the organization of Christian County (Bateman and Selby, eds., *Historical Encyclopedia of Illinois and History of Christian County,* 797; *Christian County,* 56).

RIDENHOWER. Johnson. Former community. Founded as Collinsburg. When the post office department rejected that name, claiming it was too similar to Collinsville, the community was renamed for site owner H. M. Ridenhower Jr. The Ridenhower church was located about one mile southeast of Vienna. Also known as Shoo Fly (Chapman, *A History of Johnson County,* 293; Mohlenbrock, "A New Geography of Illinois: Johnson County," 32). Post office established Nov. 19, 1895.

RIDGE FARM. Vermilion. Village (1874) five miles south of Georgetown. Named from Abraham Smith's Ridge Farm, located on the rise running east-west through Elwood Township (Jones, *History of Vermilion County,* 396, 398; Stapp, *History under Our Feet,* 15). Post office established May 17, 1841.

RIDGWAY. Gallatin. Village (1886) ten miles west of Eldorado. Founded in the late 1860s as a construction camp for workers building the Springfield and Illinois Southeastern Railroad from Shawneetown to Beardstown. Named for Thomas A. Ridgway, first president of the S&IS (*History and Families of Gallatin County,* 257). Post office established Feb. 3, 1870.

RIDOTT [REYE daht]. Stephenson. Village (1874) seven miles east of Freeport. Established about 1852 as a station on the Galena and Chicago Union Railroad as Nevada, named for Nevada City, Calif. About 1860 J. S. Cochran convinced the railroad to move the station a mile east and rename it Cochranville. For unknown reasons, the name was changed to Ridott shortly thereafter. An earlier Ridotts [*sic*] post office operated from April 11, 1848, until Nov. 2, 1860. The source of the name is unknown (Tilden, comp., *History of Stephenson County,* 517). Post office established April 4, 1854, as Nevada; changed to Cochransville Sept. 5, 1860; changed to Ridott May 8, 1861.

RIGGSTON. Scott. Nine miles west-southwest of Jacksonville. Founded in 1871 on the line of the Rockford, Rock Island and St. Louis Railroad and named Prairie Center by Mary Riggs. To avoid duplication of post offices, she changed the name to honor her father, postmaster Milton W. Riggs (*Scott County Bicentennial Book,* 213). Post office established April 25, 1871.

RILEYVILLE. Saline. Ten miles northwest of Harrisburg. Surveyed for Mrs. L. M. Riley. She and her husband were early postmasters (*Saline County,* 73). Post office established Feb. 3, 1874.

RINARD [REYE nuhrd, ri NAHRD]. Wayne. Seven miles south of Flora. Laid out in 1870 by Adam Rinard and Ed Bonham as a station on the Ohio and Mississippi Railroad (*History of Wayne and Clay Counties,* 238). Post office established March 1, 1871.

RINGWOOD. McHenry. Village (1994) three miles north-northwest of McHenry. Founded in the early 1850s. The traditional account is that the community was named Ringwood by Mrs. John Gray because it was surrounded by a ring of woods. More likely, however, the name is a transfer from Ringwood Park in Chesterfield, England, reportedly the former home of a Judge Reynolds, an early settler in Richmond Township (Stennett, *A History of the Origin,* 118). Post office established Aug. 2, 1845, as Ring Wood.

RIO [REE o]. Knox. Village (1958) eleven miles north of Galesburg. Laid out in 1871 as Coburg, named for postmaster Nelson Coe and his brother Lewis. The township was named Rio about 1850 at the suggestion of Lewis Coe, apparently a reference to the Rio Grande River. As an early county history puts it,

"The Grande part of the name was deemed a superfluous appendage, and was dropped" (*Portrait and Biographical Album of Knox County*, 1086). Post office established Aug. 19, 1843, as North Prairie; changed to Rio Feb. 10, 1871.

RIPLEY. Brown. Village (1837, 1874) eleven miles west of Beardstown. Laid out as Centerville in 1836 by John Ebey and Fielding T. Glenn. When Brown County was organized in 1839, the name was changed to Ripley, likely in honor of Gen. Eleazer Wheelock Ripley, an officer in the War of 1812 and recognized for his participation in the indecisive battle of Lundy's Lane near Niagara Falls in 1814. The name may, however, be a transfer from Ripley County, Ind., which was named for the same general (Baker, *From Needmore to Prosperity; History of Brown County*, 651). Post office established May 27, 1837.

RISING. Champaign. Four miles northwest of Champaign. Originally a station on the Cleveland, Cincinnati, Chicago and St. Louis (Big Four) Railroad. Named either for John Rising, a local farmer, or for postmaster George H. Rising (Adams, comp., *Illinois Place Names;* Bateman and Selby, eds., *Historical Encyclopedia of Illinois and History of Champaign County*, 815). Post office established June 22, 1874, as Rising Station; changed to Rising March 3, 1882.

RIVERDALE. Cook. Village (1892). Developed from a site known as Riverdale Crossing where George Dolton and J. C. Matthews operated a ferry across the Little Calumet River in the late 1830s (Lauerman, "River Life with Touch of the City"). Post office established Feb. 16, 1874.

RIVER FOREST. Cook. Founded in 1836 as Thatcher, named for Daniel Cunningham Thatcher, a Chicago business executive and the site owner. Part of the Thatcher estate is now the Thatcher's Woods section of the Cook County Forest Preserve. The name of the community was changed from Thatcher to River Forest in 1872 in order to promote residential development (Hansen, ed., *Illinois*, 579). Post office established Aug. 10, 1882.

RIVER GROVE. Cook. Village (1888). Created about 1888 through the merger of two unincorporated areas, Turner Park and River Park (*Illinois Guide*). Post office established Nov. 11, 1873, as River Park; changed to Turner Park Oct. 30, 1884; changed to River Grove Feb. 4, 1889.

RIVERSIDE. Cook. Village (1875). Founded in 1869 by the Riverside Improvement Corporation, a consortium of business executives who engaged Frederick Law Olmstead, who designed New York's Central Park and at the time was the most prominent landscape architect in America, to create a new community as a model suburb along the Des Plaines River. In the words of a recent village history, it was to be "a perfect village in a perfect setting" (Bassman, *Riverside Then and Now*, 76). Post office established Nov. 7, 1870.

RIVERTON. Sangamon. Village (1873) three miles northeast of Springfield. Founded in 1837 as Jamestown by James F. Reed, a veteran of the Black Hawk War and proprietor of a furniture manufacturing plant on the Sangamon River. To avoid duplication of post offices, the name was changed about 1864 to Howlett for Parley L. Howlett, a local brewer who was the first to recognize the significance of the coal deposits in the area. It was subsequently changed to Riverton about 1874 (Bateman and Selby, eds., *Historical Encyclopedia of Illinois and History of Sangamon County*, 709). Post office established Nov. 21, 1864, as Howlett; changed to Riverton April 23, 1874.

RIVOLI. Mercer. Township. The source of the name is unknown. The only other Rivoli in the United States is in Bibb County, Ga., near Macon.

ROACHES. Jefferson. Eight miles west of Mount Vernon. Founded in 1870 by site owner David Roach. Formerly known as Roach Town and Roachville (Perrin, ed., *History of Jefferson County*, 402).

ROACHTOWN. St. Clair. Three miles southwest of Belleville. Named for Samuel P. Roach and his son Matthew, who operated a saw mill and grist mill at the site in the 1860s (*History of St. Clair County*, 255).

ROANOKE. Woodford. Village (1874) six miles north-northeast of Eureka. Founded in the late 1840s and formally laid out in 1872 with construction of the Chicago, Pekin and Southwestern Railroad. The name was suggested by John Gish, a Dunkard minister, for Roanoke, Va., the former home of a number of early settlers, including the Gish family (Kenyon, ed., *Roanoke Centennial History*, 3). Post office established March 22, 1858.

ROBBINS. Cook. Village (1917). Founded about 1910 by Henry E. Robbins. Developed by Robbins and his son, Eugene (Schoon, *Calumet Beginnings*, 128; Hansen, ed., *Illinois*, 428). Post office established July 24, 1923.

ROBBS. Pope. Twenty miles southwest of Harrisburg. Founded about 1902 by Albert L. Robbs as Robbsville, a station on the Illinois Central Railroad. The IC shortened the name to Robbs (*Pope County*, 36).

ROBERTS. Ford. Village (1886) eleven miles northwest of Paxton. Probably named by and for Francis Alonzo Roberts, who surveyed the site in 1871 for the Gilman, Clinton and Springfield Railroad. The choice of the name may have been influenced by James Roberts, who had extensive landholdings in the area (Gardner, *History of Ford County*, 174; *Roberts Area Centennial*, 8). Post office established Jan. 22, 1872.

ROBERTS. Marshall. Township. Named for Jesse and Livingston Roberts, generally recognized as the first permanent settlers (Burt and Hawthorne, *Past and Present of Marshall and Putnam Counties*, 53).

ROBINSON. Crawford. City (1875). Named for John McCracken Robinson (1794–1843), U.S. senator from Illinois from 1830 to 1841. Robinson has been the seat of Crawford County since 1843, when it was moved from Palestine (Perrin, ed., *History of Crawford and Clark Counties*, 107). Post office established Jan. 10, 1845.

ROB ROY CREEK. Kendall. Stream. By local tradition, in the 1830s some travelers were having trouble crossing the creek because of recent heavy rains. One was riding an especially fine horse named Rob Roy, which carried him across and gave his name to the stream (Dickson, "Geographical Features and Place Names").

ROCHELLE [ro SHEL]. Ogle. City (1861, 1872). Founded about 1853 as Lane, named for Robert P. Lane of Rockford, one of several investors who purchased a tract of land for a station on the Dixon Air Line Railroad. In 1861 a fire destroyed several elevators and warehouses, and an itinerant named Burke was accused, tried, and lynched vigilante style. This incident gave the community of Lane the nickname "Hangtown," by which it was known through much of northern Illinois. A group of concerned citizens thought the best way to separate Lane from the Hangtown image would be to change the name. As they discussed alternative names in the drug store, someone noticed a bottle of Rochelle Salts, a purgative, on a shelf. That would be, it was suggested, an appropriate name because "what this town needs is a good cleaning out." Lane officially became Rochelle in 1865. The choice of the name may have been influenced by settlers from New Rochelle, Westchester County, N.Y. (*Bicentennial History of Ogle County*, 260). Post office established Feb. 12, 1850, as Story; changed to Lane Depot April 22, 1854; changed to Rochelle March 23, 1865.

ROCHESTER. Sangamon. Village (1873) six miles southeast of Springfield. More than sixty communities or townships in the United States are named Rochester. Some are transfers from Rochester, Kent, England, but most are transfers from Rochester, N.Y., itself named for Col. Nathaniel Rochester. Rochester, Ill., was probably named by settlers from a Rochester further east, perhaps Rochester, N.Y., or Rochester, Ohio, itself named for Rochester, N.Y. (Miller, *Ohio Place Names*; Vasiliev, *From Abbotts to Zurich*). Post office established June 18, 1834.

ROCK. Pope. Nineteen miles north-northeast of Metropolis. Formerly called Birdseye. The origins of both names, *Rock* and *Birdseye*, are unknown (personal communication with Mildred B. McCormick). Post office established Sept. 19, 1853.

ROCKBRIDGE. Greene. Village (1881) twelve miles northeast of Jerseyville. Founded in 1870 as Sheffield, a station on the Rockford, Rock Island and St. Louis Railroad, named for G. T. W. Sheffield, proprietor of the local general store. When the RRI&StL merged with the Chicago, Burlington and Quincy, the name was changed to agree with that of the Rockbridge post office (Miner, *Past and Present*, 176). Post office established Sept. 23, 1850.

ROCK CITY. Stephenson. Village (1882) twelve miles northeast of Freeport. Founded in 1859 by George Raymer as Rock Run City on the line of the Racine and Mississippi Railroad. Raymer took the name from the Rock Run Mills, established earlier on Rock Run Creek (*Along the Trail,* 17). Post office established Jan. 9, 1840, as Rock Run; changed to Rock City Nov. 3, 1879.

ROCK FALLS. Whiteside. City (1889). Formerly called Rapids City and proposed as the site of a canal and lock to enable water traffic to bypass the rapids on the Rock River. The project was abandoned in the 1830s. Rock Falls, named for the same rapids, was subsequently founded by A. P. Smith (Davis, *History of Whiteside County,* 218). Post office established March 11, 1868.

ROCKFORD. Winnebago. City (1852, 1880). Founded by Germanicus Kent, who settled on the west side of the Rock River in 1834. He was joined the following year by Daniel Haight, who settled on the east side. The site was first named Midway by Kent, who thought it was about half way between Chicago and Galena, then the two most prominent communities in northern Illinois. In 1836 a road from Chicago to Galena was authorized, to run through "Midway at the ford on Rock river," from which the city takes its name. Dr. Josiah C. Goodhue, one of the commissioners of the Chicago-Galena road, is credited with changing the name to Rockford later that year (Church, *Past and Present of the City of Rockford,* 17; *History of Winnebago County,* 399). Post office established Aug. 31, 1837.

ROCK GROVE. Stephenson. Thirteen miles north-northeast of Freeport. Laid out about 1850 by Samuel Guyer. Named from the stream called Rock Run (Tilden, comp., *History of Stephenson County,* 485). Post office established Jan. 9, 1840.

ROCK ISLAND. County. Created Feb. 9, 1831 from Jo Daviess County. Named for Rock Island, a two-mile-long, thousand-acre block of limestone in the Mississippi River between the cities of Rock Island–Moline, Ill., and Davenport–Bettendorf, Iowa. Construction of Fort Armstrong built to protect settlers from Indian incursions and named for John Armstrong, secretary of war under James Madison, began in 1816. From about 1861 the site was known as the Rock Island arsenal, a facility used to store army supplies and produce artillery and its components. Today the site is generally referred to as Arsenal Island.

ROCK ISLAND. Rock Island. City (1841, 1879). First known as Farnhamsburg, named for Russell Farnham (or Farnam), a trader and business partner of George Davenport, the founder of Davenport, Iowa, in the 1820s. Stephenson, named for Col. Benjamin Stephenson, the namesake of Stephenson County, was laid out adjacent to Farnhamsburg in 1835 and renamed Rock Island, taking its name from the county, in 1841 (Tweet, *Quad Cities,* 12–13). Post office established April 4, 1834, as Farnamsburgh; changed to Stephenson Nov. 9, 1835; changed to Rock Island April 13, 1841.

ROCK RIVER. Empties into the Mississippi River at Rock Island. A translation through French of Miami-Illinois *assinissippi* (rock river).

ROCKTON. Winnebago. Village (1847, 1872) nine miles north of Rockford. Formerly known as Pecatonica. The name was changed about 1846 for the community's location on the Rock River. Thomas B. Talcott, one of the first county commissioners, is generally credited with suggesting the name (Carr, *The History of Rockton*, 28; Teeman, *Postal Saga of Jo Daviess*, 21). Post office established Dec. 26, 1838, as Pekatonica; changed to Rockton Feb. 26, 1846.

ROCKVILLE. Kankakee. Township. Named for Rock Creek, which empties into the Kankakee River near Altorf (Bateman and Selby, eds., *Historical Encyclopedia of Illinois and History of Kankakee County*, 734). Post office established July 24, 1835, as Forked Creek; changed to Reids Store July 24, 1838; changed to Rockville Oct. 26, 1838.

ROCKWELL. LaSalle. Former community. Founded in 1836 by a temperance colony from Massachusetts. The Rockwell Cemetery is one mile southeast of LaSalle. The source of the name is unknown (Nelson, *The Role of Colonies*, 11).

ROCKWOOD. Randolph. Village (1865, 1891) eight miles southeast of Chester. Known in the 1800s as Jones Creek for early settler Emsley Jones. Formally established as Liberty, probably so named because it provided a rest stop for escaping slaves on the Underground Railroad. Upon incorporation in 1865 the name was changed to Rockwood, reportedly named for the rocky bluff beside the Mississippi River and for the wood yard that supplied fuel for steamboats. Because of a shift in the course of the Mississippi, Rockwood is now more than a mile from the river (Allen, *Legends and Lore*, 336). Post office established June 11, 1836, as Jones' Creek; changed to Rockwood April 7, 1865.

RODDEN [RAHD n]. Jo Daviess. Eight miles southeast of Galena. Named for postmaster John Rodden (Adams, comp., *Illinois Place Names*). Post office established July 16, 1891.

RODEMICH. St. Clair. Seven miles north of Waterloo. Named for Philip W. Rodemich, supervisor of Millstadt Township in the 1870s (*History of St. Clair County*, 259).

ROGERS PARK. Cook. Chicago community. Founded about 1870. Named for site owner Phillip Rogers, an Irish immigrant who settled in Illinois in the mid-1840s. Founded by Rogers's daughter, Catherine, and her husband, Capt. Patrick Touhy, with construction of the Chicago and North Western Railroad about 1873 (Goodspeed and Healy, eds., *History of Cook County*, 260). Post office established July 2, 1873.

ROGERS. Ford. Township. Named for Jeremy W. Rogers, the first township supervisor (Gardner, *History of Ford County*, 183).

ROHRER. Morgan. Eighteen miles northwest of Carlinville. Named for postmasters Mary and Jonathan (or Judson) Rohrer (Adams, comp., *Illinois Place Names;*

Bateman and Selby, eds., *Historical Encyclopedia of Illinois and History of Morgan County*, 929). Post office established June 10, 1889.

ROLAND. White. Twelve miles northeast of Eldorado. Laid out in 1856. Named from the Roland post office, itself named for postmaster Roland G. Rice. Post office established Nov. 5, 1849.

ROLLING MEADOWS. Cook. City (1955). The ridges and valleys of the area reportedly suggested the name to Kimball Hill, who developed the site in the early 1950s (Perica, *They Took the Challenge*, 41).

ROLLINS. Lake. Northeast of Round Lake Beach. Named for Gen. John A. Rawlins, Ulysses S. Grant's chief of staff and later his secretary of war. On the post office application the name was written *Rollins,* an accurate representation of the local pronunciation of Rawlins (Dretske, *What's in a Name?*). Post office established June 22, 1874.

ROLLO. DeKalb. Fifteen miles northeast of Mendota. Reportedly named for the Rollo books (*Rollo at Play, Rollo in Europe*), a series of popular adventure and instructional children's books of the mid-nineteenth century written by Jacob Abbott (Stennett, *A History of the Origin,* 119). Post office established March 27, 1886.

ROME. Jefferson. Township. Named for the community of Rome, now called Dix (q.v.), founded in 1849 by Arba Andrews and named for Rome, N.Y., near Andrews's former home (Perrin, ed., *History of Jefferson County,* 364). Post office established July 20, 1835, as Jordan's Prairie; changed to Rome Feb. 24, 1852.

ROME. Peoria. Laid out about 1832 and probably named for Rome, Italy, by Isaac Underhill, who would later become president of the Peoria and Bureau Valley Railroad. The original streets bore such classical names as Caesar, Pompey, Octavius, and Brutus (Rice, *Peoria City and County,* 297; www.chillicothehistorical.org/rock_island_history.htm). Post office established July 20, 1832, as LaSalle; changed to Rome Oct. 16, 1835.

ROMEOVILLE. Will. Village (1895). Established about 1835 as a port on the Illinois and Michigan Canal near a housing development known as Rairdon's Subdivision, which became Romeo, perhaps as a complement to Juliet (now Joliet), several miles south. When Juliet was changed to Joliet in 1845, Romeo responded by adding *-ville* to its name. Post office established June 29, 1833, as Juliet; changed to Romeo Oct. 29, 1833.

ROMINE. Marion. Township. Named for Abram Romine, an early settler who introduced Thoroughbred horses to the area (*History of Marion and Clinton Counties,* 282). Post office established March 1, 1860.

ROODHOUSE [ROOD haws]. Greene. City (1876) three miles northeast of White Hall. Founded in 1866 by site owner John Roodhouse as a division point on the Alton Railroad (*Illinois Guide*). Post office established Jan. 29, 1867, as Road

House Station, a popular etymology of the name *Roodhouse;* changed to Roodhouse Dec. 12, 1876.

ROOKS CREEK. Livingston. Three miles west of Pontiac. Named from the stream called Rooks Creek, itself named for first settler Frederick Rook (*History of Livingston County* [1878], 436). Post office established Nov. 2, 1847.

ROOTS. Randolph. Thirteen miles south of Red Bud. Named for postmaster John P. Roots (Adams, comp., *Illinois Place Names*). Post office established Dec. 13, 1902.

ROSAMOND [ROZ uh muhnd]. Christian. Three and a half miles west of Pana. Reportedly named for the profusion of wild roses in the spring and early summer. The spelling was changed from Rosemond in the early 1920s (Bateman and Selby, eds., *Historical Encyclopedia of Illinois and History of Christian County,* 801). Post office established March 20, 1856, as Rosemond; changed to Rosamond Sept. 14, 1923.

ROSCOE. Winnebago. Village (1965). Several histories of Winnebago County claim the Roscoe post office, and subsequently the village and township, were named for William Rosco (1753–1831), the eminent English attorney and historian. They may, however, have been named for a source much closer to home: Charlie Roscoe, a friend of Amos Tuttle. Tuttle was an early settler who laid out the community about 1840 (Church, *Past and Present of the City of Rockford,* 11; *History of Winnebago County,* 450; Nelson, comp., *Sinnissippi Saga,* 41). Post office established July 26, 1837.

ROSE. Township. Shelby. Named for the Rose family, especially for John Rose, whose family emigrated from Kentucky about 1810 (Bateman and Selby, eds., *Historical Encyclopedia of Illinois and History of Shelby County,* 966).

ROSEBUD. Pope. Twelve miles northeast of Metropolis. Founded by William King, who established the first general store in the area about 1892. The local story is that the community was named for a particularly lush red rosebush that grew outside the window of King's store (McCormick, "The Significance of Pope County Place Names," 27; *Pope County,* 37). Post office established Aug. 10, 1869, as Rose Bud; changed to Rosebud June 13, 1893.

ROSECRANS. Lake. Five miles north-northwest of Zion. Named for William Starke Rosecrans (1819–98), a Union general in the Civil War. Rosecrans played a large part in Union victories at Iuka and Corinth, Miss., in 1862 (Dretske, *What's in a Name?*). Post office established March 13, 1863.

ROSE HILL. Cook. Named from the tavern operated by Hiram Roe as a rest stop for travelers bound to and from Chicago. The tavern was located on what was known as "Roe's Hill," which by popular etymology became Rose Hill. Now part of Chicago (Karlen, *Chicago's Crabgrass Communities,* 197). Post office established Dec. 13, 1860.

ROSE HILL. Jasper. Village (1901) eight miles north of Newton. Founded in 1839 as Harrisburg, named for A. S. Harris, later to become the first postmaster. In the late 1870s the station on the Peoria, Decatur and Evansville Railroad was established as Rose Hill, taking its name from the Rose Hill post office, itself reportedly named for the roses that grew wild on Keach Hill (*Jasper County*, 15; Robins, *Historical Development of Jasper County*, 24; Sunderland, *New and Complete History*, 84). Post office established April 24, 1846.

ROSELLE [ro ZEL]. Cook, DuPage. Village (1922). Named for Roselle M. Hough (1819–92), perhaps best known as supervisor of construction of the Chicago Union Stockyards in the 1860s. About 1873 Hough had the Chicago and Pacific Railroad rerouted from Bloomingdale so it would pass through his property. The station became the nucleus for the village of Roselle, which was formally organized by Barnard Beck in 1875 (Bateman and Selby, eds., *Historical Encyclopedia of Illinois and History of DuPage County*, 666; Knoblauch, ed., *DuPage County*, 220; Moore and Bray, *DuPage at 150*, 71). Post office established Dec. 8, 1873.

ROSEMONT. Cook. Village (1956). Rosemont incorporated after being refused annexation by Schiller Park, Des Plaines, and Park Ridge. The name *Rosemont* was reportedly drawn from several possible others that had been tossed into a hat, including O'Hare, for the nearby airport; Scott, for Scott Street, a major entry into Rosemont; and Thorndale. "Rosemont" may have been suggested by the Chicago street of that name (Lucadamo, "Visitor-Oriented Village").

ROSEVILLE. Warren. Village (1875) twelve miles south of Monmouth. First known as Hat Grove, reportedly because the grove of trees near the town was shaped "like the hemisphere crown of a Mormon's hat" (*Illinois Guide*). The name was changed to Roseville about 1853 with construction of the Rockford, Rock Island and St. Louis Railroad (Lieurance, *History of Roseville*). Post office established March 2, 1838, as New Lancaster; changed to Hat Grove Jan. 4, 1843; changed to Roseville June 23, 1853.

ROSICLARE [ROZ i KLEHR]. Hardin. City (1874) thirty miles northeast of Metropolis. Probably named for Rose and Clare, daughters of an early settler who were drowned in a boating accident. An early account, however, claims that the community was named by Polly Pell, who chose the name *Rosi Clare*, saying that it meant "red earth." The community was established as Rose Clare and by the 1890s had become Rosiclare (*Hardin County*, 19). Post office established July 13, 1824, as Twitchell's Mills; changed to Rosiclare March 13, 1844.

ROSS. Edgar. Township. Probably named by James Gaines for his former home in Ross County, Ohio. Several early settlers, however, were named Ross, and they may have influenced the choice of the name (Bateman and Selby, eds., *Historical Encyclopedia of Illinois and History of Edgar County*, 642; *History of Edgar County*, 442).

ROSS. Pike. Township. Formed from Atlas Township in 1879 as Spring Lake. The name was changed shortly thereafter in honor of Col. William Ross, one of the founders of Atlas (q.v.) (*History of Pike County*, 795).

ROSSVILLE. Vermilion. Village (1872) six miles south of Hoopeston. Laid out about 1857 by Alvan Gilbert and named for Jacob T. Ross, a local sawmill operator. Previously, the community had been known as Bicknell's Point, Liggett's Grove, North Fork, and Henpeck (Tuggle, comp., *Stories of Historical Days*, 13; Williams, *History of Vermilion County*, 298). Post office established April 1, 1836, as North Fork; changed to Rossville Jan. 31, 1861.

ROUND KNOB. Massac. Six miles north of Metropolis. Named from its location north of Round Knob Hill (May, *History of Massac County*, 176). Post office established Jan. 29, 1889.

ROUNTREE. Montgomery. Township. Named for Judge Hiram Rountree of Hillsboro, a prominent citizen of early Montgomery County and a delegate to the Illinois constitutional convention of 1847 (Traylor, *Past and Present of Montgomery County*, 713).

ROWE. Livingston. Four miles north-northwest of Pontiac. Established as a station on the Chicago and Paducah Railroad in 1871 by site owner and postmaster James M. Rowe (*History of Livingston County* [1878], 547). Post office established Jan. 15, 1872.

ROXANA. Madison. Village (1921) south of Wood River. Established about 1918 for employees of the Roxana Petroleum Company. The source of the name is uncertain. One account claims the community was named for Roxana, reportedly the wife of the owner of Royal Dutch Shell, the parent company of Roxana Petroleum; another credits the name to Marcus Abrahams, the owner of the Roxana Petroleum Company, who reportedly named the community for Roxane, the wife of Alexander the Great (Underwood, "A New Geography of Illinois: Madison County," 32). Post office established March 3, 1926.

ROYALTON. Franklin. Village (1907) ten miles west of West Frankfort. Founded about 1907 as Royal Village, named for the Royal Coal Company, owned by William J. Royal (Jurich, *This Is Franklin County*, 28). Post office established May 18, 1906, as Pierce, named for postmasters Henry and Ada Pierce; changed to Royalton May 24, 1910.

RUARK. Lawrence. Twelve miles southwest of Lawrenceville. Named for the Ruark family. James and Elizabeth Ruark emigrated from Geauga County, Ohio, about 1816 (*Combined History of Edwards, Lawrence, and Wabash Counties*, 301). Post office established Oct. 19, 1840.

RUBICON. Township. Greene. Named from Rubicon Creek. The reason for the name is not known. Perhaps the namer saw some resemblance between this stream and the Rubicon River in Italy that Julius Caesar famously crossed in 49 B.C., precipitating a Roman civil war.

RUDEMENT. Saline. Six miles south of Harrisburg. Named for Hankerson Rude from Virginia, one of the first settlers to officially enter land in the county, in September 1814 (*History of Gallatin, Saline,* 152). Post office established May 6, 1896.

RURAL HILL. Hamilton. Twelve miles east-southeast of Benton. The source of the name is unknown. The post office was established as Rurell Hill, the spelling of which would suggest that it was named for an individual or family named Rurell, which became "Rural" through popular etymology (*Hamilton County,* 47). Post office established July 14, 1874, as Rurell Hill; changed to Ruell Hill July 29, 1874; changed to Rural Hill July 13, 1876.

RUSH. Jo Daviess. Township. Named from Big Rush Creek and Little Rush Creek. Big Rush Creek was supposedly so named because of the speed of its discharge (Bateman and Selby, eds., *Historical Encyclopedia of Illinois and History of Jo Daviess County,* 634). Post office established April 25, 1848.

RUSHVILLE. Schuyler. City (1839, 1898). Founded in Feb. 1826 as Rushton, the seat of Schuyler County. The name was changed to Rushville by the county commissioners court the following month. Rushville is probably named for Richard Rush (1780–1859), a Philadelphia lawyer, public official, and diplomat whose father was Dr. Benjamin Rush, surgeon general of the Continental Army. When Rushville was founded, Richard Rush was secretary of the U.S. Treasury in the administration of John Quincy Adams and nationally known (Bateman and Selby, eds., *Historical Encyclopedia of Illinois and History of Schuyler County,* 687; *Combined History of Schuyler and Brown Counties,* 234, 241; Russ, "The Export of Pennsylvania Place Names," 208; *Schuyler County,* 7). Post office established Oct. 17, 1826, as Beardstown; changed to Rushville Jan. 18, 1827.

RUSSELL. Lake. Four miles northwest of Zion. Named for Russell Sage, a stockholder in the Chicago, Milwaukee and St. Paul Railroad (Dretske, *What's in a Name?*). Post office established Sept. 13, 1847, as Mortimer; changed to Newport April 1, 1851; changed to Russell July 10, 1876.

RUSSELLVILLE. Lawrence. Village (1875) ten miles east-northeast of Lawrenceville. Established about 1835 on the site of an Indian encampment known as Little Village. Named for August, Andrew, and Clement Russell, brothers from Kentucky who built the first sawmill in the area about 1835 (*Combined History of Edwards, Lawrence, and Wabash Counties,* 271). Post office established Feb. 19, 1835.

RUST. Franklin. Eight miles east of Benton. Named for the Rust family (originally Röst) (*Franklin County,* 149).

RUTLAND. Kane. Township. Named in 1850 for Rutland, Vt., by Evelyn R. Starks, for whom Starks is named. Starks was an early settler and the first township supervisor (*Biographical and Historical Record of Kane County,* 1067). Post office established Jan. 7, 1854.

RUTLAND. LaSalle, Marshall. Village (1876) fifteen miles southwest of Streator. Named for Rutland, Vt. Founded in 1855 as New Rutland and settled by members of the Vermont Emigration Association, some two hundred of whom paid $10 each for a building lot in a city "to be located in the West." The name was proposed by William B. Burns, a member of the locating committee (Burns, *A Link to the Past*, 352; *History of LaSalle County*, 295, 301). Post office established Feb. 26, 1877, as New Rutland; changed to Rutland Feb. 26, 1877.

RUTLEDGE. DeWitt. Township. Originally known as Douglas, probably named for Stephen A. Douglas. The name was changed in 1859 in honor of William J. Rutledge, an early settler (*History of DeWitt County, Illinois, 1839–1968*, 22).

RUYLE. Jersey. Township. Named for Col. William L. Ruyle, who was instrumental in the formation of the township (*History of Greene and Jersey Counties*, 457). The Ruyle post office operated from May 13, 1901, until Sept. 15, 1903.

RYDER. Jefferson. Former community in McClennan Township. Founded about 1892 by site owners and postmasters Philena and Frank W. Ryder (Adams, comp., *Illinois Place Names*). Post office established Jan. 4, 1895.

S

SABINA. McLean. Six miles east of Le Roy. Named for Mrs. Sabina Moore, who, with her husband, operated a grain elevator in West Township (*Heritage of the Prairie*, 28). Post office established Dec. 30, 1878.

SACRAMENTO. White. Nine miles southwest of Carmi. Named for Sacramento, Calif., by Joel Rice, who ventured to the California gold fields in 1849 and founded the community upon his return (Land, comp., *History of Enfield*, 47). Post office established March 18, 1852, as Rattle Snake; changed to Sacramento Dec. 2, 1861.

SADORUS [suh DOR uhs]. Champaign. Village (1873) nine miles southwest of Champaign. Founded about 1856 and named for Henry Sadorus from Bedford County, Penn., who settled at what became known as Sadorus Grove in 1824 (*History of Champaign County*, 122). Post office established April 2, 1855, as Sodorus; changed to Sadorus Dec. 22, 1884.

SAG BRIDGE. Cook. Recorded as early as 1812 where present Saganashkee Slough appears on Gen. William Hull's map as "Ausagaunashke Swamp." The name was progressively shortened, to Saganee by 1830 and to Sag by 1844. Possibly from Potawatomi *ausagaunaskee*, perhaps meaning "tall grass valley" (Bright, *Native American Placenames*; Vogel, *Indian Place Names in Illinois*). Post office established Feb. 23, 1872.

SAIDORA. Mason. Sixteen miles east-northeast of Beardstown. Founded about 1868 and according to local tradition named for pioneer women known only as Sadie and Dora (Lynn, *Prelude to Progress*, 286). Post office established May 26, 1868.

SAILOR SPRINGS. Clay. Village (1892) ten miles northeast of Flora. Named for the dozen or so mineral springs bought by Thomas and Rebecca Sailor about 1870. The Sailors developed the site into a spa featuring steam baths and mud baths in addition to the mineral waters. The springs were first known as the "milk-sick springs" because they were thought to be toxic to cows and to humans who drank the cows' milk (*Prairie Echo*, 121). Post office established Feb. 21, 1881.

SALEM. The first Salem in the United States was in Massachusetts, founded and named in the 1620s by Puritans, who took the name from the biblical Salem, mentioned in Genesis. The word *Salem* is from the same source as Hebrew *shalom* and Arabic *salam* (peace) and is often considered a shortened form of "Jerusalem." The religious associations made Salem a desirable name in the nineteenth century, especially for churches, from which many communities took their names. There are currently some fifty churches and eleven communities or townships in Illinois named Salem, and many are transfers from Salems further east.

SALEM. Marion. City (1837, 1894). Laid out about 1813 and probably named by Mark Tully for his former home, Salem, Ind., itself named for Salem, Mass. Salem has been the seat of Marion County since its formation in 1823 (Seibel, *My Home Town*, 1). Post office established May 3, 1825.

SALINE. County. Created Feb. 25, 1847, from Gallatin County. Named from the Saline River or from the local salt springs. In Mississippi Valley French, any salt spring, salt lick, or salt works was called a saline. The springs feeding what is now the Saline River were referred to by early French explorers as *l'eau de salle* (the salt water). The county seat was established at Raleigh and moved to Harrisburg in 1859 (McDermott, *A Glossary of Mississippi Valley French*).

SALT CREEK. Cook, DuPage. According to a local story, the name came about from the following incident: A teamster named John Reid was engaged to haul merchandise between Chicago and the lead mining areas around Galena. He would transport salt and other supplies from Chicago to Galena and return with a load of ore. On one occasion, Reid, his wagon loaded with salt, attempted to ford a stream swollen by unusually heavy spring rains. By the time he crossed, the current had washed all the salt from the wagon. The stream reportedly ran brine for several days (Usher, *This Is Itasca*, 6). Post office established Jan. 29, 1874.

SALT CREEK. Logan. The name was recorded in the early 1820s as *Onaquispasippi*, reportedly from Miami-Illinois for "salt water" or "salt river" (Stringer, *History of Logan County*, 12). Post office established July 6, 1826.

SALUDA. Knox. Five miles south of Galesburg. Laid out as Louisville in 1836 by John Garrett. For unknown reasons the name was changed to Saluda in the mid-1850s. Probably a transfer from Saluda, S.C., or Saluda, Ind. The Saluda, reported to be a small native tribe related to the Shawnee, lived along the Saluda (Corn) River in South Carolina in the early eighteenth century (Bright, *Native American Placenames;* Vogel, *Indian Place Names in Illinois*). Post office established May 15, 1844, as Farmers' Hall; changed to Saluda July 12, 1856.

SAMOTH. Massac. Twelve miles north of Metropolis. A reverse spelling (as nearly as possible) of *Thomas*. Named from the Samoth post office, itself named for John Robert Thomas (1846–1914), who was elected to the U.S. House of Representatives in 1879 (May, *History of Massac County,* 174). Post office established April 9, 1880.

SAMSVILLE. Edwards. Eighteen miles northeast of Fairfield. Named for the Sams family, early settlers. Lot Sams arrived in the vicinity about 1815, and Philip H. Sams was an early postmaster (Harper, ed., *History of Edwards County,* 63). Post office established Feb. 1, 1865.

SANDERSVILLE. Christian. Two miles southeast of Stonington. Named for early settler Nicholas Sanders, who established the general store in 1852 that formed the nucleus of the community (Bateman and Selby, eds., *Historical Encyclopedia of Illinois and History of Christian County,* 810).

SANDOVAL [san DO vuhl]. Marion. Village (1859, 1873) five miles north of Centralia. Established by the Illinois Central Railroad in 1855. The source of the name is unknown. According to Ackerman, the village was named "after an old Mexican or Spanish chief" (*Early Illinois Railroads,* 152). Post office established Dec. 22, 1854.

SAND RIDGE. Jackson. Six miles west-southwest of Murphysboro. Named from the low sandy prominence running parallel to the Big Muddy River. First called Dutch Ridge for a colony of German settlers, the name was changed to Sand Ridge at the time of township formation in 1871. Sand Ridge, founded by William Boone about 1807, is claimed to be the first community established in what is now Jackson County (*History of Jackson County,* 22; Mohlenbrock, "A New Geography of Illinois: Jackson County," 33). Post office established April 9, 1872.

SANDUSKY. Alexander. Fourteen miles north-northwest of Cairo. A transfer from Sandusky, Erie County, Ohio, itself named from a Wyandot word that referred to a source of pure water. First recorded by French traders in Ohio as *ot-san-doos-ke* (Stewart, *American Place-Names;* Vogel, *Indian Place Names in Illinois*). Post office established July 21, 1875, as Helena; changed to Sandusky April 25, 1876.

SANDWICH. DeKalb. City (1859, 1872). Named from the Sandwich post office, itself named in 1850 by Dr. A. L. Merriam for Sandwich, N.H., the birthplace of John Wentworth, at the time a U.S. representative from Illinois who was instrumental in securing the post office. The community was first known as Newton and formally laid out as Almon, named for site owner Almon Gage, in 1854. Apparently, the name *Almon* was chosen without Gage's knowledge or consent. When he refused to allow it to be used, the plat was renamed for the post office. The Burlington station was established as Newark and changed to Sandwich in 1856 (Gross, *Past and Present of DeKalb County,* 319; *Portrait and Biographical Album of DeKalb County,* 870). Post office established March 7, 1850.

SANFORDVILLE. Ogle. Former community about four miles south-southwest of Polo. Named for Cyrenes Sanford and his seven sons, Albion, Alhira, Bennett, Harrison, Joel, Vernon, and Warren, who established a sawmill on Buffalo Creek about 1836 (*Bicentennial History of Ogle County,* 241). Post office established March 24, 1854, as Sanfordsville.

SANGAMO. Sangamon. Former community. Named from the Sangamon River or for Sangamon County. Once considered for the seat of Sangamon County, Sangamo prospered through the 1830s and then went into decline; the plat was vacated in 1845. The Sangamo Center school was located about six miles northeast of Springfield (Campbell, *The Sangamon Saga,* 49–50).

SANGAMON [SANG guh muhn]. County. Created Jan. 30, 1821, from parts of Madison and Bond counties. Named from the Sangamon River.

SANGAMON RIVER. The origin of the name is uncertain. It is generally assumed that Sangamon is derived from a Native American language, although no satisfactory source has been found. The name of the river was first recorded by the Jesuit priest Charlevoix in 1721 as Saguimont and subsequently recorded as Sagamond, Sanquemin, Sanguemon, and Sangamo, among others. There has been no dearth of "explanations" of the source and meaning of the name. Among them are that Sangamon was the name of a local Indian leader who lived near the river; that it evolved from St. Gamoin, a name that reportedly appears in early Macon County land records; that it means "good hunting grounds"; and that it means "where there is plenty to eat." According to a recent interpretation, the word *Sangamon* may be related to an Ojibwa word with the general meaning "at the inlet" (Bright, *Native American Placenames*) (Bateman and Selby, eds., *Historical Encyclopedia of Illinois and History of Cass County,* 621; Gannett, *The Origin of Certain Place Names;* Richmond, *Centennial History of Decatur;* Vogel, *Indian Place Names in Illinois*).

SAN JOSE [SAN JOZ]. Logan, Mason. Village (1876) fifteen miles northwest of Lincoln. Founded about 1857 by Alexander W. Morgan, Dr. Silas Parker, Daniel Dillon, and Z. B. Kidder. Named by Morgan for San Jose, Calif., upon his return from the California gold fields (Lynn, *Prelude to Progress,* 250; *San Jose Centennial,* 37). Post office established Oct. 6, 1858.

SANKOTY [SANG kuh ti]. Peoria. East Peoria suburb. Origin unknown. Possibly a transfer from Sankaty Head, the highest point on Nantucket Island, Mass. (Stewart, *American Place-Names*).

SANTA FE. Clinton. Township. Reportedly named for Santa Fe, N.M., where Richard Slade died. Slade was the son of early settler Charles Slade of Carlyle and a veteran of the Mexican War (*Commercial History of Clinton County*, 32).

SARAHVILLE. Williamson. Founded in the 1830s and named by John T. Davis for his daughter, Sarah. Davis was a veteran of the Black Hawk War, an Illinois state representative in the mid-1840s, and the namesake of Davis Prairie. The Davis Prairie Church is about five miles east of Marion (Hubbs, *Pioneer Folks and Places*). Post office established Aug. 2, 1837.

SARATOGA. Grundy. Six miles north of Morris. Named by Joshua and Harriet Collins for their former home, Saratoga, N.Y. (Bateman and Selby, eds., *Historical Encyclopedia of Illinois and History of Grundy County*, 744; Ullrich, *This Is Grundy County*).

SARATOGA. Union. Six miles northeast of Anna. Founded in 1841 by a Dr. Penoyer who sought to capitalize on the local mineral springs by turning the area into a fashionable resort, a spa of the West, much like Saratoga Springs, N.Y., for which it was named (Perrin, ed., *History of Alexander, Union, and Pulaski Counties*, 428). Post office established March 13, 1844, as Western Saratoga.

SARATOGA CENTER. Marshall. Eleven miles west of Henry. Named by early settler George Scholes for Saratoga Springs, N.Y. (*History Marshall County*, 54). Post office established May 30, 1860.

SARGENT. Douglas. Township. Named for Snowden Sargent, a business executive and justice of the peace (Niles, *History of Douglas County*, 75).

SATO [SAY to]. Jackson. Ten miles north-northwest of Murphysboro. Origin unknown. Probably from a family of that name. The only other Sato in the United States is in South Carolina. Formerly known as Gassville (Adams, comp., *Illinois Place Names*). Post office established Jan. 10, 1889.

SAUGANASH. Cook. Chicago neighborhood. Named for a Native American leader known among the Potawatomi as Sauganash (The Englishman) and among Europeans as Billy Caldwell. Caldwell was of mixed ancestry. His father, William Caldwell, was an Irish officer in the British Army, and his mother may have been Mohawk. Caldwell presented himself in many guises; he is best known as Sauganash, representative for the Potawatomi in the 1820s and 1830s. In the 1840s Mark Beaubien kept a tavern near Chicago, the Sauganash House, named in honor of Billy Caldwell. A variant, Saganosh, is the name by which George Davenport, the founder of Davenport, Iowa, was known among the Sauk and Meskwaki. Davenport was born in Lincolnshire, England (Edmunds, *The Potawatomis*, 172; Tweet, *Quad Cities*, 5; Vogel, *Indian Place Names in Illinois*).

SAUGET [SO juht, so ZHAY]. St. Clair. Village (1926) west of East St. Louis. Founded in 1926 as Monsanto, named for the Monsanto Chemical Company, the major local employer. Renamed in 1967 in honor of Leo Sauget, the first mayor of Monsanto, who served from 1926 until 1969 (*News-Democrat*).

SAUK VILLAGE. Cook, Will. Village (1957). Named for the Sauk (Sac) people of the Great Lakes region. From French *saki,* a shortening of the Sauk self-designation /*Asaakiiwaki*/ (People of the Outlet), referring to the Saginaw River in Michigan, generally considered the ancestral home of the Sauk (Bright, *Native American Placenames*).

SAUNEMIN [SAW nuh muhn]. Livingston. Village (1883) twelve miles east of Pontiac. Named by Franklin C. Oliver for Saunemin (Osanamon) "Yellow Paint," a Kickapoo (or Miami) leader of the early nineteenth century. From Potawatomi for "yellow ochre," perhaps borrowed from Miami-Illinois *oonsaalamooni* (bloodroot, yellow paint) or Potawatomi for "yellow ochre." The variants, Salamonia and Salamonie, occur nearby in western Indiana (Baker, *From Needmore to Prosperity;* personal communication from Michael McCafferty; Vogel, *Indian Place Names in Illinois*). Post office established July 30, 1869.

SAVANNA. Carroll. City (1874). Laid out and named by Luther Bowen in 1836. The source of the name is uncertain. Bowen was a Galena surveyor originally from western New York state, and he may have transferred the name from New York, where Savannah is a community near Rochester; or, he may have chosen the name because the landscape reminded him of the literal meaning of savanna: "a treeless, grassy plain." In addition to Savanna in Carroll County, there have been at least four other communities named Savannah in Illinois: in McLean County (now Downs), in Warren County (now Coldbrook), and in Coles and Iroquois counties. The spelling *Savannah* in Iroquois, Coles, and Warren counties may indicate a different origin from Savanna in Carroll County. Savannahs in Iroquois and Coles counties in particular may be transfers from Savannah, Ohio (Bourland, *Savanna Pioneers,* 15; *History of Carroll County;* 225; Thiem, ed., *Carroll County,* 145, 147). Post office established Nov. 2, 1835.

SAVOY. Champaign. Village (1956) two miles south of Champaign. Named for Princess Clotilde of the Alpine Duchy, the House of Savoy, who visited Illinois in 1861 with her husband, Prince Napoleon; the French minister, Baron Mercier; and Mercier's wife, the Countess of Lostant (*see* Lostant) (Ackerman, *Early Illinois Railroads,* 126). Post office established March 30, 1868.

SAYBROOK. McLean. Village (1867, 1872) eight miles west-southwest of Gibson City. Originally called Cheney's Grove. The name was changed about 1865, probably by settlers from Old Saybrook, Middlesex County, Conn., possibly influenced by Saybrook, Ohio. Saybrook, Conn., is the first "manufactured" name to appear in the United States, created about 1635 by blending the name of Lord Say and Sele with that of Lord Brooke (Stewart, *American Place-Names*). Post office established April 9, 1850, as Cheney's Grove; changed to Saybrook Sept. 7, 1865.

SCALES MOUND. Jo Daviess. Village (1877) ten miles northeast of Galena. Formerly called Baltimore by settlers from Baltimore, Md. Laid out in 1853 as Scales by Samuel Scales, who in the 1830s kept a public house on the Chicago and Galena stage line near the large mound now bearing his name (*History of Jo Daviess County,* 556). Post office established Sept. 3, 1843, as Baltimore; changed to Scales Mound April 27, 1854.

SCHAUMBURG [SHAWM berg]. Cook. Village (1956). Founded by German settlers in the 1840s. At the time of township formation in 1850, the name *Schaumburg,* for Schaumburg-Lippe, then a state in northwestern Germany, was chosen over Lutherville and Lutherberg at the insistence of Frederick "Fritz" Nerge. A century later, in the early 1950s, Bob Atcher, a Chicago radio and television personality and future village president, approached Robert Wood, then president of Sears, Roebuck, with the idea of building the world's largest shopping mall in Schaumburg. Wood collaborated with Marshall Field in the construction of Woodfield Mall, which was the largest shopping center under one roof at the time it opened in 1971 (Christian, "An Invitation"; Gould, *Schaumburg*). Post office established March 24, 1848, as Shaumburgh; changed to Schaumburg June 13, 1888; changed to Schaumberg June 20, 1892.

SCHICK. DuPage. Three miles west of Bloomingdale. Established in 1888 by the Illinois Central Railroad as Schick's Crossing, named for Fred Schick, a local grocer and postmaster (Blatchford, *An Honorable Heritage,* 48). Post office established Feb. 25, 1901.

SCHILLER PARK. Cook. Village (1914). Named from its proximity to Schillers Woods, part of the Cook County Forest Preserve, itself named for the Schiller Liedertafel German singing society that often sang in the woods and took its name from Johann Christoph Friedrich von Schiller (1759–1805), the German playwright and poet (Adams, comp., *Illinois Place Names;* Papajohn, "It's a Workin' Town"). Post office established Feb. 11, 1891, as Kolze, named for postmasters George H. and Robert H. Kolze; changed to Schiller Park Nov. 10, 1922.

SCHNELL. Richland. Eleven miles southwest of Olney. Named for postmaster John C. Schnell (Adams, comp., *Illinois Place Names*). Post office established July 16, 1898.

SCHOHARIE PRAIRIE. Williamson. According to a local story, a band of vigilantes was whipping a hog thief on the prairie, and members of the group would call out, "Score him, Harry!" The site became known as "Scoreharry" and then "Schoharrie," perhaps, as Hubbs suggests, "When one of the fine scholars who came to the county to teach had his way with the spelling" (*Pioneer Folks and Places,* 209). Most likely, however, the name is a transfer from eastern New York, where Schoharie is the name of a city, a county, and several natural features (Vogel, *Indian Place Names in Illinois*).

SCHRAM CITY. Montgomery. Village (1907) northeast of Hillsboro. Founded about 1904 by Henry Schram, owner of the Schram Automatic Sealer Company, manufacturers of self-sealing glass jars. The company was bought by the Ball brothers in 1925 (Bateman and Selby, eds., *Historical Encyclopedia of Illinois and History of Montgomery County*, 862).

SCHUYLER [SKEYE ler]. County. Created Jan. 13, 1825, from parts of Fulton and Pike counties. Named for Philip John Schuyler (1733–1804), a Revolutionary War officer and one of George Washington's immediate subordinates. Schuyler was also a member of the Continental Congress and a U.S. senator from New York. The county seat was established at Beardstown and moved to Rushville in 1826.

SCHWARMS. Fayette. Former community. Probably named for John Schwarm, an early settler who arrived about 1847. The Schwarms school was located about five miles east of Vandalia (Hanabarger, "Fayette County Place Names," 52).

SCHWER [SHWIHR]. Iroquois. Eight miles south-southwest of Watseka. Named about 1887, either for John Schwer, blacksmith and shoemaker; Louis Schwer, postmaster; or both. Formerly known as Queen City (Adams, comp., *Illinois Place Names*; Dowling, *History of Iroquois County*, 26).

SCIOTA [seye O duh]. McDonough. Village (1877) seven miles northwest of Macomb. Laid out in 1867 as Clarkesville by William B. Clarke. The village and the post office took the name of the township in 1869. The name *Sciota* is probably from Wyandot meaning "deer" and as a place name was given first in New York and then in Pennsylvania. The Illinois name may be a transfer from one of these states but most likely is from Scioto, Ohio, a variant (Bright, *Native American Placenames*; Chenoweth and Semonis, comps., *The History of McDonough County*, 121; Frazer and Frazer, "Place Name Patterns," 31). Post office established Feb. 7, 1868, as Amicus; changed to Sciota Sept. 20, 1869.

SCIOTO MILLS [seye O duh MILZ]. Stephenson. Three miles north of Freeport. Founded by Levi Wilcoxon and his brothers Rezin and Thompson, who emigrated from Scioto County, Ohio. The name was originally Scioto. The word *Mills* was added to avoid confusion with Sciota in McDonough County (*History of Stephenson County*, 88). Post office established June 22, 1888, as Cockrell; changed to Scioto Mills April 28, 1902.

SCOTLAND. McDonough. Township. Named for the Scottish immigrants living in the area when the township was formed about 1867 (Shadwick, *History of McDonough County*, 229).

SCOTT. Champaign. Township. Probably named for General Winfield Scott (*see* Winfield) (*History of Champaign County*, 164).

SCOTT. County. Created Feb. 16, 1839, from Morgan County. Several Scott families were early settlers, and a number of Scotts were active in the affairs of the county in its early years. Scott Riggs, a member of one of the first Illinois General Assemblies, has been proposed as the source of the name, as have early settlers James Scott and John Scott. In all likelihood, however, the name is a transfer by settlers from Scott County, Ky., itself named for Gen. Charles Scott, an officer in the Revolutionary War and governor of Kentucky from 1808 to 1812 (*Atlas, History, and Plat-Book of Scott County,* 17; Rennick, *Kentucky Place Names*).

SCOTTLAND. Edgar. Fourteen miles northeast of Paris. Founded in 1872. Named for William Scott, who donated half of the town site to the Indianapolis, Decatur and Springfield Railroad, which then sold the building lots (*History of Edgar County,* 517). Post office established Feb. 13, 1853 as Bonwell; changed to Scott Land Dec. 3, 1872.

SCOTTSBURG. McDonough. Four miles west of Bushnell. Established as Scottsburg Station on the Toledo, Peoria and Western Railroad in 1870. Named for site owner John Scott (Frazer and Frazer, "Place Name Patterns," 33; *History of McDonough County,* 1043). Post office established Oct. 23, 1872.

SCOTTSVILLE. Wayne. Formerly known as Wabash, a stop on the stage line between Fairfield and Albion where horses were changed. Laid out by Robert Monroe and named for a local Scott family. Four Scott brothers were early settlers (Allison, *History of Leech Township,* 91).

SEATON. Mercer. Village (1907) seven miles south-southwest of Aledo. Laid out about 1883 by site owner George Seaton with construction of the Iowa Central Railroad (Bassett and Goodspeed, *Past and Present of Mercer County,* 496). Post office established April 23, 1883, as Sully; changed to Seaton June 19, 1883.

SEATONVILLE. Bureau. Seven miles east of Princeton. Founded as Seaton by site owners James H. and Isom Seaton (Leonard, ed., *Big Bureau,* 70). Post office established July 14, 1886, as Mac; changed to Seatonville June 3, 1889.

SEBASTOPOL. Madison, Clinton. Four miles east-southeast of Highland. Settled in the 1850s, largely by emigrants from the French cantons of Switzerland. Sebastapol (Sevastopol) in Ukraine was in the news at the time, under siege by British and Allied forces during the Crimean War. The local story is that the name came about when Timothy Grauz, owner of the town plat, asked Norris Ramsey to provide a name, warning that if he did not, "Those Frenchmen around here will invent some long, outlandish, and jaw-breaking name, Sebastopol, for instance." The next day, Ramsey came into Grauz's store and asked, "How is Sebastopol today?" (*History of Madison County,* 435). Post office established April 2, 1884.

SECOR [SEE kor]. Woodford. Six miles west of El Paso. Laid out by site owner Isaac Underhill and named for Charles A. Secor, a partner in the firm of Cruger, Secor, and Company, which held the contract for construction of the eastern extension of the Peoria and Oquawka Railroad, and Zeno Secor, a director of the P&O (*El Paso Story,* 236). Post office established Sept. 3, 1857.

SEFTON. Fayette. Ten miles northeast of Vandalia. Named for Hugh and John Sefton, early settlers (Bateman and Selby, eds., *Historical Encyclopedia of Illinois and History of Fayette County,* 657).

SELLERS. Hardin. Former community. Named about 1856 for George Eschol Sellers, an engineer from Pennsylvania who built a wharf on the Ohio River near Sturgeon Island (Adams, comp., *Illinois Place Names; Hardin County*, 22). Post office established April 6, 1864, as Sellers Landing.

SENACHWINE [SNACH weyen]. Putnam. Township. Named for Senachwine, reported to mean "swift water," an early-nineteenth-century Potawatomi leader whose main village was near Chillicothe (Vogel, *Indian Place Names in Illinois*). Post office established May 21, 1857, as Snatchwine.

SENECA. Grundy, LaSalle. Village (1865, 1874) ten miles west-southwest of Morris. Laid out about 1848 as Crotty or Crotty Town by Jeremiah Crotty, a contractor for the Illinois and Michigan Canal. About 1853 the Rock Island Railroad established a station as Seneca, which became the popular name of the village as well. The name of the post office was changed from Crotty in 1865, but the village name was not changed officially until the 1950s (*Illinois Guide*). Post office established Feb. 18, 1854, as Crotty; changed to Seneca Aug. 10, 1865.

SENECA. McHenry. Township. Probably a transfer by settlers from Seneca, N.Y.; possibly a transfer from Seneca County in north central Ohio, itself named for Seneca, N.Y. Both areas contributed a significant number of early settlers to McHenry County. From the name of the Seneca Tribe (Nye, ed., *McHenry County Illinois*, 860; Vogel, *Indian Place Names in Illinois*).

SEPO. Fulton. Four miles northwest of Havana. Founded as Manning in 1898 by site owner Edward Mann and named by his daughter Laura. Renamed for the Sepo post office. The name *Sepo* is a form of *sipi* (*sippi*), Algonquian for "river" (Bright, *Native American Placenames*; Irwin, *A to Z Fulton County*). Post office established March 3, 1880.

SEQUOIT CREEK. Lake. Stream. Probably a form of Sauquoit and a transfer from New York, where Sauquoit is the name of a community, a stream, and a valley in Oneida County. Probably Iroquoian, but the specific language from which it was taken and its meaning are unknown. Proposed interpretations include "winding" and "smooth pebbles in the bed of a stream" (Halsey, ed., *A History of Lake County*, 393; Vogel, *Indian Place Names in Illinois*).

SERENA [suh REE nuh]. LaSalle. Eleven miles north-northeast of Ottawa. Possibly named for Serena Beresford, whose father, an Illinois militiaman, was killed in action during the Black Hawk War (Rasmusen, *LaSalle County Lore*, 51). Post office established May 15, 1848.

SESSER. Franklin. City (1906) nine miles northwest of Benton. Founded about 1904 and named for John C. Sesser, a surveyor for the Burlington Railroad. According to the traditional account, Sesser promised to donate a city lot to the parents of the first male child born in the community, provided they named him Sesser. The first boy, born in 1907, the son of John Q. and Emaline Bates, was named Sesser Bates (*Franklin County,* 21; *Illinois Guide*). Post office established March 21, 1906.

SEVEN HICKORY. Coles. Township. Named from the prominent grove of hickory trees in the southwestern part of the township, which served as a landmark for travelers. Reportedly, the grove consisted of seven unusually large trees that stood alone (Perrin, Graham, and Blair, *History of Coles County,* 463).

SEWARD. Kendall. Township. Named for William H. Seward, former governor of New York, a strong opponent of slavery, and, at the time the township was formed, a newly elected U.S. senator. Seward was later secretary of state in Lincoln's administration and probably best known for his purchase of Alaska from Russia in 1867, an act derided at the time as "Seward's Folly." Seward and Seward Township in Winnebago County are probably named for the same William H. Seward (Farren, ed., *A Bicentennial History,* 83).

SEYMOUR. Champaign. Six miles south of Mahomet. Reportedly named from the Seymour and Company general store (*History of Champaign Couunty,* 164). Post office established March 8, 1872.

SHABBONA [SHAB uh nuh, SHAB nuh]. DeKalb. Village (1875) thirteen miles south-southwest of DeKalb. Founded about 1872 and named for Shabbona (Burly Shoulders), a Potawatomi leader of the late eighteenth and early nineteenth centuries. Shabbona fought against the United States at the Battle of Tippecanoe and beside Tecumseh at the Battle of the Thames in Ontario during the War of 1812. He then became loyal to the United States, convincing the Potawatomi to remain neutral during the Black Hawk War and warning settlers of impending attacks. For his service, Shabbona was given two sections of land near present Shabbona Grove by the Treaty of Prairie du Chien in 1829. His name has also been recorded as Shaubena, Shau-bon-ni-agh, Chamblee, Cha-ba-nee, Shabbony, Shaubena, Shau-bee-nay, and Shaub-e-nee, among others. (Edmunds, *The Potawatomis,* 172; Vogel, *Indian Place Names in Illinois*). Post office established June 6, 1860, as Malma; changed to Cornton Jan. 19, 1872; changed to Shabbona Nov. 29, 1872.

SHANNON. Carroll. Village (1869, 1876) eleven miles southwest of Freeport. Founded in 1860 by land developer and promoter William Shannon (Thiem, ed., *Carroll County,* 106). Post office established Dec. 13, 1853, as Spring Valley; changed to Shannon Dec. 5, 1861.

SHARPSBURG. Christian. Five miles north-northwest of Taylorville. Founded about 1870 by brothers H. H. and G. R. Sharp; the latter was the first postmaster (Goudy, *History of Christian County,* 135). Post office established Sept. 19, 1870, as Sharpsburgh; changed to Sharpsburg Aug. 31, 1893.

SHASTA. Alexander. Former community about three miles west of the Horseshoe Lake Conservation Area. The name is probably a transfer from a geographic feature in northern California, perhaps Mt. Shasta, itself named for a California Indian tribe.

SHATTUCK'S GROVE. Boone. Former community. Named for first settlers Alfred and Harlyn Shattuck, who emigrated from Ohio about 1835. The Shattuck's Grove Cemetery is about six miles southeast of Belvidere (*Past and Present of Boone County*, 317).

SHAWNEETOWN. Gallatin. City (1814, 1874) nineteen miles east of Harrisburg. Also Shawnee Township. Named from the Shawnee Tribe, the "southern people," members of which migrated to the area from southern Ohio around 1745. Their stay in Illinois was brief, lasting fewer than twenty years. Their principle village was near the site of Old Shawneetown, established by the U.S. government in 1810 to administer the sale of public land in that part of what was then Indiana Territory. Present Shawneetown is several miles northwest of Old Shawneetown, which was largely abandoned by the 1930s because of repeated flooding from the Ohio River. Shawneetown was the seat of Gallatin County from its formation in 1812 until 1827, when it was moved to Equality. The seat was moved back to Shawneetown in 1848 (Bright, *Native American Placenames*; Miller, "Building Towns," 31; Vogel, *Indian Place Names in Illinois*). Post office established April 1, 1811.

SHEFFIELD. Bureau. Village (1861, 1882) twelve miles northeast of Kewanee. Established by the Chicago, Rock Island and Pacific Railroad about 1850 and named for Joseph E. Sheffield from New Haven, Conn., a stockholder in the CRI&P and a site owner (Bradsby, ed., *History of Bureau County*, 434). Post office established Aug. 12, 1853.

SHELBY. County. Created Jan. 23, 1827, from Fayette County. The county may have been named directly for Isaac Shelby but was probably named for Shelby County, Ky., itself named for Isaac Shelby. Shelby (1750–1826), a highly respected military leader and public official, served in the Revolutionary War and the War of 1812, notably with William Henry Harrison at the Battle of the Thames in Ontario in 1813. He was twice governor of Kentucky.

SHELBYVILLE. Shelby. City (1839, 1889). Established as the seat of Shelby County in 1827 and located by the appointed commissioners, Levi Casey, John Whitley, and William F. Weager. Named from Shelby County, strongly influenced by Shelbyville, the seat of Shelby County, Ky. (*Atlas of Shelby County*, 5). Post office established Dec. 4, 1827.

SHELDON. Iroquois. Village (1901) eight miles east of Watseka. Established about 1859 as a switch on the Toledo, Peoria and Warsaw Railroad. Named for a director of the TP&W (Hansen, ed., *Illinois*, 648). Post office established Oct. 30, 1860.

SHELDONS GROVE. Schuyler. Thirteen miles northeast of Beardstown. Named for Daniel Sheldon, formerly of Rhode Island, the first postmaster and the first teacher. Previously known as Butlersville (Bateman and Selby, eds., *Historical Encyclopedia of Illinois and History of Schuyler County*, 702). Post office established Aug. 12, 1853.

SHERBURNVILLE. Kankakee. Seven miles east-northeast of Momence. Laid out about 1861. The origin of the name is unknown. The community may have been named for early settlers named Sherburn or by settlers from Sherburne, Vt., or Sherburne, N.Y. The area was previously known as Six-Mile Grove, reportedly because travelers could ride for six miles south to the Kankakee River without leaving the shade of the forest (Houde and Klasey, *Of the People*, 31). Post office established Oct. 30, 1850.

SHERIDAN. LaSalle. Village (1903) eight miles south-southwest of Sandwich. Named for Gen. Philip H. Sheridan (1831–88), the Civil War cavalry officer for whom Fort Sheridan in Lake County was also named. Post office established Feb. 9, 1866.

SHERMAN. Mason. Township. The original legislation creating the township in 1866 called for the name *Jackson,* for Andrew Jackson. For unknown reasons the name was changed to honor Civil War general William Tecumseh Sherman (Lynn, *Prelude to Progress*, 411).

SHERRARD. Mercer. Village (1896) eleven miles south of Moline. Founded in 1894 by David Sherrard, superintendent of mining operations for the Coal Valley Mining Company (Bassett and Goodspeed, *Past and Present of Mercer County*, 475). Post office established Oct. 6, 1894.

SHETLERVILLE. Hardin. Twenty-six miles northeast of Metropolis. Founded about 1866 by Joseph Shetler, known as "Potato Joe" because the majority of his farm crop consisted of potatoes (*Hardin County*, 23). Post office established July 11, 1867, as Parkinson's Landing; changed to Parkinson May 14, 1883; changed to Shetlerville Nov. 5, 1883.

SHICK SHACK HILL. Cass. Summit north of Newmansville, near where Fancher Creek joins Middle Creek. Shick Shack (Nine) was a Potawatomi leader of the 1820s and 1830s whose main village was on the Sangamon River near New Salem. For many years the summit was called Shickshack's Knob, and early reports describe it as "a high, dome-shaped hill" (Bateman and Selby, eds., *Historical Encyclopedia of Illinois and History of Cass County*, 829; Vogel, *Indian Place Names in Illinois*).

SHIELDS. Lake. Township. Named for James Shields (1806–79), a general in the Mexican War, a member of the Illinois General Assembly, judge of the Illinois Supreme Court in the 1840s, governor of Oregon, and U.S. senator from Illinois, Minnesota, and Missouri. Upon being notified that the township was named in his honor, Shields visited the area in 1852 (Halsey, ed., *A History of Lake County*, 475; *Past and Present of Lake County*, 302).

SHILOH. St. Clair. Village (1905). Also Shiloh Valley Township. Laid out by Martin Stites and James Atkins in the late 1840s. The name was taken from the Shiloh Methodist Evangelical Church, established at what was then known as Three Springs by William McKendree, later Bishop McKendree, for whom McKendree University in Lebanon is named. The church developed from a camp meeting held at the site in 1807, organized by McKendree and the Rev. Jesse Walker. The name *Shiloh,* mentioned several times in the Bible, is a popular name for churches, more than thirty churches in Illinois are so named (Walton, *Centennial, MeKendree College,* 506–7). Post office established March 20, 1821, as Cherry Grove; changed to Rock Spring July 12, 1827; changed to Shiloh May 15, 1850.

SHILOH HILL. Randolph. Ten miles east of Chester. Laid out in the mid-1850s on land granted by the Illinois legislature for the purpose of establishing a school to be called Shiloh College (Montague, *Directory,* 233). Post office established Jan. 15, 1859.

SHINN. Pike. Eleven miles east-southeast of Hannibal, Mo. Named for Daniel Shinn, who emigrated from Batavia, Ohio, about 1820 (*History of Pike County,* 200). Post office established July 8, 1880.

SHIPMAN. Macoupin. Village (1867, 1885) fourteen miles southwest of Carlinville. Founded about 1852 on the line of the Chicago and Alton Railroad by site owner John H. Shipman (Walker, *A History of Macoupin County,* 405). Post office established Feb. 2, 1853.

SHIPPINGSPORT. LaSalle. Former community near Oglesby. Settled in the early 1830s by Simon, James, and William Crosier from Pennsylvania. Later named for the Shippingsport Wagon Bridge built across the Illinois River by Harvey J. Shippingsport in 1874 (*Oglesby,* 218).

SHIRLEY. McLean. Six miles southeast of Bloomington. Reportedly named by Mrs. Corydon Weed for the heroine in a novel that she was reading (Carpenter and Johnson, *History of Shirley Christian Church,* 8, 11). Post office established March 21, 1857.

SHOBONIER [sho buh NIHR]. Fayette. Six miles south of Vandalia. Laid out for the Illinois Central Railroad about 1855 and named for Shobonier, a Potawatomi leader of the 1830s. The name *Shobonier* is an English rendering of a Potawatomi adaptation of French *chevalier* (horseman, knight). Shobonier was a member of a prominent Potawatomi family that had either adopted the surname *Chevalier* or been given it as an honorary title. In early records he is listed both as François Shobonier and François Chevalier (Vogel, *Indian Place Names in Illinois*). Post office established Sept. 24, 1856.

SHOKOKON. Henderson. Four miles southeast of Burlington, Iowa. Founded about 1836 by Robert McQueen, Harrison Barnes, and Henry Babcock. Probably from Meskwaki (Fox) *shock-o-con* (flint hills), apparently a Native American name for the bluffs on the Iowa side of the Mississippi River near Burlington (*see* Carman) (Bright, *Native American Placenames;* Vogel, *Indian Place Names in Illinois*).

SHOREWOOD. Will. Village (1957). Founded as a residential subdivision by Horace Haff, from Troy, N.Y. In the 1930s the Shorewood Beach Improvement Association was formed to manage the Shorewood subdivision. The name became official at the time of incorporation in 1957 (Buck, "'Hideway' Is Now a Hub").

SHORT. Greene. Former community. Named for postmasters William S. and Lawrence F. Short. The Short Cemetery is eight miles east of White Hall (Adams, comp., *Illinois Place Names*). Post office established May 1, 1896.

SHUMWAY. Effingham. Village (1895) seven miles northwest of Effingham. Founded by the Chicago and Paducah Railroad about 1874 and named for P. B. Shumway, an official of the C&P (Banbury, comp., *The Sesquicentennial of Effingham*, 157; Feldhake, *Effingham County*, 48). Post office established April 16, 1872, as Tolerance; changed to Shumway April 7, 1879.

SIBLEY. Ford. Village (1880) eight miles north of Gibson City. Laid out for Michael L. Sullivant (q.v. Sullivant) in 1877. The following year Sullivant sold several thousand acres to Hiram Sibley, who laid out an addition that he named for himself (*Centennial Salute; Ford County History*, 141). Post office established Oct. 3, 1873, as Burr Oaks (the name of Sibley's estate); changed to Sibley March 8, 1880.

SIDELL [seye DEL]. Vermilion. Village (1889) eleven miles southwest of Georgetown. Laid out by site owner John Sidell, an Illinois state representative in the 1870s and a community benefactor (Stapp and Sullenberger, *Footprints in the Sands*, 34; Williams, *History of Vermilion County*, 317). Post office established Sept. 26, 1876, as Sidell's Grove.

SIDNEY. Champaign. Village (1874) eight miles southeast of Urbana. In 1837 James M. Lyon and Joseph Davis recorded the plat as Sydney, named for Davis's daughter. The county clerk caught the "misspelling" and corrected it accordingly (Bateman and Selby, eds., *Historical Encyclopedia of Illinois and History of Champaign County*, 681). Post office established June 27, 1837.

SIGEL. Shelby. Town (1867) seven miles northeast of Effingham. Established on the line of the Illinois Central Railroad in 1863 by Theodore Hoffman. Named for Franz Sigel, a German career soldier who emigrated to the United States in 1850. He joined the Union Army in 1861 and rose to the rank of general of volunteers (Ackerman, *Early Illinois Railroads*, 129). Post office established April 22, 1863, as Hooker; changed to Sigel June 27, 1871.

SILOAM. Brown. Ten miles southwest of Mount Sterling. Formally established about 1884 and named from Siloam Springs, themselves named in the late 1860s by the Rev. Reuben K. McCoy, who claimed that the springs suggested to him the miracle of Jesus healing the blind man at the pool of Siloam (John 9:11) (*History of Brown County,* 221, 224). Post office established Dec. 15, 1882.

SILVIS. Rock Island. City (1906). East Moline suburb. Named for the Silvis family, especially R. S. Silvis, who established the Silvis coal mines around 1900. Silvis sold a portion of his farm to the Rock Island Railroad for the town site (*Illinois Guide*). Post office established March 17, 1906.

SIMPSON. Johnson. Village (1893) twenty-two miles north of Metropolis. Established about 1888 for the St. Louis, Alton, and Terre Haute Railroad on the farm of J. M. Simpson. Simpson was a descendant of William Simpson, the first permanent settler in the area (Chapman, *A History of Johnson County,* 281, 291; Mohlenbrock, "A New Geography of Illinois: Johnson County," 42). Post office established March 1, 1871, as Cross Roads; changed to Simpson April 6, 1888.

SIMS (Simms). Wayne. Village (1909) nine miles west of Fairfield. Laid out about 1882 on land belonging to John Simms. Formerly called Arrington (*History of Wayne and Clay Counties,* 263). Post office established Sept. 26, 1882.

SINCLAIR. Morgan. Eight miles northeast of Jacksonville. Founded about 1857 by Samuel Sinclair (*History of Morgan County,* 436). Post office established April 21, 1858.

SINNISSIPPI. Whiteside. Park. From Miami-Illinois *assinissippi* (rock river).

SINSINAWA RIVER. Jo Daviess. Several incompatible interpretations have been offered, including "rattlesnake" for the nearby Indian mound in the form of a snake and "home of the eagle." The name is probably from Ojibwa meaning "rocks in the middle" (*History of Jo Daviess County,* 226; Stewart, *American Place-Names;* Vogel, *Indian Place Names in Illinois*).

SISTER CREEK, Big and Little. Fulton. In 1833 Isaac Clark built a sawmill at the junction of what he called the Sister Creeks, named for his twin daughters. The larger became known as Big Sister Creek and the smaller as Little Sister Creek (Irwin, *A to Z Fulton County*).

SIX MILE. Township. Franklin. Named from Six Mile Prairie, reportedly six miles long (Aiken, *Franklin County History,* 16).

SIX MILE CREEK. Pike. Stream. Reportedly so called because it was approximately six miles east of Atlas (Massie, *Past and Present of Pike County,* 49).

SKILLET FORK. Wayne. Stream. According to a local story, the name stems from an incident in 1824 when a man named Dewey, with all his worldly goods, was coming up the creek in a small boat when his skillet fell overboard and was swept away (*History of Wayne and Clay Counties,* 262).

SKOKIE. Cook. Village (1888). Founded as Niles Centre, taking its name from Niles Township. The spelling was changed to Niles Center in the early 1900s, reportedly by a telephone directory publisher who wanted to Americanize the name. Confusion between Niles Center and neighboring Niles led to a naming contest in which there was no clear winner. An appointed committee then recommended Skokie, named from the Skokie River. The name *Skokie* is from Potawatomi "great swamp," recorded as Chewab Skokie, apparently a reference to the wetlands that were the source of the north branch of the Chicago River (Kirby, "Diversity"; Reichelt, *History of Deerfield,* 8; Whittingham, *Skokie,* 16; Vogel, *Indian Place Names in Illinois*). Post office established Feb. 10, 1863, as Niles Center; changed to Skokie in 1931.

SLABTOWN. Slabtown is an informal, self-deprecatory name for a community in which houses were constructed from slabs, the rough, irregular first cuts of logs, rather than boards. There have been a number of Slabtowns in Illinois. Slabtown in Adams County is now Spring Valley; Slab Town in Woodford County is now Congerville; and Slab City in Carroll County is now part of Mount Carroll. Slabtown, a former community northeast of Monticello, was founded about 1850 at the site of John Mosgrove's Slabtown Mill, itself named for the Slabtown Mill operated by his uncle in Mosgrove, Pa. (Adams, comp., *Illinois Place Names;* West, *A Heritage Reborn*).

SLAPOUT. Hamilton. Former community eleven miles northeast of McLeansboro, two miles past Blairsville. Local folklore claims that the name developed from an expression used by the local storekeeper, who, when short of stock, would say, "I'm slap out of that." This same naming story is told of Slapouts in other states. The community was deserted by 1912 (*Hamilton County,* 40; Sneed, *Ghost Towns of Southern Illinois,* 58).

SLEEPY HOLLOW. Kane. Village (1958) northwest of Elgin. Named from the Sleepy Hollow Farm owned by J. H. McNabb, chair of the Bell and Howell board. The farm was probably named from a Washington Irving story, "The Legend of Sleepy Hollow." Sleepy Hollow Farm was sold to Floyd T. Falese, who subdivided its fields and marketed the lots as Sleepy Hollow Manor in the mid-1950s (DuPre, Braden, and Bullinger, *Dundee Township,* 167).

SLOCUM CORNERS. Lake. Five miles northeast of Lindenhurst. Named either for B. W. Slocum, an early settler who arrived in the area about 1836, or for Thomas L. Slocum, the first postmaster at Cornelia (now Wauconda) in 1843 (Dretske, *What's in a Name?;* Halsey, ed., *A History of Lake County,* 39).

SMACKOUT. Pope. Reportedly, Smackout was the nickname of Mealer and Mealer's general store. "I am smack out of that!" Meredith Mealer would say when he ran out of stock (Sneed, *Ghost Towns of Southern Illinois,* 155).

SMITHBORO. Bond. Village (1889) three miles east of Greenville. Founded in 1870 as Henderson Station on the line of the Vandalia Railroad by site owner and first postmaster Henry Hedrick Smith (Wilson, *Tales, Trails and Breadcrumbs,* 287). Post office established July 28, 1871, as Smithborough; changed to Smithboro July 6, 1893.

SMITHDALE. Livingston. Four miles southeast of Streator. Founded in 1879 as a station on the western extension of the Chicago and Alton Railroad and named from the Smithdale post office, itself named for John Smith, an early settler and postmaster (Bateman and Selby, eds., *Historical Encyclopedia of Illinois and History of Livingston County*, 793; *History of Livingston County* [1878], 539). Post office established April 29, 1870.

SMITHFIELD. Fulton. Village (1889) nine miles northwest of Lewistown. Laid out in 1868 by James N. Smith (Irwin, *A to Z Fulton County*). Post office established Sept. 15, 1868.

SMITHTON. St. Clair. Village (1878) six miles south of Belleville. Founded in 1854 by Benjamin Smith. Smithton absorbed the adjacent community of Georgetown, platted in 1853 by George Fischer and George Storger (*Tapestry of Time*, 153). Post office established Dec. 28, 1839.

SMITHVILLE. Peoria. Eight miles southwest of Peoria. Founded by Thomas P. Smith, county commissioner and postmaster (Bateman and Selby, eds., *Historical Encyclopedia of Illinois and History of Peoria County*, 745). Post office established Jan. 21, 1847.

SNEAK OUT. Franklin. Former community. Supposedly named for the otherwise respectable citizens who would sneak out of their houses, get drunk, and sneak back home. According to Sneed (*Ghost Towns of Southern Illinois*, 30), Sneak Out had one jail in the 1870s as well as one sawmill, two stores, and six saloons. Now part of Parrish.

SNICARTE. Mason. Thirteen miles east-northeast of Beardstown. Named from Snicarte Island and Snicarte Slough, themselves named from *chenail écarté*, from Canadian French, literally "lonely channel" (*see* Sny). Post office established Nov. 13, 1861.

SNIDER. Vermilion. Five miles northwest of Danville. Named for postmaster George B. Snider (Adams, comp., *Illinois Place Names*). Post office established July 24, 1886.

SNOWFLAKE. Franklin. Former community in Northern Township. Named by postmaster Joseph Wesley Kern, who reportedly took the name from a sack of Snowflake Flour (Goss, *A History of Northern Township*, 41). Post office established June 10, 1886.

SNY. A sny is primarily a side channel running parallel to the main course of a river, which creates an island of what would otherwise be a point; secondarily, it is a narrow waterway that connects two larger bodies of water, a "gut." The area along the Mississippi bottom in Pike and Calhoun counties is honeycombed with sloughs, channels, and cutoffs with such names as The Sny and Old Sny, all apparently from the earlier *snycartee*, an adaptation of Canadian French *chenail écarté* (lonely channel). Melish's map of 1819 labels the area in Calhoun County across the Mississippi from Clarksville, Mo., "Snicarke [*sic*] Chenal Ecarté" (Avis, *A Dictionary of Canadianisms*).

SOLDIER CREEK. Kankakee. Stream. Empties into the Kankakee River at Kanka-kee. Named for Sham-a-gaw or She-mor-gar, a Potawatomi leader of the 1820s and 1830s known as Soldier because of his love of military display, especially his fondness for military dress (Houde and Klasey, *Of the People*, 28; Vogel, *Indian Place Names in Illinois*).

SOLLITT. Kankakee. Thirteen miles south of Park Forest. Established in the late 1880s on the line of the Chicago and Eastern Illinois Railroad on land owned by James and John Sollitt (Johnson, comp., "Kankakee County Communities"). Post office established March 31, 1884.

SOLOMON. Dewitt. Nine miles northeast of Clinton. Named for postmaster Solomon F. Merrifield (Adams, comp., *Illinois Place Names*). Post office established July 8, 1884.

SOLON MILLS [SOL uhn MILZ]. McHenry. Four miles northwest of Pistakee Highlands. Laid out in 1843 by Henry "Solon" White, reportedly so named for his business acumen (*McHenry County*, 864). Post office established Oct. 25, 1843.

SOMER. Champaign. Township. Named for the Somers family from Mount Airy, N.Y. Early settlers in the 1840s included Wrightman Somers and Dr. Winston Somers (Bateman and Selby, eds., *Historical Encyclopedia of Illinois and History of Champaign County*, 1029).

SOMERSET. Jackson. Township. Named for Somerset County, Pa., the former home of a number of early settlers (*History of Jackson County*, 107).

SOMERSET. Saline. Six miles south-southeast of Harrisburg. Founded about 1815 and probably named by Stephen Stilley, a Baptist minister born in Somerset County, Md. Stilley founded a number of churches in Illinois, Missouri, and Kentucky in the early nineteenth century (*History of Saline County*, 163, 175). Post office established Nov. 19, 1851.

SOMONAUK [SAH muh nahk]. DeKalb, LaSalle. Village (1865, 1872) three miles west of Sandwich. Laid out about 1849 by site owner Alvarus Gage. Named from Somonauk Creek. The 1828 Treaty of Prairie du Chien granted to Awn-kote, a Potawatomi leader, four sections of land at Saw-meh-naug. The name may be an adaptation of Potawatomi *as-sim-in-eh-kon* (paw paw grove) (*see* Paw Paw) (Anderson, Marshall, and Sherman, eds., *The Beelman Story*, 7; Stewart, *American Place-Names*). Post office established March 29, 1836.

SONGER [SAWNG er]. Clay. Township. Named for the Songer family, early settlers. Samuel Songer arrived in 1828 and Giles Songer in 1830 (*History of Wayne and Clay Counties*, 439), Post office established June 24, 1886.

SONORA. Hancock. Township. Named for Sonora Johnson, the wife of John Johnson, one of the crew that surveyed the township about 1850 (*History of Hancock County,* 541, 544). Post office established March 17, 1860.

SOPERVILLE. Knox. Five miles northwest of Galesburg. Named by and for George Soper, a local justice of the peace (Hallberg, "Soperville," 51). Post office established March 3, 1893.

SORENTO [suh REN to]. Bond. Village (1885) eleven miles northwest of Greenville. Laid out by site owner August Scharf in 1882 and named for Sorrento, Lake County, Fla., which Scharf had recently visited (Bateman and Selby, eds., *Historical Encyclopedia of Illinois and History of Bond County,* 648). Post office established Dec. 7, 1882.

SOUTH BELOIT [buh LOYT]. Winnebago. City (1917). Named for its location south of Beloit, Wis., itself founded in the mid-1830s by Caleb Blodgett as New Albany, named for Albany, Vt. According to a first-hand account, a committee to choose a new name was appointed, and "we proposed several [names] and finally agreed to place the alphabet in a hat and see if we could not get a combination of letters that would give us a name. . . . While proposing this, Mr. Johnson undertook to sound a French word for handsome ground and in trying he spoke 'Bolotte,' and I said after him 'Beloit,' like Detroit in sound and pretty and original I think. All sounded it and liked it and . . . it was unanimously adopted" (Fisher, "Pioneer Recollections," 274, 279).

SOUTH ELGIN. Kane. Village (1897). Clintonville was established on the east side of the Fox River about 1836 by Dr. Nathan Collins and named for DeWitt Clinton, governor of New York. A second community, Clinton, named for either DeWitt Clinton or for James Clinton, an early settler, was founded on the west side of the river opposite Clintonville by Dr. Joseph Tefft and Benjamin W. Raymond on the projected line of the Galena and Chicago Union Railroad. The post office was established as Clintonville in 1851 and changed to South Elgin in 1876. The community followed suit in 1907 (Alft, *South Elgin,* 3–5, 13; Stennett, *A History of the Origin,* 126).

SOUTH FORK. Christian. Township. Named from the south fork of the Sangamon River (Bateman and Selby, eds., *Historical Encyclopedia of Illinois and History of Christian County,* 805).

SOUTH GROVE. DeKalb. Township. Originally known as Driscoll's Grove for first settler William Driscoll and later called Vernon, probably named by settlers from Vernon, Oneida County, N.Y. The name was changed at the time of township formation in 1850 for the stand of timber known as South Grove, the first copse south of the Kishwaukee River (Boies, *History of DeKalb County,* 467, 469; Gross, *Past and Present of DeKalb County,* 126). Post office established May 23, 1840 as Killbucks; changed to South Grove Feb. 23, 1841.

SOUTH HOLLAND. Cook. City (1894). First called Low Prairie and later known as the Dutch Settlement. Formally established in 1870 and named for the province of Zuid Holland (South Holland) in the Netherlands, the home of a number of early settlers (Cook, *South Holland, Illinois,* 61). Post office established March 22, 1870.

SOUTH WHEATLAND. Macon. Township. Named at the suggestion of Robert Carpenter for Wheatland, the Pennsylvania home of James Buchanan, a candidate for president when the county was organized into townships (Nelson, *City of Decatur,* 372; Richmond, *Centennial History of Decatur,* 95).

SPANKEY. Jersey. Twelve miles west-northwest of Jerseyville. According to a local story, two families, the Clendenins and the Clarks, were contending for the right to name the post office. Members of each were arguing over the name at a local tavern when one—which one is unclear—picked up the other, turned him over his knee, and swatted him. At that, a bystander called out, "I know what we'll call this place. We'll call it Spankey." This is the only Spankey in the United States (Postlewait, ed., *History of Jersey County,* 134). Post office established Aug. 24, 1891.

SPARKS HILL. Hardin. Eighteen miles southeast of Harrisburg. Named for postmaster James M. Sparks (Adams, comp., *Illinois Place Names*). Post office established Oct. 22, 1860.

SPARLAND. Marshall. Village (1867, 1904) eight miles north of Chillicothe. Founded in 1855 by George Sparr, who purchased land in the area in the mid-1840s (Ford, *History of Putnam and Marshall Counties,* 120). Post office established Jan. 24, 1857.

SPARTA. Randolph. City (1847, 1873). Laid out about 1829 by John Armour, a miller, as Columbus, the name suggested by postmaster Robert G. Shannon. To avoid duplication of post offices, the name was changed to Sparta at the suggestion of James Morrow in 1839. The reason for the name choice is unknown (*Combined History of Randolph, Monroe, and Perry Counties,* 386; personal communication with Carol Pirtle; Pirtle, *Where Illinois Began*). Post office established Dec. 13, 1827, as Shannon's Store; changed to Sparta Feb. 7, 1940.

SPAULDING. Cook. Southeast of Elgin. Named for Shepard Spaulding, an early settler from Steuben County, N.Y., who arrived in the area about 1843. The community developed around a railroad siding established on the Spaulding farm by the Chicago and Pacific Railroad about 1873 (www.elginhistory.com).

SPECIE GROVE. Kendall. Woods southeast of Yorkville. Named for Peter Specie, a French-Indian settler, businessman, and real estate promoter. A second Specie Grove (perhaps an extension of the first) was reported in DeKalb County and named for Peter "Specie" Lamsett, so called because he refused to accept the paper money of the day. The Specie post office operated in Kendall County from July 15, 1857, until April 7, 1868 (Bateman and Selby, eds., *Historical Encyclopedia of Illinois and History of Grundy County,* 699; Farren, ed., *A Bicentennial History,* 101).

SPEER. Stark. Ten miles northwest of Chillicothe. Named from the Chicago and North Western station, built on the John Speers farm in 1901 (*Township Histories,* 124). Post office established Jan. 23, 1902.

SPENCER. Will. Southeast of New Lenox. Laid out in 1856 with construction of the railroad for site owners Frank Goodspeed and Albert Mudge. Goodspeed was mayor of Joliet in the early 1860s. The particular Spencer or Spencer family for whom the community was named is unknown (Maue, *History of Will County,* 315). Post office established Sept. 5, 1857.

SPILLERTOWN. Williamson. Village (1900) one mile northeast of Marion. Named for the Spiller brothers, Elijah, Benjamin, Warrenton, and William, who emigrated from Tennessee about 1816 (Hale, comp. and ed., *Williamson County,* 119, 142). Post office established March 5, 1898.

SPOON RIVER. Empties into the Illinois River at Havana. The source of the name has generated a number of "explanations," most of which are figments of their authors' imaginations. One writer claims that the name comes from an incident in the early days of settlement when a group of fishermen, while eating lunch on their boat, lost their spoons overboard. Another says the name was given by a Dr. Davison, a local hermit, for a wetland near the river that was shaped like a spoon. Still another claims the river was so named because its course took the shape of a spoon. Rather, Spoon River is a translation of the Miami-Illinois name for the stream, which was recorded as A-ma-quon-sip-pi and glossed as "Mussel Shell River." A more accurate gloss is "Pumpkin River" or "Squash River." Apparently, *a-ma-quon* came to mean "spoon" among Native American groups such as Ojibwa, where *emikwaan* means "ladle." It was this form that early settlers translated. It is quite possible that the meaning ranged over both "squash" and "spoon," because Native Americans often used hollowed-out gourds as ladles. Maquon (q.v.) is a variant. About 1821 the ethnologist Henry Rowe Schoolcraft recorded the name as "Amequon, or Spoon River," and the Melish map of 1819 labels the stream "Micouenne or Spoon River." The Spoon River post office was in operation from Feb. 20, 1838, until April 28, 1847, when it was changed to Otto (Bright, *Native American Placenames;* Irwin, *A to Z Fulton County;* Muelder, "The Naming of Spoon River"; personal communication with Michael McCafferty; Vogel, *Indian Place Names in Illinois*).

SPRING BAY. Woodford. Village (1849, 1938) seven miles northeast of Peoria. Laid out about 1836, taking its name from the small bay on the east bank of the Illinois River north of Peoria and springs that discharge into the river at that point (Perrin and Hill, *Past and Present,* 309). Post office established April 20, 1848.

SPRINGERTON. White. Village (1890) twelve miles northwest of Carmi. Laid out in 1857 as Springerville, named for James Springer or John Springer, each of whom owned a general store near the site (*History of White County*, 905). Post office established June 15, 1870.

SPRINGFIELD. Sangamon. City (1840, 1882). Established as the temporary seat of Sangamon County in 1821 by commissioners Zachariah Peter, William Drennan, and Rivers Cormack on land owned by John Kelley on Spring Creek; thus the name, which undoubtedly resonated with Peter, who had lived for a time in Washington County, Ky. where Springfield is also the county seat. Formally laid out about 1823 by Elijah Iles, Pascal P. Enos, and Thomas Cox as Calhoun, named for John C. Calhoun of South Carolina, but the name reverted to Springfield when the site was made the permanent seat of Sangamon County in March 1825. There was a good deal of sentiment to change the name; some argued that there were too many Springfields already and claimed that letters addressed to Springfield, Ill., were often misdirected to Springfields in other states. Proposals for a new name included Sangamo, Illini, and Illinopolis, but these came to naught. Indeed, Springfield is a popular place name in the United States; thirty-two states have a least one Springfield, and many have several. Virginia alone has eleven (Angle, *"Here I Have Lived,"* 5, 12–13, 15; Campbell, *The Sangamon Saga*, 18; Wallace, *Past and Present*, 7). Post office established Jan. 26, 1822, as Sangamon Courthouse; changed to Springfield Feb. 19, 1828.

SPRING GARDEN. Jefferson. Ten miles south-southeast of Mount Vernon. Laid out in 1848 by James F. Duncan and John S. Lucas. Spring Garden Township was formerly known as Compton Springs, a spa of its time, named for site owner Uriah Compton (Perrin ed., *History of Jefferson County*, 371). Post office established June 13, 1838.

SPRING VALLEY. Bureau. Village (1886). Named by William L. Scott, owner of the Spring Valley coal mine, which was named from nearby Spring Creek (Stennett, *A History of the Origin*, 126). Post office established Feb. 1, 1886.

SQUAW GROVE. DeKalb. Township. Probably so named because Indian women and children were seen in the grove on a number of occasions. The name was possibly given by a Mr. Hollenback (or Hollenbeck) who laid claim to the grove and noted that Indian women and children camped there when the men went on hunting trips. The word *squaw* is from a New England Algonquian language and meant "woman," but over the years it has acquired derogatory connotations and is now considered offensive by many Native Americans and others. Names including "squaw" have, by law, been changed in several states. In August 1996 the Prairie Grove village board, after receiving several letters of concern, changed the name of Squaw Creek Road to Half Mile Trail, and in 1997 the Crystal Lake Park District changed the name of Squaw Creek Open

Area to the Prairie Ridge Conservation Area. Still, several features in Illinois have "squaw" as part of their name, including Laughing Squaw Sloughs near Palos Park in Cook County and Squaw Island near the southern tip of Calhoun County (Boies, *History of DeKalb County,* 349; Humphrey, "No Offense"; Vogel, *Indian Place Names in Illinois*). The Squaw Grove post office operated from Jan. 27, 1853, until Aug. 12, 1872, when it was changed to Hinckley.

ST. ALBANS. Hancock. Township. Named about 1839, probably by members of the Jonathan Todd family, early settlers from St. Albans, Franklin County, Vt., itself named for the original St. Albans in Hertfordshire, England, northwest of London, where St. Alban was martyred early in the third century (*Historic Sites,* 316). Post office established July 1, 1839.

STANDARD. Putnam. Village (1907) six miles south-southwest of Peru. Originally called Berry, named for the B. F. Berry Coal Company, which began operations in the early twentieth century, and later known as Taft. The origin of the name is unknown (Alleman and Immel, *A Putnam County History,* 54). Post office established Dec. 8, 1908, as Taft; changed to Standard Oct. 19, 1914.

STANFORD. Clay. Township. Named for the Stanford family, early settlers and prominent citizens. Six Stanford brothers, Samuel, David, William, Mordecai, Isaac, and Abraham, along with their widowed mother, arrived from Indiana in the 1830s (*History of Wayne and Clay Counties,* 413).

ST. ANNE. Kankakee. Village (1872) nine miles southeast of Kankakee. Founded about 1851 as the Mission of Sainte Anne by Father Charles Pascal Telesphore Chiniquy. The name is probably a transfer from one of the several St. Annes in Quebec, Canada. The church reportedly houses a relic claimed to be a fragment of a finger bone of St. Anne, the mother of Mary (*Illinois Guide;* Johnson, comp., "Kankakee County Communities").

STANTON. Champaign. Township. Created from St. Joseph Township in 1862. Named for Edwin M. Stanton, at the time secretary of war in Lincoln's cabinet (Bateman and Selby, eds., *Historical Encyclopedia of Illinois and History of Champaign County,* 831).

STARK. County. Created March 2, 1839, from Knox and Putnam counties. At its 1836–37 session, the Illinois legislature approved formation of a new county to be created from Henry, Knox and Putnam counties and to be called Coffee for Gen. John Coffee, who served under Andrew Jackson at the Battle of New Orleans in 1815. The voters of Henry and Knox counties, however, rejected the formation of the new county. Much of the area to have been included in Coffee County is now in Stark County, named for Gen. John Stark (1728–1822), a hero of the French and Indian War and also of the Revolutionary War, where he served with distinction at Trenton and Princeton, N.J. The seat has always been at Toulon (Leeson, *Documents and Biography,* 133–34; Sublett, *Paper Counties,* 32–39).

STARKS. Kane. Three miles east of Hampshire. Named for Evelyn R. Starks, who also founded Rutland.

ST. AUGUSTINE. Knox. Village (1878) twelve miles northeast of Bushnell. Possibly a transfer from an eastern state but most likely named directly for St. Augustine, the Christian theologian of the fourth and fifth centuries (Bateman and Selby, eds., *Historical Encyclopedia of Illinois and Knox County,* 934). Post office established Sept. 13, 1837.

STAUNTON [STANT uhn]. Macoupin. City (1859, 1872). Founded about 1817. By one account, Staunton was named for early settler Hugh Staunton, who agreed to pay all necessary legal expenses provided the community would be named for him. By another account, the city was named for the Stanton family, but when the relevant documents for organization were returned the name had been respelled Staunton, perhaps by someone familiar with Staunton, Va. James and Thomas Stanton were early settlers (Harder, *Illustrated Dictionary of Place Names;* Kilduff, *Staunton in Illinois,* 31). Post office established April 1, 1837.

STAVANGER [stuh VENG ger]. LaSalle. Ten miles west-northwest of Morris. Named by Norwegian settlers for Stavanger, the seaport in southwestern Norway. The community of Norway is five miles northwest of Stavanger. Post office established April 16, 1887.

ST. CHARLES. Kane. City (1839, 1874). Founded about 1835 by Ira Minard and Read Ferson as Charleston, named for Charleston, Vt., near their hometowns. When it was learned that there was an existing Charleston in Illinois, attorney Stephen S. Jones suggested the variant St. Charles. A local story claims that the community was to have been named Ithaca, for Ithaca, N.Y., but some German settlers objected, claiming that [th] was too hard to pronounce (Pearson, *Reflections of St. Charles,* 10, 22; Seits, "The Names of Kane County," 169). Post office established Nov. 23, 1838, as Waterville; changed to St. Charles Feb. 28, 1839.

ST. CLAIR. County. Arthur St. Clair created the county and named it after himself in April 1790. St. Clair (1734–1818) was a Revolutionary War general who served with Washington in New Jersey. After a rather undistinguished military career, he was appointed the first governor of the Northwest Territory and served in that capacity from 1787 until 1802. At the time of its creation, St. Clair County comprised about one-third of the present state of Illinois. Because of its size, the county had three concurrent seats from 1790 until 1814: Cahokia, Kaskaskia, and Prairie du Rocher. In 1814 a single, permanent seat was established at Belleville.

ST. DAVID. Fulton. Village (1885) five miles southwest of Canton. Named by Welsh miners for St. David, the patron saint of Wales. The name was likely proposed by David Williams, who was instrumental in developing local coal mines (Irwin, *A to Z Fulton County*). Post office established Dec. 11, 1865.

STEEL CITY. Franklin. East of Benton. Named for the United States Steel Company, which bought the Middle Fork Mine in 1919 (*Franklin County,* 21).

STEELEVILLE. Randolph. Village (1851, 1888) eight miles south of Sparta. Named for John Steele, the first miller and probably the first settler, who had established Steele's Mills by 1810. Steele's son George founded the community as Georgetown about 1825. The present village is the result of a merger between Georgetown and Alma (Montague, *Directory*, 209–10; *Randolph County*, 15). Post office established July 20, 1827, as Steele's Mills; changed to Steeleville March 6, 1882.

STEGER [STEE ger, STAY ger]. Cook, Will. Village (1896). Laid out by James Keeney in 1891 as Dearborn Heights. Keeney subsequently changed the name to Columbia Heights in honor of the Chicago Columbian Exposition of 1893. At about the same time, John Valentine Steger emigrated from Germany and established the Steger Piano Company. Steger offered to pay all costs if the community would change its name to Steger, which it did about 1896 (Hayes, "Old Piano Capital"; Schoon, *Calumet Beginnings*, 139–140). Post office established July 28, 1892, as Columbia Heights; changed to Steger Jan. 5, 1900.

ST. ELMO. Fayette. City (1896) fourteen miles northeast of Vandalia. Probably a transfer by settlers from St. Elmo, Christian County, Ky. Ultimately from St. Elmo, the third-century patron saint of sailors (*Illinois Guide*). Post office established July 9, 1840, as Howard's Point; changed to St. Elmo Dec. 15, 1869.

STE. MARIE. Jasper. Village (1873) eight miles east-southeast of Newton. Founded as the Colonie des Frerès (Colony of Brothers) by Joseph Picquet, who led a group of settlers from Alsace, France, to Jasper County in 1837, where he had purchased some ten thousand acres. The colony, placed under the protection of the Virgin Mary, was known as St. Mary's. The village was formally laid out by Picquet in 1847 (*Countries of Cumberland, Jasper, and Richland*, 484–86; Hartrich, *Quasquicentennial History*, 7). Post office established Nov. 23, 1838, as St. Marie; changed to Ste. Marie June 20, 1892.

STEPHENSON. County. Created March 4, 1837 from parts of Jo Daviess and Winnebago counties. Named for Benjamin Stephenson (1769–1822), a friend and political associate of territorial governor Ninian Edwards, a colonel in the Illinois militia during the War of 1812, and a U.S. representative from Illinois Territory from 1814 to 1816. The seat has always been at Freeport.

STERLING. Whiteside. City (1841, 1884). Chatham was founded on one side of the Rock River by William Kirkpatrick, and Harrisburg was founded on the other by Hezekiah Brink and probably named for Capt. D. S. Harris, who brought his steamer, *Pioneer*, up the Rock River to this point in 1836. Harrisburg and Chatham contended for commercial and political influence along this part of the river until 1843 when they merged in an attempt to attract the county seat. One name suggested for the consolidated community, Pipsissiway, was quickly rejected in favor of Sterling, probably proposed by Hugh Wallace on behalf of his friend Col. Samuel Sterling of Pennsylvania (Bastian, *A History of Whiteside*

County, 371; Harder, *Illustrated Dictionary of Place Names;* Russ, "The Export of Pennsylvania Place Names," 210). Post office established June 8, 1837, as Rock River Rapids; changed to Sterling May 15, 1843.

STEUBEN. Marshall. Township. A transfer from Steuben County in western New York state. Informally known as Yankeeland for the large number of settlers from New England. The choice of the name is generally credited to Timothy Atwood, a prominent early settler (*History of Marshall County*, 55). Post office established Oct. 9, 1851.

STEVENS CREEK. Macon. Stream. Named for Leonard Stevens, reportedly the first settler in Macon County, who arrived from New York City about 1822 (Richmond, *Centennial History of Decatur*, 9).

STEVENSON. Marion. Township. Named for Samuel E. Stevenson. According to an early county history Stevenson was "the leading citizen of this township at its formation" in 1873 (Brinkerhoff, *Brinkerhoff's History*, 210).

STEWARD. Lee. Village (1903) five miles south-southeast of Rochelle. Founded in 1870 by Wesley Steward, a local official and site owner (Bateman and Selby, eds., *Historical Encyclopedia of Illinois and History of Lee County*, 632). Post office established Aug. 3, 1871, as Heaton, named for Judge William Heaton; changed to Steward April 12, 1876.

STEWARDSON. Shelby. Village (1874) ten miles north-northwest of Effingham. Founded by William Stewardson Jr. in 1874 as a station on the Wabash, St. Louis and Pacific Railroad (*Combined History of Shelby and Moultrie Counties*, 319). Post office established Feb. 24, 1874, as Stewartson; changed to Stewardson June 25, 1883.

ST. FRANCISVILLE. Lawrence. City (1843, 1873) nine miles south of Lawrenceville. Laid out about 1835 by the widow of Joseph Tougas (or Tugaw) on the site of a stockade called Fort Tougas, built by Joseph Tougas in the early 1810s. Named for St. Francis Xavier, possibly by Tougas but more likely by Jesuit missionaries who were in the area by the 1830s (*Combined History of Edwards, Lawrence, and Wabash Counties*, 287; *Illinois Guide; On the Banks of the Wabash*, 51). Post office established Dec. 12, 1838.

ST. GEORGE. Kankakee. Six miles northeast of Kankakee. Settled and named in the late 1840s by French Canadians from St. George, Henriville, Quebec (Houde and Klasey, *Of the People*, 54). Post office established Jan. 30, 1866.

STICKNEY. Cook. Village (1913). Named in the late 1880s for Alpheus Beede Stickney (1840–1916), founder and first president of the Chicago Great Western Railroad (Cohen, "Suburb Clears the Air").

STILLHOUSE HOLLOW. Saline. Valley. Southeast of Harrisburg. Named for the tradition that a still for brewing illegal whiskey was located there (Bonnell, *The Illinois Ozarks*, 8).

STILLMAN VALLEY. Ogle. Village (1911) eleven miles southwest of Byron. Named from Stillman Creek, previously known as Flint Creek and Mud Creek. The stream was renamed for Isiah Stillman, commander of a troop of Illinois militia that engaged Black Hawk in one of the first skirmishes of the Black Hawk War in May 1832. Stillman's forces were routed by a much smaller band of Sauk warriors in what became known as the Battle of Stillman's Run (Vogel, *Indian Place Names in Illinois*). Post office established May 1, 1851 as Hale; changed to Stillman Valley Oct. 29, 1877.

STILLWELL. Hancock. Thirteen miles southeast of Carthage. Laid out in 1870 on the line of the Carthage, Burlington and Quincy Railroad by site owners Arthur Stillwell and William H. Zinn (Bateman and Selby, eds., *Historical Encyclopedia of Illinois and History of Hancock County*, 1099). Post office established July 1, 1839, as St. Albans; changed to Stilwell Feb. 28, 1871; changed to Sillwell Aug. 5, 1887.

STIRITZ. Williamson. Four miles east-northeast of Herrin. Founded in the early 1900s and named for business executive Albert Christopher Stiritz of Johnson City (Hale, comp. and ed., *Williamson County*, 119; Hubbs, *Pioneer Folks and Places*).

STITES. St. Clair. Township. Founded as the City of East St. Louis in Feb. 1888. The name was changed to Brooklyn in March 1888 and to Stites the following month. Named for John R. Stites, one of the first non-African Americans to live in Brooklyn, now a suburb of East St. Louis (Cha-Jua, *America's First Black Town*, 228).

ST. JACOB. Madison. Village (1875) five miles west of Highland. In 1851 farmer Jacob Schutz, shopkeeper Jacob Schroth, and blacksmith Jacob Willi agreed to name the post office for themselves, with *St.* added for effect—ironically as it turned out because Schroth kept a tavern and Schutz sold whiskey by the gallon (Norton, ed., *Centennial History of Madison County*, 599). Post office established May 13, 1851.

ST. JOHNS. Perry. Village (1903) north of Du Quoin. Named in 1856 by the Order of Masons, whose celebration was held on St. Johns Day, June 24 (Ackerman, *Early Illinois Railroads*, 134).

ST. JOSEPH. Champaign. Village (1881) eight miles east of Urbana. Old St. Joseph was established about 1856 a mile or so south of the present community and named for Joseph Kelly, keeper of the Kelly House Tavern. The traditional account is that on one occasion Kelly was especially kind to a customer, to the point of refusing payment for his services. The customer turned out to be well-connected in government circles and used his influence in securing a post office, which was named for Kelly, who was appointed the first postmaster. With the coming of the railroad, the community that had grown around the Kelly

House was moved to its present location (*Illinois Guide;* Johnson, *Medicine in Champaign County,* 73). Post office established May 13, 1851, as St. Josephs.

ST. LIBORY. St. Clair, Washington. Village (1895) ten miles southeast of Mascoutah. Formerly known as Mud Creek. The St. Laborious Catholic Church was established about 1838 by settlers from Glandorf in western Germany. The church was probably named for the St. Laborious Church in Paderborn, Germany, named for St. Laborious, Bishop of Le Mans, France, in the last half of the fourth century. The community was formally laid out as Hermanntown by John Wessels in 1866 and renamed for the St. Laborious Church in 1874 (*History St. Clair,* 369; *Tapestry of Time,* 151; www.stlibory.com/churchhistory.htm). Post office established Jan. 3, 1850, as Mud Creek; changed to St. Libory Jan. 21, 1874.

ST. MARY. Hancock. Fourteen miles southwest of Macomb. Founded about 1835 as St. Mary's by Walter R. Hurst and Wesley Williams. Reportedly named for Hurst's deceased fiancée, whose name was Mary (*History of Hancock County,* 539). Post office established Feb. 13, 1894.

ST. MORGAN. Madison. Five miles south of Highland. Named for E. M. Morgan, an early settler, storekeeper, and postmaster. The origin of *St.* is unknown, although the *Centennial History of Madison County* calls Morgan a "good man" (Norton, ed., *Centennial History of Madison County,* 527). Post office established June 26, 1861.

STOCKDALE. Grundy. Three miles west of Morris. Named for the cattle and sheep fattened in the local feed lots and then shipped to the Chicago stockyards (Ullrich, *This Is Grundy County,* 179). Post office established June 17, 1893.

STOCKLAND. Iroquois. Ten miles northeast of Hoopeston. Formerly called Crab Apple. The name was changed in 1864 at the suggestion of Alba Honeywell. The reasons for the choice of the name are unknown (*Iroquois County History,* 148). Post office established Nov. 2, 1891.

STOCKTON. Jo Daviess. Village (1890) eighteen miles west-northwest of Freeport. Founded about 1890 with construction of the Chicago Great Western Railroad. Named about 1853 by Alanson Parker. Possibly a transfer from Stockton in another state but also chosen with the expectation that the area would prosper by feeding and transporting livestock (*History of Jo Daviess County,* 599). Post office established Oct. 6, 1853.

STOKES. Union. Precinct. Named for John Stokes, an early settler from Kentucky who arrived in the 1810s (Perrin, ed., *History of Alexander, Union, and Pulaski Counties,* 430).

ST. OMER. Coles. Historical community. Laid out in 1854 by site owner and first postmaster John W. Hodge. Probably named for St. Omer, the city in Flanders that grew around the monastery founded in the seventh century by St. Omer, Bishop of Thérouanne. The St. Omer Cemetery is about ten miles northeast of

Charleston (Redlich, *The Postal History of Coles County,* 47). Post office established Oct. 24, 1849, as Modrell's Point; changed to St. Omer Oct. 7, 1852.

STONEFORT. Saline, Williamson. Village (1875) twelve miles southwest of Harrisburg. Stonefort takes its name from a rock fortification described in 1807 as already "ancient." The original Stonefort, now known as Oldtown, was laid out in 1858 a mile or so southeast of the present community. When the Cairo and Vincennes Railroad was completed most of the buildings were dismantled and moved to trackside. The new location took the name of Bolton, a community just over the Williamson County line and now part of Stonefort. The name was changed to Stonefort in June 1934 (*Saline County,* 70–71). Post office established Feb. 15, 1858, as Stone Fort.

STONINGTON. Christian. Village (1885) eight miles northeast of Taylorville. Named by settlers from North Stonington, Conn., where the Stonington Colony, a land association established for the purpose of founding a model religious-educational community in the West, was formed in 1836. Formerly known as Covington, named for one of the site owners, R. W. Covington. The name was changed to Stonington when the post office was established in 1844 (Bateman and Selby, eds., *Historical Encyclopedia of Illinois and History of Christian County,* 111; Beloit and Beloit, *History of Stonington,* 1, 6). Post office established April 29, 1844.

STOY. Crawford. Village (1907) five miles west of Robinson. By local accounts, a Judge Maxwell of Robinson was asked to provide a name for the community. Maxwell found it difficult to think of a good name because he was constantly being interrupted by his son, Stoy Maxwell. In telling Stoy to settle down, the judge realized that he had found the name he sought. This is the only Stoy in the United States (*History of Crawford County,* 161). Post office established June 17, 1889.

ST. PAUL. Fayette. Eleven miles southeast of Vandalia. Named from the Saint Paul Lutheran Church, established in the early 1860s (Hanabarger, "Fayette County Place Names," 52). Post office established Feb. 1, 1876.

ST. PETER. Fayette. Village (1909) fourteen miles east-southeast of Vandalia. Named from St. Peter's Evangelical Church, established by German settlers about 1869 (Hanabarger, "Fayette County Place Names," 52). Post office established Jan. 25, 1894.

STRADDLE CREEK. Carroll. Stream. Straddle Creek reportedly was named from an incident involving a corpulent man named Chambers who was assisting a surveying party. When they came to the banks of the stream, he wagered he could step across, planted one foot on one bank, and stepped across with the other. He was stuck, one foot on one side and one on the other. After a short struggle Chambers lost his balance and fell into the water, to the great amusement of the surveyors. From that time on, the story goes, the stream was known as Straddle Creek (*History of Carroll County,* 330–31).

STRASBURG. Shelby. Village (1877) ten miles east-southeast of Shelbyville. Founded about 1874 with construction of the Wabash railroad. Site owner Charles Ostermeier donated land for the station with the understanding that it would be named for his former home, Strasburg, Germany (Radloff, *125 Strasburg Stories,* 3). Post office established Feb. 11, 1874, as Strasburgh; changed to Strasburg July 13, 1893.

STRATFORD. Ogle. Four miles east-northeast of Polo. Founded in 1886 with construction of the Chicago, Burlington and Quincy Railroad. Presumably named for Stratford, Warwickshire, England. According to an early county history the name was "bestowed by a reader of the great dramatist, the place of whose birth it suggests to all lovers of Shakespeare's verse" (Bateman and Selby, eds., *Historical Encyclopedia of Illinois and History of Ogle County,* 815). Post office established Nov. 14, 1887.

STRATTON. Edgar. Township. Formerly known as Wayne. The name was changed in 1857 for John Stratton, said to be the first European settler in Edgar County to eat his evening meal in his own house (*History of Edgar County,* 480; *Our First 150 Years,* 12).

STRAWN. Livingston. Village (1879) nine miles southeast of Fairbury. Laid out in 1873 by David Strawn, a director of the Fairbury, Pontiac and Western Railroad (*History of Livingston County* [1991], 24). Post office established Oct. 6, 1873.

STREAMWOOD. Cook. Village (1957). Named for the family of developer Jay Stream (see Carol Stream) (Harder, *Illustrated Dictionary of Place Names*).

STREATOR. LaSalle, Livingston. City (1874). John O'Neil, an early miner and proprietor of the general store, is usually credited with giving Streator its first name, Hardscrabble. After watching two teams labor to pull a loaded wagon up the hill from the landing on the Vermilion River, O'Neil remarked that it was a hard scrabble (hard struggle) and then stenciled "Hard Scrabble" on the front of his store (the Streator High School yearbook is still called *The Hardscrabble.*) During the Civil War the community was known as Unionville. About 1865 some coal samples from the area were sent to Worthy L. Streator, a physician and financier in Cleveland, Ohio. Streator was immediately struck by the quality of the coal, and he and others formed the Vermilion Coal Company, which opened several mines in the 1860s. The community was officially named for Streator in 1867 (Franklin, *A Biography in Black,* 24–29). Post office established June 12, 1844, as Eagle; changed to Streator Nov. 26, 1867.

STRONGHURST. Henderson. Village (1894) sixteen miles southwest of Monmouth. Established in 1887 and named for William B. Strong, president, and R. D. Hurst, vice president of the Santa Fe Railroad (*Stronghurst Centennial History,* 3, 5). Post office established March 2, 1888.

ST. ROSE. Clinton. Five miles north of Breese. Perhaps named from the St. Rose Catholic Church, organized in 1868 (*History of Marion and Clinton Counties,* 162). Post office established May 14, 1872.

STUBBLEFIELD. Bond. Four miles southwest of Greenfield. Named for Wyatt Stubblefield, a miller and early settler (Peterson, "Place Names of Bond County," 43). Post office established Jan. 31, 1872.

SUBLETTE [suhb LET]. Lee. Eight miles northwest of Mendota. Named by the Illinois Central Railroad about 1854. The source of the name is unclear. Ackerman and others claim that the name arose through the practice of "subletting" contracts for grading sections of the railroad, but that explanation is in error because the town plat was recorded as Soublette. Soublette or Sublette is a French family name, and the community was likely named for an early settler or someone involved in the construction of the IC. Coulet du Gard attributes the name to five Soublette brothers, Andrew, Solomon, Milton, Pinkacy, and William, who supposedly were trappers and traders in the early 1800s, although there is no evidence they were ever in the area—if they even existed. Thomas Sublette, an Illinois militiaman in the Black Hawk War, has also been proposed as the source of the name. On his gravestone, however, his name is spelled *Sublette,* raising the question, if indeed he is the namesake, why the community was laid out as Soublette. Sublette Township was originally called Hanno, named for Hanau, Germany (then in Prussia). The name was changed in 1857 to match that of the IC station (Bateman and Selby, eds., *Historical Encyclopedia of Illinois and History of Lee County,* 692; Coulet du Gard, *Dictionary of French Place Names; Sublette, Illinois,* 7–8). Post office established June 15, 1855.

SUCKER. Illinois is known as the "sucker state," and Illinoisans are known as "suckers." The nickname probably dates from the early years of the nineteenth century. In 1833 a newspaper editor visiting from New York sent a letter home, reporting that he had met "a couple of smart-looking 'suckers' from the southern part of Illinois." A number of possible origins have been suggested. By one, the nickname was given derisively to subsistence farmers of southern Illinois, a large number of whom were emigrants from Kentucky, where sprouts from the tobacco plant, "suckers," were stripped and discarded before they could drain nutrients from the main stalk. Like the suckers of the tobacco plant, the poor farmers were claimed to have stripped themselves from the main stem. By another account, early Illinoisans learned to drink from scum-covered pools by means of long straws that did not disturb the surface scum. By still another, when babies were left alone their mothers would tie one end of a string around a piece of pork and the other end to the baby's toe. The baby would suck on the meat, but should the child try to swallow it, the natural kicking impulse, along with a taut string, would bring the pork back up. The most likely source of the name, however, is the buffalo fish, a kind of sucker. Southern Illinoisans would travel north each spring to work the lead mines around Galena and return south each fall. Both journeys coincided with the migrations of the sucker fish, well known to miners because it was a substantial part of their diet. Miners already in camp would announce the arrival of both the Illinoisans and the fish by saying, "Here come the suckers!" In the 1850s and 1860s, a steamboat called *Sucker State* operated on the Mississippi River north of St. Louis. The name is now little used and unknown to most younger Illinoisans (Read Collection).

SUEZ. Mercer. Township. Named about 1854 at the time of township formation, probably for Suez, Egypt, because the proposed Suez Canal was in the news in the 1850s. The area was also known as Utah and Palmyra. Post office established May 12, 1838, as Pope Creek; changed to Suez March 23, 1866.

SUGAR GROVE. Kane. Village (1957). Named for the nearby stands of maple trees. Possibly a translation of a native name for the sugar maple (Vann, "The Sweet Life"). Post office established Aug. 18, 1840.

SUGAR LOAF. St. Clair. Township. Also Sugarloaf Heights three miles north of Columbia. The name apparently comes from the shape of an Indian mound within the township, called by the French *le pain de sucre* (the loaf of sugar) (Brown, "French Place Names in Illinois," 464).

SULLIVAN. Livingston. Township. A mishearing or mistranscription of Sullivant. Named for Michael L. Sullivant (*History of Livingston County* [1878], 639).

SULLIVAN. Moultrie. City (1869, 1872). Most sources agree that Sullivan was named for Sullivan's Island in the Charleston, S.C., harbor, which Gen. William Moultrie (the namesake of Moultrie County) defended during the Revolutionary War. The Moultrie County Historical and Genealogical Society dismisses an alternative account—that Sullivan was named for the Revolutionary War hero Gen. John Sullivan of New Hampshire—as "just a story" (Martin, *Notes on the History*, 24; personal communication with Mary L. Storm). Post office established March 22, 1839, as East Nelson; changed to Sullivan Aug. 12, 1845.

SULLIVANT. Ford. Township. Named for Michael L. Sullivant, who owned some eighty thousand acres in Champaign, Ford, and Livingston counties, including the twenty-three thousand acres of Broadlands, the Sullivant estate (*Ford County History*, 142).

SUMMERFIELD. St. Clair. Village (1869, 1872) three miles east of Lebanon. Laid out in 1854 by Thomas Casad and B. T. Kavanaugh. The source of the name is unknown (Bateman and Selby, eds., *Historical Encyclopedia of Illinois and History of St. Clair County*, 777). Post office established April 19, 1855.

SUMMIT. Cook. Village (1890). Named for its location on the low ridge between the Chicago and Des Plaines rivers. The portage of Marquette and Jolliet from the Des Plaines River to Lake Michigan in 1673 began near Summit (*Illinois Guide*).

SUMMUM [SUHM uhm]. Fulton. Eleven miles west-southwest of Havana. Laid out in 1851 by James M. Onion and named for the Summum post office, itself probably named for Peter Summy, an early postmaster (*History of Fulton County,* 940; Irwin, *A to Z Fulton County*). Post office established April 13, 1836.

SUMNER. Kankakee. Township. Previously called Union. Renamed in June 1856 in honor of Sen. Charles Sumner of Massachusetts, well known for his raging antislavery speeches. After one particularly vituperous tirade opposing the Kansas-Nebraska Act in May 1856, he was severely beaten while at his desk in the Senate by a member of Congress from South Carolina. This incident created the necessary sympathy for Senator Sumner to change the name of the township (Houde and Klasey, *Of the People,* 55).

SUMNER. Lawrence. City (1887) nine miles west of Lawrenceville. Laid out in 1854 with construction of the Ohio and Mississippi Railroad. Named for Benjamin Sumner, who arrived about 1817 and is generally acknowledged as the first permanent settler in the area (Bateman and Selby, eds., *Illinois Historical Lawrence County Biographical,* 632). Post office established May 25, 1852, as Black Jack; changed to Sumner Sept. 4, 1855.

SUMPTER. White. Former community. Named for John and James Sumpter. John Sumpter was the first postmaster. The Sumpter Cemetery is about three miles northwest of Carmi (Sneed, *Ghost Towns of Southern Illinois,* 235). Post office established July 16, 1889.

SUNBURY. Livingston. Four miles west of Dwight. Named by William K. Brown for his former home, Sunbury, the seat of Northumberland County, Pa. (Bateman and Selby, eds., *Historical Encyclopedia of Illinois and History of Livingston County,* 639). Post office established July 1, 1840.

SUNFIELD. Perry. Three miles north of Du Quoin. Founded in 1864 as Diamond Town, named from the Black Diamond Coal Mine. Subsequently called Diamond City and renamed with establishment of the Sunfield post office in 1886. The source of the name is unknown (*Perry County,* 20).

SUNNYSIDE. McHenry. Between Johnsburg and Pistakee Highlands. Founded in 1940 as a residential subdivision built on Sunnyside Farm (Nye, ed., *McHenry County Illinois,* 766).

SUNNYSIDE. Williamson. West of Herrin. Founded about 1899 and named for the Sunnyside Coal Mine, which began operations that same year. The mine was named for the chief clerk, W. H. "Sunnyside" Brown (Hale, comp. and ed., *Williamson County,* 119; Hubbs, *Pioneer Folks and Places*).

SWANGO. Edgar. Former community. Established as a station on the Paris and Danville Railroad. Named for Jesse Swango, proprietor of the general store. The Swango Cemetery is about four miles south of Paris (*History of Edgar County,* 471). Post office established Nov. 19, 1874.

SWANSEA [SWAHN see]. St. Clair. Village (1895) north Belleville suburb. Named New Swansea by coal miners from Swansea, West Glamorgan, Wales in the mid-1800s. The word *New* was dropped from the name at the time of incorporation in 1895 (Harder, *Illustrated Dictionary of Place Names*). Post office established Oct. 5, 1894.

SWANWICK. Perry. Ten miles northwest of Pinckneyville. Laid out in 1871 by Thomas Swanwick, a tobacconist from Chester, England, who emigrated about 1818 (Dearinger, "A New Geography of Perry County," 28). Post office established Jan. 25, 1871.

SWEDONA. Mercer. Thirteen miles south of Moline. Founded as Berlin by German immigrants in 1836. To avoid duplication of post offices, the name was changed by popular vote in January 1869 to Swedona, a form of Sweden, at the suggestion of Leander Chilberg (Bassett and Goodspeed, *Past and Present of Mercer County*, 471; Landelius, *Swedish Place-Names*). Post office established March 2, 1855, as Centre Ridge; changed to Swedona Jan. 15, 1869.

SWEET WATER. Menard. Nine miles east-northeast of Petersburg. Named about 1853 for the Sweet Water post office. The popular choice for a name was Sugar Grove, but several Sugar Groves existed so postmaster William Engle created the name *Sweet Water* for the syrup drawn from the local sugar maples (*History of Menard and Mason Counties*, 365). Post office established Aug. 4, 1850.

SWETT CREEK. Madison. Stream. Named for David Swett, the first permanent settler in Omph-Ghent Township, who arrived about 1820 (Norton, ed., *Centennial History of Madison County*, 590).

SYCAMORE. DeKalb. City (1859, 1872). Founded as Orange, named for Orange, N.Y., by the New York Company, a land investment consortium that dammed the Kishwaukee River, built the first mill in the area, and laid out the community in 1836. By 1839 the name had been changed to Sycamore, a translation of Meskwaki (Fox) *kishwaukee* (sycamore), the Native American name for Sycamore Creek, now called the Kishwaukee River. Sycamore was the seat of DeKalb County from 1837 until 1839 (as Orange) and again from 1840 to the present (Boies, *History of DeKalb County*, 488). Post office established Sept. 27, 1836.

T

TABLE GROVE. Fulton. Village (1881) fourteen miles east-southeast of Macomb. Platted in 1837 as Laurel Hill. The name was changed at the time of incorporation in 1881, presumably because of the relatively flat summit of the hill on which Table Grove is located (Irwin, *A to Z Fulton County*). Post office established Sept. 27, 1837.

TALKINGTON. Sangamon. Township. Named in the early 1860s for Joseph "Job"

Talkington, one of the first settlers in the area (Bateman and Selby, eds., *Historical Encyclopedia of Illinois and History of Sangamon County,* 737).

TALLULA [tuh LOO luh]. Menard. Village (1873) fifteen miles northwest of Springfield. Laid out in 1857 by William G. Greene, J. G. Greene, Richard Yates, T. Baker, and W. G. Spears. Several engaging but fanciful stories have been created to explain the name. By one, Tallula was the name of an Indian princess; by another, in a local Indian language *tallula* meant "softly falling or dripping water," referring to the local springs around which Indians were supposed to have camped. More likely the name is a transfer from the southeastern United States, perhaps from Tallula, Issaquena County, Miss., where Tallula is derived from Choctaw *talola* (bell) (Bright, *Native American Placenames; Illustrated Atlas Map of Menard County,* 15, 27; *Menard County,* 312; Miller and Leavey, *Past and Present of Menard County,* 52). Post office established Dec. 19, 1851, as Rushaway; changed to Tallula May 10, 1858.

TAMALCO [tuh MAL ko]. Bond. Ten miles southeast of Greenville. The name *Tamalco* was created about 1884 from the names of three prominent citizens of Bond County: W. H. Taylor, John McLaren, and Frank Colwell. Taylor was Tamalco's first postmaster (Bateman and Selby, eds., *Historical Encyclopedia of Illinois and History of Bond County,* 632). Post office established April 25, 1884.

TAMARAWA RIDGE. Monroe. A variant of *Tamaroa.* The Tamarawa Ridge runs through southern St. Clair and northern Monroe counties southwest of New Athens. Also called the Tomorrowway Ridge. Post office established Nov. 13, 1837.

TAMAROA [tam uh RO uh]. Perry. Village (1867, 1875) eight miles north of Du Quoin. Founded in 1855 as a station on the Illinois Central Railroad. Named for the Tamaroa, one of the tribes of the Illinois Confederacy. Credit for proposing the name is usually given to Mrs. Nelson Holt, wife of the IC agent at Tamaroa, and Mrs. Benaiah Guernsey Roots, whose husband was chief surveyor for the IC. Reportedly, Holt and Roots first named the community Kiawkashaw, claiming it to be a French name for the Tamaroa. They reconsidered, however, and chose Tamaroa because it was "more polite and euphonious." Maroa (q.v.) is a variant (*Combined History of Randolph, Monroe, and Perry Counties,* 362; Dearinger, "A New Geography of Perry County," 22; Vogel, *Indian Place Names in Illinois*). Post office established March 14, 1855.

TAMMS. Alexander. Village (1905) fourteen miles north of Cairo. Established about 1900 as a station on the Chicago and Eastern Illinois Railroad by site owners Theodore and Oscar Tamm (*Alexander County,* 17). Post office established April 23, 1893, as Idlewild; changed to Tamms March 9, 1900.

TAMPICO [TAM puh ko]. Whiteside. Village (1875) eleven miles south-southwest of Rock Falls. Founded in 1861 by John W. Glassburn. Named from the city of Tampico in Tamaulipas state on the east coast of Mexico. In 1846 Tampico was occupied by U.S. troops under the command of Zachary Taylor, and returning veterans of the Mexican War brought the name to Illinois. The Third Independent Company of Illinois Mounted Volunteers (the Marmaluke Legion), commanded by Michael K. Lawler, scouted for the Department of Tampico in 1847–48. From Huastec, a Mayan language, meaning "place of the dogs" (Bastian, *A History of Whiteside County*, 434, 471; Bright, *Native American Placenames*). Post office established July 27, 1870.

TATE. Saline. Township. Named for the Tate family. Both John Tate, a Revolutionary War veteran and his son, John V. Tate, a veteran of the War of 1812, are buried in the cemetery of Tate Chapel north of Galatia (*History of Saline County*, 115).

TATER CREEK. Fulton. Stream. Also Tater Holler. Named Potato Hollow by Philip Aylesworth, one of the founders of Meredosia and Babylon, in 1835 (Irwin, *A to Z Fulton County*).

TAYLOR HILL. Franklin. Ten miles northeast of Benton. Named for the Taylor family. Hering and Alvis Taylor were early postmasters. Post office established Aug. 8, 1867 (Adams, comp., *Illinois Place Names*).

TAYLOR RIDGE. Rock Island. Eight miles southwest of Rock Island. Founded about 1876 and named for James Taylor, who donated land for a station on the Rock Island and Mercer County Railroad (*Past and Present of Rock Island County*, 231). Post office established March 7, 1877.

TAYLORVILLE. Christian. City (1881). Founded in 1839 as the seat of Christian County (then called Dane County). Named for John Taylor of Springfield. Taylor, along with Dr. Richard F. Barrett, Marvellous Eastham, and Robert Allen were the commissioners charged with locating the county seat (Bateman and Selby, eds., *Historical Encyclopedia of Illinois and History of Christian County*, 81; Goudy, *History of Christian County*, 187). Post office established April 17, 1841, as Taylorsville.

TAZEWELL [TAZ wel]. County. Created Jan. 31, 1827, from Fayette County. Named for Littleton W. Tazewell (1774–1860), a Virginia lawyer, U.S. representative from 1800 to 1801, and a U.S. senator at the time the county was created.

TEMPLE HILL. Pope. Twelve miles north-northeast of Metropolis. Founded by Dr. George Dodd and named for his former home in Barren County, Ky. (*Pope County*, 38). Post office established Jan. 12, 1888.

TENNESSEE. McDonough. Village (1872) eight-and-a-half miles southwest of Macomb. Founded in 1854 by Larkin C. Bacon, Thomas K. Waddill (Waddle), and Steven Cockerham as a station on the Chicago, Burlington and Quincy Railroad. Named by Bacon for his home state of Tennessee (*History of McDonough County*, 565). Post office established April 1, 1856.

TERRA COTTA. McHenry. Four miles south of McHenry. Named for the factory established by William D. Gates in the 1880s that originally made terra-cotta drain tiles used for "tiling," a process that effectively drained many wetlands in northern Illinois (Stennett, *A History of the Origin,* 129). Post office established Jan. 28, 1886.

TERRAPIN RIDGE. Jo Daviess. Ridge near Elizabeth. "Terrapin," an Eastern Algonquin word, refers to the small turtles found in the Middle and South Atlantic states. It was probably brought to Illinois by settlers from Maryland or Virginia. The name also appears in Madison and Bond counties.

TERRE HAUTE. Henderson. Twenty-three miles southwest of Monmouth. Founded about 1854 and named by the Joseph Genung family for their former home, Terre Haute, Vigo County, Ind. French for "high land" (*History of Mercer and Henderson Counties,* 1277). Post office established Aug. 24, 1857.

TEUTOPOLIS. Effingham. Village (1845, 1874) three miles east of Effingham. Organized in Cincinnati, Ohio, in 1838 by the Deutche Land-Compagnie (German Land Company) as a colony for persecuted German Catholics. Several names were considered, including New Cincinnati, Muenster, Hanover, and Germantown. The Rt. Rev. John B. Purcell, Bishop of Cincinnati, suggested Teutopolis because it was to be a "city of the Germans." It is the only community so named in the United States (Banbury, comp., *The Sesquicentennial of Effingham County,* 41; *Teutopolis Illinois Quasquicentennial,* 3). Post office established July 8, 1842.

TEXAS. About a dozen features in Illinois have been named for the state of Texas. Texas City in Saline County reportedly was named by a group of settlers headed for Texas in a one-horse wagon. When the horse dropped dead from exhaustion, they decided to stay where they were and call the place Texas. The Cairo, Vincennes and Chicago Railroad formally established the community as Texas about 1859. Texas Township in DeWitt County was reportedly so named when Daniel Newcomb of Clinton sold all his property with the intention of moving to Texas but changed his mind and decided to stay where he was, saying it was good enough for him and as close to Texas as he ever wanted to get. Other Texas-inspired names include Texas Junction, now a part of Murphysboro, and Old Texas Cemetery, named for the now-vanished town of Texas near Eastburn in Iroquois County. A Texas post office operated in Randolph County from Aug. 13, 1850, until Jan. 30, 1857, when it was changed to Laurel Hill (Adams, comp., *Illinois Place Names; History of DeWitt County* [1882], 337; *History of Saline County,* 131).

TEXICO. Jefferson. Eight miles north of Mount Vernon. Founded about 1905. A blend of *Texas* and *Mexico.* The name was probably transferred from Texico, Curry County, N.M., by officials of the Chicago and Eastern Illinois Railroad. The area was earlier known as Beehive (Sneed, *Ghost Towns of Southern Illinois,*104). Post office established May 12, 1892, as Beehive; discontinued Dec. 24, 1895; reestablished as Texico July 27, 1898.

THACKERAY [THAK uh ree]. Hamilton. Five miles east of McLeansboro. Established about 1871 by the Louisville and Nashville Railroad. Probably named for the English novelist William Makepeace Thackeray (1811–63), although the name was spelled Thackery on the original post office petition, probably a misspelling by David Hammill, the first postmaster (*Hamilton County*, 41; *History Gallatin, Saline*, 309; Sneed, *Ghost Towns of Southern Illinois*, 59). Post office established Dec. 11, 1871, as Thackery.

THAWVILLE. Iroquois. Village (1903) fifteen miles north of Paxton. Founded about 1870 and named for William K. Thaw of Pittsburgh, Pa., a major stockholder in the Gilman, Clinton and Springfield Railroad. Thaw was later vice president of the Pennsylvania Railroad and a community benefactor (Dowling, *History of Iroquois County*, 108). Post office established Jan. 22, 1872.

THEBES. Alexander. Village (1852, 1899) seven miles southeast of Cape Girardeau, east of Illmo, Mo. Founded about 1835 and probably named for Thebes, the ancient capital of Upper Egypt, motivated by the village's location in Egypt (q.v.). Formerly known as Sparhawk's Landing, named for the Sparhawk brothers, local lumbermen. Thebes was the seat of Alexander County from 1845 until 1860. This is one of two Thebes in the United States; the other is in Snyder County, Ark. (*Alexander County*, 18; Perrin, ed., *History of Alexander, Union and Pulaski Counties*, 497). Post office established Dec. 13, 1845.

THIRD LAKE. Lake. Village (1959) two miles east of Round Lake Beach. The village of Third Lake includes the subdivisions of Sunshine, founded about 1920, and Mariner's Cove, founded about 1980, on opposite sides of Third Lake, itself so named for its position in the series of lakes extending northwestward from First Lake (Gage's Lake) to Fourth Lake, near Venetian Village (Dretske, *What's in a Name?*; Youngman, "A Tale of Two Subdivisions").

THOMAS. Bureau. Eighteen miles south-southwest of Rock Falls. Named for postmaster Washington Thomas. Formerly known as Sodtown (Leonard, ed., *Big Bureau*, 67). Post office established Dec. 22, 1888.

THOMASBORO. Champaign. Village (1900) five miles south of Rantoul. Founded about 1863 on the line of the Illinois Central Railroad by Englishman and site owner John Thomas (Ackerman, *Early Illinois Railroads*, 126). Post office established March 7, 1865, as Thomasborough; changed to Thomasboro Oct. 14, 1893.

THOMPSON. Jo Daviess. Township and former community. Named for early settlers Christopher Columbus Thompson and his brothers, Hiram and Icabod. The Thompson Cemetery is about sixteen miles east of Galena (*History of Jo Daviess County*, 610).

THOMPSONVILLE. Franklin. Village (1880) eight miles east of West Frankfort. Named for Richard Thompson, who established the first general store in the

1870s (Henson, *History of Franklin County,* 87; Jurich, *This Is Franklin County*). Post office established Sept. 27, 1847, as Cave, named for U.S. postmaster general Cave Johnson; changed to Thompsonville March 26, 1879.

THOMSON. Carroll. Village (1865, 1873) twelve miles northwest of Morrison. Established as a station on the Western Union Railroad in 1864. Named for G. A. Thompson, a principle investor and promoter of the railroad. Formerly known as Sandville and York (Thiem, ed., *Carroll County,* 220). Post office established March 29, 1856, as Sandville; changed to Thomson May 5, 1865.

THORNTON. Cook. Village (1900). Named for William F. Thornton, one of the first commissioners of the Illinois and Michigan Canal and later president of the canal board (Bateman and Selby, eds., *Historical Encyclopedia of Illinois Cook County Edition,* 793). Post office established Jan. 28, 1837.

TICE. Menard. Four miles southeast of Petersburg. Named for the Tice family. Jacob and Jane Tice emigrated from Maryland in the late 1820s; Wilson Tice established a general store on the railroad line between Petersburg and Athens in the late 1870s; and Anderson W. Tice was an early postmaster (*Menard County,* 313; Miller and Leavey, *Past and Present of Menard County,* 87). Post office established March 3, 1863, as Oak Ridge; changed to Tice June 25, 1883.

TICONA. LaSalle. Eight miles south of LaSalle. An anagram of *Tonica* (q.v.) (Barge and Caldwell, "Illinois Place-Names").

TILDEN. Randolph. Village (1904) six miles north of Sparta. Founded about 1870 by William Edmiston, Robert Matthews, and William G. Crawford. Named for Samuel J. Tilden, at the time a leader of the Democratic Party in New York and candidate for the presidency in 1876 (www.randolphcountyillinois.net/sub88 .htm). Post office established March 4, 1870, as Sadowa; changed to Tilden May 16, 1871.

TILTON. Vermilion. Village (1884) southwest Danville suburb. Laid out in 1854 by the Northern Cross Railroad as Bryant, named for an assistant surveyor for the NC. Renamed for L. Tilton of New York, manager of the Northern Cross from 1861 until the mid-1870s (Tuggle, comp., *Stories of Historical Days,* 13). Post office established June 11, 1864.

TIME. Pike. Village (1874) five miles east-southeast of Pittsfield. The second smallest incorporated community in Illinois, with a population of twenty-nine (Valley City is the smallest with a population of fourteen). The source of the name is unknown. Post office established Feb. 27, 1854.

TIMEWELL. Brown. Six miles northwest of Mount Sterling. Laid out about 1862 as Mound Station on the line of the Wabash Railroad by Martin McNitt. Confusion with Mounds in Pulaski County led to a name change about 1903 to Timewell, for C. A. Timewell, a station agent for the Wabash (*History of Brown*

County, 253). Post office established Dec. 28, 1860, as Mound Station; changed to Timewell July 28, 1903.

TIMOTHY. Cumberland. The origin of the name is unknown. According to a local story, when the post office was established in 1887 Frank Ormsby, the first postmaster, chose the name *Timothy* from a list of names submitted by the post office department (Lindsay, *Cumberland County,* 148). Post office established March 16, 1887.

TINCHERTOWN. Vermilion. Founded in the 1840s by John L. Tincher, an Illinois state representative and senator in the 1860s and 1870s. Now part of Danville (Stapp, *History under Our Feet,* 59).

TINLEY PARK. Cook, Will. Village (1892). Formerly known as New Bremen, named for Bremen, Germany. The name was changed by popular vote in June 1892, for Samuel Tinley Jr., who served as the first station agent for the Rock Island Railroad, beginning in 1854 (Trebe, "Tinley Park Has Come a Long Way"). Post office established May 15, 1848, as Cooper's Grove; changed to New Bremen May 30, 1850; changed to Tinley Park Oct. 6, 1890.

TIOGA [teye O guh]. Hancock. Twelve miles south of Hamilton. Founded by George Ensminger about 1855. Probably a transfer from Tioga, Pa., or Tioga, N.Y., themselves named from a Mohawk word meaning "junction" or "fork" (Bright, *Native American Placenames;* Gregg, *History of Hancock County,* 565). Post office established April 25, 1873.

TIPTON. Monroe. Six miles west-northwest of Red Bud. An adaptation of earlier Tip Town, itself short for Tipperary, named for Tipperary, Ireland, the former home of a number of settlers in the mid-nineteenth century (Allen Collection). Post office established July 24, 1871.

TISKILWA [TIS kil wah]. Bureau. Village (1840, 1890) six miles southwest of Princeton. Created in 1840 through the merger of Windsor and West Windsor and located on the site of a Native American village called Indiantown, now the name of the township. Tiskilwa appears to be a native name, but its source and meaning are unknown. Several origins have been proposed. By one more fanciful account, two Indian men, Tis and Wa, were in love with the same Indian princess. In the course of contending for her hand in marriage, Tis killed Wa (i.e., Tiskilwa). By a more serious accounts, apparently first proposed by Nehemiah Matson in the 1870s, Tiskilwa was the name of a Potawatomi leader whose village was near the site. His existence, however, can not be verified. A number of meanings have been suggested, including "plover," "gem of the valley," "beautiful valley," "many waters," and even "old bachelor" (Barge and Caldwell, "Illinois Place-Names"; Bradsby, ed., *History of Bureau County,* 431; Bright, *Native American Placenames;* Leonard, ed., *Big Bureau,* 74; Mitchell, *Historical Fragments,* 55; Vogel, *Indian*

Place Names in Illinois). Post office established Aug. 4, 1835, as Indiantown; changed to Windsor Feb. 4, 1836; changed to Tiskilwa March 1, 1852.

TODDS MILL. Perry. Eight miles north of Pinckneyville. Named for Joseph Todd, an Irish immigrant and a founder of the Todds Mill Catholic church in the early 1820s (*Perry County,* 24).

TODDS POINT. Shelby. Seven miles west of Sullivan. Laid out about 1867. Named for William Todd, who built a cabin on a point of timber along the Okaw River in 1835 (*Atlas of Shelby County,* 5; *Combined History of Shelby and Moultrie Counties,* 249). Post office established Sept. 20, 1865.

TOLEDO [tuh LEE do]. Cumberland. Village (1857) thirteen miles west of Casey. Founded about 1854 as Prairie City. The name was changed in 1874, probably by settlers from Toledo, the seat of Lucas County, Ohio, itself named for Toledo, Spain. Toledo has been the seat of Cumberland County since 1855 (*Counties of Cumberland, Jasper, and Richland,* 217). Post office established Nov. 29, 1856, as Majority Point; changed to Toledo Sept. 1, 1881.

TOLONO [tuh LO no]. Champaign. Village (1873). Founded in 1856 by the Illinois Central Railroad where the tracks of the IC crossed those of the Chicago Great Western. The origin of the name is unknown, but there is no want of naming legends, conjectures, and popular etymologies. According to one story, in the early 1850s, when the route for the IC was being planned, one of the surveyors asked a colleague if the site was too low. The reply was, "No"; thus, "Too low no." According to another, an Indian hunting party pursuing game was looking for a spot to camp for the night. After considering a site, the leader said, "Too low, no." Several writers have suggested that the namesake is Chief Tolony, a leader of the Soghonate (Sognati), a subtribe of the Wampanoag of Massachusetts in the 1670s. An early newspaper story claims that the IC purchased the site of Tolono from three men whose surnames were Todd, Logan, and Noyes. One of the requirements of the sale was that the first part of each man's name was to be used in the name of the town. Ackerman, a president of the Illinois Central, states that J. B. Calhoun, a land agent for the IC, created the name by "placing the vowel o three times thus, o-o-o, and filling in with the consonants t-l-n, forming *T-o-l-o-n-o*" (*Early Illinois Railroads,* 127) (Moore, *Tolono Topics,* 4; Vogel, *Indian Place Names in Illinois*). Post office established June 8, 1857.

TOLUCA [tuh LOO kuh]. Marshall. City (1894) seventeen miles southwest of Streator. Founded about 1890 as a station on the Santa Fe Railroad. Named for the city of Toluca de Lerdo west of Mexico City. The circumstances surrounding the naming are unknown. According to one account, however, Mexican workers building the railroad came across a packing crate addressed to Toluca. Homesick, they took the board on which the address was written and nailed it to a post in the switchyard, thus giving the community its name. A Toluca post office operated in Madison County from Aug. 18, 1853, to March 9, 1864

(Burt and Hawthorne, *Past and Present of Marshall and Putnam Counties,* 60; *Illinois Guide*). Post office established Sept. 21, 1888.

TOMPKINS. Warren. Township. Named for Benjamin Tompkins, who was instrumental in the organization of the township (Rowley, *The History of Kirkwood, Illinois*).

TONICA [TAHN uh kuh]. LaSalle. Village (1859, 1873). Laid out about 1853 for the Illinois Central Railroad by postmaster A. J. West. Ultimately named for the Tonica or Tunica Indians who were reported in the lower Mississippi Valley in the eighteenth century. The immediate source of the name, however, was probably a story that appeared in *Sartain's Magazine* in 1851 in which Tonika, a Natchez Indian princess, fell in love with an Illinois leader named Chikagou. Both the Natchez and the Illinois were against the match, and Tonika and Chikagou eloped to New Orleans, where they married. Ticona, northeast of Tonica, is an anagram (Richardson, *Ray Richardson's History of Tonica*, 1, 14; Vogel, *Indian Place Names in Illinois*). Post office established April 27, 1883, as Vermillion; changed to Point Republic April 6, 1836; changed to Tonica Station March 7, 1854.

TONTI. Marion. Three miles northwest of Salem. Named for Henri de Tonti (Tonty), LaSalle's second in command. Tonti explored the Illinois country with LaSalle in 1679 and 1680. Together they built Fort Creve Coeur at Lake Peoria and Fort St. Louis at Starved Rock. As a teenager Tonti lost his right hand in a grenade explosion, and because of his metal prosthesis he was known among the Indians as Iron Hand (Hansen, ed., *Illinois,* 548, 657). Post office established Oct. 2, 1866.

TOPEKA. Mason. Town (1869) seven miles northeast of Havana. Named for Topeka, Kans., in the early 1850s by organizers of the Santa Fe Railroad (Vogel, *Indian Place Names in Illinois*). Post office established June 14, 1861.

TORONTO. Sangamon. South Springfield suburb. Transferred by settlers from Toronto, Ontario, Canada. Ultimately from a Mohawk word meaning "trees standing in the water," referring to the weirs Indians used to trap fish (Rayburn, *Dictionary of Canadian Place Names*).

TOULON [TOOL uhn]. Stark. City (1859, 1873) ten miles south-southeast of Kewanee. Originally known as Miller's Point, named for early settler John Miller. Formally established about 1841 and named by county commissioner William H. Henderson for his former home, Toulon, Haywood County, Tenn., itself probably named for Toulon in southern France. Toulon has been the seat of Stark County since 1841 (Leeson, *Documents and Biography,* 260). Post office established July 28, 1844.

TOVEY [TO vee]. Christian. Village (1914) eight miles northwest of Taylorville. Formerly known as Georgetown and also as Humphrey, the name of the Chicago and Illinois Midland railroad station. The source of the name is unknown. The local story is that the name was drawn from a hat in which several potential others had been placed (Goudy, *History of Christian County*, 301). Post office established May 3, 1915.

TOWANDA. McLean. Village (1875) five miles northeast of Normal. Laid out in 1854 with construction of the Chicago and Mississippi Railroad by Peter Badeau and Jesse W. Fell, founder of the Illinois State Normal University (now Illinois State University). Named by Fell for his birthplace, Towanda, Bradford County, Pa. Ultimately from a Delaware word meaning "burial ground" (Hasbrouck, *History of McLean County*, 118; Vogel, *Indian Place Names in Illinois*). Post office established June 7, 1843, as Money Creek; changed to Towanda Aug. 3, 1855.

TOWER HILL. Shelby. Village (1872) six miles east of Pana. Formerly known as Pilot Knob, named for a navigational landmark. Formally established as Tower Hill about 1857 by Simeon Ryder and P. C. Huggins. The area was also known as Manyawper, a name of unknown origin (*see* Westminster) (*Atlas of Shelby County*, 5; *Combined History of Shelby and Moultrie Counties*, 276). Post office established Oct. 21, 1849, as Westminster; changed to Tower Hill May 11, 1857.

TOWER LAKES. Lake. Village (1966) two miles south of Wauconda. Originally planned as a religious retreat. The retreat did not materialize, however, and in the 1920s a community was established around an artificial lake and a combination transmitting tower and beacon light; thus the name (Dretske, *What's in a Name?*; Martin, "Residents Think It Would Be a Crime").

TREMONT [TREE mahnt]. Tazewell. Village (1841, 1878) seven miles southeast of Pekin. Several local histories claim that the name was derived from the three hills that border the village on the northeast, southeast, and southwest. The source, however, is most likely the Tremont section of The Bronx, New York. About 1834 the Tremont Colony was formed in New York City and Providence, R.I. By the end of 1835 the community had been platted and accommodated some fifty colonists (Blue, ed., *Historical Program*, 6; *History of Tazewell County*, 653). Post office established Dec. 30, 1835.

TRENTON. Clinton. City (1865, 1887) eight miles west of Breese. Founded about 1836 by A. W. Casad on land owned by his brother-in-law, William Lewis. Formally laid out in May 1855. Named for Trenton, N.J., the former home of Casad, Lewis, and other early settlers (*Trenton Centennial*, 5–6). Post office established Feb. 24, 1853.

TRICKELS GROVE. Ford. Former community. Named from the copse called Trickels Grove, itself named for first settlers Joshua and Robert Trickel, who arrived in 1836. The Trickel Grove Cemetery is about three miles southeast of Paxton. A Trickels Grove Township was authorized in Vermilion County in 1851 but never formally organized (Gardner, *History of Ford County*, 127).

TRILLA. Coles, Cumberland. Seven miles south of Mattoon. Established in 1882 on the line of the Cloverleaf Railroad by Jacob Fickes. Named for Trilla Toles, who accompanied her father, Jerry, to the meeting at which the name was chosen. This is the only Trilla in the United States (Lindsay, *Cumberland County,* 148). Post office established June 28, 1882.

TRIMBLE. Crawford. Five miles northeast of Robinson. Named for the Trimble family. James Baird Trimble, an early settler in 1829, was later appointed county judge by Governor Ninian Edwards. John R. Trimble was an early postmaster. The Trimbles donated land for the station on the Paris and Danville Railroad in 1874, and at that point the name of the community was changed from Harmony to Trimble (*History of Crawford County,* 344). Post office established Feb. 20, 1878.

TRINITY. Alexander. Former community south of Mound City near the mouth of the Cache River. Founded in 1816 by a consortium of land speculators that included James Riddle, Nicholas Berthend, Henry Bechtel, and Elias Rector. Trinity disappeared in the 1830s. The source of the name is unknown (Fults, Chisholm, and Novella, *Promised Land in Southern Illinois,* 36). Post office established Jan. 31, 1827.

TRIUMPH. LaSalle. Seven miles southeast of Mendota. Laid out in 1836 by Stephen R. Beggs as La Fayette and informally known as Hard Scrabble. La Fayette failed to prosper, and the community was reestablished in the 1850s as Triumph, taking its name from the Triumph post office. The reason for the name is unknown. Stennett (*A History of the Origin,* 131) suggests that Triumph was an appropriate name because the citizens "triumphed" over the opposition and after a long struggle secured a post office (*History of LaSalle County,* 491; *Past and Present of LaSalle County,* 352). Post office established May 21, 1857.

TRIVOLI [TRIV uh lee, tri VOL ee]. Peoria. Eleven miles west of Peoria. Formally laid out about 1841 and named for the Trivoli post office, but who chose the name—and for what reason—are unknown. The community was known as Trivoli by at least 1839, when the Trivoli Social Library was organized. The name is possibly a variant of "Tivoli" and if so may be a transfer from New York or Pennsylvania. It may also be a variant of "Tripoli" and, if so, again may be a transfer from New York or Pennsylvania. The only other Trivoli in the United States, in Kansas, is probably a transfer from Illinois (Bateman and Selby, eds., *Historical Encyclopedia of Illinois and History of Peoria County,* 837). Post office established May 5, 1837.

TROUBLESOME CREEK. McDonough. Stream. The local story is that a government surveyor laying out congressional townships had a particularly difficult time crossing this creek because of its steep banks and declared it to be "the most troublesome stream he ever saw" (Clarke, *History of McDonough County,* 602).

TROUT HOLLOW. Monroe. Valley north and east of Valmeyer. Named for Jacob Trout, a tanner (*Combined History of Randolph, Monroe, and Perry Counties,* 333).

TROY. Madison. City (1857, 1892) five miles northwest of Collinsville. Modern Troy had its beginnings in the late 1810s as a cluster of three communities: Columbia, Mechanicsburg, and Brookside. In 1819 a group of land speculators purchased Columbia and renamed it Troy. Mechanicsburg merged with Troy in 1857, and Brookside merged in 1891. The name was probably chosen by James Riggin, one of the founders of Troy, who would lay out Athens in Menard County a decade later (Hansen, ed., *Illinois,* 697; Norton, ed., *Centennial History of Madison County,* 557; Underwood, "A New Geography of Illinois: Madison County," 33). Post office established Oct. 21, 1822.

TROY. Will. Township. Founded about 1837 as West Troy by Horace Haff and named for his former home, Troy, N.Y. (Maue, *History of Will County,* 353).

TROY GROVE. LaSalle. Village (1886) eight miles north of LaSalle. Laid out about 1836 as Homer by Cyrus Colton, an early settler from Homer, N.Y. Renamed by James Reed and Warren Root for their former home, Troy, N.Y. (O'Byrne, *History of LaSalle,* 383; Rasmusen, *LaSalle County Lore,* 73). Post office established March 21, 1837.

TRURO. Knox. Fifteen miles east of Galesburg. The source of the name is uncertain. Truro is a transfer, but whether from Truro, Mass., Truro, Ohio, or Truro, Nova Scotia is unknown. Ultimately from Truro in Cornwall, England. Post office established Dec. 10, 1849 as Littleton; changed to Truro Aug. 5, 1850.

TUCKER. Formerly known as La Prairie. The name was changed to Martin in 1873 and to Tucker in 1876 for J. F. Tucker, general superintendent of the Illinois Central Railroad (Ackerman, *Early Illinois Railroads,* 123).

TUCKERS CORNERS. Hamilton. Eight miles south-southwest of McLeansboro. Named for Johnny Tucker, who established a general store at the site in 1931 (*Hamilton County,* 39).

TUNBRIDGE. DeWitt. Five miles southwest of Clinton. Probably a transfer by settlers from Tunbridge, Orange County, Vt., itself named in 1761 for William Henry Nassau de Zuylstein (1717–81), Fourth Earl of Rochford, Viscount Tunbridge, Baron Enfield and Colchester. Tunbridge, officially Royal Tunbridge Wells, is a borough in Kent, England (*History of DeWitt County* [1882], 243; Stewart, *American Place-Names*). Post office established Dec. 22, 1854.

TUNNEL HILL. Johnson. Sixteen miles south of Morrison. Named for the train tunnel blasted through the hill in 1871–72 (Mohlenbrock, "A New Geography of Illinois: Johnson County," 33). Post office established Feb. 28, 1873.

TURPIN. Macon. South Decatur suburb. Established as Turpin Station, a stop on the Illinois Central Railroad, by site owner Jerry Turpin (Richmond, *Centennial History of Decatur,* 97).

TUSCARORA. Peoria. South Peoria suburb. Tuscarora is the name of an Iroquoian tribe originally from North Carolina, now associated with New York state. Tuscarora is found as a place name throughout the Appalachian mountain region.

Tuscarora, Ill., is probably a transfer from New York or Pennsylvania (Bright, *Native American Placenames*).

TUSCOLA [tuhs KOL uh]. Douglas. City (1861, 1872). Named by the Illinois Central Railroad in the 1850s. The origin of the name is uncertain. Perhaps a transfer from Tuscola in Leake County, Miss., or a transfer with shortening from Tusco-lameta, Miss., both of which are derived from Choctaw *tashka* (warrior). It may also be a transfer from Michigan, where the word *Tuscola* was coined by the nineteenth-century ethnologist Henry Rowe Schoolcraft, who created a number of pseudo-Indian names based loosely upon native materials. At one time Schoolcraft claimed that Tuscola meant "warrior prairie" and at another that it meant "level lands" (Bright, *Native American Placenames;* Gresham, comp., *Historical and Biographical Record,* 94; Stewart, *American Place-Names*). Post office established Dec. 13, 1857.

TWIGG. Hamilton. Township. Named for James Twigg, an early settler from Rutherford County, Tenn. (*History of Gallatin, Saline,* 243).

TYRONE. Franklin. Township. Named after the *Tyrone,* a Mississippi River steamboat whose captain, Charles Tinsley, settled in the township (Henson, *History of Franklin County,* 57).

U

UDINA. Kane. Two miles west of Elgin. The origin of the name is uncertain. Udina may be a form of Udine, a city northeast of Venice, Italy, brought to the area by Italian settlers, or it may be from a Russian personal name or a transfer from Udina, the name of a river and volcano in Russia. It may also be a transfer from Scotland or given in memory of Scotland. There were a significant number of Scottish settlers in the area, as evidenced by such nearby place names as Dundee and Caledonia. Furthermore, as Ghrist notes (23), in several of his poems Robert Burns refers to Edinburgh as Edina, which may have been altered to Udina (Ghrist, *Junction 20,* 12–32). Post office established Dec. 30, 1839.

ULAH. Henry. Three miles southeast of Cambridge. Laid out by site owner C. A. Morris about 1873. Probably named for the heroine of one of the pseudo-Indian "Starved Rock" legends popular in the nineteenth century (*see* Oconee) (Vogel, *Indian Place Names in Illinois*). Post office established June 5, 1868.

ULLIN [UHL uhn]. Pulaski. Village (1900) thirteen miles south-southeast of Anna. Although Ackerman (*Early Illinois Railroads,* 137) claims that the name was taken from Ossian's poems, in which Ullin is described as the "stormy son of war," the source is more likely the Ulen family. Samuel Ulen was an early settler from Greenup County, Ky., and also the first postmaster (*Pulaski County,* 327). Post office established Jan. 5, 1856.

UNION. Union is one of the most popular place names in the United States; GNIS shows some seven hundred populated places or civil divisions with that name. Among current Illinois communities there are five Unions, three Unionvilles, two Uniontowns, two Union Hills, and one each Union Center, Union Grove, and Union Point as well as Union County and the seven townships or precincts named *Union*. In addition, there have been several dozen Union post offices and settlements that have disappeared or been absorbed into other communities. Many Unions, such as Union Hill in Kankakee County and Union Township in Livingston County, were named during the Civil War in honor of the federal union of states. A few have unique origins. Unionville in Massac County was named for its location at the union (junction) of the five roads coming from New Liberty, Bay City, Fairplay, Metropolis, and Brookport. Union Grove in Whiteside County took its name from two nearby groves that were so similar they were called the "Union Groves" (*History of Massac County*, 37; Stennett, *A History of the Origin*, 132).

UNION. County. Created Jan. 2, 1818, from Johnson County. Named for a joint revival meeting of the Baptists and Dunkards held near Dongola in 1816 or 1817. When George Wolfe, a Dunkard minister, and his Baptist counterpart, a Reverend Jones, realized that they would be holding concurrent revival meetings, they decided to hold a common service, a "union meeting." The seal of Union County shows Wolfe and Jones shaking hands. Although Union County was named primarily in recognition of this joint service, a strong sense of the federal union likely contributed to the appeal of the name, given that Illinois was being considered for statehood at the time (Perrin, ed., *History of Alexander, Union and Pulaski Counties*).

UNION. McHenry. Village (1897) three miles east-southeast of Marengo. Founded in 1851 in anticipation of a station on the Chicago and North Western Railroad by site owner William Jackson. Named for the federal union or a transfer from Union, N.Y. (Stennett, *A History of the Origin*, 132). Post office established April 17, 1852.

UNIVERSITY PARK. Cook, Will. Village (1967) two miles south of Park Forest. Founded as Park Forest South in 1967 by Nathan Manilow, one of the developers of Park Forest. Renamed for Governors State University and Governors Gateway, a large industrial park on the west side of the village (Leroux, "Metra Service Part of University Park Plan").

URBANA. Champaign. City (1833, 1873). Founded about 1822. The name was transferred by settlers from Urbana, the seat of Champaign County, Ohio. Ultimately from Latin "of the city." Urbana has been the seat of Champaign County since its formation in 1833. Post office established Sept. 2, 1836.

URSA [ER suh]. Adams. Village (1963) nine miles north of Quincy. The area bounded by Bear Creek to the north of Ursa and Rock Creek to the south was known as "Bear Creek country." By the mid-1830s the *bear* of Bear Creek had been translated into Latin *ursa* (female bear), likely influenced by the constellations Ursa Major and Ursa Minor, probably by Richard M. Johnson, who was instrumental in securing the Ursa post office (Genosky, ed., *People's History,* 729, 736–37). Post office established March 12, 1836.

USTICK [YOO stik]. Whiteside. Five miles north of Morrison. Named for Henry Ustick (Eustick), who emigrated from western Pennsylvania in 1845. The post office was established in 1850 as Hemlo, reportedly named by drawing letters randomly from a hat. When the first five drawn were *h, e, m, l,* and *o* (and fearing that the next letter would be *c* or *k*), the namers stopped (Bastian, *A History of Whiteside County,* 456). Post office established Nov. 19, 1850, as Hemlo; discontinued May 17, 1870; reestablished as Ustick March 16, 1854.

UTAH. Warren. Five miles northwest of Galesburg. Established in 1850 and named for the present state of Utah, which at the time had recently been organized as Utah Territory. Post office established Aug. 9, 1841, as Tylerville; changed to Utah Oct. 30, 1850.

UTICA [YOO tuh kuh]. LaSalle. Three miles east of LaSalle. A transfer from Utica, Oneida County, N.Y., by land speculators or by officials of the Illinois and Michigan Canal. Utica, N.Y., was the first Utica in the United States, named for the ancient city near modern Tunis. Post office established June 26, 1834 (*Past and Present of LaSalle County,* 333).

V

VALIER [vuh LIHR]. Franklin. Village (1918) six miles west of Benton. Founded in 1905 by H. B. Scott on land owned by Albert and William Valier. Valier Patch, formerly known as the Cactus Patch, is just north of Valier. In parts of southern Illinois a "patch" was a temporary community, usually near a coal mine. When the mine was worked out or no longer profitable the "patch" usually disappeared. Valier Patch is one of the few that endured (*Franklin County,* 22; Harris, "Illinois Place-Name Lore," 219; Henson, *History of Franklin County,* 83). Post office established May 9, 1906.

VALLEY CITY. Pike. Village (1955) ten miles northeast of Pittsfield. The smallest incorporated community in Illinois, with a population of fourteen. Post office established Feb. 1, 1856, as Flint; changed to Valley City Aug. 17, 1877.

VALMEYER. Monroe. Village (1909) eight miles west of Waterloo. Founded in 1902 as Meyer City by members of one or more Meyer families. The name was changed in 1903 to Valmeyer, a blend of *valley* and *Meyer,* at the suggestion of Dr. E. J. Lee, the postmaster at Harrisonville (Klein, ed., *Arrowheads to Aerojets,* 548). Post office established Jan. 10, 1903.

VANCE. Vermilion. Township. Changed from Union in 1851 to honor John W. Vance, an Illinois state senator of the late 1830s who was instrumental in the organization of Champaign County (Stapp and Sullenberger, *Footprints in the Sands,* 6).

VANCIL BEND. Williamson. The loop in the Big Muddy River northwest of Herrin in Blairsville Township. Named in honor of Isaac Vancil, an early settler whose legacy took an ironic turn when he was hanged by a vigilante group for refusing to leave the area that had been named for him (Hale, comp. and ed., *Williamson County,* 119; Hubbs, *Pioneer Folks and Places*).

VANDALIA. Fayette. City (1821). Founded in 1819 as the second capital of Illinois by Samuel Whiteside (for whom Whiteside County is named), Thomas Cox, Levi Compton, and William Alexander. Stewart calls Vandalia "a curiously popular name of uncertain origin." The source of the Illinois name is indeed unknown, although a number of sources have been proposed. One, offered in jest but apparently taken seriously, claimed that the Vandals were a local Indian tribe; another held the name to be a blend of *van,* suggesting that the city was in the "vanguard" of progress, and *dalia,* for the dales within the surrounding hills; and still another claimed that Vandalia (or Van Dale) was the name of an early hunter or explorer. These suggestions are without merit. The founders, though, may have been familiar with the name because Vandalia was a potential place name for many years. As early as the 1760s the name, derived from the word *vandal,* which designated a group of Germanic tribes and also coincidentally honored the Germanic heritage of both King George III of Britain and his wife, Charlotte, was proposed for a fourteenth English colony in America, to consist largely of the territory now comprising the state of West Virginia. The American Revolution brought an abrupt and permanent halt to the Vandalia Colony but not necessarily to the name. Further, there is evidence that the name (or a similar one) was in use locally several decades before 1819. A hand-drawn map, probably dating from the early 1800s, shows a "Vanne Delai" (perhaps derived from French *vanne* [floodgate]) near the site of present Vandalia. Another map, drawn several years later, shows the same site as "Vandla," which may have been adapted to Vandalia through popular etymology. Whether the surveyors of 1819 drew the name from, or were even aware of, these maps is unknown. Vandalia was the capital of Illinois from 1819 until 1839 (personal communication with Linda Hanabarger; Strobel, *High on the Okaw's Western Bank,* 13, 136). Post office established Dec. 8, 1820.

VANDERVILLE. Christian. Eleven miles west of Pana. Founded about 1891 by William Fines as Vandeveerville, named for Judge Horatio M. Vandeveer (Goudy, *History of Christian County,* 148). Post office established July 16, 1894.

VAN ORIN. Bureau. Thirteen miles northeast of Princeton. Named for Van Orin Cresap, a local farmer and prominent citizen (Bradsby, ed., *History of Bureau County,* 160). Post office established Jan. 15, 1872.

VAN PETTEN. Lee. Six miles southeast of Rock Falls. Named for site owner A. G. Van Petten (Barge and Caldwell, "Illinois Place Names"). Post office established Nov. 14, 1901.

VARNA. Marshall. Village (1873) twenty miles west-southwest of Streator. Laid out in Sept. 1870. By his own account, Joseph Maleham was at the railroad station when someone pitched a newspaper from a passing train. The paper included an article about a war being fought in Varna, Bulgaria. Maleham was fascinated by the name and suggested Varna for the name of the community, which was then in the early stages of development. The choice of the name may have been influenced by settlers from Varna, Tompkins County, N.Y. (Ellsworth, *Records of the Olden Times,* 404; *History of Marshall County,* 53). Post office established April 20, 1871.

VELMA. Christian. Four miles southeast of Taylorville. Founded in the late 1890s and named for Velma Shumway by her father, postmaster Hiram Shumway (*Christian County History,* 44). Post office established Oct. 24, 1894.

VENEDY [VEN uh dee]. Washington. Village (1881) eleven miles southeast of Mascoutah. Founded in the late 1830s by German settlers and known as Brockschmidt's Town, for G. H. Brockschmidt, from Hanover, Germany. Formally laid out as Venedy about 1860. Perhaps named for Venedig, the German name for Venice, or for Jacob Venedy (1805–71), author, friend, and associate of Karl Marx (*Washington County,* 79). Post office established July 2, 1861.

VENICE [VEN uhs]. Madison. City (1873) east of St. Louis, Mo. Named in the early 1840s by Dr. Cornelius Campbell of St. Louis, who had a financial interest in a Mississippi River ferry. Probably named for Venice, Italy, perhaps because Venice, Illinois, like Venice, Italy, had to contend with persistent and often severe flooding (*History of Madison County,* 521; *Illinois Gazetteer*). Post office established Sept. 29, 1838, as Six Mile; changed to Venice March 15, 1843.

VERA. Fayette. Five miles north of Vandalia. The source of the name is unknown. Several early writers suggest the name is derived from Latin *veritas* (truth) or that the community was named for the Italian philosopher Augusto Vera (1813–85). Just as likely but much less exotic, Vera may also have been the name of the wife or daughter of a postmaster, railroad official, or site owner (Ackerman, *Early Illinois Railroads,* 150). Post office established May 16, 1862.

VERGENNES [ver JENZ]. Jackson. Village (1887) nine miles north of Murphysboro. Originally called Middletown and informally known as the Yankee Settlement for the large number of settlers from New England. Named by site owner Daniel B. Tuthill for his wife's former home, Vergennes, Addison County, Vt., itself named during the post-Revolutionary infatuation for all things French in honor of Charles Gravier, Count de Vergennes, the French minister of foreign affairs under Louis XVI who negotiated the Treaty of Paris that officially ended the

Revolutionary War in 1783 (Allen, *Jackson County Notes,* 37; *History of Jackson County,* 120). Post office established Feb. 23, 1846.

VERMILION. County. Created Jan. 18, 1826. Named from the Vermilion River.

VERMILION RIVER. Empties into the Illinois River north of Oglesby. The name *Vermilion* is a French translation of Miami-Illinois *aramoni,* which referred to the red clay, often called "red ochre," Native Americans used to decorate their bodies. The Vermilion River is called the Aramoni on Coronelli's map of about 1683 (personal communication with Michael McCafferty).

VERMILION RIVER. Empties into the Wabash River in Indiana, south of Danville. Known to early French explorers as Vermillion Jaune (Yellow Vermilion), a translation of *osanamon* (yellow ochre) from Potawatomi (see Saunemin) (Baker, *From Needmore to Prosperity;* personal communication with Michael McCafferty).

VERMILION. Edgar. Village (1869, 1873) six miles southeast of Paris. Laid out about 1856 as Vermillion, named for James S. Vermillion, the first postmaster. The spelling was changed to Vermilion about 1949 to agree with that of the river and county (*Prairie Progress,* 298). Post office established July 24, 1856, as Vermillion; changed to Vermilion June 23, 1892.

VERMONT. Fulton. Village (1857, 1879) seventeen miles southeast of Macomb. Founded by James and Joseph Crail in 1835. According to the traditional naming story, the community was to be called Meridian for its location on the fourth principle meridian. Abitha Williams, however, offered the Crails a gallon of whisky in return for the naming rights. The Crails accepted Williams's offer and passed the jug around to those bidding for town lots. Williams then announced that the name would be Vermont, in honor of his home state (*History of Fulton County,* 899). Post office established Aug. 23, 1837.

VERNON. Lake. Township. Named for George Washington's estate, Mt. Vernon, Va. Other names considered at the time of township formation were Rome, for Rome, N.Y., and Half Day (q.v.) (*Past and Present of Lake County,* 314).

VERNON. Marion. Village (1809) eleven miles south of Vandalia. Established by the Illinois Central Railroad in 1872 and named for William Vernon, an auditor for the IC (Ackerman, *Early Illinois Railroads,* 152). Post office established March 21, 1873.

VERNON HILLS. Lake. Village (1958) south of Libertyville. Developers Barney Loeb and Quinn Hogan named the community in the mid-1950s for its location in Vernon Township (Dretske, *What's in a Name?*).

VERONA [vuh RO nuh]. Grundy. Village (1903) ten miles south-southwest of Morris. Established about 1876 as a station on the Chicago, Pekin and Southwestern Railroad by George D. Smith and named for his birthplace, Verona, Oneida County, N.Y. (Ullrich, *This Is Grundy County,* 258). Post office established July 13, 1866, as Highland Town; changed to Verona July 18, 1876.

VERSAILLES [ver SAYLZ]. Brown. Village (1861, 1917) eight miles southeast of Mount Sterling. Founded in the 1830s by Henry Casteen and named for his former home, Versailles, Woodford County, Ky., itself named in 1792 for Lafayette's birthplace near Paris, France (*Combined History of Schuyler and Brown Counties*, 241, 299; Rennick, *Kentucky Place Names*). Post office established Dec. 21, 1835, as Sugar Grove; changed to Versailles Oct. 17, 1837.

VERSAILLES. Woodford. Former community. Platted in 1836 by Thomas Bullock and named for his former home, Versailles, Ky. Versailles was the first seat of Woodford County, serving from 1841 until 1843, when it was moved to Metamora. The railroads isolated Versailles, and it has now disappeared. The Versailles School was located about two miles southeast of Eureka (Yates, *The Woodford County History*, 121).

VEVAY PARK. Cumberland. Four miles west-southwest of Casey. Originally known as Long Point Station, established by the Vandalia Railroad about 1869. Renamed by Grant Pickett, who operated a pumping station for the Vandalia line, for his former home, Vevay, Ind., itself named for Vevay, Switzerland (Baker, *From Needmore to Prosperity*; Lindsay, *Cumberland County 1843–1993*, 151). Post office established Nov. 15, 1883, as Vevay; changed to Vevay Park Oct. 19, 1887.

VICTOR. DeKalb. Township and former community. Created from Clinton Township about 1852 and probably named for Victor, Ontario County, N.Y. The Victor Cemetery is three miles north of Leland. The Victor Centre post office operated from April 13, 1863, until July 7, 1879, and the Victor post office from Sept. 9, 1896, until Sept. 13, 1902 (Gross, *Past and Present of DeKalb County*, 137).

VICTORIA. Knox. Village (1886) seventeen miles southwest of Kewanee. Founded about 1839 and named for the Victoria post office, itself probably named for Queen Victoria of Great Britain, whose coronation was in 1837, the year the post office was established. Victoria Township is abutted on the west by Copley Township, which was formerly known as Prince Albert (*Annals of Knox County*, 184). Post office established Dec. 6, 1837.

VIENNA [veye EN uh]. Johnson. City (1837, 1877) 20 m nw of Metropolis. Laid out in 1818 as the permanent seat of Johnson County, succeeding Elvira, the temporary seat. One account attributes the name to Vienna McFatridge, claimed to be the daughter of William McFatridge, but her existence has not been verified. Perhaps named for Vienna, Austria (Allen Collection; Chapman, *A History of Johnson County*, 295). Post office established Feb. 3, 1815, as Johnson Courthouse; changed to Vienna Oct. 22, 1821.

VIENNA. Grundy. Township. Probably a transfer by settlers from Vienna, Oneida County, N.Y. (Bateman and Selby, eds., *Historical Encyclopedia of Illinois and History of Grundy County*, 746).

VILLA PARK. DuPage. Village (1914). Founded about 1908 by the Chicago real estate firm of Ballard and Pottinger, which in 1910 established Ardmore, reportedly named for a Philadelphia suburb adjacent to Villa Park. Several years later, Ardmore and Villa Park merged as Ardmore. The name was changed to Villa Park by popular referendum in 1917. The source of the name is unclear. It may be a developer's promotional name, or it may have been proposed by Chicago business executive Charles Heisen, whose Florida estate was called Villa Park (*Recollections: Story of Villa Park,* 28, 34, 45–46). Post office established Nov. 30, 1917.

VILLA RIDGE. Pulaski. Three miles north of Mounds. Established by the Illinois Central Railroad in 1852 and named by the daughter of a Dr. Arter for their family farm, Villa Ridge. The IC supply station was known as the Villa (Ackerman, *Early Illinois Railroads,* 137–38). Post office established Aug. 12, 1853, as Valley Forge; changed to Villa Ridge June 26, 1861.

VILLAS. Crawford. Six miles south of Robinson. Originally called Ono, possibly for the biblical city Ono mentioned in First Chronicles 8:12, but probably a transfer from Ono, Russell County, K.Y. For unknown reasons the name was changed to Villas in the late 1880s (*History of Crawford County,* 22). Post office established April 23, 1888.

VINEGAR HILL. Jo Daviess. Township. Created as Mann Township, named for Harvey Mann, chair of the first board of supervisors of Jo Daviess County and the oldest resident at the time of township formation in 1852. The name was changed in 1857 for Vinegar Hill, County Wexford, in southeast Ireland. Local stories claim that a group of miners, "while in a state of spiritual hallucination," christened an Indian mound by pouring whisky over it and declaring, "Henceforth and forever, this placed shall be called Vinegar Hill" (Bateman and Selby, eds., *Historical Encyclopedia of Illinois and History of Jo Daviess County,* 633; *History of Jo Daviess County,* 609). Post office established Jan. 15, 1852.

VIOLA. Mercer. Village (1870, 1873). Eight miles east of Aledo. Laid out about 1856 and named for Viola Perkins, daughter of one of the site owners (Bateman and Selby, eds., *Historical Encyclopedia of Illinois and History of Mercer County,* 644). Post office established July 9, 1856.

VIOLA. Lee. Township. Formed as Stockton in February 1861. The name was changed to Viola in September 1861. The source of the name is unknown (*History of Lee County,* 611).

VIRDEN [VERD n]. Macoupin. City (1861, 1872). Founded in 1852 by John Virden, proprietor of the local hotel (*History of Macoupin County,* 238). Post office established Feb. 10, 1852.

VIRGIL. Kane. Village (1990) seven miles east-southeast of Sycamore. Probably a transfer from Virgil, Cortland County, N.Y., itself named for the Roman poet Virgil. Post office established Jan. 9, 1893.

VIRGINIA. Cass. City (1857, 1872) twelve miles east-southeast of Beardstown. After a tour that included the United States, Dr. Henry Hammond Hall, a surgeon in the British navy, resigned his commission and established a medical practice first in Baltimore and later in Virginia. Hall migrated to Illinois and founded Virginia in 1836, naming it in honor of the state of Virginia. It was the seat of Cass County from 1839 until 1843 and again from 1867 (Bateman and Selby, eds., *Historical Encyclopedia of Illinois and History of Cass County*, 831). Post office established April 3, 1826, as Horns, for postmaster Reddick Horn; changed to Sylvan Grove Nov. 16, 1827; changed to Virginia Feb. 26, 1839.

VOLLENTINE. Christian. Former community. Probably named for the Vollentine (Vollintine) family. George Wesley Vollintine was an early settler. The Vollentine School was northwest of Taylorville (Bateman and Selby, eds., *Historical Encyclopedia of Illinois and History of Christian County*, 1002).

VOLO. Lake. Five miles east of McHenry. First known as The Forks and later as Forksville for its location at the fork of the McHenry-Chicago and Little Fort (Waukegan) roads. The name was formally changed to Volo in 1868, possibly at the suggestion of Greek immigrants for Volo (Volos) in eastern Greece (Gowen, "After the Birth"; *Past and Present of Lake County*, 318). Post office established March 24, 1848, as Forksville; changed to Volo Nov. 27, 1868.

VOORHIES. Piatt. Seventeen miles east of Decatur. Laid out as Voorhies Station on the line of the Wabash Railroad by Jack and William Voorhies (Morgan, ed., *The Good Life in Piatt County*, 113). Post office established Feb. 8, 1878.

W

WABASH. County. Created Dec. 27, 1824, from Edwards County. Named for the Wabash River. From Miami-Illinois meaning "shining white," referring to the limestone bed of the river's upper reaches. Early French explorers recorded the name as Ouabache. The county seat was established at Centreville and moved to Mount Carmel in 1829 (Baker, *From Needmore to Prosperity*; Bright, *Native American Placenames*).

WACKER. Carroll. Six miles southeast of Savanna. The community grew around a creamery established on land owned by farmer John Wacker (Thiem, ed., *Carroll County*, 120). Post office established Dec. 12, 1894.

WADDAMS GROVE. Stephenson. Fifteen miles northwest of Freeport. Also Waddams Township. Named for William Waddams, generally acknowledged as the first permanent settler in Stephenson County. Waddams emigrated from New York with his sons Hiram and Nelson about 1830 (*History of Stephenson County*, 199; Tilden, comp., *History of Stephenson County*, 520). Post office established March 31, 1838.

WADE. Township. Jasper. Named for Hiram Wade, clerk of the circuit court and Jasper county recorder in the 1840s. The name was changed from Newton in 1860 (*Counties of Cumberland, Jasper, and Richland*, 410).

WADSWORTH. Lake. Village (1962) three miles west of Zion. Laid out in 1874 by John Lux as a station on the Chicago, Milwaukee and St. Paul Railroad. Named for Julius Wadsworth, vice president of the CM&StP; or for Elisha Wadsworth, a major shareholder in the railroad whose estate was near Waukegan; or for both (Dretske, *What's in a Name?*; Goodley, *The Wire Mill*, 9). Post office established Feb. 9, 1874.

WADY PETRA. Stark. An alternate name for the community of Stark. Wady Petra was laid out about 1875 and perhaps named by Philander Chase, who founded the Jubilee School. The reason for the name is unknown. Wady is Arabic for "valley, arroyo," and Petra is the famous ruined city in southwestern Jordan (*Township Histories*, 120). Post office established Sept. 29, 1871.

WAGGONER [WAG ner]. Montgomery. Village (1895) fourteen miles northeast of Carlinville. Named for George Waggoner, an early settler from Kentucky (Traylor, *Past and Present of Montgomery County*, 744). Post office established Dec. 29, 1886.

WAISH-KEE-SHAW. Kendall. Reserve. Three miles south of Oswego on Reservation Road. Also Waa Kee Sha Park. Named for Waish-kee-shaw, the Potawatomi wife of David Laughton. By the Treaty of Prairie du Chien in 1829, Waish-kee-shaw was granted one and one-half sections of land at the village of Naausay. She sold the land to white settlers a few years later (Farren, ed., *A Bicentennial History*, 46, 106).

WAKEFIELD. Richland. Eleven miles northwest of Olney. Laid out by Thomas Wakefield and Pleasant M. Stanley in 1853 (*Counties of Cumberland, Jasper, and Richland*, 722). Post office established May 27, 1856.

WALDO. Livingston. Twelve miles southwest of Pontiac. Laid out about 1880 by site owners Elijah Filly and Jacob Keller. Named by Parker Jewett for his former home, Waldo, Maine. Waldo Township, originally called Kansas, was formed from Nebraska Township in 1860 (*History of Livingston County* [1878], 287). Post office established Sept. 6, 1900.

WALKER. Hancock. Township. Named for George Walker, an early settler and county commissioner (Gregg, *History of Hancock County*, 565). Post office established Feb. 23, 1857.

WALKER. Macon. Eleven miles south of Decatur. Named for John W. Walker, a stock and grain dealer. The Illinois Central station was called Willow Branch until 1882 (Ackerman, *Early Illinois Railroads*, 148). Post office established April 5, 1881.

WALKERVILLE. Greene. Five miles southwest of White Hall. Founded about 1835 by site owner John Walker (Clapp, *History of Greene County*, 429). Post office established March 7, 1865.

WALL. Ford. Township. Formed from Patton Township in 1867 and named for Abraham Wall, the first permanent settler (Gardner, *History of Ford County*, 168).

WALLA WALLA. Cumberland. Thirteen miles southwest of Casey. A transfer from Walla Walla in Washington state; itself from a Native American source meaning "little rivers" (Bright, *Native American Placenames*). Post office established Nov. 5, 1889.

WALLINGFORD. Will. Former community ten miles southwest of Frankfort. Probably named by settlers from Wallingford, New Haven County, Conn. Post office established July 22, 1847.

WALNUT. There are more than one hundred Walnut place names in Illinois. Most were given in recognition of the walnut groves that provided lumber, food, and shelter to early settlers and served as landmarks for pioneers traversing the prairies. Walnut Grove is the most popular, followed by Walnut, Walnut Point, Walnut Hill, and an assortment of Walnut Prairies, Walnut Ridges, Walnut Shades, and Walnut Valleys.

WALPOLE. Hamilton. Thirteen miles north of Harrisburg. Laid out in 1857 by postmaster Gilbert Griswold. Probably named for Horace Walpole, the eighteenth-century English novelist whose works Griswold reportedly admired (*Hamilton County,* 45). Post office established April 16, 1832, as Griswold; changed to Walpole Sept. 22, 1873.

WALSH. Randolph. Eight miles southwest of Sparta. Originally called Muerville. Renamed about 1899 by John R. Walsh, who was instrumental in attracting a railroad station to the site (*Randolph County,* 101). Post office established May 12, 1899.

WALSHVILLE. Montgomery. Village (1863, 1891) seven miles south-southeast of Litchfield. Founded about 1854 by site owner Michael Walsh (Perrin, ed., *History of Bond and Montgomery Counties,* 374). Post office established Dec. 11, 1840, as Mount Kingston; changed to Walshville April 28, 1854.

WALTERSBURG. Pope. Twenty miles north-northeast of Metropolis. The post office was established in July 1878 as Wallersburg, probably an errant transcription of Walkersburg, presumably named for Andrew Walker, the first postmaster. Later in 1878 the name was changed to Waltersburg for postmaster Adolph Walter (Allen, *Pope County Notes,* 86). Post office established June 12, 1878, as Wallersburg; changed to Waltersburg July 1, 1878.

WALTHAM. LaSalle. Seven-and-a-half miles northeast of LaSalle. Named by settlers from the Boston suburb of Waltham, Mass. (O'Byrne, *History of LaSalle,* 423). Post office established March 31, 1852.

WAMAC. City (1916). South Centralia suburb. An acronym formed from the names of the three counties in which the community lies: Washington, Marion, and Clinton (*Illinois Guide*).

WAMPUM. Cook. Lake. Wampum is an Algonquian word referring to the strings of shells offered as gifts and later as mediums of exchange. Perhaps a transfer from Pennsylvania or Massachusetts (personal communication with Michael McCafferty).

WANBOROUGH. Edwards. Former community west of Albion. Founded in 1818 by Morris Birkbeck and named for Birkbeck's estate in Surry, near London, England. The growth of Albion as the county seat and the death of Birkbeck in 1825 led to Wanborough's decline and ultimate demise. The Wanborough (Wanboro) Cemetery is fifteen miles east of Fairfield (*see* Albion) (Harper, ed., *History of Edwards County*, 63–64). Post office established Aug. 20, 1821.

WANLOCK. Mercer. Seven miles east of Aledo. Founded by Hugh Gilchrist as a residential community for mine employees and named by Gilchrist for his birthplace, Wanlockhead, Dumfries and Galloway, Scotland (Bateman and Selby, eds., *Historical Encyclopedia of Illinois and History of Mercer County*, 643, 742). Post office established March 12, 1895.

WAPELLA [wah PEL uh]. DeWitt. Village (1876) four miles north of Clinton. Founded in 1854 by David A. Neal, vice president of the Illinois Central Railroad, and named for Wapella (Little Bird), a Meskwaki (Fox) leader of the 1820s and 1830s. Wapella was neutral during the Black Hawk War and for this reason was looked upon favorably by European settlers. He died in Iowa in 1842. Wapello, a variant, is the seat of Louisa County, Iowa (Bright, *Native American Placenames*; Vogel, *Indian Place Names in Illinois*). Post office established April 6, 1855.

WARD'S GROVE. Jo Daviess. Township. Named for Bernard Ward, the first permanent settler in the area (*History of Jo Daviess County*, 601). Post office established June 15, 1848.

WARE. Union. Eight miles west of Anna. Founded by Jesse Ware, an attorney whose practice was in Anna (Mohlenbrock, "A New Geography of Illinois: Union County," 36). Post office established June 8, 1893.

WARREN. County. Created Jan. 13, 1825. Probably named directly for Joseph Warren (1741–75), a Massachusetts political leader and general in the Revolutionary War. It was Joseph Warren who dispatched Paul Revere and William Dawes to Lexington to warn of the approach of British troops. He was killed at Bunker Hill on June 17, 1775. Possibly named by, or at least influenced by, settlers from Warren County, Tenn., itself named for Joseph Warren.

WARREN. Jo Daviess. Village (1859, 1876) twenty-two miles northwest of Freeport. First known as Burnett's Corners for early settler Alexander Burnett. About 1854, with construction of the railroad from Rockford to Galena, the community was formally laid out as Courtland [*sic*], named for Cortland, N.Y. Shortly thereafter the name was changed to Warren, taking the name of the Warren post office, previously named by Burnett for his son, Warren, who was named for Warren, Ohio, the Burnetts' former home. The name of the township was changed from Courtland about 1865 (Bateman and Selby, eds., *Historical Encyclopedia* of Illinois and History of Jo Daviess County, 633; Carson and Gray, History of Warren, 10). Post office established June 4, 1849.

WARREN. Lake. Township. The name was chosen by popular vote at the time of township formation about 1850 at the suggestion of Alexander Druce (for whom Druce Lake is named) and Amos Wright for their former home, Warren, Herkimer County, N.Y., itself named for the same Gen. Joseph Warren for whom Warren County was named (Dretske, What's in a Name?; Past and Present of Lake County, 316–17).

WARRENSBURG. Macon. Village (1880) six miles northwest of Decatur. Founded in 1872 and named for John K. Warren, mayor of Decatur in 1867 and a director of the Pekin, Lincoln and Decatur Railroad (Richmond, Centennial History of Decatur, 96). Post office established Dec. 12, 1871, as Warrensburgh; changed to Warrensburg April 26, 1886.

WARRENVILLE. DuPage. City (1967). Founded about 1844 by Julius Morton Warren (1810–93). Named for himself and for his father, Daniel. Julius Warren was the city's first postmaster and a member of the Illinois General Assembly in the 1840s and 1850s (Moore and Bray, DuPage at 150, 132). Post office established May 2, 1838, as Warrensville; changed to Warrenville Aug. 29, 1883.

WARSAW. Hancock. City (1837, 1906) three miles southwest of Keokuk, Iowa. Laid out in 1834 by John R. Wilcox, Mark Aldrich, John Montague, and John W. Vineyard. Named from an early-nineteenth-century novel, Thaddeus of Warsaw, by Jane Porter. Not everyone was taken with the name. About 1870, John M. Hay, one of Abraham Lincoln's secretaries, observed, "Towns are sometimes absurdly named. . . . Some idiots, just before I was born, who had read Miss Porter's novel 'Thaddeus of Warsaw,' a romance, thought 'Warsaw' would be . . . genteel, and so we are Nicodemussed into nothing for the rest of time" (quoted in Climer, Fornell and Havens, Welcome to Warsaw, 30) The novel also gave its name to the Thaddeus of Warsaw, a ferry that ran between Warsaw, Ill., and Alexandria, Mo. (Albers, Van Pappelendam, and Worthen, comps., History of Warsaw, 2). Post office established Jan. 30, 1833, as Fort Edwards; changed to Warsaw Nov. 14, 1834.

WARTBURG. Monroe. Four miles southwest of Waterloo. Settled largely by German immigrants and named either directly for Wartburg Castle in Eisenach, Germany, where Martin Luther translated the Bible, or for the Wartburg Evangelical Lutheran Church, first established about two miles south of Waterloo, itself named for Wartburg Castle (Allen Collection; Combined History of Randolph, Monroe, and Perry Counties, 422). Post office established May 24, 1881.

WARTRACE. Johnson. Sixteen miles north-northwest of Metropolis. According to one local story, a veteran, on his way home from the Civil War, stole a horse and killed its owner. He was shortly apprehended, given a quick trial, and promptly hanged. Residents of the previously unnamed community decided to call it Wartrace in the hope that this incident would be the last trace of the Civil War. A second story claims that the town was built on an old Indian war path or war trace. More likely, the name is a transfer from Wartrace, Bedford County, Tenn., itself named for a trace ("trail") reportedly used by Indian war parties (Chapman, *A History of Johnson County*, 287; Miller, *Tennessee Place Names*). Post office established March 13, 1891.

WASCO [WAHS ko]. Kane. Four miles northwest of St. Charles. A shortened form of Owasco. Probably transferred by settlers from Owasco, Cayuga County, N.Y., or possibly by settlers from Owasco, Carroll County, Ind., itself named for Owasco, N.Y. Wasco, Ore., the only other Wasco in the United States, is from a different source (Baker, *From Needmore to Prosperity*). Post office established Oct. 20, 1887.

WASHBURN. Marshall, Woodford. Village (1857, 1873) ten miles east of Chillicothe. Laid out about 1851 by site owner Hiram Echols as Uniontown, reportedly so named because the community straddled the boundary between Marshall and Woodford counties, thus uniting them. The name was changed about 1857, possibly at the suggestion of Alonson Howard, to agree with that of the Washburn post office (Ford, *History of Marshall and Putnam Counties*, 120; Perrin and Hill, *Past and Present*, 360). Post office established June 13, 1851.

WASHINGTON. County. Created Feb. 28, 1818, from St. Clair County. Named for George Washington (1732–99), first president of the United States. The county seat was established at Covington and moved to Nashville in 1831.

WASHINGTON. Tazewell. City (1857, 1878). Founded in 1834 by the first permanent settler, William Holland, and named for George Washington (*Early History of Washington*, 12, 70). Post office established Feb. 12, 1833, as Holland's Grove; changed to Washington Sept. 13, 1837.

WASSON. Saline. Five miles northeast of Harrisburg. First known as Rathbone Station, a flag stop on the Big Four Railroad named for Valentine Rathbone, and later known as Dooley's Station. Formally established about 1906 by Charles M. Wasson of Harrisburg as a company town for employees of the Wasson Mine (*History of Saline County*, 6). Post office established April 25, 1908.

WATAGA [wah TAH guh]. Knox. Village (1874) seven miles northeast of Galesburg. Laid out about 1854. Probably a variant of "Watauga" and a transfer from Watauga, North Carolina, Tennessee, or Kentucky. Watauga is from Cherokee and was first recorded in the early 1770s as the name of a Cherokee village (Bright, *Native American Placenames*; Stewart, *American Place-Names*). Post office established Nov. 17, 1853, as Urn; changed to Wataga June 15, 1855.

WATERFORD. Township. Fulton. Named from the former community of Waterford, laid out by James Johnson about 1825 and reportedly so named because this was a shallow spot where one could cross Spoon River with ease; thus it was a convenient "water ford." Waterford is also a popular place name, however, occurring in about two dozen states, and may be a transfer, perhaps from Waterford, N.Y. The Waterford Cemetery is about four miles south of Lewistown (Irwin, *A to Z Fulton County*).

WATERLOO. Monroe. Village (1849, 1888). Founded in 1818 by George Forquer and Daniel Cook through the merger of two small communities, Bellefontaine and Peterstown, the latter named for Peter Rogers, a Massachusetts teacher and proprietor of the local general store. Named by Forquer and Cook for the village in Belgium where Napoleon was defeated in 1815 by a British and allied force under the command of the Duke of Wellington. Waterloo has been the seat of Monroe County since 1825 (Allen Collection; Allen, *Legends and Lore*, 47). Post office established Oct. 26, 1818.

WATERMAN. DeKalb. Village (1877) ten miles south of DeKalb. Founded about 1872 and named for Daniel B. Waterman of Aurora, then general solicitor for the Chicago and Iowa Railroad, which established a station at the site about 1870 (www.rootsweb.com/~ildekalb/places.htm). Post office established Oct. 31, 1860, as Prairie Pond; changed to Waterman Station May 9, 1871; changed to Waterman May 14, 1883.

WATSEKA [waht SEE kuh]. Iroquois. City (1867, 1872). Founded about 1859 as South Middleport. Renamed about 1864 for Watseka, or Watch-e-kee, the niece of the Potawatomi leader Tamin and wife of Gurdon Hubbard, a trader for the American Fur Company. Watch-e-kee bore the name of a legendary Potawatomi woman who had rallied the survivors of a particularly vicious Iroquois attack and formed a women's fighting unit to mount a counterattack. This display of bravery shamed the Potawatomi men to action, and the Iroquois were routed. From that time, and from generation to generation, the name *Watch-e-kee* was passed to a highly respected woman of the tribe. The meaning of the name is unknown (Kern, *Past and Present*, 672; Vogel, *Indian Place Names in Illinois*). Post office established April 8, 1864.

WATSON. Effingham. Village (1882) six miles south of Effingham. Named for George Watson, division superintendent of the Illinois Central Railroad in the 1850s (Ackerman, *Early Illinois Railroads*, 129). Post office established Jan. 13, 1859, as Salt Creek; changed to Watson Oct. 7, 1868.

WAUBANSEE [wuh BAHN see, wuh BAHN zee]. Grundy. Township. Named for Waubansee, a Potawatomi leader of the first half of the nineteenth century whose village was near Aurora. The name *Waubansee* is reported to mean "daybreak," "morning," or "half light." Waubansee is supposed to have received his name through an act of great courage on an overcast morning when he boarded an American supply vessel on the Wabash River, killed one of the crew, and escaped unharmed. Waubansee became popular with white settlers because he was neutral during the Winnebago War of the 1820s and actively campaigned with the Illinois militia in the Black Hawk War of 1832. For this service he was awarded five sections of land in the Aurora-Batavia area. Wauponsee is a variant (Vogel, *Indian Place Names in Illinois*).

WAUCONDA [wah KAHN duh]. Lake. Village (1877). Founded on Bangs Lake in the 1840s by Justus Bangs. Wauconda was the name of an Indian character in a popular novel of the day. Reports vary on who suggested the name for the village. Some say it was Bangs himself; others credit a local teacher, perhaps Lafayette Mills. From Dakota (Siouan), meaning "to worship" (Bright, *Native American Placenames; Illinois Guide; Past and Present of Lake County*, 318). Post office established March 30, 1843, as Cornelia; changed to Wauconda June 27, 1849.

WAUKARUSA CREEK. Carroll. Stream. Reported to be a Native American name for Carroll Creek. The source of the name is unknown (Thiem, ed., *Carroll County*, 117).

WAUKEGAN [waw KEE guhn]. Lake. City (1852, 1890). The first settlement at the site of present Waukegan grew around a small fort built by French traders perhaps as early as 1700. The "Riviere du Vieux Fort or Wakaygagh" appears on a 1778 map drawn by Thomas Hutchins, the supervisor in charge of surveying the Northwest Territory and later geographer general of the United States. By the 1820s Riviere du Vieux Fort (Old Fort River) was being called Small Fort River, and the settlement became known as Little Fort. Some settlers apparently felt that name to be inappropriate, even disparaging, for a progressive community, and John H. Kinzie and Solomon Juneau were asked to provide a new one. Starting from Wakaygagh, they created Waukegance and then Waukegan, which they claimed meant "Trading Place" and was more appropriate than the name *Waukegance*, which, they said, meant "Little Trading Place." In 1849 the name *Little Fort* was changed to Waukegan by popular vote. Kinzie and Juneau were essentially correct in their etymology. "Waukegan" likely has its roots in Potawatomi *wakaigin* (fort). Waukegan (first as Little Fort) has been the seat of Lake County since 1841 (Bright, *Native American Placenames*; Halsey, ed., *A History of Lake County*, 587; Vogel, *Indian Place Names in Illinois*). Post office established Aug. 28, 1841, as Little Fort; changed to Waukegan June 27, 1849.

WAUPECAN CREEK. Grundy, LaSalle. Stream. Possibly named for Waupekee, a Potawatomi subchief of the 1820s whose village was nearby. Possibly meaning "white" or "clear." Waupaca County, Wis., is likely a variant (Vogel, *Indian Place Names in Illinois*).

WAVERLY. Morgan. City (1867, 1878) eighteen miles southwest of Springfield. Laid out about 1836 by Cleveland J. Salter, James D. B. Salter, and others from New Haven, Conn., who sought to build a community around a theological school.

Named by James Salter, who admired the Waverley novels of Sir Walter Scott. Through scribal error or intent to Americanize the spelling, the name was entered as Waverly on the post office application (Hageman, comp., *Partial Encyclopedia of Waverly*, 9; *History Morgan County*, 422). Post office established Dec. 19, 1832, as Apple Creek; changed to Waverly April 15, 1847.

WAYNE. County. Created March 26, 1819, from Edwards County. Named for Gen. Anthony Wayne (1745–96), a distinguished officer of the Revolutionary War and perhaps best known for defeating the Miami leader Little Turtle at Fallen Timbers in Ohio in 1794. Wayne became famous as a result of this battle, and dozens of communities and townships, especially in the Midwest, were named in his honor. In Illinois, Wayne and Wayne Center in DuPage County, Waynesville in DeWitt County, as well as several townships were named for "Mad Anthony" Wayne, so called for his personal courage and boldness on the field of battle.

WEBER. Cook. Named by and for brickyard owner Barney Weber. Now part of Evanston (Stennett, *A History of the Origin*, 137).

WEBSTER. Hancock. Seven-and-a-half miles northeast of Carthage. Founded by William Wrightman in 1840 as a Mormon community, Ramus. Three years later, Macedonia was laid out on a site that included Ramus. Following the Mormon War in Illinois and the migration of Mormons to the West, Macedonia went into rapid decline. The name was changed about 1860 to agree with that of the Webster post office. The particular Webster or Webster family for whom the post office was named is not known (Bateman and Selby, eds., *Historical Encyclopedia of Illinois and History of Hancock County*, 1077). Post office established March 13, 1844, as Macedonia; changed to Webster July 23, 1847.

WEDGES CORNER. Lake. Five miles northeast of Round Lake Beach. Named for C. E. Wedge, proprietor of a general store at the junction of Routes 45 and 132 in the 1930s (Dretske, *What's in a Name?*).

WEDRON [WE druhn]. LaSalle. Seven miles north-northeast of Ottawa. According to a local story, the crews of the Chicago, Burlington and Quincy Railroad called the area the "weed run." The person sent to paint the name on the CB&Q station had only a small amount of paint left from earlier jobs, so instead of painting *Weed Run*, he conserved by painting only a single *e*. This, along with an indistinct *u* being interpreted as an *o*, resulted in the name *Wedron*. A nice bit of folklore, but the true origin of the name is unknown (Rasmusen, *LaSalle County Lore*, 101). Post office established Nov. 13, 1871.

WEEDMAN. DeWitt, McLean. Nine miles east-southeast of Le Roy. Named for John Weedman, site owner and early township supervisor. Formerly called Weedman Station (*History of McLean County*, 665). Post office established Jan. 21, 1879.

WELDON. DeWitt. Village (1892) eleven miles northwest of Monticello. Founded about 1872. Named for Lawrence Weldon of Bloomington, an attorney for the

Illinois Central Railroad (*History of DeWitt County* [1882], 328). Post office established Sept. 3, 1867, as Nixon; changed to Weldon Sept. 27, 1874.

WELGE [WELJ]. Randolph. Seven miles northeast of Chester. Named for the Welge family. Roger Welge was a sawmill operator, and Samuel Welge was an early postmaster (*Randolph County*, 52). Post office established Oct. 12, 1881, as Welga; changed to Welge May 16, 1925.

WELLER. Henry. Township. Reportedly named for an Ohio friend by John Piatt, one of the commissioners appointed to establish townships in Henry County about 1856 (Kiner, *History of Henry County*, 620). Post office established March 20, 1858.

WELLINGTON. Iroquois. Village (1902). Five miles north of Hoopeston. Laid out in 1872 by site owners J. L. Hamilton and R. T. Race. The source of the name is unknown (*Iroquois County History*, 133). Post office established Jan. 22, 1872.

WENDELIN. Clay. Twelve miles northwest of Olney. First known as St. Wentel. The name was changed to Saint Wendel in 1878 and to Wendelin in 1899. Named for St. Wendelin of Trier, Germany (late sixth and early seventh centuries), the patron saint of country people and herders (*Prairie Echo*, 121). Post office established July 8, 1899.

WENONA [wuh NO nuh]. LaSalle, Marshall. City (1867, 1872) twelve miles southwest of Streator. Established by the Illinois Central Railroad about 1852. Wenona is the Lakota (Siouan) name given to a first-born female. The name was popularized by Henry Wadsworth Longfellow's *The Song of Hiawatha,* in which Wenona is the daughter of Nokomis and the mother of Hiawatha (Vogel, *Indian Place Names in Illinois*). Post office established Oct. 31, 1853, as Wenona Station; changed to Wenona June 17, 1873.

WERTENBERG. Clinton. Seven miles east-southeast of Mascoutah. Laid out as Wertemburg by Andrew Eisenmayer in 1856. Named for the German state of Württemberg (now part of Baden-Württemberg), the home of Eisenmayer's ancestors (*History of Marion and Clinton Counties*, 103, 260)

WESLEY. Will. Township. Probably named by Methodist settlers for John Wesley, the founder of Methodism (Stevens, *Past and Present of Will County*, 117).

WEST. Effingham. Township. Originally the voting precinct on the west side of the county (Perrin, ed., *History of Effingham County*, 263).

WEST. McLean. Township. The original proposal called for the township to be named Kickapoo, for the large Kickapoo village previously in the area. Because of an existing Kickapoo Township, the name was changed to honor Henry West, an early settler and the first township supervisor (*History of McLean County*, 663–64).

WESTCHESTER. Cook. Village (1925). Founded about 1924 and named for Chester, England, by Samuel Insull, the founder of Northfield. Insull, born in London, intended to build a typical English-style village in the west Chicago suburbs. The depression of the 1930s, however, put a damper on the project (Harder, *Illustrated Dictionary of Place Names*; Peterson, "'A Good Place to Live'").

WEST CITY. Franklin. Village (1911). Named for its location west of Benton (*Franklin County*, 22).

WESTERN SPRINGS. Cook. Village (1886). Named for the local mineral springs thought to have curative powers. The springs were heavily promoted in the 1880s (*Illinois Gazetteer*). Post office established Sept. 12, 1873.

WESTERVELT. Shelby. Five miles north-northeast of Shelbyville. Founded in 1903 and named for Dr. C. J. Westervelt, who, along with John G. Root, operated a grain elevator at the site (Gordon, *Here and There in Shelby County*, 95). Post office established Nov. 28, 1904.

WEST HALLOCK. Peoria. Seven miles west of Chillicothe. Named for Lewis Hallock, generally regarded as the first permanent settler in the area. The name was chosen by popular vote about 1859 (*History of Peoria County*, 592). Post office established Nov. 17, 1860, as Blue Ridge; changed to Hallock Dec. 13, 1860.

WEST JERSEY. Stark. Township. Named about 1856 by Jacob Young for his home state of New Jersey (Leeson, *Documents and Biography*, 705). Post office established March 16, 1839, as Walnut Creek; changed to West Jersey Dec. 10, 1849.

WESTMINSTER. Shelby. Former community. Laid out in 1848 as Manyawper, possibly named by Washburn Wade for Manyopper Run, another name for Spring Run in Adams County, Ohio. When the Indianapolis and St. Louis Railroad was built through Tower Hill some three miles away, many of the buildings in Westminster were disassembled and moved to trackside (*Combined History of Shelby and Moultrie Counties*, 275). Post office established Oct. 2, 1849; changed to Tower Hill May 11, 1857.

WESTMONT. DuPage. Village (1921). Originally known as Gregg's Milk Station, a stop on the Burlington Railroad, and later as Gregg's Corners, for William L. Gregg, who established a kiln for manufacturing bricks to assist in rebuilding Chicago after the great fire of 1871. Formally laid out by developer Arthur W. McIntosh as Westmont, named for its location west of Chicago and for the positive associations of the name, which implies "western mountain" (Cutshall, *A Gazetteer*; Knoblauch, ed., *DuPage County*, 207). Post office established June 7, 1922.

WEST POINT. Hancock. Village (1893) eleven miles south of Carthage. Formerly known as Pumpkinville and then as Wigletown, named for early settler David Wigle. Renamed in 1856 for their former home, West Point, N.Y., by Wigle's wife, who felt this was a more dignified name than Wigletown (*Historic Sites*, 320). Post office established March 31, 1858.

WEST SALEM. Edwards. Village (1857, 1914) fifteen miles south of Olney. Settled in the late 1820s by Moravians from Salem, N.C. (now part of Winston-Salem).

Formally laid out in 1849 (*Combined History of Edwards, Lawrence, and Wabash Counties*). Post office established Jan. 17, 1855.

WEST SANFORD. Edgar. Nine miles southeast of Paris, directly across the state line from Sanford, Ind. Founded by Hiram Sandford in 1856 and named either for himself or for his father, Isaac Sandford (*History of Edgar County*, 409–10).

WESTVILLE. Vermilion. Village (1896) five miles south of Danville. Founded in 1873 by William P. and Elizabeth A. West as a station on the Danville and Southwestern Railroad (*Illinois Guide*). Post office established Jan. 12, 1874.

WETAUG [WEE tawg]. Pulaski. Ten miles southeast of Anna. According to several local accounts, Wetaug was the name of a Cherokee leader or the name of a subtribe of Cherokee who dropped out of the Trail of Tears during their forced march across southern Illinois in 1838. Some accounts even give directions to Chief Wetaug's grave. These tales (pure folklore) were repeated throughout much of the twentieth century even though Ackerman (*Early Illinois Railroads*, 137) had it nearly right in the 1880s when he said that Wetaug was named for a community in Massachusetts by George Watson, division superintendent of the Illinois Central Railroad. The name is, in fact, a transfer from Litchfield County, Conn., where the spelling is Weatogue (Hansen, ed., *Illinois*, 510; Harris, "Wetaug"; Moyer, *Moyers' Brief History*, 71; *Pulaski County*, 20; Vogel, *Indian Place Names in Illinois*). Post office established Dec. 6, 1856.

WETHERSFIELD. Henry. Township and former community. Founded in 1836 in Wethersfield, Conn., by the Connecticut Association, a stock company organized by the Rev. Ithamar Pillsbury (whose New York Association founded Andover) and the Rev. Caleb J. Tenney, a Congregational minister, for the purpose of bringing religion and free education to the West. Settlement of the colony began in 1836, but its growth was curtailed when the railroad bypassed it and ran through Kewanee instead. Weathersfield became part of Kewanee in 1924 (Colby, "Historic Spots in Henry County," 169; Hansen, ed., *Illinois*, 621; Polson, *Corn, Commerce*, 47). Post office established 6/6/1839.

WETZEL. Edgar. Six miles north of Paris. Named for storekeeper and postmaster Jacob Wetzel. Formerly known as Wetzel Station (*History of Edgar County*, 537). Post office established Feb. 3, 1879.

WHEATFIELD. Clinton. Township. Originally called Beaver Township, named for its location on Beaver Creek. The name was changed to Wheatfield in 1874 at the suggestion of Henry Zieren (*History of Marion and Clinton Counties*, 283).

WHEATLAND. Bureau. Township. A local story is that a maverick farmer, instead of planting the usual corn, planted wheat and had such a good crop that he declared, "This is good wheatland" (Leonard, ed., *Big Bureau*, 74).

WHEATLAND. Will. Township. Named for Wheatland Center, near Rochester, N.Y. (*"Where There's a Will,"* 49).

WHEATON. DuPage. City (1859, 1890). Founded about 1848 by Warren Lyon Wheaton, who emigrated from Pomfret, Windom County, Conn., with his brother, Jesse, in 1837. Warren Wheaton was the first president of the village of Wheaton and instrumental in securing a station on the Galena and Chicago Union Railroad, which was named Wheaton in his honor. Wheaton has been the seat of DuPage County since 1867, when county records were forcibly removed from the courthouse at Naperville (Hansen, ed., *Illinois,* 601; *Illinois Guide;* Knoblauch, ed., *DuPage County,* 168). Post office established Jan. 20, 1846, as Langdon; changed to Wheaton Feb. 16, 1852.

WHEELER. Jasper. Village (1894) nine miles west-northwest of Newton. Founded about 1861 as Mason, named for storekeeper John Mason. Formally laid out in 1883 by site owner Nancy J. Carter and named for her first husband, who was killed in the Civil War (*Counties of Cumberland, Jasper, and Richland,* 491). Post office established March 17, 1881.

WHEELING. Cook. Village (1894). A transfer from Wheeling, Ohio County, W.V., itself from a native American language, but the source and meaning are unknown (Vogel, *Indian Place Names in Illinois*). Post office established May 1, 1837

WHITE. County. Created Dec. 9, 1815, from Gallatin County. The source of the name is uncertain. There are two candidates as possible namesakes: Leonard White and Isaac White. Each played a significant political and developmental role in early southeastern Illinois, and each is a credible source of the county's name. County historians and descendants of early settlers are unable to settle the issue. As William D. Hay, a grandson of one of the founders of Carmi, says, "The county had been named 'White' in honor of Capt. Isaac White of St. Clair county; he was quite a prominent man and his life was such that it was a proper mark of respect that his name be given in the new county," although, "I was long under the impression that the county was named in honor of Leonard White, who was a pioneer citizen of the county." Both Leonard and Isaac White were representative of the men for whom counties were named in the early nineteenth century. Leonard White, one of the site owners of Carmi, was a captain in the Illinois Fourth Regiment during the War of 1812, a delegate to the Illinois constitutional convention of 1818, and an Illinois state senator in the 1820s. Isaac White was a supervisor of the salt works on the Saline River in the early 1800s and a colonel in the Illinois militia. He fought in Indiana with William Henry Harrison and was killed at the Battle of Tippecanoe in 1811. Many counties and communities were named for local luminaries such as Leonard White, and many others for public servants and military leaders such as Isaac White. Of the two, Leonard White was more closely associated with the area, but Isaac White was perhaps better known. One cannot discount the attractiveness of naming a county for a young officer who died in battle; White County, Ind., was named for Isaac White, and Jo Daviess County (q.v.) was named for Col. Joseph Hamilton Daveiss [*sic*], who also fell at Tippecanoe. As Lecta Hortin of the White County Historical Society observes, there is "still no definitive answer to the question" of whether the county was named for Isaac White or for Leonard White (personal communication with Lecta Horton).

WHITEASH. Williamson. Village (1905). Three miles north of Marion. Founded in 1903 as White Ash, the trade name of the coal mined by the Chicago and Marion Coal Company (Hubbs, *Pioneer Folks and Places*). Post office established Feb. 29, 1904.

WHITEFIELD. Bureau, Marshall. Seven miles west-northwest of Henry. Named for John B. White, the first township supervisor (Burt and Hawthorne, *Past and Present of Marshall and Putnam Counties*, 39). Post office established March 15, 1851.

WHITE HALL. Greene. City (1837, 1884). Founded in the 1820s by David Barrow. According to one local story, the name derives from a long white building that housed an entertainment hall and conveniences for the traveling public in the 1830s. Stage drivers would supposedly call out, "Next stop, the white hall!" According to another source, the "white hall" was the whitewashed house of postmaster Beverly Holliday, a waystop on the stagecoach line between Alton and Peoria; by still another, Zecheriah Allen's blacksmith shop was painted white and became known as the "white hall." White Hall (or Whitehall) is a popular place name in the United States, occurring in more than half of the continental states. It is especially common east of the Appalachian Mountains, and one or more of these may have influenced the naming of White Hall, Ill. (Anderson, *Yesterday's Heritage*, 13; Cunningham, *Lower Illinois Valley*, 32; Cutshall, *A Gazetteer*). Post office established July 12, 1827.

WHITE HEATH. Piatt. Five miles northeast of Monticello. Laid out about 1872 and named for land owner Frank White and entrepreneur Porter Heath (Piatt, *History of Piatt County*, 565). Post office established Jan. 20, 1873.

WHITE OAK. McLean. Township. Named from White Oak Grove, a tract of timber along the Mackinaw River (*History of McLean County*, 680).

WHITE PIGEON. Whiteside. Seven miles northeast of Morrison. Perhaps named for one of several Potawatomi leaders of the first half of the nineteenth century who were named Wapmeme (White Pigeon); perhaps a transfer from White Pigeon, St. Joseph County, Mich. (Vogel, *Indian Place Names in Illinois*). Post office established Sept. 26, 1876.

WHITE ROCK. Ogle. Nine miles northwest of Rochelle. Named from a prominent white rock on the bank of Stillman Creek (*History of Ogle County*, 296). Post office established Oct. 21, 1846.

WHITESIDE. County. Created Jan. 16, 1836, from Jo Daviess County. Named for Samuel Whiteside, commander of the Illinois militia during the War of 1812 and one of the first Illinois state representatives, serving from 1818 to 1820. Whiteside was in command of the militia that destroyed the Prophet's village at the outset of the Black Hawk War in 1832 (*see* Prophetstown). The county seat was established at Lyndon in 1839, moved to Sterling in 1841, moved back to Lyndon in 1842, was located at the courts and county commissioners' offices in 1846, moved to Sterling in 1847, and finally to Morrison in 1857.

WHITLEY. Moultrie. Township. Named for John Whitley, an early settler who emigrated from Maryland about 1826 (*Combined History of Shelby and Moultrie Counties,* 209). Post office established May 14, 1847, as Whitley's Grove.

WHITMORE. Macon. Township. Named for John Whittemore, an early settler from Connecticut. By the time of township formation in 1859, Whittemore's descendants had changed the spelling to Whitmore (Richmond, *Centennial History of Decatur,* 94).

WHITTINGTON. Franklin. Six miles north of Benton. Laid out with construction of the Chicago and Eastern Illinois Railroad in the 1890s and named for William J. Whittington (Henson, *History of Franklin County,* 89). Post office established Jan. 16, 1895.

WICHERT [WICH ert]. Kankakee. Nine miles southeast of Kankakee. Named for the Henry Wichert Pickle Works, which moved from Chicago in 1892 (Houde and Klasey, *Of the People,* 190). Post office established Sept. 29, 1893.

WILBERTON. Fayette. Ten miles southeast of Vandalia. Founded about 1825 and named for Justice of the Peace Willis Wilbern (Bateman and Selby, eds., *Historical Encyclopedia of Illinois and History of Fayette County,* 664). Post office established Aug. 4, 1890.

WILCOX. Hancock. Township. Named for Maj. John R. Wilcox, an officer at Fort Edwards (now the site of Warsaw), itself constructed in 1817 and named for Ninian Edwards, for whom Edwards County is named (Gregg, *History of Hancock County,* 637; *History of Hancock County,* 599).

WILDWOOD. Lake. West side of Gage's Lake, four miles southeast of Round Lake. This, the latest of several Wildwoods in the area, takes its name from the Wildwood subdivision established by J. L. Shaw about 1900 (Dretske, *What's in a Name?*).

WILL. County. Created Jan. 12, 1836, from Cook and Iroquois counties. Named for Dr. Conrad Will (1779–1835), a physician from Pennsylvania who settled at Kaskaskia in 1815. Will was one of the first commissioners of Jackson County, a delegate to the first Illinois constitutional convention in 1818, and a long-time member of the Illinois legislature.

WILLEFORD. Williamson. Former community. Founded at the confluence of Cana and Little Cana creeks by the Illinois Central Railroad as Canaville (q.v.) about 1889. The name was changed by the IC in 1904 for postmaster William H. Willeford (Hubbs, *Pioneer Folks and Places*). Post office established May 31, 1888, as Canaville; changed to Willeford Feb. 12, 1906.

WILLEYS. Christian. Four-and-a-half miles northeast of Taylorville. Laid out by Israel Willey, the first local storekeeper (Bateman and Selby, eds., *Historical Encyclopedia of Illinois and History of Christian County,* 775). Post office established June 23, 1871, as Willey Station; changed to Willey May 14, 1883.

WILLIAMS. Sangamon. Township. Named for Col. John Williams, Springfield merchant and community benefactor (Bateman and Selby, eds., *Historical Encyclopedia of Illinois and History of Sangamon County,* 738).

WILLIAMSBURG. Jefferson. Eight miles southwest of Mount Vernon. Laid out in 1867. With construction of the railroad about 1892 most of the buildings of Williamsburg were disassembled and moved a mile south to Waltonburg (Dearinger, "A New Geography of Illinois: Jefferson County," 25).

WILLIAMSBURG HILL. Shelby. Nine miles southeast of Pana. Laid out in 1839 as Williamsburg by Dr. Thomas H. Williams (Bateman and Selby, eds., *Historical Encyclopedia of Illinois and History of Shelby County,* 649).

WILLIAMSFIELD. Knox. Village (1896) thirteen miles east of Knoxville. Laid out in 1888 by E. B. Purcell. Reportedly named for a contractor for the Santa Fe Railroad named Williams (Bateman and Selby, eds., *Historical Encyclopedia of Illinois and Knox County,* 887; Marshall, *Santa Fe,* 357). Post office established March 1, 1888.

WILLIAMSON. County. Created Feb. 28, 1839, from Franklin County. Probably named for Williamson County, Tenn., itself named for Dr. Hugh Williamson, a signer of the U.S. Constitution and a member of the Continental Congress. A local tradition, however, claims the county was named for William Benson, who donated twenty acres of land for the county seat, and the name was derived by blending the words *William* and *Benson* (Hubbs, *Pioneer Folks and Places;* Miller, *Tennessee Place Names*).

WILLIAMSON. Madison. Village (1907) two miles south-southwest of Staunton. Named for site owners John and Matthew Williamson (Norton, ed., *Centennial History of Madison County,* 589).

WILLIAMSVILLE. Sangamon. Village (1884) ten miles northeast of Springfield. Founded in 1853 as Benton, named for Thomas Hart Benton, U.S. senator from Missouri. The name was changed shortly thereafter to honor Col. John Williams of Springfield. Informally known as Billtown (Wallace, *Past and Present,* 36). Post office established April 4, 1854.

WILLISVILLE. Perry, Randolph. Village (1900) thirteen miles east-northeast of Chester. Established about 1893 by the Willis Coal and Mining Company (Neville, comp., *Student's History of Perry County,* 20). Post office established July 15, 1896.

WILLOW BRANCH. Piatt. Township. Named from Willow Branch, itself reportedly named for a particularly prominent willow tree that stood near the spot where the stream was easily forded. Previously known as Liberty (Bateman and Selby, eds., *Historical Encyclopedia of Illinois and History of Piatt County,* 701).

WILLOWBROOK. DuPage. Village (1960). Named by Anton Borse, president of the homeowners' association. Faced with a deadline, Borse was asked what name to put on the incorporation documents. He reportedly looked out the window, noticed some willow trees growing along a nearby stream, and the name *Willowbrook* sprang to mind (Gregory, "A Suburb Where Stereotypes Haven't Found a Home").

WILMETTE [wil MET]. Cook. Village (1872). Platted in 1869 and named by Judge H. W. Blodgett of Waukegan for Archange Ouilmette, the Potawatomi wife of Antoine Ouilmette, a French trader and representative of the American Fur Company and also one of the first European settlers in what is now Chicago. Archange Ouilmette was granted two sections of land along Lake Michigan by the 1829 Treaty of Prairie du Chien (Stennett, *A History of the Origin,* 139; Vogel, *Indian Place Names in Illinois*). Post office established April 19, 1870.

WILMINGTON. Will. City (1837, 1902). Laid out as Winchester in 1836 by Thomas Cox, who built the first sawmill and operated the first corn cracker in the area. To avoid duplication of post offices, the name was changed the following year at the suggestion of settlers from Wilmington, Ohio, itself named for Wilmington, N.C. (Hansen, ed., *Illinois,* 672; *History of Will County,* 444). Post office established March 21, 1837.

WILSMAN. LaSalle. Six miles northwest of Streator. Established in 1885 by the Chicago, Burlington and Quincy Railroad on land owned by Henry Wilsman (Rasmusen, *LaSalle County Lore,* 258). Post office established Oct. 27, 1890.

WILSON. DeWitt. Township. Named for one or more Wilson families. Brothers Thomas, Edward, and James Wilson were early settlers from Ohio about 1834 (*History of DeWitt County, Illinois, 1839–1968,* 22).

WINCHESTER. Scott. City (1843, 1876) twelve miles southeast of Jacksonville. Laid out in 1830 by J. P. and M. A. Wilkinson. The traditional story is that the Wilkinsons offered the naming rights to whomever would treat to a gallon of whiskey. A. T. Hite, who ran a combination dry goods store and saloon, produced the whiskey and announced, after everyone had taken a heavy pull on the jug, that the name would be Winchester, for his former home in Clark County, Ky. (*Atlas, History, and Plat-Book of Scott County,* 14; *Scott County Bicentennial Book,* 219). Post office established June 8, 1829, as Sandy Bluffs; changed to Winchester Feb. 16, 1833.

WINDSOR. Shelby. City (1865, 1908) eleven miles west-southwest of Mattoon. Founded in 1856 with construction of the Terre Haute, Alton and St. Louis

Railroad as Illiopolis (Illinois City). The name was changed to Windsor later in 1856. The source of the name is unknown (Gordon, *Here and There in Shelby County*, 68). Post office established Nov. 4, 1831, as Cochran's Grove; changed to Windsor July 8 1856.

WINE HILL. Randolph. Nine miles east-northeast of Chester. Named by early German settlers who established several local vineyards in the area (Allen, *Randolph County Notes*, 18). Post office established Sept. 10, 1867, as Lakeville; changed to Wine Hill Jan. 12, 1874.

WINFIELD. DuPage. Village (1921). Previously known as Garys Mill, named for the grist mill established in the 1830s by early settlers Erastus and Jude Gary. Formally laid out by J. P. Doe in 1853 as Fredericksburg. Renamed for Winfield Township, itself probably named in honor of Gen. Winfield Scott, a hero of the War of 1812 who led a contingent of U.S. Army troops to the area to reinforce the Illinois militia during the Black Hawk War in 1832. The ruts left by the heavy army wagons created a track for early settlers that was later called Army Trail Road and is now DuPage County Route 11, from Addison to St. Charles. At a meeting to choose a name for the township, votes were divided between LeRoy and Greenwood. Commissioner E. O. Hills suggested Winfield as a compromise (Knoblauch, ed., *DuPage County*, 192; Richmond and Vallette, *A History of the County of DuPage*, 145, 147; Spanke, comp., *Winfield's Good Old Days*, 17). Post office established July 12, 1852.

WING. Livingston. Seven miles northeast of Fairbury. Founded in 1883 by a man named Byrd. According to a local story, there was already a Byrd in Illinois so there ought to be a Wing as well (*History of Livingston County* [1991], 36). Post office established Sept. 28, 1881.

WINKEL. Tazewell. Four miles west-southwest of Delavan. Named for postmaster and shopkeeper Christian C. Winkel Jr. (Adams, comp., *Illinois Place Names*). Post office established April 2, 1898.

WINKLE. Perry. Six miles northwest of Pinckneyville. Founded by William Craig in 1871 as Craig, a station on the St. Louis branch of the Illinois Central Railroad. The name was changed about 1903 when Joseph Winkle purchased the site and established the Bald Eagle Mine and a company store, the Winkle Mercantile and Agricultural Company (*Perry County*, 7, 8, 24). Post office established Feb. 17, 1871, as Craig.

WINNEBAGO [win uh BAY go]. County. Created Jan. 16, 1836, from Jo Daviess County. Named for the Winnebago, a Siouan people whose villages extended from near Moline northward along the Rock River into south central Wisconsin. Winnebago is probably from a Potawatomi word meaning "people of the stinking water," a reference to the fact that many Winnebago lived along the Fox River in Wisconsin, which became polluted with rotting fish each summer. The Winnebago call themselves the Ho-chunk. The county seat was established at Winnebago and moved to Rockford in 1839 (Bright, *Native American Placenames*).

WINNEBAGO. Winnebago. Village (1855, 1877) five miles west of Rockford. Laid out about 1854 with construction of the Galena and Chicago Union Railroad. Named for its location in Winnebago County. Formerly known as Elyda or Elida (*History of Winnebago County*, 227). Post office established July 3, 1854, as Winnebago Depot; changed to Winnebago Jan. 29, 1871.

WINNEMAC. Cook. Chicago park. Named for Wi-na-mak, a Potawatomi leader of the early nineteenth century for whom Winamac in Pulaski County, Ind., is also named. Literally, "mudfish" (i.e., catfish) (Baker, *From Needmore to Prosperity*; Vogel, *Indian Place Names in Illinois*).

WINNESHIEK. Stephenson. Six miles northeast of Freeport. Named for a Winnebago leader of the late eighteenth and early nineteenth centuries whose main village was near Freeport. A number of places in Iowa and Wisconsin as well as Illinois are named for this Winneshiek or for his descendants. Freeport was known as Winneshiek until the late 1830s (Ackerman, *Early Illinois Railroads*, 140; Vogel, *Iowa Place Names*). Post office established March 31, 1854.

WINNETKA [wuh NET kuh]. Cook. Village (1869). Founded in 1854 by Charles E. Peck and Walter S. Gurnee as Wynetka. According to the traditional account, the name was chosen by Peck's wife, Sarah, who proposed Wynetka as an alternative to Pecktown. She said Wynetka was a native name that she found in a story she was reading and that it meant "beautiful land." The name is apparently based on Algonquian *winne* (beautiful) (Bright, *Native American Placenames*; Dickinson, *Story of Winnetka*, 58). Post office established July 19, 1850, as New Trier; changed to Winnetka March 9, 1857.

WINSLOW. Stephenson. Village (1889) fifteen miles north-northwest of Freeport. Founded in 1844 by the Boston Western Land Company, a Massachusetts corporation that purchased some seventy thousand acres in the Midwest. Winslow, chosen as the name of the community some years earlier by W. S. Russell, an agent for the land company, honored Edward Winslow, a founder of Plymouth Colony and governor of Massachusetts in the 1630s and 1640s (Tilden, comp., *History of Stephenson County*, 550). Post office established Sept. 26, 1837, as Brewster's Ferry; changed to Winslow April 2, 1845.

WINTERROWD. Effingham. Sixteen miles southeast of Effingham. Laid out in 1863 by Washington Winterrowd (Perrin, ed., *History of Effingham County*, 249). Post office established July 27, 1870.

WINTHROP HARBOR. Lake. Village (1901) one mile north of Zion near the Wisconsin state line. Originally known as Spring Bluff, the name of the Northwestern Railroad station. In the 1880s J. H. Van Vlissengen of Chicago purchased the site and resold it to the Winthrop Harbor and Dock Company, which planned an industrial park beside Lake Michigan. The relationship of Van Vlissengen to the company and his role in the naming of Winthrop Harbor are unclear. By one account, the company pressured the community, then unincorporated, to change its name from Spring Bluff to Winthrop Harbor; by another, Van Vlissengen named the community (and possibly the company as well) for Winthrop, Mass. (Dretske, *What's in a Name?*; Stennett, *A History of the Origin,* 140). Post office established Jan. 23, 1871, as Spring Bluff; changed to Winthrop Harbor March 3, 1894.

WISETOWN. Bond. Alternate name for Beaver Creek. Founded in 1860 by site owner David W. Wise. The Wisetown Cemetery is just south of Beaver Creek (Peterson, "Place Names of Bond County," 44).

WITT. Montgomery. City (1898) ten miles northeast of Hillsboro. Founded by William Wood about 1869 with construction of the Indianapolis and St. Louis Railroad. According to a local account, Wood purchased the site, laid it out, and named it Chance because it represented his best chance for financial success. Success did not come to Wood, however, and he was forced to sell at a substantial loss. The new owner renamed the site Witt because he had "outwitted" Wood on the deal. The city of Witt includes Paisley, where George W. Paisley established a coal mine in the early 1890s (Bateman and Selby, eds., *Historical Encyclopedia of Illinois and History of Montgomery County,* 979). Post office established June 15, 1869, as Chance; changed to Witt Sept. 22, 1869.

WOBURN. Bond. Six miles northeast of Greenville. Laid out by John Hughes in 1856 as Newport, named for his former home, Newport, Va. When the post office was established in 1860 the name was changed at the suggestion of J. B. Reid for his former home, Woburn, Middlesex County, Mass. (Bateman and Selby, eds., *Historical Encyclopedia of Illinois and History of Bond County,* 635; Peterson, "Place Names of Bond County," 44). Post office established May 29, 1860.

WOLF. GNIS lists some sixty-five features in Illinois named Wolf, twenty-two of which are named Wolf Creek. Although some take their name from settlers named Wolf (such as Wolfs in Kendall County, a shortening of Wolf's Crossing, named for postmaster Leonard Wolf), most take their name either from a place where the presence of wolves was noted or where an incident involving wolves took place. Wolf Prairie in Jefferson County was reportedly so named because a pack of wolves pursued a settler and forced him to spend the night in a tree.

WOLF POINT. Cook. Located at the forks of the Chicago River. Probably a translation of Moaway, the name of a local Potawatomi leader (*see* Moahway) (Vogel, *Indian Place Names in Illinois*).

WOMAC. Macoupin. Five miles east of Carlinville. Founded in 1870 as a station on the Chicago and North Western Railroad. Named for shopkeeper John J. Womac (Stennett, *A History of the Origin,* 140). Post office established May 8, 1888.

WONDER LAKE. McHenry. Village (1974) four miles northwest of McHenry. Named from Wonder Lake, an artificial lake created in 1929 by damming Nippersink Creek. Formerly known as Sunrise Ridge (*Illinois Guide*).

WOODBURN. Macoupin. Twelve miles north of Wood River. Founded in 1833 by site owner B. F. Edwards of Edwardsville. Named for the Wood family. Several Wood brothers emigrated from Kentucky about 1830. J. M. Wood was a county assessor, and R. H. Wood was a justice of the peace. It is unclear how "burn" came to be attached to the Wood name. The only known accounts of the naming are popular etymologies along the lines of "the Wood brothers camped in the area and their large campfire was called the 'Wood Burn,' which became Woodburn" (Redford and Triplett, comps., *Reflections*, 13). Post office established May 5, 1837.

WOODBURY. Cumberland. Fifteen miles northeast of Effingham. Founded in 1835 by site owners William C. Greenup and George Hanson. Named for George Woodbury, the first permanent settler, who arrived about 1831. An alternate spelling is Woodberry (*Montrose Centennial*, 7). Post office established May 18, 1835.

WOOD DALE. DuPage. City (1928). Present Wood Dale developed from a community first called Sagone (perhaps named for Sagone, Italy) and later known as Lester's Station, a stop on the Chicago and Pacific Railroad named for the first postmaster, Edward Lester. The station took the name of the Wooddale subdivision in 1899 (Mittell, "Wood Dale," 266). Post office established Jan. 29, 1874, as Salt Creek; changed to Wooddale June 15, 1895.

WOODFORD. County. Created Feb. 27, 1841, from McLean and Tazewell counties. The county and its first seat, Versailles, were named by Thomas Bullock for his former home, Woodford County, Ky., itself named for William Woodford, an officer in the Revolutionary War who died in British custody in 1780, and its seat, Versailles (Moore, *History of Woodford County*, 38; Rennick, *Kentucky Place Names*).

WOODHULL. Henry. Village (1860, 1875) fourteen miles north of Galesburg. First named Heath Land for the Heath family and later known as Leoti, claimed to be a native name meaning "flower." Formally laid out by Maxwell Z. V. Woodhull, a land speculator from New York City, in 1857 (*History of Henry County*, 537; Polson, *Corn, Commerce*, 32) Post office established Dec. 24, 1852, as Heath Land; changed to Leoti May 14, 1857; changed to Woodhull March 1, 1858.

WOODRIDGE. DuPage, Will. Village (1959). Founded as the Woodridge subdivision by Albert Kaufmann and Surety Builders about 1958. A previous settlement near the site was called Woodridge, but the immediate source of the name is the Woodridge Golf Course (Kagann and Kagann, "Woodridge," 269).

WOOD RIVER. Madison. City (1908). Named from Wood River, which empties into the Mississippi three miles south of Alton. Contrary to appearances, Wood River is not named for the local stands of timber. Rather, the source of the name is Rivière à Dubois (Dubois' River), named for an early French explorer or trader named Du Bois (from *bois,* "wood"). Many, including William Clark, translated Rivière à Dubois as "Wood River" rather than "Wood's River." Wood River was the embarkation point for the Lewis and Clark expedition of 1804–6. An alternate name is River Dubois (McDermott, "William Clark's Struggle," 144). Post office established Oct. 26, 1907, as Woodriver; changed to Wood River Feb. 6, 1925.

WOODSON. Morgan. Village (1894) seven miles south of Jacksonville. Founded about 1858 by Richard Henry and Joseph Adams. Named for David Meade Woodson, a Carrollton lawyer, circuit court judge, state representative in the early 1840s, and at the time the community was established president of the Chicago and Alton Railroad (Bateman and Selby, eds., *Historical Encyclopedia of Illinois and History of Morgan County,* 665; *History of Morgan County,* 429). Post office established June 8, 1863.

WOODSTOCK. McHenry. City (1852, 1873). Founded in 1844 as Centreville. The name was changed in 1845 at the request of Joel H. Johnson, a director of the Northwestern Railroad, for his former home in Woodstock, Windsor County, Vt. The original Woodstock is in Oxfordshire, England (Nye, ed., *McHenry County, Illinois,* 546; Stennett, *A History of the Origin,* 26). Post office established March 13, 1845, as Dorr; changed to Woodstock April 3, 1852.

WOODY. Greene. Twelve miles northwest of Jerseyville. Also Woodville Township. Laid out in 1835 as Woodville by Amon Wood, Seanright Wood, and others (Clapp, *History of Greene County,* 429). Post office established March 5, 1883.

WOOSUNG [WOO SUHNG]. Ogle. Four miles north-northwest of Dixon. Originally called Juniata City, named from Juniata County and the Juniata River in Pennsylvania. Formally established by retired sea captains Harvey Roundy, John Anderson, and Samuel Brimblecorn, who had sailed in the China trade in the early nineteenth century. When they retired here in 1856, they named the community Shanghai, one of their ports of call. When the Illinois Central Railroad objected to that name, the captains suggested Woosung, for Wusong (Wusung) China, just north of Shanghai (*Bicentennial History of Ogle County,* 450). Post office established Dec. 26, 1855.

WORDEN. Madison. Village (1877) ten miles northeast of Edwardsville. Founded as New Hampton by Hampton Wall about 1860. The site was purchased from Wall by an Englishman, John C. Worden, in 1867. With completion of the Decatur and East St. Louis Railroad in 1870, the station was named for Worden, the first station agent and postmaster (Norton, ed., *Centennial History of Madison County,* 591; Underwood, "A New Geography of Illinois: Madison County," 33). Post office established June 19, 1851, as Lamb's Point; changed to New Hampton Jan. 4, 1869; changed to Worden Sept. 6, 1870.

WORTH. Cook. Village (1914). Named for William Jenkins Worth (1794–1849), who served under Gen. Winfield Scott during the Black Hawk War and was later commander of the Eighth Infantry and a general in the Mexican War. Worth Township in Woodford County is named for the same General Worth, as is Ft. Worth, Tex. (Harder, *Illustrated Dictionary of Place Names;* Perrin and Hill, *Past and Present,* 374).

WRIGHTS. Greene. Eight miles northeast of Carrollton. Laid out by Andrew J. Wright in 1872. Wright was the first postmaster, first justice of the peace, and first station agent for the Chicago, Burlington and Quincy Railroad (Cunningham, *History of the Carrollton, Illinois, Area,* 33; *History of Greene and Jersey Counties,* 957). Post office established Feb. 16, 1871, as Wrightsville; changed to Wrights Aug. 27, 1905.

WYANET [weye uh NET]. Bureau. Village (1869, 1891) six miles west of Princeton. Founded in the mid-1850s as Kingston by site owners Mary and Henry King. The name was changed to Wyanet by officials of the Chicago, Burlington and Quincy Railroad in 1855. Although it is usually claimed that Wyanet is from Potawatomi, the name has no known etymology and was apparently created from what Stewart calls "vaguely Indian materials." In 1905 Gannett claimed that Wyanet was "an Indian word meaning 'beautiful.'" This interpretation has been dutifully copied for more than a century although there is little to support it (Gannett, *The Origin of Certain Place Names;* Stewart, *American Place-Names;* Trotter, *"Our Town,"* 10). Post office established Aug. 20, 1855.

WYCKLES. Macon. West of Decatur. Established as Wyckles Station. Named for site owner Joseph Wycle (Richmond, *Centennial History of Decatur,* 96). Post office established Dec. 7, 1895.

WYNOOSE. Richland, Wayne. Twelve miles southwest of Olney. Probably an adaptation and transfer of Wynooska, from Pike County, Pa. This is the only Wynoose in the United Sates. Post office established May 10, 1881.

WYOMING. Stark. City (1865, 1873). Also Lee County Township. A transfer from the Wyoming Valley near Wilkes-Barre in northeastern Pennsylvania. The name is from Delaware (Algonquian) meaning "at the big river flat." An 1809 poem, "Gertrude of Wyoming: A Pennsylvanian Tale," by Thomas Campbell, which told the highly romanticized story of a conflict between British soldiers and the Iroquois, popularized the name and influenced its spread from Pennsylvania to New York and other states. Wyoming Township in Lee County was formally named in 1851 at the suggestion of James Goble, later to become county sheriff, whose family was from the Wyoming Valley in Pennsylvania. The city of Wyoming in Stark County was platted by Samuel Thomas in 1836. Thomas had spent much of his life in the Wyoming Valley; he served in the War of 1812 and was appointed a brigadier general by the governor of Pennsylvania before settling in Illinois in 1834 (Bateman and Selby, eds., *Historical Encyclopedia of Illinois and History of Lee County*, 698; Leeson, *Documents and Biography*, 294; Stevens, *History of Lee Valley*, 498; *Wyoming through the Years*, 4). Post office established April 20, 1832, as Spoon River; changed to Goshen Nov. 18, 1834; changed to Wyoming Dec. 14, 1835.

WYSOX. Carroll. Township. A transfer from Wysox, a community, stream, and township in Bradford County, northeastern Pennsylvania, home of a number of early settlers. From Delaware (Algonquian) possibly meaning "place of the grapes" (Stewart, *American Place-Names;* Vogel, *Indian Place Names in Illinois*).

WYTHE. Hancock. Township. The name was suggested by George Washington Davidson Harris in honor of George Wythe (1726–1806), Virginia statesman, signer of the Declaration of Independence, and member of the Constitutional Convention of 1787. The Wythe Cemetery is about five miles east-southeast of Warsaw (Gregg, *History of Hancock County*, 629; *History of Hancock County*, 611). Post office established May 15, 1851.

XENIA [ZIN yuh]. Clay. Village (1865, 1875) nine miles west of Flora. The original Xenia was founded in 1834 several miles from the present community, which was laid out in 1854 for the Ohio and Mississippi Railroad. There are several stories to explain the origin of the name: that it was brought to Illinois by settlers from Xenia, Ohio; that it was named for a Princess Xenia of Greece; and that it was taken from the Greek word *xenien* (hospitable), suggested by a visiting member of the clergy who had been treated kindly by townspeople. Several of the same stories are told to explain the naming of Xenia, Ohio, contributing to the probability that both the name and the naming lore were transferred from there (Miller, *Ohio Place Names; Xenia Then and Now*, 143). Post office established May 5, 1834, as Cato; changed to Xenia May 1, 1848.

YANKEE. Vermilion. Named from Yankee Point, itself named for the large number of settlers from New England, collectively called "Yankees." The Yankee Point Cemetery is about three miles northeast of Ridge Farm (Beckwith, *History of Vermilion County*, 561).

YANTISVILLE. Shelby. Ten miles northwest of Shelbyville. Named for Henry Yantis, the first postmaster (*Combined History of Shelby and Moultrie Counties*, 301). Post office established Sept. 27, 1880.

YATES. McLean. Township. Formerly known as Union Township. Renamed in 1863 in honor of Richard Yates (1815–73), governor of Illinois from 1861 to 1864 (*History of McLean County,* 730).

YATES CITY. Knox. Village (1869, 1911) fifteen miles north of Canton. Laid out in 1857 by site owners Amos and William Babcock and named for their former home in Yates County in western New York state (*Yates City Community Centennial,* 3). Post office established Feb. 14, 1859.

YELLOWHEAD. Kankakee. Township. Named for Ozanotap (Yellow Head), a Potawatomi leader of the early nineteenth century whose village was north of Momence (Vogel, *Indian Place Names in Illinois*). Post office established Aug. 26, 1842

YELROME. Hancock. Laid out by the Mormon Prophet Joseph Smith in 1844 and named for Smith's attorney, Isaac Morley, spelled backward. Yelrome was burned by a mob during the Mormon war of 1845 (*History of Hancock County,* 562).

YORK. There are more than forty Yorks, present and past, in Illinois, the majority of which are named for the city or state of New York. Settlers from New York were so numerous in parts of Illinois, especially the northern third, that they were referred to simply as "Yorkers." The ultimate source of the name is either the Duke of York or the city of York, England.

YORK. Carroll. Township. The name of the township was to have been Argo but was changed by settlers from New York before the township was officially organized (Thiem, ed., *Carroll County,* 82).

YORK. Clark. Twelve miles north-northeast of Robinson. Founded as New York by John R. Ritch and Ezekiel Bishop. West York, one mile west of York, was established in the mid-1870s with construction of the railroad (*History of Crawford County,* 56; Perrin, ed., *History of Crawford and Clark Counties,* 330).

YORKVILLE. Kendall. City (1873). Founded about 1834 as Bristol by Lyman and Burr Bristol. The townsite was purchased by Rulief Duryea and James Cornell, who laid out Yorkville in 1836 and named it for New York state, their former home. Yorkville was the seat of Kendall County from 1841 until 1845, when the county seat was moved to Oswego, and again since 1864 (Hicks, *History of Kendall County,* 169; Tio and Farren, *A History of Yorkville,* 11). Post office established April 18, 1864.

YOUNG AMERICA. Edgar. Township. In the middle of the nineteenth century, a number of communities in the Midwest took the name *Young America* to show they were part of the promise and exuberance of a young, dynamic country. The name is found in Ohio, Indiana, Minnesota, and several other states. A Young America post office operated in Warren County from May 19, 1856, until June 11, 1874, when it was changed to Kirkwood (Stewart, *American Place-Names*).

YOUNG HICKORY. Fulton. Township. Originally called Hickory in honor of Andrew Jackson, known as "Old Hickory." Because there was an existing Hickory Township, this one, being newer, was logically Young Hickory (*History of Fulton County*, 969).

YOUNGSDALE. Kane. Three miles west of South Elgin. Named for postmaster Smith Youngs (Adams, comp., *Illinois Place Names*). Post office established June 9, 1890.

ZANESVILLE. Montgomery. Nine miles north of Litchfield. Founded about 1828 by George Brewer as Leesburg, named for Brewer's friend, Robert E. Lee, a St. Louis merchant. Renamed by settlers from Zanesville, Ohio, itself named for early settler Ebenezer Zane (Bateman and Selby, eds., *Historical Encyclopedia of Illinois and History of Montgomery County*, 982; Traylor, *Past and Present of Montgomery County*, 746). Post office established June 26, 1838, as Hamlet; changed to Zanesville March 23, 1839.

ZEARING. Bureau. Nine miles northeast of Princeton. Named for the Zearing family. Martin Zearing was an early settler from PA, arriving about 1835 (Bradsby, ed., *History of Bureau County*, 703). Post office established Aug. 14, 1902.

ZEIGLER [ZIG ler]. Franklin. City (1914) seven miles west of West Frankfort. A company town named for Levi Zeigler Leiter by his son, Joseph Leiter, founder of the Zeigler Coal Company, which opened the first coal mine in Franklin County in 1904 (Henson, *History of Franklin County*, iii). Post office established May 12, 1903.

ZIF. Wayne. Township. Apparently the name *Zif* was submitted for consideration as a township name by J. C. Patterson and W. R. Barker, delegates from the northeastern portion of Wayne County, at the township convention of 1859. The source of the name is unknown. It may be from a family named Zif or Zipf, or it may be from Zif or Ziv, the old Hebrew month corresponding to present Iyar, the eighth month of the Jewish calendar. This is the only Zif in the United States (*History of Wayne and Clay Counties*, 255). Post office established June 3, 1856.

ZION. Lake. City (1902). Named for Mount Zion, a hill in the eastern part of Jerusalem, by John Alexander Dowie in 1901. Dowie (1847–1907), a Scottish fundamentalist preacher and faith healer, organized the Christian Catholic Apostolic Church in 1896. Zion was founded as a community where church law prevailed and there were to be "no breweries or saloons, gambling halls, houses of ill fame, hog raising, tobacco shops, hospitals [or] theaters" (Cook, *Zion City*, 55). Original street names maintained the biblical theme and included

Lebanon Avenue, Shiloh Boulevard, and Horeb Avenue. The city was theocrati-
cally governed until 1935. Post office established March 10, 1902, as Zion City;
changed to Zion Oct. 24, 1918.

ZOOKVILLE. Livingston. Former community. Named for a B. Zook, who opened
the first store in the area in 1872. The Zooks Cemetery is seven miles northwest
of Pontiac and south of Cornell (*History of Livingston County* [1878], 471).

ZUMA. Rock Island. Township and former community. Zuma Center was laid out
by A. F. Russell about 1857, when the name of Walker Township was changed
to Zuma Township, probably for Zuma Creek. The derivation of the name is
unclear. It is presumably a shortening of Montezuma, although Zuma was also
a reasonably popular given name for females at the time. The historical Zuma
School was located about ten miles east-northeast of Moline (*Historic Rock
Island County*, 99).

NAMES OF UNKNOWN ORIGIN

I have found little or nothing on the sources of the following names. I would appreciate hearing from anyone with information on the origins of the names or the circumstances surrounding the naming. Please direct correspondence to one of the following addresses:

email: ecallary@niu.edu
surface mail:
    Edward Callary
    English Department
    Northern Illinois University
    DeKalb IL 60115

Adams County: Marcelline
Alexander County: Diswood, Frog City, Golden Lily, Olive Branch
Bond County: Bunje
Brown County: Damon, Fargo
Bureau County: Macon Township
Carroll County: Ashdale Junction, Zier Cors
Champaign County: Augerville, Giblin

Christian County: Sicily, Zenobia
Clark County: Allright, Moriah
Clay County: Riffle
Clinton County: Marydale
Coles County: Loxa, Magnet, St. Omer
Cook County: Alpine, Lyons, Maine Township
Crawford County: Marco
DeKalb County: Clare
DeWitt County: Ospur
Douglas County: Chicken Bristle
DuPage County: Auvergne, Utopia
Edgar County: Hildreth, Melwood, Raven
Effingham County: Bethlehem
Fayette County: Confidence

Ford County: Harpster
Franklin County: Cambon, Frisco, Macedonia
Fulton County: Enion
Hamilton County: Aden, Macedonia, Nipper Corner
Hancock County: Disco
Henderson County: Rozetta
Henry County: Phenix Township
Iroquois County: Alonzo, Loda
Jackson County: Sato
Jasper County: Advance, Shamrock
Jo Daviess County: Aiken, Elmoville
Jefferson County: Cravat
Jersey County: Beltrees
Kankakee County: First Pommier, Flickerville
LaSalle County: Altmar, Fitchmoor, Milla
Lee County: Viola Township
Livingston County: Eylar, Katy Did, Lodemia, Missal, Munster, Rugby
Logan County: Eminence Township, Laenna, Oran
Macon County: Bulldog Crossing
Madison County: Alan Dale, Formosa Junction
Marion County: Sandoval
Marshall County: Choctaw, Lacon
Mason County: Buzzville, Teheran
Massac County: Brooklyn
McDonough County: Shoo Fly
McHenry County: Coral, Lilymoor
McLean County: Eldorado Township, Glen Avon, Shamrock
Menard County: Bobtown

Mercer County: Arpee, Rivoli Township
Monroe County: Madonnaville
Ogle County: Carthage, Loose Pully Junction, Lost Nation, Luda
Peoria County: Medina, Olio
Pike County: Aladdin, Fishhook
Pope County: Leisure City
Putnam County: Florid
Rock Island County: Ginger Hill
Richland County: Amity, Elbow, Passport, Wynoose
Sangamon County: Bando, Beamington, Cascade, Glen Arm, Loami, Zenobia
Schuyler County: Ray
Scott County: Oxville
Shelby County: Dollville, Mode, Pleak
St. Clair County: Lebanon, Rodemish
Stephenson County: Afolkey, Loran
Tazewell County: Gardena, Harvard Hills
Union County: Moscow
Vermilion County: Hustle, Vernal, Walz
Wabash County: Orio
Warren County: Nemo
Washington County: Biddleborn, Bolo Township, Clarmin, Pyramid
Wayne County: Crisp, Orel Township, Sock Nation
Whiteside County: Denrock
Will County: Arbury Hills, Ballou, Brisbane, Tokio
Williamson County: Fopal

NOTES

Note to the Preface

1. Information regarding the American Name Society and the Toponymy Interest Group is available online at www.wtsn.binghamton.edu/ANS and www.wtsn.binghamton.edu/plansus, respectively. Accessed March 13, 2008.

Notes to the Introduction

1. GNIS is the national digital gazetteer. It currently contains more than two million names and related information such as the type of feature named, its location, and its elevation. GNIS includes the names of populated places, lakes, summits, streams, and the like but not street names, the names of neighborhoods, or the names of most subdivisions, nor does it typically include etymological, cultural, or historical information. GNIS can be accessed, and the databases of both foreign and domestic names searched online, at www.geonames.usgs.gov.

2. The twentieth century developed its own naming patterns. The number of features requiring names grew exponentially, especially after World War II, with the founding of an increasing number of subdivisions and their associated streets, schools, churches, parks, and public buildings. Subdivisions tended to be named "promotionally," with names such as The Meadows, Heatherwood, and Nature's Edge chosen by developers to appeal to young parents by projecting a rural, bucolic image where children could roam freely and safely, far from the concerns and cares of urban life. These names represent a sixth layer, but one that is beyond the scope of this book.

3. Although the number of indisputably Native American names in Illinois is small, it continues to grow due to a resurgence of interest in Native American languages in general and in the Miami-Illinois language in particular, primarily through the work of David Costa and Michael McCafferty, both of whom are often cited in this book.

Note to the Form of Entries

1. In Illinois a community can choose to incorporate as a city, a village, or a town; the designation is not related to size but to the type of corporate charter. Thus there are considerable differences in size among cities, villages, and towns. Arlington Heights has a population of some eighty thousand and Valley City has a population of fourteen, but both are villages. Cities range from Chicago, with about three million people, to Nason with 234. Incorporation status leads to some odd collocations of official names, such as the Village of Fairmont City, the City of Granite City, and the Village of Elk Grove Village.

BIBLIOGRAPHY

Ackerman, William K. *Early Illinois Railroads*. Chicago: Fergus, 1884.

Adair, Anna B., and Adele Sandberg. *Indian Trails to Tollways. The Story of the Home-wood-Flossmoor Area*. Homewood, Ill.: Fremouw, 1968.

Adams, James N., comp. *Illinois Place Names*. Springfield: Illinois State Historical Society. Occasional Publications no. 54. (1969, repr.1989); originally published in *Illinois Libraries* 50 (April, May, June, 1968): 275–596.

Aiken, Hiram M. *Franklin County History*. N.p.: Franklin County Centennial Committee, 1918.

Albers, Adelaide, Virginia Van Pappelendam, and Marie Worthen, comps. *History of Warsaw*. Warsaw, Ill.: Warsaw Bulletin, 1960.

Alexander County, Illinois: History and Families, 1819–1889. Paducah, Ky.: Turner, 1989.

Alft, E. C. *South Elgin: A History of the Village from its Origin as Clintonville*. South Elgin, Ill.: South Elgin Heritage Commission, 1979.

Alhambra, Illinois Sesquicentennial, 1849–1999: Moving Forward into the Next Century. Shawnee Mission, Kans.: Kes-Print, 1999.

Alleman, Jeanne, and Elizabeth Immel. *A Putnam County History for Young People*. Granville, Ill.: Putnam County Record, 1996.

Allen Collection. The John W. Allen Papers. Special Collections. Morton Library. Southern Illinois University, Carbondale.

Allen, John W. "Golconda Got Its Name in 1817." *Daily Register* (Harrisburg, Ill.), July 19, 1961, 8.

———. *Jackson County Notes*. Contribution 21. Carbondale, Ill.: Museum of Natural and Social Sciences, 1945.

———. *Legends and Lore of Southern Illinois.* Carbondale: Southern Illinois University Press, 1963.

———. *Pope County Notes.* Contribution 22. Carbondale, Ill.: Museum of Natural and Social Sciences, 1949.

———. *Randolph County Notes.* Contribution 20. Carbondale, Ill.: Museum of Natural and Social Sciences, 1944.

Allison, Leah. *History of Leech Township.* Fairfield, Ill.: Wayne County Record, 1954.

Along the Trail: In Memory of Rock City Pioneers Rock City Centennial, 1859–1959. Rock City, Ill.: N.p., 1959.

Alpha: Century of Progress, 1872–1972. Alpha, Ill.: Centennial Book Committee, 1972.

Anderson, Francis P. *Yesterday's Heritage, Tomorrow's Promise: White Hall, Illinois Sesquicentennial, 1832–1982.* White Hall, Ill.: Sesquicentennial Book Committee, 1982.

Anderson, Hazel, Bernice Marshall, and Edna Sherman, eds. *The Beelman Story: A History of Somonauk, 1843–1970.* Somonauk, Ill.: N.p., 1970.

Anderson, Vernon. *Matherville History.* Aledo, Ill.: Times Record, 1983.

Anderson, Wilbur W., and Kenneth M. Norcross. *A History of Orion, Illinois: Nineteenth Century.* N.p.: N.p., 1953.

Andreas, A. T. *History of Cook County Illinois: From the Earliest Period to the Present Time.* Chicago: Andreas. 1884.

Angle, Paul M. *"Here I Have Lived": A History of Lincoln's Springfield.* New Brunswick, N.J.: Rutgers University Press, 1935.

Annals of Knox County. Galesburg, Ill.: Republican Register Print, 1921.

Arimond, Joseph. "Oraville: A Jackson County Settlement." *Southern Illinoisan* (Carbondale), May 6, 1973, 36.

Armstrong, Ken. "Carpentersville Looking to 'Dundee' for Renewal." *Chicago Tribune,* Aug. 3, 1995, 1, 16.

Arnold, Myrtle Foster. *Buda Our Home Town, 1828–1975.* N.p.: N.p., 1975.

Arpee, Edward. *Lake Forest Illinois: History and Reminiscences, 1861–1961.* Lake Forest, Ill.: Rotary Club of Lake Forest, 1964.

Atlas, History and Plat-Book of Scott County, Illinois. Winchester, Ill.: Winchester Times, 1903.

Atlas Map of Fulton County, Illinois. Davenport, Iowa: Andreas, Lyter, 1871.

Atlas Map of Schuyler County, Illinois. Davenport, Iowa. Andreas, Lyter, 1872.

Atlas of Shelby County, and the State of Illinois. Chicago: Warner and Beers, 1875.

Ava: From Headquarters to City, the Early Years. N.p, n.d.

Avis, Walter S. *A Dictionary of Canadianisms on Historical Principles.* Toronto: Gage, 1967.

Aviston Quasquicentennial. Millstadt, Ill.: Schaefer-Mollman, 1989.

Azbell, Wayne, ed. *A History of Ipava.* Astoria, Ill.: Stevens, 1986.

Baker, Ronald L. *From Needmore to Prosperity.* Bloomington: Indiana University Press, 1995.

Baker, Ronald L., and Marvin Carmony. *Indiana Place Names.* Bloomington: Indiana University Press, 1975.

Bakken, Timothy H. *Hinsdale.* Hinsdale, Ill.: Hinsdale Doings, 1976.

Baldwin, Elmer. *History of LaSalle County, Illinois*. Chicago: Rand McNally, 1877.

Balesi, Charles J. *The Time of the French in the Heart of North America, 1673–1818*. Chicago: Alliance Français Chicago, 1992.

Banbury, Larry Francis, comp. *The Sesquicentennial of Effingham County, 1831–1981*. Effingham, Ill.: Banbury, 1982.

Bandy, Gail M., comp. *Moro: The Story behind the Town*. N.p.: N.p., 1993.

Barge, William D. *Early Lee County*. Chicago: Barnard and Miller, 1918.

———. "Illinois County Names." *Magazine of History* 9 (Jan.–June 1909): 273–77.

Barge, William D., and Norman W. Caldwell. "Illinois Place-Names." *Journal of the Illinois State Historical Society* 29 (April 1936–Jan. 1937): 189–311.

"Barreville, Once Thriving Business Center, Still Rich in History." *Herald* (Crystal Lake, Ill.), April 13, 1961, 4:1.

Bassett, Isaac Newton, and Weston A. Goodspeed. *Past and Present of Mercer County, Illinois*. Chicago: Clarke, 1914.

Bassman, Herbert J. *Riverside Then and Now*. Chicago: University of Chicago Press, 1958.

Bastian, Wayne. *A History of Whiteside County, Illinois*. Morrison, Ill.: Whiteside County Board of Supervisors, 1968.

Bateman, Newton, and Paul Selby, series eds. *Historical Encyclopedia of Illinois and History of Bond County*. Edited by Warren E. McCaslin. Chicago: Munsell, 1915.

———. *Historical Encyclopedia of Illinois and History of Boone County*. Edited by Richard V. Carpenter. Chicago: Munsell, 1909.

———. *Historical Encyclopedia of Illinois and History of Carroll County*. Edited by Charles L. Hostetter. Chicago: Munsell, 1913.

———. *Historical Encyclopedia of Illinois and History of Cass County*. Edited by Charles Æ. Martin. Chicago: Munsell, 1913.

———. *Historical Encyclopedia of Illinois and History of Champaign County*. Edited by Joseph O. Cunningham. Chicago: Munsell, 1905.

———. *Historical Encyclopedia of Illinois and History of Christian County*. Edited by Henry L. Fowkes. Chicago: Munsell, 1918.

———. *Historical Encyclopedia of Illinois and History of Clark County*. Edited by H. C. Bell. Chicago: Middle-West, 1907.

———. *Historical Encyclopedia of Illinois and History of Coles County*. Edited by Charles Edward Wilson. Chicago: Munsell, 1906.

———. *Historical Encyclopedia of Illinois Cook County Edition*. Chicago: Munsell, 1905.

———. *Historical Encyclopedia of Illinois and History of DuPage County*. Chicago: Munsell, 1913.

———. *Historical Encyclopedia of Illinois and History of Edgar County*. Edited by H. Van Sellar. Chicago: Munsell, 1905.

———. *Historical Encyclopedia of Illinois and History of Fayette County*. Edited by Robert W. Ross and John J. Bullington. Chicago: Munsell, 1910.

———. *Historical Encyclopedia of Illinois and History of Grundy County*. Chicago: Munsell, 1914.

———. *Historical Encyclopedia of Illinois and History of Hancock County.* Edited by Charles J. Scofield. Chicago: Munsell, 1921.

———. *Historical Encyclopedia of Illinois and History of Henderson County.* Edited by James W. Gordon. Chicago: Munsell, 1911.

———. *Historical Encyclopedia of Illinois and History of Jo Daviess County.* Edited by William Spensley. Chicago: Munsell, 1904.

———. *Historical Encyclopedia of Illinois and History of Kane County.* Edited by John S. Wilcox. Chicago: Munsell, 1904.

———. *Historical Encyclopedia of Illinois and History of Kankakee County.* Edited by William F. Kenaga and George R. Letourneau. Chicago: Middle-West, 1906.

———. *Historical Encyclopedia of Illinois and History of Kendall County.* Chicago: Munsell, 1914.

———. *Historical Encyclopedia of Illinois and Knox County.* Edited by W. Selden Gale and George Candee Gale. Chicago: Munsell, 1899.

———. *Historical Encyclopedia of Illinois and History of Lee County.* Edited by A. C. Bardwell. Chicago: Munsell, 1904.

———. *Historical Encyclopedia of Illinois and History of Livingston County.* Edited by Christopher C. Strawn, Fordyce B. Johnson, and George H. Franzen. Chicago: Munsell, 1909.

———. *Historical Encyclopedia of Illinois and History of McLean County.* Edited by Ezra M. Prince and John H. Burnham. Chicago: Munsell, 1908.

———. *Historical Encyclopedia of Illinois and History of Mercer County.* Edited by William A. Lorimer. Chicago: Munsell, 1903.

———. *Historical Encyclopedia of Illinois and History of Montgomery County.* Edited by Alexander T. Strange. Chicago: Munsell, 1918.

———. *Historical Encyclopedia of Illinois and History of Morgan County.* Edited by William F. Short. Chicago: Munsell, 1906.

———. *Historical Encyclopedia of Illinois and History of Ogle County.* Edited by Horace G. Kauffman and Rebecca H. Kauffman. Chicago: Munsell, 1909.

———. *Historical Encyclopedia of Illinois and History of Peoria County.* Edited by David McCulloch. Chicago: Munsell, 1902.

———. *Historical Encyclopedia of Illinois and History of Piatt County.* Edited by Francis M. Shonkwiler. Chicago: Munsell, 1917.

———. *Historical Encyclopedia of Illinois and History of Rock Island County.* Chicago: Munsell, 1914.

———. *Historical Encyclopedia of Illinois and History of Sangamon County.* Chicago: Munsell, 1912.

———. *Historical Encyclopedia of Illinois and History of Schuyler County.* Edited by Howard F. Dyson. Chicago: Munsell, 1908.

———. *Historical Encyclopedia of Illinois and History of Shelby County.* Edited by George D. Chafee. Chicago: Munsell, 1910.

———. *Historical Encyclopedia of Illinois and History of St. Clair County.* Edited by A. S. Wilderman and A. A. Wilderman. Chicago: Munsell, 1907.

———. *Historical Encyclopedia of Illinois and History of Tazewell County.* Edited by Ben C. Allensworth. Chicago: Munsell, 1905.

———. *Historical Encyclopedia of Illinois and History of Warren County.* Edited by Hugh R. Moffet and Thomas H. Rogers. Chicago: Munsell, 1903.

———. *Illinois Historical Crawford County Biographical.* Chicago: Munsell, 1909.

———. *Illinois Historical Douglas County Biographical.* Edited by John W. King. Chicago: Munsell, 1910.

———. *Illinois Historical Effingham County Biographical.* Chicago: Munsell, 1910.

———. *Illinois Historical Lawrence County Biographical.* Edited by John William Mc-Cleave. Chicago: Munsell, 1910.

———. *Illinois Historical Wabash County Biographical.* Edited by Theodore G. Risley. Chicago: Munsell, 1911.

Bates, William H. *Souvenir of Early and Notable Events in the History of the North West Territory, Illinois, and Tazewell County.* Pekin, Ill.: Bates, 1916.

Baxter, Jack L. *Yesterday, Today: History of New Milford, 1835–1975.* Rockford, Ill.: Rockford Map Publishers, 1976.

Beadles, John Asa. *A History of Southernmost Illinois.* Des Peres, Mo.: Gateway, 1990.

Beal, Elsie, and Dolores Trost. *Portrait of Yesterday: A History of Dupo, Illinois.* Dupo, Ill.: Dupo State Bank, 1976.

Beaver, Paul J. *History of Logan County, Illinois.* Lincoln, Ill.: Logan County Heritage Foundation, 1982.

Becker, Anthony. *The Biography of a Country Town: U.S.A.* N.p.: N.p., 1954.

Beckwith, H. W. *History of Iroquois County.* Chicago: H. H. Hill, 1880.

———. *History of Vermilion County.* Chicago: H. H. Hill, 1879.

Beloit, Philip G., and Carroll L. Beloit. *History of Stonington Illinois: 1871–1971.* N.p.: n.d.

Benedetti, Rose Marie, and Virginia C. Bulat. *Portage, Pioneers, and Pubs: A History of Lyons, Illinois.* Chicago: Angel Guardian Orphanage Press, 1963.

Benson, Ethel. *Leland "66."* Waterman, Ill.: Waterman Press. 1974.

Bent, Charles, ed. *History of Whiteside County, Illinois.* Morrison, Ill.: Allen, 1877.

Bentley, Martha A. *There the Heart Is: A History of Brighton, Illinois.* Greenfield, Ill.: N.p., 1965.

Berens, Helmut Alan. *Elmhurst: Prairie to Tree Town.* Elmhurst, Ill. Elmhurst Historical Commission, 1968.

Berko, Casey. "In These Parts Change Is Almost Unheard Of." *Chicago Tribune,* Oct. 24, 1992, 4:1, 4.

Betsanes, Susanne. "Miniature Building Boom." *Chicago Tribune,* Dec. 25, 1993, 3:1, 4.

Bicentennial History of Ogle County. Oregon, Ill.: The Commission, 1976.

Biggsville 1854–1979. Monmouth: Kellogg, 1979.

Bigolin, Steve. "Landmarks of Barb City." *Daily Chronicle* (DeKalb, Ill.), March 3, 2003, A3.

Biographical and Historical Record of Kane County, Illinois. Chicago: Beers, Leggett, 1888.

Biographical Directory of the Tax-Payers and Voters of McHenry County. Chicago: C. Walker, 1877.

Black Hawk: An Autobiography. Edited by Donald Jackson. Urbana: University of Illinois Press. 1955.

Blades, John. "Fields of Dreams." *Chicago Tribune,* Sept. 2, 1989, 1, 4.

Blatchford, Tannisse T. *An Honorable Heritage: A Biography of Wayne Township, Illinois, 1834–1984.* N.p.: Wayne Community Association, 1984.

Blevins, Don. *Peculiar, Uncertain, and Two Egg.* Nashville, Tenn.: Cumberland House, 2000.

Bliss, Dorothy, and Tom Bliss. *Hillsboro, a History.* Hillsboro, Ill.: Montgomery County News, 1989.

Blue, Harold M., ed. *Historical Program Commemorating the One Hundredth Anniversary of Tremont, Illinois.* N.p.: N.p., 1935.

Boden, Robert. *History of the Town of Young Hickory, Amarugia, and the Village of London Mills.* London Mills, Ill.: London Mills Community Association, 1975.

Boies, Henry L. *History of DeKalb County, Illinois.* Chicago: O. P. Bassett, 1868.

Bond County History. Greenville, Ill.: Bond County Historical Society, 1979.

Bonnell, Clarence. *The Illinois Ozarks.* Harrisburg, Ill.: Register, 1946.

Borcover, Alfred. "Not Much Happens Here, and That's Its Appeal." *Chicago Tribune,* Jan. 22, 1994, 4:1, 4.

Bordner, Marjorie Rich. *From Cornfields to Marching Feet: Camp Ellis, Illinois.* Dallas, Tex.: Curtis Media, 1993.

Boss, Henry R. *Sketches of the History of Ogle County, Illinois.* Polo, Ill.: Boss, 1859.

Bourland, Richard D. *Savanna Pioneers.* Morrison, Ill.: Shawver Press, 1978.

Bradley, Jack L. *History of Chillicothe, Illinois.* Chillicothe, Ill.: Chillicothe Historical Society, 1995.

Bradsby, H. C., ed. *History of Bureau County, Illinois.* Chicago: World, 1885.

Brady, David M. *Divernon: Its Place in Time.* Divernon, Ill.: Emerson Press, 2000.

Brass, Louise. "Ashton." *Telegraph* (Dixon, Ill.), Aug. 27, 1988, 13.

Brewer, John M. *Steal Easy, My Home Town: A Memoiric History of Crab Orchard, Illinois.* Rolla, Mo.: J. M. Brewer, 1985.

Brieschke, Walter L. *Notes on Makanda.* Makanda, Ill.: Brieschke, 1983.

Bright, William. *Native American Placenames of the United States.* Norman: University of Oklahoma Press, 2004.

Brinkerhoff, J. H. G. *Brinkerhoff's History of Marion County.* Indianapolis, Ind.: B. F. Bowen, 1909.

Brinkman, Grover, ed. *This Is Washington County, Its First 150 Years, 1818–1968.* Nashville, Ill.: Historical Society of Washington County, 1968.

Brown, Margaret Kimball. "French Place Names in Illinois." In *450 ans de noms de lieux Français en Amérique du Nord,* 463–65. Québec: Les Publications du Québec, 1986.

Brown, Margaret Kimball, and Lawrie Cena Dean. *The Village of Chartre in Colonial Illinois 1720–1765.* New Orleans, La.: Polyanthos, 1977.

Brown, Virginia Sparr, ed. *Grundy County, Illinois, Landmarks.* Morris, Ill.: Grundy County Historical Society, 1981.

Bucciferro, Rose Parker, ed. *Parker's History of Johnson County, Illinois.* Hartford, Ky.: McDowell, 1977.

Buck, Genevieve. "'Hideaway' Is Now a Hub." *Chicago Tribune,* June 9, 1990, 4:1, 4.

Buffalo Centennial Souvenir Program. N.p.: N.p., 1954.

Bureau County Centennial 1828–1928. Princeton, Ill.: N.p., 1929.

Burns, Robert T. *A Link to the Past: The Saga of LaSalle County.* Mendota, Ill.: Butler, 1968.

Burt, John Spencer, and W. E. Hawthorne. *Past and Present of Marshall and Putnam Counties, Illinois.* Chicago: Pioneer, 1907.

Burton, Charles Pierce. *Aurora: From Covered Wagon to Stream-Lined Zephyr.* Aurora, Ill.: Finch and McCullouch, 1937.

Callary, Edward, ed. *Place Names in the Midwestern United States.* Lewiston, N.Y.: Mellen, 2000.

Calumet Region Historical Guide. Gary, Ind.: German, 1939.

Campbell, Bruce Alexander. *The Sangamon Saga.* Springfield, Ill.: Phillips, 1976.

Carlock, Where History Is Still Being Made. N.p.: N.p., 1976.

Carpenter, George W. *—and They Changed the Name to Gilead.* Hardin, Ill.: N.p., 1976.

———. *Calhoun Is My Kingdom.* N.p.: Merkle Print, 1967.

Carpenter, Ruth, and Theodora Karr Johnson. *History of Shirley Christian Church and Shirley, Illinois.* N.p.: N.p., 1984.

Carr, Edson I. *The History of Rockton, Winnebago County, Illinois 1820 to 1898.* Rockton, Ill.: Herald Office Print, 1989.

Carr, Kay J. *Belleville, Ottawa, and Galesburg: Community and Democracy on the Illinois Frontier.* Carbondale: Southern Illinois University Press, 1996.

Carroll, S. R. "In the Name of . . . How Our Townships Got Their Monikers." *Chicago Tribune,* June 12, 1994, 4:1, 8.

Carson, May Hawley, and Zoe Lenore Gray. *History of Warren, Illinois.* 1928. Reprint. N.p.: Jo Daviess County Republican Central Committee, 1993.

Cates, Michael. "Despite Changes, Residents Won't Lay Tradition to Rest." *Chicago Tribune,* Jan. 26, 1991, 4:1, 4.

Cawiezel, Marilyn W. "Lisle." In *DuPage Roots.* Edited by Richard A. Thompson, 184–90. Wheaton, Ill.: DuPage County Historical Society, 1985.

Cedeck, Mark J., and Joan Foster, eds. *A History of Glen Carbon.* Glen Carbon, Ill.: Glen Carbon Centennial, 1992.

Centennial Celebration New Baden Illinois. New Baden, Ill.: New Baden Centennial Committee, 1955.

Centennial History of Crossville and Phillips Township. N.p.: N.p., 1995.

Centennial History of Litchfield, Illinois: One Hundred Years. N.p.: N.p., 1953.

Centennial History of Morrisonville, Illinois, 1872–1972. Morrisonville, Ill.: Morrisonville Centennial Corporation, 1972.

Centennial Salute to the Village of Sibley, Illinois, and Sullivant Township in Ford County, 1877–1977. Melvin, Ill.: Ford County Press, 1977.

Century of a Town, Bismarck, Illinois, 1872–1972. Potomac, Ill.: Westcove, 1972.

Cerro Gordo Centennial 1855–1955. N.p.: N.p., 1955.

Cha-Jua, Sundiata Keita. *America's First Black Town: Brooklyn, Illinois, 1830–1915.* Urbana: University of Illinois Press, 2000.

Chapin, Charles A. "Newton and Jasper: A Search for Their Stories." *Illinois Heritage* 1 (Winter 1988): 12–16.

Chapman, Mrs. P. T. *A History of Johnson County, Illinois.* Herrin, Ill.: Herrin News, 1925.

Chatsworth Area Centennial Celebration. Chatsworth, Ill.: The Association, 1967.

Chavez, Donna, "Nothing but a Memory." *Chicago Tribune,* Oct. 27, 1996, 17:4.

Chenoweth, Ruth, and Sara Wisslead Semonis, comps. *The History of McDonough County, Illinois.* Dallas, Tex.: Curtis Media, 1992.

Christian County History. Taylorville: Christian County Historical Society, 2000.

Christian, Sue Ellen. "An Invitation to Stop Shopping Long Enough to Look Around." *Chicago Tribune,* Aug. 7, 1993, 3:1, 4.

———. "It's Not Cutting-Edge but Residents Like It That Way." *Chicago Tribune,* March 21, 1992, 1:22, 23.

———. "Living Here Can Prove a Moving Experience." *Chicago Tribune,* Sept. 5, 1991, 4:1, 4.

Church, Charles A. *Past and Present of the City of Rockford and Winnebago County, Illinois.* Chicago: S. J. Clarke, 1905.

Cissna Park, Illinois 1882–1982: A Great Past with a Greater Future. Cissna Park, Ill.: Cissna Park News, 1984.

City of Harvey, 1890–1962: History. Harvey, Ill.: First National Bank of Harvey, 1962.

City of LaSalle Sesquicentennial, 1852–2002. N.p.: City of LaSalle, 2002.

Clapp, Clement L. *History of Greene County, Illinois: Its Past and Present.* Chicago: Donnelley, Gassette and Loyd, 1879.

Clark, Helen Hollandsworth, ed. *A History of Fulton County, Illinois, in Spoon River Country, 1818–1968.* N.p.: Fulton County Board of Supervisors, 1969.

Clarke, S. J. *History of McDonough County Illinois.* Springfield, Ill.: Lusk. 1878.

Clayton, John. *The Illinois Fact Book and Historical Almanac, 1673–1968.* Carbondale: Southern Illinois University Press, 1970.

Climer, Ruth E., Sandra Fornell, and Mary Ellen Havens. *Welcome to Warsaw.* Warsaw, Ill.: Warsaw Historic District Commission, 1984.

Clinton 1835–1985, DeWitt County 1839–1985, Illinois. Clinton, Ill.: The Committee, 1985.

Coates, James. "Rollicking Roots." *Chicago Tribune,* April 3, 1993, 4:1, 4.

Coats, Betty Spindler, and Raymond Jurgen Spahn. *The Swiss on Looking Glass Prairie: A Century and a Half, 1831–1981.* Edwardsville, Ill.: Lovejoy Library, 1983.

Cochrane, Joseph. *Centennial History of Mason County.* Springfield, Ill.: Rokker's Steam Printing House, 1876.

Cofield, Jewell Russell. *Memories of Lakeview.* N.p.: N.p., 1976.

Cohen, Laurie. "Suburb Clears the Air: We're Close-Knit and We Like It." *Chicago Tribune,* Jan. 12, 1991, 1:1, 4.

Colby, Lydia. "Historic Spots in Henry County, Illinois." *Journal of the Illinois State Historical Society* 28 (Oct. 1935): 164–87.

Colson, U. O. *Souvenir History of Edgar County 1823–1893*. Paris, Ill.: Colson, 1892.

Combined History of Edwards, Lawrence and Wabash Counties, Illinois. Philadelphia, Pa.: J. L. McDonough, 1883.

Combined History of Randolph, Monroe and Perry Counties, Illinois. Philadelphia, Pa.: J. L. McDonough, 1883.

Combined History of Schuyler and Brown Counties, Illinois. Philadelphia, Pa.: Brink, 1882.

Combined History of Shelby and Moultrie Counties, Illinois. Philadelphia, Pa.: Brink, McDonough, 1881.

Commemorative Biographical and Historical Record of Kane County, Illinois. Chicago: Beers, Legget, 1888

Commercial History of Clinton County and Its Thriving Cities. East St. Louis, Ill.: East St. Louis Gazette, 1913.

Condon, Sidney S. *Pioneer Sketches of Union County, Illinois*. Anna, Ill.: Gazette-Democrat, 1987.

Condor, Bob. "A Place Where Old Meets New—and It Works." *Chicago Tribune*, Aug. 28, 1993, 4:1, 4.

Conibear, R. C. *Morton Illinois Centennial, 1877–1977*. Morton, Ill.: Morton Historical Society, 1977.

Cook Philip. *Zion City, Illinois: Twentieth-Century Utopia*. Syracuse, N.Y.: Syracuse University Press, 1996.

Cook, Richard A. *South Holland, Illinois: A History 1846–1966*. South Holland, Ill.: South Holland Trust and Savings Bank, 1966.

Cooper, Marshall M. *History of Jerseyville, Illinois, 1822 to 1901*. Jerseyville, Ill.: Jerseyville Republican Print, 1901.

Costa, David J. "Illinois." *Society for the Study of the Indigenous Languagues of the Americas Newsletter* 25 (Jan. 2007): 9–12.

Coulet du Gard, René. *Dictionary of French Place Names in the U.S.A*. Newark, Del.: Editions des Deux Mondes et Slavuta, 1986.

Counties of Cumberland, Jasper and Richland, Illinois, Historical and Biographical. Chicago: F. A. Battey, 1884.

County of Douglas, Illinois. Chicago: F. A. Battey, 1884.

Cox, S. V., comp. *A History of Hoopeston—"World's Greatest Corn Canning Center."* Hoopeston, Ill.: Chronicle Herald. 1925.

Crawford, William B. "'The City on Wheels' Still Rolling Along." *Chicago Tribune*, July 13, 1991, 1:22, 23.

Crisler, Amy E. "Glendale Heights." In *DuPage Roots*. Edited by Richard A. Thompson, 166–71. Wheaton, Ill.: DuPage County Historical Society, 1985.

Cromie, William J., Edward J. F. Young, and Helen T. Young. *La Grange Centennial History*. La Grange, Ill.: La Grange Area Historical Society, 1978.

Cross, Robert. "You Can't Get Past the Wealth, but the Locals Sure Try." *Chicago Tribune*, Nov. 6, 1993, 4:1, 2.

Cruitt, Lois Riley, and Betty J. Coventry, comps. *Findlay, Illinois*. N.p.: N.p., 1992.

Cumberland County History. Olney, Ill.: Taylor Print Shop, 1973.

Cunningham, Eileen Smith. *History of the Carrollton, Illinois Area, 1821–1989.* Dallas, Tex.: Curtis Media, 1989.

———. *Lower Illinois Valley: Color Me Greene.* Greenfield, Ill.: Cole, 1980.

Cutshall, Alden D. *A Gazetteer of the Origin of Illinois Nomenclature.* N.p.: N.p., 1930.

Danvers Illinois Community History. N.p.: Danvers Historical Society, 1987.

Davis, Lucille Wilderman, comp. *Freeburg's Centennial Celebration, 1859–1959.* Mascoutah, Ill.: Jenkins, 1959.

Davis, William W. *History of Whiteside County, Illinois.* Chicago: Pioneer, 1908.

Deardorff, Julie. "Their Appetite for This Place Seems almost Insatiable." *Chicago Tribune,* July 25, 1992, 1:22–23.

Dearinger, Lowell A. "A New Geography of Brown County." *Illinois Magazine* 17 (Oct. 1978): 21–37.

———. "A New Geography of Illinois: Jefferson County." *Outdoor Illinois* 13 (Oct. 1974): 15–38.

———. "A New Geography of Perry County." *Outdoor Illinois* 9 (Aug.–Sept. 1975): 19–43.

Deason, Everett L., Donna Esker, Charles Meier, William Riechmann, and Warren Stieg, eds. *Okawville, Illinois.* N.p.: N.p., 1988.

Deep Are the Roots. Henry, Ill.: Riverside Press, 1976.

Dell'Angela, Tracy. "Nothing but a Memory." *Chicago Tribune,* Oct. 27, 1996, 17:6.

Derry, Elsie May. *Through the Years in an Early Pioneer Town, Bernadotte.* Lewistown, Ill.: Mid-County. 1969.

Dickinson, Burrus. *History of Eureka, Illinois.* Eureka, Ill.: Dickinson, 1985.

Dickinson, Lora Townsend. *Story of Winnetka.* Winnetka, Ill.: Winnetka Historical Society, 1956.

Dickson, Elmer. "Geographical Features and Place Names of Kendall County." www.rootsweb.com/~ilkendal/placenames/kcplacenames.htm. Accessed March 13, 2008.

Dionne, Edward C. *Olympia Fields 1927.* Chicago Heights, Ill.: Signal.

Dole, Mrs. Joseph C. "Pioneer Days in Coles County, Illinois." *Journal of the Illinois State Historical Society* 14 (April–July 1921): 107–21.

Donovan, Frank P., Jr. "Named for Railroad Presidents." *Railroad Magazine* (Feb. 1965): 24–27.

Dooley, Raymond, ed. *The Namesake Town: A Centennial History of Lincoln, Illinois.* Lincoln, Ill.: Feldman's Print Shop, 1953.

Dotterer, Lori. "Potosi, My Neighborhood Ghost Town." *Illinois History* 42 (Oct. 1988): 12.

Dowling, John W. *History of Iroquois County.* Watseka, Ill.: Iroquois County Board of Supervisors, 1968.

Dretske, Diana. *What's in a Name? The Origin of Place Names in Lake County, Illinois.* Wauconda, Ill.: Lake County Discovery Museum, 1996.

Drury, John. *This Is Brown County, Illinois.* Chicago: Loree, 1955.

Dugan, Hugh G. *Village on the County Line: A History of Hinsdale, Illinois.* N.p.: N.p., 1949.

Dunning, Mildred Robinson. *The Story of Lombard 1833–1955.* N.p.: N.p., 1955.

Dupre, Irma, Beatrice Brittain Braden, and Carolyn J. Bullinger. *Dundee Township 1835–1985*. Carpentersville, Ill.: Crossroads Communications, 1985.

Dwight Centennial, 1854–1954: A Great Past—a Greater Future. N.p.: N.p., 1954.

Early History of Washington, Illinois and Vicinity. Washington, Ill.: Tazewell County Reporter, 1929.

Edmunds, R. David. *The Potawatomis, Keepers of the Fire*. Norman: University of Oklahoma Press, 1978.

Eggemeyer, Frankie. *Bricktown Illinois, Randolph County, U.S.A.* 1976. Reprint. Ellis Grove, Ill.: N.p., 1991.

Ekberg, Carl J. *French Roots in the Illinois Country*. Urbana: University of Illinois Press, 1998.

El Paso Story: The Centennial Book of El Paso, Illinois. El Paso, Ill.: El Paso Public Library Board, 1954.

Elbe, Anita, and Eisenhower Junior High Social Studies Department. "Darien." In *DuPage County Roots*. Edited by Richard A. Thompson, 138–43. Wheaton, Ill.: DuPage County Historical Society, 1985.

Ellsworth, Spencer. *Records of the Olden Times; Or, Fifty Years on the Prairies*. Lacon, Ill.: Home Journal Steam Printing Establishment, 1880.

Elmira, Illinois, Centennial and Scottish Pioneers, 1838–1938. Elmira, Ill.: Centennial, 1938.

Ely, Salem. *A Centennial History of the Villages of Iroquois and Montgomery and the Township of Concord, 1818 to 1918*. Chicago: Regan, 1918.

Engelke, Georgia McCormick. *Looking Back at Granite City's Heritage, 1801–1893*. St. Louis, Mo.: C. Sarne, 1993.

Eno, Joel N. "A Tercentennial History of the Towns and Cities of New York: Their Origin, Dates and Names." *Proceedings of the New York State Historical Association* 15 (1916): 225–64.

"Eola." *Beacon-News* (Aurora, Ill.), Aug. 23, 1984, D13.

Evans, Don. *Ellsworth's Hundredth Year: Early Settlement: Dawson, Arrowsmith, Empire, Bluemound, Old Town Townships*. N.p.: N.p., 1971.

Fabian, William M. *Chautauqua, Illinois: A Brief History*. Leaflet 5. Elsah, Ill.: Historic Elsa Foundation, 1975.

Facts and Folks: A History of Jefferson County, Illinois. Mount Vernon, Ill.: Jefferson County Historical Society, 1978.

Farren, Kathy, ed. *A Bicentennial History of Kendall County, Illinois*. Yorkville, Ill.: Kendall County Bicentennial Commission, 1976.

Feeley, Ralph. *From Camelot to Metropolis: The History of Ontarioville–Hanover Park*. S l: N.p., 1976.

Fegelman, Andrew. "It's Not Chicago." *Chicago Tribune*, Dec. 9, 1989, 3:1, 6.

Feldhake, Hilda Engbring. *Effingham County, Illinois—Past and Present*. Effingham, Ill.: Effingham Regional Historical Society, 1968.

———. *The Lords Effingham and the American Colonies*. Effingham, Ill.: Effingham County Bicentennial Commission, 1976.

Fennessy, Florence, and Grace Woods, comps. *Centennial History of Avon*. Avon, Ill.: Avon Sentinel, 1937.

Ferguson, Gillum. "'He Acted Well His Part': Hamlet Ferguson and Southern Illinois." *Journal of Illinois History* 6 (Winter 2003): 271–95.

Fiftieth Anniversary Souvenir of Effingham, Illinois, 1853–1903. Effingham, Ill.: Effingham Democrat, 1903.

Fishback, Woodson W. *A History of Murphysboro, Illinois, 1843–1982.* Brandon, Miss.: Quail Ridge. 1982.

Fisher, Lucius G. "Pioneer Recollections of Beloit and Southern Wisconsin." *Wisconsin Magazine of History* 1 (March 1918): 262–75.

Fitzgerald, Mike. "Centreville Pushes for Alorton Annexation." *News-Democrat* (Belleville, Ill.), July 19, 2000, 1A+.

Fliege, Stu. *Tales and Trails of Illinois.* Urbana: University of Illinois Press, 2002.

Ford County History: Ford County, Illinois. Dallas, Tex.: Taylor, 1984.

Ford, Henry A. *History of Putnam and Marshall Counties, with Some Accounts of Bureau and Stark Counties.* Lacon, Ill.:. Ford, 1860.

Fortier, John B. "New Light on Fort Massac." In *Frenchmen and French Ways in the Mississippi Valley.* Edited by John Francis McDermott, 57–71. Urbana: University of Illinois Press, 1969.

Franck, Fred. *Landmarks, the Story of Boone County.* Belvidere, Ill.: Boone County Heritage Days Committee, 1985.

Franke, Judith. *French Peoria and the Illinois Country, 1673–1846.* Springfield: Illinois State Museum, 1995.

Frankfort Centennial. Frankfort, Ill.: Historical Program Committee, 1955.

Franklin County, Illinois, 1818–1997. Paducah, Ky.: Turner, 1996.

Franklin, Paula. A. *Biography in Black: A History of Streator, Illinois.* Streator, Ill.: Weber, 1962.

Frazer, Timothy C., and June M. Frazer. "Place Name Patterns in McDonough County, Illinois." In *Place Names in the Midwestern United States.* Edited by Edward Callary, 35–42. Lewiston, N.Y.: Mellen, 2000.

Fulton County Heritage. Dallas, Tex.: Curtis Media, 1988.

Fulton County Historical Society. *Historic Fulton County: Sites and Scenes—Past and Present.* Lewistown, Ill.: Mid-County Press, 1973.

Fults, Florence Chism, Leslie Chisholm, and Ruth Kirkham Novella. *Promised Land in Southern Illinois.* Wickliffe, Ky.: Magee, 1985.

Fulwider, Addison L. *History of Stephenson County, Illinois.* Chicago: S. J. Clarke, 1910.

Galena Guide. Federal Writers' Project. Galena, Ill.: City of Galena, 1937.

Gannett, Henry. *The Origin of Certain Place Names in the United States.* Washington, D.C.: U.S. Geological Survey, 1905.

Gardner, E. A. *History of Ford County, Illinois, from Its Earliest Settlement to 1908.* Chicago: Clarke, 1908.

Gates, Paul W. *The Illinois Central Railroad and Its Colonization Work.* Cambridge, Mass.: Harvard University Press, 1934.

Genosky, Landry, ed. *People's History of Quincy and Adams County, Illinois: A Sesquicentennial History.* Quincy, Ill.: Jost and Kiefer, 1974.

Ghrist, John Russell. *Junction 20: The Story of Udina.* Dundee, Ill.: JRG Communications, 1995.

———. *Plato Center Memories.* Dundee, Ill.: JRG Communications, 1999.

Gilbert, Barry. "KI-RO? KAY-RO? CARE-O?" *Journal of the Illinois State Historical Society* 33 (1940): 359–60.

Gilman Centennial: The First Hundred Years, 1855–1955. N.p.: N.p., 1955

Goodley, Mary W. *The Wire Mill That Created North Chicago.* N.p.: N.p., n.d.

Goodspeed, Weston Arthur, and Daniel D. Healy, eds. *History of Cook County, Illinois.* Chicago: Goodspeed Historical Association, 1909.

Gordon, Beulah. *Here and There in Shelby County.* N.p.: N.p., 1973.

Goss, David E. *A History of Northern Township, Franklin County, Illinois.* N.p.: N.p., 2001.

Goudy, Calvin. *History of Christian County.* Philadelphia, Pa.: Brink, McDonough, 1880.

Gould, Alice J. *Schaumburg: A History of the Township.* Schaumburg: Schaumburg Township Historical Society, 1982.

Gowen, Anne. "After the Birth Come Growing Pains." *Chicago Tribune,* Aug. 13, 1994, 4:1, 2.

Grady, William. "County No Longer Has Space to Du More With Its Name." *Chicago Tribune,* March 9, 1994, 2:1.

Greenblatt, Miriam. *History of Itasca.* Itasca, Ill.: Itasca State Bank, 1976.

Green Valley, Illinois 1872–1972. Astoria, Ill.: Stevens, 1972.

Gregg, Thomas. *History of Hancock County, Illinois.* Chicago: Chapman, 1880.

Gregory, Ted. "A Burb Where Stereotypes Haven't Found a Home." *Chicago Tribune,* Nov. 4, 1992, 4:1, 4.

Gresham, John, comp. *Historical and Biographical Record of Douglas County, Illinois.* Logansport, Ind.: Wilson, Humphries, 1900.

Griffith, Katharine, and Will Griffith. *Spotlight on Egypt.* Carbondale, Ill.: Egypt Book House, 1946.

Griffith, Will. "Egyptian Place-Names." *Egyptian Key* 2 (March 1947): 29–33.

Gross, Lewis M. *Past and Present of DeKalb County, Illinois.* Chicago: Pioneer, 1907.

Grubbs, Jim. "Origins of Auburn." *State Journal-Register* (Springfield, Ill.), July 23, 1991, 2.

Hadley, George D. "A History of Boone County, Illinois." M.Ed. thesis. Colorado State College of Education, Greeley, 1942.

Hagan, William T. *The Sac and Fox Indians.* Norman: University of Oklahoma Press, 1958.

Hageman, Lucille, comp. *Partial Encyclopedia of Waverly.* Jacksonville, Ill.: Jacksonville Courier, 1968.

Hale, Stan J., comp. and ed. *Williamson County, Illinois Sesquicentennial History.* Paducah, Ky.: Turner, 1993.

Hallberg, Carl V. "Soperville: An Immigrant Community in Knox County." *Journal of the Illinois State Historical Society* 74 (Spring 1981): 51–57.

Halpert, Herbert. "'Egypt'—a Wandering Place-Name Legend." *Midwest Folklore* 4 (Fall 1954): 165–68.

Halsey, John J., ed. *A History of Lake County, Illinois*. Philadelphia, Pa.: R. S. Bates, 1912.

Hamilton County, Illinois: Celebrating 175 Years. Paducah, Ky.: Turner, 1996.

Hamilton, Oscar Brown. *History of Jersey County, Illinois*. Chicago: Munsell, 1919.

Hanabarger, Linda. "Fayette County Place Names." *Fayette Facts* 23 (1994): 43–54.

Handley, John. "Boomtown." *Chicago Tribune*, Jan. 12, 2003, 16:1, 5.

———. "Old Not Stuffy Tony Suburb Features Wealth of the Unexpected." *Chicago Tribune*, Oct. 23, 1992, 4:1, 3.

Hanford, Carolyn M., and Mary Jane O'Hara. *Menard County, Illinois History*. Petersburg, Ill.: History of Menard County, 1988.

Hansen, Harry, ed. *Illinois: A Descriptive and Historical Guide*. 1939. Rev. ed. New York: Hastings House, 1974.

Harder, Kelsie B. *Illustrated Dictionary of Place Names: United States and Canada*. New York: Facts on File, 1985.

Hardin County, Illinois. Paducah, Ky.: Turner, 1987.

Harmon, Ada Douglas. *The Story of an Old Town—Glen Ellyn*. Glen Ellyn, Ill.: Glen Ellyn News Printing, 1928.

Harper, Terry L., ed. *History of Edwards County, Illinois*. Dallas, Tex.: Curtis Media, 1993.

Harrelson, Ralph S. *Hoodville, Illinois*. McLeansboro, N.p.: N.p., 1975.

Harrington, George B. *Past and Present of Bureau County, Illinois*. Chicago: Pioneer 1906.

Harris, Jesse W. "Illinois Place-Name Lore." *Midwest Folklore* 4 (Winter 1954): 217–20.

———. "Wetaug—A Place-Name Puzzle." *Names* 9 (1961): 126–28.

Hartrich, Mary Clotilde Huber. *Quasquicentennial History of Sainte Marie, Saint Mary's Church and Sainte Marie Township*. N.p.: N.p., 1962.

Harvey, Daniel G. *The Argyle Settlement in History and Story*. Beloit, Wis.: Beloit Daily News, 1924.

Hasbrouck, Jacob L. *History of McLean County, Illinois*. Indianapolis, Ind.: Historical, 1924.

Hatton, Jim. "Once It Was a Thriving Produce Center." *Southern Illinoisan* (Carbondale), March 1, 1970, 8.

Havens, Catherine. *Marietta, Illinois: Past and Present and Harris Township*. Astoria, Ill.: K. K. Stevens, 1987.

Havighurst, Walter. "The Way to Future City." *Journal of the Illinois State Historical Society* 69 (Aug. 1976): 224–37.

Hay, William D. . . . . *a Matter of History* . . . . Carmi: White County Historical Society, 1996.

Hayes, Charles. "For Village, Store Is Another Selling Point." *Chicago Tribune*, Oct. 5, 1991, 1:18–19.

———. "Old Piano Capital Now Keyed to Affordability." *Chicago Tribune*, Nov. 27, 1993, 4:1, 4.

Hayner, Don, and Tom McNamee. *Streetwise Chicago: A History of Chicago Street Names*. Chicago: Loyola University Press, 1988.

Heisler, James, Susan Riegler, and Roberta Smith, eds. *Crystal Lake, Illinois: A Pictorial History.* Crystal Lake, Ill.: The Committee, 1986.

Henson, Winifred Nooner. "History of Franklin County, Illinois." M.Ed.thesis. Colorado State College of Education, Greeley, 1942.

Heritage of the Prairie: A History of Le Roy and of Empire and West Townships. N.p.: Kramer, 1976.

Hermann, Brenda. "Town Thrives on Industry, Family Life." *Chicago Tribune,* July 24, 1993, 1:20–21.

Hicks, E. W. *History of Kendall County, Illinois.* Aurora, Ill.: Knickerbocker and Hodder, 1877.

Highlights of Fairview Heights, 1776–1976. Fairview Heights, Ill.: B and W Print, 1976.

Hillsboro Guide. Works Progress Administration. Hillsboro, Ill.: Montgomery News, 1940.

Historic Rock Island County. Rock Island, Ill.: Kramer, 1908.

Historic Sites and Structures of Hancock County, Illinois. Carthage, Ill.: Hancock County Historical Society, 1979.

Historic Sketch and Biographical Album of Shelby County, Illinois. Shelbyville, Ill.: Wilder, 1900.

History of Adams County, Illinois. Chicago: Murray, Williamson and Phelps, 1879.

History of Atlanta, 1853–1953. Atlanta, Ill.: Stewart-Finks, 1953.

History of Brown County, Illinois, 1880–1970. Astoria, Ill: Stevens, 1972.

History of Carroll County, Illinois. Chicago: Kett, 1878.

History of Carroll Township, History of Casey, Illinois, and Western Clark County. Shawnee Mission, Kans.: Kesler, 1981.

History of Champaign County, Illinois. Philadelphia, Pa.: Brink, McDonough, 1878.

History of Columbia and Columbia Precinct, Monroe County, Illinois, 1859–1959. N.p.: Clarion, 1959.

History of Crawford County, Illinois, 1980. Robinson, Ill.: Crawford County Historical Society, 1981.

History of DeWitt County, Illinois. Chicago: Pioneer, 1910.

History of DeWitt County, Illinois. Philadelphia, Pa. W. R. Brink, 1882.

History of DeWitt County, Illinois, 1839–1968. Clinton, Ill.: The Committee, 1968.

History of Edgar County, Illinois. Chicago: Le Baron, 1879.

History of Edwards County, Illinois. Albion, Ill.: Edwards County Historical Society. 1980.

History of Eureka College. St. Louis, Mo.: Christian Publishing Company, 1894.

History and Families of Gallatin County, Illinois. Paducah, Ky.: Turner, 1988.

History of Fulton County, Illinois. Peoria, Ill.: Chapman, 1879.

History of Gallatin, Saline, Hamilton, Franklin and Williamson Counties, Illinois. Chicago: Goodspeed, 1887.

History of Girard, Illinois "from Then till Now," 1855–1955. Girard, Ill.: Historical Committee, 1955.

History of Greene and Jersey Counties, Illinois. Springfield, Ill.: Continental Historical, 1885.

History of Grundy County, Illinois. Chicago: Baskin, 1882.

History of Hancock County, Illinois. Carthage, Ill.: Board of Supervisors of Hancock County, 1968.

History of Henry County (Its Tax-Payers and Voters). Chicago: Kett, 1877.

History of Jackson County, Illinois. Philadelphia, Pa.: Brink, McDonough, 1878.

History of Jo Daviess County, Illinois. Chicago: Kett, 1878.

History of LaSalle County. Chicago: Inter-state Printing, 1886.

History of Lee County. Chicago: H. H. Hill, 1881.

History of Livingston County, Illinois. Chicago: Le Baron, 1878.

History of Livingston County, Illinois. Dallas, Tex.: Curtis Media, 1991.

History of Logan County, Illinois. Chicago: Donnelley, 1878.

History of Logan County, Illinois. Chicago: Inter-state Printing, 1886.

History of Macon County, Illinois. Philadelphia, Pa.: Brink, McDonough, 1880.

History of Macoupin County, Illinois. Philadelphia, Pa.: Brink, McDonough, 1879.

History of Madison County, Illinois. Edwardsville, Ill.: W. R. Brink, 1882.

History of Maquon and Vicinity, 1827–1976. Maquon, Ill.: The Assn., 1976.

History of Marion and Clinton Counties, Illinois. Philadelphia, Pa.: Brink, McDonough, 1881.

History of Marshall County, Illinois. Lacon, Ill.: Marshall County Historical Society, 1983.

History of Marshall, Illinois and Eastern Clark County. N.p.: N.p., 1978.

History of Massac County, Illinois. Paducah, Ky.: Turner, 1987.

History of McDonough County, Illinois. Springfield, Ill.: Continental Historical, 1885.

History of McHenry County, Illinois. Chicago: Inter-state Printing, 1885.

History of McHenry County, Illinois. Chicago: Munsell, 1922.

History of McLean County, Illinois. Chicago: Le Baron, 1879.

History of Menard and Mason Counties, Illinois. Chicago: Baskin, 1879.

History of Mercer and Henderson Counties. Chicago: Hill, 1882.

History of Morgan County, Illinois. Chicago: Donnelley, 1878.

History of Ogle County, Illinois. Chicago: Kett, 1878.

History of Park Ridge, 1841–1926. Chicago: Edison Press, 1926.

History of Payson, Illinois, 1835–1976. N.p.: Payson Bicentennial Book Committee, 1976.

History of Plainfield, Then and Now. Plainfield, Ill.: Plainfield Historical Society, 1977.

History of Peoria County, Illinois. Chicago: Johnson, 1880.

History of Pike County, Illinois. Chicago: Chapman, 1880.

History of Saline County. Harrisburg, Ill.: Saline County Genealogical Society, 1997.

History of Sangamon County, Illinois. Chicago: Inter-state Printing, 1881.

History of St. Clair County, Illinois. Philadelphia, Pa.: Brink, McDonough, 1881.

History of Stephenson County, Illinois 1970. Mount Morris, Ill.: Kable, 1972

History of Tazewell County, Illinois. Chicago: Chapman, 1879.

History of Washington County, Illinois. Philadelphia, Pa.: Brink, McDonough, 1897.

History of Wayne and Clay Counties, Illinois. Chicago: Globe, 1884.

History of Westfield, Illinois, and Northwest Clark County. Shawnee Mission, Kans.: H. Kesler, 1981.

History of White County, Illinois. Chicago: Inter-state Printing, 1883.

History of Will County, Illinois. Chicago: Le Baron, 1878.

History of Winnebago County, Illinois. Chicago: Kett, 1877.

Hobbs, Richard Gear. *Glamorous Galena.* Galena, Ill.: Galena Gazette Print, 1939.

Hochstetter, Nancy, ed. *Guide to Illinois' Historical Markers.* Verona, Wis.: Guide Press, 1985.

Hoffman, Muriel Martens. *History of Lawndale, Martin, and Anchor Townships and the Villages of Colfax and Anchor.* Fairbury, Ill.: Cornbelt Press, 1976.

Hoffman, U. J. *History of LaSalle County, Illinois.* Chicago: Clarke, 1906.

Holt, Douglas. "A Lovely Town for Trees, Friends and Fights." *Chicago Tribune,* May 21, 1994, 4:1, 4.

Hosmer, Charles B., Jr., and Paul O. Williams. *Elsah: A Historic Guidebook.* 4th ed. Elsah, Ill.: Historic Elsa, 1979.

Houde, Mary Jean, and John Klasey. *Of the People: A Popular History of Kankakee County.* Chicago: General Print, 1968.

Hubbs, Barbara Burr. *Pioneer Folks and Places: An Historic Gazetteer of Williamson County.* 1939. Reprint. Marion, Ill.: Williamson County Historical Society, 1979.

Huizenga, Pat. *Dolton, 1892–1976.* N.p.: N.p., 1976.

Humphrey, Marles. "No Offense but 'Squaw' Taken out of Park Name." *Chicago Tribune,* Jan. 17, 1997, 2:1, 2.

Husband, Will W. *Old Brownsville Days.* 1935. Reprint. Murphysboro, Ill.: Jackson County Historical Society, 1973.

Hutchison, Florence. "Old Morgan County Village and Town Settlements in the Earliest Days." www.rootsweb.com/~ilmorgan/morgan/htm.

Illinois Atlas and Gazeteer. 4th ed. Yarmouth, Maine: DeLorme, 2003.

Illinois Blue Book 2005–2006. Springfield: Illinois Secretary of State, 2006.

Illinois Counties and Incorporated Municipalities. Springfield: Illinois Secretary of State, 2003.

Illinois Gazetteer, 1981. Wilmington, Del.: American Historical Publications, 1981.

Illinois Guide and Gazetteer. Chicago: Rand McNally, 1969.

Illustrated Atlas Map of Iroquois County, Illinois. Edwardsville, Ill.: Brink, 1884.

Illustrated Atlas Map of Menard County, Illinois. Edwardsville, Ill.: Brink, 1874.

Illustrated Historical Atlas Map of Randolph County, Ills. Edwardsville, Ill.: Brink, 1875.

Iroquois County History. Dallas, Tex.: Taylor, 1985.

Irwin, Betty J. *A to Z Fulton County, Illinois Place Names.* N.p.: Fulton County Historical and Genealogical Society, 1993.

James, Frank. "Southern Isle." *Chicago Tribune,* Oct. 21, 1989, 3:1, 4.

James, Georgia. *History of Raleigh, Illinois. 1847–1979.* Hartford, Ky.: McDowell, 1979.

"James T. Gifford and the Founding of Elgin, Illinois." *Transactions of the Illinois State Historical Society* 29 (1922): 69–78.

Jasper County, Illinois. Paducah, Ky.: Turner, 1988.

Johnson County, Illinois: History and Families. Paducah, Ky.: Turner, 1990.

Johnson, Allan. "The Real Name Here Is 'Change.'" *Chicago Tribune,* April 17, 1993, 4:1, 4.

———. "Where You Can Visit the Country without Leaving the City." *Chicago Tribune,* June 29, 1991, 1:17, 19.

Johnson, Charles B. *Medicine in Champaign County.* Champaign, Ill.: Gazette Press, 1909.

Johnson, K. C. "Village's Friendliness Is the Stuff of Legends." *Chicago Tribune,* Feb. 22, 1992, 4:1, 4.

Johnson, Rosemarie. *From Oats to Roses: The History of Berkeley.* Berkeley, Ill.: Friends of Berkeley Library, 1974.

Johnson, Steve. "For Its Residents, City More Than Lives Up To Its Name." *Chicago Tribune,* Sept. 28, 1991, 1:20–21.

Johnson, Vic, comp. "Kankakee County Communities." www.visitkankakeecounty.com/kankakee_communities.htm. Accessed May 6, 2006.

Johnston, Donna Gowin, comp. *Our Crawford County, Illinois Heritage.* Casper, Wyo.: Mountain States Lithographing Company, 1983.

Johnston, William J. *Sketches of the History of Stephenson County, Ill.* Freeport, Ill.: Burnside, 1854.

Jones, Lottie E. *History of Vermilion County, Illinois.* Chicago: Pioneer, 1911.

Jones, Martha Kirker. *Bensenville.* Bensenville, Ill.: Village of Bensenville, 1976.

Joslyn, R. Waite, and Frank W. Joslyn. *History of Kane County, Illinois.* Chicago: Pioneer, 1908.

Jurich, Joseph F. *This Is Franklin County.* Benton, Ill.: Benton Evening News Print, 1954.

Kabbes, Elise D., and Mary GiaQuinta. *Flossmoor, Illinois.* Charleston, S.C.: Arcadia, 1999.

Kable, Harry G., and Harvey J. Kable. *Mount Morris: Past and Present.* 1900. Reprint. Mount Morris, Ill.: Kable, 1938.

Kagann, Joel, and Laurie Kagann. "Woodridge." In *DuPage Roots.* Edited by Richard A. Thompson, 269–73. Wheaton, Ill.: DuPage County Historical Society, 1985.

Karlen, Harvey M. *Chicago's Crabgrass Communities.* Chicago: Collectors' Club of Chicago, 1992.

Keister, Philip L. *Kent for a Century and a Quarter, 1827–1952.* Mount Vernon, Ill.: Windmill, 1952.

Kelly, Sheila. *County and Township Gazetteer.* Springfield: Illinois State Archives, 1988.

Kennedy, Inez A. *Recollections of the Pioneers of Lee County.* Dixon, Ill.: Kennedy, 1893.

Kenyon, Franklin N., ed. *Roanoke Centennial History, 1874–1974.* Roanoke, Ill.: Logan, 1974.

Kerch, Steve. "Village Has an Appetite for the Variety of Life." *Chicago Tribune,* July 6, 1991, 1:17, 18.

Kern, J. W. *Past and Present of Iroquois County, Illinois.* Chicago: Clarke, 1907.

Kewanee Story, 1854–1954. N.p.: N.p., 1954.

Kilduff, Mary Dorrell. *Staunton in Illinois*. N.p.: N.p., 1988.

Kiner, H. L. *History of Henry County*. Chicago: Pioneer, 1910.

Kinmundy: Railway to Thruway, 1857–1957. Kinmundy, Ill.: Centennial Board, 1957.

Kinnear, John B. *Brief History of McLeansboro, Illinois*. N.p.: N.p., 1938.

Kirby, Joseph A. "Diversity: Bagels Just Part of the Appeal of High-Profile Suburb." *Chicago Tribune*, Feb. 19, 1994, 4:1, 4.

Kitagawa, Evelyn M., and Karl E. Taeuber, eds. *Local Community Fact Book Chicago Metropolitan Area 1960*. Chicago: University of Chicago, Chicago Community Inventory, 1963.

Klein, Helen Ragland, ed. *Arrowheads to Aerojets*. Valmeyer, Ill.: Myron Roever, 1967.

Knoblauch, Marion, ed. *DuPage County: A Descriptive and Historical Guide, 1831–1839*. Elmhurst, Ill.: I. A. Ruby, 1948.

Koziol, Ronald. "Two Syllables or Three: Pronounce This Village Ready to Grow Again." *Chicago Tribune*, May 22, 1993, 4:1, 4.

Land, Mrs. Chalon T. (Margaret Davis), comp. *History of Enfield, Illinois*. Carmi, Ill.: Carmi Times, 1953.

Ladd, Martha Cates, and Constance Schneider Kimball. *History of Coles County, 1876–1976*. N.p.: Charleston and Mattoon Bicentennial Commission, 1976.

Landelius, Otto Robert. *Swedish Place-Names in North America*. Translated by Karin Franzén. Edited by Raymond Jarvi. Carbondale: Southern Illinois University Press, 1985.

Lauerman, Connie. "River Life with Touch of the City." *Chicago Tribune*, Dec. 11, 1993, 4:1, 4.

Lavin, Cheryl. "Water Water Everywhere in This McHenry Town." *Chicago Tribune*, May 26, 1990, 4:1, 4.

Lawler, Lucile. *Gallatin County: Gateway to Illinois*. Crossville, Ill.: Gregg, 1968.

Lazaros, Ettarose, and Phyllis Monks. *Crete*. N.p.: Crete Area Historical Society, 1980.

Lebanon. N.p.: Lebanon Centennial Committee, 1974.

Leeson, M. A. *Documents and Biography Pertaining to the Settlement and Progress of Stark County, Illinois*. Chicago: Leeson, 1887.

Lemont, Illinois: Its History in Commemoration of the Centennial of Its Incorporation. Des Plaines, Ill.: King-Mann, 1973.

Leonard, Doris Parr, ed. *Big Bureau and Bright Prairies*. N.p.: Bureau County Board of Supervisors, 1968.

———. *A Pioneer Tour of Bureau County, Illinois*. Princeton, Ill.: Bureau County Republican, 1954.

Leonard, Lulu. *History of Union County*. Anna, Ill.: N.p., 1941.

Leptich, John. "Residents Enjoy a Real-Life Mayberry." *Chicago Tribune*, Dec. 28, 1991, 4:1, 3.

Leroux, Charles. "Metra Service Part of University Park Plan." *Chicago Tribune*, Sept. 1, 2006, 5:4.

Lewis, Edward R., Jr. *Reflections of Canton in a Pharmacist's Show Globe*. N.p.: N.p., 1967.

Lexington Centennial: 1855–1955. N.p.: N.p., n.d.

Lieurance, L. B. *History of Roseville.* 1948. Reprint. Roseville, Ill.: Roseville Independent, 1969.

Light, Ivan. *This Blooming Town.* Bloomington, Ill.: Light House Press, 1956.

Lill, Herbert F. *An Early History of Mascoutah.* 1963. Reprint. N.p.: N.p., 1988.

Lillyville Centennial Book. N.p.: N.p., n.d.

Lindsay, Mildred Gentry. *Cumberland County, Illinois, 1843–1993.* Shawnee Mission, Kans.: KES-Print, 1992.

Lockport Has a Birthday: 1830–1930. N.p.: N.p., n.d.

Long, Jeff. "'Mouthful Name Gets a Makeover." *Chicago Tribune,* Oct. 10, 2002, 2:1, 6.

Lonngren, B. Monroe. "Glacial Lake Spawns Town." *Chicago Tribune,* June 12, 1985, 8:17.

Loomis, Spencer. *Pictorial History of Ela Township.* N.p.: Walworth, 1994.

Loos, Ronald W. *A Walk through Marine: From the Past to the Present.* N.p.: N.p., 1988.

Lossau, Carl S. "Leclaire, Illinois: A Model Industrial Village." *Gateway Heritage* 8 (Spring 1988): 20–31.

Lucadamo, John. "Visitor-Oriented Village Is a Place to Call Home, Too." *Chicago Tribune,* June 27, 1992, 4:1, 4.

Lynn, Ruth Wallace. *Prelude to Progress: The History of Mason County, Illinois, 1818–1968.* N.p.: Mason County Board of Supervisors, 1968.

Lyon, Jeff. "A Town Poised to Rise above Its Hard-Luck Past." *Chicago Tribune,* Feb. 2, 1994, 4:1, 4.

Majorowiz, Amelia, comp. *History of Norton Township.* N.p.: Kankakee County Bicentennial Commission, 1976.

Mann, Roberts. *Origins of Names and Histories of Places . . . in the Forest Preserve District of Cook County, Illinois.* Chicago: Forest Preserve District of Cook County, 1965.

Marissa, Its People and History. N.p.: N.p., 1967.

Markel, Diane. "Township Residents to Live Elsewhere." *Telegraph* (Dixon, Ill.), Oct. 10, 2002, A12.

———. "Township to Change Name." *Telegraph* (Dixon, Ill.), Jan. 23, 2003, A1–2.

Marshall, Bruce E. "The History of Cordova, Illinois." http://cordova.lib.il.us/history_of_cordova.htm. Accessed April 1, 2008.

Marshall, James. *Santa Fe.* New York: Random House, 1945.

Martin, Andrew. "Residents Think It Would Be a Crime If This Place Changed." *Chicago Tribune,* Nov., 14, 1992, 4:1, 4.

Martin, Larry. "An Elburn History." www.sarah/eebond.com/elburnhistory.html. Accessed April 1, 2008.

Martin, R. Eden. *Notes on the History of Moultrie County and Sullivan, Illinois.* Edited by I. J. Martin. Sullivan, Ill.: Martin, 1990.

Massie, Melville D., *Past and Present of Pike County, Illinois.* Chicago: Clarke, 1906.

Matson, N. *Map and Sketches of Bureau County, Illinois.* Chicago: Tribune Company, 1867.

Maue, August. *History of Will County.* Indianapolis, Ind.: Historical, 1928.

Maxey, Mima, ed. *Annals of Carlyle, Illinois, 1809–1956.* N.p.: N.p., 1956.

May, George W. *History of Massac County, Illinois.* Galesburg, Ill.: Wagoner, 1955.

———. *Massac Pilgrimage.* Ann Arbor, Mich.: Edwards, 1964.

McBride, J. C. *Present and Past of Christian County, Illinois.* Chicago: Clarke, 1904.

McCafferty, Michael. "Correction." *Names* 52, no. 1 (2004): 44.

———. "A Fresh Look at the Place Name 'Chicago.'" *Journal of the Illinois State Historical Society* 96, no. 2 (2003): 116–29.

———. "'Kankakee': An Old Etymological Puzzle." *Names* 52, no. 4 (2004): 287–304.

———. "On the Birthday and Etymology of the Placename 'Missouri.'" *Names* 51, no. 2 (2003): 111–25.

———. "Peoria." *Society for the Study of the Indigenous Languages of the Americas Newsletter* 25 (Jan. 2007): 13–14.

———. "Revisiting Chicago." *Journal of the Illinois State Historical Society* 98, nos. 1, 2 (2003): 82–98.

McCarthy, Mary J. *Elk Grove: The Peony Village.* Elk Grove Village, Ill.: Elk Grove Village Public Library, 1981.

McCormick, Mildred. "The Country Store as Community Center." *Springhouse* 2 (Jan.–Feb. 1985): 6–7.

———. "The Significance of Pope County Place Names." *Springhouse* 12 (June 1995): 26–28.

McDermott, John Francis. "The French Impress on Place Names in the Mississippi Valley." *Journal of the Illinois State Historical Society* 72, no. 3 (1979): 225–34.

———. *A Glossary of Mississippi Valley French 1673–1850.* St. Louis, Mo.: Washington University Press, 1941.

———. "William Clark's Struggle with Place Names in Upper Louisiana." *Missouri Historical Society Bulletin* 34 (1978): 140–50.

McHenry County in the Twentieth Century, 1968–1994. Union City: McHenry County Historical Society, 1994.

McIntosh, Charles F., ed. *Past and Present of Piatt County, Illinois.* Chicago: Clarke, 1903.

McRoberts, Flynn. "Residents Love One-Campus Schools, Laid-Back Living." *Chicago Tribune,* Jan. 29, 1994, 4:1, 5.

———. "Where Residents Take Life One Improvement at a Time." *Chicago Tribune,* Dec. 22, 1990, 4:1, 2.

Mechanicsburg Sesquicentennial, 1832–1982. Mechanicsburg, Ill.: Mechanicsburg Women's Club, 1982.

Menard County, Illinois History. Petersburg, Ill.: History of Menard County, 1988.

Meredosia Bicentennial Book. Bluffs, Ill.: Jones, 1976.

Michels, Bert. *History of Olney.* Olney, Ill.: Olney Daily Mail, 1962.

Millenson, Michael L. "Rich in Hope." *Chicago Tribune,* Jan. 6, 1992, 4:1, 6.

Miller, Bryan. "This Place Is Known by the Company It Keeps." *Chicago Tribune,* March 14, 1992, 1:20–21.

Miller, Dan A. *History of Arthur, Illinois.* Arthur, Ill.: Miller, 1975.

Miller, Keith Linus. "Building Towns on the Southeastern Illinois Frontier." Ph.D. diss., Miami University of Ohio, 1976.

Miller, Larry L. *Ohio Place Names.* Bloomington: Indiana University Press, 1996.

———. *Tennessee Place Names.* Bloomington: Indiana University Press, 2001.

Miller, Robert Don Leavey. *Past and Present of Menard County, Illinois.* Chicago: S. J. Clarke, 1905.

Miller, Sandy. *Life and Times of Cerro Gordo, Cisco, Hammond, La Place, Milmine, Oakley.* Dallas, Tex.: Curtis Media, 1989.

Miller, Terry J. *Hanover: A Portrayal of a Northwestern Illinois Village's Changes from 1827 through 1976.* Hanover, Ill.: Miller, 1976.

Miller-Mathis, Averil. *History of Eldorado, Illinois.* Eldorado, Ill.: Miller-Mathis, 1994.

Milne, Muriel Mueller. *Our Roots Are Deep: A History of Monee, Illinois.* South Holland, Ill.: South Suburban Genealogical and Historical Society, 1973.

Miner, Ed. *Past and Present of Greene County, Illinois.* Chicago: Clarke, 1905.

Misenheimer, Freda Landrus. *The Johnstown Story.* N.p.: N.p., 1976.

Mitchell, Betty. *Carbondale: A Pictorial History.* St. Louis, Mo.: G. Bradley, 1991.

Mitchell, Harley Bradford. *Historical Fragments of Early Chicagoland.* Chicago: Atwell, 1928.

Mittell, Mary Lou. "Wood Dale." In *DuPage Roots.* Edited by Richard A. Thompson, 262–68. Wheaton, Ill.: DuPage County Historical Society, 1985.

Modesto Centennial Book. N.p.: Modesto Centennial Committee, 1996.

Mohlenbrock, Robert H. "A New Geography of Iliinois: Jackson County." *Outdoor Illinois* 13 (Feb. 1974): 15–38.

———. "A New Geography of Illinois: Johnson County." *Outdoor Illinois* 14 (Jan. 1975): 15–47.

———. "A New Geography of Illinois: Union County." *Outdoor Illinois* 13 (June–July 1974): 11–43.

———. "A New Geography of Williamson County." *Outdoor Illinois* 15 (Jan. 1976): 13–44.

Montague, E. J. *Directory, Business Mirror, and Historical Sketches of Randolph County.* Alton, Ill.: Courier Steam Book and Job Printing House, 1859.

Montrose Centennial, 1870–1970. Teutopolis, Ill.: Worman, 1970.

Moon, June. *"Multum in Parvo": A History of Colchester, Illinois.* Colchester, Ill.: Colchester Chronicle, 1956.

Moore, Jean. *Build Your Own Town . . . the Carol Stream Story.* West Chicago, Ill.: West Chicago Printing Company, 1984.

Moore, Jean, and Hiawatha Bray. *DuPage at 150 and Those Who Shaped Our World.* Wheaton, Ill.: DuPage County Sesquicentennial Steering Committee, 1989.

Moore, Marion. *Tolono Topics.* N.p.: N.p., 1979.

Moore, Roy L. *History of Woodford County.* Eureka, Ill.: Woodford County Republican, 1910.

Moorhead, Virginia B., ed. *Boone County, Then and Now, 1835–1976.* N.p.: Boone County Bicentennial Commission, 1976.

Morgan, Jessie Borror, ed. *The Good Life in Piatt County*. Moline, Ill.: DeSaulniers, 1968.

Morris, Margaret E. *Allerton, Illinois, 1887–1987*. Allerton, Ill.: Allerton Historical Society, 1987.

Moweaqua Remembers. Moweaqua, Ill.: Moweaqua Bicentennial Committee, 1976.

Moyer, William Nelson. *Moyers' Brief History of Pulaski County*. Mound City, Ill.: Pulaski Enterprise, 1944.

Muelder, Hermann R. "The Naming of Spoon River." *Western Illinois Regional Studies* 4 (1981): 105–14.

Mulberry Grove, Illinois Community Sesquicentennial, 1834–1984. N.p.: Mulberry Grove Lions Club, 1984.

Munsell, Malinda G. "A History of Hamilton County, McLeansboro, Illinois." Typescript. St. Charles, Ill., Public Library, 1966.

Murphy, Jean Powley, and Mary Hagen Wajer. *Mount Prospect*. Mount Prospect, Ill.: Mount Prospect Historical Society, 1992.

Musgrove, Jon. "Saline County Gazetteer." *Daily Register* (Harrisburg, Ill.) on-line edition. www.dailyregister.com/articles/2003//08/30.

Nebelsick, Alvin Louis. *A History of Belleville*. Belleville, Ill.: Belleville High School and Junior College, 1951.

Nelson, C. Hal, comp. *Sinnissippi Saga: A History of Rockford and Winnebago County, Illinois*. Mendota, Ill.: Wayside, 1968.

Nelson, Ronald E. "The Role of Colonies in the Pioneer Settlement of Henry County, Illinois." Ph.D. diss., University of Nebraska, Lincoln, 1969.

Nelson, William E. *City of Decatur and Macon County, Illinois*. Chicago: Pioneer, 1910.

Neponset's One Hundred Years, 1855–1955. N.p.: N.p.

Neville, J. Wesley, comp. *Student's History of Perry County*. N.p.: N.p., 1947.

News-Democrat (Belleville, Ill.) on-line edition, Nov. 8, 2003. www.bnd.com.

Newsome, Edmund. *Historical Sketches of Jackson County, Illinois*. Carbondale, Ill.: E. Newsome, 1894.

Nichols, Kay Folsom. *The Kankakee*. Brooklyn, N.Y.: Theo. Gaus' Sons, 1965.

Niles Centennial History, 1899–1999. Marceline, Mo.: Walsworth, 1999.

Niles, Henry C. *History of Douglas County, Illinois*. Tuscola, Ill.: Converse and Parks, 1876.

Norton, Louise James, and Thomas L. Anderson. *The History of Alto Pass, Illinois*. Dallas, Tex.: Thomas L. Anderson, 1989.

Norton, W. T., ed. *Centennial History of Madison County, Illinois, and Its People, 1812–1912*. Chicago: Lewis, 1912.

Nye, Lowell Albert, ed. *McHenry County Illinois, 1832–1968*. Woodstock, Ill.: McHenry County Board of Supervisors, 1968.

O'Byrne, Michael Cyprian. *History of LaSalle, Illinois*. Chicago: Lewis, 1924.

Oglesby, Our Home Town, 1902–2002. Oglesby, Ill.: Oglesby Historical Society, 2002.

Oliver, Edward. *Norris City and Indian Creek Township Illinois*. Norris City, Ill.: Norris City Lions Club, 1980.

One Hundred Golden Years, Brief History of Golden, Illinois. N.p.: N.p., 1963.

One Hundred Years of Progress: The Centennial History of Anna, Illinois. Cape Girardeau, Mo.: Missourian Printing, 1954.

"One Hundred Years of Progress": *Mt. Olive Centennial, 1865–1965.* N.p.: N.p., 1965.

On the Banks of the Wabash: St. Francisville Centennial. N.p.: N.p., 1962.

Onstot, T. G. *Pioneers of Menard and Mason Counties.* Forest City, Ill.: Onstot, 1902.

Oreana, Illinois: Golden Yesterdays, 1873–1973. N.p.: N.p., 1973.

Orland Story: From Prairie to Pavement. Orland Park, Ill.: Orland Heritage Book Association, 1991.

Orr, Richard. "Goofy Ridge Eludes Even the Mapmakers." *Chicago Tribune,* July 7, 1983, 2:11

Our First Hundred Years: Kansas, Illinois. Charleston, Ill.: Prather, 1953.

Our First 150 Years: Hunter, Stratton, Elbridge Townships, 1818–1968. Vermilion, Ill.: Sesquicentennial Committee, 1968.

Paddock, Stuart R. *Palatine Centennial Book.* Palatine, Ill.: Quasquicentennial Committee, 1991.

Page O. J. *History of Massac County, Il.* Metropolis, Ill.: N.p., 1900.

Papajohn, George. "Air Burnham." *Chicago Tribune,* Aug. 4, 1990, 4:1, 4.

———. "It's a Workin' Town with No Flights of Fancy." *Chicago Tribune,* Feb. 10, 1990, 4:1, 4.

Parrott, Gerta Jean, ed. *Village of Bath, Illinois, 125th Anniversary, 1836–1961.* N.p.: S.n., 1961.

Past and Present of Boone County, Illinois. Chicago: Kett, 1877.

Past and Present of the City of Decatur and Macon County, Illinois. Chicago: Clarke, 1903.

Past and Present of Kane County, Illinois. Chicago: Le Baron, 1878.

Past and Present of Lake County, Illinois. Chicago: Le Baron, 1877.

Past and Present of LaSalle County, Illinois. Chicago: Kett, 1877.

Past and Present of Rock Island County, Ill. Chicago: Kett, 1877.

Past and Present of Warren County, Illinois. Chicago: Kett, 1877.

Past to Present: Elizabeth, Illinois Centennial. N.p.: N.p., 1968.

Pearson, Ruth Seen. *Reflections of St. Charles.* St. Charles, Ill.: St. Charles Historical Society, 1976.

Pekin Sesquicentennial: A History, 1824–1974. Pekin, Ill.: Chamber of Commerce, 1974.

Peotone on Parade, 1856–1956. N.p.: N.p., n.d.

Perica, Esther. *They Took the Challenge: The Story of Rolling Meadows.* Rolling Meadows, Ill.: Rolling Meadows Public Library, 1979.

Perkins, Margery. *Evanstoniana.* Chicago: Chicago Review Press. 1984.

Perkins, Thomas J., Jr., and Patti Lee Perkins. "Bloomingdale." In *DuPage Roots.* Edited by Richard A. Thompson, 118–25. Wheaton, Ill.: DuPage County Historical Society, 1985.

Perrin, William Henry, ed. *History of Alexander, Union, and Pulaski Counties, Illinois.* Chicago: Baskin, 1883.

———, ed. *History of Bond and Montgomery Counties*. Chicago: Baskin, 1882.

———, ed. *History of Cass County, Illinois*. Chicago: Baskin, 1882.

———, ed. *History of Crawford and Clark Counties, Illinois*. Chicago: Baskin, 1883.

———, ed. *History of Effingham County, Illinois*. Chicago: Baskin, 1883.

———, ed. *History of Jefferson County, Illinois*. Chicago: Globe, 1883.

Perrin, William Henry, A. A. Graham, and D. M. Blair. *History of Coles County, Illinois*. Chicago: Le Baron, 1879.

Perrin, William Henry, and H. H. Hill. *Past and Present of Woodford County, Illinois*. Chicago: Le Baron, 1878.

Perry, A. J. *History of Knox County, Illinois*. Chicago: Clarke, 1912.

Perry County, Illinois. Paducah, Ky.: Turner, 1988–98.

Peterson, Clarence. "'A Good Place to Live' Still Has Some Drive." *Chicago Tribune*, May 6, 1989, 3:1, 4.

Peterson, Gordon E. "Place Names of Bond County, Illinois." *Bond County Genealogical Society Bulletin* 20 (Winter 2002): 38–44.

Peterson, Marna E. *Story of Loda, Illinois*. 1968. Reprint. Danville, Calif.: Mimo Majic, 1975.

Petro, Angie. "Lawndale." *Logan County Genealogical and Historical Bulletin* (Spring 2002): n.p.

Peyron, Ernest A. *LaHarpe*. N.p.: N.p., 1970.

Piatt, Emma C. *History of Piatt County*. Chicago: Shepard and Johnson, 1883.

Pirtle, Carol. *Where Illinois Began: A Pictorial History of Randolph County*. Virginia Beach, Va.: Donning, 1995.

Pitman, Florence. *Story of Mokena*. N.p.: N.p., 1963.

Poage, George Rawlings. "The Coming of the Portuguese." *Journal of the Illinois State Historical Society* 18 (April 1925): 101–35.

Polson, Terry Ellen. *Corn, Commerce and Country Living: A History of Henry County, Illinois*. Moline, Ill.: Desaulniers, 1968.

Pope County, Illinois, 1986. Paducah Ky.: Turner, 1986.

Popik, Barry. "Coinage of 'The Windy City.'" *Comments on Etymology* 34 (Dec. 2004): 2–19.

Portrait and Biographical Album of Champaign County, Illinois. Chicago: Chapman, 1887.

Portrait and Biographical Album of DeKalb County, Illinois. Chicago: Chapman, 1885.

Portrait and Biographical Album of Henry County, Illinois. Chicago: Biographical, 1885.

Portrait and Biographical Album of Knox County. Chicago: Biographical, 1886.

Portrait and Biographical Album of Rock Island County, Illinois. Chicago: Biographical, 1885.

Portrait and Biographical Album of Warren County, Illinois. Chicago: Chapman, 1886.

Postlewait, Ruby, ed. *History of Jersey County, Illinois*. Dallas, Tex.: Curtis Media, 1991.

Prairie Echo. Flora, Ill.: Flora Kiwanis Club and Clay County Regulators, 1976.

Prairie Progress: A History of Edgar County, 1888–1975. Dallas, Tex.: Taylor, 1976.

Puckett, Judith. *Mount Erie, Illinois: The Village on the Hill.* N.p.: N.p., 2003.

Pulaski County, Illinois. Paducah, Ky.: Turner, 1987.

Pulliam, Peggy, ed. *Towns of Effingham County, Illinois.* N.p.: Effingham County Bicentennial Commission, 1975.

———, ed. *Townships of Effingham County, Illinois.* N.p.: Effingham County Bicentennial Commission, 1975.

Purnell, Isabelle S. *An Unofficial History of Mahomet, Illinois: 150 Years.* Mahomet, Ill.: Mayhaven, 2000.

Putnam Past Times. Hennepin, Ill.: Putnam County Historical Society, 1983.

Pyle, "Judge." "History of Carmi—1810–1820." Ms. Mary Smith Fay Genealogy Library, Carmi, Ill. N.p., 1955(?).

Quaid, Laurel. *A Little Square of Prairie: Stories of Cooksville and Blue Mound Township, Illinois.* Cooksville, Ill.: Cooksville Centennial Committee, 1983.

Radloff, Ramona. *125 Strasburg Stories and Then Some.* Sullivan, Ill.: Depot Services, 1999.

Ramsay, Robert L. *Our Storehouse of Missouri Place Names.* Columbia: University of Missouri Press, 1973.

Ramsey, Susie M., and Flossie P. Miller. *The Heritage of Franklin County, Illinois.* 1965. Reprint. Sesser, Ill.: Print Shop, 1993.

Randall, Gregory C. *America's Original GI Town.* Baltimore: Johns Hopkins University Press, 2000.

Randolph County, Illinois. Paducah, Ky.: Turner, 1995.

Rasmusen, Marilyn. *LaSalle County Lore.* Utica, Ill.: LaSalle County Historical Society, 1992.

Rayburn, Alan. *Dictionary of Canadian Place Names.* New York: Oxford University Press, 1997.

Raymond Centennial, 1871–1971. Raymond, Ill.: Centennial Book Committee, 1971.

Read, Allen Walker. "The Recognition of Patterning in American Place-Naming." In *America: Naming the Country and Its People.* Edited by R. N. Ashley, 241–50. Lewiston, N.Y.: Mellen, 2001.

Read Collection. The Allen Walker Read Papers. Western Historical Manuscript Collection, University of Missouri, Columbia.

Reardon, Patrick T. "No Frills on State's Highest Hill." *Chicago Tribune,* July 25, 2006, 5:1.

Recollections Illustrated, Orangeville, Illinois—From Millstream to Jetstream. N.p.: The Historical Committee, 1967.

Recollections: Story of Villa Park. Villa Park, Ill.: Villa Park Bicentennial Commission Heritage Committee, 1976.

Redford, Carol, and Betty Triplett, comps. *Reflections: A History of the Bunker Hill–Woodburn Area.* Bunker Hill, Ill.: Bunker Hill Publications, 1993.

Redlich, Paul R. *The Postal History of Coles County, Illinois.* Des Plaines: Illinois Postal History Society, 1986.

Reich, Howard. "The Suburb That Growth Forgot." *Chicago Tribune*, Jan. 16, 1993, 4:1, 4.

Reichelt, Marie Ward. *History of Deerfield, Illinois*. Glenview, Ill.: Glenview Press, 1928.

Rennick, Robert M. *Kentucky Place Names*. Lexington: University Press of Kentucky, 1984.

———. "On the Success of Efforts to Retain the Names of Several American Communities in the Two World Wars." *Names* 32, no. 1 (1984): 26–32.

Reynolds, John. *The Pioneer History of Illinois*. Chicago: Fergus, 1887.

Rhodes, Steve. "So Little Space, So Much Action." *Chicago Tribune*, May 7, 1994, 4:1, 4.

Rice, James M. *Peoria City and County, Illinois*. Chicago: S. J. Clarke, 1912.

Rice, William. "Tradition Still Calls This Home." *Chicago Tribune*, Oct. 13, 1990, 4:1, 4.

Richardson, Ray. *Ray Richardson's History of Tonica: The First Hundred Years*. 1953. Reprint. Utica, Ill.: LaSalle County Historical Society, 1990.

Richmond, C. W., and H. F. Vallette. *A History of the County of DuPage, Illinois*. Chicago: Scripps, Bross and Spears, 1857.

Richmond, Mable E. *Centennial History of Decatur and Macon County*. Decatur, Ill.: Decatur Review, 1930.

Ritzert, Kenneth. "Bensenville." In *DuPage Roots*. Edited by Richard A. Thompson, 111–17. Wheaton, Ill.: DuPage County Historical Society, 1985.

Roberts Area Centennial, 1872–1972. N.p.: N.p.

Roberts, Pearl. *Glimpses of the Past in Johnson City, Illinois, 1894–1945*. Johnson City, Ill.: Johnson City Business and Professional Women's Club, 1977.

Roberts, Penny. "Growth Goes Rural with a Clash." *Chicago Tribune*, May 14, 1994, 4:1, 4.

Robins, Martha. *Historical Development of Jasper County, Illinois*. N.p.: N.p., 1938.

Robinson, Marilyn. *Sidewalks of Elburn*. Elburn, Ill.: Village of Elburn, 2005.

Roop, Anne. *History of Fox River Grove*. Fox River Grove, Ill.: Community Methodist Church, 1951.

Ross, George E. *Centralia, Illinois: A Pictorial History*. St. Louis, Mo.: G. Bradley, 1992.

Roth, Donald F., and Ruth C. Roth. *Morton: A Pictorial History*. St. Louis, Mo.: G. Bradley, 1988.

Rowley, Mildred L. *The History of Kirkwood, Illinois and Tompkins Township, Warren County*. N.p.: N.p., 1976.

Ruebke, Genevieve Dudenbostel. *Do You Remember Campbell Hill?* Cape Girardeau, Mo.: Missourian Lithograph and Printing, 1978.

Russ, William A., Jr. "The Export of Pennsylvania Place Names." *Pennsylvania History* 15 (Jan.–Oct. 1948): 194–214.

Saline County: A Century of History, 1847–1947. Harrisburg, Ill.: Harrisburg Register, 1947.

San Jose Centennial, 1858–1958. San Jose, Ill.: The Association, 1958.

Scheetz, George H. "Peoria." In *Place Names in the Midwestern United States*. Edited by Edward Callary, 43–70. Lewiston, N.Y.: Mellen, 2000.

Schoon, Kenneth J. *Calumet Beginnings: Ancient Shorelines and Settlements at the South End of Lake Michigan.* Bloomington: Indiana University Press, 2003.

Schulze, Franz, Rosemary Cowler, and Arthur H. Miller. *Thirty Miles North: A History of Lake Forest College, Its Town, and Its City of Chicago.* Lake Forest, Ill.: Lake Forest College, 2000.

Schuyler County, Illinois History. Dallas, Tex.: Taylor, 1983.

Scoby, Maranda Cavanas. *The Story of Carterville: Its Hundred Years.* New York. Vantage, 1972.

Scott, Barbara Sample, and Virginia Elder Anderson. *Travels in Time: Milan, Illinois.* Mediapolis, Iowa: New Era Print, 1982.

Scott County Bicentennial Book. N.p.: Bluff Times and Winchester Times, 1976.

Seibel, Clark W. *My Home Town: A Brief History of Central City, Illinois.* Ann Arbor, Mich.: Edwards, 1952.

Seits, Laurence E. "The Names of Kane County, Illinois." In *Place Names in the Midwestern United States.* Edited by Edward Callary, 163–72. Lewiston, N.Y.: Mellen, 2000.

Sesquicentennial Carmi, Illinois, 1816–1966. N.p.: N.p., 1966.

Shadwick, George W., Jr. *History of McDonough County, Illinois.* Moline, Ill.: Desaulniers, 1968.

Simon, Stephanie. "Being Dull Can't Take the Edge Off Living in This Village." *Chicago Tribune,* Aug. 25, 1990, 4:1, 6.

Six Score and Five: A Brief but Exciting History of Farmer City. Farmer City, Ill.: N.p., 1962.

Smith, C. Henry. *Metamora.* Bluffton, Ohio: College Book Store, 1947.

Smith, George Owen. *A History of Princeton.* Princeton, Ill.: Matson Public Library, 1966.

Smith, Hermon Dunlap. *The Des Plaines River 1673–1940.* N.p.: N.p., 1940.

Smith, Sid. "But There's No Shortage of Good Neighbors Here." *Chicago Tribune,* Sept. 12, 1992, 4:1, 4.

Sneed, Glenn J. *Ghost Towns of Southern Illinois.* Royalton, Ill.: Sneed, 1977.

Snively, Marian C., comp. and ed. *Lee County Historical Yearbook.* Dixon, Ill.: Print Shop, 1977.

Souter, Gerry, ed. *Chronicle of a Prairie Town.* Arlington Heights, Ill.: Arlington Heights Historical Society, 1997.

Souvenir History for the Bethalto Centennial. Bethalto, Ill.: Clausen, 1954.

Souvenir History of Edgar County, 1823–1893. Paris, Ill.: Colson, 1893.

Souvenir of Settlement and Progress of Will County, Ill. Chicago: Historical Directory, 1884.

Spanke, Louise, comp. *Winfield's Good Old Days.* Winfield, Ill.: Winfield Public Library, 1978.

Spelman, Walter Bishop. *Town of Cicero: History, Advantages, and Government.* Cicero, Ill.: Author-published, 1923.

Spencer, A. P. *Centennial History of Highland, Illinois, 1837–1937.* Highland, Ill.: Highland Historical Society, 1978.

Stapp, Katherine Elizabeth. *History under Our Feet: The Story of Vermilion County, Illinois.* Danville, Ill.: Interstate Printers, 1968.

Stapp, Katherine, and Betty Sullenberger. *Footprints in the Sands: Founders and Builders of Vermilion County Illinois.* Danville, Ill.: Interstate Printers, 1975.

Stark, Mary E., and Donald L. Brown. *Paths from the Past: A History of Georgetown, Vermilion County, Illinois.* Danville, Ill.: Printing Techniques, 1977.

Stehman, Lucille M. *Collinsville, Illinois: A Pictorial History.* St. Louis, Mo.: G. Bradley, 1992.

Stennett, W. H. *A History of the Origin of the Place Names Connected with the Chicago and North Western and Chicago, St. Paul, Minneapolis, and Omaha Railways.* Chicago: N.p., 1908.

Stephenson, Andrew, Jr. "Many Towns Named for Santa Fe Men." *Santa Fe Magazine* 22 (Aug. 1928): 55–56.

Sterling, Robert E. *Joliet: A Pictorial History.* St. Louis, Mo.: G. Bradley, 1986.

Stern, Ron. *A Centennial History of Madison, Illinois, 1891–1991.* St. Louis, Mo.: Bunn Winter, 1991.

Stevens, Darlene Gavron. "High Pride Keeps Low Profile." *Chicago Tribune,* Sept. 25, 1993, 1:16–17.

Stevens, Frank E. *History of Lee County, Illinois.* Chicago: S. J. Clarke, 1914.

Stevens, W. W. *Past and Present of Will County, Illinois.* Chicago: S. J. Clarke, 1907.

Stewart, George R. *American Place-Names.* New York: Oxford University Press, 1970.

Stokes, Bill. "Ask Anyone: The Focus of This Town Is Kids." *Chicago Tribune,* March 25, 1989, 3:1, 4.

Story of Marseilles. N.p.: N.p., 1976.

Story of Oregon, Illinois, Sesquicentennial, 1836–1986. Oregon, Ill.: The Book Committee, n.d.

Stringer, Lawrence B. *History of Logan County, Illinois.* Chicago: Pioneer, 1911.

Strobel, Paul E., Jr. *High on the Okaw's Western Bank.* Urbana: University of Illinois Press, 1992.

Stronghurst Centennial History, 1887–1987. Stronghurst, Ill.: Stronghurst Centennial Publications Committee, 1987.

Sublett, Michael D. *Paper Counties: The Illinois Experience, 1825–1867.* New York: Peter Lang, 1990.

Sublette, Illinois, Our Bit of U.S.A: Sublette Centennial. N.p.: N.p., 1957.

Suess, Adolph B. *Glimpses of Prairie du Rocher.* Belleville, Ill.: Buechler, 1942.

Sunderland, Sarah Taylor. *New and Complete History of Jasper County, Illinois.* 1976. Reprint. Washington, Ill.: Bookworks, 1984.

Sutton, Robert P. *Rivers, Railways, and Roads: A History of Henderson County.* Raritan, Ill.: Henderson County Historical Society, 1988.

Swan, Alonzo M. *Canton: Its Pioneers and History.* Canton, Ill.: N.p. 1871.

Swank, George. *Historic Henry County.* Galva, Ill.: N.p., 1941.

Swenson, John F. "Chicagoua/Chicago: The Origin, Meaning, and Etymology of a Place Name." *Illinois Historical Journal* 84, no. 1 (1991): 235–48.

Syfert, Vernon A. "The Naming of Bloomington." *Journal of the Illinois State Historical Society* 29 (April 1936–Jan. 1937): 161–67.

Tapestry of Time: A Bicentennial History of St. Clair County, Illinois, in Pictures. Belleville, Ill.: St. Clair County Bicentennial Commission, 1991.

Taylor, Carolyn. *Salina, a Prairie Township.* Kankakee, Ill.: Kankakee County Bicentennial Commission, 1976.

Teeman, Charles M. *Postal Saga of Jo Daviess County, Illinois.* Des Plaines, Ill.: Illinois Postal History Society, 1985.

Tennison, Patricia. "Quite a Find." *Chicago Tribune,* May 20, 1989, 3:1, 4.

Teutopolis, Illinois Quasquicentennial Celebration, 1839–1964. N.p.: N.p., 1964.

Thiem, E. George, ed. *Carroll County—a Goodly Heritage.* Mount Morris, Ill.: Kable, 1968.

Thompson, Anna B., and Stewart C. Thompson. *Byron Centennial Souvenir Booklet.* Byron, Ill.: Byron Tribune, 1935.

Thompson, Cheryl. "A Town of Regular Joes." *Chicago Tribune,* July 31, 1993, 1:20–21.

Thompson, Jess M. "Pike County Settled 1820; One Hundred Years Ago." *Journal of the Illinois State Historical Society* 13, no. 1 (1920): 71–84.

———. *The Jess M. Thompson Pike County History.* Pittsfield, Ill.: Pike County Historical Society, 1967.

Tilden, M. H., comp. *History of Stephenson County, Illinois.* Chicago: Western Historical, 1880.

Times (Carmi, Ill.) *Sesquicentennial Edition,* Dec. 9, 1965.

Tio, Lucinda, and Kathy Farren. *A History of Yorkville, Illinois, 1836–1986.* Yorkville, Ill.: N.p., 1986.

Tisler, C. C. *Story of Ottawa Illinois.* Ottawa, Ill.: Tisler, 1953.

"Town of Dupo Ponders Change Back to Original Name." *News-Gazette* (Champaign, Ill.), Jan. 5, 1997, A2.

Townley, Wayne C. *Historic McLean.* Bloomington, Ill.: McLean County Historical Society, 1945

Towns and Families of Randolph County, Illinois. N.p.: Randolph County Genealogical Society, 2000.

Township Histories Princeville, Millbrook, Hallock, Jubilee, Radnor. Peoria, Ill.: Hine, 1906.

Traylor, Jacob L. *Past and Present of Montgomery County Illinois.* Chicago: S. J. Clarke, 1904.

Trebe, Patricia. "Tinley Park Has Come a Long Way since 1854." *Chicago Tribune,* May 21, 2003, 1:23.

Trenton Centennial, 1855–1955. Trenton, Ill.: Centennial Historical Committee, 1955.

Trotter, Maxine. *"Our Town": A History of Wyanet, 1828–1973.* N.p.: N.p., 1973.

Tucker, Sara Jones. *Indian Villages of the Illinois Country: Atlas.* Springfield: Illinois State Museum, 1942.

Tuggle, L. A., comp. *Stories of Historical Days in Vermilion County, Illinois.* Danville, Ill.: Interstate Printers, 1940.

Turner, Brett. "The Lumaghi Family's Impact on Collinsville." *Illinois History* 53, no. 1 (1999): 20.

Tweet, Roald. *Quad Cities: An American Mosaic.* Rock Island, Ill.: East Hall Press, 1996.

Ullrich, Helen Stine. *This Is Grundy County.* Dixon: Rogers Print, 1968.

Underwood, Larry D. "A New Geography of Calhoun County." *Outdoor Illinois* 14 (June–July 1975): 13–42.

———. "A New Geography of Illinois: Adams County." *Outdoor Illinois* 13 (Dec. 1974): 15–43.

———. "A New Geography of Illinois: Madison County." *Outdoor Illinois* 13 (Aug.–Sept. 1974): 15–39.

———. "A New Geography of Illinois: Vermilion County." *Outdoor Illinois* 13 (Nov. 1974): 21–42.

Usher, Joyce M. *This Is Itasca.* N.p.: N.p., n.d.

Van, Jon. "It's Keeping Alive Small-Town Feeling." *Chicago Tribune,* Nov. 21, 1992, 4:1, 4.

Van Matre, Lynn. "Its Rural Feeling Can Grow on You." *Chicago Tribune,* July 18, 1992, 1:22, 24.

Vann, Sonya C. "Entrepreneurial Spirit Blooms along with the Lilacs." *Chicago Tribune,* Feb. 26, 1994, 4:1, 4.

———. "The Sweet Life." *Chicago Tribune,* Jan. 1, 1994, 4:1, 4.

Vasiliev, Ren. *From Abbotts to Zurich: New York State Placenames.* Syracuse, N.Y.: Syracuse University Press, 2004.

Vermilion County, Illinois. Danville, Ill.: Interstate Printers, 1986.

Village of Elkhart City. Lincoln, Ill.: Feldman's Print Shop, 1955.

Villarosa, Lori. "The Whole Town Is a Neighborhood." *Chicago Tribune,* April 13, 1991, 4:1, 4.

Vogel, Virgil J. *Indian Place Names in Illinois.* Springfield: Illinois State Historical Society Pamphlet Series no. 4 (1963); originally published in the *Journal of the Illinois State Historical Society* 1 (Spring 1962): 45–71; 1 (Summer 1962): 157–80; 1 (Autumn 1962): 271–308; and 1 (Winter 1962): 385–458.

———. *Iowa Place Names of Indian Origin.* Iowa City: University of Iowa Press, 1983.

———. "Some Illinois Place-Name Legends." *Midwest Folklore* 9 (1963): 155–62.

Voters and Tax-Payers of Bureau County, Illinois. Chicago: Kett, 1877.

Wabash County, Illinois. Marion, Ky.: Riverbend, 1993.

Wade, Richard C. *The Urban Frontier: The Rise of Western Cities, 1790–1830.* Cambridge, Mass.: Harvard University Press, 1959.

Walker, Charles A. *History of Macoupin County, Illinois.* Chicago: S. J. Clarke, 1911

Walker, Margaret, ed. 1968. *Bainbridge Township of Schuyler County, Illinois.* Rushville, Ill.: Schuyler County Historical Museum, 1968.

Wall, John A. *Wall's History of Jefferson County, Illinois.* Indianapolis, Ind.: B. F. Bowen, 1909.

Wallace, Joseph. *Past and Present of the City of Springfield and Sangamon County, Illinois.* Chicago: Clarke, 1904.

Walthall, John A., and Elizabeth D. Benchley. *The River L'abbe Mission*. Springfield: Illinois Historic Preservation Agency, 1987.

Walton, William Clarence. *Centennial, McKendree College, with St. Clair County History*. Lebanon, Ill.: McKendree College, 1928.

Washington County, Illinois, 1979 History. Nashville, Ill.: Historical Society of Washington County, 1980.

Watson, W. W. *History of Barry*. N.p.: N.p., 1903.

Weber, Carl J. "A Critique of the Swenson/McCafferty Linguistic Analysis of the Word 'Chicago.'" *Journal of the Illinois State Historical Society* 97, no. 2 (2004): 169–85.

West, Larry. *A Heritage Reborn*. Monticello, Ill.: West, 1966.

"Where There's a Will . . .". Joliet, Ill.: Will County 125th Anniversary Committee, 1961

Whittingham, Richard. *Skokie: A Centennial History*. Skokie, Ill.: Village of Skokie, 1988.

Wilcox, David F., supervising ed. *Quincy and Adams County*. Chicago: Lewis, 1919.

Wilkey, Harry L. *The Story of a Little Town: A History of Paloma, Illinois*. N.p.: W. A. Shanholtzer, 1934.

Will County Places Old and New. Lockport, Ill.: Will County Historical Society, 1982.

Williams, Jack Moore. *History of Vermilion County, Illinois*. Topeka, Kans.: Historical Publishing, 1930.

Wilson, Kathryn Eleanor. *Tales, Trails, and Breadcrumbs, 1838–1938: One Hundred Years, Bond County, Illinois*. Greenville, Ill.: K. W. Wilson, 1993.

Wiltz, Ken. "History of Black Partridge." Accessed April 1, 2008: genealogytrails.com/ill/woodfordBlackPartridge.html.

Wittelle, Marvyn. *Twenty-eight Miles North: The Story of Highwood*. Highwood, Ill.: Highwood History Foundation. 1953.

Word and Picture Story of Hampshire, Illinois, 1876–1976. N.p.: Hampshire Centennial Corp., 1976.

Wright, John W. D. *A History of Early Carbondale, Illinois, 1852–1905*. Carbondale: Southern Illinois University Press, 1977.

Wyoming through the Years. Wyoming, Ill.: Wyoming Chamber of Commerce, 1986.

Xenia Then and Now, 1834–1984. Flora, Ill: Martin, 1984.

Yates City Community Centennial 1857–1957. N.p.: N.p., n.d.

Yates, William. *The Woodford County History*. Bloomington, Ill.: Woodford County Board of Supervisors, 1968.

Young, David. "One Animal Threatens This Valley—the Human." *Chicago Tribune*, April 15, 1989, 3:1, 4.

Young, Linda. "A Quiet Place with Come-Back Spirit." *Chicago Tribune*, Sept. 18, 1993, 1:22–23.

Youngman, Owen. "A Tale of Two Subdivisions." *Chicago Tribune*, April 21, 1990, 4:1, 4.

Zimmerman, Jacob Fredrich. *History of Incorporated Municipalities of Thornton Township*. 1938. Reprint. N.p.: N.p., 1979.

Zorn, Eric. "Ode to a Spot—or Is It a Plot?" *Chicago Tribune*, Sept. 11, 1993, 4:1–2.

———. "Small-Town USA Knows Its Own Mind." *Chicago Tribune*, June 23, 1990, 4:1, 4.

http://archiver.rootsweb.ancestry.com/th/read/ILKNOX/2000–08/0966128168. Accessed April 1, 2008.

www.bolingbrook.com. Accessed March 13, 2008.

www.cardunal.com/lake.htm. Accessed March 14, 2008.

www.chathampresbyterian.org. Accessed March 14, 2008.

www.chillicothehistorical.org/rock_island_history.htm. Accessed March 14, 2008.

www.elginhistory.com. Accessed March 14, 2008.

www.genealogytrails.com/ill/bureau/Township/#Ohio. Accessed March 14, 2008.

www.genealogytrails.com/ill/jefferson/ghostowns.html. Accessed March 14, 2008.

www.genealogytrails.com/ill/lasalle/Earlville.html. Accessed March 14, 2008.

www.genealogytrails.com/ill/randolph/t4r7.htm. Accessed March 14, 2008.

www.genealogytrails.com/ill/randolph/t6r9.htm. Accessed March 14, 2008.

www.genealogytrails.com/ill/randolph/t7r5.htm. Accessed March 14, 2008.

www.iltrails.org/mchenry/majormchenry.htm. Accessed March 14, 2008.

www.machesney-park.il.us. Accessed March 14, 2008.

www.medinahcc.org. Accessed March 14, 2008.

www.outfitters.com/illinois/bureau/communities_bureau.html. Accessed March 14, 2008.

www.outfitters.com/illinois/logan/communities_logan.html. Accessed March 14, 2008.

www.outfitters.com/illinois/pike/communities_pike.html. Accessed March 14, 2008.

www.papadocs.com/villages/damiansville/dvilhist.htm. Accessed March 14, 2008.

www.park-ridge.il.us. Accessed March 14, 2008.

www.randolphcountyillinois.net/sub88.htm. Accessed March 14, 2008.

www.rootsweb.com/~iladams/places/placenames.htm. Accessed March 1, 2008.

www.rootsweb.com/~ilbureau/towns.htm. Accessed April 8, 2008.

www.rootsweb.com/~ildekalb/places.htm. Accessed March 14, 2008.

www.rootsweb.com/~ilschuy/BioCassSchuyler/CTJokisch.htm. Accessed March 14, 2008.

www.stlibory.com/churchhistory.htm. Accessed March 14, 2008.

www.vil.maryville.il.us/maryville%20history.html. Accessed March 14, 2008.

EDWARD CALLARY is associate professor of English at Northern Illinois University in DeKalb and an editor of several books on naming, most recently *Place Names in the Midwestern United States.*

The University of Illinois Press
is a founding member of the
Association of American University Presses.

Composed in 10.25/13 Adobe Minion Pro
with Frutiger LT Std display
by Jim Proefrock
at the University of Illinois Press
Designed by Kelly Gray
Manufactured by Sheridan Books, Inc.

University of Illinois Press
1325 South Oak Street
Champaign, IL 61820-6903
www.press.uillinois.edu